Learning with Adults

A Reader

Edited by

Peter Mayo
University of Malta, Malta

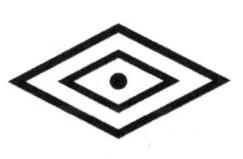

SENSE PUBLISHERS
ROTTERDAM/BOSTON/TAIPEI

A C.I.P. record for this book is available from the Library of Congress.

ISBN: 978-94-6209-333-1 (paperback)
ISBN: 978-94-6209-334-8 (hardback)
ISBN: 978-94-6209-335-5 (e-book)

Published by: Sense Publishers,
P.O. Box 21858,
3001 AW Rotterdam,
The Netherlands
https://www.sensepublishers.com/

Printed on acid-free paper

All Rights Reserved © 2013 Sense Publishers

No part of this work may be reproduced, stored in a retrieval system, or transmitted in any form or by any means, electronic, mechanical, photocopying, microfilming, recording or otherwise, without written permission from the Publisher, with the exception of any material supplied specifically for the purpose of being entered and executed on a computer system, for exclusive use by the purchaser of the work.

Learning with Adults

INTERNATIONAL ISSUES IN ADULT EDUCATION

Volume 13

Series Editor:
Peter Mayo, *University of Malta, Msida, Malta*

Editorial Advisory Board:
Stephen Brookfield, University of St Thomas, Minnesota, USA
Waguida El Bakary, American University in Cairo, Egypt
Budd L. Hall, University of Victoria, BC, Canada
Astrid Von Kotze, University of Natal, South Africa
Alberto Melo, University of the Algarve, Portugal
Lidia Puigvert-Mallart, CREA-University of Barcelona, Spain
Daniel Schugurensky, Arizona State University, USA
Joyce Stalker, University of Waikato, Hamilton, New Zealand/ Aotearoa
Juha Suoranta, University of Tampere, Finland

Scope:
This international book series attempts to do justice to adult education as an ever expanding field. It is intended to be internationally inclusive and attract writers and readers from different parts of the world. It also attempts to cover many of the areas that feature prominently in this amorphous field. It is a series that seeks to underline the global dimensions of adult education, covering a whole range of perspectives. In this regard, the series seeks to fill in an international void by providing a book series that complements the many journals, professional and academic, that exist in the area. The scope would be broad enough to comprise such issues as 'Adult Education in specific regional contexts', 'Adult Education in the Arab world', 'Participatory Action Research and Adult Education', 'Adult Education and Participatory Citizenship', 'Adult Education and the World Social Forum', 'Adult Education and Disability', 'Adult Education and the Elderly', 'Adult Education in Prisons', 'Adult Education, Work and Livelihoods', 'Adult Education and Migration', 'The Education of Older Adults', 'Southern Perspectives on Adult Education', 'Adult Education and Progressive Social Movements', 'Popular Education in Latin America and Beyond', 'Eastern European perspectives on Adult Education', 'An anti-Racist Agenda in Adult Education', 'Postcolonial perspectives on Adult Education', 'Adult Education and Indigenous Movements', 'Adult Education and Small States'. There is also room for single country studies of Adult Education provided that a market for such a study is guaranteed.

An extremely useful collection of articles on adult education. This book expands and elevates our understanding of this underestimated modality of education and its role in social change by bringing together multiple aspects – from culture, gender, identity, and policy to instruments and sites for knowledge transmission and production. *Learning with Adults: A Reader* constitutes the most valuable practical and theoretical reflection on adult education I have seen in a long time.
Nelly P. Stromquist, Professor, International Education Policy, College of Education University of Maryland, College Park

This book provides an opportunity at a very appropriate moment to discuss adult education issues during challenging times. It includes discussions on lifelong learning, the learning society, diversity of practices, learning in everyday life and policies. Therefore, the reader might find an engaged debate upon relevant subjects and an interesting problematization of contemporary dilemmas.
Paula Guimarães, University of Lisbon

This Adult Education Reader is unusual and remarkable. It is not usual to have renowned social theorists who are situated outside the field of adult learning included with many prominent adult learning theorists. Readers are invited to a large table filled with delectable goods from many cultures and contexts. Read and savour delights and surprises.
Michael Welton, University of British Columbia and Athabasca University

This is an important book Peter Mayo has put together with an impressive range of articles and with many of the more important names in adult education. It satisfies everything one could desire of a reader on the subject.
Kenneth Wain, University of Malta

TABLE OF CONTENTS

1. Introduction: The Multivaried Nature of Adult Education Provision and Learning
   Peter Mayo 1

Part I: Lifelong Learning and the Learning Society

2. Learning to Walk on Quicksand: Lifelong Learning and Liquid Life
   Zygmunt Bauman 9

3. Youth and Adult Education and Lifelong Learning in Latin America and the Caribbean
   Rosa Maria Torres 19

4. The Learning Society: Past, Present and Future Views
   D. W. Livingstone 33

Part II: Adult Learning, Difference and Identity

5. "We Must Believe in Ourselves": Attitudes and Experiences of Adult Learners with Disabilities in Kwazulu-Natal, South Africa
   Peter Rule & Tadi Ruth Modipa 57

6. Women, Sport and Adult Education: Shortchanging Women and Girls
   Cynthia Lee A. Pemberton & Eileen Casey White 77

7. Queering the Discourse: International Adult Learning and Education
   Robert Hill 87

8. Migration, Education, Gender
   Ursula Apitzsch 99

9. Adult Education and European Identity
   Oskar Negt 113

10. Anti-colonial Subaltern Social Movement (SSM) Learning and Development Dispossession in India
    Dip Kapoor 131

TABLE OF CONTENTS

Part III: Sites and Instruments of Practice

11. ICTs and Adult Learning 153
    Behrang Foroughi & Leona English

12. Radio as Public Pedagogy: A Critical Adult Education of the Airwaves 161
    Antonia Darder

13. Adult Education and Film/Television 175
    Asoke Bhattacharya

14. Literacies, Naratives and Adult Learning in Libraries 185
    Jim Elmborg

15. Community Development and the Arts: Towards a More Creative Reciprocity 195
    Mae Shaw & Rosie Meade

16. The Use of Aesthetic Experience in Unearthing Critical Thinking 205
    Alexis Kokkos

17. The Folk High School: Denmark's Contribution to Adult Education 219
    Palle Rasmussen

18. Four Decades of Universities of the Third Age: Past, present, Future 229
    Marvin Formosa

19. The European Agenda for Education in Prison 251
    Joseph Giordmaina

Part IV: Learning in Everyday Life

20. Transformative Learning 267
    Patricia Cranton

21. Adult Literacies 275
    Lyn Tett

22. Learning (through) Consumption: Shopping as a Site of Adult Education 285
    Kaela Jubas

23. Social Creation 293
    Antonia De Vita & Anna Maria Piussi

Part V: Policy and Regions

24. Adult Education and Poverty Reduction — 309
    Julia Preece

25. Cinderella and the Search for the Missing Shoe: 1990s Latin American Adult Education Policy and Practice — 317
    Daniel Schugurensky & John P. Myers

26. Adult Citizenship Education and Political Engagement in Sub-Saharan Africa: Critical Analysis — 341
    Edward Shizha & Ali A. Abdi

27. Adult Education policy in Micro-States: The Case of the Caribbean — 355
    Didacus Jules

28. Globalisation, Southern Europe and European Adult Education Policy — 371
    Carmel Borg & Peter Mayo

Name Index — 393

Subject Index — 397

PETER MAYO

1. INTRODUCTION: THE MULTIVARIED NATURE OF ADULT EDUCATION PROVISION AND LEARNING

I write this introduction almost a year after the launch of Leona English and my co-authored book, *Learning with Adults: A Critical Pedagogical Introduction* for the same series in which we broached a variety of topics widely deemed pertinent to the fields of adult education and adult learning. Both Leona and I made a strong effort to combine our expertise, as well as draw on previous separate publications of ours, to furnish material for an introductory graduate text in adult education. Needless to say, despite the broad ranging book, our combined expertise has its limits and we could not possibly cover most of the issues one would expect to include in an introductory course. Readers of the book were told in the Introduction, that:

> The volume broaches a variety of themes though we recognise important absences which deserve greater treatment elsewhere, including issues such as sexual orientation, transformative learning, literacy, consumer-rights education, and disability. The selection of themes was conditioned by the areas that fall within our combined expertise based on our previous writings, areas of ongoing research and teaching commitments, and our own adult education practice. (English & Mayo, p. 4)

It is this consideration that prompted me, as we finalized the text for our joint contribution, to suggest to the publishers, and specifically Peter de Leifde, the idea of an edited companion volume. We actually announced this in the Introduction to the 2012 volume. I have remained true to our word with the publication of this Reader which serves two purposes

1. To provide chapters by relevant authorities on important areas not broached in the earlier volume. These included consumption, literacy, sexual orientation transformative learning, ICT (this topic was given adequate treatment in the context of different topics in the previous book, especially university continuing education, but I felt that it deserves a chapter unto itself) and disability, in addition to other topics including those of libraries, poverty, micro-states, social creation, the 'learning society,' social film, community arts, education in prisons, community radio, sport, aesthetic experience, Folk High Schools, larger supranational identities, among others. Furthermore, I also sought

to introduce a section focusing on policy and regional issues with special reference to Africa, Europe and specifically Southern Europe, Latin America and the Caribbean.
2. To provide different perspectives on issues already dealt with in the earlier, 2012 volume, some in chapters focusing specifically on the theme itself, e.g. social movements or lifelong learning, and others in connection with different themes e.g. women and sport, citizenship and African adult education, workers' education and the learning society.

As with the previous and now companion volume, I tried, in my selections of themes and chapters, to be as inclusive as possible but once again there are limits to the extent to which one can be successful here. Regions covered include Africa, Asia (a particular focus on India), the Caribbean, Europe and Latin America. It is impossible to include each of the world's regions and perhaps one requires an entire book on its own providing regional foci. Readers will agree that the volume at hand is very large as it is and space restrictions became an important consideration. I feel however that we have a variety of perspectives, from North and South, to render the book reasonably inclusive.

Many of the authors are household names in the adult education literature. There are also a few relative newcomers to the field. There are others who have made their mark in other disciplines especially sociology and comparative education. As Leona and I stated in the introduction to the companion volume, adult education, while having its own literature, draws from a variety of fields. The selection of authors for this reader was deliberately carried out in a manner that illustrates this point. It is worth noting that sociology, a discipline that is strongly represented in this reader, perhaps reflecting my own personal bias as someone trained in sociology of education, lends itself to empirical research and theoretical ruminations on adult education and learning. We have managed to attract work by some of the finest exponents in this area. It is amazing, and perhaps surprising to some, to notice how such areas as adult learning and the larger all-embracing domain of lifelong learning feature in the work of major social theorists, some even combining their sociological work in universities and research institutes with engagement in the fields of workers' education, trade union education and adult education in general. We are fortunate to have contributions from a few of these persons in this reader.

Furthermore, the Reader contains contributions from writers whose first language is not English. I sought to enrich this volume by providing space for issues that take us beyond the reductive Anglocentric (used in its widest possible context) perspective which dominates the mainstream adult education literature, especially that literature which finds itself (in journals from different disciplines) in the much celebrated International Social Science Citation Index. Even in its 'europeanness,' and possibly, but very arguably, its 'eurocentrism,' this literature can broaden boundaries for some readers.

INTRODUCTION

All this is meant to capture the variegated nature of adult education, an amorphous field with porous areas, the loosely defined boundaries being both a perceived strength and 'weakness'(for disciplinary purists) of the field.

For solely heuristic purposes, I have grouped the various contributions to the Reader according to the following rubrics:

- Lifelong Learning and the Learning Society
- Learning, Difference and Identity
- Sites and Instruments of Practice
- Learning in everyday life
- Policy and Regions.

The first section accommodates the broader chapters dealing with the theme of Lifelong Learning and the related issue of the Learning Society. It includes a discussion by Zygmunt Bauman focused on Europe and the European Union within the context of his notion of Liquid Modernity and another by D. W. Livingstone viewing lifelong learning within a broad and historical notion of the 'learning society' and critique of the 'Knowledge economy' a discussion worth viewing alongside that of other writers.[1] We have a third contribution, this time from a Latin American perspective, by the prominent Ecuadorian policy analyst, Rosa Maria Torres. This is followed by the section on social difference including areas sorely missing from the previous volume, notably sexual orientation, tackled by activist and well known adult education writer and former editor of *Convergence* (the ICAE journal), Bob Hill, and disability, the latter, by Peter Rule and Tadi Ruth Modipa written from the perspective of people working in an African context. The chapter on sport can easily fit into the 'Sites of Practice' section but the contribution by Cynthia Lee Pemberton and Eileen Casey White stresses the identity perspective and focuses very much on women and gender construction.

Also connected with identities is the issue of social movements and, in this case, the contribution by Dip Kapoor on subaltern social movements. This chapter focuses on dispossessed people, the Adivasis and Dalits. The section also contains the contribution by prominent German sociologist, Oskar Negt, dealing with the construction of a 'European identity,' a recurring if controversial issue in Europe and across the European Union for quite some time now. Another prominent German sociologist from the University of Frankfurt, Ursula Apitzsch, deals with identity issues with respect to the situation of immigrant women in Germany. As with Pemberton and Casey White's paper, the issue of women and adult education is here discussed with regard to another important social topic in adult education: Migration. Migration featured in the previous volume, in the chapter on Racism, while an entire chapter was devoted to Women and Adult Education.

Many of these chapters can easily fit Section 3 dealing with sites of practice, which testifies to the fluidity of these sections. I sought to provide discussions around more specific learning contexts here. One chapter, by Mae Shaw and Rosie Meade, concerns the community arts and community development settings.

Another, a contribution from Denmark by Palle Rasmussen, focuses on the Danish Folk High Schools, foregrounding Nikolaj Frederik Severin Grundtvig and Kristen Kold. Importance is also attached to the prison as an important site of learning, not only for a host of brilliant political figures such as Gramsci, Castro and Mandela but for inmates in general, We have a chapter by Joseph Giordmaina who has for years been active in the field in his native country, EU Prison Education projects and the European Prison Education Association (EPEA). This section also foregrounds work, by Jim Elmborg, concerning adult learning in that most important of adult learning spaces, the library (the multimedia library these days), which, in the words of Canadian sociologist, D. W. Livingstone, in this volume, constitutes a venue for the "increasing socialization of the forces of knowledge production."

Prominent sites of learning include centres for *cinefora* such as those found in Kolkata, West Bengal, India, with their social purpose adult education provision as described and analysed by Asoke Bhattacharya. From film we move to the ever important medium of community radio with its potential to allow space for subaltern insurrectional voices contrasting with those deriving from the corporate media. In this chapter, well known critical pedagogue, Antonia Darder writes about community radio as a source of public pedagogy for adults, drawing on her own involvement in a project she helped set up. One cannot talk about sites and media and not mention the all pervasive nature of ICT in adult education, dealt with in the previous volume but given specific treatment here by Behrang Foroughi and Leona English from that important historical centre of Canadian Adult Education that is St Francis Xavier University in Nova Scotia, Canada, which houses the Coady Institute. Then we also venture into the area of aesthetic education and experience to foster critical thinking. The piece in question by Alexis Kokkos, from the Hellenic Open University, draws on the Frankfurt School's critical theory (Adorno, Horkheimer and Marcuse in particular), Dewey, Bourdieu, Freire and others. to show how the use of aesthetic experience in the learning context is connected to the process of engaging in a critical approach to challenging the status quo. Mention of Bourdieu brings to mind Marvin Formosa's discussion around Universities of the Third Age and their class and status politics, also serving, in certain places, as a means of social distinction and a source of provision of positional goods.

The world of everyday living cannot be underestimated as a means to constantly unfurl before our eyes different sites of adult learning. Antonia De Vita and Anna Maria Piussi from the University of Verona highlight the many different projects involving 'social creation' that constitute a groundswell of grassroots adult education in Northern Italy, especially the Veneto region. The authors discuss projects concerning consumption, the Roma people and the social solidarity economy, among other things. They, however, do not confine themselves to their immediate context and extend their reach to highlight projects in the same vein including those carried out by the *Madres* of the *desaparecidos* in Argentina. The consumption issue, broached by Piussi and De Vita, warrants sole treatment in a volume such as this. Kaela Jubas obliges, viewing this important issue from the lenses of critical theory, feminism, Gramscian social theory and poststructuralism. I decided to include Lyn Tett's chapter on literacy in this section because of the strong connection between this aspect of learning or lack of it and people's quotidian experience, a connection strongly highlighted by the author. I also included Patricia Cranton's chapter on transformative learning here because of her inclusion of the personal anecdotal experience of perspective transformation alongside an overview of the theory deriving from such key figures as Jack Mezirow.

The final section of the book brings together chapters which have a policy and/or regional focus. One policy issue, discussed by Julia Preece, concerns poverty. Three other policy discussions have a specific regional focus. These are Daniel Schugurensky and John Myers' paper on the 'Cinderella element' in adult education policy making in Latin America, Carmel Borg and my paper on European adult education policy in adult education, viewed from a Southern European and Mediterranean vantage point, and finally Didacus Jules' discussion of adult education policy making in small island states. Jules focuses specifically on the Caribbean. As someone who, like Didacus Jules and Carmel Borg, also hails from a micro-island state which poses specific challenges for adult education, I could not leave out this perspective. Jules has massive experience of educational policy making in the region, having also been the Coordinator of the Grenadian Literacy Campaign in the 80s. The other regionally focused work, which also connects with policy making in adult education but which extends its reach to discuss other issues, notably that of citizenship, is Edward Shizha and Ali A. Abdi's chapter. It focuses on the struggles involved in adult education for citizenship in Africa, drawing insights from radical educators who adopt a Southern, decolonizing perspective, such as Freire and African thinkers such as Julius K. Nyerere and Jomo Kenyatta.

I would like to think that this volume provides the reader with a varied, comprehensive perspective of the field, without any assumptions on my part, as editor, of its being exhaustive. I finally would like to thank all authors for their contributions, for going out of their way to make the editorial changes and updates requested of them and for being so prompt in obtaining authorization to republish in cases when the chapter had appeared in a journal, book or edited volume. I also take this opportunity to thank the original publishers of the works involved for allowing republication, often with modifications, without any conditions attached save for acknowledgement of prior publication in their outlet.

NOTE

[1] See for instance, Welton, M. (2005). *Designing the Just Learning Society: A Critical Inquiry*, Leicester: NIACE.

REFERENCE

English, L., & Mayo, P. (2012). *Learning with adults. A critical pedagogical introduction*, Rotterdam, Boston & Taipei: Sense Publishers.

AFFILIATION

Peter Mayo
Professor, Department of Education Studies, Faculty of Education, University of Malta

PART I

LIFELONG LEARNING AND THE LEARNING SOCIETY

ZYGMUNT BAUMAN

2. LEARNING TO WALK ON QUICKSAND: LIFELONG LEARNING AND LIQUID LIFE[1]

It took more than two millennia from the time the ancient Greek sages invented the notion of *paidea* for the idea of 'lifelong education' to turn from an oxymoron (a contradiction in terms) into a pleonasm (akin to a 'buttery butter' or 'metallic iron' …). That remarkable transformation occurred quite recently, in the last few decades, under the impact of the radically accelerated pace of change in the social setting in which both the principal actors of education the teachers and the learners alike – had to act.

The moment a bullet is fired from a ballistic weapon, its direction and the distance it will travel have already been decided by the shape and position of the gun and the amount of gunpowder in the shell; one can calculate with little or no error the spot where the missile will land, and one can choose that spot by shifting the barrel of the gun or changing the amount of gunpowder. These qualities of ballistic missiles made them ideal weapons for use in positional warfare-when the targets stayed dug into their trenches or bunkers and the missiles were the sole bodies on the move.

The same qualities make them useless, however, once targets that are invisible to the gunner start to move- particularly if they move faster than the missiles can fly, and even more so if they move erratically, in an unpredictable fashion that plays havoc with the preliminary calculation of the required trajectory. A smart, intelligent missile is needed then, a missile that can change its direction in mid-flight depending on changes in circumstances, that can immediately spot movements of the target, learn from them whatever cal'l be and needs to be learnt about the target's latest direction and speed and extrapolate from the information gathered the exact spot where their trajectories will cross. Such smart missiles cannot suspend the gathering and processing of information as it travels, let alone finish them – its target never stops moving and changing direction and speed, so that plotting the place of encounter needs to be constantly updated and corrected.

We may say that smart missiles will follow a strategy of 'instrumental rationality'' though in its liquidized, fluid version, so to speak; that is, dropping the assumption that the end will be given, steady and immovable for the duration and so only the means will need to be calculated and manipulated. Missiles that are even smarter won't be confined to a preselected target at all but will choose targets as they go. What will guide them is rather the consideration of what the most is that they can achieve given their technical capacities, and which of the potential targets around are the ones they are best equipped to hit. This would be, we may say, a case of 'instrumental rationality' in reverse: targets are selected while the missile travels, and it is the available means that decide which 'end' will eventually be selected. In this case the 'smartness' of the flying missile and its effectiveness would benefit if its equipment was of a rather 'generalist' or 'uncommitted' nature, unfocused on any specific category of ends, not overly adjusted to the hitting of any particular kind of target.

Smart missiles, unlike their ballistic elder cousins, *learn as they go*. So what they need to be supplied with at the outset is the *ability* to learn, and learn fast. This is obvious. What is less visible, however, though no less crucial than the skill of learning quickly, is the ability to instantly *forget* what was learned before. Smart missiles wouldn't be smart if they were not able to 'change their mind' or revoke their previous 'decisions' without a second thought and without regret ... They must not overly cherish the information they acquire and on no account should they develop a habit of behaving in the way the information suggested. All the information they acquire ages rapidly and if it is not promptly dismissed it may be misleading instead of providing reliable guidance. What the 'brains' of smart missiles must never forget is that the knowledge they Acquire is eminently *disposable,* good only until further notice and only temporarily useful, and that the warrant of success is not to overlook the moment when acquired knowledge is of no more use and needs to be thrown away, forgotten and replaced.

Philosophers of education of the solid modern era saw teachers as launchers of ballistic missiles and instructed them how to ensure that their products would stay strictly on the predesigned course determined by the original momentum. And no wonder; at the early stages of the modern era ballistic missiles were the highest achievement of human technical invention. They gave flawless service to anyone wishing to conquer and master the world as it then was; as Hilaire Belloc confidently declared, referring to the African natives, 'Whatever happens, we have got The Maxim Gun, and they have not' (the Maxim gun, let's recall, was a machine to launch great numbers of bullets in a short time, and was effective only if there were very many such bullets to hand).

As a matter of fact, though, that vision of the teacher's task and the pupil's destiny was much older than the idea of the 'ballistic missile' and the modern era that invented it – there is an ancient Chinese proverb that precedes the advent of modernity by two millennia but is still quoted by the Commission of the European Communities in support of its programme for 'Lifelong Learning' at the threshold of the twenty-first century: 'When planning for a year, plant corn. When planning for a decade, plant trees. When planning for life, train and educate people.' It is only with the entry into liquid modern times that the ancient wisdom lost its pragmatic value and people concerned with learning and the promotion of learning known by the name of 'education' had to shift their attention from ballistic to smart missiles.

More to the point, in the liquid modern setting, education and learning, to be of any use, must be continuous and indeed life long. No other kind of education and/or learning is conceivable; the 'formation' of selves or personalities is unthinkable in any fashion other than that of an ongoing and perpetually unfinished re-formation.

In a crisp and pithy rendition by Leszek Kolakowski, the freedom that transforms every step into a (potentially fateful) choice 'is given to us along with our humanity, and is the foundation of that humanity, it gives uniqueness to our very existence'(Kolakowski, 1999, p. 98). But it can be said that at no other time has the necessity to make choices been so deeply felt. At no other time have the acts of choosing been so poignantly self-conscious as they are now, conducted as they are under conditions of painful yet incurable uncertainty, under the constant threat of 'being left behind' and of being excluded from the game with any return barred because of a failure to rise to the new demands.

What separates the present-day agony of choice from the discomforts which have always tormented *homo eligens,* the 'man choosing', is the discovery or suspicion that there are no preordained rules or universally approved objectives that can be steadfastly followed whatever happens, thereby relieving the choosers from responsibility for any adverse consequences of their choices. Nothing prevents those reference points and guidelines that seem trustworthy today from being debunked and condemned tomorrow (and retrospectively!) as misleading or corrupt. Allegedly rock-solid companies are unmasked as figments of the accountants' imagination. Whatever is 'good for you' today may be reclassified as your poison tomorrow. Apparently firm commitments and solemnly signed agreements may be overturned overnight. And promises, or most of them, seem to be made solely to be broken or denied, counting on the short span of public memory. There seems to be no stable, secure island among the tides.

So where does this leave the prospects and the tasks of education? Jacek Wojciechowski, the editor of a Polish periodical dedicated to the academic profession, observes that 'once upon a time a university degree offered a safe conduct for practising the profession until retirement – but this is now history. Nowadays, knowledge needs to be constantly refreshed, even the professions need to be changed, otherwise all effort to earn a living will come to nothing.' (Wojciechowski, 2004) In other words, the impetuous growth of new knowledge and no less rapid ageing of the old combine to produce human ignorance on a massive scale, and continuously replenish, perhaps even beef up, its supplies. Wojciechowski warns: where there is a problem that people struggle to resolve, the market will promptly come to their rescue. This comes at a price, of course. In this case, the problem is people's ignorance – a stroke of good fortune for the sellers, bad luck for the buyers. For skilful school managers, this offers a not-to-be-missed opportunity to garner extra funds by patching together courses in the skills currently sought after, even if teachers with the skills needed to impart them are conspicuous mostly by their absence. This is a supplier's market, prospective clients being by definition in no position to judge the quality of the commodities on offer or to be choosy if they risk making a judgement. Knowledge that is inferior or useless, sometimes outdated or even downright misleading, is easily sold, and the more of it is bought, the less likely are the cheated to call the suppliers' bluff. Wojciechowski suggests that the only 'continuous education' courses that should be experimentally, allowed to be offered by an institution with no proper credentials are courses in dentistry – on condition that the teachers register as patients in their graduates' surgeries.

Preying on human ignorance and gullibility promises swift and secure returns, and there will always be some fortune-seekers around who are unable to resist such a promise. But even leaving aside the genuine, widespread and growing danger of dishonest trade, the speed with which the acquired skills are devalued and the demands of labour markets drift allows even impeccably honest dealers to contribute (even if this time by default rather than design) to the unsavoury social repercussions of the new and massive knowledge-dependence. As Lisa Thomas found recently, the commercialization of the mid-career education that has become indispensable is everywhere deepening the economic and social divisions between a highly educated and skilled labour elite and the rest of the labour force, as well as between skilled and unskilled labour, erecting new barriers to social mobility that are difficult to negotiate, and adding to the volume of unemployment and poverty. Once established, the divisions tend in addition to be self perpetuating and self-enhancing.[2]

In the US, for instance, only 19 per cent of people on low incomes who need professional training are likely to complete the course, while 76 per cent in higher income groups probably will. In a relatively small country like Finland, it has recently been discovered that about half a million adults in employment need education but cannot afford it. It is becoming increasingly clear that, left to its own logic, the 'teaching market' will magnify· rather than mitigate inequity and multiply its potentially catastrophic social consequences and side-effects. A political intervention is unavoidable if the bane is to be avoided.

This much has been assumed by the Commission of European Communities and confirmed in the communication already mentioned, 'Making a European area of lifelong learning a reality', issued on 21 November 2001 – though it is by no means certain that the *social* consequences of the ongoing commercialization of further education were the main worry prompting the initiative; the dominant motif re-emerging throughout the document is the suspicion that market-administered continuous education will not supply what the 'economy' truly needs and may therefore adversely affect the efficiency and competitiveness of the European Union and its member states.

The authors of the document are worried that the advent of the 'knowledge society' portends enormous risks alongside its potential benefits; it 'threatens to bring about greater inequalities and social exclusion', because only 60.3 per cent of people between 25 and 64 in the EU have attained at least upper secondary level education, while almost 150 million people in the EU are without such a basic level of education and 'face a higher risk of marginalization'. But the need to expand lifelong education/learning is argued, from the start of the document, in terms of the 'competitive advantage' that is 'increasingly dependent on investment in human capital', and on knowledge and competences becoming 'a powerful engine for economic growth'. According to the Commission, the importance of and the need for lifelong learning consist in its role 'in promoting a skilled, trained and adaptable workforce'. The task of achieving a 'more inclusive, tolerant and democratic' society marked by 'greater civic participation, higher reported well-being and lower criminality' enters the reasoning mostly as an afterthought and is represented as a side-effect: it is hoped it will be fulfilled as a natural consequence when more of the people who were inadequately trained thus far 'enter the labour market' thanks to improved training.

The document bears all the marks of a 'committee product', collating concerns whose heterogeneous origins and potentially conflict-prone relations can only be concealed by painstaking editorial work. But time and again the main concern and *argumentum crucis* around which the rest of the text is wrapped shows through clearly. Viviane Reding, then the European Commissioner for Education and Culture, stated in her preface to the 'Communication' that its purpose is to 'adjust our educational systems to the requirements of the economy and the knowledge society', while in the Cedefop / Euridice commentary, published a year later, one can read that the 'identification of skills needed by the labour market' needs to become a 'highly significant aspect of curriculum provision'. As Kenneth Wain observes in a paper prepared for the National Consultation Conference on Lifelong Learning held in Malta in 2001, the document may suggest 'that what is valued is *only* this kind of learning, vocational learning for the purposes of the economy and the job market'.(Wain, in Borg & Mayo, 2004, p.22) Similarly, Carmel Borg and Peter Mayo conclude their thorough analysis of the document's message by pointing out that 'the memorandum's messages ought to be read against an economic backdrop characterised by a market-oriented definition of social viability. As educational change is becoming increasingly linked to the discourse of efficiency, competitiveness, cost effectiveness and accountability' its declared aim is to impart to the 'labour force' the virtues of flexibility, mobility and 'basic, employment-related skills' (Borg & Mayo, 2004, p. 23).

The apprehensions are well founded. It is easy to trace a remarkable affinity between the approach taken by the European Commission and the overtly stated intentions and demands made by authors writing explicitly in the name of and for the benefit of business managers. The latter follow, with little variation, the pattern of reasoning exemplified by a highly popular and influential compendium of corporation thinking, according to which the purpose of education is 'developing employees to enhance their current performance at work as well as to prepare them to perform in positions they may hold in the future', while the aims of such development need to be at all times determined by 'identification of needed skills and active management of employee learning for the long-range future in relation to explicit corporate and business strategies'.(Fombrun, *et al,* 1984, p. 41, 159). Raili Moilanen, having analysed the contents of those papers submitted to the 3rd International Conference of Researching Work and Learning that represented the employers' point of view, found out that 'learning and development seem to be important for organizations mostly for the reasons of effectiveness and competitiveness' while 'the viewpoint of human being as such does not seem to be important' (Moilanen, 2004, p. 38). One could hardly expect different findings...

Let me add that however doubtful the approach of the authors of the 'Communication' may appear to people concerned with the ethical and social consequences of the unquestioned priority accorded to economic (in the last account, profit-making) considerations (as Borg and Mayo point out, while the profit-making capacity of companies improves, 'socio-economic inequalities and corresponding asymmetrical relations of power continue to intensify'), it also seems unsound in purely pragmatic terms.

Appeals to the guiding role of 'Human Resources Development' based on the 'identification of skills needed by the labour market' have been made with exemplary consistency in the past, and with a similarly monotonous regularity the managers of 'human resources' have failed to anticipate what the 'labour market' would 'need' when the currently trained 'labour force' completed their instruction and were presumably ready for employment. Future twists of market demand are not easily predictable, however artful the forecasters and methodologically refined their prognoses. Errors are, to be sure, a notorious and probably incurable ailment of all 'scientific predictions' of social trends, but in this case, when people's life prospects are at stake, mistaken judgments are exceptionally damaging. Surrendering human efforts of self-assertion and self-improvement to essentially unpredictable and so known to be unreliable visions of the future needs of volatile and chaotic markets portends a lot of human suffering – of frustration, dashed hopes and wasted lives. Calculations of 'human power' claim an authority they do not possess, make promises that cannot hold up and as a result assume responsibilities they are unable to bear.

This is probably why programmes of 'lifelong education' tend to be recast, imperceptibly and with no explicit explanation, into exhortations to 'lifelong learning' – 'subsidiarizing' thereby the responsibility for skills selection and their acquisition, and for the consequences of wrong choices, to those on the receiving end of the notoriously fluid and fickle 'labour markets'. Borg and Mayo are precisely on target when they conclude that 'in these stringent neo-liberal times, the notion of self-directive learning lends itself to a discourse that allows the State to abdicate its responsibilities in providing the quality education to which every citizen is entitled in a democratic society.' Let me point out that this is not the first nor the last function which the state would gladly remove from the realm of politics, and thereby from its responsibilities. Let me add as well that the shifting emphasis from 'education' to 'learning' chimes well with another tendency, common among contemporary managers: the inclination to 'subsidiarize' from their own on to their employees' shoulders responsibility for all effects, but above all the negative ones, and more generally responsibility for 'failing to rise to the challenge'.

Given the continuing convergence of two overwhelming trends that shape power relations and the strategy of domination in liquid modern times, the prospects for the twisted and erratic itinerary of market developments to be straightened up, and so for 'Human Resources' calculations to be made more realistic, are poor at best, and most probably nil. In a liquid modern setting 'manufactured uncertainty' is the paramount instrument of domination, while the policy of *precarisation,* to use Pierre Bourdieu's term (a concept referring to the ploys that result in the situation of the subjects becoming more insecure and vulnerable and therefore even less predictable and controllable), is fast becoming the hard core of the domination strategy. 'Planning for life' and the market are at loggerheads, and once state politics surrenders to the guidance of the 'economy,' understood as the free play of market forces, the balance of power between the two switches decisively to the advantage of the second.

This does not augur well for the 'empowering of citizens'; named by the European Commission as the primary objective of lifelong learning. By widespread consent, 'empowerment' (a term used in the current debates interchangeably with that of 'enablement') is achieved when people acquire the ability to control, or at least significantly influence the personal, political, economic and social forces by which their life trajectory would otherwise be buffeted; in other words, to be 'empowered' means to be *able to make choices and act effectively on the choices made,* and that in turn signifies the *capacity to influence the range of available choices and the social settings in which choices are made and pursued.* To put it bluntly, genuine 'empowerment' requires the acquisition not only of the skills needed to successfully play a game designed· by others, but also of the *powers* to influence the game's objectives, stakes and rules; not only the personal skills, but also the *social* powers.

'Empowerment' requires the building and rebuilding of inter human bonds, the will and the ability to engage with others in a continuous effort to make human cohabitation into a hospitable and friendly setting for the mutually enriching cooperation of men and women struggling for self-esteem, for the development of their potential and for the proper use of their abilities. In short, one of the decisive stakes of lifelong education aimed at 'empowerment' is the *rebuilding of the now increasingly deserted public space* where men and women may engage in a continuous translation between the individual and the common, the private and the communal interests, rights and duties.

'In light of fragmentation and segmentation processes and increasing individual and social diversity,' writes Dominique Simone Rychen, 'strengthening social cohesion and developing a sense of social awareness and responsibility have become important societal and political goals.' (Simone Rychen, 2004, p. 29). In the workplace, in the immediate neighbourhood and in the street, we mix daily with others who, as Rychen points out, 'do not necessarily speak the same language (literally or metaphorically) or share the same memory or history'. Under such circumstances, the skills we need more than any others in order to offer the public

Z. BAUMAN

sphere a reas[...] [th]e skills of interaction with others – of conductin[g ...] [ga]ining mutual understanding and of managing or [...] [eve]ry instance of shared life.

Let me re[peat my warn]ing: in the liquid modern setting, education ar[...] be continuous and indeed lifelong. I hope we ca[...] the decisive, reason why it must be continuous and lifelong is the nature of the task we confront on the shared road to 'empowerment' – a task which is exactly as education should be: continuous, never ending, lifelong.

This is indeed how education should be so that the men and women of the liquid modern world can pursue their life goals with at least a modicum of resourcefulness and self-confidence, and hope to succeed. But there is another reason, less often discussed, though more powerful than the one argued thus far: this is not to do with adapting human skills to the fast pace of the world's change, but with making the fast changing world more hospitable to humanity.

That task also calls for continuous, lifelong education. As Henry A. Giroux and Susan Searls Giroux have recently reminded us –

> Democracy is imperiled as individuals are unable to translate their privately suffered misery into broadly shared public concerns and collective action. Civic engagement now appears impotent and public values have become expendable as a result of the growing power of multinational corporations to shape the content of most mainstream media...For many people today, citizenship is about the act of buying and selling commodities (including political candidates) rather than broadening the scope of their freedoms and rights in order to expand the operations of a substantive democracy.(Giroux and Searls Giroux, 2004, p. 1)

The consumer is an enemy of the citizen...All over the 'developed' and affluent part of the planet signs abound of people turning their backs on politics, of growing political apathy and loss of interest in the running of the political process. But democratic politics cannot survive for long in the face of citizens' passivity arising from political ignorance and indifference. Citizens' freedoms are not properties acquired once and for all; such properties are not secure once they are locked in private safes. They are planted and rooted in the sociopolitical soil and it needs to be fertilized daily and will dry out and crumble if it is not attended to 'day in day out' by the informed actions of a knowledgeable and committed public. It is not only the *technical* skills that need to be continually refreshed, not only the *job-focused* education that needs to be lifelong. The same is required, and with still greater urgency, by education in *citizenship*.

Most people would agree today without much prompting that they need to refresh their professional knowledge and digest new technical information if they wish to avoid 'being left behind' and don't wish to be thrown overboard from the fast accelerating 'technological progress'. And yet a similar feeling of urgency is conspicuously missing when it comes to catching up with the impetuous stream of political developments and the fast changing rules of the political game. The authors quoted above have collated some survey results testifying to the rapid widening of the gap that separates public opinion from the central facts of political life:

> Soon after the invasion of Iraq, *The New York Times* released a survey indicating that 42 percent of the American public believed that Saddam Hussein was directly responsible for the September 11 attacks on the World Trade Center and the Pentagon. CBS also released a news poll indicating that 55 percent of the public believed that Saddam Hussein directly supported the terrorist organization *Al Qaeda*. A Knight Ridder / Princeton Research poll found that '44 percent of respondents said they thought "most" or "some" of the September 11, 2001 hijackers were Iraqi citizens.' A majority of Americans also believed already that Saddam Hussein had weapons of mass destruction, and that such weapons had been found, that he was about to build a nuclear bomb, and that he would unleash it eventually on an unsuspecting American public. None of these claims had any basis in fact, as no evidence existed to even remotely confirm these assertions. A poll conducted by *The Washington Post* near the second anniversary of the September 11 tragedy indicated that 70 percent of Americans continued to believe that Iraq played a direct role in the planning of the attacks.[3]

In such a landscape of ignorance, it is easy to feel lost and hapless – and easier still to be lost and hapless without feeling it. As Pierre Bourdieu memorably remarked, the person who has no grip on the present wouldn't dream of controlling the future- and most Americans must have only a misty view of what the present holds. This suspicion is amply confirmed by some incisive and insightful observers. 'Many Americans', Brian Knowlton of the *International Herald Tribune* notes, 'said the hot-cold-hot nature of recent alerts had left them unsure just how urgently, and fear fully, they should react'.[9]

Ignorance leads to paralysis of the will. One does not know what is in store and has no way to count the risks. For authorities impatient with constraints imposed on power-holders by a buoyant and resilient democracy, this kind of impotence of the electorate produced by ignorance, and the widespread disbelief in the efficacy of dissent and an unwillingness to get politically involved are much needed and welcome sources of political capital: domination through deliberately cultivated ignorance and uncertainty is more reliable and comes cheaper than rule grounded in a thorough debate of the facts and a protracted effort to agree on the truth of the matter and on the least risky ways to proceed.

Political ignorance is self-perpetuating, and a rope that is plaited of ignorance and inaction comes in handy whenever the voice of democracy' is to be stifled or its hands tied.

We need. lifelong education to give us choice. But we need it even more to salvage the conditions that make choice available and within our power.

NOTES

1. This chapter appeared previously as Chapter 6 Learning to Walk on Quicksand in Zygmunt Bauman's 2005 book *Liquid Life*, Polity Press. Permission to republish obtained from author and from Polity Press.
2. See www.staffs.ac.uk.journal/volume 6(1)editor.htm.
3. See 'Hot-cold-hot:terror alert left America uncertain', International Herald Tribune, 5 August.

REFERENCES

Borg, C., & Mayo, P. (2003). 'Diluted wine in new bottles: The key messages of the memorandum' *LLinE: Lifelong Learning in Europe, 1*, 18–25.

Fombrun, C. J, Tichy, N. M., & Devanna, M. A. (1984). *Strategic human resources management*, New York: John Wiley.

Giroux, H., & Searls Giroux, S. (2004). *Take back higher education: Race, youth, and the crisis of democracy in the post-civil rights era,* New York & Hampshire: Palgrave-Macmillan.

Kolakowski, L. (1999). *Freedom, fame, lying and betrayal: Essays in everyday life*, Harmondsworth: Penguin.

Moilanen, R. (2004). HRD and learning – for whose well being? *LLinE: Lifelong Learning in Europe, 1*, 34–39.

Simone Rychen, D. (2004). Lifelong learning – but learning for what? *LLinE: Lifelong Learning in Europe, 1*, 26–33.

Wojciechowski, J. (2004). Studia podyplomowe, *Forum Akademickie, 3.* http://www.forumakad.pl/archiwum/2004/05/10-agora-studia_podyplomowe.htm

AFFILIATION

Zygmunt Bauman
Emeritus Professor in the Department of Sociology,
University of Leeds, England

ROSA MARIA TORRES

3. YOUTH AND ADULT EDUCATION AND LIFELONG LEARNING IN LATIN AMERICA AND THE CARIBBEAN[1]

INTRODUCTION

This paper draws from various studies I have conducted on adult education and on lifelong learning in Latin America and other regions. Two such studies (written in English) serve here as main references (Torres, 2004; 2009).

Latin America and the Caribbean is a highly heterogeneous region, comprising two sub-regions (Latin America, the Caribbean) and 41 countries and territories with very different political, cultural, economic, social and educational realities. Some 600 languages are spoken; Spanish and Portuguese are the two most widespread official languages. Any regional generalization would be abusive, and space does not allow us to elaborate here more on each country. Also, the situation is very dynamic; trends may change considerably in a short period of time. In the current international context, and *vis a vis* the world and European crisis, Latin America appears strong and united, with economic and social indicators improving over the past few years.[2] On the other hand, Mexico and Chile, the two Latin American countries that are members of OECD, are facing major turmoil, their education systems being exposed and under heavy social scrutiny and criticism.

In most Latin American countries, the term used is 'Youth & Adult Education' (henceforth YAE). The term "youth" was incorporated in the 1980s, acknowledging the increased presence of young people in adult education programmes as well as the need to address the specificity of youth in such programmes.

The information and analysis presented below refers basically to the twelve year period between CONFINTEA V (1997) and CONFINTEA VI (2009).

REACTIVATION OF YOUTH AND ADULT EDUCATION IN THE REGION IN THE PAST FEW YEARS

Between the late 1980s and the late 1990s, YAE practically disappeared in most countries, following World Bank recommendations to governments in "developing countries" in the sense of giving priority to primary education and to children as opposed to adults (The World Bank later also rectified its argument about the failure of adult literacy, which was ill-documented). The Education for All (henceforth EFA) world initiative coordinated by UNESCO (1900-2000-2015) has followed the same trend: out of the six EFA goals, Goal 2 referred to primary education, has received the most attention while Goals 3 and 4 referred to youth and adult education, have received the least attention, as acknowledged every year by EFA Global Monitoring Reports (henceforth EFA GMR). In fact, the 2009 EFA GMR, coinciding with the year of CONFINTEA VI, continued to ignore YAE, not considered of strategic importance to the achievement of EFA by 2015.

For various reasons, since the late 1990s there has been a visible reactivation of YAE in the region. CONFINTEA V contributed to enhance social mobilization and networking around YAE, both before and right after the Hamburg conference. Later on, we have witnessed the emergence of new supranational and international actors engaged in YAE, notably the Cuban government and its '*Yo Sí Puedo*' (Yes, I Can) literacy programme, and the Organization of IberoAmerican States (OEI) which organized the Ibero-American Plan for Youth and Adult Literacy and Basic Education (PIA) 2007–2015. (OEI, 2006)

Such reactivation is reflected among others in the following:

Renewed emphasis on youth/adult literacy. A new wave of 'illiteracy eradication' has taken over the region. Many countries resumed national literacy programmes or campaigns, even some countries with very low illiteracy rates (lower than 3%) such as Argentina and Uruguay. The exception is Cuba, declared a 'territory free of illiteracy' almost half a century ago (1961), as well as several countries in the English-speaking Caribbean where governmental focus on literacy is on the formal system. There are also sub-national and local programmes run by local governments, religious groups, NGOs, social organizations and movements, and teacher unions.

Clearer institutionalization of YAE. There are advances in legislation and policy in most countries. There is increased recognition of the right to (free) education as well as to linguistic and cultural diversity and to inter-culturality as a comprehensive approach to education. In Cuba and Mexico for a long time, and more recently in countries such as Chile, Venezuela, Bolivia or Paraguay, YAE becomes more institutionalized, pointing towards the building of a *system* or *subsystem*, rather than the usual and discontinued *ad-hoc* interventions.

New actors and partnerships. In most countries, there are government partnerships with NGOs, universities, religious groups and the private sector. In a few countries, partnerships have included teacher unions and strong social movements (e.g. in Argentina and Brazil). There are also several international actors engaged in YAE in the region. As indicated, the most active in recent times are the Spanish government/ OEI and the Cuban government/IPLAC. Others include the *Convenio Andrés Bello* (Andrés Bello Agreement – CAB), an international inter-governmental organization focused on supranational integration (twelve countries), based in Bogota and linked to OEI; and the Organization of American States (OAS), based in Washington, which coordinates the Summits of the Americas.

More and better information and knowledge on YAE. There is considerable growth in research and documentation at national, sub-regional and regional level in recent years. Of course, there are also major differences between countries in terms of quantity, quality, topics and approaches related to research. Big countries such as Brazil and Mexico and also Chile report many surveys and studies.

Advances in evaluation. Evaluation has become a central piece of school systems and reforms in the region since the 1990s, but its incorporation in YAE is rather recent. In Brazil, a Functional Literacy Indicator (INAF), based on actual evaluation of reading, writing and numeracy skills of the adult population (15–64 years of age), has been developed annually since 2001 by two private institutions. In Mexico, the National Institute for Adult Education (INEA) has its own evaluation system. In Chile, evaluation of student outcomes is under a National System for the Evaluation of Learning and Certification of Studies, which includes YAE. Both Mexico and Chile have adopted results-based schemes for paying the institutions and/or teaching staff hired for YAE programmes.

Linkages between education/training and work as a field of research, policy and action. The linkages between education, the economy and work have become a field of concern, policy and action, within the overall concern with poverty, unemployment and social exclusion. *Social Economy* gains increased attention as an alternative economic model that generates also alternative approaches to education and training linked to production, commercialization, barter and other income-generation activities by families, cooperatives, and organized communities.

Increased attention to 'special groups'. Visible attention has been given in recent years to the disabled, migrants and prison inmates. The use of traditional and modern technologies has facilitated this task, especially with the disabled and with the migrant population. Prison education has been enhanced since 2006 in the framework of the EUROsociAL programme of the European Commission. Initiatives aimed at the blind, the visually challenged and hearing impaired have been developed in recent years in many countries. (UNESCO-OEI, 2008).

New technologies reaching the field. Radio has been a powerful ally of YAE for several decades and continues to be in many countries, especially in some of the poorest ones such as Haiti, Bolivia, and Paraguay. In the past few years, audiovisual media have become widespread mainly through the Cuba-assisted *Yo Sí Puedo* literacy and post-literacy programme operating in several countries since 2003. Computers and the Internet are also reaching YAE, particularly for the younger population. *Tele-centers* or *info-centers* (different from *cybercafes*, privately owned and for-profit) are part of basic education programmes in several countries. In remote rural areas, energy plants or solar panels are being installed. In many places today it is easier to find a cybercafe or a tele-center than a library, a computer than a book.

SOME OLD AND NEW WEAKNESSES AND LIMITATIONS. CHALLENGES FOR THE FUTURE

The 'Agenda for the Future' approved at CONFINTEA V, its wide vision and ambitious proposals for adult learning, is not the one that has been implemented in this region since 1997. Neither is the 2000–2010 YAE Regional Framework for Action prepared as a follow up to CONFINTEA V. Advances coexist with old and new limitations related to governmental and non-governmental action as well as to international agencies intervening in the field.

Sectoral approaches and interventions. Despite advances in cross-sectoral policies and collaboration with other government actors, YAE continues to be perceived as pertaining to the 'education sector', unconnected with major economic, political and social issues. YAE is in fact a transversal issue, but invisible unless it falls directly under an education authority and refers somewhere explicitly to the term *'adult'*.

Continued low status of YAE. The traditional low status of YAE is related to: (a) age (vis a vis children), and (b) socio-economic status. Estimations of costs of programmes and plans rarely consider infrastructure, equipment or even remunerated work. In many cases, YAE continues to be considered a 'special regime' together with other areas that challenge conventional classifications, such as bilingual intercultural education, special education, and multigrade schools.

Activism and discontinuity of efforts. Activism has been a characteristic of YAE, often related to 'one-shot' and isolated activities lacking continuity, monitoring, systematization, evaluation and feedback. Countries engage from time to time and over and over again in 'illiteracy eradication' or 'illiteracy reduction' initiatives. So far, policies have been unable to deal with literacy/basic education in a sustained and integral manner, linking school and out-of-school, children's and adults' education as part of one single strategy towards education for all.

Big distances between policies and implementation. The right to free, quality education continues to be denied to a large portion of the population. National reports prepared for CONFINTEA VI say little about actual implementation. One key conclusion I drew from the field study on literacy and written culture by out-of-school youth and adults in nine countries of the region is that "policies in this field have become autonomous, with little or no contact with actual practice on the ground."

High political, financial and administrative vulnerability of YAE YAE continues to be highly vulnerable to national/local political and administrative changes as well as to changes in international priorities. This implies a permanent threat to the continuity of policies and programmes, and to the building of national capacities and accumulated practical experience. A key component of such vulnerability are the meager financial resources available for education in general and for YAE in particular. Few national reports and studies provide concrete information on YAE funding and costs. This is marked in the case of the private sector. In many countries, YAE budget represents less than 1% of educational spending. Brazil calculates that, budget-wise, an adult learner counts as 0.7% of a primary school child (Brazil CONFINTEA VI report).

Funding comes from various sources: government, churches, the private sector, social movements, and international agencies. There is scarce information on the financial contribution of bilateral and multilateral agencies to YAE, its uses and impact. In most countries, government plays the major role, especially in basic education levels.

Government programmes generally do not charge fees and many of them provide access to free equipment and materials. Also, various countries have been adopting compensation policies or plans tied to studying.

Rise of for-profit spirit and market mechanisms. There is an important decline in volunteerism, social mobilization and political commitment traditionally linked to YAE. In many countries, NGOs are hired and paid by governments to implement programmes. On the other hand, the trend towards accreditation and certification (completion of primary/basic/secondary education) has attracted the for-profit private sector, introducing fees and other market mechanisms into the field.

Low attention to professionalization of adult educators. The low status, poor training and bad working conditions of adult educators is an old vicious circle in YAE. Training is generally poor and short, and its deficits are even more visible in the case of indigenous educators prepared for intercultural bilingual education programmes. Availability of audiovisual and digital technologies are contributing to further reduce the importance of professionalization and of initial and in-service training,

Requisites for adult educators have been "upgraded" in some countries, including a professional teaching title or completion of secondary education rather than primary education only; such requisites tend to loosen in rural areas and in literacy programmes, which continue to operate in most cases with community volunteers. The question that remains concerns the desired profile and education/training of adult educators, and whether possessing a teacher certificate ensures good teaching.

Weak dissemination, use and impact of research and evaluation results. Research, documentation and evaluation efforts lack sufficient and opportune dissemination.

We found differentiated circuits, one closer to academic circles and another one closer to bureaucratic and government structures. Overall, there is little evidence that research results are informing and influencing policy-making, training or teaching practice. They have not contributed to modifying long-entrenched 'common sense' in the field, including negative perceptions and terminologies linked to illiteracy (e.g. 'scourge', 'plague', 'darkness', 'blindness', 'shackle', 'eradication', etc.), the association between illiteracy and ignorance, between number of years of schooling and 'functional literacy', and between adult education, non-formal and remedial education. Also, most diagnoses and recommendations are based on literature reviews, with little connection to realities and little or no empirical research. (Caruso, et.al, 2008).

Age discrimination within YAE. There is a consistent trend towards (a) giving priority to the younger segments of the adult population, establishing age limits (40, 35, in some cases less), and (b) segmenting educational opportunities by age: literacy offered to older generations and other programmes offered to youth. Cuba is the only country that has the elderly as a priority group in terms of educational and cultural attention by government. Uruguay – known for its high percentage of third age population – is also expanding the age of learners within YAE.

Continued neglect of indigenous peoples. The YAE Regional Framework for Action (2000–2010) identified four priority groups: indigenous, peasants, youth and women. Youth and women have in fact been prioritized; indigenous and afro descendant groups have not. Racism is alive despite advances in national and international legislation, including the approval in 2007 of the United Nations Declaration on the Rights of Indigenous Peoples. Brazil's national illiteracy rate (2008) was 7,1%. Among indigenous peoples it stands at 18% and 16 % among black people (Brazil CONFINTEA VI report). In Mexico, the national illiteracy rate was 8.4%. and the illiteracy rate among indigenous groups was 36.1% (Mexico CONFINTEA VI report). Also, Intercultural Bilingual Education (IBE) continues to focus on rural areas. However, indigenous populations are also settled in urban areas, especially in large Latin American cities, following strong rural-urban migration patterns.

Continued neglect of rural areas. Formal and non-formal education continue to concentrate in urban and the periphery of urban areas, thus maintaining and even deepening the urban-rural educational gap. Probabilities that youth and adults in rural areas get no or incipient education are twice as big as in urban areas, and in some countries three times bigger (SITEAL). Peru has the highest urban-rural school gap. Peru's CONFINTEA VI report acknowledged that practically all educational institutions doing adult education are located in cities. In Brazil, illiterates in urban areas are 9.7 million as against 4.7 million in rural areas; however, in percentile terms, rural areas have almost three times more illiterates – 26.3% against 8.7% in urban areas.

Low coverage of programmes. YAE programmes are very limited for actual needs. Despite being a prioritized age group, by 2007 less than 10% of 20–29 year olds who had not completed secondary education attended some educational programme. In large countries such as Brazil and Mexico, all efforts seem small and advances slow. According to Brazil's CONFINTEA VI report, only 10% of the demand was served in 2008. Chile calculated that it would take 20 years to reach the 4 million people who have not completed basic education (Chile CONFINTEA VI report).

Quality and **learning** *remain distant issues.* Quantitative indicators (enrolment and retention, number of groups organized, materials or equipments distributed, etc.) predominate as indicators of achievement and success. A minimum number of participants is often established as a requisite to start a programme or a center, thus often leading to cheating (e.g. manipulating the statistics, completing the list with family members, friends or persons who are not part of the target population, etc.). In literacy programmes, goals continue to be set in terms of 'eradicating' or 'reducing' illiteracy rates, rather than in terms of learning and effective use of reading and writing. Only in very few cases have adult literacy programmes and campaigns been thoroughly evaluated. One such example is Ecuador's National Literacy Campaign '*Monsignor Leonidas Proaño*' (1988–1990).

Continued weaknesses of technical and vocational education/training programmes. There is skepticism in relation to the effectiveness of these programmes; several international organizations have commissioned studies and impact evaluations of the programmes they support. The "solution" of keeping or 're-inserting' adolescents and youth in schools (often against their will) – the same unchanged schools that expelled them in the first place – is also debatable. An IIEP study of 52 programmes in fourteen Latin American countries concluded that education/training programmes intended to prepare young people for work (a) take a simplistic view of youth inclusion in the labor market, (b) reach only a small portion of the potential population, (c) adopt a narrow approach focused on specific training, and (d) do not take sufficiently into account the importance of formal education, the competitiveness of the labor market and the scarcity of decent jobs (Jacinto, 2007, 2008).

"Best practices" selected without clear criteria. Many practices selected as 'good' or 'best' practices in education and in YAE in particular are outdated, are based on documents, experts' opinions or self-evaluation by their own actors, and lack evidence of their implementation, results and actual perceptions by participating learners. Few of them would pass the test of the four As – *availability*, *accessibility*, *adaptability* and *acceptability*. On the other hand, many relevant experiences remain un-systematized and unknown because of chronic lack of time and of resources in the field, their commitment to action and their many urgencies. Also, it is important to remember that 'innovative' does not necessarily mean 'effective,' or generalizable.

Innovations are specific, generally local and small-scale, and cannot be easily replicated or expanded on a massive scale.

MAJOR COORDINATION PROBLEMS AMONG NATIONAL AND INTERNATIONAL ACTORS

Decentralization processes and diversification of educational provision have increased coordination and articulation problems amongst the diverse national actors: government across sectors and at the various levels, governmental and non-governmental bodies, profit and non-profit private sector, NGOs, universities, churches, etc. The same is true for the various international actors working in YAE, and in the literacy field in particular. Each of them has its own plans, objectives, goals, timeframes, diagnoses, approaches, methodologies, reporting and financing mechanisms. See table below for the case of literacy.

Table 1. Regional and International Adult Literacy Goals (1980–2015)

MPE *Major Project for Education in Latin America and the Caribbean*	**EFA I-Jomtien** *Education for All*	**EFA II–Dakar** *Education for All*	**UNLD** *United Nations Literacy Decade*	**PIA** *Ibero-American Plan for Youth and Adult Literacy and Basic Education*
1980–2000 UNESCO-OREALC Eradicate illiteracy by 2000	1990–2000 UNESCO-UNICEF-UNDP-World Bank Reduce illiteracy by half by 2000	2000–2015 Reduce illiteracy by half by 2015	2003–2012 UNESCO Reduce illiteracy by half by 2012	2007–2015 OEI Eradicate illiteracy by 2015

Elaborated by R.M. Torres

LIFELONG LEARNING (LLL) IN LATIN AMERICA AND THE CARIBBEAN

The paradigm shift proposed worldwide – from *education* to *learning*, and from *adult education* to *adult learning* – has not been appropriated in this region. Although CONFINTEA V had strong regional resonance, the term *learning* was never introduced in its follow up. Youth and Adult Education (YAE) was the term used in the Regional Framework for Action following CONFINTEA V.

The Lifelong Learning (LLL) concept that emerged in the North, closely related to economic growth, competitiveness and employability, is understood and utilized in most diverse ways worldwide. Generally: (a) LLL continues to be used interchangeably with *Lifelong Education*, without differentiating *education* and learning³; and (b) *LLL is associated with adults* rather than to the entire lifespan – 'from the cradle to the grave'.

All this is reflected in Latin America and the Caribbean. LLL is mentioned in many legal and policy/programme documents, with the same biases and inconsistencies that are found internationally. LLL appears often as a separate line of action or goal rather than as an embracing category. In Jamaica's Ministry of Education's structure, for example, LLL has been added as a sixth section, next to the other five sections on early childhood, primary, secondary, tertiary and special education.

From the documents and websites reviewed, the LLL terminology appears to be more widespread and more embedded in recent policies and plans in the English-speaking Caribbean countries than in Latin American ones. In the Caribbean, LLL seems to follow the frameworks adopted in Europe. In Jamaica, for example, the LLL policy, devised in 2005, was decided by the Human Employment and Resource Training-HEART Trust /National Training Agency-NTA, the institutions that coordinate workforce development in Jamaica. (Warrican, 2008).

Even new initiatives such as the *Metas Educativas* 2021 (2021 Education Goals) coordinated by OEI do not refer to *Lifelong Learning* but to *Lifelong Education,* and is considered a separate goal rather than a goal including all others.

Table 2. OEI: Metas Educativas 2021 (2021 Education Goals) 2012–2021

1. Participation of society in educational action.
2. Achieve educational equality and overcome discrimination.
3. Increase supply for early childhood education.
4. Universalize primary education and lower secondary education, and expand access to upper secondary education.
5. Improve the quality of education and of the school curriculum.
6. Facilitate the connection between education and employment through technical-professional education.
7. Offer every person lifelong education opportunities.
8. Strengthen the teaching profession.
9. Expand the Ibero-American Knowledge space and strengthen scientific research.
10. Invest more and better.
11. Evaluate the functioning of education systems and the 2021 Education Goals project.

Source: http://www.oei.es/metas2021/libro.htm Translation from Spanish: Rosa María Torres

A FEW CONCLUSIONS

Some conclusions can be drawn:

- Given the big gap between rhetoric/policies/laws and practice, the inclusion of YAE in recent policies, reforms and legislative frameworks on paper should not lead to assumptions about effective implementation.

- Quantitative gains – small as they are – are usually shadowed by quality and equity problems.
- Priority given to youth has ended up marginalizing adults and the elderly, just as priority given to women ended up marginalizing men in several countries and programmes.
- The acknowledgement of the importance of literacy has traditionally placed it at the heart of YA efforts, and is currently being overemphasized in many countries with too many programmes running in parallel and poor targeting of efforts.
- Literacy achievements are rarely sustained and complemented with policies and strategies aimed at making reading and writing accessible to the population, paying attention to their specific needs, languages and cultures.
- Many vocational and technical training programmes continue to ignore the complex issues involved in the transition between education and work (not only employment), and of the world of work these days.
- The important impulse towards completion of primary/secondary education and accreditation of studies needs to be accompanied by the necessary efforts to ensure effective, meaningful and useful *learning*.
- Many hands involved often do not generate genuine 'partnerships' but rather enhanced lack of coordination, competitiveness, duplication of efforts and misuse of resources.
- Experience indicates that decentralization and outsourcing do not necessarily bring with them the advantages promised.
- Expansion of ICTs for YAE purposes is counterbalanced with improvisation, poor use of such technologies, poor criteria to decide on the best one or the best combination to use in each specific case, and – most importantly – neglect of the essential interpersonal pedagogical relationship.
- Cost-efficiency applied to YAE is often understood as 'cheaper and quicker', thus leading to an amplified vicious circle of low quality and poor results.

CHALLENGES FOR THE FUTURE

A common language. The terminological labyrinth is an old concern in the field of education and especially of YAE worldwide. Glossaries have been proposed and produced over the past few decades, but the terminological/conceptual confusion persists and becomes more acute as new terms emerge. Once again, during the CONFINTEA VI process, and specifically in the case of Latin America and the Caribbean, it was agreed that a common language is essential if we want to communicate better and also give more scientific consistency to the field.

Lack of evidence and lack of financial resources: two myths to be revisited. Two myths must be revisited with regard to YAE and for education in general: in order to receive more attention (a) more evidence and (b) more financial resources are needed. In fact, there is plenty of research evidence, for several decades now, regarding the multiple benefits of investing in YAE, for learners themselves, for their families and communities, and for citizenship-building and national democracy. Abundant research shows that YAE has positive effects on the self-esteem and life opportunities of men and women as well as on their children's wellbeing with respect to child mortality, child birth, rearing practices, access to school and learning outcomes, etc. It is clear that lack of attention to YAE is not related to insufficient data, evidence or conceptual clarity, as argued in the 2009 EFA Global Monitoring Report.[4] There is more than enough knowledge available on YAE – theoretical and empirical, regional and international – to indicate what needs to be done and to be done well. The main shortcoming concerns action, not information and knowledge.

On the other hand, the *financial deficit* is only a manifestation of a *political deficit*, namely the lack of political will to make education a priority and to invest in the poor on the basis of quality and equity. Addressing the political deficit is the real priority. Also, as evaluations in the field of school education reiterate, there is no direct and necessary connection between more financial resources and better education. What is needed is not only *more* – usually highlighted – but *better use* of available resources, precisely because they are scarce. Parameters of what is 'good spending' and 'good international co-operation' in YAE must be established.

Internationally, in 2005, the Global Campaign for Education proposed "at least 3% of the education budget" allocated to adult literacy in order to attain the EFA goal of reducing illiteracy by half by 2015. Regionally, the Final Document of the Mexico CONFINTEA VI Regional Conference (Sep. 2008) requested 3% for YAE in general, and not only for literacy. Many countries have set financial benchmarks for the education sector in their constitutions, laws and/or policies. Most of them aim at reaching, over several years, 6% of the GNP allocated to education. It is thus clear that the fight for higher financial resources devoted to YAE must be associated with the fight for more and sustained financial resources and attention dedicated to education as a whole.

Time for action and for investing in people. Lots of money are spent on research that has little relevance and impact on actual decision-making and on costly events and publications that reach only a few. They are spent on reiterated diagnoses that repeat the same problems and the same information. It is time to revise the allocation of scarce financial resources at all levels, from governments and international agencies to organizations of civil society. It is time for action, for making sure that policies and laws are effectively implemented, and that what is already known is translated into practice. It is time for investing in the people, in the capacities and qualities of those engaged in YAE at all levels, not only facilitators on the ground, but also those in planning, organizing and managerial positions.

Holistic approach. Whatever the advances or inertias, they must be attributed not solely to education in general and to YAE in particular but also and primarily to the political, social and economic contexts in which education occurs. YAE deals with the most disadvantageous situations and with the most vulnerable segments of society, those most affected by poverty, exclusion, and subordination in many aspects: political, economic, social, cultural, linguistic. How much more or better could be done under the concrete circumstances, in each case, remains an open question with at least one clear answer: unless there are important economic and social changes in the overall conditions of the population served by YAE, YAE will not be able to fulfill its mission. It is time to rethink the equation: education by itself cannot fight poverty and exclusion, unless specific and intended economic and social policies – not just compensatory programmes – are in place to deal with them in a radical manner. YAE is not an independent variable.

Recuperate the transformative role of education and of YAE specifically. The role of education is not to ensure enrolment, retention, completion and accreditation. The ultimate mission is to enhance personal and social change, to ensure relevant learning, awareness raising, critical and creative thinking, informed and committed action, citizenship building. YAE's historical critical and transformative nature has been lost and must be recuperated, challenging conformity and mere social adaptation promoted by current times and ideologies dominating the world. Learners must be educated as citizens, not only as people in need of certain basic skills, but also in need of knowing their rights and duties so as to be better able to fight for them.

From literacy to lifelong learning. "From literacy to lifelong learning" was the title chosen for the CONFINTEA VI regional preparatory conference held in Mexico (Sep. 2008). In other words, the challenge to move from the usual narrow understandings of *adult education* as equivalent to *adult literacy*, from *adult education* to *adult learning* and to *lifelong learning*, anywhere and anytime: in the family, in the community, at work, through the media, through art, social participation and through the active exercise of citizenship. The right to education today is no longer the right to basic literacy, to access school or to complete a number of years of schooling, but the right to learn and to learn throughout life, from early childhood to late adulthood.

NOTES

[1] Previously published in LLinE – Lifelong Learning in Europe, Vol. XXVI, No. 4, 2011. Permission to republish granted by KVS, Finland. (Torres, 2011).
[2] About the current situation of the region, see: ECLAC's *Social Panorama of Latin America 2011* "Poverty and Indigence Levels Are the Lowest in 20 Years in Latin America" "Good tidings from the south: Less poor, and less unequal", *The Economist*, 3 Dec. 2011.
[3] Lifelong Learning is *Aprendizaje a lo largo de toda la vida* in Spanish. Most translators continue to use *education* and *learning* in an undifferentiated manner. The Delors Report entitled "Learning, the Treasure within" was translated into Spanish as "La *educación* encierra un tesoro". The 1st World Forum on Lifelong Learning (Paris, October 2008) was translated as *Foro Mundial para la Educación y la Formación a lo largo de la vida* and into French as *Forum Mondial pour l'Education et la Formation Tout au Long de la Vie.*

[4] Also, "the fact that no clear quantitative targets were established at Dakar, apart from the main literacy target, may have contributed to a lack of urgency. In addition, the language of the commitment is ambiguous. Some read goal 3 as calling for universal access to learning and life-skills programmes, but others, including the drafters of the Dakar Framework, understand no such intent." (EFA GMR 2009, 2008: 91).

REFERENCES

Caruso, A., Di Pierro, M. C., Ruiz, M., & Camilo, M. (2008). *Situación presente de la educación de personas jóvenes y adultas en América Latina y el Caribe, Informe Regional.* (present situation concerning adult & youth education in Latin American and the Caribbean. Regional Report), Pátzcuaro, Mexico: CREFAL-CEAAL.

Jacinto, C. (2007). From education to employment: Working it out in Latin America. *IIEP Newsletter, XXV*(4).

Jacinto, C. (2008). *Enfoques y estrategias de la capacitación laboral de jóvenes desempleados en América Latina.¿Algo ha cambiado en años recientes?* (Approaches and Strategies for work empowerment of unemployed youth in latin America. What has changed in recent years?)Paris: IIPE-UNESCO. (Currently being translated into English for on-line publication as *Trends in Technical Education and Training in Latin America.*)

OEI (Organization of Ibero-American States). (2006). *Plan iberoamericano de alfabetización y educación básica de personas jóvenes y adultas 2007–2015, Documento base.* (Ibero-American plan for adult & youth basic education 2007–2015. Basic document) http://www.oei.es/alfabetizacion/documento_base.pdf.

Torres, R. M. (2004). *Lifelong learning in the south: Critical issues and opportunities for adult education,* SIDA studies 11, Stockholm: SIDA.

Torres, R. M. (2009). *Youth and adult education and learning in Latin America and the Caribbean: Trends, issues and challenges. Regional report prepared for the sixth international conference on adult education CONFINTEA VI, Belém, Brazil,* Hamburg: the UNESCO Institute for Lifelong Learning (UIL).

Torres, R. M. (2011). Youth & adult education and lifelong learning in Latin America and the Caribbean. *LLinE – Lifelong Learning in Europe, XXVI* (4), pp. 210–217.

UNESCO Brazil/OEI Brazil (2008). *Educación en prisiones en latinoamérica. Derechos humanos, Libertad y ciudadanía* (Education in Prisons in Latin America. Human Rights, Freedom ad Citizenship), Brasilia: UNESCO/OEI.

Warican, J. S. (2008). *Public policies,strategies and programmes for literacy and adult education in nations of the Caribbean 2003–2008* (working document). University of the West Indies (UWI). (mimeo)

AFFILIATION

Rosa Maria Torres
Researcher and International Adviser specialized in lifelong learning,
based in Ecuador

D. W. LIVINGSTONE

4. THE LEARNING SOCIETY: PAST, PRESENT AND FUTURE VIEWS[1]

INTRODUCTION

In this chapter, I will try to outline briefly the development of learning activities through time in human societies. I will then consider what, if anything, is distinctive about the form and extent of these activities in the current market-driven societies in which the notions of lifelong learning and learning society have become very widely promoted. Finally, I will suggest a few steps toward the fuller realization of these notions.

Continual acquisition and sharing of knowledge and skill to cope with our changing environment defines *Homo sapiens*. –urvive and gain partial control of our environment has involved the invention of powerful mediating tools and the social construction of complex systems of language and culture. Learning to use these tools and language systems has been intimately linked with the work of developing them throughout most of human history. The consequent edifices and institutions now dwarf the creations of any other species. Learning for less instrumental interests also became more common when and if our environmental adaptation became more secure. We are becoming more aware of the communicative and knowledge capacities among other animals, but the quest for knowledge has been our most distinctive intrinsic feature since the origin of our species. In this sense, human societies have always been learning societies

It is deeply ironic that the same inventive capacities that have enabled our species to flourish in the natural environment which frequently threatened our very survival now threaten the very survival of the same natural environment. Along with our unprecedented civilizational achievements, we have created a potent mix of air, water and soil pollution, global warming, widespread conditions of impoverishment, war as well as the prospects of nuclear winter, and a massive collective institutional incapacity to comprehend the long-term consequences of our interventions in our global ecosystem. In this respect, we may be <u>becoming increasingly willfully ignorant societies rather than learning ones.</u>

I will suggest that learning as a process needs to be understood at three different levels of abstraction: the intrinsic activities we all do in our lives; the institutionalized practices of any given society; and the images and ideologies of "a good education" advocated in that society. A comparative historical perspective can aid in clarifying these different views of learning and their relations.

PAST VIEWS OF THE LEARNING SOCIETY

Recently, biologists have discovered, in the DNA of chromosome 7, a genetic mutation that all *homo sapiens* share which is associated with our smaller, weaker jaws than other primates, and perhaps our bigger brains. This mutation is estimated to have occurred about 2.5 million years ago in the grasslands of East Africa, about the same time as tool-making seems to have begun (Verrengia, 2004). By that time, the hands of *homo erectus* had become free and had attained greater dexterity than any simian, hands that adapted to ever new, more complicated operations or labours. The capacity to deal proactively with the natural environment began with the development of handmade tools and associated labours of hunting and gathering which brought our ancestors closer together in joint activities. These activities required the development of speech. Harnessing of fire, domestication of animals, sedentary agriculture all massively enhanced our survival capacity. The Lascaux cave paintings in France, dating from 13,000 BC, have been widely regarded as evidence of the development of graphic representation leading to the symbolisms of writing and reckoning which are often taken as the basis of modern civilization and our capability to transcend local time and space. Recent archaeological research in the Loiyangalani river valley in Tanzania has found evidence, in the form of ostrich egg shell beads, pigment and ochre pencils, that our ancestors actually developed symbolic thinking over 40,000 years ago (Fox, 2004, p. K3) and there is some evidence emerging from over 90,000 years ago (Vianello, 2004).

In any case, spinning, weaving, metalworking, pottery and navigation all developed many millennia ago, as well as the beginnings of trade, industry, art and science. As tribes developed into hierarchically organized states, law, politics and religion, which were products of the minds of elite groups who gained control of surplus production, came to dominate human societies. As Frederick Engels (1876, p. 7) observed in one of his later writings:

> [T]he more modest productions of the working hand retreated into the background, the more so since the mind that planned the labour was able, at a very early stage in the development of society...to have the labour that had been planned carried out by other hands than its own. All merit for the swift advance of civilization was ascribed to the mind, to the development and activity of the brain. Men became accustomed to explain their actions as arising out of thought instead of their needs (which in any case are reflected and perceived in the mind); and so in the course of time there emerged that idealistic world outlook which, especially since the fall of the world of antiquity, has dominated men's (sic) minds.

There is now considerable evidence that in early human societies there was little direct teaching of youth by adults; rather, children learned in a family setting by imitating adults with older playmates leading, and took important tasks such as childcare, household chores, minor hunting and foraging early on (Herzog, 1974).

In later civilizations, while adult instruction of youths became more prominent, mainly oral and apprenticeship methods of education continued to predominate (Myers, 1960). However, at least in the major Western civilizations (e.g. Mesopotamia, Ancient Egypt, Greece, Rome) as a growing economic surplus developed, systems of writing and records were created in urban centres. A small part of the population released from primary production was trained in formal court and temple schools as professional scribes and other specialists to use these practical means to "administer" this surplus (Smith, 1955). This was the origin of formal schooling in the basic form we know it today. These schools were first to prepare the professional scribes for the ruling class and later became associated with centres of research and systemization of knowledge. But the vast majority continued to obtain their vocational training and any other knowledge through oral methods in family settings.

Throughout most of human history, most of our learning has occurred in intimate relation to our labours and the rest of our everyday lives; formal schools and abstract ideologies of learning have been of little consequence for most people. I will not dwell here on the history of formal schooling, except to note that it remained essentially the preserve of kings, priests and their minions through the Middle Ages until the emergence of industrial capitalism a few centuries ago.

As free wage labour replaced indentured serfdom and landless peasants roamed for work, traditional family apprenticeships broke down and mass compulsory public schooling emerged. Nineteenth century class struggles over control and content of schools were often intense (Simon, 1974), but they generally resulted in diluted and more coercive versions of pre-capitalist forms. The institutionalization of mass public schooling has proceeded apace until today it is generally regarded as the most common form of education, even thought of by some as identical with learning. Primary and secondary schooling have become nearly universal in advanced market societies and the little red school house has become the big centre of learning in most communities. Majorities of graduates now pursue some form of tertiary level education, and supporters of educational equity advocate the expansion of adult education programs as the next logical step in lifelong education.

The dominant ideologies of learning that emerged with hierarchically organized class societies appear to have stressed the intricacy or mystical nature of ruling specialist knowledge while subordinate group ideologies emphasized the benefits of their "really useful", practical knowledge. Industrial capitalism rent the veil of secrecy of medieval craft guilds and promised democratic access to literacy and advanced working knowledge through mass schooling. This dominant ideology has now grown into calls of lifelong learning for all. But selection for higher levels of public schooling has always discriminated against lower classes and various ethnic minorities, while the numbers of more highly credentialled specialists who continue to claim exclusive knowledge has continued to increase.

So, with regard to the different levels of abstraction of learning, our actual learning activities have generally been fused with our labour and other practical activities. Institutional learning has been the preserve of ruling elites until it became partially democratized with industrial capitalism. The dominant ideology of learning has shifted from celebrating rare brilliance and perseverance to promising something for everyone. With this brief tour of the past, we can more clearly make sense of the "learning society" claims about the present moment.

But first a word about labour per se. I have already alluded to the first major separation of learning and labour: the division of labour between direct producers and ruling "intellectual" elites which arose with sustained production of economic surpluses. From slave and feudal societies to capitalism, paid employment has become increasingly separated from household economies. Virtually every form of good or service has become vulnerable to conversion into wage labour that could produce vendible commodities for profit. Other household and community labours became increasingly devalued if not invisible.

PRESENT VIEWS

So an adequate understanding of contemporary relations between learning and labour requires careful consideration of the "underlayers" of both, that is, unpaid as well as paid forms of work, and informal as well as formal learning activities. In industrialized market societies, as Graph 1 outlines, there are at least four distinguishable forms of materially-based activity (paid employment, housework, community volunteer work and leisure including hobbies, hygiene and rest) and four forms of learning (informal training, non-taught informal learning, initial formal schooling, and further or continuing adult education).

Forms of basic activity		Forms of learning
• Paid employment • Unpaid housework • Community volunteer work • Leisure time (hygiene, hobbies, rest)	→ ←	• Informal education • Non-taught learning • Formal schooling • Further education

Graph 1. Forms of Activity and Learning.

"Work" is now commonly regarded as synonymous with "earning a living" through *paid employment* in the production, distribution and exchange of goods and services commodities. But most of us still must also do some household work and many need to contribute to community labours in order to reproduce ourselves and society. Both housework and community volunteer work are typically unpaid and underappreciated, but they remain essential for our survival and quality of life (see Waring, 1988). *Household work*, including cooking, cleaning, childcare and other often complex household tasks, has been largely relegated to women and only gained some public recognition as women have gained power through increased participation in paid employment. As community life has become more fragmented with dual-earner commuter households, time devoted to *community work* to sustain and build social life through local associations and helping neighbours has declined, and the productive importance of this work has been rediscovered as "social capital" (Putnam, 2000). All three forms of labour should be included in any careful accounting of contemporary work practices. Leisure refers to all those activities we do most immediately for ourselves, albeit often out of necessity, including personal hygiene, rest and sleep, and various hobbies.

"Learning", in the most generic sense, involves the gaining of knowledge, skill or understanding anytime and anywhere through individual and group processes. Learning occurs throughout our lives. The sites of learning make up a continuum ranging from spontaneous responses to everyday life to highly organized participation in formal education programs. The dominant tendency in contemporary thought has been to equate learning with the provision of learning opportunities in settings organized by institutional authorities and led by teachers approved by these authorities. *Formal education* has frequently been identified with continuous enrolment in age-graded, bureaucratically-structured institutions of formal schooling from early childhood to tertiary levels, ignoring other types of instruction in bodies of traditional knowledge in subordinate groups (see Illich, 1971). In addition, *further or continuing adult education* includes a diverse array of further education courses and workshops in many institutionally organized settings, from schools to workplaces and community centres. Such continuing education is the most evident site of lifelong learning for adults past the initial cycle of schooling. But we also continually engage, as we always have, in intrinsic informal learning activities to acquire knowledge or skill outside of the curricula of institutions providing educational programs, courses or workshops. *Informal education or training* occurs when mentors take responsibility for instructing others without sustained reference to a pre-established curriculum in more incidental or spontaneous situations, such as guiding them in learning job skills or in community development activities. Finally, all other forms of explicit or tacit learning in which we engage either individually or collectively without direct reliance on a teacher/mentor or an externally-organized curriculum can be termed *non-taught self-directed or collective informal learning*. As my colleague Allen Tough (1978) has observed, informal learning is the submerged part of the iceberg of adult learning activities. It is likely that, for most adults, informal learning (including both informal training and non-taught learning activities) continues to represent our most important learning for coping with our changing environment. No account of "lifelong learning" can be complete without considering peoples' informal learning activities as well as their initial formal schooling and further adult education courses through the life course.

All of these forms of human activity are relational processes rather than categorical ones. But the dominant focus on relations between paid employment and organized education ignores significant interactions between these and other forms of work and learning. Valuable transfers of knowledge and skill among these four basic forms of learning and the other forms of our activities may be unrecognized or discouraged by current workplace design, for example (see Livingstone, 2003).

Many observers have celebrated the arrival of a fundamentally new "post-industrial" or "knowledge-based economy" (KBE). Advocates of KBE generally assume the centrality of occupations requiring advanced cognitive skills in management and technical design work as well as a general imperative upgrading of the skills needed for all types of employment (Bell, 1973; Reich, 1991). The direct evidence presented to demonstrate the KBE typically has focused on showing the increasing prevalence of service sectors over primary extractive and secondary manufacturing industries, and allusions to rapid growth of specific occupations such as computer analysts. KBE advocates have not identified specific thresholds for its realization but there is usually a strong implication of the prevalence of knowledge workers engaged in complex planning and design work. As summarized in Graph 2, a Canadian census-based analysis of occupational distributions over the 1971–96 period (Lavoie & Roy, 1998) provides one of the most extensive estimates to date of the actual extent of movement toward KBE.

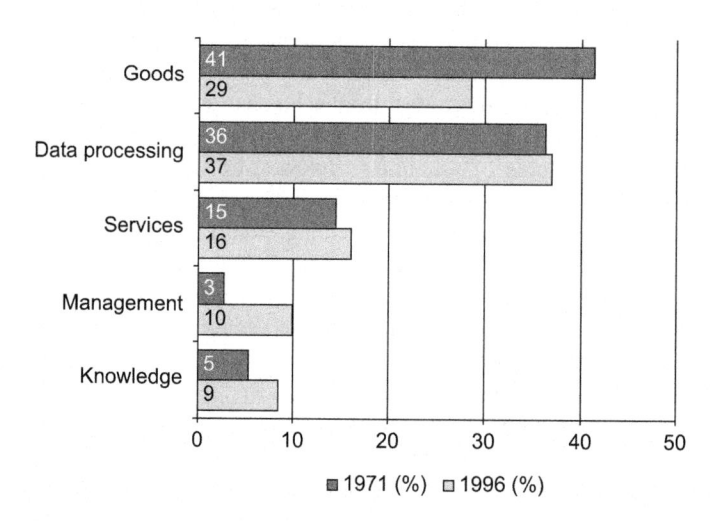

Occupation	1971 (%)	1996 (%)
Goods	41	29
Data processing	36	37
Services	15	16
Management	3	10
Knowledge	5	9

Graph 2. Employment by Type of Occupation, Canada, 1971–1996.
Source: Lavoie & Roy (1998).

There were significant changes over this period in the redistribution of jobs from goods production to services, data processing and especially management and knowledge work. The proportion of people in management occupations nearly quadrupled. But, those in knowledge-based occupations involving mainly the generation of ideas or provision of expert opinion – such as scientists, engineers, and artists – remained a very small proportion of the entire employment picture. In spite of fairly rapid growth over this period, knowledge workers still made up less than 10 percent of the labour force in 1996. While details of this occupational classification may be disputed, it is clear that the vast majority of the Canadian labour force continued to be employed in jobs that require fairly routinized transmission of data, processing of goods or provision of personal services. As the authors of this report themselves concluded (Lavoie & Roy, 1998, p. 15): "Based on this one-time snapshot of employment it is rather difficult to make the case that Canada has become a knowledge-based economy."

The rate of change in the general skill requirements of the Canadian job structure during most of this period has also been estimated based on census data on occupational composition for the 1971–91 period (Leckie, 1996). There was a gradual skill upgrading trend. On measures of the general educational development (GED) required for jobs, the length of specific vocational preparation (SVP) needed to perform the job adequately, and the levels of cognitive complexity, task diversity and responsibility in job descriptions, this analysis consistently found gradually declining proportions of the lowest skilled jobs and comparable increases in the highest skilled jobs, resulting in net skill increases of around 10 percent over this entire 20 year period. Other Canadian and international analyses based on large-scale surveys for the post-WWII era (see Livingstone, 2003 for detailed reviews) generally confirm this pattern of gradual skill upgrading. The most thorough empirical assessments of skill changes in the U.S. – which was the original source of claims about the shift to a knowledge-based economy – have also found little evidence for more than a gradual increase in job skill requirements either in the entire post WWII period or in more recent trends (Barton, 2000; Handel, 2000). U.S. Bureau of Labor Statistics' estimates project that only about 20 percent of job openings will require a university degree in the early part of this century, compared with over a third of new entrants who have one, while the vast majority of new jobs will require only short-term training (Hecker, 2001). The weight of empirical evidence clearly indicates substantially less skill upgrading of jobs than the heralds of the knowledge-based economy typically assume. Future discussions of increasing demand for more highly skilled knowledge workers should pay at least as much attention to the slower growing forest of routine data transmitting, service providing and goods processing jobs as to the faster growing knowledge work trees.

A more substantial change in the composition of the paid labour force in the past few generations has been the growing participation of women and especially married women with children. As Graph 3 indicates, male participation rates have been fairly stable, while women's have doubled since the mid-1960s.

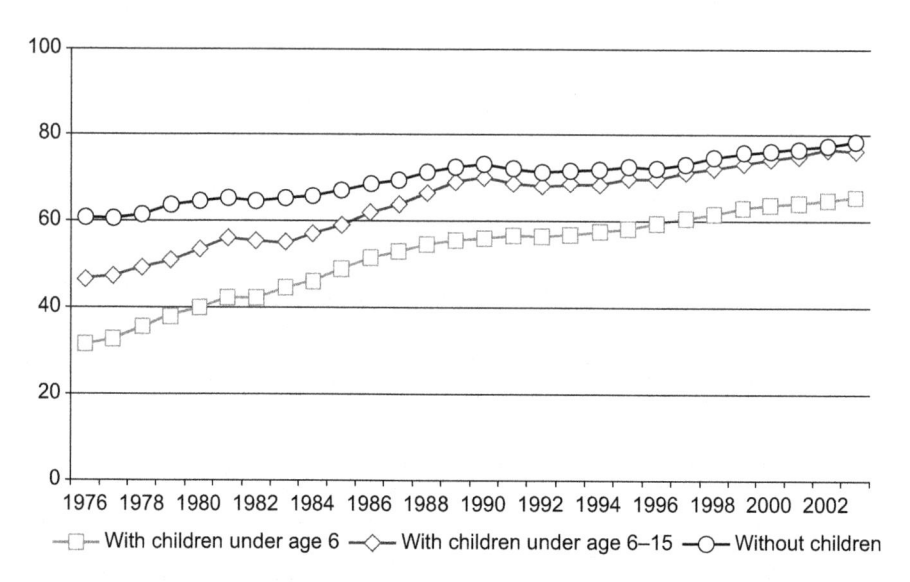

Graph 3. Percentage of Women Employed, with and without Children, Canada, 1976–2003.
Source: Statistics Canada (2004).

Working for pay is now a pervasive activity for both men and women. Our WALL national survey[2] estimates that 95 percent of the entire 18+ Canadian population have now worked for pay in their lives, 85 percent in the past decade, and half of all of those not currently in the labour force indicate they expect to look for a job in the next year. In spite of formal educational qualifications that may now exceed men's, women still face formidable barriers to job mobility. The majority of married women still do most of the housework, are much more likely to be employed part-time. Although women are now approaching half of the labour force in Canada as well as the US and UK, they make up only about a third of those in managerial posts, as Graph 4 summarizes.

What's more, women still rarely manage men. In 2004, around 15 percent of men were managed by women, up from only 5 percent a generation earlier. But the vast majority of women managers manage only women, typically in lower paid jobs. The "glass ceiling" for women is most evident at top management levels. While women may have greater token representation on corporate boards, they still only make up around 10 percent of board members and 1 percent of CEOs and the inside directors from whom CEOs are typically selected (Livingstone & Pollock, 2004). As long as women are delegated most of the housework, vital as this is, their relative chances of reaching employment levels consistent with their talents and formal qualifications will continue to be jeopardized by lack of time and energy to engage effectively in social and political networks of power. Researchers have increasingly recognized that continued informal training and untaught learning are important for success of

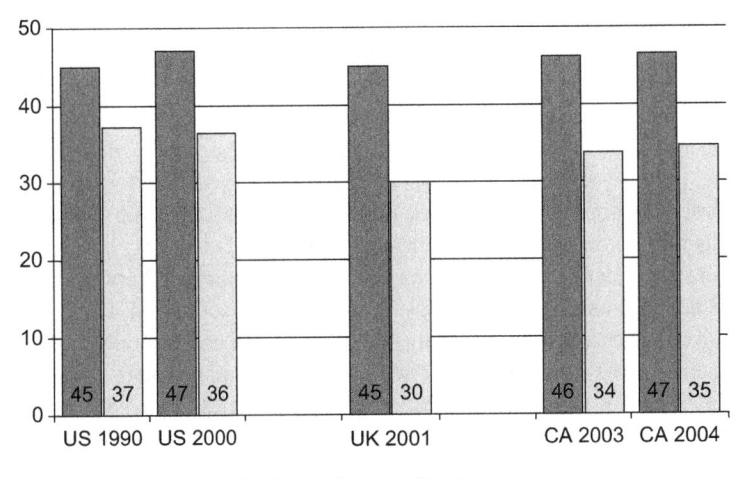

Graph 4. Women in Managerial Positions, U.S., U.K., and Canada.
Source: Livingstone & Pollock (2004).

both men and women in the context of paid workplaces (e.g. Betcherman, Leckie, McMullen, 1997; Center for Workforce Development, 1998; Matthews & Candy, 1999). By all direct accounts, through a combination of initial schooling, further adult education, informal training and non-taught learning, the vast majority of workers manage to become at least adequately qualified for their current jobs. The finding that highly qualified women are highly underrepresented in top management is probably an indicator of persistent sexism especially in informal learning networks.

Yet the dominant discourse about the rapid emergence of a "knowledge-based economy" and the frequent call for creation of "learning organizations" largely ignores or depreciates these realities of interaction between organized education, informal training and untaught learning and job performance. KBE discourse presumes that the central challenge for improved enterprise performance is for workers to become more active and motivated individual learners.

This is not a new story. Throughout the history of industrial capitalist societies, formal education has been looked to as the solution to economic problems and crises (see Curti, 1935). In this sense, current appeals for people to become greater lifelong learners continues a familiar mantra that more and better education will provide economic salvation. Of course, nobody would argue against more and better education. But to insist that more education and training are the primary solution to economic problems, to the exclusion of any serious address to economic reforms themselves—as many current politicians do—is merely to divert attention from the central problem, lack of decent jobs.

In all capitalist societies, inter-firm competition, technological innovation, and conflicts between employers and employees over working conditions, benefits and knowledge requirements all lead to incessant shifts in the numbers and types of jobs available. Population growth cycles, modified household needs and new legislative regulations also frequently serve to alter the supply of labour. At the same time, popular demand for general education and specialized training increases cumulatively as people generally seek more knowledge, different skills and added credentials in order to live and work in such a changing society.

In capitalist societies, there are always some "mismatches" between employers' aggregate demand and requirements for employees on the one hand, and the aggregate supply and qualifications of job seekers on the other. The accelerating productivity of capitalist enterprises regularly throws workers into unemployment, reproducing the most evident part of a reserve army of labour. In societies like Canada with liberal democratic state regimes that acclaim the right to equal educational opportunity, and with labour markets in which both employers and job seekers make mainly individual employment choices, the *dominant* historical tendency has been for the supply of educationally qualified job seekers to exceed the demand for most types of job. These same dynamics also generate some formal underqualification of some workers, particularly older employees who are experienced and competent in their jobs but have had few incentives to upgrade their credentialed skills.

But, the gap between workers' educational qualifications and job requirements has been growing. While there has only been very gradual net upgrading of the actual skill requirements of jobs in general over the past few generations, formal educational attainments have seen explosive growth. As Graph 5 shows, Canadian participation in post-secondary education grew about six-fold between the early 1960s and the late 1990s to world-leading levels, with nearly half of the 20–64 population having attained a post-secondary credential by 1996 and over 60 percent of the 25 to 29 age cohort getting one.

As Graph 6 shows, adult course participation in Canada expanded even more rapidly, from 4 percent in 1960 to 35 percent in the early 1990s. While the adult course participation rate may have declined a bit in the mid-1990 by some estimates, it then rebounded. Over 40 percent of adults participated in some type of formal education in 2004. This puts Canada "in the ballpark" with various other advanced capitalist societies but trailing Scandinavia. Many other advanced capitalist societies have similarly large increases in participation in post-secondary education and more gradual increase in job entry requirements (see Livingstone, 2003).

Before we look more closely at this formal education-jobs gap, we should recall that informal education and non-taught learning have remained foundational in all modern societies. Some new insights in this area have been generated by the research networks on New Approaches to Lifelong Learning (NALL) and the Changing Nature of Work and Lifelong Learning (WALL) which conducted the first inclusive Canadian surveys of work and learning in 1998 and 2004 with representative national samples of adults. Respondents were asked about their paid employment,

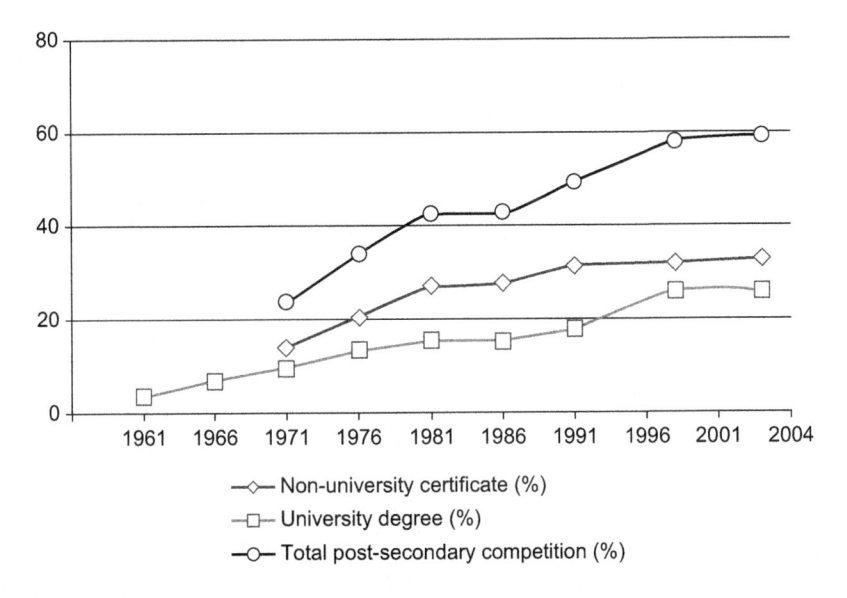

THE LEARNING SOCIETY: PAST, PRESENT AND FUTURE VIEWS

Graph 5. Post-secondary Education Completion (%) 25–29 Age Group, Canada, 1961–2004.
Sources: Livingstone (2002): WALL (2004); Special tabulations.

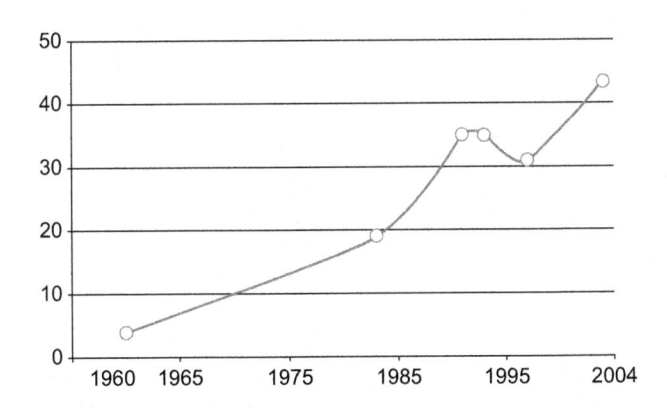

Graph 6. Participation in Further Education, Canadians Over 17, 1960–2004 (%).
Sources: Livingstone (2002); WALL (2004).

housework, community volunteer work, as well as their schooling, further education and informal learning related to each sphere of work and other general interests. (The survey design and basic findings are available at the research network website www.wallnetwork.ca)

According to these surveys, well over 80 percent of Canadian adults report devoting time to intentional informal learning activities related to their paid employment, household duties, community volunteer work and other general interests, respectively. The average time spent was over 14 hours a week. Such intentional informal learning is much more extensive than further education courses in which only a minority of all adults currently spend an average of only a few hours per week. This iceberg of adult learning also ignores the tacit learning which is probably much more extensive. It should also be underlined that the distribution of the basic incidence of intentional informal learning is quite equitable regardless of prior schooling. In the 1998 NALL survey, as Graph 7 shows, school dropouts and university graduates spent very similar amounts of time in informal learning.

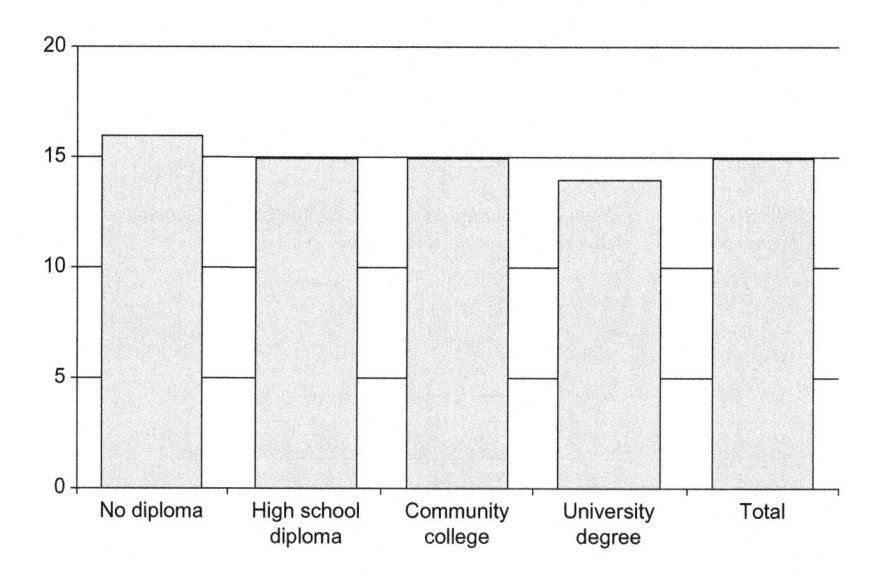

Graph 7. Informal Learning by Level of Schooling, Avg. hours per week, Canada, 1998. Source: Livingstone (2002).

Similarly, there appears to be little difference in the amount of time those in different occupational classes devote to informal learning. The vast majority of workers continue to be actively involved in quite extensive employment-related informal learning activities. Indeed, industrial workers may spend even more time in employment-related informal learning than occupational classes with higher formal educational participation rates – perhaps partly to compensate for limited access to formal courses. Much of this learning is quite creative and generates competent skills, often beyond those skills actually needed to do their jobs, as our case studies with workers in several union locals have documented (see Livingstone & Sawchuk, 2004). "Discouraged workers" and others outside the current "active" labour force also continue to be quite active informal learners in other spheres. Neither chronic unemployment nor other forms of underemployment have much diminished the pursuit of lifelong learning.

In contrast, the gap in completion of post-secondary education participation between corporate executives, professionals and managers on the one hand and industrial and service workers on the other has been stark. As Graph 8 shows, the majority of the former have obtained degrees while only a small proportion of workers have. However, the gap between them in participation in further education is much less and shrinking. In addition, the proportions of younger industrial and service workers obtaining post-secondary education has been increasing quite rapidly.

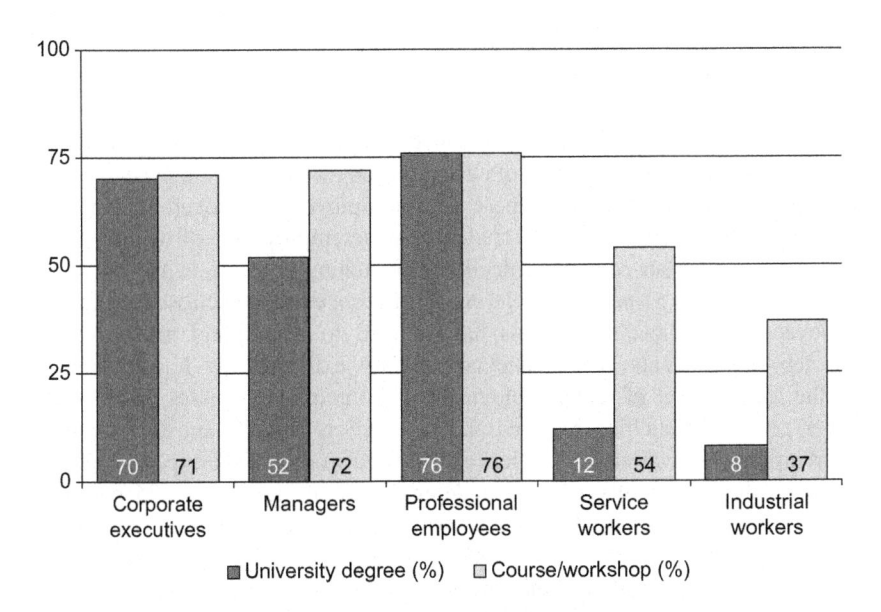

Occupational Class	University degree (%)	Course/workshop (%)
Corporate executives	70	71
Managers	52	72
Professional employees	76	76
Service workers	12	54
Industrial workers	8	37

Graph 8. Schooling and Further Education by Occupational Class, Canadian Labour Force, 1999.
Source: Livingstone (2002).

Even limiting the knowledge focus to formal education, many people now find themselves *underemployed* in the sense that they are unable to use many of their employment-related qualifications in current jobs. As I have documented in detail in several books (Livingstone, 2002, 2003, 2009), there are at least six dimensions of underemployment. The books address two time-based measures (general unemployment and involuntary reduced employment) and three skill-based measures (talent use gap, credential gap and performance gap), as well as subjective underemployment – which could reference either time or skill-based criteria or both.

[note: need post-sec ↑ 60% : 28% - 45%
# of people obtaining : 22 - 56% ↑ 150%]

e dimension, the credential gap. I have already observed have increased rapidly while changes in educational cture have been more gradual. Only 28 per cent of y degree or a college diploma to get their jobs in 1983. to 45 per cent, an increase of 60 per cent. But, during lary credential attainment more than doubled from 22 crease of over 150 per cent. Clearly, many more people ducation during this period than needed it to get their that these credentials, including a high school diploma, or entry to all manner of jobs. Such increases may well ential inflation beyond actual performance requirements in some instances. Certainly, some who entered employment prior to 1983 with lower formal education may have found that entry requirements increased, but they continued to perform their job without increased credentials. Generally, workers are keeping up with or ahead of required credential levels. This is also true of required computer skills, even though these have increased quite rapidly (Livingstone 2010).

Graph 9 summarizes the extent of education-job match with reference to levels of credential attainment and requirement for all employees. The overall change from 1983 to 2004 was an increase in credential underemployment of about 6 percent to 31 percent, and an equivalent decline in matching credentials and attainments from 57 per cent to 51 per cent. In terms of different employee classes, professional employees' specialized credentials have tended to correspond most closely to their job requirements. They have consistently exhibited the highest matching and the lowest level of underemployment of all employee classes. In 2004, over 60 per cent had matching required and attained credentials, and their credential underemployment was around 20 per cent. Service workers have experienced higher and increasing levels of credential underemployment, going from 25 per cent in 1983 to 36 per cent in 2004. Industrial workers have had consistently high levels of credential underemployment, about one-third in both 1983 and 2004. Managers show wide fluctuations during this period, with high levels of underqualification in 1983 but much lower underqualification and increasing levels of underemployment in 2004. Such fluctuations may suggest that other personal network and allegiance factors may be more pertinent than formal credentials for those in positions of formal managerial authority (see Elliot, 2000). But the most basic points are that credential underemployment has been increasing both generally and in most employees classes, and that underemployment of workers' skills and knowledge is much more likely than underqualification for their jobs.

These estimates should be taken with a grain of salt. More in-depth case studies do suggest that workers are often quite adept at adapting detailed requirements of their jobs to better match their actual skills (Livingstone, 2009). More accurate measures of people's employment-related skills and knowledge and the extent of correspondence with available jobs are certainly needed, as well as longitudinal cohort studies. But the weight of empirical evidence, on credential match and other

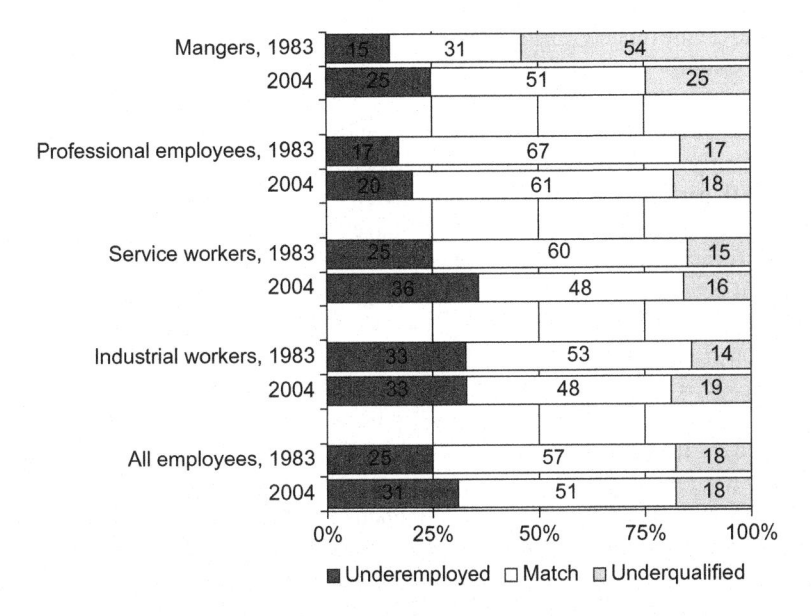

Employee Class	Year	Underemployed	Match	Underqualified
Managers	1983	15	31	54
	2004	25	51	25
Professional employees	1983	17	67	17
	2004	20	61	18
Service workers	1983	25	60	15
	2004	36	48	16
Industrial workers	1983	33	53	14
	2004	33	48	19
All employees	1983	25	57	18
	2004	31	51	18

Graph 9. Credential Match, by Employee Class, Canada, 1983–2004 (%).
Source: Livingstone (2009).

measures, continues to suggest that the actual skill development of the employed workforce generally exceeds job requirements.

Even more pertinently, the greatest discrepancies are clearly experienced by those with the least economic or political power to define the appropriate requirements for their work. The highest levels of underutilization of working knowledge is in jobs held by those in lower occupational class positions, as well as among those whose general subordination in society has put them at a disadvantage in negotiations over working conditions, especially women, younger people, ethnic and racial minorities, recent immigrants and those labelled as "disabled". This constitutes a major waste of talent.

The relative correspondence between different types of work and relevant *informal* learning activities also may vary according to how much discretionary control people can exercise over their work. There may be greater levels of correspondence between unpaid work and informal learning because of less pronounced power hierarchies in these spheres of activity than in paid work and formal education settings. In particular, since people are not generally compelled to do community volunteer work, relevant informal learning activities have been found to be more closely associated with involvement in this sort of work than either hierarchically structured employment or necessary domestic labour (Livingstone, 2001). This may suggest that a most effective way to increase correspondence between jobs learning may be to increase job control through workplace [democratization.]

[In summary, there] appear to have been only gradual changes in skill upgrading [of the occupational str]ucture and incremental gains in the proportion of jobs [actually performin]g the knowledge work of planning and design during the [post-WWII period, wh]ile rates of completion of post-compulsory schooling and participation in further education courses have grown exponentially. Employment-related informal learning remains even more extensive. Rates of underemployment– in terms of general unemployment, involuntary reduced employment and educational attainments exceeding job requirements– have also grown significantly during this period (Livingstone, 2003). Such evidence suggests that we already live in a "learning society" in both formal and informal educational terms, but not yet in an effectively "knowledge-based economy."

In any case, further empirical studies of the full range of learning and work relations are likely to provide a more effective guide to policy making in the "new economy" of today than the simple assumptions of human capital theory or a knowledge-based economy perspective fixated on exhorting greater investments in formal education to the exclusion of serious attention to learning and work relationships.

FUTURE VIEWS

Conversion of more aspects of everyday production and consumption into saleable commodities continues, along with commercialization of further aspects of both domestic labour and previously voluntary community labours. But *limits to indefinite further capitalist expansion are becoming evident* in terms of environmental degradation and various forms of global underemployment. In addition, many people are recognizing the social value of their own housework and child care work and are beginning to renegotiate and effectively juggle domestic divisions of paid and unpaid labour rather than conceding the conversion of more intimate aspects of housework into profit-seeking activity. Similarly, volunteer community work is frequently valued precisely because it is freely chosen in relation to our strongest interests and people are generally loathe to pay others to perform their most fulfilling activities. As environmental and social limits to expansion of capitalist production and associated wage labours become more apparent, we need to look more closely at the changing nature of paid and unpaid work in capitalist societies, their associations with different types of learning activities, and the significance of these learning and work relations for continuity and change in global capitalism.

The oversupply of qualified people for many existing jobs continues to encourage employers to inflate required entry credentials as a means of selection. Indeed, credential underemployment may serve to stimulate still greater individual efforts to obtain further educational credentials and related skills to enhance relative chances in competitive job markets—a sort of educational arms race. The pursuit of knowledge is never a bad thing per se. It continues to be an intrinsic feature of our species. But the underemployment of acquired knowledge and skills in current paid workplaces is becoming a very serious social problem. The reasonable solution to this problem is not to restrict access to educational institutions through higher fees or other means. This merely increases social inequities between those from affluent family origins and the rest of society (see Livingstone & Stowe, 2003). Besides, as the analysis of underemployment and learning activities shows, those who are underemployed would continue to seek further knowledge through informal means and their actual underemployment would persist. The only effective solutions to current underemployment problems are likely to be found in economic reforms that encourage an increasingly highly educated labour force to make fuller use of their skills and knowledge in their workplaces.

As Graph 10 illustrates, three basic economic alternatives currently available to us are: *shareholder capitalism; stakeholder capitalism and economic democracy*. I have examined these economic alternatives and their basic learning and work links more fully elsewhere (see Livingstone 2003). Here I can only note that unless we have clear visions of the work alternatives that actually exist, that are preferable and that are feasible, we are unlikely to contribute to sustainable, progressive workplace change. The basic thesis is that greater genuine democratic participation will be associated with lower levels of underemployment, as well as enhanced creative capacity to cope with our increasingly threatened and threatening environment.

	Shareholder capitalism	Stakeholder capitalism	Economic democracy
Ownership	People's capitalism	Profit sharing	Socialized market
Labour process	Re-engineering	Co-determination	Self-management
Work redistribution	Flexible labour force	Reduced workweek	Full employment
New forms of work	Workfare	Guaranteed income	Green work

Graph 10. Economic Alternatives.
Source: Livingstone (2003).

The most feasible immediate work reforms include *work redistribution* and *workplace democratization*. In light of the increasing polarization of paid employment between those who feel compelled to work over 50 hours per week and those involuntarily working under 30 hours or unemployed, an obvious response is to redistribute employment hours among them, where general skills are compatible.

But even with significant paid work-time reduction measures, credential and performance-based conditions of underemployment are likely to persist among the employed labour force. If the measures of mismatch cited above are even remotely accurate, democratic workplace reorganization is greatly needed to allow many workers to use their skills and knowledge more fully in their jobs. There are multitudes of specific innovations (including work teams, job rotation, job enrichment, incentive pay, flexible scheduling, etc.) that have sometimes been successful in enhancing both the quality of working conditions and productivity per worker—but to be sustained they need to be based on decent living standards, safe tasks in safe environments and open democratic decision-making.

Both survey data and ethnographic studies (see Livingstone & Sawchuk, 2004; Livingstone, 2009) confirm that we are now living in an "information age" in terms of the accessibility of employment-related knowledge from multiple sources, and in a "learning society" in terms of the continuing learning efforts of most workers. Although extensive underemployment contradicts the frequent claims that we are also living in a "knowledge-based economy", the lack of immediate opportunities to use their knowledge in available jobs has not dissuaded most workers from continuing to seek ever more of it. We now have a lifelong learning culture in the labour force but one which is insufficiently recognized in the design of many paid workplaces. Educational reforms should always be encouraged for human enrichment. We will surely continue to strive to do this. But only economic reforms that address basic dimensions of work reform, including the *redistribution of paid work time* to reduce current polarization and the *democratization of paid work* to give more workers' greater opportunities to apply their extensive acquired knowledge, can substantially enhance the quality of employment. Without such major paid work reforms, the underemployment of most working people may continue to grow and their latent power to flourish in more democratic workplaces may wither.

In this context, the profuse rhetoric about a learning society and a knowledge-based economy that engulfs current public discourse at least can offer some ingredients for a useful way forward. With all due respect to materially grounded wisdom, all historical societies have been guided in significant ways by dominant ideologies and normative images of the "good society" and "good citizen"; the prevalence of cynical and negative imagery has often been associated with the decline of earlier civilizations (Polak, 1973).

Transformative images of a learning society in which all citizens have enhanced opportunities to combine learning with their everyday lives and more democratized work, have been promoted by social activists such as Paulo Freire, Clodomir Santos de Morais, as well as UNESCO. Such progressive images now contend for the hearts and minds of concerned citizens against instrumental vocationalist views of training deficits advocated by heralds of the knowledge-based economy, such as the OECD, myriads of human capital theorists and many elected politicians (see Wain, 2004). These normative images may be seen as expressions of a fundamental contradiction of education and learning in advanced capitalist societies. The increasing socialization of the forces of knowledge production (especially through the availability of free voluntary forms such as public libraries, trade union schools, and now electronic information networks) continue to provide major sources of independent knowledge for ordinary people. The ready availability of such information and knowledge presents a continual challenge to private capitalist efforts to shape and privatize the social relations of knowledge production (e.g. via conglomerate ownership of mass media, commodified information packages) for narrower economic purposes. The debate between transformative and narrower vocationalist versions of lifelong learning could be very consequential, not only for educational policy and programs but our very survival.

The credibility of those incessantly advocating more instrumental formal education as economic salvation is wearing thin in the wake of mounting underemployment of a more and more highly educated labour force, coupled with other persistent ecological, economic and political challenges. Arnold Toynbee (1960, p. 278), distinguished historian of the challenges and responses of earlier civilizations, concluded that:

> Every man, woman and child that is alive today is living in a world in which mankind is now faced with the extreme choice between learning to live together as one family and committing genocide on a planetary scale. Neither the human race nor any living member of it can afford to ignore the present human situation. We must cope with it if we are not to destroy ourselves; in order to cope with it we must understand it [through the pursuit of knowledge].

Lester Milbraith (1989, p. 379–80), director of the environment and society program at SUNY Buffalo, concluded a wide-ranging general assessment of prospects for more democratic governance and a sustainable relationship with the ecosystem by noting:

> We do not need to sit idly by. [We should] do everything we can to promote *social learning*. We can try to reorient or redesign our institutions so they learn more readily. [for example, development of highly consultative and informed councils for long-range societal guidance] We can study and do research. We can speak up against injury, foolishness, selfishness, injustice, waste and tyranny. We can try to help our friends and neighbours think anew about things…learning to be in the world with an open mind and a quiet heart.

Such exhortations might be misinterpreted as yet more of a liberal version of the "formal education for secular salvation" mantra. But both authors are at great pains to point to informal leaning activities deeply integrated with and responsive to their environmental contexts — and this surely must include our paid and unpaid work — as our only real hope. It is now time for local, national and international level forums which bring together major interest groups and social networks in open, informed debate about the most preferable, feasible economic alternatives to address underemployment, nurture development of a genuine knowledge-based economy and fulfilling individual and collective lifelong learning, and to provide sustainable living conditions for all citizens. Our times require no less.

NOTES

[1] This chapter is an updated version of the R.W. B. Jackson Memorial Lecture delivered at the Ontario Institute for Studies in Education on October 14, 2004.
[2] For an overview of the WALL surveys and case studies, see Livingstone (2010) and www.wallnetwork.ca.

REFERENCES

Barton, P. E. (2000). *What jobs require: Literacy, education and training, 1940–2006*. Princeton, NJ: Educational Testing Service.
Bell, D. (1973). *The coming of post-industrial society*. New York, NY: Basic Books.
Betcherman, G., Leckie, N., & McMullen, K. (1997). *Developing skills for the Canadian workplace: The results of the EKOS workplace training survey*. Ottawa: Canadian Policy Research Networks.
Center for Workforce Development. (1998). *The teaching firm: Where productive work and learning converge*. Newton, MA: Education Development Center.
Curti, M. (1935). *The social ideas of American educators*. Paterson, NJ: Littlefield, Adams and Co.
Engels, F. (1876). The part played by labor in the transition from ape to man. Works of Frederick Engels. Retrieved September 17, 2004 from http://www.marxists.org/archive/marx/works/1876/part-played-labour/
Fox, M. (2004, April 10). Stone age ancestors may have had flair. *Toronto Star*. p. K3.
Handel, M. (2000). *Trends in direct measures of job skill requirements*. Working paper No. 301, Jerome Levy Economics Institute. Retrieved October 2, 2004 from http://www.levy.org/pubs/wp/301.pdf
Hecker, D. (2001). Occupational employment projections to 2010. *Monthly Labor Review, 124*(11), 57–84.
Herzog, J. (1974). The socialization of juveniles in primate and foraging societies: Implications for contemporary education. *Council on Anthropology and Education Quarterly, 5*, 170–177.
Illich, I. (1971). *Deschooling society*. New York, NY: Harper and Row.
Lavoie, M., & Roy, R. (1998). *Employment in the knowledge-based economy: A growth accounting exercise for Canada*. Ottawa: Applied Research Branch, Human Resources Development Canada.
Leckie, N. (1996). *On skill requirements trends in Canada, 1971–1991*. Ottawa: Canadian Policy Research Networks.
Livingstone, D. W. (2001). Worker control as the missing link: Relations between paid/unpaid work and work-related learning. *Journal of Workplace Learning. 13*(7/8), 308–317.
Livingstone, D. W. (2002). *Working and learning in the information age: A profile of Canadians*. Ottawa: Canadian Policy Research Networks.
Livingstone, D. W. (2003). *The education-jobs gap: Underemployment or economic democracy*. (2nd revised edition). Toronto, ON: Garamond Press & Clinton Corners, NY: Percheron Press.
Livingstone, D. W. (Ed.). (2009). *Education and jobs: Exploring the gaps*. Toronto: University of Toronto Press.
Livingstone, D. W. (Ed.). (2010). *Lifelong learning in paid and unpaid work: Survey and case study findings*. London: Routledge.
Livingstone, D. W., & Stowe, S. (2003). Class and university education: Inter-generational patterns. In A. Scott & J. Freeman-Moir (Eds.), *Yesterday's dreams: International and critical perspectives on education and social class*. (pp. 40–59). Auckland: Canterbury University Press.
Livingstone, D. W., & Sawchuk, P. (2004). *Hidden knowledge: Organized labour in the information age*. Toronto: Garamond Press & Lanham, MA: Rowman & Littlefield.
Livingstone, D. W., & Pollock, K. (2004). No room at the top. Paper presented at conference on "Maximizing existing talent", task force on the hidden brain drain: Women and minorities as unrealized assets, center for work-life policy, New York, September 8–9.

Matthews, J., & Candy, P. (1999). New dimensions in the dynamics of learning and knowledge. In D. Boud & J. Garrick (Eds.), *Understanding learning at work*.(pp. 47–64), London: Routledge.

Milbraith, L. W. (1989). *Envisioning a sustainable society: Learning our way out*. Albany: State University of New York Press.

Myers, E. D. (1960). *Education in the perspective of history*. (1st ed.). New York, NY: Harper.

Polak, F. (1973). *The image of the future*. San Francisco: Jossey-Bass.

Putnam, R. D. (2000). *Bowling alone: The collapse and revival of American community*. New York, NY: Simon & Schuster.

Reich, R. B. (1991). *The work of nations: Preparing ourselves for 21st capitalism*. New York, NY: Vintage.

Simon, B. (1974). *Studies in the history of education*. London: Lawrence & Wishart.

Smith, W. A. (1955). *Ancient education*. New York, NY: Greenwood Press.

Statistics Canada. (2004). *Women in Canada: Work chapter updates 2003*. Catalogue no. 89F0133XIE. Ottawa: Ministry of Industry. Retrieved September 12, 2004 from http://publications.gc.ca/Collection/Statcan/89F0133X/89F0133XIE2003.pdf

Tough, A. (1978). Major learning efforts: Recent research and future directions. *Adult Education, 28*, 250–263.

Toynbee, A. J. (1960). *Concluding chapter: Education in the perspective of history*. In E. D. Myers, (1960). *Education in the perspective of history*. (1st ed.). New York, NY: Harper & Brothers.

Verrengia, J. (2004, March 25). Genetic mutation may have separated man, apelike kin. *Toronto Star*. p. A12.

Vianello, A. (2004). Stone age symbolic behaviours: Questions and prospects. Paper at graduate school of Archaeology, University of Sheffield. Retrieved October 12, 2004, from http://www.semioticon.com/virtuals/symbolicity/behaviours.html

Wain, K. (2004). *The learning society in a postmodern world. The Education Crisis*. New York, NY: Peter Lang.

WALL. (2004). Basic findings of the 2004 WALL survey of learning and work in Canada. Retrieved October 5, http://www.wallnetwork.ca

Waring, M. (1988). *If women counted: A new feminist economics*. San Francisco: Harper & Row.

AFFILIATION

D.W. Livingstone
Professor Emeritus and Canada Research Chair in Lifelong Learning and Work,
Department of Humanities, Social Sciences and Social Justice,
Ontario Institute for Studies in Education,
University of Toronto, Canada

PART II

ADULT LEARNING, DIFFERENCE AND IDENTITY

PETER RULE & TADI RUTH MODIPA

5. "WE MUST BELIEVE IN OURSELVES": ATTITUDES AND EXPERIENCES OF ADULT LEARNERS WITH DISABILITIES IN KWAZULU-NATAL, SOUTH AFRICA[1]

INTRODUCTION

Adult basic education is a marginalized sphere of activity within the South African education system, receiving less than 1% of the annual education budget and actually declining in provision over the last decade (Aitchison, 1999; Baatjes, 2003). Within the adult basic education sector, adult learners with disabilities are a further marginalized group to the extent that they are all but invisible in the realm of formal Adult Basic Education and Training (ABET) provision, although some progress has been made in recruiting learners with disabilities to the Kha Ri Gude mass literacy campaign (Department of Education, 2008). The 2001 census revealed that people with disabilities constituted 5% of the population but were disproportionately represented (10.5%) in the category of people with no education, and underrepresented in successively higher levels of education: primary (5.2%), secondary (3.9%), and higher (3.0%; Statistics South Africa, 2005). There is therefore a large adult population of people with disabilities that is illiterate or semiliterate, significantly larger in percentage terms than the general adult population. Because of the apartheid system and wider sociocultural practices of discrimination against people with disabilities, many Black people with disabilities in particular either never attended school or dropped out at an early stage.

KwaZulu-Natal, the setting of this study, is situated on South Africa's eastern seaboard. It was the most populous province in South Africa in 2001, although the population of Gauteng province is now estimated to be larger (Statistics South Africa, 2009). Of KwaZulu-Natal's population of 9,426,017 in 2001, 470,588 were classified as disabled (Statistics South Africa, 2005). KwaZulu-Natal is experiencing an acute HIV epidemic and has the highest HIV prevalence (15.8%) in South Africa (Human Sciences Research Council, 2009). HIV prevalence among people with disabilities, categorized as a "most at risk group" (MARG), is estimated nationally at 14.1% (Human Sciences Research Council, 2009). Although there are thriving industrial centres in Durban, Richards Bay, and Pietermaritzburg, much of the KwaZulu-Natal population is still rural, and the prevalence of poverty is high.

Of the approximately half a million people with disabilities in the province, therefore, many are unschooled, live in poverty, and have HIV. On the other hand, there are many disabled people's organizations that exist at a community level, and the government's system of disability grants provides some relief to unemployed people with disabilities (Emmett, 2006). In this chapter, we present and reflect on an action research study into the attitudes and experiences of adults with disabilities regarding education in KwaZulu-Natal, South Africa. The research team included six members, two nondisabled members from the University of KwaZulu-Natal, four persons with disabilities from a nongovernmental organization (NGO), three with visual impairments, and one with a physical impairment. The study took place under the auspices of the Enable Education, Training and Development Initiative (hereafter "Enable"), at the beginning of the study a program within an adult literacy NGO and by the end an independent NGO in its own right. Enable is based in the South African province of KwaZulu-Natal. It provides ABET to adults with disabilities and raises awareness of disability in their communities. Enable works with disabled people's organizations in setting up and running projects, and adheres to the principle of people with disabilities being involved at all levels—as learners, educators, and steering committee members. The research team conceptualized the study collaboratively and attempted to conduct it along collaborative lines, although the exigencies of keeping the organization alive during a funding crisis placed de facto limits on collaboration.

PURPOSE OF THE STUDY

The study had three primary purposes: to generate knowledge about the educational attitudes and experiences of adult learners with disabilities in KwaZulu-Natal, to build the research capacity of people with disabilities, and to improve the curriculum of the Enable program. This article focuses primarily on the first and third of these purposes. The study arose from a need within the Enable program to find out more about the attitudes toward, and experiences of, education among adult learners with disabilities who were attending adult basic education classes in English, Zulu, and numeracy within the program. This purpose was related to the problem of a lack of knowledge about the educational attitudes and experiences of adult learners with disabilities, both in Enable and more widely in South Africa. An enhanced understanding of adult learners with disabilities would then feed into the development and implementation of the Enable program curriculum as the "action" component of the research.

FRAMING THE STUDY IN LITERATURE AND THEORY

The Convention of the Rights of Persons with Disabilities (United Nations, 2006, Article 24) asserts the right of people with disabilities to education, including "vocational training, adult education and lifelong learning without discrimination and on an equal basis with others." However, the hiatus regarding adult education and disability is both national (Glaser & Lorenzo, 2006) and international (M. Clark, 2006), with links between the two in the south only beginning to emerge, for example, in the context of international development (Weigt, 2007) and calls for the inclusion of people with disabilities in HIV and AIDS campaigns and programs (Africa Campaign on Disability and HIV & AIDS, 2008). There have been some valuable studies on disability and schooling in South Africa—a focus promoted by the government's promulgation of Education White Paper 6 on inclusive education (Philpott & Sait, 2001; Soudien & Baxen, 2006).

However, besides the works of Aarons and Glaser (2002) and Glaser and Lorenzo (2006) on deaf adult literacy projects, and by Ram and Muthukrishna (2001) on the voices of deaf adults, very little has been written about adult learning and disability in a South African context. The works of Corley and Taymans (2001) on adults with learning disabilities and Rocco (2001) on disability, diversity, and power has contributed importantly to an understanding of disability and adult education in North American contexts. The present study focuses on adult learners with physical and visual impairments. Writing in *Adult Education Quarterly*, M. Clark (2006) calls for an "interdisciplinary relationship between adult education and disability studies as a way to investigate the disability experience within the adult learning context" (p. 308). The present study draws on key theories and concepts from the ambit of disability studies regarding models of disability, and disability and research, as well as embodied notions of cognition.

INTERACTIONAL MODEL OF DISABILITY

There has been a great deal of discursive contestation around the notion of disability and what disablement means, ranging from a positivist medical approach to a politicized social model promulgated by the disability movements; more recently, postmodern interpretations of disability as a discursive and textual construct have begun to emerge (Oliver, 1983, 1996; Shakespeare, 2006; Smith, 2009; Thomas & Corker, 2002; Williams, 2001). The social model developed in the United Kingdom in the 1960s and 1970s provided a radical challenge to conventional medical notions that located disability in persons with disabilities themselves as "illness" and/or "personal tragedy." Instead, advocates of the social model, drawing on critical disability theory (Rocco, 2002), argued that people with impairments "are disabled by society's failure to accommodate their needs" (Barnes, Oliver, & Barton, 2002, p. 5). The South African government's *Integrated National Disability Strategy* (Republic of South Africa, 1997) narrows the discursive contest around disability to these two competing models: the medical model and the social model. The former identifies people with disabilities as "ill, different from their able-bodied peers, and in need of care". In contrast, the social model shifts the emphasis from people with disabilities to the society that constructs them as disabled: "if society cannot cater for people with disabilities, it is society that must change." The strategy goes on to assert that a key principle of this model is "the involvement of people with disabilities in the process of transformation" (p. 1). As with much other legislation, there is a critical gap between policy and implementation—this is especially the case regarding the lack of state provision for adult learners with disabilities.

Although it has contributed to mobilizing people with disabilities and removing social barriers, the social model of disability has been criticized at a number of levels: for asserting unsustainable dichotomies between impairment and disability, and between the individual and society; for downplaying the role of impairment; for downplaying the different experiences of oppression within the population of people with disabilities; and for neglecting the personal experience of pain and the body (Mercer, 2002; Scully, 2008; Shakespeare, 2006; Siebers, 2008). A more holistic, interactional view of disability explains disability as a function of the relationship between an individual and his or her environment, including biological, cultural, psychological, and sociopolitical aspects (Schneider, 2006; Shakespeare, 2006). This view is holistic in the sense that it strives to accommodate not only biological aspects (medical model) and sociopolitical aspects (social model) of disability but also the cultural and psychological aspects within the lived bodily experiences of persons with disabilities. It is interactional in that it interrogates the relations among these aspects in context. Within this model, therefore, disability is not a purely individual or social phenomenon but arises from the often complex relationship among various factors in a dynamic context. We adopt a holistic interactional view of disability to frame this study.

RESEARCH AND DISABILITY

In his trenchant critique of research on disability, Oliver (1992) highlights the relations between power and knowledge. He argues that research has discriminated against people with disabilities in two important ways: by using theoretical models that are alien to their experience and by contributing nothing to the improvement of their lives (Oliver 1992, p. 105). He calls for a transformation of the social relations of research production—people with disabilities should be involved in all stages of the research process. Oliver frames these transformed relations of research production within an emancipatory approach and underlines the research process itself rather than simply its outcomes or products, the actual relationships of knowledge production. As Barnes (2003) elaborates, "emancipatory disability research is about the empowerment of disabled people through the transformation of the material and social relations of research production" (p. 6).

As a practitioner-based research approach, action research combines action and research in attempting to change and improve situations. It is guided by principles such as participation, collaboration, self-criticism, praxis, and uses the methodological mechanism of a self-reflective spiral of planning, acting, observing, and reflecting (Cohen, Manion, & Morrison, 2007; Kemmis & McTaggart, 1992;

McNiff, Lomax, & Whitehead, 2003). The emancipatory version of action research roots its epistemology in critical theory, identifies explicitly with the cause of oppressed groups, and challenges oppressive interpersonal and structural constraints in its quest for a more just social order (Barton, 1998; Grundy, 1987; Torres, 1992). The attempt at an emancipatory action research approach that involved people with disabilities in our study is consistent with Oliver's call to facilitate empowerment through research. However, as Barnes (2003, p. 8) points out, relations between university-based researchers, who are under pressure within market-led academic environments, and disabled people's organizations, which are typically "hand-to-mouth operations with very limited resources," are sometimes difficult to maintain. This was the case in this study, which achieved limited levels of collaboration, as we explain under the Method section.

COGNITION AND EMBODIMENT: A CHALLENGE TO KNOWLEDGE PRODUCTION

Alongside the interactional model of disability and an emancipatory approach to disability research, this project draws on insights from the emerging field of cognitive science known as embodied cognition. This is an interdisciplinary approach, which charts the important role of embodiment, for example, bodily movement, posture, and position, in shaping cognition (A. Clark, 1997; Gallagher, 2005; Lakoff & Johnson, 1999; Varela, Thompson & Rosch, 1991). An embodied approach to cognition insists that "the mind must be understood in the context of its relationship to a physical body that interacts with the world" (Wilson, 2002, p. 625). This view of cognition and cognitive processes as embodied rather than as free-floating challenges the Cartesian dualism of mind and body, which has fundamentally shaped Western thinking for the past three centuries, and the concept of mind as a "mental thing" as opposed to the body as a "physical thing." Embodied cognition sees bodily situatedness as central to the way that humans perceive and conceive of the world. The generation of knowledge is not a function simply of the relation between mind and world but of real living bodies interacting with the world and other bodies in social contexts (Gibbs, 2006). Thus, the way that we are embodied affects the way that we know the world. Within adult education scholarship, the role of the body in adult learning has been considered only over the past few decades. This includes the acknowledgement that somatic knowing contributes to the ways that adult learners make meaning of their lives (Merriam, Caffarella, & Baumgartner, 2007).

Regarding embodied cognition and disability, Scully (2009) raises the possibility that those with anomalous bodies think and moralize in nonstandard ways related to their particular embodiment. However, Scully rejects the essentialist position that there is a "disability mind" or a "disability morality," unlike the minds or moralities of "normal people" (p. 70). She posits that social, cultural, and environmental factors are as formative of moral cognition as bodily factors—a position that is consistent with the interactional approach to disability discussed above—and argues that more empirical data are needed if progress is to be made in the philosophical engagement with bodily difference. Drawing on the emerging field of embodied cognition, we employ Gallagher's (2005) notion of *body image* to understand adult learners' attitudes toward and experiences of education and society more broadly. For Gallagher, body image consists of three elements: body percept (the subject's perceptual experience of his or her own body); body concept (the subject's conceptual understanding, including folk and/or scientific knowledge, of the body in general); and body affect (the subject's emotional attitude toward his or her body; p. 25). The strength of this approach is that it takes into account the centrality of the body to meaning making and knowledge creation in a way that acknowledges perceptions, thoughts, and feelings holistically in relation to the environment. We use this schema of body image to analyze interview and focus group data gathered from adult learners with disabilities.

METHOD

The emancipatory action research approach (Kemmis & McTaggart, 1992; McNiff *et al.*, 2003) adopted in the study is consistent with the requirements of the social and interactional models of disability concerning the involvement of people with disabilities at all stages of the research process. A number of studies have explored the use of an action research approach within a disability context, pointing to its efficacies and limitations (Balcazar, Keys, Kaplan, & Suarez-Balcazar, 1998; Barnes, 2003; Radermacher, 2006; Sample, 1996; Van Niekerk, Lorenzo & Mdlokolo, 2006). Some of the limitations around collaboration were experienced in this study.

The research project progressed through one cycle of action research: (a) problem identification, (b) research design, (c) data collection and analysis, and (d) application of findings to practice. Although ideally action research is an iterative process, this project did not repeat the research cycle for practical and logistical reasons elaborated below. The six-member research team participated fully in Phases 1 and 2. The problem identified was the lack of knowledge within the Enable program, and in the country as a whole, about adult learners with disabilities. As coordinator of the research team, one of the nondisabled researchers presented the following draft research topic for consideration by the team.

INVESTIGATING THE NEEDS AND RESPONSES OF ADULT LEARNERS WITH DISABILITIES

People with disabilities in the research team pointed out that the wording of the topic made assumptions about people with disabilities which might be detrimental to the research project as a whole. In particular, the term *needs* had implications of deficit and inadequacy: people with disabilities were "in need" of the interventions of professionals and caregivers, and thus dependent on others to fulfill their needs. The *able-bodied* researchers came to see that this formulation tacitly deferred to the medical and charity discourses, which position the person with a disability as helpless, passive, and dependent. In the field of adult education, this approach is underpinned by what Armstrong (1982) refers to as "the needs-meeting ideology"—it is an ideological construct that serves the interests of professionals by naturalizing "need" as the intrinsic state of people with disabilities. The term *responses* also suggested a certain passivity people with disabilities being expected to respond to what others do for them rather than initiating ideas and actions themselves. The team reformulated the research topic to allow for a more open-ended and active role for the research participants in creating their own meanings.

INVESTIGATING THE ATTITUDES AND EXPERIENCES OF ADULT LEARNERS WITH DISABILITIES

The team adopted a qualitative research design using in-depth interviews, focus groups, and educators' written accounts (Cohen et al., 2007; McNiff et al., 2003) to collect data from adults with disabilities and their educators involved in basic education projects in KwaZulu-Natal. The interview and focus group instruments were drafted, piloted, and revised by the team. The use of interviews gave the team an opportunity to explore in some depth the educational experiences and attitudes of individual adult learners in the context of their biographies. On the other hand, the use of focus groups provided an opportunity to explore the collective perceptions of adult learners with disabilities. All the interviewees and focus group participants were learners with disabilities participating in the Enable program. They were indigenous IsiZulu speakers and were interviewed in IsiZulu. Twelve in-depth interviews were conducted with participants in the projects. Interviewees volunteered to be interviewed after each project group was briefed about the research study. This was done in order not to exclude anyone from the particular group who was interested in participating in interviews. Each interview lasted approximately 45 minutes. The interviews were conducted by a pair of interviewers: a nondisabled researcher and a researcher with a visual or physical impairment, who, as an indigenous IsiZulu speaker, also acted as translator. A semistructured interview format was used that covered the participant's family background, attitudes toward and experiences of disability, and educational experiences as a child and an adult. Interviewees ranged in age from 17 to 49, with the visually impaired learners tending to be in their late teens or twenties and the physically impaired learners mainly in their 30s and 40s. This was possibly because the learners with physical impairments had been part of preexisting craft-making groups for some time before basic education was introduced to their groups, and so came to adult basic education at a later age, whereas the project for the visually impaired began as a basic education project, thus attracting younger learners who had not completed schooling for various reasons. There were six men and six women interviewed. In terms of their educational background, three had never attended school, whereas two had reached the early years of high school. The remainder had 3 to 5 years of primary schooling. They were thus spread across the levels of basic education, from Level 1 to Level 4. Six of the interviewees had a physical impairment and five a sensory impairment, whereas one had multiple impairments.

Four focus group discussions were conducted—two in urban areas and two in rural areas. The selection of focus groups in both urban and rural areas provided a geographical spread of Enable learners from contexts where urban/rural differences can be significant regarding community profiles, access to education, and barriers to participation for people with disabilities. One of the focus groups, located in an urban area, consisted of 13 learners with visual impairments, whereas the other 3, each consisting of 8 to 9 participants, were for learners with mobility impairments. The focus groups all comprised both men and women, with a similar range of ages and educational levels to the interviewees. The topics included the experiences of adults with disabilities in their communities, attitudes of communities toward people with disabilities, and the participants' views about education for people with disabilities. The focus groups were conducted in IsiZulu.

The focus group method was adopted to give an opportunity for adult learners with particular disabilities to discuss ideas together and interact with each other. The method sought to tap into the collective experiences and attitudes of these learners that might not emerge from individual interviews (Babbie & Mouton, 2001). The focus groups gave participants the opportunity to speak of "we" in addition to "I" regarding their attitudes and experiences. This is important in an African context where identity is construed not just or primarily as individual but also as collective (Merriam & Ntseane, 2008).

In addition, Enable educators were asked to write short accounts of their experiences in the program. These processes generated data from people with disabilities regarding their subjective experiences of disability in education and society, and so were able to "contribute to understanding the experience of disability from the inside" (Scully, 2009, p. 59). The interviews and focus groups were tape-recorded, transcribed, and translated from IsiZulu into English by members of the research team. All participants quoted in the findings below are given pseudonyms to protect their anonymity.

The data collection phase of the research was interrupted by the exigencies of keeping a nongovernmental adult literacy organization afloat in difficult financial circumstances.

This was part of the wider continuing struggle of adult literacy organizations to survive in the post-apartheid era in South Africa. Aitchison, Houghton, and Baatjes (2000) found that by 2000 only 38 of 150 ABET NGOs surveyed in 1997 were still in operation. The members of the research team were also members of Enable's management committee, and research took a back seat to the imperatives of organizational survival as the Enable program's parent organization collapsed because of lack of funding. The committee had to reconstitute Enable as an independent nonprofit organization and salvage the funds specifically directed toward the Enable program to keep it going.

In this context, the data analysis phase of the study reverted to the ablebodied researchers who, from their relatively privileged university location, were able to analyze the data and write up the findings while the Enable committee pursued its primary objective of keeping the organization going and so continuing to provide basic education to adults with disabilities. Although this situation was far from ideal given the requirements of emancipatory action research (Barnes, 2003; Oliver, 1992), it was the only way to save the research from oblivion. The researchers remained accountable (Barnes, 2003) to Enable as an organization of and for people with disabilities by presenting the findings to the organization, engaging in dialogue about their implications for the curriculum, and working on an action plan for implementation with the Enable committee as the fourth phase of the process. The data were analyzed using three strategies. The first was thematic content analysis using open coding, which coded, categorized, compared, and summarized themes from the three data sources together: interview transcripts; focus group transcripts; and educator's accounts (Babbie & Mouton, 2001; Lichtman, 2006).

Although the parameters for data analysis were set by the overall focus of the study on the attitudes and experiences of adult learners with disabilities, the actual themes for coding the data arose inductively from the data themselves (Babbie & Mouton, 2001). Fifteen key themes emerged, through coding, categorizing, and forming concepts, and combining concepts where necessary to avoid duplication (Lichtman, 2006), which in turn led to a more refined process of coding. These themes are indicated in **Table 1 (further down)**. The second data analysis strategy consisted of an analysis of the discourse of interview and focus group data using the three elements of Gallagher's notion of body image discussed above: body percept,

Table 1. Themes and Codes

Theme	Code
Adult basic education and training	A
Abuse	AB
Barriers to learning	B
Benefits of education	BE
Disability	D
Finances	F
Illiteracy	I
Income generation	IG
Medical	M
Participation	P
Poverty	PY
Reasons for learning	R
Schooling	SC
Skills development	SK
Support	SU

Note. Each theme encompassed a number of subthemes that were also coded. For example, the theme of Barriers to learning (B) spanned 14 subthemes, including Transport (BT), Access (BA), Poor vision (BV), Family attitudes (FA), and Teacher capacity (TC).

body concept, and body affect. These elements served as categories that allowed us to examine the larger chunks of data that made up mini-narratives and to link these mini-narratives in new ways (Strauss & Corbin, 1990).

A third strategy involved selective coding, which meant identifying "core" categories that concern the primary phenomenon around which the other categories are integrated (Strauss & Corbin cited in Babbie & Mouton, 2001, p. 501). These three categories were "Experiences of schooling," "Disability in family and community," and "Education and transformation." These overarching categories allowed us to integrate a number of categories around a central theme. For example, "Experiences of schooling" drew on categories such as "Schooling," "Barriers to learning," and "Abuse." It is these three categories that we used to organize the findings below. These analytical strategies together allowed for a triangulation of sources and methods as a way of checking the trustworthiness of data. We then reached conclusions based on an interpretation of emerging patterns (Cohen et al, 2007).

FINDINGS: CRITICAL THEMES IN THE RESEARCH DATA

In this section, we examine some of the primary themes that emerged from the interview and focus group data. The process of content analysis elicited three key thematic clusters: experiences of schooling, disability in family and community, and education and transformation. The data indicated that it was not possible to isolate the adult learners' attitudes toward and experiences of education from their broader social experiences of disability. We present key insights into these thematic clusters, drawing on excerpts from the data and analyzing them with tools drawn from our theoretical framing.

EXPERIENCES OF SCHOOLING

Some adult learners never attended school because of their disability. A number of factors were at play here: parents keeping their children at home because of the shame attached to having a child with a disability, schools simply not catering for children with disabilities, impoverished family circumstances, illness and poor health, or a combination of these factors. One such adult learner, Themba, describes his experiences:

> A bad event which happened during the time I was growing up is that I did not get an opportunity to go to school because of the reason that my parents were poor and could not afford sending me to school. I was also old. I did not have good health. I would be continuously ill and lived a disabled life and felt despised by my disability until today. (Themba)

For those who did attend, many had negative experiences, which resulted in them dropping out of school at an early age. For some, this was related to the "spoiled identity" (Goffman, 1968) of disability and the consequent discrimination experienced at the hands (and mouths) of "normal" teachers and learners. The following excerpts are from the learners Bathabile, Zodwa, and Fikile who left school for various reasons:

> We were isolated by both teachers and learners and that is why we failed to [achieve] with our schooling like other kids. The learners would tease us and reports to teachers proved futile. That is why I stopped schooling and now I am uneducated. (Bathabile)

> I could not see the board and exercise books. I was not able to continue with schooling. (Zodwa)

> I walked a long distance from home to school and I would be constantly punished for being late. The problem was that I could never walk fast to avoid being late. (Fikile)

Some of the adult learners left school as a result of barriers to education that affected children more widely, including poverty and gender discrimination. This points to the intersectionality of factors such as race, gender, and class in relation to disability, which creates a matrix of oppression (Collins, 2009). One female learner with a disability left school for reasons related to gender:

> Even at school I attended up to standard 6 because in olden days girls were not allowed to learn to the high standards. At home they took me out of school because of that. (Busi)

Table 2. Body Image and Social Discrimination in Three Interview Excerpts

Body Percept	Body Concept	Body Affect
Jabulani Awareness of scars on head	Spurned body: the impaired body does not belong with the able-bodied	Negative feelings
Zandile Awareness of difference and "abnormality" of own body as a blind person	Body as public curiosity: Disabled people should stay out of the public eye	Loss of confidence
Thoko Awareness of words directed over/across her body but not to her despite capacity	Dependent body: Disabled people cannot speak or decide for themselves	Passivity and dependence to hear and understand

DISABILITY IN FAMILY AND COMMUNITY

Although some participants experienced supportive family and community environments, many suffered as a result of discrimination and marginalization in ways that reflect their schooling experiences, and the school as an exemplar of wider social values and practices. This reflects the prevalence of stigma around disability within the communities that adult learners live in and come from. Stigma around disability takes on a number of forms in the data: disability as a divine curse or punishment; disability as a sign of bewitchment; disability as insanity; disability as a mark of an abnormal and subhuman status. The following excerpts reflect the experiences of disability of three adult learners, two with physical impairments (Jabulani and Thoko), and one with a visual impairment (Zandile). Of interest is the particular embodied nature of their experiences of discrimination. We analyze their stories using Gallagher's notion of body image (see **Table 2, above**).

> I still have scars on my head which I sustained from those young people who said I walked like a dog and I should not walk next to them because they will be like me. There are those who called me names then and are still doing that . . . That made me feel very bad and I still feel bad about that. (Jabulani)

> The community still discriminates against us, more especially the youth. They always say, "Look at this young girl. She is blind, as young as she is," and that makes me to lose my confidence. Take for instance the discussion we had with our teacher this morning, when she asked us if we attend funerals. To be honest I do not attend funerals because, if I do try to attend the funeral, I would be told "Zandile where are you going? Sit down and do not go to the funeral because all eyes will be on you, you are disabled." What I would like to say though is that we as people with disabilities must believe in ourselves and then the community will believe in us too. (Zandile)

> When I was growing up people never spoke to me, they would speak to me through my mother. They would ask her my name and if I was fine. Even at the age of fifteen the doctor asked my mother if I was doing well at school, and I was there, he could have just asked me. This shaped the way I communicated with people. I always expected someone to speak on my behalf. It took years for me to be able to make my own decisions. I would expect my mother and other people to make them. (Thoko)

In all three cases, the impairment is linked directly to social discrimination, and this shapes the body percepts, body concepts, and body affects of the three interviewees. All three respondents reported incidents in which they were recipients of the words and actions of others: they were acted upon, against, or on behalf of; they were insulted, instructed, or ignored. In all three cases, they were silent. The excerpts underline the notion that embodied cognition is also social cognition. Through processes of discrimination, oppression, and silencing, society reproduces stigma inside the person as a form of internalized oppression, an imposed sense of one's own bodily deficit, which effects a particular negative body image. The spatial aspects of the three stories are also informative. For Zandile, with her strong auditory sense of the environment, social discrimination takes the form of surrounding voices that isolate and peculiarize her: "they always say"; "I would be told"; and the almost tactile sense of being the object of scrutiny: "all eyes will be on you, you are disabled". For Jabulani, the voices and blows come from above ("I still have the scars on my head") and the sense of being looked down upon, both literally and figuratively ("who said I walked like a dog"). For Thoko, the voices communicate "over her head," as if she, a third person, is absent; or somewhere below the levels of agency and responsibility expected of a "normal" person. Interestingly, for Zandile the adult learning classroom provides a dialogic space for reflection on her own experiences of oppression, as does the research interview for all three respondents. The safe collective learning space of the classroom enables Zandile to move from her own experience to a sense of collective agency in countering oppression: "We must believe in ourselves."

EDUCATION AND TRANSFORMATION

Transformation is an enduring and developing theme in adult education theory and practice (Freire, 1972, 1998; Merriam & Ntseane, 2008; Mezirow, 1991) but little if anything exists on transformative learning and adults with disabilities (M. Clark, 2006; Taylor, 2007). There is evidence in the data of transformation at a number of levels—among adult educators in the Enable projects, among learners, within the organization and in the wider community in which projects are located. First, nondisabled educators express views about disability that have been shaped by their experiences of participating in the Enable program and educating learners with disabilities. In the case of Nonhlanhla, the mother of a child with a disability, her views of disability were shaped by its cultural stigmatization as a curse, or a sign of bewitchment:

> When I was eighteen I dropped out of school and in 1980 I had a disabled child—he was physically challenged . . . In those days I thought it is the curse of God for me. But now all things and my mind have changed . . . Now I never think that when I have a disabled child it is the curse of God, no, all people are the gift of God . . . I like to [raise] awareness [of] our communities—do not discriminate and abuse disabled people because you can get [a] disability anytime and anywhere. I love my child and other disabled people. I think now I have more information and knowledge about disability. (Nonhlanhla)

The educator shows a shift in her body concept of the disabled child from a "curse of God" to a "gift of God," and in her affect regarding the impaired body from implied isolation and exclusion to love, inclusion, and commonality with the nondisabled ("you can get a disability anytime and anywhere"). Although there is not enough evidence here to claim a thorough-going Mezirow-style perspective transformation, there are indications of a change in attitude and approach that has spiritual ("all people are a gift of God"), cognitive ("all things and my mind have changed"), affective ("I love my child and other disabled people"), and agentive ("[raise] awareness [of] our communities") dimensions.

The following extract from an interview with a rural woman learner with a physical impairment, Bongekile, reveals something of how disablement worked within a family situation and the process of empowerment that occurs through collective action of people with disabilities. Again, we analyze the extract in terms of the components of body image (see **Table 3. further down**).

> The problem was with my mother at home. When she was around at home she would stop me from going to school even during exams and I would stay at home. The school was also very far and she would not give me bus fare. She was not interested in getting me an education; I think she thought I did not need an education because no job would be suitable for me. But now she can see that she was wrong because I joined other people and we started community projects. We negotiated with the headman and the chief to get a piece of land and now we are doing hand crafts. (Bongekile)

The negative agency of the mother and the passivity of the girl child are apparent in the first three sentences of the extract: "she would stop me"; "she would not give me bus fare"; "she was not interested"; "I would stay at home." The mother's attitudes reflect wider lay perceptions of people with disabilities as in deficit, nonproductive, incapable. There is then a remarkable change in the discourse marked by the disjunction "But" in the fifth sentence. It is characterized by a shift from the individual to the collective and from the passive to the active: "*I joined* other people and *we started* community projects." Here the political potential of participation in a learning group is visible. It also indicates a spatial shift from confinement of the disabled body to the home to engagement in public, generative activity in the civic and economic spheres: "We negotiated with the headman and the chief to get a piece of land and now we are doing hand crafts." The transformation here is not only in the body image of the speaker but also, pivotally, in Bongekile's perceptions of her mother: "But now *she can see that* she was wrong."

Table 3. Body Image and Empowerment in a Mini Narrative

	Body Percept	Body Concept	Body Affect Initial Body Image
Initial body image	Experience of restriction Confinement to home	Disabled body as not suitable for school/work	Sense of oppression, hopelessness
Revised body image	Experience of body with others, doing things, in collective spaces	Body as capable, interactive, envoiced	Sense of capability and empowerment

Data from other adult learners in the study confirm that they experienced a boost in their levels of skills and knowledge, as well as in their self-esteem and sense of capability, through participating in adult education. They take this back into their families and communities, challenging the conventional ways that they are perceived. An elderly blind woman, Thokozani, described this process as follows:

> [My family and friends] are amazed and say: "Are you learning?" I say yes, I am learning. "Who are these people who can teach you, being old and blind?" I say some of our teachers are blind and some are sighted. "You are joking!" When there is something said in English and I respond to it, my children will say, "Our mother is really learning." I will be happy. (Thokozani)

A striking feature in this quotation is the affective impact of learning, the sense of confidence and joy that arises from the recognition of one's learning by others. There is a shift from the monological oppression of a society that tells people with disabilities what they cannot do and be, to a dialogic engagement and assertiveness that comes from a sense of voice and capability among the adult learners. This suggests that a liberating education can play a role in transforming the way people with disabilities see themselves and interact with others. This is not to argue that education is the magic bullet that ends all problems, or that other factors such as the creation of employment opportunities, the social activism and advocacy of the disability movement, and the development of progressive policies are unimportant, but rather that education has an important role to play alongside other interventions, and that authentic transformation is unlikely without an educational component.

FROM RESEARCH TO ACTION: PHASE 4—APPLYING FINDINGS TO PRACTICE

The research findings were presented to the Enable committee once the new organization had found its feet and the research agenda could be resurrected. In accordance with the action research approach, the evidence from the research challenged Enable to consider its education program more broadly in light of the widespread stigma surrounding disability in communities. The study plainly revealed widespread discrimination in families and communities against the people with disabilities involved in Enable's projects. In addition to its adult basic education program, Enable thus extended its curriculum by initiating a series of awareness-raising workshops in communities in an endeavor to change attitudes toward people with disabilities. This marked a shift from providing education only to adults with disabilities to educating the communities in which they live as well. This shift corresponds with Article 8 of the Convention on the Rights of Persons with Disabilities (United Nations, 2006), which calls for awareness raising throughout society, including at a family level; countering of negative stereotypes; and emphasizing the capabilities and contributions of people with disabilities.

Such workshops typically adopt a participatory methodology, using activities such as group discussion and report backs, case studies and role play, and are conducted in the predominant local language, IsiZulu. They focus on issues such as social barriers encountered by people with disabilities, the rights of people with disabilities, and questions from the community concerning disability, such as disability and marriage. One activity involved able-bodied people having to spend time in a wheelchair or blindfolded negotiating certain obstacles, and then discussing what they learnt from the experience about disability and how to relate to people with disabilities. Workshops are attended by both people with disabilities and able-bodied community members, thus creating a space for dialogue and interaction, which is often unprecedented. This is exemplified in the Enable Director's report on a workshop: At one of the workshops, the local *induna* [traditional leader] told the community about the difficulties faced by his eldest son. He said he was sharing this with the community for the first time. His son could not succeed whilst at school. They tried everything from prayer to changing schools but nothing happened.

They eventually gave up and the son dropped out whilst in primary school. The *induna* knows that his son, who can do things on his own, has the mind of a child, but he was too embarrassed to tell it to anyone, and did not even confide in the men who assist him. He ended by saying he is grateful to Enable for giving him an opportunity to talk about this as it felt so good to talk about his son without shame. (Enable, 2007, p. 5)

An *induna* is a headman in the traditional authority structure of rural KwaZulu-Natal, and plays an important role, under the chief, in community matters such as land allocation and dispute resolution. The workshop facilitator recalls that for a person with the social status of an *induna* to open up about his son's disability was a shock to the community. The community expected him and his life to be exemplary and to hear him talk about it in a public arena was unexpected. The *induna* talked about his son's disability that everyone in the community knew of implicitly but would not dare talk about, out of respect for his position. He created a platform where he not only encouraged his community but also his equals and superiors to talk openly about disability. This outcome indicated that awareness-raising workshops can provide people from all walks of life in the community with an opportunity to learn and share. However, further research is required to assess the longer term impact of such interventions on the quality of life of persons with disabilities.

CONCLUSION: FROM THE PERSONAL BODY TO THE SOCIAL BODY AND BACK AGAIN

The data suggest that the engagement of adults with disabilities in collective learning and action can be transformatory. One way of understanding this transformatory potential is through the metaphor of movement. This movement can happen at a number of interrelated levels, which might vary from one learner to the next. First, there is a movement from the personal body, perceived by society, and, consequently, the person with the disability, as abnormal, abhorrent, pitiful, to engagement with the social body of people with disabilities, in the form of self-help groups, adult learning groups, and advocacy groups. It is a movement from an "I" to a "We". This movement is a physical movement from the isolation of the home to a public space in which people with disabilities engage in public activities. It can also be a spiritual, emotional, and political movement from dependency to activity, from isolation to solidarity, from silence to dialogue, and from passivity to assertiveness. The movement is not only outward but also inward. The return from the corporate learning and acting body of people with disabilities is to a personal body, in terms of a transformed body image, that is capable and interconnected—"and now *we are doing* hand crafts"—and so to a new sense of identity and self-worth.

This is not to assert that involvement in the disability movement is an unqualified panacea. The damage of discrimination is internalized ("I still feel bad about that"), and the struggle continues ("we must believe in ourselves and then the community will believe in us too"). In addition, there is a need for further research on issues such as power differentials among people with disabilities, between disabled and able-bodied researchers (a factor clearly evident in this research study), and the ways in which the intersectionality of disability, gender, race, class, and other factors articulate in contexts of learning and action. However, the data suggest that collective learning and action have distinct transformatory potential at both the personal and social levels. Using an embodied cognition frame, this study points to the relation between the individual body of the person with a disability and the corporate body of the disability movement. It indicates that the engagement of people with disabilities in collective learning and action has the potential to transform their body images, and indicates a close relation between embodied cognition in both its personal and social senses. It also points to the importance of learning about disability in society as a whole to counter discriminatory beliefs and practices. In this regard, the disability movement has a crucial role to play in challenging and transforming social perceptions of disability so that people can "talk without shame" in a society that is truly for all.

NOTE

[1] *Acknowledgments*: This chapter was previously published by the authors with the same title in *Adult Education Quarterly 62*(2) 138–158. Permission to republish granted by Sage. http://aeq.sagepub.com The authors would like to acknowledge the contribution of the learners, educators, staff and committee members of the Enable Education, Training and Development Initiative to this study. This chapter was presented as a paper at the Kenton Phumula conference, South Coast, KwaZulu-Natal, South Africa, October 25–28, 2007, titled "Adults With Disabilities: Perspectives on and Experiences of Education."

REFERENCES

Aarons, D., & Glaser, M. (2002). A deaf adult literacy collective. *Stellenbosch Papers in Linguistics, 34*, 1–18.

Africa campaign on disability and HIV&AIDS. (2008). *Kampala declaration on disability and HIV/AIDS*. Retrieved from http://www.heard.org.za/downloads/disability-kampala-declaration.pdf

Aitchison, J. (1999). Literacy and adult basic education and training in South Africa: A quick survey. *Adult Education and Development, 53*, 99–120.

Aitchison, J., Houghton, T., & Baatjes, I. (2000). *University of natal survey of ABE and training: South Africa*. Pietermaritzburg, South Africa: University of Natal, Centre for Adult Education.

Armstrong, P. (1982). The "needs-meeting" ideology in liberal adult education. *International Journal of Lifelong Education, 1*, 293–321.

Baatjes, I. (2003). The new knowledge-rich society: Perpetuating marginalisation and exclusion. *Journal of Education, 29*, 179–204.
Babbie, E., & Mouton, J. (2001). *The practice of social research*. Oxford, England: Oxford University Press.
Balcazar, F., Keys, C., Kaplan, D., & Suarez-Balcazar, Y. (1998). Participatory action research and people with disabilities: Principles and challenges. *Canadian Journal of Rehabilitation, 12*, 105–112.
Barnes, C. (2003). What a difference a decade makes: Reflections on doing "emancipatory" disability research. *Disability & Society, 18*, 3–17.
Barnes, C., Oliver, M., & Barton, L. (2002). Introduction. In C. Barnes, M. Oliver & L. Barton (Eds.), *Disability studies today* (pp. 1–17). Oxford, England: Blackwell.
Barton, L. (1998). Developing an emancipatory research agenda: Possibilities and dilemmas. In P. Clough & L. Barton (Eds.), *Articulating with difficulty: Research voices in inclusive education* (pp. 29–39). London, England: Paul Chapman.
Clark, A. (1997). *Being there: Putting brain, body, and world together again*. Cambridge: MIT Press.
Clark, M. (2006). Adult education and disability studies, an interdisciplinary relationship. *Adult Education Quarterly, 56*, 308–322.
Cohen, L., Manion, L., & Morrison, K. (2007). *Research methods in education* (6th ed.). New York, NY: Routledge.
Collins, P. (2009). *Black feminist thought*. New York, NY: Routledge.
Corley, M. A., & Taymans, J. M. (2001). Adults with learning disabilities and the role of self determination: Implications for literacy. *Canadian Journal for the Study of Adult Education,15*, 149–167.
Department of Education. (2008). *Kha Ri Gude mass literacy campaign. Report to Portfolio Committee on Education, 19 August*. Retrieved from http://www.pmg.org.za/files/docs/080819kharigude.pdf
Emmett, T. (2006). Disability, poverty, gender and race. In B. Watermeyer, L. Swartz, T. Lorenzo, M. Schneider, & M. Priestley (Eds.), *Disability and social change: A South African agenda* (pp. 207–233). Cape Town, South Africa: HSRC Press.
Enable Education, Training and Development Initiative. (2007). *Annual Report 2006–7*. Durban, South Africa: Author.
Freire, P. (1972). *Pedagogy of the oppressed*. London, England: Penguin Books.
Freire, P. (1998). *Pedagogy of hope: Reliving pedagogy of the oppressed*. New York, NY: Continuum.
Gallagher, S. (2005). *How the body shapes the mind*. Oxford, England: Clarendon Press.
Gibbs, R. W. (2006). *Embodiment and cognitive science*. Cambridge, England: Cambridge University Press.
Glaser, M., & Lorenzo, T. (2006). Developing literacy with deaf adults. In B. Watermeyer, L. Swartz, T. Lorenzo, M. Schneider, & M. Priestley (Eds.), *Disability and social change: A South African agenda* (pp. 192–205). Cape Town, South Africa: HSRC Press.
Goffman, E. (1968). *Stigma: Notes on the management of spoiled identity*. Harmondsworth: Penguin Books.
Grundy, S. (1987). *Curriculum: Product or praxis*. Lewes, England: Falmer.
Human Sciences Research Council. (2009). *South African national HIV prevalence, incidence, behaviour and communication survey, 2008: A turning tide among teenagers?* Cape Town, South Africa: Human Sciences Research Council Press.
Kemmis, S., & McTaggart, R. (1992). *The action research planner* (3rd ed.). Geelong, Victoria, Australia: Deakin University Press.
Lakoff, G., & Johnson, M. (1999). *Philosophy in the flesh*. New York, NY: Cambridge University Press.
Lichtman, M. (2006). *Qualitative research in education: A user's guide*. Thousand Oaks, CA: Sage.
McNiff, J., Lomax, P., & Whitehead, J. (2003). *You and your action research project* (2nd ed.). London, England: RoutledgeFalmer.
Mercer, G. (2002). Emancipatory disability research. In C. Barnes, M. Oliver, & L. Barton (Eds.), *Disability studies today* (pp. 228–249). Oxford, England: Blackwell.
Merriam, S. B., Caffarella, R. S., & Baumgartner, L. M. (2007). *Learning in adulthood: A Comprehensive guide* (3rd ed.). San Francisco, CA: Jossey-Bass.
Merriam, S. B., & Ntseane, G. (2008). Transformational learning in Botswana: How culture shapes the process. *Adult Education Quarterly, 58*, 183–197.

Mezirow, J. (1991). *Transformative dimensions of adult learning.* San Francisco, CA: Jossey-Bass.
Oliver, M. (1983). *Social work with disabled people.* Basingstoke, England: Macmillan.
Oliver, M. (1992). Changing the social relations of research production. *Disability, Handicap, & Society, 7,* 101–115.
Oliver, M. (1996). *Understanding disability: From theory to practice.* Basingstoke, England: Macmillan.
Philpott, S., & Sait, W. (2001). Disabled children: An emergency submerged. In M. Priestley (Ed.), *Disability and the life course: Global perspectives* (pp. 151–165). Cambridge, England: Cambridge University Press.
Radermacher, H. (2006). *Participatory action research with people with disabilities: Exploring experiences of participation* (Unpublished doctoral dissertation). Victoria University, Melbourne, Australia.
Ram, A., & Muthukrishna, N. (2001). Voices of deaf adults in South Africa. *Perspectives in Education, 19,* 39–52.
Republic of South Africa. (1997). *Integrated national disability strategy* (White Paper). Pretoria, South Africa: Office of the Deputy President.
Rocco, T. S. (2001). Helping adult educators understand disability disclosure. *Adult Learning, 12,* 10–12.
Rocco, T. S. (2002, October). *The invisible people: Disability, diversity, and issues of power in adult education.* Paper presented at the Midwest Research-to-Practice conference in Adult, Continuing, and Community Education, Northern Illinois University, DeKalb.
Sample, P. (1996). Beginnings: Participatory action research and adults with developmental disabilities. *Disability & Society, 11,* 317–332.
Schneider, M. (2006). Disability and the environment. In B. Watermeyer, L. Swartz, T. Lorenzo, M. Schneider, & M. Priestley (Eds.), *Disability and social change: A South African agenda* (pp. 8–18). Cape Town, South Africa: HSRC Press.
Scully, J. (2008). *Disability bioethics: Moral bodies, moral difference.* Lanham, MD: Rowman & Littlefield.
Scully, J. (2009). Disability and the thinking body. In K. Kristiansen, S. Vehmas, & T. Shakespeare (Eds.), *Arguing about disability: Philosophical perspectives* (pp. 57–73). London, England: Routledge.
Shakespeare, T. (2006). *Disability rights and wrongs.* London, England: Routledge.
Siebers, T. (2008). *Disability theory.* Ann Arbor: University of Michigan Press.
Smith, S. (2009). Social justice and disability: Competing interpretations of the medical and social models. In K. Kristiansen, S. Vehmas, & T. Shakespeare (Eds.), *Arguing about disability: Philosophical perspectives* (pp. 15–28). London, England: Routledge.
Soudien, C., & Baxen, J. (2006). Disability and schooling in South Africa. In B. Watermeyer, L. Swartz, T. Lorenzo, M. Schneider, & M. Priestley (Eds.), *Disability and social change: A South African agenda* (pp. 149–163). Cape Town, South Africa: HSRC Press.
Statistics South Africa. (2005). *Prevalence of disability in South Africa.* Pretoria, South Africa: Author.
Statistics South Africa. (2009). *Mid-year population estimates, 2009.* Retrieved from http://www.statssa.gov.za/PublicationsHTML/P03022009/html/P03022009.html
Strauss, A., & Corbin, J. (1990). *Basics of qualitative research.* Newbury Park, CA: Sage.
Taylor, E. (2007). An update on transformative learning theory: A critical review of the empirical research (1999–2005). *International Journal of Lifelong Education, 26,* 173–191.
Thomas, C., & Corker, M. (2002). A journey around the social model. In M. Corker & T. Shakespeare (Eds.), *Disability/postmodernity: Embodying disability theory* (pp. 18–31). London, England: Continuum.
Torres, C. A. (1992). Participatory action research and popular education in Latin America. *International Journal of Qualitative Studies in Education, 5,* 51–62.
United Nations. (2006). *Convention on the rights of persons with disabilities.* Retrieved from http://www.un.org/disabilities/default.asp?id=150
Van Niekerk, L., Lorenzo, T., & Mdlokolo, P. (2006). Understanding partnerships in developing disabled entrepreneurs through Participatory Action Research. *Disability and Rehabilitation, 28,* 323–331.
Varela, F., Thompson, E., & Rosch, E. (1991). *The embodied mind: Cognitive science and human experience.* Cambridge: MIT Press.

Weigt, G. (2007). Inclusive development: The rights of persons with disabilities to equal participation. *Adult Education and Development, 68*, 7–12.

Williams, G. (2001). Theorizing disability. In G. L. Albrecht, K. D. Seelman, & M. Bury (Eds.), *Handbook of disability studies* (pp. 123–144). Thousand Oaks, CA: Sage.

Wilson, M. (2002). Six views of embodied cognition. *Psychonomic Bulletin & Review, 9*, 625–636.

AFFILIATIONS

Peter Rule
Senior lecturer in the Centre for Adult Education,
University of KwaZulu-Natal in Pietermaritzburg, South Africa

Taadi Ruth Modipa
A materials developer for Learn with Echo, *a weekly adult education newspaper supplement, in the Centre for Adult Education,*
University of KwaZulu-Natal in Pietermaritzburg, South Africa

CYNTHIA LEE A. PEMBERTON & EILEEN CASEY WHITE

6. WOMEN, SPORT AND ADULT EDUCATION: SHORTCHANGING WOMEN AND GIRLS

INTRODUCTION

In 1992 the American Association of University Women (AAUW) released a report titled *How Schools Shortchange Girls*. The report challenged the assumption that girls and boys were being treated equally and/or receive an equitable education in American public schools. The report showed that despite 40 years of existing United States (U.S.) federal educational equity legislation (i.e., Title IX of the 1972 Education Amendments) girls were not receiving the same quality or quantity of education as their brothers. More recently in her 2008 book *The Gender Gap in College: Maximizing the Developmental Potential of Women and Men*, Linda Sax noted that although "…[s]ome…education statistics do paint a rosy picture for women, who now make up the majority of undergraduates (up to 58 percent nationally), earn better college grades than men do, and are more likely than men to complete college" (p. 1), educational equity is about more than numbers. According to Sax:

> …gender shapes not just the characteristics of women and men entering college but also the way in which women and men *experience* college. In various ways and to varying extents, gender influences how women's and men's interactions with people, programs, and services on campus ultimately contribute to their academic success, their beliefs about themselves, and their outlook on life. (p. 217)

It is the intersection of this gender-differentiated educational experience with adult education and the life and learning skills attributed to and gained through emotionally connected experiential learning opportunities—like sport, that provide the thematic focus of this chapter.

GENDER BIAS IN SCHOOL

Historically, "[t]o say that schools have had a 'gender bias,'" according to Nicholson (1980) "…is not to say that schools have excluded women. It is rather to say that schooling has been primarily intended for young men and only secondarily for young women" (p. 231). According to Nicholson, "Schools, rather than providing a fair means for channeling young people of different capacities into different classes, legitimize existing class, [and gender] divisions, [as well as stereotypes] constructed on the basis of differences in inheritance" (p. 225). Schools and schooling by their very nature have and continue to reinforce gender-differentiation and gender bias classroom-by-classroom across all levels of the educational system (Orenstein, 1994; Sadker & Sadker, 1994; Sadker, Sadker, & Zittleman, 2009).

At the classroom level, gender bias in education permeates curricular content and context through text books, assignments, assessments, teacher-student and student-student interactions, and language. In terms of text books, assignments and assessments, research shows that the language, examples and even images are quantitatively and qualitatively biased in favor of men and boys (Blumberg, 2007; Klein, 2007; Rosser, 1989; Sadker & Sadker, 1994; Sadker, et al., 2009). As a result, females see themselves and their experiences reflected in and through curricular content vehicles not only less often than males, but as less valued. These early age perceptions of the learning environment often continue into adulthood. The positionality implied by the expression, "Where you stand depends on where you sit" is applicable to how students perceive and experience the classroom environment. While students' views of family, peers and teachers do impact the learning process, their ideas, memories, dreams, values, and responding behaviors do as well (Doloz, 1986).

Relative to teacher-student and student-student interactions, according to Sadker, et al. (2009): "Male students frequently control classroom conversations. They ask and answer more questions. They receive more praise for the intellectual quality of their ideas...They get help when they are confused. They are the heart and center of interaction" (p. 65). The researchers went on to say that in the "typical classroom...male students are more often heard and female students more often stifled" (p. 69). Further, the quality of interaction varies by gender, with male students praised for what they do, while female students' praise is too often focused on how they look (Sadker, et al., 2009). These gender-differentiated educational experiences carry forward into and through middle-school and high school where "...even boys not doing well in school believe they are better, [and] more valued, than girls" (Sadker, *et al.,* 2009, p. 125). In terms of adult education, the cumulative impact of these interactions often results in diminished perceptions of potential. According to Knowles (1984), the learners' experiences build their ways of thinking and behaving, becoming the source of their self-identities. The result may be that if female students' contributions to the learning process are ignored or suppressed, "it is not just the experience that is being rejected; it is the person" (p.11).

The relevance of language regarding how we come to understand the world is well documented. According to Pitkin (1972) "What we can say and think is very largely determined by the language we have available" (p. 194). Language literally encodes our thinking based on cultural metaphors (Lakoff & Johnson, 1980) which then colors and contextualizes perceptions and understanding, thereby framing and informing perceived reality. With this in mind it becomes increasingly important that educators are aware of the patterns and impact, not only of their behaviors, but of the language they use. Research by Richmond and Dyba (1982) showed that: "...not only are male terms cited much more frequently in dictionaries and textbooks, but children's books include seven times as many men as women, with the male appearing as the dominant figure" (p. 266). Further, work by Flanagan and Todd-Mancillas (1982) on *Teaching Inclusive Generic Pronoun Usage* demonstrated that "...instructor language choices can have an effect on [the] student's own use of language" (p. 276). As an example, Flanagan and Todd-Mancillas drew attention to the inappropriateness of the continued use of third person masculine pronouns as generic substitutes for references of non-specific gender (p. 275). Considering the relevance of education communication through language and imagery in a more contemporary framework, the advent of social networks and use of "avatars," or social personas in education prompt the question of how women's interactions in these theoretically more gender-neutral settings impact learning. There has been some dispute (AAUW, 2000; Kramarae, 2001) in the early research as to whether computer-mediated education creates a more equal balance between the genders. In the report *The Third Shift: Women Learning Online,* nearly 25% of students asserted that online courses were not gender-neutral and, that men and women interact in different ways, with differing priorities and styles (Kramarae, 2001). According to one teacher interviewed in the report, Most male students are quite skilled at putting

> up a façade of confidence and self-assurance even if they haven't grasped the content of a lecture. Women tend not to ask questions in mixed-gender groups for fear of appearing stupid, thinking that everyone else has understood the subject matter. (p. 44)

Despite these cautions the report noted that women were generally optimistic that technology could balance or reduce the bias and/or discrimination they experienced in a traditional classroom. Research suggests, however, that may not be possible at this stage of online learning development. Rodino (1997) as cited in the AAUW's report (Kramarae, 2001) noted that even when individuals take on another persona (such as an avatar or screen name) "users who present maleness online (whether or not they are male) generally have more power than those who present femaleness" (p. 46). These contemporized e-learning environment findings reinforce the gender-differentiated and gender biased behavior roles that have historically and traditionally typified traditional classroom settings (Blumberg, 2007; Klein, 2007; Rosser, 1989; Sadker & Sadker, 1994; Sadker, et al., 2009).

WOMEN, GIRLS AND SPORT

To overcome gender bias in education, Fagot (1981) urged that "...rather than just presenting a nonsexist environment, an active environment designed to break through sex-stereotypes without threatening gender identity needs to be created..." (p. 270). A medium through which this might be achieved is that of sport participation. However, athletics and sport, like education and schools, have been and are not only gender-differentiated and biased, but have historically and persistently shortchanged women and girls.

Historically there have been three major reasons why women and girls have not had equal sport opportunities to those of men and boys. These are: (a) physiological differences between the sexes ("The longest race allowed for women in the 1972 Olympics was the 1500 metres, a hold-over from the belief that females could not physically or mentally cope with the competitive demand of longer events" [Weiss & Glenn, 1992, p. 139]); (b) societal norms and attitudes; and (c) organizational rules and support (Lumpkin, 1984). Continuing research has provided evidence that (a) there are no medical reasons to justify restricting competition for females based on potential physical and/or psychological harm; (b) cultural attitudes are changing (albeit still slowly) relative to women and girls in sport; and (c) although historically females have gotten the short end of the stick regarding athletic opportunities, equipment, facilities and budgets, equity legislation and ongoing litigation are beginning to force more equitable sport-related support allocations (Acosta & Carpenter, 2012; Lumpkin, 1984; Yasser, McCurdy, Gopelerud, & Weston, 2011; Zimmerman & Reavill, 1998).

LEGISLATING EQUITY: A NECESSARY BUT INSUFFICIENT CONDITION

Using the United States (U.S.) as an example of educational equity legislation, Title IX derives from the 1972 Education Amendments to the 1964 Civil Rights Act, and is "...a statutory remedy for gender-based classifications in education" (Yassser, *et al.*, 2011, p. 136). Among other things Title IX applies to interscholastic (K-12) and intercollegiate athletics in education settings. Title IX states: "No person in the United States shall, on the basis of sex, be excluded from participation in, be denied the benefits of, or be subjected to discrimination under any education program or activity receiving Federal financial assistance" (Title IX, 20 U.S.C. Section 1681). It was signed into law in June of 1972 by President Richard Nixon, and then more fully described and operationalized through the 1975 *Title IX Rules and Regulations* and again in even more detail in the 1979 *Policy Interpretations* propagated by the Department of Health, Education, and Welfare (HEW).

Since the passage of Title IX the percentage of women participating in athletics has increased considerably (Acosta & Carpenter, 2012). That said, even though women and girls represent over half of school enrollments at all levels, male sport participation still dramatically outnumbers that of females (AAUW, 2012; Acosta & Carpenter, 2012; National Coalition for Women & Girls in Education, 2008).

At the high school level, despite growth in female athletics the male favored participation gap has actually widened over the past decade (National Federation of State High School Associations [NFHS], 2007–2008; National Women's Law Center

[NWLC], 2008; Women's Sports Foundation [WSF], 2007). Girls receive just over 40% of all interscholastic athletic opportunities, and lag behind boys in terms of sport-related operating budgets, benefits, services, equipment and facilities (NFHS, 2007–2008; NWLC, 2008; WSF, 2007). Similarly, at the collegiate level, four decades after legislating equity: (a) only about 45% of college athletes are women, (b) women receive a similar percentage of college scholarship dollars and only about a third of athletic department budgets, (c) the ranks of women college coaches have declined from 90% in 1972 to just over 42% in 2010, and (d) female coaches are paid significantly less than their male counterparts (AAUW, 2012; Acosta & Carpenter, 2012; National Coalition for Women & Girls in Education 2008).

Equity matters. The 1975 *Title IX Rules and Regulations* established an initial compliance deadline of July, 1978. Using this compliance deadline as the end-point starting point, roughly 47.26% of the U.S. population has been born since sex-based educational equity was supposed to have been achieved (http://www.census.gov/prod/cen2010/briefs/c2010br-03.pdf). This translates to approximately 145,917,503 people, nearly 61 million of them girls and women who have endured and are still receiving less school sport educational access and opportunity; and as a result less in terms of the chance "...to achieve, to [learn to] overcome obstacles, to practice to the point of proficiency....[to] learn [through school sport participation] about sacrifice, commitment to a greater good, [and] responsibility to others...." (Zimmerman & Reavill, 1998, p. 138). That's a lot of folks, generations of girls and boys, women and men, moving through an education system wherein sex-based discrimination persists.

Legislating equity matters. It provides structural scaffolding for pursuing and establishing educational equity. It is however, a necessary but insufficient condition to actually achieving equity. Achieving equity requires emotional connection—it needs to matter to us practically, morally and ethically—we need to care about it.

Sport and fitness matter. Women and girls are shortchanged in athletics through socialization. As defined by Weiss and Glenn (1992), socialization is "...the process whereby individuals learn the skills, values, norms and behaviors enabling them to function competently in many different social roles within their group or culture" (p. 140). They go on to say that the "...socialization of girls into competitive sport roles is influenced by three interacting factors" (p. 140). These factors are: modeling/mentoring and reinforcement by significant others, available opportunities and personal attributes. Regarding significant others and modeling/mentoring, research shows "...a positive relationship between female self-confidence [and self-esteem] and participation in physical activity..." but, "...girls may not get the same verbal encouragement or prodding [i.e., coaching] in sport that boys may get, and as a consequence girls self-confidence and future achievement levels may suffer" (Lirgg, 1992, p. 164–165). In reference to available opportunities and personal attributes,

Weiss and Glen (1992) suggested that "...performance differences often observed between males and females in sport settings may be a function of experience and practice advantages enjoyed by males because of their earlier introduction into sport, encouragement to become actively involved, and the importance communicated by significant others of being a good athlete" (p. 148). Boys are encouraged and coached to engage and succeed in sport, while girls are often not only not encouraged and coached to be athletically successful, but must overcome society's "...lower expectations of women in sport activities..." (Weiller & Higgs, 1989, p. 65). They must also face stereotypes that haunt them regarding the incompatibility of traditional female roles and success in sport (Weiller & Higgs, 1989).

In a 1993 study conducted by the University of Wisconsin titled: *My Worst Nightmare... Wisconsin Students' Perceptions of Being the Other Gender,*

> ...sport involvement was the most frequently mentioned subject coded under the category of the school and the second most frequently mentioned item in the entire survey...most girls thought that more opportunities for sports participation would be a positive outcome of being a boy and most boys indicated they thought less opportunity to participate in sports would be a negative outcome of being a girl. (p.7)

According to Greendorfer (1987) "...the domain of sport has been ignored all too often as a potential source of rich social learning experiences for females (p. 339)." In terms of the playing field of life, qualities associated with sport participation have been linked to leadership (Aburdene & Naisbitt, 1992; Cantor & Bernay, 1992). As an example, Cantor and Bernay (1992) interviewed 25 female government leaders asking what qualities and/or strengths they believed contributed to their success in getting elected and persevering in government/ political leadership positions. Time and again, the women interviewed noted sport participation as a "training ground" (p. 62) for effective participation on the "playing field of power" (p. 50).

Sport and fitness activities are important physically, mentally and emotionally (Lopiano, 1994; Weiss & Glenn, 1992). Women and girls who participate in sports are more achievement-oriented, independent and confident (Sabo, 1993). "[G]irls who are athletes do better in school...[earn] higher grades and [get] better standardized test scores...are less likely to drop out of high school and more likely to go on to college than their nonathletic counterparts" (Zimmerman & Reaville, 1998, p. 21). Girls who play sports are less likely to have unwanted pregnancies, and less likely to become involved in drugs than their non-athletic peers (Lopiano, 1994; Sadker & Sadker, 1994; Sadker, et al., 2009).

Sport and fitness matter. Through the emotionally connected learning opportunities inherent in these activities, women and girls, like men and boys, build strong and capable "...ways of thinking and behaving..." (Knowles, 1984, p. 11). As young women move into adulthood, learning experiences can and do build on the strengths developed through their participation in sport. Through these experiences the learner's self-agency is empowered, enabling her to choose to make her own interpretations, rather than responding subconsciously to the judgments and biases of others. This empowerment is a core goal of adult education.

CONNECTING THE DOTS – WOMEN, SPORT AND ADULT EDUCATION

Through empowerment, adult education promotes changes, encouraging growth and development and enabling agency for the learner (Caffarella, 1994; Merriam & Caffarella, 1999; Wilson & Hayes, 2000). Adult learning is grounded in experience; that is, the experiences adults bring to the learning environment, the experiences that motivate them to engage in learning, and the experiences they engage in as part of the learning process (Caffarella, 1994, Caffarella & Barnett, 1994; Merriam & Caffarella, 1999; Wilson & Hayes, 2000). Adults need to have their experiences acknowledged by, applied to and included in the learning process. They need to be actively involved in the learning process, not just passive recipients of knowledge. Adults need to have concrete experiences, make reflective observations, engage in abstract conceptualization, and actively experiment (Kolb's learning process, as cited in Lewis & Williams, 1994, Wilson & Hayes, 2000).

Malcom Knowles (1984), an early adult education theorist, described and defined adult learning in terms of what he called "andragogy." According to Knowles, andragogy is ". . . a label for the growing body of knowledge and technology in regard to adult learning . . . [i.e.,] . . . the art and science of helping adults learn" (p. 6). Knowles (1984) and Brookfield (1986, 1995) described and defined andragogy as separate and distinct from pedagogy. They distinguished pedagogy's core tenant in terms of content planning, while noting andragogy as being experientially grounded in process design. In contrast to pedagogy, andragogy's process design is learner centered, learner driven, fully grounded in the learner's experience, and requires the educator to facilitate and/or coach the learner in and through the transformative changes, growth and development inherent in the learning process.

Transformative learning is the process of creating change within a frame of reference (Mezirow, 1997; 2003). A young woman who participates in sport has gained a body of experiences that defines her world and sense of self-agency. This includes the significant socialization factors cited by Weiss and Glenn (1992) as well as other values, concepts and responses (i.e., ways of thinking and behaving) through which she has learned to interpret her experiences (Aburdene & Naisbitt, 1992; Cantor & Bernay, 1992; Lopiano, 1994; Sadker & Sadker, 1994; Sadker, et al., 2009; Zimmerman & Reaville, 1998). This frame of reference encompasses multiple aspects, including thinking, behavior and emotion, and is comprised of two dimensions: habits of mind and points of view. Habits of mind, which are ways of thinking, feeling and acting, have been strongly influenced by and through the female sport experience. This experience creates a set of codes that shapes one's point of view. While habits of mind are generally deeply rooted in past interactions and culture, points of view can be changed or modified through adult learning practices.

As adults, women learn through four processes that can enhance and strengthen the positive aspects of their youth experiences, and change or eliminate the preconceptions and fallacies about their abilities or roles (Mezirow, 1997). One process is to build on an existing point of view; for example, reinforcing the belief that women can successfully lead and compete in multiple arenas in life, including the male-dominated "playing field of power" (Cantor & Bernay, 1992, p. 50). A second way adults learn is to create new points of view. Female learners can take on new boundary-crossing experiences (e.g., welding) and create alternate understandings about women's opportunities in male-dominated industries. Transforming/changing a point of view is the third way adults learn. An adult learner can experience another culture where women have more dominant or submissive roles in society, for example, which can result in her critically reflecting on her own misconceptions and assumptions, along with more broadly evidenced gender-differentiated/ male-dominated norms, values and beliefs. These processes and their associated experiences can ultimately impact and even transform deeply rooted habits of mind.

Grounded in emotionally connected experiential learning, sport provides women and girls with a vehicle to engage and practice transformative learning processes—processes that serve to challenge and change the limiting frames of reference that can and do guide and prescribe learners' "ways of thinking and behaving" (Knowles, 1984, p. 11). In this way, among others, sport matters for women, girls and adult education. Ultimately sport participation can be and is "…an important feature [and vehicle] of social and political movements struggling for change…" (Mayo, 2009, p.269 ;English & Mayo, 2012, p.215), and a potentially more just world (Brookfield & Holst, 2011).

REFERENCES

AAUW. (2012). *TitleIX athletics statistics.* Available: http://www.aauw.org/act/laf/library/ athletic Statistics.cfm

AAUW. (2000). *Tech-savvy: Educating girls in the new computer age.* Available:www.aauw.org/learn/ research/upload/TechSavvy.pdf

AAUW. (1992). *Executive Summary.* Washington DC: Author.

AAUW. (1992). *Shortchanging girls, shortchanging America: A call to action. AAUW Initiative for Educational Equity.* Washington DC (ERIC Document Reproduction Services No. ED 340 658).

AAUW. (1992). *How schools shortchange girls. A study of major findings on girls and education.* Washington DC. (ERIC Document Reproduction Services No. ED 339 674).

Aburdene, P., & Naisbitt, J. (1992). *Megatrends for women.* New York, NY: Villard Books.

Acosta, V., & Carpenter, L. J. (2012). *Women in intercollegiate sport: A longitudinal, national study thirty five year update.* Available: http://www.acostacarpenter.org/

Blumberg, R. L. (2007). *Gender bias in textbooks: A hidden obstacle on the road to gender equality in education.* Paper commissioned for the EFA Global Monitoring Report 2008, Education for All by 2015: will we make it. United Nations Educational, Scientific and Cultural Organization.

Brookfield, S. D. (1986). *Understanding and facilitating adult learning.* San Francisco, CA: Jossey-Bass.

Brookfield, S. (1995). *Adult Learning: An overview.* Available: http://www. serprofessoruniversitario.pro. br/m%C3%B3dulos/ensino-n%C3%A3o-diretivo/adult-learning-overview.

Bookfield, S. D., & Holst, J. D. (2011). *Radicalizing learning: Adult education for a just world.* San Francisco, CA: Wiley & Sons Inc.

Caffarella, R. S. (1994). *Planning programs for adult learners: A practical guide for educators, trainers, and staff developers.* San Francisco, CA: Jossey-Bass.

Caffarella, R. S., & Barnett, B. G. (1994). Characteristics of adult learners and foundations of experiential learning. In L. Jackson & R. W. Caffarella (Eds.), *Experiential learning: A new approach* (pp. 29–42). San Francisco, CA: Jossey-Bass.

Cantor, D. W., & Bernay, T. (1992). *Women in power: The secrets of leadership.* Boston, MA: Houghton Mifflin Company.

English, L., & Mayo, P. (2012). *learning with Adults. A Critical pedagogical Introduction,* Rotterdam and Taipei: Sense.

Fagot, B. (1981). Male and female teachers: Do they treat boys and girls differently? *Sex Roles, 7*(3) 263–271.

Flanagan, A. M., & Todd-Mancillas, W. R. (1982). *Teaching inclusive gender pronoun usage: The effectiveness of an authority innovation-decision, 31*(4). 275–284.

Greendorfer, S. L. (1987). Gender bias in theoretical perspectives: The case of female socialization into sport. *Psychology of Women Quarterly, 11*(3), 327–340.

Klein, S. S. (2007). *Handbook for achieving gender equity through education* (2nd ed.). New York, NY: Lawrence Erlbaum Associates, Taylor & Francis Group.

Knowles, M. S. (1984). *Andragogy in action.* San Francisco, CA: Jossey Bass.

Kramarae, C. (2001). *The third shift: Women learning online.* Washington, DC: AAUW Educational Foundation.

Lakoff, G., & Johnson, M. (1980). *Metaphors we live by.* Chicago, IL: The University of Chicago Press.

Lewis, L. H., & Williams, C. J. (1994). Experiential learning: Past and present. In L. Jackson & R.S. Caffarella (Eds.), *Experiential learning: A new approach* (pp. 5–16). San Francisco, CA: Jossey-Bass.

Lopiano, D. A. (1994). Equity in women's sports: A health and fairness perspective. *The Athletic Woman, 13*(2), 281–296.

Lumpkin, A. (1984). *Historical perspectives of female participation in youth sport.* Paper Presented at: The annual convention of the American alliance for health, physical education, recreation and dance. Washington DC (ERIC Document Reproduction Services No. ED 243 878).

Mayo, P. (2009). Flying below the Radar? Critical approaches to adult education. In M. Apple, L. Gandin & W. Au. *The routledge international handbook of critical education* (pp. 269–280), new York & London: Routledge.

Merriam S. B., & Caffarella, R. S. (1999). *Learning in adulthood: A comprehensive guide.* San Francisco, CA: Jossey-Bass.

Mezirow, J. (1997). Transformative learning: Theory to practice. *New directions for adult and continuing education, 74,* p. 5–12. http://www.hrdmax.com/images/ column_1325932983/Mezirow%20 Transformative%20Learning.pdf

Mezirow, J. (2003). Transformative learning as discourse. *Journal of Transformative Education, 1*(1), 58–63.

National Coalition for Women & Girls in Education (2008). *Beyond the headlines: A report of the National Coalition for Women and Girls in Education.* Available: www.ncwge.org/PDF/TitleIXat35.pdf

National Federation of State High School Associations (NFHS). 2007–2008 High school athletics participation survey. Available: http://www.nfhs.org

National Women's Law Center. (2008, June). *The battle for gender equity in athletics in elementary and secondary schools.* Available: http://www.nwlc.org/pdf/Battle%20 final.pdf

National Center for Education Statistics (NCES). (2012). *Fast facts.* Available: http://nces.ed.gov/fastfacts/display.asp?id=98

Nicholson, L. (1980). Women and schooling. *Educational Theory, 30* (3), 225–234.

Orenstein, P. (1994). *School girls: Young women, self-esteem and the confidence gap.* New York, NY: Anchor Books.

Pitkin, H. F. (1972). *Wittgenstein and justice: On the significance of Ludwig wittgenstein for social and political thought.* Berkeley, CA: University of California Press.

Richmond, V. P., & Dyba, P. (1982, October). The roots of sexual stereotyping: The teacher as model. *Communication Education. 31*, 265–273.
Rosser, P. (1989). *Gender and testing*. Berkeley, CA: National Commission on Testing and Public Policy—Graduate School of Education, University of California at Berkeley.
Sabo, D. (1993). Psychosocial impacts of athletic participation on American women: Facts and fables. In D. S. Eitzen (Ed.). *Sport in Contemporary Society: An Anthology* (pp. 374–87). New York, NY: St. Martin's Press.
Sadker, M., & Sadker, D. (1994). *Failing at fairness: How our schools cheat girls*. New York, NY: Simon & Schuster Publishers.
Sadker, D., Sadker, M., & Zittleman, K. R. (2009). *Still failing at fairness: How gender bias cheats girls and boys in school and what we can do about it*. New York, NY: Scribner.
Title IX of the Education Amendments of 1972, 20 U.S.C. § 1681 (2000).
U.S. Census Bureau (2010). *Age and Sex Compositions: 2010 U.S. Census Briefs*. http://www.census.gov/prod/cen2010/briefs/c2010br-03.pdf
United States Department of Health, Education, and Welfare. (1980). Rules and regulations. *Federal Register, 45*(92), 30-955-30, 965.
United States Department of Health, Education, and Welfare. (1979). Policy interpretation. *Federal Register, 44*(239), 71, 413–71423.
United States Department of Health, Education, and Welfare. (1990). *Title IX Athletics Investigator's Manual*. Washington D.C.: Office for Civil Rights, Department of Education.
Weiller, K. H., & Higgs, C. T. (1989, August). Female learned helplessness in sport. An analysis of children's literature. *Journal of Physical Education, Recreation, and Dance. 60*(6), 65–67.
Weiss, M. R., & Glenn, S. D. (1992, August). Psychological development and females' sport participation: An interaction perspective. *Quest, 44*(22), 138–157.
Wilson, A. L., & Hayes, E. R., (2000). *Handbook of adult and continuing education*. San Francisco, CA: Jossey-Bass Higher & Adult Education Series.
Wisconsin Univ.-Stout, Menomonie. Center for vocational, technical and adult education. (1993). *"My worst nightmare..." Wisconsin students' perceptions of being the other gender. A statewide study to document current gender perceptions of Wisconsin students*. Menomonie, WI: Wisconsin state dept. of public instruction. (ERIC Document Reproduction Service No. ED 356 426).
Women's Sports Foundation. (2007, December 12). *Women's sports & physical activity facts & statistics*. Available: http://www.womenssportsfoundation.org/binary-data/WSF_ARTICLE/pdf_file/191.pdf
Yasser, R., McCurdy, J. R., Goplerud, C. P., & Weston, M. A. (2011). *Sports law cases and materials* (7th ed.). San Francisco, CA: Mathew Bender - Lexis Nexis Law School Publishing.
Zimmerman, J., & Reavill, G. (1998). *Raising our athletic daughters: How sports can build self-esteem and save girls' lives*. New York, NY: Doubleday Publishing.

AFFILIATIONS

Cynthia Lee A. Pemberton
Provost & Vice President for Academic Affairs,
Professor of Education,
Dickinson State University, Dickinson, ND 58601

Eileen Casey White
President, Connections Consulting,
Salem, Oregon

ROBERT HILL

7. QUEERING THE DISCOURSE: INTERNATIONAL ADULT LEARNING AND EDUCATION[1]

INTRODUCTION

In 1997, Merriam and Brockett pointed out that,

> through conscious or benign neglect, women, racial minorities, homosexuals, older individuals, and so on have had little if any say in determining what counts as adult education. These voices have not been acknowledged in the construction of the official knowledge base, in the preparation of professionals, or in activities of the profession. (p. 243)

A decade after they penned these lines, Baird (2007) would write that sexual orientation remained a controversial issue in most technologically-developing nations. This could also have been claimed for most of the (so-called) technologically-developed countries as well. Across time and space the topics of sexual orientation, gender identity and gender expression—sexual minority[2] issues that involve lesbian, gay, bisexual, transgender, Two Spirit, intersex and Queer people—have been taboo terrain in international adult learning and education.

As a backdrop to this chapter, internationally, as many as 78 nations, approximately 40% of United Nations membership, still outlaw "homosexuality[3]" (Itaborahy, 2012). South Sudan became the most recent, in 2008 under the moral code and religious law of Islam, known as Sharia. And, at least seven countries prescribe death for convictions of same-sex behavior (O'Flaherty & Fisher, 2008). Furthermore, it is not safe to assume that the remaining 60% of countries, where sexual minorities are not listed in the penal code, are free from discrimination and violence. In fact, extra-judicial and non-state actors often play roles that equal the oppression of state-sponsored inequity. Problems cut across the spectrum of life events and geographies. So, whether it is the murder of transsexuals, where globally one is killed every three days (Balzer, 2009); discrimination in employment in Turkey (Ozturk, 2011); bullying, unfair treatment in housing, or property crimes in the United States (Herek, 2009); intolerance toward HIV-positive gay men in South Africa (Cloete, Simbayi, Kalichman, & Henda, 2008); intimidation, arrests, and discrimination in education in Guyana (*Human rights violations in Guyana*, 2012); speech inciting attacks on sexual minorities in Armenia (*Human rights violations in Armenia*, 2012); the inadequacy of the official ombudsman in Lithuania (*Human rights violations in Lithuania*, 2012); the jailing, beating, and ridicule (including by family members) of women and men in the Middle East (Whitaker, 2006); to Singapore's state and moral-religious entrepreneurs who have ideologically mobilized a conservative majority to mete out caning and imprisonment (Tan & Jin, 2007)—sexual minorities remain the objects of scorn and repression. The spectrum of treatment ranges from repression through criminalization that at times leads to death. This multifarious exclusion significantly impacts the public and private spheres of sexual minorities who are disenfranchised from the rights and privileges of citizenship in democratic societies. Perhaps the most current compilation of sexual minority rights is the report, *Discriminatory laws and practices and acts of violence against individuals based on the sexual orientation and gender identity* (2011), commissioned by the UN Office of the High Commissioner for Human Rights. This study shows the violence, silencing, and discrimination that have been ongoing for nearly two decades that human rights treaty bodies and special procedures of the Human Rights Council have documented.

This chapter is written from the sociopolitical landscape of the United Nation's (UN) Universal Declaration of Human Rights (UDHR), various UN and UNESCO events, and several government policies and practices. The chapter situates libratory education for sexual orientation and gender identity in the context of the right to learn: to be, to become, to belong, to know, to do, and to live together. These "pillars" are derived from UNESCO's *Delors Report, The International Commission on Education for the Twenty-first Century*. This report advocates that, all societies desire a necessary Utopia in which none of the talents, hidden like buried treasure in all people, are left fallow (Delors, et al., 1996). Libratory pedagogy is one that works against violence. As defined by Freire (1970), "An act of violence is any situation in which some [people] prevent others from the process of inquiry.... Any attempt to prevent human freedom is an 'act of violence.' Any system which deliberately tries to discourage critical consciousness is guilty of oppressive violence (p. 74)."

We sexual minorities—and our allies—both challenge, and in many instances are changing, social and public policies, employment, and cultural attitudes toward human rights and social justice for our communities. This has implications for all people, regardless of sexual orientation or gender identity. There is also "pushback" against the individual and social transformation we are generating (Hill, 2009). This work argues that education must counteract resistance to change.

THE UNITED NATIONS: A QUEER GLANCE

There has been positive movement at the UN for action supportive of sexual minorities in the past decade and a half. This history is far too complex to fully address here. I will mention only a few movements that have taken place in this direction. For a number of years, domestic partner benefits for UN workers were on the agenda. And, in 2003 Brazil moved to add sexual orientation to human rights protection documents of the UN. An epic moment in the battle for sexual minority rights was the promulgation of the *Yogyakarta Principles on the application of international human rights law in relation to sexual orientation and gender identity* (2006). This set of twenty six principles addresses sexual orientation, gender identity and intersexuality, with the intent to apply international human rights law to redress abuses; principles 12–18 include the role of education. The earlier *Vienna Declaration and Programme of Action* (1993), a human rights declaration promulgated at the *World Conference on Human Rights* in Vienna, was the prelude to the *Yogyakarta Principles*. Although the *World Conference* did not mention sexual minorities, it unambiguously reaffirmed fundamental human rights, the dignity and worth of the every human, and in the equal rights of men and women and of all nations. The *Yogyakarta Principles,* however, identify state obligations "to respect, protect, and fulfill the human rights of all persons regardless of their sexual orientation or gender identity" (O'Flaherty & Fisher, 2008, p. 207). These documents call on all nations and institutions to include human rights as a subject in the curricula of all learning institutions in formal and non-formal settings.

In 2008 and subsequent years, the UN took positive actions to extend the promotion and protection of human rights based on sexual orientation and gender identity (See, for example, Angell-Hansen, 2010; *UN: General Assembly to address sexual orientation and gender identity,* 2008; and *UN Human Rights Council passes first-ever resolution,* 2011).

In a landmark speech on sexual minority rights, delivered on Human Rights Day, December 10, 2010, Ban Ki-moon, the Secretary-General of the UN noted that, "As men and women of conscience, we reject discrimination in general, and in particular discrimination based on sexual orientation and gender identity….Where there is tension between cultural attitudes and universal human rights, universal human rights must carry the day" (*Speak up,* 2012). In fact, the Office of the High Commissioner for Human Rights has issued supportive statements periodically throughout that past half-decade (*Justice and equality for all,* 2009).

In June 2011, the action by the UN Human Rights Council, Agenda item 8, *Follow-up and implementation of the Vienna Declaration and Programme of Action* (2011) was notable in its request for the UN High Commission on Human Rights to draft a report detailing the global situation of sexual minorities, and to act on the *Vienna Declaration and Programme of Action*. Thus, the fight at the UN, from 2003–2011 for universal protection of sexual minorities had gained ground. In March, 2012, the Human Rights Council held a watershed formal UN inter-governmental debate on violence and discrimination against sexual minorities. The panel session, titled, "Ending Violence and Discrimination based on Sexual Orientation and Gender Identity," was a response to the June 2011 call of the UN Human Rights Council resolution 17/19 that articulated "grave concern" (*UN Human Rights Council: Landmark Report and Panel,* 2012, para 3) at the discrimination and violence based on sexual orientation and gender identity. The meeting also called for a panel discussion at the 19th session of the Human Rights Council to discuss the findings of the report in a "constructive, informed and transparent dialogue" (para 3).

UNESCO: A QUEER GLANCE

A main interest for educationists is understandably the pedagogical aspect of the United Nation's Educational, Scientific, and Cultural Organization's (UNESCO) mission, and in particular the youth and adult learning and education (ALE) dimension. In the context of education generally, and adult education specifically, from its founding UNESCO has been slow to address sexual minority issues. One of the first documents on the topic was the paper, "Turning a gay gaze on citizenship. Sexual orientation and gender identity: Contesting/ed terrain" (Hill, 2003). This work was published by UNESCO's Institute for Lifelong Learning in celebration of the 50th Anniversary of UNESCO.

CONFINTEA MEETINGS: A QUEER GLANCE

UNESCO has sponsored conferences every twelve years since 1949 "centering on policy dialogue and advocacy in the field of adult education and learning" titled, *CONFérence INTernationale sur l'Education des Adultes,* or the International Conference on Adult Education (CONFINTEA). It is the only conference of its kind at a global level (see: *Welcome to the CONFINTEA portal,* 2010–2011). CONFINTEA meetings are thought by many educators to be the most important international event for youth and adult education. CONFINTEA gatherings are attended officially by UNESCO member states' representatives, mainly Ministries of Education, or their representatives, and work to establish international guidelines for education policies. In recent years, advocacy by civil society organizations has influenced various stages of this process, with the intent to influence the language of the final policy document and the commitments (actions) agreed upon by the governments present at the meetings.

One such conference was the fifth meeting, CONFINTEA V, convened in Hamburg, Germany in 1997. More than 1,500 representatives of governments and non-governmental organizations (NGOs) developed ten themes to promote the assertion that adult learning is the key to the 21st century. These themes included notions about adult learning, democracy, peace, and critical citizenship; improving conditions and quality of adult learning; literacy and basic education; promoting the empowerment of women; the changing world of work; the environment; health, and population; special needs groups; media, culture and information and communication technologies (ICTs); aging populations; migrants; prisoners; persons with disabilities; indigenous communities and cultural minorities; the economics of adult learning and enhancing international co-operation; and solidarity and networking for and through adult learning. More than a decade later, most government policymakers, as well as educators working in adult and lifelong learning had neither interpreted nor applied *any* of these themes in consideration of the rights and needs of sexual minorities. For example, lesbian, gay, bisexual, transgender, and indigenous expressions of gender non-conformity remain silenced, marginalized, and invisible—often driven underground—in most countries around the world. Sexual minorities had clearly fallen into the rank of second-class citizens.

At CONFINTEA V in 1997, sexual orientation and gender identity were not on the agenda. However, participants,

> Developed…thematic areas which [had] direct relevance to sexual minorities…as persons, citizens, learners, and workers. Yet…most government policymakers as well as educators working in adult and lifelong education… neither interpreted nor applied any of these themes in consideration of the rights and needs of sexual minorities. For example…under the theme of adult learning, democracy, peace, and critical citizenship, sexual minorities clearly fall into the rank of second-class citizens in most countries of the world. Sexual-minority individuals and communities are denied full and equal rights, justice and equality, free will, and the right to organise. They usually do not have full opportunity to participate in civil society and to openly engage in economic development in the formal and informal economies. This composite exclusion deeply impacts the wellbeing and public and personal health of sexual-minority citizens who are disenfranchised from the access and accommodation that go hand in hand with the rights and privileges of citizenship in democratic cultures and societies. (Hill, 2007, p. 171)

Hill (2003, 2007) has pointed out that CONFINTEA meetings from 1948 to 1997 had not discussed the rights of sexual minorities. CONFINTEA V, however, had a 'midterm' evaluation (2003), which, although not an official decision-making meeting, was convened in Bangkok, Thailand, six years into the cycle to assess whether countries were meeting the commitments made in Hamburg. At the midterm evaluation, new ideas were permitted for discussion—ideas that had not been covered six years prior. Advocates partnered with others to organize a movement to challenge participants to think about sexual minorities. Robert Hill from the United States introduced language that added sexual minorities into the midterm evaluation closing document, "Call to Action," which was immediately opposed by some members of the delegation from Uganda. A brief but very heated debate erupted, and Justin Ellis, from Angola, the convener of the closing session, called a recess. During the break, with the assistance of Alan Tuckett (NIACE), Hill spoke to the Uganda leadership and compromise language was decided. When reconvened, the simple insertion calling for rights of LGBT people—in countries where such rights were legal—was accepted. The official, and historic, wording found in the document, *Recommitting to Adult Education and Learning. Synthesis Report of the CONFINTEA V Midterm Review Meeting* (September 6–11, 2003, Bangkok, Thailand), is, "We therefore call upon Member States, bi- and multilateral agencies, non-governmental and civil- society organizations, social movements and the private sector...to adopt inclusive policies and take concrete measures and provide adequate resources in support of education programs mainstreaming and catering to the learning demands of...marginalized groups such as indigenous people, migrants and refugees, minorities (including *sexual minorities*, where licit), prisoners etc...." (*italics* not in original; the underscored phrase was the compromise).

In preparation for CONFINTEA VI (held in Belém, Brazil in 2009), the International Council for Adult Education (ICAE) published a special issue of the international journal, *Convergence*. In it appeared an article, "Finding a voice for sexual minority rights (lesbian, gay, bisexual, transgender, indigenous / Two-Spirit, and Queer): Some comprehensive policy considerations" (Hill, 2007). Although success was achieved at the CONFINTEA V midterm evaluation in Bangkok, the next arena was to move the agenda for sexual minority rights to the official CONFINTEA VI. Missing this opportunity would mean waiting until 2021 for the next chance. Some adult education scholar-activists were determined to not let this opportunity slip by.

Hill continued to lobby and work for the time when CONFINTEA VI in 2009 would provide the opportunity for the coalition of proponents to move the agenda of Queer rights forward. This work included a Panel Presentation and a workshop at the International Civil Society Forum (FISC for its Portuguese acronym) that preceded CONFINTEA VI, also in Belém. In December 2009, 156 member states of the UN endorsed the definition of adult education, first laid down in the Nairobi Recommendation on the Development of Adult Education of 1976, and further developed in the Hamburg Declaration of 1997, namely, adult education denotes,

> the entire body of ongoing learning processes, formal or otherwise, whereby people regarded as adults by the society to which they belong develop their abilities, enrich their knowledge, and improve their technical or professional qualifications or turn them in a new direction to meet their own needs and those of their society. (*CONFINTEA VI: Living and Learning for a Viable Future*, 2009, p. 1)

At CONFINTEA VI, one more step toward LGBTQ freedom was achieved when, in the Final Belém Framework, sexual minority rights were added to the official language of the conference. It declared under the section "Participation, inclusion and equity" point 15,

> Inclusive education is fundamental to the achievement of human, social and economic development. Equipping all individuals to develop their potential contributes significantly to encouraging them to live together in harmony and with dignity. There can be no exclusion arising from age, gender, ethnicity, migrant status, language, religion, disability, rurality, *sexual identity or orientation*, poverty, displacement or imprisonment. Combating the cumulative effects of multiple disadvantage is of particular importance. Measures should

be taken to enhance motivation and access for all. (*CONFINTEA VI: Living and learning for a viable future*, 2009: 5).

It is unfortunate that "sexual identity" was used rather than "sexual orientation," but a victory was ours!

ICAE: A QUEER GLANCE

Perhaps these musings should have begun with the International Council for Adult Education (ICAE), for it was through this important and supportive organization that Queer advocacy in lifelong learning, began in earnest in 2001, in Ocho Rios (Jamaica) at ICAE's 6th World Assembly of Adult Education. Prior to the World Assembly, ICAE requested the North American Alliance for Popular and Adult Education (NAAPAE) to arrange a "Banner/Mural Making Project." The Jamaican host community was invited to select local community activists and artists to participate in the mural project and to work collaboratively with conference participants for ideas and images for the mural. The artists were to assist in executing the mural. The mural was to function as a pedagogical tool. Clover (2000, p. 19) reminds us that "over the years, the arts, and in particular community arts, have become important learning tools for adults, feminists, and popular educators world-wide to nurture the 'spirit,' to encourage 'conscientization' and to mobilize the community." In support of Queer activism, I sketched a graphic for the mural that included symbols and words linked to sexual minority communities and added the phrase, "Difference Is A Human Right." A controversy unfolded, that has been documented (Hill, 2001). This "art-attack" and other tensions surrounding work on sexual minority rights were an opportunity for workshop participants to raise the issue of organizational intolerance on the basis of sexual orientation and gender presentation.

It was in Jamaica that I learned of the serious consequences of our work; my life was threatened for what was characterized as gay activism. The President of the Caribbean Island Adult Education Association, and sponsor of the World Assembly, told me that I was in danger and that the organization could not vouch for my safety. It was kindly recommended that I leave the island. I stayed...we fought...we won recognition at this important assembly! I thought that this experience would ensure that future ICAE World Assemblies would take up pedagogical action in support of sexual minorities. Sadly, I was wrong.

After the happenings in Jamaica in summer 2001, support for sexual minority rights was most often generous and generative. Some opposition came from conservative right-wing Christians in the U.S., and "Christianized" African countries, such as Uganda, as well as from some Islamic states. In general, capacity building and energy were derived from Canada, the U.S., Europe—especially Northern Europe—the Pacific region (e.g., the Philippines), and Latin America. Latin America, particularly the women of Latin America, was the most supportive. In addition to writing and publishing about ICAE's "Jamaica experience," Hill (2007) also wrote about what seemed like the very best opportunity to move an agenda forward at the UNESCO sponsored event, CONFINTEA VI (Brazil) in 2009.

ICAE's 8th World Assembly, titled, "A World Worth Living In" with the subtitle "Adult Learning and Education: A Key to Transformation," was held in Malmö, Sweden, in June 2011. The goals of the Assembly were,

> to provide a collective space to strongly affirm the right to lifelong learning and education *for all* (emphasis added) and to assert the immense value of adult education and learning in enabling citizens to build a world worth living in [and] to identify the priorities of lifelong learning and education and to develop proposals for action at a global, regional and local level. (*A world worth living in*, 2011, para. 2)

Despite the lessons learned at the Sixth World Assembly in Jamaica surprisingly the *Report from the ICAE VIII World Assembly* (2011) and the *Final Declaration from the VIII ICAE World in Malmö* (2011) said nothing directly about sexual minorities. They are brilliant documents that speak eloquently for the rights of youth and adults, and women, for indigenous people, for ecological stability and resistance to economic discourses that privilege the few over the many, and those who would have us careen toward dramatic and devastating climate change. There is the call for a new economic order, the creation of forces to balance the uneven distribution of learning provisions, and so much more. The documents speak of environmental justice, climate justice and biodiversity justice, of women farmers, fisher-folk and policy makers—but not of sexual minorities. The outcome of Malmö has opened unexpected opportunities to ponder the efforts of we who have toiled for more than a decade to resist heterosexism and homo- and transphobia, and who struggled to build "a world worth living in" for sexual minorities.

CONCLUSION

Heterosexual privilege, the notion that heterosexuality is "normal" (and therefore unimpeachable), and homophobia create a hostile public sphere, that often offers the contexts for misguided policies at the national and personal levels. Despite gains in civil rights and sociocultural attitudes in some countries that view sexual minorities in more favorable ways (see, Mizzi, 2008), other nation states and civil society actors still oppress, silence, and marginalize, lesbians, gay men, bisexuals, transgender, intersex, Two-Spirit and Queer peoples and communities. And, in countries where tolerance or celebration of sexual and gender identities and orientations occur, right-wing political movements, "religious" discourse, local traditions and cultural norms may still place sexual minorities in jeopardy. International adult education apparatus and institutions slowly have been assuming a pedagogical role in challenging the trends that have historically rendered invisible, or worse mete out violence on our communities. Institutions, include the United Nations, especial the Human Rights Council; UNESCO, particularly the Institute for Lifelong Learning; and the

International Council for Adult Education have mobilized to challenge this. The role of youth and adult education and learning remains critically important as tools for liberation and for equal implementation of supra-governmental agreements and declarations such as the UN's Universal Declaration for Human Rights.

A QUEER POSTSCRIPT

"Only after I came out broadly did this pressure ease. Once I was irrevocably gay, the fight for my soul was over—angels and demons alike looked for other quarry" (Yoshino, 2006: 44).

The focus of this chapter was to situate liberatory education for sexual orientation and gender identity in the context of the right to learn: to be, to become, to belong, to know, to do, and to live together. These are "pillars" derived from UNESCO's Delors Report, The International Commission on Education for the Twenty-first Century. This report advocates that, "all societies aim to move towards a necessary Utopia in which none of the talents hidden like buried treasure in every person are left untapped" (Delors, *et al.*, 1996).

We sexual minorities – and our allies—both challenge, and in many instances are changing, social and public policies and cultural attitudes toward human rights and social justice for our communities. This has implications for all people, regardless of sexual orientation or gender identity. There is also "pushback" against the individual and social transformation we are generating; youth and adult education and learning must work against this resistance.

It is with both deep joy and profound sadness that I reflect on Queer rights in the international context of adult education and lifelong learning. There have been hard fought victories and disappointing moments. The most recent was to witness the silence on sexual minority rights at the ICAE 8th World Assembly in Malmö, Sweden. I received a number of notes from friends and colleagues regarding the muteness at the 8th World Assembly. One colleague wrote to me, "When I heard that you were not attending the ICAE World Assembly, the first thing that came to my mind was: who will take care of the sexual orientation issue?" I was also told, "There is no justification [for the missing Queer voice]....You know that, like in the case of women, you have to be there, otherwise the issue is left aside." Another colleague wrote, "I didn't think about putting sexual orientation and gender identity issues in the document at Malmö. I'm now recalling how happy you were to put the issue in the Belém [CONFINTEA VI] document." The message went on to say that sexual minority rights are really "issues for all of us." I agree. In closing I'd like to share with all scholar-activists a lesson that has emerged from my personal Queer international journey: *presence makes a difference*. If not at the table, despite the support of countless friends and vital allies, the possibility of invisibility still haunts us. No one can speak for us—we must continue to speak for ourselves. In the end, it's all about a "pedagogy of presence"!

95

NOTES

[1] This chapter is derived from two primary sources: The modification of a paper written by the author, published in the online journal, *Voices Rising, IX* (404), "From Ocho Rios to Rio Amazonas: Musings of a Queer scholar-activist" (December 2, 2011); used with permission. The second source is an unpublished paper presented at the 55th Annual Comparative International Education Society (CEIS) meeting, Montreal, Canada, May 2011, titled, "Education to Be, to Become, to Belong: Sexual Minorities Challenging and Changing the World."

[2] The term "sexual minorities" is meant to indicate people and communities that have same-gender desires and behaviors and/or that have gender identity and expression that is discordant with their societies expected gender constructions. The term "Two Spirit" is employed to signify multiple gender roles with/in aboriginal, First Nation or Native American communities. The word "Queer" has multiple meanings, including a category that encompasses all sexual minorities, and also a term that speaks to a more radically dissident politics the challenges structures that tend to "normalize" and make all discourse (seemingly) unimpeachable. For a fuller elaboration of all sexual minority terms, see Hill & Grace (2009).

[3] The term "homosexuality" is seldom employed in gay, lesbian and Queer studies today. It has: (a) medical/clinical connotations that do not fully embrace the constellation of characteristics of same-gender desires, (b) often meant only genital or erotic behavior, and (c) historically been linked to pathologizing people rather than celebrating them.

REFERENCES

A world worth living in. Adult learning and education: A key to transformation. (2011) ICAE VIII World Assembly. Available at http://aworldworthlivingin.se/about-icae/

Angell-Hansen. (2010, June). *Report of the Human Rights Council on its seventeenth session.* Publication A/HRC/17/L.30. Available at http://www2.ohchr.org/english/bodies/hrcouncil/docs/17session/A.HRC.17.L.30AUV.pdf

Baird, V. (2007). *The no-nonsense guide to sexual diversity, revised edition.* Toronto: New Internationalist Publications.

Balzer, C. (2009, July). Every 3rd day the murder of a trans person is reported. *Liminalis, 3.* Available at http://www.liminalis.de/2009_03/TMM/tmm-englisch/Liminalis-2009-TMM-report2008–2009-en.pdf

Cloete, A., Simbayi, L. C., Kalichman, S. C., & Henda, N. (2008). Stigma and discrimination experiences of HIV-positive men who have sex with men in Cape Town, South Africa. *AIDS Care, 20*(9), 1105–1110. doi: 10.1080/09540120701842720

Clover, D. (2000). Community arts as environmental education and activism: A labour and environment case study. *Convergence, 33*(4), 19–31.

CONFINTEA VI: Living and learning for a viable future. (2009). Available at http://www.unesco.de/fileadmin/medien/Dokumente/Bildung/CONFINTEA_VI_Belem_Framework_for_Action_Final.pdf

Delors, J., et al., (1996). *Learning: The treasure within.* Paris: UNESCO. Available at http://www.unesco.org/delors/delors_e.pdf

Discriminatory laws and practices and acts of violence against individuals based on the sexual orientation and gender identity. (2011). Available at http://www2.ohchr.org/english/bodies/hrcouncil/docs/19session/A.HRC.19.41_English.pdf

Final declaration from the VIII world assembly in Malmö. (2011, June 19). Available at http://aworldworthlivingin.se/final-declaration-from-the-viii-icae-world-assembly-in-malmo/

Follow-up and implementation of the vienna declaration and programme of action (2011, June 15). A/HRC/17/L.9/Rev. 1. Available at http://ilga.org/ilga/static/uploads/files/2011/6/17/RESOLUTION%20L9rev1.pdf

Freire, P. (1970). *Pedagogy of the oppressed.* NY: Herder and Herder.

Herek, G. M. (2009). Hate crimes and stigma-related experiences among sexual minority adults in the United States. *Journal of Interpersonal Violence, 24*(1), 54–74. doi: 10.1177/0886260508316477

Hill, R. J. (2001). Contesting discrimination based on sexual orientation at the ICAE Sixth World Assembly: 'Difference' is a fundamental human right. *Convergence, 34*(2–3), 100–116.

Hill, R. J. (2003). Turning a gay gaze on citizenship. Sexual orientation and gender identity: Contesting/ed terrain. In C. Medel-Anonuevo et al. (Eds.), *Citizenship, democracy and lifelong learning* (pp. 99–139). UNESCO Institute for Lifelong Learning (ULL), Hamburg, Germany. Available at http://www.unesco.org/education/uie/pdf/uiestud35.pdf

Hill, R. J. (2007). Finding a voice for sexual minority rights: Some comprehensive policy considerations. *Convergence, 40*(3/4), 169–180. Available at http://www.icae2.org/files/convergence34.pdf

Hill, R. J. (2009). In Corporating queers: Blowback, backlash and other forms of resistance to workplace diversity initiatives that support sexual minorities. In T. S. Rocco, J. Gedro & M. B. Kormanik (Eds.), Gay lesbian, bisexual, and transgender issues in HRD: Balancing inquiry and advocacy. *Advances in Developing Human Resources, 11*(3), 37–53.

Hill, R. J., & Grace, A. P. (2009). Queer silence no more—Let's make some noise. In R. J. Hill & A. Grace. (Eds.), *Adult education in Queer contexts: Power, politics, and pedagogy* (pp. 1–10). Chicago: Discovery Association Publishing House.

Human rights violations of lesbians, bisexual, and transgender (LBT) people in Guyana: A shadow report. (2012, July 10). Available at http://www2.ohchr.org/english/bodies/cedaw/docs/ngos/GuyanaLGBTSubmission_for_the_session.pdf

Human rights violations of lesbians, gay, bisexual, and transgender (LGBT) people in Armenia: A shadow report. (2012, July). Available at http://www2.ohchr.org/english/bodies/hrc/docs/ngos/LGBT_Armenia_HRC105.pdf

Human rights violations of lesbians, gay, bisexual, and transgender (LGBT) people in Lithuania: A shadow report. (2012, July). Available at http://www2.ohchr.org/english/bodies/hrc/docs/ngos/LGBT_Lithuania_HRC105.pdf

Itaborahy, L. P. (2012, May). *State sponsored homophobia: A world survey of laws criminalizing same-sex sexual acts between consenting adults.* Available at http://old.ilga.org/Statehomophobia/ILGA_State_Sponsored_Homophobia_2012.pdf

Justice and equality for all regardless of gender or sexual orientation. (2009, May 15). United nations office of the high commissioner for human rights. Available at http://www.ohchr.org/EN/NewsEvents/Pages/JusticeEqualityforallGenderorSexualorientation.aspx

Merriam, S. B., & Brockett, R. G. (1997). *The profession and practice of adult education.* San Francisco: Jossey-Bass.

Mizzi, R. (Ed.). (2008). *Breaking free: Sexual diversity and change in emerging nations.* Toronto: QPI Publishing.

NAAPAE. (2001). *Special edition for the world assembly of adult education, Jamaica, August 9–11.*

O'Flaherty, M., & Fisher, J. (2008). Sexual orientation, gender identity and international human rights law: Contextualizing the Yogyakarta Principles. *Human Rights Law Review, 8*(2), 207–248.

Ozturk, M. B. (2011, August). Sexual orientation discrimination: Exploring the experiences of lesbian, gay and bisexual employees in Turkey. *Human Relations, 64*(8), 1099–1118. doi: 10.1177/0018726710396249

Recommitting to adult education and learning. Synthesis report of the CONFINTEA V midterm review meeting. (2003). Available at http://www.iiz-dvv.de/index.php?article_id=540&clang=1

Report from the ICAE VIII world assembly. (2011, June 18). Available at http://aworldworthlivingin.se/report-from-the-icae-viii-world-assembly/

Speak up. Stop discrimination. (2012). UN office of the high commissioner for human rights. Available at http://www.ohchr.org/EN/Issues/Discrimination/Pages/LGBT.aspx

Tan, K. P., & Jin, G. L. J. (2007). Imagining the gay community in Singapore. *Critical Asian Studies, 39*(2), 179–204. doi: 10.1080/14672710701339311

UN: General Assembly to address sexual orientation and gender identity. (2008, December 11). Available at http://www.hrw.org/news/2008/12/11/un-general-assembly-address-sexual-orientation-and-gender-identity

UN Human Rights Council: Landmark Report and Panel. (2012, March 7). Available at http://www.iglhrc.org/cgi-bin/iowa/article/pressroom/pressrelease/1494.html

UN Human Rights Council passes first-ever resolution on sexual orientation and genderidentity. (2011, June 17). Available at http://www.wluml.org/node/7296
Universal Declaration of Human Rights (UDHR). (1948). Available at http://www.un.org/en/documents/udhr/
Vienna Declaration and Programme of Action. (1993, July 12). A/CONF.157/23. Available at http://www.unhchr.ch/huridocda/huridoca.nsf/(symbol)/a.conf.157.23.en
Welcome to the CONFINTEA portal. (2010–2011). Available at http://uil.unesco.org/home/programme-areas/adult-learning-and-education/confintea-portal/
Whitaker, B. (2006). *Unspeakable love: Gay and lesbian life in the middle east.* Berkeley: University of California Press.
Yogyakarta Principles on the application of international human rights law in relation to sexual orientation and gender identity. (2006). Available at http://www.yogyakartaprinciples.org/
Yoshino, K. (2006). *Covering: The hidden assault on our civil rights.* NY: Random House.

AFFILIATION

Robert J. Hill
Associate Professor of Adult Education,
University of Georgia, Athens, GA USA

URSULA APITZSCH

8. MIGRATION, EDUCATION, GENDER

INTRODUCTION

Until the 1990s, mainstream sociology and pedagogy failed to recognise that the main constituting and transforming element of migration flows – both to Europe and inward Europe – is not the success or failure to assimilate individuals to the norms of Western industrial societies, but rather a process I call the 'dialectics of family-migration'. Through the focal position that women hold in the family project, a position they have acquired historically in virtually all societies, women play a dominant as opposed to a peripheral role within the migration process. Although apparently more traditional, young women with closer ties to the family experience a modernisation impulse by which they try to combine the demands of the society of arrival with a gain in personal autonomy. In this endeavour, the ethnic colony is not perceived as a help. In summary, we could say that, for women of the second migrant generation, having education and an occupation is perceived as both a means of achieving family objectives and as a legitimate opportunity to escape from traditional ties.

In the following discussion, I should like, firstly, to briefly recapitulate 'the sociological perspective' on women's migration. Secondly, I shall present some empirical studies that identify women as subjects and protagonists of migration processes. Thirdly, I shall address the role of migrant women in occupation and educational processes, advancements through education in the transnational space and the gender gap within the second generation. Finally, I will draw some conclusions regarding the concept of intercultural education.

1. THE SOCIOLOGICAL PERSPECTIVE ON WOMEN'S MIGRATION

The central issues in Western European migration research since the early 1970s have been acculturation, assimilation and deculturation – i.e. research has been based in key respects on the assumption that migrants should be understood as members of certain cultures of origin. The concept of assimilation draws on the notion of 'culture change' inspired by cultural anthropology and commonly entertained in the USA since the 1930s. Acculturation, in the classic definition formulated by Redfield, Linton and Herskovits in 1936, encompasses certain phenomena that are generated through direct and persistent contact between groups from different cultures, with such contact giving rise to changes in the cultural models of one or both groups.¹ This very definition is itself an illustration of the basic problems inherent in applying the notion of culture to the migration debate. There is an underlying assumption that cultures should be understood as monolithic and separate. Internal gender differentiation, for example, is generalised from the outset, if referred to at all; women, through their special ties to family and tradition, are seen as bearers of the culture of origin in its purer form. This conception leads on to the idea of migration causing 'culture shock', 'culture change stress' and 'cultural lag'. Attention is focused on the 'deficits' that arise through migration, while migration theories are conceived of as the basis on which to compensate for or surmount cultural deficits. Family-centeredness is thus viewed as a special obstacle to modernisation.

The first West German studies that explicitly addressed the situation of women migrants – especially in the context of social work and migration research on children – were based on this cultural paradigm. This led to stereotypes in terms of differentials in modernity, discontinuities in modernity and the more or less successful assimilation to Western values.[2] Women appear doubly disadvantaged on account of their culture and gender. Orientation to employment and the family are viewed as two diametrically opposite poles on the modernisation scale.[3]

If we look beyond the situation in Germany, we can discern a decisive change since the mid-1970s in the approach taken by researchers to the social situation of women migrants. 1984 saw the publication in Paris of a first comprehensive international bibliography on *'Les femmes migrantes 1965–1983'*, in which the author, Louis Taravella, saw the immigration controls imposed since the economic crisis of 1974 as a crucial factor behind a new awareness of immigration problems.

This crisis of the global economy was accompanied by attempts to stop the very migration flows from countries on the European periphery to the major cities that had previously been encouraged by government immigration agencies. These efforts to stem immigration have an unintended social effect similar to those that had been observed previously in Great Britain after immigration from Commonwealth countries was subjected to strict controls. Restrictive legislation in Great Britain since 1962 'compelled migrants to take decisions in favour of permanent settlement that they would probably not have taken otherwise'.[4] Temporary migration becomes final emigration, because a return from the country of origin to the host country was now beset with problems. As a result, other members of the family come to join those who have already emigrated, while second- and third-generation youths attend schools in the host country and try to gain access to the indigenous labour market.

2. THE DIALECTICS OF FAMILY-CENTEREDNESS – WOMEN AS PROTAGONISTS OF THE MIGRATION PROJECT

What, empirically speaking, is the relationship between work and family among women of the first and second generation? In Taravella's description of the 'feminisation' of European migration since the mid-1970s, one is struck by the fact that the presence of migrant women in the labour market was not really acknowledged until these women were perceived as having a Muslim culture. In fact, women in post-war Europe were often protagonists of internal migration and migration flows within the EC that were not subject to immigration controls. In French sociology, this was remarked upon here and there *en passant* as early as the 1960s, as in Bourdieu's 1962 study on predominantly female migration from rural areas of France.[5] In the 1980s, Piselli[6] and Arlacchi[7] studied the kinship structures and cultural roots of the Calabrian Mafia in Italy, showing that migration is often chosen (especially by women) as an alternative to falling victim to regressive developments in the regions of origin. Mirjana Morokvasic's 1987 study in the former Yugoslavia found that 'in a milieu where unwritten laws have drawn the boundaries of acceptable behaviour for women, where only certain categories of women are socially accepted..., survival is very difficult for those women who have violated these rules or who do not fall into one of the socially accepted categories. If this situation is coupled with the impossibility of an independent livelihood, many women see emigration as one or even the only way to escape from this predicament'.[8]

A biographical study I carried out with 40 Italian families in the Rhine-Main area of Germany showed, however, that it is quite typical for women in extreme situations, also with several small children of infant and school age, to provide the crucial impetus for the whole family to migrate, even for the second and third time after the return home proved fruitless, or that they migrate with several small children before the husband and take on work.[9]

There is also very clear and statistically documented evidence of the widespread resistance offered by women to any return to their regions of origin. Most first-generation women migrants will verbally profess that they intend to return home at some stage, at the latest when they retire. The statistics suggest otherwise, however. According to a UN study already carried out in 1979 entitled 'Labour Supply and Migration in Europe',[10] for about every 100 men of a particular nationality who return home, there were 82 women in the case of Greeks, and only 44 Italian women. It is obvious that this trend has not weakened to this day, as shown by the current statistics on male and female migrants leaving the host country on reaching retirement age. Women seem to prefer living with their children and grandchildren in migration, even in cramped living quarters, to a life in their own house in their home village.[11]

What factors account for this peculiarly ambivalent orientation of women to the family project, on the one hand, and to the host society, on the other? From the results of the biographical study I conducted, I would no longer speak of a 'field-specific orientation' (to family and occupation) among second-generation women migrants, but rather a 'dialectic of family orientation'. Whereas male youths are exempted from all duties within the family and orient themselves very early on to their peer group – mostly within the particular ethnic colony- girls, especially the oldest ones in each family, bear the main burden of domestic labour when both parents work.

Katharina Ley has shown that the employment rate of women migrants during the family phase was always much higher than that of Swiss women. A declining employment rate in Germany in the eighties is due, as Czarina Wilpert and Maria Eleonora Karsten have shown, not to a lack of employment orientation, but to factors that push such women into insecure employment.[12]

A peculiar development occurs among girls of the second generation: the more intensive their responsibility for the family, the more likely they are to evaluate the emigration project on their own terms, to perform a summary evaluation of their situation and to take corrective action. In other words, those young people who realise through their involvement in the family that each year of emigration diminishes further their chances of successfully returning home are under more pressure to seek a successful outcome to the migration project in the host society by education. Girls are quite clear in their own minds that they cannot expect any assistance from the ethnic colony.

By contrast, those young people who are traditionally exempted from family duties and responsibilities – and we have every reason to assume that this applies for the majority of males – can often utilise their scope for action under the conditions of migration only by casting themselves in the role of outsiders, by playing with deviance careers, etc. In any case, they can be quite certain that the institutions of the ethnic colony will at least provide them with a basic livelihood in casual, temporary jobs. Many of these young men attempt at an early age to form ties through traditional marriage, and in this way escape from the nascent anomie in their situation. Biographical studies have also shown, however, that second-generation women migrants are reluctant to accept such traditional ties, and that they try to engineer a 'contract' in which they have a strong position.

These observations offer a plausible hypothesis for interpreting the astonishing differences in school performance between migrant boys and girls. Whereas second-generation migrant girls attain virtually the same standards as German girls by the time they leave school, according to all existing statistics, migrant boys display enormous deficits.

Mothers try, through their daughters, to achieve their own frustrated hopes of escaping the eternal cycle of subordination. Very often, the father's refusal to allow his daughter an appropriate education leads to full-blown rebellion within the family. It is not unusual in such cases for women to leave their husbands and take the children with them. Women migrants from EU countries, for example, are not reliant on their husband having a residence permit (Immigrant women from non-EU countries are dependent on their husbands having such a permit, which means they lack the autonomy to determine their place of residence).

These observed cases of 'family revolts', particularly in connection with a daughter's education, are by no means confined to non-Muslim families. Violaine des Villers's film about young Algerian women in Brussels, *'La tête à l' envers'*, which was produced already in 1993 for 'Arte', the German-French TV channel, provides some beautiful examples. One of the young women portrayed in the film was born in Belgium; her parents are from the Maghreb, and illiterate. The mother decides to leave her Muslim husband when he refuses to buy his daughter the things she needs for school. The daughter is now a sports teacher in the St. Gil district of Brussels, where the film shows her training young people from the district – predominantly of North African origin – on the flying trapeze. 'Teaching little Moroccan boys ... was difficult', she says, 'the children can't look you in the eyes at first ... they have not been brought up to look up to women, but their view changes...' Their view has to change, because the boys must trust their teacher if they do not want to fall from the trapeze. One of the assistants in the gymnasium had left her Kabyle village with her family only four years previously (i.e. before the interview took place) and had come to Brussels via Torino. 'There are things where I wouldn't give in ...', she says, 'for example, if my husband tried to push me into giving up my career and my independence'. She also indicates, quite clearly, that such rebellious thinking had developed prior to emigrating. Back in her home village, she tries to relate to tribal traditions in a very reflective manner. This woman migrant is proud of her Berber traditions and shows some very beautiful photographs of her grandmother in traditional dress. She is equally proud of a picture showing a piece of Berber graffiti on a police station wall: 'If my thoughts were a man, they would have to imprison me'.

Another common feature in these narratives is the hope that education will increase women's chances on the labour market. All these girls share a diffuse anxiety that they have no real chances of being integrated into the labour market according to universalist criteria, but they are unsure about how best to respond.

The gender-specific segmentation of the labour market, as also applies for German women, operates more intensively in their case. Indeed, German women need the domestic services of immigrant women as a prerequisite for getting the good jobs.

3. CONSEQUENCES FOR THE ROLE OF MIGRANT WOMEN IN OCCUPATION AND EDUCATIONAL PROCESSES

3.1. Migration and Ethnic Subordination

Although there are approximately six million women migrants in Europe, migration studies and women's studies, particularly in Germany, during the 1980's and 1990's till today have directed little or no attention to the relationship between migration and ethnic subordination by the receiving society.

The 'housewife' thesis, which viewed all women without distinction as victims of patriarchal relations, thereby neglecting economic dependencies and the specific mechanisms of racial subordination, operated for a long time as a barrier to any wider perspective. In Veronica Bennholdt-Thomsen's 1987 study on employment among immigrant Turkish women, for example, we read that 'within this framework, the financial independence acquired by women with their own source of income has very little value. Their powerlessness to determine their own lives is paralleled by an inability to dispose of their own labour power'.[13] Empirical examples for the oppression of Islamic women (which includes physical violence) serve only to substantiate such a thesis; there is no attempt to analyse the way in which biographies differ. The discrimination experienced by immigrant women in the modern host society in the form of ethnifying distinctions in the entire occupational structure is interpreted as a further level of oppression, additional to the sexist oppression experienced by all women.

The 'race, culture and difference' debate in Great Britain and the USA in the 1990's[14] has shown, very convincingly, that gender-based social inequalities are not just reinforced by social inequalities based on origin, but that these inequalities are produced anew and in a very specific way by the receiving society. The social definition of gender and the ascription of 'cultural identity' by the host society are interwoven in a complex way – the issue, however, is always the specific ways in which social power is used to oppress others. When marginalised groups adopt the same definitions of themselves, they are effectively supporting such subordination mechanisms.

Giovanna Campani, in her study on Philippine women in Italy,[15] has put forward the thesis that Italian women owe their higher qualifications to more than 100,000 Philippine and other immigrant women from the 'Third World' who care for their families as domestic servants. In Germany, the situation is probably no different. According to estimates by the Collaborative Research Centre 333 in Munich ('Changes in the individual division of labour'), there were already at the beginning of the 1990's about 2.4 million women in West Germany working in private households in insecure jobs that do not appear in the official statistics. Immigrant women probably account for a high proportion of that total. Maria Rerrich[16] has put forward the thesis (very similar to Campani's for Italy) that West German women have only been able to establish a presence for themselves on the primary labour market at the expense of increasing employment of illegal women migrants (and she refers to similar trends in the USA, as exposed in the several 'Nannygate' affairs). The question, therefore, is whether the successful German, English or Italian woman with her immigrant care workers to look after her children (and who may even be a sociologist conducting research on these immigrant women) can show forms of 'women's' solidarity. This seems a rhetorical question, but there is nothing rhetorical about its converse. Does this state of affairs mean that there can only be particular agreement between women along the boundaries of social and ethnic origin? [17][18]Could the social subordination of immigrant women be combated in this way at all? Or would the best alternative consist in a general denunciation of private social services with no personal 'blame' attached to such exploitation of others?

Caroline Knowles and Sharmila Mercer from Great Britain have described beautifully the social impacts of the typical moralist reaction among the leftwing middle class to this problem. The latter demand that men and women share domestic labour and be active in 'parent run community nurseries'. What is actually achieved, however, by the parents' initiative in Hackney used as an example? The only parents who can effectively join the initiative are teachers, other people with good public-service jobs, or the self-employed. Women in full-time employment, especially single mothers, are systematically excluded, and yet single mothers account for the majority of immigrant families. This leads to the paradox problem that immigrant women are in particular need of the very same professionalised social services that they themselves provide at present – often in insecure employment. If indigenous and immigrant women were to share a common aim, this would consist, for example, in securing and socialising personal social services instead of moralistically demanding their abolishment, and ensuring that such services are also available to the providers themselves. The same principle could apply, moreover, to hospital services, private households and community initiatives.

3.2. THE SITUATION OF THE SECOND GENERATION OF "GUEST WORKERS" IN GERMANY

What, in general terms, is the social situation of this second generation of "guest workers" born in the 1970s? The original "Gastarbeiter" in Germany, the workers who had arrived from the mid-1950s onwards, were at first mostly men over 18 years old. However, as soon as the members of this group had settled in Germany and found jobs for their wives, the children joined their parents. Because both parents were often working in exhausting jobs, the children frequently travelled to and fro between their country of origin and Germany (see Apitzsch 2006a). A transnational space of life was thus established, which certainly increased access to recent resources but also became a trap for some members of this second generation. The receiving society exhibited tendencies to close itself off: access to higher education was blocked, and social insecurity increased. As a consequence, the second generation experienced much worse discrimination than their parents. This was the generation that was labelled "disadvantaged", and it was branded further by state programmes designed to benefit the "disadvantaged" and "disillusioned" with regard to its life chances. The first generation immigrants, especially those who had found their way to the target countries after being signed up by state recruitment commissions, were usually able both to find work and to get involved in the social structures of the country to which they had emigrated as a result of their involvement in functioning trade union organisations. As this happened, though, the social and political traditions of their country of origin remained valid because the emigration phase was always thought of as temporary. The immigrants were still rooted in the history of their society of origin. By the beginning of the 1980s, none of this applied any longer to the members of the second generation. One can say that young people belonging to this generation often found themselves in a "modernisation trap" and on a negative "trajectory" (see Apitzsch, 2000). In their country of origin, certain modernisation processes had come to an end and did not offer those who had emigrated any improved prospects of participation. However, only a small proportion of young people from the second generation could hope for success by orienting themselves towards professional advancement in the receiving society. The rest of them experienced identification with the modernisation goal of professional advancement as an illusion, but they no longer had the option of retreating to the ethnic colony that had been available to their parents in times of crisis.

Despite this potentially negative trajectory affecting a whole generation, one can also identify a counter-dynamic which was at least as strong as the first one and took the form of well-thought-out strategies against exclusion. Many members of the first generation had undertaken the migration project principally because they wanted their children to have professional opportunities unavailable to them. These parents understood very well that they needed to give their children the chance of getting a better education in the receiving country. Only by doing this could they bring the family migration project, which had also been a protest against the living conditions in their society of origin, to a successful conclusion. In this way, many biographies embodying an upward trend came to fruition even though they were statistically unlikely (see Apitzsch, 1990).

How could this happen, given the immigrants' unfavourable initial social situation, as described above, and the tendency of the receiving society to close itself off? One factor that was certainly important was the setting up of networks within the immigrant communities. This trend was supported by a new wave of immigration in the framework of freedom of movement as guaranteed by the European Community as it established itself. Soon the second generation also produced university graduates, and the staff of consulates, schools, cultural organisations, and educational institutions outside the school system were recruited from the ranks of these graduates. In addition, a number of self-organised measures to counteract exclusionary mechanisms in the German school system were successfully implemented. In the Italian community these were predominantly designed to counter selection processes in the German system, while the Greek communities successfully set up their own schools. The Greek national schools were set up as early as the 1960s, as a result of intensive efforts by Greek parents and after heated debates about teaching methods. They are structured on the same lines as the Greek school system, and are financed by the Greek state and coordinated by the Greek diplomatic missions in Germany (see Paraschou, 2001). For pupils who are unable to obtain a higher-level qualification in the German system, the national schools offer a way of making the transition to either the German or the Greek university system. One can say that the discovery and use of a transnational European educational space made it possible to circumvent the exclusionary mechanisms of the German education system much more effectively than through unconditional assimilation into that system.

The political associations among the bodies set up by immigrants, which, in the 1970s and 80s, were mostly of a left-wing orientation, gave rise to communication networks between intellectuals, the new self-employed, and a trade union and political working-class elite (see Apitzsch, 2006a). Because the German labour market was now offering fewer opportunities, some of the new arrivals set themselves up in self-employment, in many cases without any intermediate phase of employment with existing companies. They became "ethnic entrepreneurs" by occupying economic niches that had been abandoned by German society (see Apitzsch, 2005a, 2005b). The two concluded EU-projects on "Self employment activities concerning women and minorities (acronym: SEM)" and on "The chances of the second generation in families of ethnic entrepreneurs (acronym: EthnoGeneration)" have evaluated social policies in relation to the self-employment activities of migrant women (Mason 2002; Apitzsch and Kontos 2003). These research projects have been focusing on immigrant self employment and informal work from the gender and intergenerational policy perspective. In these research networks the situation of the new generations of the children of migrants in the countries of former recruitment of guest-workers (UK, Sweden, Denmark, Germany, France) as well as the situation of newly arriving informal and illegal migrants have been investigated. In contrast to what has been said about the second generation of ethnic entrepreneurs in the US and also in Europe our observations astonishingly show that – generally speaking- the involvement of children in the family business has not been interpreted as a disadvantage by the interviewees themselves. Both Generations – parents and children- typically agree that money earned in the business has mostly been invested in enabling mobility for the children, either through their education as qualified workers, technical or academic studies or else through buying, for example, a whole sale business where the children can apply what they have learned. Also teachers whom we asked as experts did not consider children from migrant entrepreneur families as having particular problems at school. On the contrary, involvement and socialization within the family business is seen as an advantage even when the children decide against taking over the business. Involvement in the parents' business and developing their own professional perspectives outside of it are not experienced as contradictory.

All European teams had difficulties to locate members of the second generation who worked full time in their parents' business and were planning to take it over later. Obviously, this type of involvement of the second generation was not a predominant phenomenon. This finding already modifies a possible research hypothesis that the quality of life of the second generation might deteriorate when compared with that of their parents, as their chances would be tied to their parents' project. On the contrary, parents attempt to secure their children's independence from the family business. In those cases, however, where the children were not successful in finding their vocational pathway outside the family business or where they really liked to take it over, the parents very often in diverse ways tried to improve their children's situation, for example, by formalizing their work as an approved apprenticeship that would keep their chances open for finding work elsewhere. The family business is considered as a "safe haven" when children do not want to or when they fail to secure an income through other means of work. In some cases, the second generation has founded new businesses that cooperate with their parents' businesses. The cultural capital of establishing a business is thus not tied to the parents' business or its clientele. In our findings it appears that keeping the same business, such as a restaurant in the family for several generations cannot be expected as "the normal case".

We could also formulate some observations about specific gender differences in the second generation. Researchers found out that typically in migrant families boys are less involved in family issues and mostly do worse in school than girls. Also, one found different orientation patterns for boys, who sometimes tend to see ethnic peer groups as an alternative to educational efforts, while girls see themselves more responsible for the family success, even though this translates not in terms of them wanting to stick to traditional ways of life, but rather as a step towards their own educational career. In families of ethic entrepreneurs, however, we cannot find a clear reproduction of this pattern. We have several cases of boys who do well at school which seems due to their new responsibility in the family migration project. (Apitzsch, 2003).

3.3. ADVANCEMENT THROUGH EDUCATION IN THE TRANSNATIONAL SPACE

It is only in the last few years that the phenomenon of advancement through education in migration has begun to receive explicit attention in qualitative empirical migration research (see, for example, Hummrich, 2002). Scholars investigating this question define advancement through education in migration as a distinctive form of upward mobility in the generation succeeding labour migration, which involves reaching the highest possible rung on the educational career ladder, i.e. obtaining the highest possible secondary school qualification and entering the German university system (for Turkish immigrants, see Pott, 2002).

Most studies of educational success in migration operate with a definition and categorisation of advancement through education which relies exclusively on the classical nation-state model of immigration. It is almost impossible to bring successful educational careers between different nation states into focus from this perspective. Unsurprisingly, therefore, migration research has treated the "commuting phenomenon" in the second generation as something that triggers problems, leading to the failure of educational careers and low levels of achievement at school (see Damanakis 1982; Diehl 2002; Auernheimer 2006). Particularly in the case of the second generation of Italian immigrants, the commuting mentality of the parents has been put forward as an explanation for the lack of educational success of the second generation (Auernheimer 2006, p. 3). Diehl (2002) has treated the commuting phenomenon as a "strategy which swallows up resources". In connection with the educational success of pupils from Turkish and Italian families, she carried out a quantitative investigation of the effects of commuting on success at school and found that, although commuting "does not independently have a negative effect on success at school", it affects pupils' secondary education "indirectly" because of its consequences for their language skills (Diehl 2002, p. 181).

Only in more recent empirical investigations, transnational research perspectives have been introduced in such a way that "commuting", i.e. travelling to and fro between different national contexts and education systems, can be treated as a resource rather than a deficit (Fürstenau, 2004; Ruokonen-Engler and Siouti 2006; Siouti 2003; for pupils with Greek and Italian background, see Apitzsch/Siouti 2008; 2012).

Fürstenau (2004) has investigated the educational careers and future orientations of young people from Portuguese families in Hamburg who have been educationally successful. Researchers like Hartmut Esser (2001), according to the acculturation scheme, had strictly assumed that social integration into the receiving society is only possible by means of assimilation processes which rule out any simultaneous integration into the ethnic community or the society of origin. Fürstenau found that, contrary to this assumption, "social integration into the receiving society need not contradict a high level of self-organisation within an ethnic community" (Fürstenau, 2004, p. 51). These young people orient themselves transnationally during the phase in which they make the transition from school to the labour market. Transnational secondary education divided between Portugal and Germany functions within the Portuguese community as a successful model according to which planning for the future can be oriented (Fürstenau, 2004, p. 49).

In my view, the concept of transnational social spaces is a way of grasping the phenomenon of the biographical knowledge (Apitzsch, 2009; 2012) of subjects interacting with one another. This knowledge is accumulated and symbolised in the course of individual lives and of the lives of groups. On the basis of past, continuing and necessary future separations and border crossings, this knowledge constitutes different and partly overlapping social spaces understood as coordinates of orientation for individual and group action. This biographical knowledge introduces the time axis into the constitution of social spaces, in the sense that accumulated experience represents the dimension of the past and biographical learning and planning represents the anticipated future. The structures and effects of such border crossings and of the ways in which people cope with them in psycho-social and pedagogical terms in their biographies are linked to one another and interact with one another. Family members involved in a migration process experience this process in different ways depending on their age, gender, whether they have older or younger siblings, etc. Although each individual has his or her own biography, there are typical sequences of events which are specific to migrants and which tell us a great deal about the invisible, but very real, structures of the immigration society.

SOME CONCLUSIONS

If our previous observations are correct, then the issue for intercultural adult education is neither to assimilate 'foreigners' to 'indigenous' traditions, nor to exercise a form of tolerance that is essentially indifferent to foreigners. The point is to recognise that those who are marginalised in a variety of spheres (e.g. in social security, education, etc.) actually shape the socio-ecological foundations of shared social reality to a major extent, without themselves often having an opportunity to address and process the specific knowledge that they acquire through their own activities. This is the case in both the social and cultural domains.

However, it would be wrong to ignore the fact that the potential autonomy to act on the part of migrants – as acquired, for example, through education and career success – is certainly very limited, and that these constraints are closely interwoven with the cumulative effects of social re-stratification and gender-specific disadvantages. We often see among women migrants that the greater level of motivation to acquire education generated by their specific social knowledge is not accompanied by appropriate opportunities to plan their educational careers in a competent manner. Although the host society expects them to take advantage of the very autonomy that migration promises, the double character of education as an agency of modernisation and at the same – time as a system of social ascription of roles is often overlooked.[18]

For educational work, however, it is important to realise the capacity of migrants and especially of women to link modern dispositions to their own biographical resources and to utilise as well as change and dissolve traditional social forms, and hence to exert a type of feedback that changes the underlying structures of the host society.

NOTES

[1] R. Redfield, R. Linton & M. J. Herskovits (1936) "Memorandum for the Study of Acculturation" in *American Anthropologist* XXXVIII, p. 149.
[2] Cf. Angelika Schmidt-Koddenberg (1989) *Akkulturation von Migrantinnen. Eine Studie zur Bedeutsamkeit sozialer Vergleichsprozesse zwischen Türkinnen und deutschen Frauen.* Opladen.
[3] Louis Taravella (1984) *Les femmes migrantes. Bibliographie analytique internationale*, 19651983. Paris.
[4] James L. Watson (1980) "*Arbeitsimmigrantinnen in Großbritannien – neuere Entwicklungen*" in Jochen Blaschke & Kurt Greussing (Eds.) "*Dritte Welt*" *in Europa*. Frankfurt/Main, p. 43f.
[5] Cf. Pierre Bourdieu (1962) "Célibat et condition paysanne" in *Etudes rurales*, pp. 67–106.
[6] F. Piselli (1980) *Parentela ed emigrazione. Mutamenti e continuità in una comunità calabrese.* Torino.
[7] Pino Arlacchi (1989) *Mafiose Ethik und der Geist des Kapitalismus.* Frankfurt am Main.
[8] Mirjana Morokvasic (1989) *Jugoslawische Frauen. Die Emigration – und danach?* Frankfurt am Main, p. 77f.
[9] Ursula Apitzsch (1990) *Migration und Biographie.* Bremen.
[10] In Economic Survey of Europe, Part 11. Geneva 1979
[11] Amt für multikulturelle Angelegenheiten der Stadt Frankfurt (Ed.) (1992) *Eine statistische Erfassung der älteren Arbeitsmigrantinnen und – migranten in Frankfurt.* Frankfurt am Main. Donald Vaughan (1996) Migration and Biography: Elder Migrants in Frankfurt am Main. (Manuscript).
[12] Cf. Maria Eleonora Karsten (1987) "*Migrantinnen*. Traditionelle Frauenarbeit in ungeschützten Arbeitsverhältnissen. Hamburg, pp. 9–18.
[13] Veronica Bennholdt-Thomsen (Ed.) (1987) *Frauen aus der Türkei kommen in die Bundesrepublik.* Bremen, p. 28.
[14] Cf. Avtar Brah (1993) "*Difference, diversity and differentiation*" in James Donald & Ali Rattsani (Eds.) 'Race', Culture and Difference. London, pp. 126–145.
[15] Giovanna Campani (1992) *Transnational perspectives in migrant women's employment.* Paper presented to the "Migrant Women in the 1990s" symposium. Barcelona.
[16] Maria S. Rerrich (1992) *Auf dem Weg zu einer neuen internationalen Arbeitsteilung der Frauen in Europa?* Beharrungs- und Veränderungstendenzen in der Verteilung der Reproduktionsarbeit. Paper

presented to the 26th Annual Conference of the German Sociological Association. Düsseldorf. (Manuscript).
[17] Cf. Caroline Knowles & Sharmila Mercer *"Feminism and antiracism: an exploration of the political possibilities"* in Donald & Rattansi, op. cit., p. 111.
[18] Cf. Ursula Apitzsch (1990) "Besser integriert und doch nicht gleich. Bildungsbiographien jugendlicher Migrantinnen als Dokumente widersprüchlicher Modernisierungsprozesse" in Ursula Rabe-Kleberg (Ed.) *Besser gebildet und doch nicht gleich! Frauen und Bildung in der Arbeitsgesellschaft.* Bielefeld.

REFERENCES

Amt für multikulturelle angelegenheiten der stadt frankfurt (Ed.) (1992). *Eine statistische erfassung der älteren arbeitsmigrantinnen und – migranten in frankfurt.* Frankfurt am Main.

Apitzsch, U. (1990 a). Besser integriert und doch nicht gleich. Bildungsbiographien jugendlicher migrantinnen als dokumente widersprüchlicher modernisierungsprozesse. In U Rabe-Kleberg (Ed.). *Besser gebildet und doch nicht gleich! Frauen und Bildung in der Arbeitsgesellschaft.* Bielefeld: USP Publishing Kleine Verlag.

Apitzsch, U. (1990 b). *Migration und Biographie.* Bremen: Universität.

Apitzsch, U. (2000). Biographische, unordnung' und, caring work'. *Feministische Studien extra: Fürsorge – Anerkennung – Arbeit,* 102–116.

Apitzsch, U., & Kontos, M. (2003). Self-emplyment, gender and migration. *International Review of Sociology, 13*(1). 67–235.

Apitzsch, U. (2005). The chances of the second generation in families of migrant entrepreneurs. *Revue Européenne des Migrations Internationales, 21*(3), 83–95.

Apitzsch, U. (2005b). Dal "lavoro ospite" al "lavoro autonomo". Esperienze generazionali e differenze sociali nei lavoratori migranti e nei loro figli. *Studi Emigrazione XLII* (158), 349–367.

Apitzsch, U. (2006a). Esperienze e differenze sociali in tre generazioni di migranti italiani: Conseguenze della creazione di uno spazio transnazionale fra l'Italia e la Germania. In F. Carchedi & E. Pugliese: *Andare, Restare, Tornare. Cinquant' anni di emigrazione italiana in Germania* (pp. 99–106), Isernia: Fondazione Nicola e Giulia Iannone,.

Apitzsch, U. (2009). Transnationales biographisches wissen. In H. Lutz (Ed.). *Gender Mobil? Geschlecht und Migration in transnationalen Räumen* (pp.122–142). Münster: Westfälisches Dampfboot.

Apitzsch, U. (2012). The concept of ethnicity and its relevance for biographical learning. In Zvi Bekerman/Thomas Geisen (Eds.), *International handbook of migration, minorities and education. Understanding cultural and social differences in processes of learning* (pp. 53–66), Dordrecht-Heidelberg-London-New York: Springer.

Apitzsch, U., & Siouti, I. (2008). Transnationale biographien. In Homfeldt, Günther et al. (Eds.) *Soziale arbeit und transnationalität* (pp. 97–112). Weinheim-München: Beltz Juventa.

Apitzsch, U., & Siouti, I. (2012). Die entstehung transnationaler Familienbiographien in Europa. Transnationales biographisches Wissen als zentrales Schlüsselkonzept zum Verständnis von transnationalen mehrgenerationalen migrationsprozessen. In D Bender, *et al.* (Eds.) *Transnationales Wissen und soziale Arbeit* (pp. 144–158). Weinheim-Basel: Beltz Juventa.

Arlacchi, P. (1989). *Mafiose Ethik und der Geist des Kapitalismus.* Frankfurt am Main: Cooperative.

Auernheimer, G. (2006). Schüler und eltern italienischer herkunft im deutschen schulsystem. In M. Libbi, N. Bergmann, and V. Califano (Eds.) (pp. 56–71). Düsseldorf,

Bennholdt-Thomsen, V. (Ed.) (1987). *Frauen aus der Türkei kommen in die Bundesrepublik.* Bremen: Ed. Con.

Bourdieu, P. (1962). "Célibat et condition paysanne" in *Etudes rurales, 5*(6), 67–106.

Brah, A. (1993). Difference, diversity and differentiation. In J. Donald & A. Rattsani (Eds.), *'Race', Culture and Difference* (pp. 126–145). Thousand Oaks: Sage.

Campani, G. (1992). *Transnational perspectives in migrant women's employment.* Paper presented to the "Migrant Women in the 1990s" symposium. Barcelona.

Damanakis, M. (1982). Ausbildungsprobleme junger griechen in deutschland – forderungen, einflussfaktoren, Konsequenzen. In J. Ruhloff (Ed.). *Aufwachsen im fremden Land. Probleme und Perspektiven der „Ausländerpädagogik* (pp. 54–86). Frankfurt a.M./Bern: Peter Lang.

Diehl, C. (2002). Die auswirkungen längerer herkunftslandaufenthalte auf den bildungserfolg türkisch- und italienischstämmiger schülerinnen. In *Zeitschrift für Bevölkerungswissenschaft, 2,* 165–185.

UNECE (1979). *Economic survey of Europe,* Part 11. Geneva: United Nations Economic Commission for Europe.

Esser, H. (2001). Kulturelle pluralisierung und strukturelle assimilation: Das problem der ethnischen schichtung. *Schweizerische Zeitschrift für Politikwissenschaft, 2,* 97–108.

Fürstenau, S (2004). Transnationale (Aus)bildungs- und zukunftsorientierungen. Ergebnisse einer Untersuchung unter zugewanderten Jugendlichen portugiesischer Herkunft. *Zeitschrift für Erziehungswissenschaft, 7,* 33–57.

Granato, M. (1994). *Bildungs- und lebenssituation junger Italiener.* Ed. Bonn: Bundesinstitut für Berufsbildung.

Hummrich, M. (2002). *Bildungserfolg und migration. Biographien junger Frauen in der Einwanderungsgesellschaft.* Opladen: VS Verlag für Sozialwissenschaften.

Vaughn, D. (1996). *Migration and biography: Elder migrants in frankfurt am main.* (Manuscript).

Karsten, M. E. (1987). *Migrantinnen. traditionelle frauenarbeit in ungeschützten arbeitsverhältnissen.* Hamburg: VSA.

Knowles, C., & Mercer, S. (1992). Feminism and antiracism: An exploration of the political possibilities. In J. Donald & A. Rattansi (Eds.), *Race, Culture and Difference,* Thousand Oaks: Sage.

Ley, K. (1979). *Frauen in der emigration. Eine soziologische untersuchung der lebens- und arbeitssituation italienischer frauen in der schweiz.* Frauenfeld/Stuttgart: Huber.

Mason, J. (2002). *Qualitative researching,* Thousand Oaks: Sage.

Morokvasic, M. (1989). *Jugoslawische Frauen. Die Emigration – und danach?* Frankfurt am Main: Roter Stern.

Paraschou, A. (2001). *Remigration in die heimat oder emigration in die fremde?* Frankfurt: Peter Lang.

Piselli, F. (1980). *Parentela ed emigrazione. Mutamenti e continuità in una comunità calabrese.* Torino: Einaudi.

Pott, A. (2002). *Ethnizität und raum im Aufstiegsprozess: Eine untersuchung zum bildungsaufstieg in der zweiten türkischen Migrantengeneration.* Köln: VS Verlag für Sozialwissenschaften.

Redfield, R., & Herskovits, M. (1936). Memorandum for the study of acculturation. *American Anthropologist XXXVIII,* 149.

Rerrich, M. S. (1992). *Auf dem Weg zu einer neuen internationalen Arbeitsteilung der Frauen in Europa? Beharrungs- und Veränderungstendenzen in der Verteilung der Reproduktionsarbeit.* Paper presented to the 26th Annual Conference of the German Sociological Association. Düsseldorf. (Manuscript).

Ruokonen-Engler, M., & Siouti, I. (2006). *Biographies dispersed? Interpreting narrations of transnational belongings.* paper presented at the World Congress of Sociology in Durban, South Africa, July.

Schmidt-Koddenberg, A. (1989). *Akkulturation von migrantinnen. Eine studie zur bedeutsamkeit sozialer vergleichsprozesse zwischen Türkinnen und deutschen Frauen.* Opladen: Leske + Budrich.

Siouti, I. (2003). *Migration, bildung und biographie. eine biographieanalytische Untersuchung von transnationalen Bildungswegen bei griechischen migrantInnen der zweiten generation.* Diplomarbeit. Fachbereich Gesellschaftswissenschaften, Frankfurt: Universität Frankfurt a.M.

Taravella, L. (1984). Les femmes migrantes. *Bibliographie analytique internationale,* 19651983. Paris.

Watson, J. L. (1980). Arbeitsimmigrantinnen in Großbritannien – neuere Entwicklunge. in J. Blaschke & K. Greussing (Eds.) *"Dritte Welt" in Europa.* Frankfurt/Main: Promedia.

AFFILIATION

Ursula Apitzsch
Professor in the Faculty of Sociology and Political Economy,
Wolfgange Goethe University of Frankfurt

OSKAR NEGT

9. ADULT EDUCATION AND EUROPEAN IDENTITY[1]

EUROPE AS A PROJECT

For the first time in modern history, will and consciousness are used for bringing political, social and cultural unity to the European continent. It is neither self-evident nor a natural phenomenon.

For 500 years this continent has been a theatre of bloody wars and harsh competition. Europe has now become one of the most amazing historical projects being constructed. Peoples and governments that were fighting against one another in military alliances in the first half of the twentieth century, leading to 50 million deaths and the commission of unspeakable mass crimes by individual states, have willingly and consciously set out on the taxing path of establishing rules to govern a social peace based on mutual recognition and equality.

This is not meant as a pathetic exaggeration but as a factual statement of the situation. This historic project is unique because the two attempts to unite Europe by force which served the exploitative interests of a dominant great power, the France of Napoleon and the Germany of Hitler, were attended by untold numbers of victims and the protectionist reinforcement of nation-states. The pathology of the nation-state is crumbling, and even de Gaulle's peaceful notion of a 'Europe des patries' is no more than a faded memory for the younger generation of Europeans.

In his *Philosophy of History*, Hegel says that the only thing we can learn from history is that we learn nothing from it (Hegel, 1994: 19). This bitter realisation is usually apposite. But it is not the whole truth; what is happening in Europe at present must be seen as historic learning. Certain governments and outstanding individuals have given decisive momentum to the unification of Europe, and have set the political course. But if its peoples had not gone through an underlying process of learning, if they had not revised their accustomed world views and perceptions of potential enemies, if individual concepts of life had not undergone fundamental change, such a unification project would have had no firm foundations.

An example of such changes in awareness is the fact that the Finnish President, Ahtisaari, made a successful contribution as a negotiator and peacemaker in an area of conflict far on the southern fringes of Europe, in Yugoslavia in the late 1990s. That is a hopeful symbol, a sign that the small countries of Europe are able to gain greater credibility and trust among many people than the European

Great Powers, whose history in the twentieth century is burdened with colonial adventures, war and obsession with race. This very example demonstrates that the virtue of solidarity throughout Europe has taken root. I regard a different element as the key, however.

There can be no lasting peaceful settlement in Europe if new threats of violence are looming on its borders. We know that ethnic cleansing is largely occurring where old power struggles between ethnic groups are being revived, where the authoritarian state that ruled vast territories in the name of Soviet communism is collapsing along with its satellite system.

It should be remembered, however, that it took centuries for the wars of religion and tribal vendettas to come to an end in Europe. The edicts of tolerance which removed political meaning from tribal allegiance and religious opinion, and gave greater recognition to actual behaviour than to opinion, were an essential part of the civilising process of bourgeois society. President Ahtisaari had good reason to involve Russia in his peace mission; it will not be the last time that this is necessary, and perhaps the Russian option is more important in the long term for the peace of Europe than, for example, the admission of Turkey.

I will freely admit that I had doubts about the sense of military intervention in Yugoslavia, but I was unable to make alternative suggestions to my friends in the federal government. I should nonetheless like to pick out one lesson born of experience: that violence achieves nothing. Not even counter-violence, for it too causes an astonishing amount of destruction to property and human relations. Therefore my reflections on the opportunities and requirements of a European civil society primarily concern a level below that of the formal provisions of relevant policy agreements between governments and the contractual niceties of the nexus between economic and fiscal affairs. To me, Europe is a working project, and it may be sensible to begin the unification agenda with monetary union, using money as a cold medium of human interchange right at the outset, in order to accelerate the creation of one society. The very name 'euro' may contribute to changes in awareness.

I am skeptical, however, about whether the agreements reached under their various names – Rome, Maastricht, Paris, Berlin, and so on – while absolutely necessary as individual steps, are sufficient in themselves to bring about anything approaching a general and well-founded European consciousness. There therefore arises, in my view, the vital problem of how these government decisions, and the measures and proposed legislation of the European Parliament and the EU Commission in Brussels, are to be internalised, processed and accepted in people's everyday lives. In a word, how will they become the raw material of critical judgment? We are, after all, talking about collective learning processes of a quite particular nature. They are not restricted merely to the level of factual knowledge about Europe. People will quickly learn how to handle euros and, in the long term, the laws and regulations of the EU Commission will also present no problem. But the dangerously low voter turnout at European Parliament elections, as well as the abstention of considerable numbers of voters in elections in Germany, clearly demonstrate a reluctance to participate, to take an interest and become involved in the fortunes of the community. This directs our attention forcefully to a contradiction that we must address and resolve if we wish to found a European civil society that is free from violence. It is a fundamental question which everyone in Europe asks about life, and must legitimately ask: What do I gain, in addition to what I have already, from joining in a European community and treating it as a necessary part of my existence? The answer need not be material benefits, but it must be more than the removal of passport controls at borders.

In this article I single out five critical issues as specific areas for work and action. The global challenge is not simply that posed by the stock exchange in Tokyo or New York, but relates to quite different problems: How do we shape and preserve our ecological system? How do we equip the new generation to dispose of the refuse that we leave behind, and to pay off the debts that we have incurred? These are critical issues which we have created ourselves, which have come about at the heart of societies of a high order of development; they are areas of extremely tense conflict in which there will be a growing potential for violence unless they are resolved.

These critical issues are to be met, in degrees of severity that vary from region to region and at differing stages of evolution, in every European country. They are not merely the leftovers of the nation-states, and they can no longer be attributed to a single, specific cause in the varied cultural landscape of Europe. I should like to emphasise strongly that the debate about the economic situation, and the outlook for business and growth, give the impression that human happiness and misery hang by a silken thread from the economy. Viviane Forrester rightly called attention to the paradoxicality of the present situation in speaking of the 'terror of the economy' (Forrester, 1999). Day and night we worry about economic concerns although it is plain to all that our societies are overflowing with wealth and that the goods which we have accumulated prevent us from thinking about the aims of culture, the purpose of humanity and consequent processes of learning.

We live in a world of radical change: traditional values and directions are no longer taken for granted without question, while new, reliable and binding values and directions have yet to be found. They are being sought, however, with the result that this is an age of anomie, as the French sociologist Durkheim has called this in-between world (Durkheim, 1984), an age of intensive search. In such an in-between world in search of a direction, huge efforts are required of the adult generation in order to cope with the vast amount of learning called for by the following critical issues.

GLOBALISATION, CAPITAL AND CIVIL SOCIETY

One critical issue is currently referred to by the term globalisation. At no time in modern history has so much changed in so short a time as in the last 15 years. In a time of peace, that is, rather than war. An entire imperial system has collapsed, and individual peoples have freely returned to the European scene. The simplistic division of the world into a First World, a Second World and a Third World has vanished; we are witnesses to this process of upheaval, but has it really penetrated into people's consciousness and lifestyles?

The factors governing the new order that have remained are, first, the logic of the marketplace and capitalism and, second, the western military bloc. When the Soviet Union existed as a powerful reality, the image of a free and more just society in the West was alive. The authoritarian system in the East served as a distinctive warning: we did not want our society to look like that! Democratic socialists, as well as liberals and conservatives, worked actively to create rights to social liberty and to build up the post-war social systems. In the heads and hearts of many people in Europe, a democratic civil society provided the sole firm foundation, even for those who organised themselves in socialist parties and trade unions.

Now we have to learn anew. The military threat to our existence from outside has disappeared, and the peaceful laws of capital accumulation and the market are rising while the social systems of all western countries are at the same time being turned upside down, cut back and radically transformed. Yet at the same time, wealth production in these countries has grown immensely. What has been going on? The crucial change is in the relationship between capital and state: the state founded on taxation is dying, and major companies in Germany, such as Daimler and Allianz Insurance, proudly pay no more taxes. Although they make extensive use of infrastructures, the German education system and transport facilities, they pay less and less into the common purse.

It is not globalisation that is new about the present form of capitalism; what is totally new is that capital can operate with complete freedom for the first time in history, without encountering borders or barriers. Bourgeois society and capitalism were never identical, since the development of a bourgeois civil society consisted in limiting the effects of capitalist and market thinking, but when neither the state nor the power of trade union opposition is any longer capable of protecting the basic requirements of a civil society based on tolerance and rights to social liberty, and when those with economic power decline to take on any responsibility for the economy of the entire house, for the common weal, on their own initiative, then the whole of Europe is in the gravest danger. It is necessary, as is evident from the increasingly loud calls made in all countries, for economic activity once more to be brought within the bounds of cultural aims and purposes. We are dealing not with an economic crisis, but with a crisis in the cultural significance of economic activities.

Only a European solution can be found to this critical issue, since individual states are being blackmailed by the argument of the needs of globalisation: those with economic power say that they will leave Germany or France if they are obliged to pay taxes. They may certainly go on looking for ways of avoiding taxes, but not in the European economic area. The need for such changes calls for active learning, as it is difficult to explain to people in Europe that the powerful are paying less and less into the common purse, while the powerless are paying ever more.

THE CRISIS OF WORK

The civil society that we want cannot be achieved without a restructuring of work and paid employment. This is the second critical issue that we have to consider. It has been known for a long time, at least since the early 1980s, that the principle no longer applies whereby today's profits are the investments of tomorrow and the jobs of the day after tomorrow. Since 1980, profits in Germany have increased by about 100% and wages and salaries have risen only to a certain degree; but unemployment has more than doubled during this time of economic prosperity and long-term wage restraint.

Such huge mass unemployment as is presently seen in Europe is not a problem that can be solved by technical adjustments; it touches on many issues of culture, morality and the ethics of responsibility in a civil society. At a European employment conference held in Hannover in 1999 a depressing finding was published: 50,000 people were becoming unemployed in Europe each day. At the same time, academics and politicians are eager to declare in front of television cameras that many new jobs are also being created. This is true; the whole structure of employment is in turmoil. But it is not enough. The wave of rationalisation brought about by microelectronics is affecting all sections of society, including the service industries. While one new job may be created, two or three are destroyed. We can change little about this epoch-making trend if we go on leaving social development with almost religious faith tothe logic and laws of the market and capital.

The human problems of mass unemployment go deeper. They affect individual people's lives. We know from surveys of the unemployed that personal identity, social recognition and individual dignity are still essentially defined by work, at least in the European context. It is necessary to stress forcefully that unemployment is an act of violence, an attack on physical and spiritual integrity, on the freedom from bodily harm of the people concerned; it is theft and dispossession of skills and qualities which have generally been acquired through a laborious and costly process of education within the family, and at school and college, but which are suddenly cut off from the opportunity to be applied in society, and are in danger of rotting and causing serious personality disturbances. The Berlin artist Heinrich Zille once said that people can just as surely be killed by losing the roof over their heads as by an axe.

In this critical issue we have to learn anew about work and unemployment. The popular cries of lean production, lean management, just-in-time delivery, and so on suggest a process of sensible rationalisation of production and trade, but they disguise the reality. If companies rationalise, they push the costs saved on to others. Every government department is proud of making savings, but the burden of cost simply moves elsewhere. Money saved, for example, in education, family support, primary socialisation, and so on, means more money spent a few years later on police, prisons and the building of psychiatric units. I am therefore arguing for a carefully considered balancing of the economy of the entire house (cf. Negt, 2001, p. 308ff.) This will produce a balance sheet that is quite different from what is produced merely by totalling the balance sheets of every individual enterprise. In this economy of the entire house (and I am thinking of the Greek concept of *oikos*), categories such as education – learning and training – take priority. I do not mean only general education but also vocational training, although I doubt whether vocational training alone will enable us to resolve the critical issue of unemployment.

In many companies, including the service industries, a radical 'deskilling' of jobs is taking place. As Richard Sennett shows in his challenging book *The Corrosion of Character* (Sennett, 1998), flexibility (job fragmentation or the combining of several different jobs) is increasingly leading to the fragmentation of human lives, especially family relationships, the very resources that have nourished capitalism until now.

It is not only young people, who may not yet have had a job at all, who are affected, but to an increasing extent older people as well. Can there still be any doubt about the huge cultural importance of adult education at such times? When people cannot understand the fragmentation of their lives, when they remain unaware of it, there is a palpable danger of their declining into psychiatric conditions such as depression and loss of a feeling of self-worth, and into illness, alcoholism and drug-dependency. We often behave as though the drugs problem had nothing to do with this difficult restructuring of employment. However, the problems that this leaves unresolved are the breeding ground for people's tendency to retreat from reality and to develop an addiction.

There are no quick practicable solutions. But I do believe it would be worthwhile to take this critical issue of work and unemployment seriously, so that we can reach a real decision as to whether we have a Europe-wide society that is culturally viable. One consideration I must point out: that the insane vision of a collective planned economy collapsed of its own accord; it was its own irrationality that brought this about. This is a good thing and was overdue. But it would be fatal to deduce from this that we can do without collective solutions to our self-induced problems. Democratic socialism and the European trade unions have a long tradition of fighting for a balance between private property and collective forms of living. A great cooperative movement grew up: production collectives, and self-help trading and loan organisations guided by solidarity, cooperation and mutual aid rather than profit. It developed further in Europe than in other parts of the world. I find it of great importance to preserve a collective memory of these social experiments for the future. Movements to found cooperatives are once again stirring, especially in Italy, and while they are certainly market-oriented, they are far from obsessed with mergers and acquisitions, or even with profit.

In Europe we have had in the past a vast range of social experiments, and will perhaps have yet more in the future, associating individual freedoms and independence with the need to safeguard the community. We must learn once again that while economic activity is necessary and jobs have to be secured, we should not lose sight of human goals. A European society needs a new ethic of responsibility for the community.

THE CRISIS OF SOCIAL LIFE

A structural change in the relations between places of upbringing and education is taking place in Europe before our eyes. We may regret the fact that the old bourgeois family no longer exists; but it may be that this ideal type of family based on marriage, property and children as a viable unit did not exist before the fifteenth century and will no longer exist in the twenty-first century. The divorce rate is high in every country, and some children grow up with single parents. In the United States more than a third of all children and adolescents are living with only one parent. What interests me is where children in these circumstances learn the basic social skills that are so important for life in society. Where do people learn today to share and to compromise? Where do they experience absolute reliability and security?

Without such essential virtues, a democratic society cannot remain stable in the long term. But this is just one aspect of growing up for the new generation. It is not only in Brazil or Thailand that masses of children are impoverished; the fragmentation of family relationships also means that child poverty has reached huge proportions even in a rich country such as Germany. Cynics might say that if two thirds of a society is doing well, then it still has a firm basis. But this is false. When a third of the population is to all intents and purposes disconnected from a good, well-ordered society, there is not only the potential for unrest but also an enduring denial of the self-proclaimed values of justice of that society. Augustine, who lived during the decline of the Western Roman Empire, said once in his famous book *The City of God*: 'What are empires without justice but large bands of robbers?' (Augustine, 1950, Book IV, p. 112–113). If we speak of a civil society, we imply the need for compensatory justice, and this means protection and care for those groups and classes in society that cannot help themselves because of their circumstances. The trade unions still have a historic task that is by no means accomplished. If people's primary experiences are so fragmented but no one can grow up without close personal relationships and physical touch – that is, without human contact – we must look more closely at the social institutions that convey and provide opportunities to practise these social virtues. In this connection I see an increasing role for schools, which have the task not only of teaching reading, writing and arithmetic, and familiarity with computers – the technical skills required in our culture – but also of fostering and structuring social and emotional learning. There is a need for a balance between cognitive, emotional and social learning processes. I have, incidentally, discovered on training courses for managers of major companies that emotional and social learning is not regarded as a superfluous addition even in those circles – on the contrary, it is absolutely necessary and is what makes factual knowledge stick.

There is nowadays so much inflated talk about the information and learning society that one becomes quite giddy. But this link between cognitive training and the development of personality in the sense of identity, purpose and social competence in intercourse with other people, including strangers, is crucial to learning in an information society. Where else are people to acquire the ground rules that will enable them to learn to learn? How will anyone who is not encouraged to indulge his or her curiosity in childhood and adolescence, anyone who has not experienced reliable relationships in childhood and adolescence, anyone for whom the primary institution of the family and the school are alien, cold institutions, be able to defend the democratic, civil community as though it were his or her own?

In all three critical issues discussed so far, I have set out to portray both dangers and solutions. That is the meaning of the Greek word from which 'crisis' is derived: *krino* means separating, dividing, distinguishing (judging), and also deciding. A crisis means a moment of radical change, in which there may be both fatal developments and renewal. I am banking on renewal, which is why I stress the issue of the community.

NEW TECHNOLOGY AND HUMAN EXISTENCE

This is a critical issue directly affecting the human condition; it goes to the core of the integrity and identity of human life. I refer to the altered relationship between technology, particularly medical techniques, and the growing importance of ethical issues arising from the fact that humanity sees itself with the aid of technical intervention as a kind of prosthetic god, as Sigmund Freud once appositely expressed it (Freud, 2005). It is not only the rapidly increasing prolongation of life which is bringing about progress in the history of our northern culture. The overcoming of diseases and the postponement of dying have been cultural, utopian ideals since ancient times. But we are entering a new stage. Growing old and dying with dignity are surely among the basic civilising attributes of a society that is proud of its cultural tradition. But if we do not wish to upset the contract between the generations, about which there is so much talk, then social wealth must be redistributed. Children and young people may have caring representatives in this world, but they have no real power. In this society, young people arouse attention only in two fields: as perpetrators of violence, and as consumers. Have we reached the point in Europe where we can take seriously and recognise their interests and needs as social and political beings? We are far from it. Care for the elderly in this society lies in their own hands, however; initiatives to make small reductions in pensions usually lead to considerable punishment by the electorate.

This is only one aspect associated with technology. The health service is the only sector in our societies where costs are consistently growing. There is even talk of a sixth Kondratieff, a long period of economic prosperity (named after the Russian economist of the 1920s; cf. Kondratieff, 1984), taking over from the age of microelectronics that has already exhausted its power of innovation. Medical techniques, on the other hand, gene technology, antenatal diagnostics, cloning and embryo technology, all these possible micro-interventions into the body and the very substance of the human species, have developed so spectacularly within a few decades that they are having a profound effect on our image of the human being. The Greek physician Hippocrates forbade the cutting of organs, and Kant said that only the removal of a diseased human organ was permissible, anything else degrading the human being to the level of material and infringing human dignity (Kant, 1996). Transplant technology means that people can more or less be rebuilt out of alien parts. Are we aware of what this means for our perception of integrity, for the human feeling of self-worth and personal identity?

We let all these processes continue as though they were a matter of course. We discuss the economic situation, company mergers and atomic power stations with great passion, and I am not saying that these are unimportant. But out of public view, in realms of hidden reality, processes are taking place with the potential for interventions in the nature of human beings which would be an abuse of gene technology by those in power. A code of bioethics is therefore urgently needed, going beyond the boundaries of national borders. The manipulation of genes may certainly have a place in eliminating diseases. But the notion that a commercial company can intervene through gene technology in the inherited substance of a human being in order to produce individuals with specific characteristics can only be regarded as a nightmare. Yet it is far from unimaginable. European regulation has specific tasks in this field. Laws are certainly necessary to forbid and punish such actions. But that is no longer enough. Europe must develop a cultural awareness that such misuse of the power of technology contradicts our understanding of a cultured, civil society.

Such an ethical consensus is an essential requirement for a Europe that is free from violence, as Jürgen Habermas and Pierre Bourdieu have constantly suggested (Bourdieu, 1998; Habermas, 2001). Discussion of such an ethic is crucial to the shaping of life in Europe; the funding of discussions and recommendations concerning such awareness should be on the agendas of political parties and trade unions. This is a real task for them. If they come to grips with these vital issues, they will have no need to worry about electors and members. The soil of right-wing radicalism is fertile: the seeds of violence grow best where problems and conflicts are unresolved. It is true that once technologies are discovered, they cannot be forgotten again. It is therefore all the more urgent that people become culturally aware that such technologies can be rejected. This applies equally to atomic technology, which may be profitable as long as it is used economically. But it is no stain on the honour of a cultural community to decline things that are not really necessary for a satisfying standard of living, but which impinge on the very basis of our existence, on nature, on our physical integrity, and on the other creatures on earth. I am sure that a single massive explosion of the size of Chernobyl in the heart of Europe would have shut down nearly all atomic power stations in these latitudes. We need not, I believe, wait for such a collective misfortune. We can also learn from the mistakes of others.

IDENTITY AND DEMOCRACY

At the core of this critical issue lies the balance between democracy and public life. To me, civil society is another expression for a functioning democratic society. I prefer the term democracy because it is unmistakably associated with a whole series of issues that have arisen during its history. Civil society sounds more neutral; but in Europe it has lost its opposite pole, which consisted originally of absolutist feudal regimes, and then authoritarian and militarised forms of society. Neither the land-owning classes nor the military have decisive influence in present-day Europe. The issue of democracy is still on the European agenda. Here, too, we face radical change in the old institutions associated with the democratic polity – parliament, the division of powers into three, civilian control of the military, political parties and trade unions – all of which are involved in their visible forms of expression. Increasing numbers of people doubt whether all is well with these institutions and whether it makes sense to vote in elections in order to influence events as a whole.

All constitutional organs may be functioning, but the question nonetheless has to be asked, and within the institutions there are growing feelings of discouragement, frustration and anxiety about life, and a desire to escape from these institutions and to go quite different ways; I see these as political black market fantasies. Countries with widely differing democratic traditions are now expected to grow together in Europe. This requires that these countries each come to terms with their own past. Some, such as Spain and Portugal, only joined the major democratic nations in the mid-1970s. Earlier, in the 1920s and 1930s, they had attained a high level of democracy, but Franco and Salazar are part of the past that must also be dealt with. In Germany, the wound which fascism inflicted on Europe has still not healed. In other countries that were victims, there is doubtless also much that is not forgotten.

However, this is not the main threat to democracy in Europe. I see another danger approaching: in the huge tension between growing globalisation and increasing individualisation, which are currently discerned as the two main trends by sociologists, vital intermediate levels are being threatened or destroyed. I would term this: the need for viable units. By that I mean readily comprehensible contexts in which people recognise themselves in their thoughts and actions, and find acknowledgement and confirmation in their personal and material environments. They may be neighbourhoods, trade union centres of communication, or public places where young people meet. Where such viable units (organisations and institutions) disappear, people lose interest in the community. People need solidarity that can be grasped with the senses, but this is only created if they feel a need for society and community. Only if young people discover, for example, that those who damage the community and society damage their own individuality, will they develop a sense of community, a social sense.

I should therefore like to argue that many institutions are too small, such as the family or relations with partners, and many are too large and too remote. The balance between proximity and remoteness is disturbed. For many people in Europe, the bodies that have a say in their fate are too far away, too abstract. They therefore do not know whether their vote in an election and their interests have been taken into account and have influenced the decisions of those bodies. This trend of creeping depoliticisation harbours two dangers. In the national parliaments, increasing attention is called to the fact that the real decisions are taken in the European context.

On the other hand, Europe has not yet acquired any true political identity that provides a sense of direction. Here, too, I must reiterate my basic precept: that democracy starts where people live, work and acquire their initial experiences in social intercourse. The fostering and development of this primary socialisation should be the basis for the use of technical media for the purpose of shaping life. Where the media take on the suggestive power of a second reality which overlays or suppresses the initial experience of reality, a substitute world of illusions and self-deception is the result. Mere access to the Internet or other information networks does not make people enlightened and unprejudiced world citizens; nor does such an access to a network directly increase political judgement; more information is made available, but the real problem of learning and education today is no longer the amount of information but the ability to handle information.

Adult education in Europe has a key role and task in this regard. In order to create forms of organisation and social contexts in which human proximity and critical distance, proximity and remoteness, balance each other out, the democratic civil society in Europe needs to strengthen and promote all those collective institutions that are not chiefly profit-oriented but give people actual access to larger units, and we need to concentrate our imagination on the organisation of such social institutions. This completely contradicts the current obsession with privatisation, which is the characteristic of present-day capitalism. The major companies are caught up in a fever of mergers and are breaking all the bonds that hold people's lives together, as Ralf Dahrendorf has rightly put it (Dahrendorf *et al*, 1995). If these forces of social cohesion are loosened or weakened, there are grave consequences for people's ability to communicate since they are only willing to entertain what is different and alien in the world if they have firm ground, experience of belonging, beneath their feet.

The commercial demand for people who are flexible, adaptable and market-oriented assumes an intact personal identity. But people can only be flexible if they have developed what amounts to a core identity. That in turn benefits not only the modern economy but also a democratically structured society, which requires people to be guided from within and to have critical judgement. Both of these characteristics can only come about in people's development if they are standing on firm ground and are attached to a perceptible reality. Democracy is thus that form of social existence which cannot come about by itself but must be learnt. Lifelong learning, adult education which goes beyond narrow vocational training, is therefore a requirement for the existence of a democratic social order. Furthermore, we cannot sub-divide this notion of democracy by divorcing participation in society and the community on the level of parliamentary elections, in which free citizens rule, from the recreation of old hierarchical, authoritarian relationships in industrial enterprises, service industries, schools and universities, disenfranchising those who depend on them. In the long term, that will not work, and I am convinced that it is, in fact, economically counter-productive.

CONTRIBUTIONS TO THE EUROPEAN PROJECT

Let me divide up these critical issues roughly as follows. There is no continent on earth which can invest so many and such varied resources in a productive unification process as Europe. We can even gain something positive from the development in isolation of the nation-states in the nineteenth century, even though the eighteenth century had gone much further with the Europeanisation of our cultural area. Europe must not be a construct without a memory. Too many productive approaches to living would be lost if we failed to direct our attention to preserving our collective memory and to recognising our unique socio-cultural variety of lifestyles, which must not be reduced to a common level by money and the production of goods. Although it may sound paradoxical, the long-standing plethora of languages is an essential element of creating a European identity. The time may perhaps not be far off when children grow up in every family with a second language, and I do not mean always the same one, but Italian with German, Finnish with French, or English with Danish.

I have called Europe a working project. All countries have something of an unquestionably European nature to contribute to this project. It might, for example, be the tradition of trade union organisation, which goes back more than a hundred years, with its specific workers' culture in the individual countries. This is not the same in Italy, Germany and Finland, but it is consistently governed by the thought that there are masses of people in a capitalist society (and by no means only there) who cannot defend their rightful interests and needs individually but require collective support and solidarity. The European trade unions may be in crisis in the present state of upheaval, but there can be no doubt that there are millions of people who are poor, exploited and sick. The trade unions should, if I may be permitted a word of advice, pay far more regard to their mandate towards society as a whole and conceive of their interests as clearly concerning people's lives, which are not defined solely in terms of the workplace (cf. Negt, 1989). The struggle to democratise relations in enterprises is an essential step towards the realisation by those who work in them that they can influence what happens in society.

Europe has the traditions of the social state on which to draw for its contribution, the Nordic countries and Germany more strongly than the southern countries. A Europe which became completely Americanised in this regard would destroy the foundations of its existence, though I do not want this to be misunderstood as anti-Americanism. We must certainly restructure the existing social systems. But even then there remains something amounting to a European idea. It consists of the cultural 'human capital' which the individual countries contribute to European life. I am not only thinking here of museums and music, which have always contained an element of internationalism: what Jean Sibelius learnt from the 'Art of the Fugue' met with national barriers and narrow-mindedness. I mean the everyday cultures, which deserve to be preserved and must definitely not fix their sights solely on the global society. Even at the present time, this variety in unity provides its own extremely important dialectic of relations between the particular and the general. Political and sociological ingenuity creates many different cultural peculiarities within this unity.

A wide range of social experiments are being conducted to solve the pressing problem of unemployment in the individual countries of Europe; they are many and varied, and I will only mention a few here. Attempts are being made through self-help, with state support channelled through employment offices, not to trust market forces blindly, but to develop collective alternatives that are worthy of human beings. In Italy, social cooperatives are being set up with tax reductions and local authority grants in the initial years, and with the support of the trade unions. These cooperatives are increasingly becoming numerous. Other initiatives are being launched by major companies – for example, by the steel giant Voest-Alpine in Austria. On the day when notice is given, staff who are dismissed become members of a foundation, and they take part in a six-week orientation course, the costs of the foundation being borne by the company, and by the staff through withheld salaries. Foundations covering particular occupations or regions and involving local authorities (communes) are common in Austria. In the Scandinavian countries, there is more state support, and in France, there are occupational associations, which must be part-funded by companies. The trade unions are actively involved in all these cases, and in the so-called social enterprises in Germany. Here, too, we are therefore undergoing a European learning process, and without such mutual learning and experimentation, Europe will remain an empty economic shell.

If Europe is to grow together, leisure-time tourist visits will not be enough to ensure that people learn from an exchange of ideas. It will be necessary to carry out adult education programmes in all European countries as part of the type of projects mentioned earlier on. Mere vocational training may increase the chances of finding a job in the market place, but it does not directly help to redirect this world of radical change towards education, towards the capacity to make critical judgements and the ability to handle information – that will require a special effort, didactic skill and, of course, money. The self-awareness that I am German and European, Finnish and European, and so on, is necessary if European cohesion is to be sustainable. I am not talking about the kind of European patriotism which renders other peoples enemiesand removes recognition from the strangers in our countries. But education and learning always have a double purpose today: both conveying factual knowledge and providing guidance. People have a great interest in both. They can indeed draw their factual knowledge nowadays from technical channels such as computer programs and the Internet, but this accumulated wisdom seldom turns them into active citizens who are as concerned for the common weal as for the protection of their own interests. They might still make sacrifices for the old nation-state, but why should they do so for Europe, for other countries? What do Europeans need, then, in order to find their way successfully in this world, what guidance do they need, and what knowledge of vocational skills is required?

NEW KEY SKILLS

To conclude this article, I will try to outline some new key skills that are crucial to the citizens of Europe. I do this against the background of 30 years of involvement in workers' education, among trade unions and in general adult education. These key skills can also be regarded as learning objectives for adult education. There is a certain universalism about this approach: I cannot imagine any civil society in which people are not equipped with such guiding knowledge or, to put it more exactly, those skills which link individual interests with a perception of the community, and the whole of society. Lengthy consideration and didactic trials have led to the identification of seven such skills which can be learnt by way of exemplary learning. By 'exemplary' I mean learning processes that are determined by people's own interests and horizon of perception, so that general relationships are made comprehensible (cf. Negt, 1971).

1. Creation of Context

The oppressive alternative reality of the world of the media sets out to fragment information. Weighing, selecting and processing information is a necessary act of personality development. This is only conceivable as the object of conscious learning. If people do not combine information, they can have no concept of the world, are liable to be deceived and can in certain circumstances be politically manipulated (the externally controlled character type, to use David Riesman's term (Riesman, 2001).

2. Identity Skill

In our world of accelerating change, where a high degree of mobility is demanded of people, feelings of self-worth must be strengthened so that people have a secure sense of orientation. This calls for a large amount of knowledge. People need some form of 'identity training' to avoid succumbing to depression, illness and psychological disturbances when they are uprooted, lose their jobs and become unemployed, or suffer family break-up. Identity is not simply given but must be acquired, must be learnt, and changes as society develops. The pace at which social values are lost also has consequences for the loss of individual values of identity.

3. Ecological Skill

This is for me the caring, careful handling of nature, of things and of other people: for our quality of life we rely on the foundation of our existence remaining undamaged. Ecology in this sense has a far wider meaning than environmental issues, although it is central to these. Ecological thinking, ecological awareness, is a vital condition of the modern world, and on it depends the survival of the human species. Focusing on ecological learning is not a luxury which can be dispensed with as and when required.

4. Economic Skill

By this I mean that we need to grasp that economic activity is a social project devised by people and therefore governed by power and the vested interests of those with power. Restoring a human purpose to the economy is a matter of learning, by children of course, but also by adults, who must come to understand that economic laws are not the laws of nature.

5. Technological Skill

Here, too, our attitude is ambivalent. There are many people who say that technological development is fated, and that we can do nothing about it. Governments and bureaucracies often see it this way, and this is reflected in people's everyday lives; but that is mistaken. If we think in terms of Europe as a whole, it is very important to shed light on the cultural meaning of technology. It is through this process of enlightenment and education that people will learn to comprehend that microelectronic rationalisation both renders communication between people far easier and makes increasing numbers of real live workers superfluous. This ambivalence of technology should be addressed in the educational campaign which Europe needs, and which must be more than purely vocational.

6. Justice Skill

People have to learn to distinguish between equality and inequality, justice and injustice. We live in a society in which it looks as though there was equality of opportunity, as though we had realised the ideal of justice in the circumstances governing people's prospects in life. Market forces, with their semblance of equivalency, force their way into our brains and confirm such illusions of equality. But this is a gigantic deception; for instance, it is self-evident that we have in Europe a North–South divide, rich and poor countries. A sharpened awareness of invisible inequalities and hidden injustices has been one of the essential elements of political education and one of the basic tools of people active in public life since the times of the ancient polis, since Plato and Aristotle. One factor is the enduring asymmetry, the injustice in the relations between the genders; the fact that women are gaining increasing numbers of school and university qualifications in many European countries while their representation in senior positions remains very modest is one of the matters at issue, and it amounts to a Europe-wide scandal. This is an unjust relationship between the genders. Inequality and injustice cannot be overcome merely by acquiring the skill of being aware of them; but if we are talking about civil society, then the virtue of justice is a main objective of education.

7. Historical Skill

This refers to the power of utopian ideals and people's ability to remember. If people have no past, they have no energy and no courage to face the future, and are fearful of experimenting. In Europe, however, we are increasingly called on to involve ourselves in social experiments, and this requires us to pay far more attention to European history than we have to date in our reflections on the present. Sometimes, blind obsession with the present prevents us from opening our eyes to the potential riches of a European civil society which may lie hidden in some European country. It is also a fundamental task of adult education to make these visible and open them to discussion by the European public.

THE NEED FOR ADULT EDUCATION

Adult education is an essential means of creating a European identity; and there is a vital need for strengthening adult education by focusing the arguments which I have presented here on a number of political demands. Lifelong learning is currently a magic formula that is used in almost as indiscriminate a fashion as the concepts of individualisation and globalisation. Lifelong learning also has similarities with other slogans that are used as a form of legitimation, being easily turned into something optional. But as I have emphasised, learning throughout life is no longer a luxury which can be dispensed with in a society that is governed by rapid loss of values and the dynamics of production; it is a vital need that touches every individual. Therefore two preconditions must be fulfilled in the long term.

First, the hierarchy of values in our advanced societies must be overturned, so that the production of goods, capital and the share market are no longer the 'hard items' occupying the top positions while education, health care and learning are far down the list. The 'soft' items of education, health and well-being, and people's lifestyles increasingly point the way to the future as the real investment opportunities for a society on which depends everything associated with democracy and with what we call a citizens' or a civil society.

Second, we must finally grasp that adult learning is no longer a matter of individual needs and individual decisions about how we spend our money. The education ministers of all member countries of the Organisation for Economic Co-operation and Development (OECD) have set lifelong learning for all as a guiding principle.

If this is not to be reduced to a form of words, adult education must become a public affair, just as the struggle for general school education eventually led to the creation of public institutions.

Professional adult educators, educationists and critical contemporaries who decry the tragic state of the public school system may raise considerable objections to such an institutionalisation of adult education. I share these doubts in some respects; but the objections are only partly justified. When the attempt was made in the eighteenth and nineteenth centuries to institutionalise the acquisition of cultural skills through compulsory schools and compulsory teaching rather than leaving it to the wishes and material wealth of the parents, humanistic purposes doubtlessly played a part; but the essential thing was that an entire system of production and trade had made reading, writing and arithmetic a prerequisite for everyday dealings with engines and machinery and could not function without these cultural skills. And how do things stand today?

People are tied to technological communication systems which are constantly changing, and are subjected to systems of control governing responsibility and ethical norms. These have a deep influence on our lives and make it necessary, in the interest of finding one's own identity, not only to take further vocational training or even to choose new occupations but also to acquire knowledge in order to find some direction in life. We are confronted by a historic pace of change so that we must subjectively react to what is done to us by outside forces, to what we are drawn into, rather than merely being carried along by circumstances. We can no longer assume that what is learnt during childhood in schools will remain viable throughout life. This is no longer even the case in trade crafts, where traditional sets of skills and rules used to be handed down. My demand is therefore that compulsory institutions should be created for adults, paid for and maintained out of public funds, so that they are comparable in rank and status to the public school system. Why should it not be compulsory for an adult, who has a long life expectancy of 60, 70 or 80 years, to attend educational institutions for five or six years, and to gain certificates? This is not in fact as revolutionary as all that, since the supplementary training of managers, doctors, architects and teachers, which is currently largely funded privately or by companies, points directly to the social need for such institutionalised education. I regard the notion that informal learning might be obstructed or rejected because of this institutionalisation as a mistaken assessment of relations between institutionalised learning and so-called voluntary learning. On the contrary: the higher the place of learning in the hierarchy of public concerns, the more powerful will be the motivation to seek further education of one's own choice voluntarily.

NOTE

[1] This article is based on a paper given at the conference 'Lifelong Learning, Liberal Adult Education and Civil Society' in September 1999 in Turku, Finland. With the permission of the author, Palle Rasmussen has added subtitles and references and made minor editorial changes when it appeared

as an article, Negt, O (2008), Adult Education and European identity. *Policy Futures in Education* 6(6), 744–746. http://www.wwwords.co.uk/pdf/validate.asp?j=pfie&vol=6&issue=6&year=2008&article=7_Negt_PFIE_6_6_web Permission granted by journal publisher, Roger Osborne King and guest editor for the PFIE special issue, Palle Rasmussen..

REFERENCES

Augustine of Hippo (1950). *The City of God*. New York: Modem Library.
Bourdieu, P. (1998). *Le myte de la mondialisation et l'Etat social europeen*. Paris: Contre-feux, Liber raisons D'Agir.
Dahrendorf, R. et al. (1995). Report on wealth creation and social cohesion in a free society. London: Commission on Wealth Creation & Social Cohesion.
Durkheim, E. (1984). *The division of labour in society*. London: Macmillan.
Forrester, V. (1999). *The Economic Horror*. Cambridge: Polity Press.
Freud, S. (2005). *Civilization and its discontents*. New York: W.W. Norton.
Habermas, J. (2001). Why Europe needs a constitution, *New Left Review*, *11*, 5–26.
Hegel, G. W. F. (1994). Vorlesungen über die philosophie der weltgeschichte In J. Hoffmeister (Ed.) vol. 1, *Die Vernunft in der Geschichte* (pp.265–956). Hamburg: Felix Meiner Verlag.
Kant, I. (1996). *The metaphysics of morals*. Cambridge: Cambridge University Press.
Kondratieff, N. (1984). *The long wave cycle*. New York: Richardson & Snyder.
Negt, 0. (1971). *Soziologische phantasie und exemplarisches lernen*, 6th edn. Frankfurt am Main: Europaische Verlagsanstalt.
Negt, 0. (1989). *Die herausforderung der gewerkschaften*. Frankfurt am Main: Campus.
Negt, O. (2001). *Arbeit und menschliche würde*. Göttingen: Steidl.
Riesman, D. (2001). *The lonely crowd*. New Haven: Yale University Press.
Sennett, R. (1998). *The corrosion of character*. New York: W.W. Norton.

AFFILIATION

Oskar Negt
Former Professor of Sociology at the University of Hannover, Germany

DIP KAPOOR

10. ANTI-COLONIAL SUBALTERN SOCIAL MOVEMENT (SSM) LEARNING AND DEVELOPMENT DISPOSSESSION IN INDIA[1]

INTRODUCTION

This chapter considers the significance of a selective reading of subaltern studies for informing and understanding SSM political formations and anti-colonial SSM pedagogies of place (Kapoor, 2009a) in contexts of development-displacement and dispossession of Adivasis and Dalits in the state of Orissa, India. Adivasis account for 40 per cent of the 33 million 'development-displaced peoples' (DDPs) in the post-independence period (Fernandes, 2006: 113; Rajagopal, 2003: 195). The assumption here is that listening to Adivasi and Dalit subalterns, not as infallible communities but as comtnunities facing an unparalleled existential crisis, and who are more than qualified by virtue of their direct experiences with colonial oppression, is revealing about the 'ways of outsiders' (e.g. of the global/national agents and processes of colonial capitalism) (Kapoor, 2011, p.141) and subaltern social action and movement learning in colonial contexts.

While the term subaltern is used to refer to several marginalised social groups/classes and rural locations, including Adivasi[2], it should be noted that indigeneity, unlike in settler colonies where the demarcations between original peoples and colonial settlers is relatively conspicuous, is a contested category in India given the different waves of migration and multiple colonisations. Claims to being original inhabitants of an area are harder to establish than are definitions of indigeneity predicated on being prior peoples (Barnes, Gray & Kingsbury, 1995, p. 2). However, this article acknowledges the indigenous status of Adivasi based on self-declared claims (as recognised by indigenous peoples and the UN) to being 'mulo ntvasi' (root/original people). The government of India lists (see Ghosh, 2010 or Kapoor, 2010 for the politics of state-essentialist representations) the same peoples as constitutionally recognised Scheduled Tribes (STs) numbering some 84 million or 8.2 per cent of the total population of India as the second-largest indigenous population in the world (Ghosh, 2006: 505). The state of Orissa alone lists 62 ST groups or some 8 million Adivasi subalterns.

Subaltern is a term attributed to Antonio Gramsci to refer to peasants and the labouring poor in early 20th-century Italy and to a subaltern common sense, or the possible basis for a unifying peasant political consciousness,[3] in the context of a class hierarchy in Europe under industrial capitalism. The Subaltern Studies project (a group that initially included, under the founding editorship of Ranajit Guha and Subaltern Studies, Shahid Amin, David Arnold, Partha Chatterjee and Gyanendra Pandey), on the other hand, sought to revise the elitism of colonialist and bourgeois-nationalist historiography of Indian nationalism and elite interpretations of the Freedom Movement from two hundred years of colonial solitude under British India' (Guha, 2001: 35), underscoring the inextricable link between subalternity and colonialism. Guha's contribution was to link subalternity to coloniality and to 'redefine it as a structure of power in the (modern/colonial) interstate system' (Guha, 2001: 35). As proposed in this chapter, this is a significant link for the study and praxis of anti-colonial SSMs and the politics of political (un-civil) society in India today, if not in similar neo/colonial contexts elsewhere and for informing trans/national movements and dissident politics in imperial societies.

Notwithstanding the various critiques of subaltern studies,[4] what defines the preoccupations here with respect to informing adult education praxis and learning in anticolonial SSMs (Kapoor, 2007; 2009a), is the Gramscian-inspired regional/local focus (South Asia/India) on revisiting subaltern rebellions (Guha, 1983) and the associated conceptualisations of subaltern political space and politics addressing historical and contemporary colonial-capital-imperial imbrications (e.g. trans/national mining and dispossession of subaltern groups in Orissa who are racially-targeted in terms of caste and tribal subaltern locations) (Padel & Das, 2010). These struggles are all the more instructive and noteworthy for the study and praxis of resistance in the age of empire (Biel, 2000; Boron, 2005; Dirlik, 1994; Hardt & Negri, 2000; Harvey, 2003; Neeraj, 2007; Petras & Veltmeyer, 2001) or what Anibal Quijano refers to as the 'coloniality of power being expressed through a globalising capitalism' (2000: 215). Recognising the significance of anti-colonial politics, once aimed at the British (a preoccupation of the original Subaltern studies group), the political and educational interest here is in relation to subaltern resistance and contemporary internal and external agents and processes of post-colonial capitalist-development, including an increasingly neoliberal and corporatised Indian state since the introduction of the New Economic Policy in 1991 (Neeraj, 2007; Sanyal, 2010).

The wider significance of the pre-occupation with rural/forest-based subalterns, classes or communities in other locations and their social struggles and movements, is being variously addressed in recent place-specific scholarship attempting to register these politics and their contribution towards addressing colonialism, imperialism and the global designs of capitalism (Barua, 2009; Da Costa, 2009; Ghosh, 2006; Kwaipun, 2009; Langdon, 2011; Mookerjea, 2010, 2011; Menon, 2010; Peine, 2010; Prasant & Kapoor, 2010; Sayeed & Haider, 2010; Swords, 2010; Veissiere, 2009; Wittman, 2010). It should be noted that while all SSMs and struggles do not necessarily subscribe to an explicit anti-colonial, nor anti-developmental politics or teleology, this article focuses on those SSMs that have predominantly defined themselves as such.

SSM LEARNING AND RESEARCH: A WORD ON METHODOLOGY AND SIGNIFICANCE

The research is based on funded participatory research (Kapoor, 2009c) to explore and contribute towards Adivasi (Kondh, Saora and Panos/Dalits) social movement learning in South Orissa, specifically, the Adivasi-Dalit Ektha Abhijan or ADEA movement which germinated in the early 90s and now includes 120 villages or some 20,000 Adivasi/Dalit people as active participants, and a wider trans-local Adivasi/Dalit subaltern activism in the state between 2006 and 2009 (Kapoor, 2011). Insights are also informed by the author's engagements with the ADEA and other groups since the early 1990s. This includes several participatory action research initiatives involving education and organising in relation to food, land, forest and water issues in the Scheduled Areas (constitutionally protected areas). The work is in keeping with recent writing and research into knowledge production and social movements which foregrounds movement actor-generated knowledge and learning that emphasises political integrity and academic accountability to movements (Bevington & Dixon, 2005; Choudry, 2009; Choudry & Kapoor, 2010) through, for instance, long-term engagement and movement-actor determination in all aspects of social movement learning research, especially in relation to indigenous locations and 'insider-outsider' approaches to doing critical local research (Kapoor, 2009c; Tuhiwai-Smith, 1999: 177).

The participatory research project, 2006–2009, was jointly conceptualised with some degree of skepticism, especially on the part of ADEA movement leaders, given the numerous state survey-research experiences that did nothing to address their concerns. These reservations were re-considered after discussing the possibility of setting up a people's research institution that would actively address Adivasi/Dalit concerns and were connected to ADEA political interests as well as people's knowledge, education and social action. The end result was the establishment of a Center for Research and Development Solidarity (CRDS) that became the vehicle for the funded People's Participatory Action Research (PAR) project in to social movement learning (Kapoor, 2009c).

The research engaged ten Adivasi/Dalit community-based researchers and involved the following: joint-development of research questions; joint data collection in terms of selection of sites and sources; collective theorisation and interpretation of emergent thematics, distilled from several datasets collected over a three year period; several collaborative opportunities for writing and dissemination including in the vernacular for local popular education and politicisation through Amakatha/Our Voice. This resulted in 1000 copy distributions, on four occasions, including an eventful dissemination during *panchayat*/local government elections. Critical incident analysis of specific land occupations/conflicts, community celebrations (where Bakhanis or narratives were shared), central/regional ADEA leadership meetings, focus-group interviews with villagers threatened with land eviction, drama/political poetry and inter-SSM leadership gatherings, are all examples of data collection opportunities and related data sources that were utilised to generate insights into SSM formations, movement learning and organised action (Kapoor, 2009c).

One of the key developments from the PAR process was the germination of a trans/local SSM network/association or Lok Adhikar Manch (LAM) (Kapoor, 2011) as frequent data collection visits were utilised as opportunities for inter-SSM dialogue and collaboration for purposes of solidarity action, addressing development displacement and dispossession in the region, while continuing to inform the study.

Subaltern studies have always emphasised the politics of the lower orders and their political consciousness and the central focus of this scholarship has been on subaltern groups and classes, their struggles, movements and activities. Contrary to Western radical democratic versions of 'globalisation from below', that tend to limit the realm of 'the political' and 'resistance' to a modernist-politics of a globalising civil society (equated with globalization from below), subaltern studies extends the realm of the 'political' and 'resistance' by taking note of the myriad subaltern and/or anti-colonial un-civil politics being waged in the trenches and in the debris of rural, water and forest bodies left in the wake of a colonising capitalism.

Subsequently, SSMs need to be differentiated from NSM or OSM (see Hoist this issue) and other post/modern movement ideas for conceptual and analytical reasons and more significantly, for the purposes of political visibility and a historically persistent contribution to a radical praxis addressing colonialism and capitalist penetration (Kapoor, 2007, 2009a, 2011). The tendency to absorb, through theoretical slippage, whereby local theories/histories of Europe morph into global theories/histories (see Connell, 2007; Mignolo, 2000; Sethi, 2011) the politics of SSMs into NSM and/or OSM formations by reading them as civil-societarian ethnic/ identity, or ecology movements, or as movements concerned with what some have dismissed as the so-called mundane politics of food, survival and livelihood, dwarfs their specific political contributions. This not only misses the mark on the grounds of academic and political inaccuracy, but more egregiously perhaps, obscures the crucial historical and contemporary 'anti/ colonial politics' of ever-present subaltern constituencies; a politics which predates the histories of these contemporary strains of western political expression and activism.

CONTEXTS OF CAPITALIST COLONISATION AND DEVELOPMENT DISPOSSESSION IN INDIA

We fought the British thinking we will be equal in the independent India. (Kondh Adivasi Elder, Interview notes, January 2007).

They have the power of dhana (wealth) and astro-shastro (armaments). They have the power of kruthrima ain (artificial laws and rules)—they created these laws Just to maintain their own interests ... and where we live, they call this area adhusith (Adivasi-Dalit infested, as in "pest-infestation") ...we are condemned to the life of the ananta paapi (eternal sinners), as colonkitha (dirty/black/ stained), as ghruniya (despised and hated). (Dalit Leader, ADEA, Interview notes, February, 2007).

Historically, anti-colonial SSMs and rebellions were faced with the daunting challenge of addressing dominance predicated on the double articulation' of two types of governance: one by the British and the other by the Indian elites (Guha, 2001, p. 11). This is also the case today as the 'double articulation' ties the politics of the local (national) to the global (international, colonial, imperial) and the old and new agents of the globalisation of capitalism. Ranajit Guha acknowledges that the 'colonial experience has outlived decolonization and continues to be related significantly to the concerns of our time' (2001, p. 41–42). While Subaltern Studies recognises that, despite the formation of new social groups and institutions in rural and urban life under the aegis of British rule and post-independence modernisation and development, collectivities like the Dalits and Adivasis 'have continued to exist vigorously and to even develop new forms and content' (Ludden, 2005: 100).

The British were the first to restrict the customary rights of tribals over land and forests in 1855. The Indian Forest Act of 1878, of 1927, and then the Government of India Act of 1935, successively consolidated the power of the imperial government over forests and emphasised the revenue yield and the resource requirements of British military, commercial and industrial sectors. During 200 years of colonial rule, the British sought changes in land use patterns; exploited forest resources and mineral ores and introduced cash cropping, thus distorting the land structure, ecology, forest resources, and flora and fauna with grave implications for the Adivasi (Behura & Panigrahi, 2006: 35). British colonial rule, in other words, began the process of detribalisation of tribal land and forests, whereby the various Forest and Land Acts reduced the tribal to the status of encroachers on their own territories. This process was met with determined tribal resistance and rebellion (including Chota Nagpur, Munda, Kol, Santal, and Rampha rebellions), which did result in acts of amelioration and legislative measures to recognise some tribal rights (Guha, 1983).

The post-independence scenario in the form of the Forest Policy of 1952 was the reiteration of bureaucratic management of forests and the promotion of state capitalism in the forest sector, a major reason for continued unrest in the Adivasi areas in Orissa and elsewhere (Rath, 2006). Despite constitutional provisions in the 5th and 6th Schedules that recognise tribal ownership rights over land and forests in Scheduled/ Protected Areas (a provision that has been re-affirmed in the recent Forest Rights Act of 2006), 'people do not have the right to question the decision of the government on forceable evictions' (Asian Center for Human Rights, 2005, p. 9). In fact, the Center's report highlights the role of the Land Acquisition Act as being instrumental in the eviction of tribal peoples for more than a century and until recently, there was no provision for resettlement and 'rehabilitation', not to mention right to free, prior and informed consent (contrary to International Labour Organisation (ILO) Convention 169 requirements of which India is a signatory).

Pimple and Sethi (2005) conclude that under the recent turn towards neoliberal land policies, since the introduction of the New Economic Policy (NEP) in 1991 and the more recent plan to open over 300 corporate havens termed Special Economic Zones (SEZs), 'traditional occupiers of the land under customary law confront the prospect and reality of becoming illegal encroachers on land they have cultivated and sustained for generations—they are vulnerable and subject to summary eviction' (p.239).

The policies that encourage development-dispossession of rural subalterns appear to have crossed party political lines. For instance, the provisions of the NEP and the push to establish SEZs have 'resulted in policies pursued by the Communist Party of India (Marxist)-led Left Front government in West Bengal [unseated in 2011 state elections] that are virtually indistinguishable from those of other parties committed to the neoliberal agenda. In recent times, the Left-Front government has turned out to be more zealous than many others in dispossessing farmers of their land, and making it available for capital' (Menon & Nigam, 2007: 103). According to one estimate, the acquisition of 120,000 acres of land by the Left-Front over the past five years has been accompanied by an increase of 2.5 million landless peasants (Banerjee, 2006: 4719). In fact, 144,000 acres of land in nine districts have been earmarked for such acquisitions by private industry (Bidwai, 2007: 14).

Under the provisions of the NEP, the state of Orissa has signed Memorandums of Understanding worth $12 billion with South Korean steel giant POSCO Ltd. (single largest Foreign Direct Investment in the country), to exploit the best coal and iron ore deposits for a period of 30 years. This is being met with resistance from betel leaf farmers and several constituencies across the state and the country. The Utkal Alumina Industrial Limited (UAIL) consortium of state and trans/national mining companies, that has gradually acquired 2800 acres of land since 1993, displacing up to 60,000 Adivasi/Dalits in Kashipur Block, Rayagada district, operates an open cast bauxite mine that has met with consistent resistance over the past 17 years. Mining has become a flash-point for several subaltern struggles (Padel & Das, 2010): Adivasi/Dalit subalterns constitute 22 per cent of the population in Orissa yet account for 42 per cent of development displaced peoples (DDPs in state terminology) whilst, throughout India, Adivasi account for 40 per cent of DDPs while constituting 8 per cent of the Indian population (Fernandes, 2006: 113). Relatively better publicised subaltern movements and resistance to such developments of recent note include: Singur (Bengal), Nandigram (Bengal), Kashipur (Orissa), Lanjigarh (Orissa), Kalinganagar (Orissa), and the state level POSCO Pratirodh Manch (engaging Adivasis and Dalits) while other lesser known subaltern resistances continue to attempt to scale up activity through a coalitional trans-local politics aimed at these state-corporate, colonial-capitalist, developments and their implications for the displacement and dispossession of subalterns (Kapoor, 2011).

LOCATING POLITICAL (UN-CIVIL) SOCIETY AND ANTI-COLONIAL SSM PEDAGOGIES OF PLACE

As noted above, SSM responses to these developments have been escalating, given the import of Menon and Nigam's observation that.

> There is no understanding of communities as the subjects of dislocation or ways of life that are destroyed. There is an abyss of incomprehension on the part of the Indian elites toward rural and tribal communities. Ripping them out from lands they have occupied for generations and transplanting them overnight into an alien setting (which is the best they can expect) is understood as rehabilitation and liberation from their backward ways of life (2007: 72–73).

Conditions of impoverishment arising from displacement and dispossession then entail 'disciplining the subaltern who are presented as inhabiting a series of local spaces across the globe that, marked by the label "social exclusion", lie outside the normal civil society.... Their route back is through the willing and active transformation of themselves to conform to the discipline of the market' (Cameron & Palan, 2004: 148).

Partha Chatterjee (2001: 177), contrary to Gramsci's usage in relation to political parties/formal politics, refers to these local spaces outside normal civil society as constituting political society or populations that are not bodies of citizens belonging to the lawfully constituted civil society but are populations in need and deserving of welfare and who are not proper citizens under the law, consequently having to make collective demands on the state founded on a violation of the law, or who survive by side-stepping the law.

Anti-colonial SSMs constitute and take root in political society as movements that are primarily located outside and against the state-market-civil society nexus and the laws and institutions constructed and strategically deployed by this nexus. The impact of the latter is to legalise and normalise displacement and dispossession and to encourage post-displacement disciplining into welfare, re-settlement and rehabilitation and market-related schemes, or to subject subalterns to abject poverty in urban slums and constant migration in search of work, i.e., what Adivasi refer to as becoming 'lost peoples'. For instance, the ADEA's response to displacement and dispossession is discussed as follows:

> We are giving importance to land occupation (padar bari akthiar) and land use (chatriya chatri). We are now beginning to see the fruits of occupations. Before the government uses anawadi land to plant cashew, eucalyptus or virtually gives the land to bauxite mining companies, we must encroach and occupy and put the land to use through our plantation activities and agricultural use. This

has become our knowledge through joint land action. This knowledge is not only with me now but with all our people—what are the ways open to us—this is like the opening of knowledge that was hidden to us for ages (Kondh man. Interview notes, 2007).

They are fighting against those who have everything and nothing to lose. We will persist and as long as they keep breaking their own laws—this only makes it easier for us! That is why even after the police firing in Maikanch (South Orissa, India) in 2000, over 10,000 of us showed up to oppose the UAIL (Bauxite mine/refinery) project the very next month (ADEA Leader, Focus Group notes, February, 2008).

Adivasis have subsequently learned to take collective extra-legal action in order to achieve their ends, as the law is perceived to be a disciplining and colonial instrument of the state. For instance, there are numerous examples of state and corporate breaches of constitutional and legal stipulations pertaining to the Adivasi and Scheduled Area provisions. In the case of the UAIL project, with the help of the Orissa Mining Corporation, a state organ, the companies continued development activities despite the expiry of the lease, while environmental clearances were not obtained prior to the issuance of mining leases. When issued, site clearance was given to UAIL within 18 days by the Ministry of Environment and Forest, when the norm is closer to a year. (Kapoor, 2009b: 64–65). What's more, market violence through forced dispossession or development repression is not uncommon either when SSMs resist the project altogether, in keeping with their constitutional and human rights (Rajagopal, 2003; Kapoor, 2013a):

There were at least 5000 of us when they fired. I too was one of the 12 injured (pointing to scar on the thigh) but I never spoke up for fear of police retaliations. I have endured my lot in poverty and silence and could not get treated but we will never back down... even in Chilika, after Tatas got shut down by the Supreme court because they violated the Coastal Regulation Zone with their aquaculture project, their mafias came and destroyed people's fishing boats... it seems we act non-violently and use the law and the courts but they always respond with customary violence and break their own law (Adivasi man. Focus Group notes, February, 2008).

According to the convenor, a Dalit ADEA leader and movement representative, 'we are the most burnable (expendable) communities and by this I mean we, the Dalit, the Adivasi, the farmer and the fisherman are always forced to give up what we have and suffer and sacrifice for the sake of their development... we are in the way of their process of exploitation of natural resources for this development' (Focus Group notes, February 2008).

Following Chatterjee, it would seem that anti-colonial SSMs are agents of and simultaneously constitute political society since: a) they face unequal treatment under the law or are victims of the law, b) are expendable or burnable through multiple and racial/ethnically-targeted dispossessions and subjected to other forms of violence if need be (since they are not lawfully constituted civil society), and c) are compelled to resort to extra-legal collective activism through land occupations by stealth or un-civil activism and transgression of laws that are there to keep them out.

These movements learn to engage in an extra-legal politics by utilising, for instance, strategic knowledge gained through direct experience with land occupation and an anti-colonial politics of Adivasi/Dalit 'place' (i.e., we will not move for the mining project) with respect to the colonising and dispossessing implications of a capitalist-developmental state and a complicit, modernizing, Indian civil society. In the words of a Saora leader of the ADEA:

> If the government continues to control lands, forest and water that we have depended on since our ancestors came, then through the ADEA we will be compelled to engage in a collective struggle (ame samohiko bhabe, sangram kariba pahi badhyo hebu). ADEA is building a movement among us from village to panchayat to federation levels. I think this movement (andolan) should spread to the district and become district level struggle. The organisation is always giving us new ideas (nothon chinta), new education (ncjthon shikhya), awareness (chetna) andjojona (plans). We believe this will continue (ao yu eha kari chalibo amaro viswas).

Or in the words of a Kondh woman:

> The ADEA is there to fight collectively (sangram) to save (raksha) the forests and to protect our way of life. The ADEA is a means of collective struggle for the forest (ame samastha mishi sangram o kariba). We are all members of the ADEA and our struggle is around khadyo, jamin, jalo, jangalo o ektha (food, water, forest and unity).

As populations outside the law (political society) as opposed to 'lawfully' constituted civil society, SSMs germinate and subsequently seek to address, amongst other things, the loss of the means of reproducing their material existence as rural land/forest-based self-provisioning agri-economies, subsequently engaging in a social movement politics that resists, erodes, blocks and precludes the reproduction of capital through struggles in and around the fields, forests and water bodies targeted by global and national capitalist colonial development in the 'post-colony' (Kapoor, 2009a, 2011). According to a study on resistance to Industrial Tree Plantations in the global South, for instance, popular struggles have been successful in interrupting or stopping projects in a fifth of the cases examined (Gerber, 2010). In Chatterjee's terms,

> The usual features here are the intrusion of new extractive mechanisms into the agrarian economy, often with the active legal and armed support of colonial political authority, leading to a systematic commercialization of agriculture and the incorporation in varying degrees of the agrarian economy into a larger

capitalist world market... with varying contributions of foreign, comprador and national capital; the growth of new political institutions and processes based on bourgeois conceptions of law, bureaucracy and representation. (1983: 347)

In contrast to NSM middle-class politics of identity or sympathetic environmentalists who 'consume resources here while aiming to protect nature over there' (Kapoor, 2009a, p. 80), SSM constituencies are agents motivated by the direct and immediate material impacts of colonial trans/national developmental displacements and dispossessions e.g. dam displacement and resulting poverty, hunger and loss of meaning—the 'unique unfreedom of uprooted subalterns' or 'lost peoples' (Kapoor, 2011, p. 140). Chatterjee describes this modernising Indian civil society as 'bourgeois society... and the mark of non-Western modernity as an always incomplete project' (2001, p. 172),

set up by the nationalist elite in the era of colonial modernity (though often as part of the anti-colonial struggle) ... these institutions embody the desire of this elite to replicate ... the substance of Western modernity ...a desire for a new ethical life conforming to the virtues of the Enlightenment and bourgeois freedom and whose known cultural forms are those of Western Christianity (2001, p. 174).

Chatterjee suggests that while civil society was the most significant site of transformation in the colonial era, in the postcolonial period it is political society that is the most significant site of transformation and that in 'the latest phase of the globalization of capital, we will be witnessing an emerging opposition between civil society and political society' (2001, p. 178).

Such postulations help to assess and inform the politics and learning of dis/engagements between civil societarian social movements (NSMs) and NGOs (civil society actors) on the one hand, and anti-colonial SSMs or political society movements, on the other. The former tend to define justice and possibility as a project of inclusion and equity within modernity and a reformed capital. The latter, however, take exception to the colonial implications of the project of capital displacement, dispossession and loss of material, cultural and spiritual place and a Eurocentric modernisation (or an Indian bourgeois version of the same) that compels Adivasi/Dalit subalterns to change their ways of life/being in exchange for the mantle of civility and legal citizenship/ recognition. In the words of one ADEA member,

NGOs often try to derail the people's movement by forcing them into Constitutional and legal frameworks and by relying on the slow pace of legal avenues to make it seem like they are working in solidarity with the people but all the while using the delaying tactic to help UAIL.

... they make us into programme managers and statisticians concerned with accountability and the management of our people for the NGO... what they fail to realise is that we are engaged in an Andolan (movement struggle) and not donor-funded programmes (Focus Group notes, February 2008).

The differences between civil society and political society locations for respective movements and agents, and their politics, helps to explain and inform SSMs about what they might come to expect in such knowledge or political engagements. The ADEA has learnt, for instance, that partnerships with NGOs and NSMs can be depoliticising and disabling and have subsequently become more discerning and skeptical about the possibilities for solidarity around an anti-colonial politics."[5] For instance, a purist indigenous human rights activism that seeks to 'eco-incarcerate' (Shah, 2010:130) Adivasi/Dalit subalterns is often viewed with incredulousness and bemusement given the shrill attempts of 'Adivasi-outsiders' (civil society activists) to legally institutionalise 'subaltern spaces' (amounting to 'restriction' of Adivasi to Scheduled Areas) as physically fixed and frozen in time in cultural, social and political-economic terms; a white-stream ecological activism that has also been critiqued in North American settler colonies (see Grande, 2004). Despite these stifling implications, this civil society eco-politics can be simultaneously re-enacted in an anti-colonial SSM politics when strategically necessary (Kapoor, 2013b).

Partha Chatterjee (1983) discusses the implications of the intermingling of contradictory power systems or modes of power: communal, where entitlements are allocated on the authority of a whole community collective; feudal, where the same is derived from direct domination and the use of physical force; bourgeois, where property rights are guaranteed by general law and indirect domination through institutions of representative government. These modes of power were associated with, but not reducible to, Marxist conceptions of modes of production (communal, feudal and capitalist). Chatterjee attempts to highlight the interplay and transition between these modes since in India, different modes of production are operational simultaneously and may be discontinuous or antithetical. For example, these observations become apparent in the relations between forest-based community swidden ('cut-and-burn') cultivation, horticulture and hunting or self-provisioning moral economies, on the one hand, and agro-industrial capitalist development on the other, where capital tends towards the extinction of communal modes of power and production. This is evidenced by Adivasi/ Dalit subaltern expressions of loss'—being scattered—which is reflected in the content and socio-political directions for learning in anti-colonial SSMs.

> It is time we seriously start to think about this destruction in the name of development... otherwise, like yesterdays children of nature, who never depended upon anybody for their food, we will have no option but to go for mass transition from self-sufficient cultivators and forest and fish gatherers to migratory labourers in far away places. After displacement we stand to lose our traditions, our culture and own historical civilization...from known communities we become scattered unknown people thrown into the darkness to wander about in an unknown world of uncertainty and insecurity (Adivasi Leader, Field notes, April 2009).

The convenor of the ADEA points to the significance of learning to organise to meet this threat.

> We are forest dwellers, poor people, peasants and fisherfolks and we are in all aspects of our life, different from them. Let us get involved in campaigns to save our forests, land and water which sustain us. Let us occupy land... because I know that the government will never think about us seriously... if the companies like Tata and Vedanta ask the government for land, it is ever ready to oblige them at throw-away prices... this is how the government plans and acts against our interests.

On the other hand, as Chatterjee points out, capitalism can incorporate and intensify feudal structures of domination e.g. micro-credit interventions through NGO actors and feudal capture of labour and profit from these ventures in certain locations or multi-national corporate/feudal elite interventions in agriculture that have been partially responsible for the agrarian crises. Symptomatic of this has been the 241,679 farmer suicides connected to the introduction of genetically modified (GM) Bt cotton between 1995 and 2009, (Center for Human Rights and Global Justice, 2011, p. 3) and the neoliberal state's propensity to promote GM crops patented and produced by global agri-business. This is not unlike Stuart Hall's (1980, p. 320) description of 'an articulation between different modes of production, structured in some relation of dominance' where Hall goes further with this, suggesting that capital benefited from older forms of exploitation and ethnic and racial hierarchies constructed by pre-capitalist modes, e.g. European plantation slavery ensured the provision of cheap labour for modern European capitalist expansion. This is recognised as such by Adivasi in the current juncture—'Who wants to go to join the Oriyas and do business and open shops and be shaharis (city folk/moderns) if they make you labour like donkeys for one meal? Even if they teach us we do not want to go to the cities...' (Adivasi Elder, Interview notes, January, 2007).

> We cannot leave our forests (ame Jangale chari paribo nahi). The forest is our second home (after the huts). There is no distance between our homes and the forest. You just come out and you have everything you need.... My friends and brothers, we are from the forest. That is why we use the small sticks of the karanja tree to brush our teeth— not tooth brushes. Our relationship to the forest is like a finger nail to flesh (nakho koo mangsho)—we cannot be separated.... That is why we are Adivasi (Interview notes. Village D, 2007).

In keeping with these observations regarding multiple modes of production and power, spaces of transition and related implications for the various, shifting, structural locations of SSMs in political society (being mostly outside and beside the state--market-civil society nexus), SSM movement teleology and associated pedagogies are, out of strategic and political necessity, a multi-faceted praxis and political strategy. Anti-colonial SSMs, often located in forested/interior regions and organised in communal or semi-feudal modes of production and power, subsequently:

a) make overt political claims that might range from and between outright secession (very rarely), sovereignty, pluri-nationalism, degrees of self-determination or autonomy as these movements have become aware of the impacts of mining development in neighbouring regions for instance;
b) could decide to engage in a coalitional politics with certain political parties, usually from the Left, other SSMs (that may not openly espouse an anti-colonial position). Old Social Movements or labour (e.g. Maoist peasant movements and versions from the left) and/or NSMs (e.g. human rights and environmental NGOs) or at times, even corporate initiatives (especially with Corporate Organised NGOs (CONGOs) seeking to bait, fool or persuade Adivasi/Dalit subalterns into projects), while keeping an eye on their specific political interests by improving prospects for shutting down the projects of capital-state developmental interests; and
c) selectively engaging and some times, losing strategic/anti-colonial direction/objectives with the various politics in the locale including: class (e.g. left-peasant/Maoist guerrilla versions in Orissa); feminist/gender; environment; indigenous human rights, peace and justice; good governance; empowerment/emancipation (e.g. the World Bank strain or various NGOised-Freirean antipolitical-politics); participatory/alternative development; charity/service (e.g. humanitarian NGO versions); various religious appeals (e.g. Saffron/Hindu fundamentalisms and numerous Christian missionary possibilities in the rural districts) etc. At the core, anti-colonial SSMs subscribe to a political learning content and process that is embedded in 'our ways learning', with epistemic starting points in Adivasi ontologies. In the event that strategic deployments of outsider rights discourses help to open up political space in the interests of the anti-colonial project in the locale/region, they are taken up, despite the mutual caricaturing this often entails (Kapoor, 2013).

These insights on anti-colonial SSM political praxis are in keeping with Ranajit Guha's insights regarding the links between notions of an autonomous domain (and dominance without hegemony) and the significance of a people's politics, which is always at the core of SSM politics, i.e., 'our ways learning'. In *Dominance Without Hegemony and its Historiography*, Guha suggests that the Raj never achieved hegemony and was based on coercion and a façade of legality and that the end of the universalising tendency of bourgeois culture, based on the colonial expansion of capital, finds its limit in colonialism: 'in India subaltern politics constituted an autonomous domain which neither originated from the elite politics nor did its existence depend upon the latter' (1997). He sees 'subaltern classes and groups as having roots in the pre-colonial period and which continued to operate vigorously under the British, even to develop new strains in both form and content' (1982, p. 4), a position not dissimilar to James Scott's work (1990) on infra politics and hidden transcripts in Asian contexts (positions that have extended the realm of the political, however impotent or radical the implication of such politics).

Guha (1997) identifies the subaltern domain of politics as including a wide variety of generally autonomous modes of thought and action, expressed particularly in rebellions, riots and popular movements through the political expression of subalterti cultures and world views that are seen to be largely autonomous from the elite (British and Indian). David Hardiman, for instance, in speaking to the relative autonomy of tribal movements in India suggests that 'divine commands were a powerful programme for Adivasi assertion', what he references as 'this fundamentally religious ideology of peasant action' (cited in Ludden, 2005, p. 113) or what Alpa Shah refers to as 'democracy as sacral polity' (2010, p. 62).

SSMs demonstrate a unity of the sacred and the political that cannot be simply dismissed, as has been the case in colonial anthropology, as purely 'backward' superstition and subsequently relegated to the realm of the immaterial and irrational or an ineffectual pre-political anti-politics. As a moral politics, endorsed by the spiritual realm, the spiritual has material and non-material implications. An SSM anti-colonial pedagogy of place, then, is defined and determined by a historical and spiritual sense of place, rootedness and belonging, despite the plausible critique raised by Shah around an exaggerated human rights politics tending towards 'eco-incarceration' This sense of place is evident in a pedagogy that relies on the spiritual-intellectual resources of Adivasi/Dalit living and ancestral communities. Such appeals are marked by an emphasis on an apparent physical-metaphysics of Gods and ecology-human-animal relations, and a pragmatic sense of colonial politics concerning outsiders, that has been sharpened by a long history of direct experience with multiple colonial invasions and material dislocations (Kapoor, 2010). Contrary to certain Marxist (Brass, 2001, 2007; Das, 2007) and colonial/racist dismissals or relegations of this spiritual praxis to the sphere of irrational or mad politics Oesson, 1999) (or as non-material and therefore politically docile, mystifying, conservative, traditional, barbaric or even post-modern), the dominance without hegemony proposition and related notions of autonomous domain and a people's politics embedded in local knowledge and existence rationalities are simultaneously, and always spiritually and materially, politically relevant to subaltern ecological relations and the reproduction of subaltern political economies.

For instance, narratives, lamentations and rituals of 'our ways learning' (Kapoor, 2007, 2009a) establish a powerful historical continuity with ancestral anti-colonial struggles and current movement-motivation through spiritual sanction and political nourishment. This provides a crucial sense of political balance established through spiritual oversight with respect to an exaggerated sense of political mission and recognizes the limits to a subaltern politics. In the event of extreme conflict, violence and destruction, this spirituo-political restraint is essential at times, despite the magnitude of political and economic adversity wrought by colonial capitalist displacement and dispossession or similar invasions. It constitutes a pedagogy of the recognition of limits to what should be done in the name of the political (material), even in the face of constant provocations—an antithetical stance or understanding to a 'rational' and informed material politics of unrelenting capitalist colonisation of place, people and ecology.

> Oh friends let us go to the aggressors and bow our heads before them and also tell them that we too can become wild like oxen...
>
> Oh brothers, come to this paddy field and let us sit together with our aggressors and seek forgiveness from each other... (excerpt, from a Kondh Adivasi lamentation. Field notes, February 2007).

A SSM anti-colonial pedagogy of place is also informed by grounded-experiential theories of the wider political economy and their implications for the unfreedom of Adivasi/Dalit communities with related pointers for specific movement learning requirements including critical, strategic, tactical and informational learning (Kapoor, 2009b, 2009c, 2011). These are in constant engagement with macro-micro linking and analysis, including intra-movement critique/analyses (as with respect to the significance of Adivasi-Dalit unity OR ektha or a gender politics introduced by NGOs in the region and taken up by the ADEA as a significant politics) (Kapoor, 2009b). In the words of an ADEA leader on ADEA learning and education (Interview notes, 2007):

> Acting together has given us a different direction/vision (bhinna-diga). The ADEA has become a platform for us because we have made it so we have to teach each other (bujha-sujha), explain to each other and that is how education has happened and made things possible for us.... we have created a learning environment for our people and a political education around land, forest and water issues and we debate courses of action...

SSMs are also increasingly engaging in a scaled-up, trans-local activism, which raises the decibel level of a SSM anti-colonial pedagogy of place with other SSMs in the state of Orissa (Kapoor, 2011), to face the mammoth task of addressing the colonial capitalist development invasion for minerals and agro-industrial opportunity in the state, village by village, and region by region. As expressed in the People's Manifesto of the Lok Adhikar Manch (LAM), a trans-local alliance or loose network of 13 SSM organisations (April, 2009):

> We, the people's movements present here representing people's struggles from South and coastal Orissa have discussed and debated our issues and are hereby resolved to stand as a broad-based platform known as Lok Adhikar Manch (LAM) in support of the following manifesto (people's statement):
>
> ... we have nothing to gain from mukto bojaro (liberalisation), ghoroi korono (privatisation) and jagathi korono (globalisation), which are talked about today. We want to live the way we know how to live among our forests, streams, hills and mountains and water bodies with our culture and traditions and whatever that is good in our society intact. We want to define change and development for

ourselves (amo unathi abom parivarthanoro songhya ame nirupuno koribako chaho). We are nature's friends (prakruthi bandhu), so our main concern is preserving nature and enhancing its influence in our lives.

CONCLUDING REMARKS

Subaltern studies have attempted to make the importance of the subaltern to history known by uncovering forms of popular protest, including grain riots, small scale peasant insurgencies and struggles over forest rights and uprisings of hill and Adivasi peoples—'they have [arguably or attempted to] defined a subaltern consciousness separate from hegemonic cultural forms... realized in the practice of rural resistance' (Sivaramakrishnan, 2005, p. 217). Subalterns are recognised as subjects of history and the makers of their own history while such studies also demonstrate 'the extent to which peasant politics possessed autonomy within... encompassing structures of subordination' (Arnold, 1984, p. 169).

In other words, while SSMs need to be understood on local terms in specific contexts, they also need to be understood in relation to social orders, institutions and the history of material relations that mediate, shape and influence SSM formations (Arnold, 1984; Comaroff & Comaroff, 1992). These preoccupations are germane to a critical adult education that concerns itself with learning in social movements and struggles and questions of political consciousness, knowledge engagement, agency and social structures at local, national and global levels.

This chapter has focused on demonstrating the conceptual and political significance of a selective reading of Subaltern Studies as it pertains to understanding and informing political society SSM formations and the learning implications of an anti-colonial SSM pedagogy of place. As a source for movement learning, a site of politics in/about political society, involving partially autonomous and arguably distinct subaltern people's politics, SSMs continue to make a conspicuous case for pluri-nationalism (and pluri-modalities of production and power). They do so by exposing and resisting the machinations of colonial-capitalist dispossession in forest and rural spaces where 80 per cent or more of Orissa's 36 million people reside in 55,000 or so villages.

> ...we are laying a claim on the government who is supposed to serve all the people in this land. We are demanding a place for ourselves. ADEA's idea is that our livelihood should be protected and our traditional occupations and relationship to the land and forest be protected in the form of community control over land and forests in our areas and this is our understanding of our Constitutional rights too. There is no contradiction. Once this is understood, we can cooperate and when necessary, work with the government to take care of land and forests. If they can help the shaharis (moderns/urban peoples) destroy the forests, then they can and should help us protect it and listen to our story to. (Kondh ADEA Leader, Interview notes, 2007).

NOTES

[1] Reproduced with permission of NIACE. This article was originally published in Studies in the Education of Adults: Kapoor, D. (2012). 'Adult learning in political (un-civil) society: Anti-colonial subaltern social movement (SSM) pedagogies of place, Studies in the Education of Adults, 43(2), 128–46. Leicester: National Institute of Adult Continuing Education. http://www.niace.org.uk/publications/academic-journals/studies
The author acknowledges the assistance of the Social Sciences and Humanities Research Council of Canada (SSHRC) for this research in to 'Learning in Adivasi (original dweller) social movements in India' through a Standard Research Grant (2006–2009). Reflections and grounded discussion are both informed by this research.

[2] Using the term interchangeably with 'people' (and 'subaltern classes' where industrial/agrarian capitalism has classed subalterns) Guha acknowledges the historical specificity of this empirical judgment (2000: 7), subaltern loosely defined in the Indian context and with all its ambiguities, refers to the rural landless poor (migrant under employed labour), poor (small) peasants, pastoralists/nomads, Adivasis (original dwellers or Scheduled tribes in state parlance), Dalits ('untouchable' castes or Scheduled Castes), Other Backward Castes (OBCs) and development displaced people (DDPs) specifically from these former categories, including women in any of these groupings. Subalternity, is also understood as a social location and in terms of the dialectics of super-ordination and subordination (between these groups and class, caste, gender, urban and/or ethnically dominant/elite groups embedded in and across multiple modes of production) in global and national hierarchical social relations of exploitation (including but not restricted to those that reproduce capitalist property relations).

[3] See Peter Mayo, 1999, 2010 for the relevance of Gramsci in critical adult education.

[4] For instance, see Sumit Sarkar (2005) on critique pertaining to post-modern and cultural slippage (in later works) from founding Marxist/Gramscian structuralist (materialist) positioning and the waning of the subaltern, including Partha Chatterjee's general silence on economic themes (free markets, International Financial Institutions and MNCs) in recent works.

[5] See Kamat, 2002, 2004; Kapoor, 2005, in press; Petras and Veltmeyer, 2001 and for disabling NGO-politics in Global Justice Movements, see Choudry, 2010.

REFERENCES

Arnold, D. (1984). 'Gramsci and peasant subalternity in India', *Journal of of Peasant Studies*, *11*(4), 155–177.

Asian Center for Human Rights. (2005). 'Promising picture or broken future? Commentary and recommendations on the draft national policy on Tribals of the Government of India'. Retrieved May 29, 2011, from www.achrweb.org

Banerjee, P. (2006). 'West Bengal: land acquisition and peasant resistance in Singur.' *Economic and Political Weekly* (Kolkata) (pp. 4718–4720), 18 November.

Barnes, R., Gray, A & Kingsbury, B. (Eds.) (1995). *Indigenous peoples of Asia*. Ann Arbor, MI: Association for Asian Studies.

Barua, B. (2009). 'Colonial education and non-violent activism of rural Buddhist communities in Bangladesh', in D. Kapoor (Ed.). *Education, decolonization and development: Perspectives from Asia, Africa and the Americas* (pp. 57–74). Rotterdam: Sense Publishers.

Behura, N. & Panigrahi, N. (2006). *Tribals and the Indian constitution: Functioning of the fifth schedule in Orissa*. New Delhi, India: Rawat Publications.

Bevington, D., & Dixon, C. (2005). Movement-relevant theory: Rethinking Social Movement scholarship and activism. *Social Movement Studies*, *4*(3), 185–208.

Bidwai, P. (2007). Left faces critical choices. *Combat Law*, *6*(3), 12–16.

Biel, R. (2000). *The new imperialism: Crisis and contradictions in North/South relations*. London and New York: Zed Books.

Boron, A. (2005). *Empire and imperialism: A critical reading of michael hardt and antonio negri*. London: Zed Books.
Brass, T. (2001). 'Moral economists, subalterns. New social movements and the (re-) emergence of a (post) modernized (middle) peasant. V. Chaturvedi (Ed.). *Mapping Subaltern Studies and the Postcolonial* (pp. 127–162). New York: Verso.
Brass, T. (2007). A world which is not yet: peasants, civil society and the state. *Journal of Peasant Studies*, *34*(3–4), 582–664.
Cameron, A., & Palan, R. (2004). *The imagined economies of globalization*. London: Sage.
Chatterjee, P. (1983). More on modes of power and the peasantry. *Subaltern Studies*, *2*(3), 311–349.
Chatterjee, P. (2001). 'On civil and political society in post-colonial democracies. In S. Kaviraj & S. Khilnani (Eds.), *Civil Society: History and Possibilities* (pp. 165–178). Cambridge: Cambridge University Press.
Center for Human Rights and Global Justice (CHRGJ) (2011). *Every thirty minutes: Farmer suicides, human rights, and the agrarian crises in India*. New York: NYU School of Law.
Choudry, A., & Kapoor, D. (2010). *Learning from the ground up: Global perspectives on social movements and knowledge production*. New York: Palgrave Macmillan.
Choudry, A. (2009). Learning in social action: Knowledge production in social movements. *McGill Journal of Education*, *44*(1), 5–9.
Choudry, A. (2010). Global justice? Contesting NGOization: Knowledge politics and containment in anti-globalization networks. In A. Choudry & D. Kapoor (Eds.), Learning from the Ground Up: Global Perspectives on Social Movements and Knowledge Production (pp. 17–34). New York: Palgrave Macmillan.
Comaroff, J., & Comaroff, J. (1992). *Ethnography and the Historical Imagination*. Boulder, CO: Westview Press.
Connell, R. (2007). *Southern Theory*. Cambridge: Polity Press.
Da Costa, D. (2009). *Development dramas: Reimagining rural political action in eastern India*. New Delhi: Routledge.
Das, R. (2007). Introduction: Peasant, state and class. *Journal of Peasant Studies*, *34*(3–4), 351–370.
Dirlik, A. (1994). The postcolonial era: Third world criticism in the age of global capitalism. *Critical Inquiry*, *20*(2), 328–356.
Fernandes, W. (2006). Development-related displacement and tribal women. In G. Rath, (Ed.). *Tribal Development in India: The Contemporary Debate* (pp. 112–132). New Delhi: Sage Publications.
Gerber, J. (2010). An overview of resistance against industrial tree plantations in the global south. *Economic and Political Weekly*, *XLV*(4l), 30–34.
Ghosh, K. (2006). Between global flows and local dams: Indigenousness, locality and the transnational sphere in Jharkhand, India, *Cultural Anthropology*, *21*(4), 501–534.
Ghosh, K. (2010). Indigenous incitements. In D. Kapoor and E. Shizha (Eds.), *Indigenous knowledge and learning in Asia/Pacific and Africa: Perspectives on development, education and culture*. New York: Palgrave Macmillan.
Grande, S. (2004). *Red pedagogy: Native American social and political thought*. Lanham, MD: Rowman and Littlefield.
Guha, R. (1982). 'On some aspects of the historiography of colonial India.' In R. Guha, (Ed.). *Subaltern Studies I* (pp. 1–8). Delhi: Oxford University Press.
Guha, R. (1985). *Elementary aspects of peasant insurgency in colonial India*. New Delhi: Oxford University Press.
Guha, R. (1997). *Dominance without hegemony: History and power in colonial India*. Cambridge: Harvard University Press.
Guha, R. (2000). 'On some aspects of the historiography of colonial India'. In V. Chaturvedi, (Ed.). *Mapping the subaltern studies and the postcolonial* (pp. 1–7). London: Verso.
Guha, R. (2001). 'Subaltern studies: Projects for our time and their convergence'. In I. Rodriguez, (Ed.). *The latin American subaltern studies reader* (pp. 35–46). Durham, NC: Duke University Press.
Hall, S. (1980). Race, articulation and societies structured in dominance. In *Sociological theories, race and colonialism* (pp. 303–345). Paris: UNESCO.
Hardt, M., & Negri, A. (2000). *Empire*. Cambridge, MA: Harvard University Press.

Harvey, D. (2003). *The new imperialism*. London: Oxford University Press.
Holst, J. (2002). *Social movements, civil society and radical adult education*. Westport, Connecticut: Bergin and Garvey.
Jesson, B. (1999). *Only their purpose is mad*. Palmerston North: Dunmore Press.
Kamat, S. (2002). *Development hegemony: NGOs and the state in India*. New Delhi: Oxford University Press.
Kamat, S. (2004). The privatization of public interest: Theorizing NGO discourse in a neoliberal Era. *Review of International Political Economy*, *11*(1) 155–176.
Kapoor, D. (2005). NGO partnerships and the taming of the grassroots in rural India. *Development in Practice*, *15*(2), 210–215.
Kapoor, D. (2007). Subaltern social movement learning and the decolonization of space in India. *International Education*, *37*(1), 10–41.
Kapoor, D. (2009a). 'Globalization, dispossession, and subaltern social movement (SSM) learning in the South'. In A. Abdi, & D. Kapoor (Eds.), *Global perspectives on adult education* (pp. 71–92). NY: Palgrave Macmillan.
Kapoor, D. (2009b). 'Adivasis "in the way" of state-corporate development: Development dispossession and learning in social action for land and forests in India'. *McGill Journal of Education*, *44* (1), 55–78.
Kapoor, D. (2009c). Participatory academic research (par) and people's Participatory Action Research (PAR): Research, politicization, and subaltern social movements in India. In D. Kapoor, D & S. Jordan (Eds.), *Education, participatory action research and social change* (pp. 29–44). NY: Palgrave Macmillan.
Kapoor, D. (2010). 'Learning from adivasi (original dweller) political-ecologieal expositions of development: Claims on forests, land and place in India. In D. Kapoor & E. Shizha (Eds.), *Indigenous knowledge and learning in Asia/Pacific and Africa: Perspectives on development, education and culture* (pp. 17–34). New York: Palgrave Macmillan.
Kapoor, D. (2011). 'Subaltern Social Movement (SSM) post-mortems of development in India: Locating trans-local activism and radicalism', *Journal of Asian and African Studies*, *46*(2), 130–148.
Kapoor, D. (2013a). Colonial continuities, Neoliberal hegemony and adivasi (original dweller) space: Human rights as paradox and equivocation in contexts of dispossession in India. In S. Bagchi & A. Das (Eds.) *Towards a Third World Discourse on Human Rights* (pp. 123–144), NYC: Peter Lang.
Kapoor, D. (2013b). NGOs, compulsory industrialization and social action in the rural periphery: Explorations in to the uncivility of civil society in India. In A. Choudry & D. Kapoor (Eds.), *NGOization: Complicity, contradiction and prospects* (pp. 46–74). London: Zed.
Kwaipun, V. (2009). Popular education and organize d response to gold mining in Ghana. In A. Abdi & D. Kapoor (Eds.), *Global Perspectives on Adult Education* (pp. 175–192). New York: Palgrave Macmillan.
Langdon, J. (2011). Social Movement learning in Ghana: communal defense of resources in neoliberal times. In D. Kapoor (Ed.). *Critical Perspectives on Neoliberal Globalization, Development and Education in Africa and Asia* (pp. 153–170) Rotterdam: Sense Publishers.
Ludden, D. (2003). (Ed.) *Reading Subaltern Studies: Critical History, Contested Meaning arid the Globalization of South Asia*. New Delhi, India: Pauls Press.
Mayo, P. (1999). *Gramsci, freiré and adult education: Possibilities for transformative action*. London: Zed.
Mayo, P. (2010). (Ed.). *Gramsci and educational thought*. Sussex, UK: Wiley-Blackwell.
Menon, G. (2010). Recoveries of space and subjectivity in the shadow of violence: The clandestine politics of pavement dwellers in Mumbai. In P. McMichael (Ed.). *Contesting development: Critical struggles for social change* (pp. 151–164). New York: Routledge.
Menon, A., & Nigam, A. (2007). *Power and contestation: India Since 1989*. London: Zed Books.
Mignolo, W. (2000). *Local histories/global designs: Coloniality, subaltern knowledges, and border thinking*. Princeton, NJ: Princeton University Press.
Mookerjea, M (2010). Autonomy and video mediation: Dalitbahujan women's Utopian knowledge production. In D. Kapoor and E. Shizha (Eds.), *Indigenous knowledge and learning in Asia/ Pacific and Africa: Perspectives on development, Education and cCulture.(pp.)* New York: Palgrave Macmillan.
Mookerjea, S. (2011). On learning how to liberate the common: Subaltern biopolitics and the endgame of Neoliberalism. In D. Kapoor (Ed.). *Critical perspectives on neoliberal globalization, development and education in Africa and Asia(pp..??)*. Rotterdam: Sense Publishers.

Neeraj, J. (2007). *Globalization or Re-colonization*. Pune, India: Lokayat Press.
Padel, F. & Das, S. (2010). *Out of this earth: East India adivasis and the aluminium cartel* New Delhi, India: Orient Blackswan.
Peine, E. (2010). Corporate mobilization on the soyabean frontier of mato grosso, Brazil. In P. McMichael (Ed.). *Contesting development: critical struggles for social change*. New York: Routledge.
Petras, J., & Veltmeyer, H. (2001). *Globalization umasked: Imperialism in the 21st Century*. New York: Zed Books.
Pimple, M., & Sethi, M. (2005). Occupation of land in India. In S. Moyo and P. Years (Eds.) *Reclaiming the Land: The resurgence of rural movements in Africa, Asia and Latin America* (pp. 235–256). London: Zed Books.
Prasant, K., & Kapoor, D. (2010). Learning and knowledge production in Dalit Social Movements in rural India. In A. Choudry & D. Kapoor (Eds.) *Learning from the ground up: Global perspectives on social movements and knowledge production* (pp. 193–210). New York: Palgrave Macmillan.
Quijano, A. (2000). Coloniality of power and eurocentrism in Latin America. *International Sociology*, *15*(2), 213–232.
Rath, G. (Ed.) (2006). *Tribal development in India: The contemporary debate*. New Delhi: Sage Publications.
Rajagopal, B. (2003). *International law from below: Development, social movements and third world resistance*. Cambridge: Cambridge University Press.
Sanyal, K. (2010). *Rethinking capitalist development: Primitive accumulation, governmentality and post-colonial capitalism*. New Delhi: Routledge.
Sarkar, S. (2003). The decline of the subaltern in subaltern studies. In D. Ludden (Ed.) *Reading subalternsStudies: Critical history, contested meaning and the globalization of South Asia* (pp.). New Delhi: Pauls Press.
Sayeed, A., & Haider, W. (2010). Anjuman-e-Mazareen Punjab: Ownership or death—the struggle continues. In A. Choudry & D. Kapoor (Eds.), *Learning from the ground up: Global perspectives on social movements and knowledge production* (pp.211–226). New York: Palgrave Macmillan.
Scott, J. (1990). *Domination and the arts of resistance: Hidden transcripts*. New Haven, CT: Yale University Press.
Sethi, R. (2011). *The politics of postcolonialism: Empire, nation and resistance*. London: Pluto.
Shah, A. (2010). *In the shadows of the state: Indigenous politics, environmentalism, and insurgency in Jharkhand, India*. Durham, NC: Duke University Press.
Sivaramakrishnan, K. (2005). Situating the subaltern: History and anthropology in the subaltern studies project. In D. Ludden (Ed.), *Reading subaltern studies: Critical history, contested meaning and the globalization of South Asia*(pp.). New Delhi: Pauls Press.
Swords, A. (2010). Teaching against neo-liberalism in chiapas, Mexico: gendered resistance via Neo-Zapatista network polities. In P. McMichael (Ed.). *Contesting development: Critical struggles for social change.*(pp.) New York: Routledge.
Tuhiwai-Smith, L. (1999). *Decolonizing methodologies: Research and indigenous peoples*. London: Zed.
Veissiere, S. (2009). Notes and queries for an activist street anthropology: Street resistance, gringopolitica, and the quest for subaltern visions in Salvador da Bahia, Brazil. In D. Kapoor & S. Jordan (Eds.), *Education, participatory action research and social change* (pp.). New York: Palgrave Macmillan.
Wittman, H. (2010). Mobilizing agrarian citizenship: A new rural paradigm for Brazil. In P. McMichael (Ed.) *Contesting development: Critical struggles for social change*(pp.). New York: Routledge.

AFFILIATION

Dip Kapoor
Professor, Department of Education Policy Studies,
University of Alberta, Edmonton, Canada

PART III

SITES AND INSTRUMENTS OF PRACTICE

BEHRANG FOROUGHI & LEONA ENGLISH

11. ICTs AND ADULT LEARNING

Information and Communication Technologies (ICTs) is a term that refers to a variety of technologies that facilitate communications and information sharing. Most often they are computer-mediated forms such as the Internet, including email and the World Wide Web (popularly called *the net* or *web*). They also may refer to mobile phones, handheld computing devices, or even pre-computer technologies such as community radio (Hafkin & Huyer, 2006). The words SKYPE, Blackberry, moodle and Twitter have become the lingua franca of our world, all within a very short space of time. Despite the ubiquity of these ICTs in all facets of our life, there has been amazingly little written in our informal and critical adult education literature. We see far more in the distance education literature which tends to focus on the technical aspects of these ICTs and their use in formal education environments. Yet, it is clear to those of us in the informal and nonformal sphere that the use of ICTs to mobilize, educate and communicate is at record proportions. Only a Luddite would predict its demise or even ignore it.

Take for example these everyday examples of how these technologies are being used

> *Bobak organizes the protest in Iran from his bedroom in Copenhagen where he works in a men's health center. He uses his Blackberry to organize protests and he circulates pictures of violence against protestors from his school friends in Tehran to western media.*

> *The Association for Women's Rights in Development (AWID) partners with women's organizations in Zambia through online chatlines, e-messaging, Skype, and texts. From their centers in Toronto and Mexico City, they remain in daily contact with the women in Lusaka to fight against religious fundamentalism (see Harper, English, & MacDonald, 2010).*

> *The Coady International Institute in Nova Scotia offers online courses in microfinance to students in Egypt, India, China and Philippines. Their process is challenging as they are dealing with students in regions that have intermittent technological access.*

> *The Africa Leadership Forum, located in Nigeria, set up in 1988, has a Digital Library with full text books online such as "Empowering Women for the 21st Century," "Leadership Challenge in African Agricultural Production," "Police*

> and Society," "The Settler Question in Nigeria: the Case of Jos-Plateau," "Africa's Agenda and the Role of the USA" (1993), "The Challenge of Education in Africa" (1988), "Ethics and Professionalism in Nigerian Banking Industry," "Corruption, Democracy and Human rights," "The Media in Democracy." Also reports from the Africa Women's Forums, the National Women Peace Group, and an online newsletter, Akuko. http://www.africaleadership.org/
>
> From her work desk in the financial sector in New York City, Susan provides continuing professional education to colleagues in the Philippines. There is no travel involved, though admittedly the technology in the Philippines is often "down."

Clearly, ICTs are an integral part of how we do our work in the community sphere, especially in issues that have global implications and meanings. Yet, these ICTs are not neutral objects or inventions that stand apart from their teachers and students. Indeed, Marshall McLuhan's (1964) maxim that the medium is the message is as pertinent today as it ever was. This chapter takes on these ICTs asking critical questions about their use, misuse and the ethical implications for the practice of adult education. In the same way that Neil Postman (1993) was asking about technology in the 1980s and 1990s, when there really were only the rudiments of computers, we ask them now as a way forward for our field. We do so knowing that the ordinary sphere of adult education is the community. Although adult education does happen in higher education, its main concentration is in the informal pockets of civil society, whether it be non-profit organizations, community based groups or in social movement organizing. Communication and how it is done is a central concern then for adult education because much depends on the ability not only to transfer information but to do so in a way that builds civil society and creates community. The use of Internet-based community radio in Ghana and Uganda, for instance, has allowed local conversations about development strategies for climate change to go global. ICTs then can help further interactions among civil society, market and state actors. It must be said that the way in which we teach and learn outside higher education and official institutions may change but the concerns for people and access remain paramount.

ASSUMPTIONS IN THE FIELD

It is hard to be a naysayer in the face of such innovation. Indeed, innovation would appear to be the catchword of our times. We want there to be newness and freshness, and who could possibly say no to improvements? Indeed, the solitary professor image in front of a lecture theatre of 100 students seems somewhat quaint in the face of teaching and learning across the Internet.

One of the first assumptions is that ICTs actually improve education and learning, yet we have little evidence that is the case. One who has made a career of critically assessing the impact of technology is Neil Selwyn (2011) who makes it abundantly clear that ICTs and digital technology may or may not improve our teaching. We only know that the medium and potential access points have changed. For sure, there is increased access to learning opportunities for those who can avail of the technology; there is also increased chance of informal and incidental learning through the increased connectivity and exposure to varied viewpoints and ideas. However, we do not know how this access will affect actual retention, or result in an increase in knowledge, skills and attitudes. We know very little actually, and are aware that the steady stream of APPLE products, only produces consumers of us, as we struggle to update Ipods, Iphones, IPads, and IMacs.

There is an assumption in the use of ICTs for teaching and learning that the body no longer counts. We are disembodied people who operate apart from the reality of our bodies when we teach online and lose that face to face encounter. That is not to say that we cannot compensate but it is sometimes harder to do so. Without the embodied knowing that comes from inter- and intra- personal contact, the technology has to mediate the style, the tone, and the message of the communicator. Without the body, we must struggle harder to be present, to communicate information that includes us as people in relationship to one another. We run the risk of allowing the technology to mechanically dehumanize us. This does not occur maliciously but through benign neglect.

There is also an assumption that instantaneous is better. Though we are counselled to be cautious we are rarely if ever counselled to just slow it down and take time for critical deliberation on and in practice. With the immediacy of texting, Twitter, Facebook, and Myspace, there rarely is any mention of reflection, which for many years was a centerpiece of our field. We note that Freire's (1970) notion of praxis builds in action with reflection. Indeed, we wonder if the constant and often unconsidered use of ICTs eliminates thoughtful reflection, which is a key piece of our learning. It is possible that in reading responses to responses on Twitter for instance that I begin to absorb another's reflections as my own, and allow reflection to become situated outside of myself, removed from my own physicality (my body) and my reality. Because I have not invested myself, the reflection is more often superficial and disconnected *from* my own processes or *others'*.

ISSUES WITH ICTs

For all the promise of ICTs there are continued issues with Women and Access. While the ICTs are supposedly accessible and affordable, there remains the reality of the digital divide. Women continue to have less connectivity which is not surprising, when one considers the fact that technology generally is seen to operate within a masculinist realm (Butterwick & Jubas, 2005, 2006), which has been created by men for men. Women often are just the recipients of the latest phone or computer. Though this sounds stereotypic it is indeed the reality (Irving &

English, 2010, 2011) and it continued to be problematic, a situation that has literally always been the case with the innovation of technology. One only has to think of the image of computer geek, typists *or* call center operators to realise that normalization of gender roles, though of course exceptions apply. University of Toronto critic of science, Ursula Franklin (1999) made this point many times.

> Women also are less likely to use the computer in the home with children or men having priority of usage (Selwyn et al., 2006). Furthermore, structured gender roles which assign child care and homecare responsibilities primarily to women, cause a further divide in the home. When women, regardless of outside-the-home roles, are given or assume the bulk of domestic work, they have less time for developing computer skills and ICT capacity than their male partners. The mere presence of a computer in the home or in the community does not guarantee equal access or equal ICT capacity (Selwyn et al.). (Irving & English, 2010).

Indeed, we would not be the first to notice that even computer training is the domain of men. Even when efforts are made to have female teacher and female-friendly methods, there are issues that arise (Vehviläinen & Brunila, 2007). When men are given some roles and women are exempt from them, there is bound to be a problem. Elsewhere, we have noted (Irving & English, 2010) that there is an overrepresentation of men in occupations such as computer science, indeed the number of women is actually decreasing in this field (Stross, 2008; Fisher & Margolis, 2002) despite efforts to make these fields more female friendly. Fisher and Margolis also observe a constant "questioning of women's abilities" (p. 80) in these formal settings. They recommend that focus be placed on interactions and relationship among students and between students and faculty. They point to the need for personal connections and relationship building. With the growth of cyberfeminsm, or the efforts of women to organize online, there is some hope that the freeze on women will decline (Van Zoonen, 2001).

Interlinked with the issue of gender and technology is the whole notion of social class and ICTs. For those women who do have access, technology allows and enables voice, giving them the anonymous space to name their reality and organise for change in the case of the varied AWID actions. For instance, when an anonymous activist in Iran blogged about the low quality of female parliamentarians, she launched a national firestorm of energy and public debate that would not be possible if she were visible and named. Yet, it must be said that social class is still a big issue when it comes to having access to the Internet. We have to have money to have access, technology, etc. It is supposed to effect flattened hierarchies and this is not always true. While ICTs are popular in the Mediterranean and they played an enormous role in the Arab Spring, the same would not be true for most of the African continent. They still have challenges in terms of access, with women's access being less than men's, though neither is high. There is a direct link between GDP and connectivity, and between democracy and connectivity. Given that about 90% of the African continent does not have a steady supply of electricity it is hard to see how this entire continent can keep pace (Muller, 2009).

And as Muller notes, "In sub-Saharan Africa, where the number of female-headed households varies between 50 per cent and 80 per cent of rural households as men migrate to urban centres seeking employment, leaving their wives behind (ITDG, 2005)" (p. 33). This further disenfranchises the women who are rural poor. Writing in the same collection, Abraham (2009) notes that when husbands and wives use the same phone, which is often the case in Zambia, there may be gender based conflict and suspicion over who women are calling. She notes that poor women lack access and as a consequence it is harder for them to access women's organizations and support. Virtual social class may also be created between women who have phones and those who do not, and between those who have access to ICTs and those who do not. Clearly there are many problems associated with the development in Zambia or indeed in many other countries with similar cultural and economic conditions.

In many cases, the private funder has become implicated in supplying technology to education, without regard for local context and indigenous knowledge. The stress is mostly on increasing the total number of computers per capita and on the total number of individuals who can run the technology. For instance, with the SARI (Sustainable Access in Rural India) project, the funders were most interested in numbers and profitability of technology use (http://edev.media.mit.edu/SARI/). Another example is with the Bill and Melinda Gates Foundation which has been instrumental in funding technology for a great number of African schools. On the face of it, all seems like a good idea. Yet, Michael Edwards (2011a), former employee of the World Bank and the Ford Foundation, cautions that much of this large scale decision making, such as putting computers in schools or into development nations is increasingly being decided by large scale private donors such as Bill and Melinda Gates. Edwards questions whether any one person should be doing this. Donor driven development is an issue, making one wonder how much a private funder will be attentive to issues such as gender, social class, race, and ability. The implications of such funding need to be addressed in the public arena.

Indeed money can cause a lot of problems when it comes to technology. As Martin Carnoy (2004) of Stanford University notes, the efforts of elite universities to raise money by offering degrees online actually cost them money. For example, Columbia University lost more than 20 million dollars because it tried as a private university to make an online extension university. Carnoy contrasts this with the Massachusetts Institute of Technology, which put all its courses online free, gaining funding from private donors. Not discussed by Carnoy is the colonial mentality of spreading western knowledge to developing worlds with the hope of profit. The possibilities of global online learning systems raise the spectre of globalizing knowledge without due regard for the culture or the situation in which learners are located. The possibility, however, that those form the Global South might use these technologies to teach the west is rarely discussed though it sounds promising.

As public intellectual Michael Edwards (2011b) suggests, ICTs and social media are "thin solutions" to very complex social and economic problems, what he calls "thick" issues. He notes that these technological advances are

> less successful in bridging different interests and in counteracting the structural problems that weaken participation of every kind (especially inequality). In these areas direct, face-to-face encounters are more important, since they have more of an impact on the power structures of democracy and politics and can lead to shifts in public norms.(p. 10).

It seems that face to face contact is still superior when the issues are deep.

DISCUSSION

ICTs have never been a neutral zone. They are fraught with possibility and with challenge. If we use them with the intent to enable the creation of change for democracy as in the Arab Spring then we need to be careful to engage with them in a critical way, much as previous generations have engaged television and radio. We suggest here the use of a critical tool in the manner of the community impact assessment tools that are all the rage in environment, health and community development (see Coady & Cameron, 2012). This tool, as we see it, would consist of several critical questions that might be asked of technological innovations:

1. How are women's lives affected by this innovation?
2. What are the effects of this innovation on community life?
3. What are the impediments to its implementation?
4. What are the financial implications?
5. What content is appropriate and accessed?
6. Who produces the content accessed?

These scans and tools are helpful and they ask very good questions. Of course, we do not want to be Luddites; we want to embrace change but in a careful way. The use of impact assessment tools for such purposes has the potential to support discussion in democratic spaces that are context specific and inclusive of indigenous knowledge. The outcome of such dialogue can then feed into policy and political decision making around technology and the state.

When it comes to social movements and learning we need to be attentive to the fact that we are not only advancing the cause of the movement whether it be the Arab Spring for democracy or the environment; our technology is part of the social movement learning. We are learning before, during, and after we become involved. As such, the social movement cannot be confined only to the named issue, e.g., environment; rather the social movement needs to be critically self-reflective on the learning that is engendered and on the way in which technology has been employed in the service of the movement. It must embrace the learning that is part of being fully integrated into a wired world. The exclusion from this world, as may be the case in some developing nations, especially among rural women, is a continued concern and must be accounted for. Otherwise, the movement becomes a western exercise in exclusion and impe alism. In the same way that McLuhen (1964) was concerned in the 60s, we must continue to be concerned about the medium.

REFERENCES

Abraham, K. B. (2009). The names in your address book: Are mobile phone networks effective in advocating women's rights in Zambia? In I. Buskens & A. Webb (Eds.), *African women and ICTs: Investigating technology, gender and empowerment* (pp. 97–106). London: Zed Books.

Butterwick, S., & Jubas, K. (2005). Being a girl in the boys' club: Lessons of gender politics from the centre and fringes of the knowledge-based society. *Proceedings of the 24th national annual conference of the Canadian association for the study of adult education* (pp. 38–43). University of Western Ontario, London, ON.

Butterwick, S., & Jubas, K. (2006). The organic and accidental IT worker: Women's on-the-job teaching and learning experiences. *Proceedings of the 25th national annual conference of the Canadian association for the study of adult education* (pp. 19–24), York University, Toronto, ON.

Carnoy, M. (2004). ICT in education: Possibilities and challenges. Inaugural lecture of the 2004–2005 year. Barcelona [online]. UOC. Accessed on January 16, 2012. http://www.uoc.edu/inaugural04/eng/carnoy1004.pdf

Coady, M.J., & Cameron, C. (2012). Community health impact assessment: Fostering community learning and healthy public policy at the local level. In L. M. English (Ed.). *Adult education and health*. Toronto: University of Toronto Press.

Edwards, M. (2011a). Spirituality and development. Lecture at Coady International Institute, St. Francis Xavier University, Antigonish, NS, Canada. October, 2011.

Edwards, M. (2011b). Thick problems and thin solutions: How NGOs can bridge the gap. Retrieved on March 19, 2012 from http://www.thebrokeronline.eu/var/broker/storage/original/application/960b295f2838b63a6609cea4fdf0a51f.pdf

Fisher, A., & Margolis, J. (2002). Unlocking the clubhouse: The carnegie mellon experience. *ACM SIGCSE Bulletin, 34*(2), 79–83.

Franklin, U. (1999). *The real world of technology*. Toronto: House of Anansi.

Freire, P. (1970). *Pedagogy of the oppressed*. New York: Continuum.

Hafkin, N.J., & Huyer, S. (Eds.), (2006). *Cinderella or cyberella?: Empowering women in the knowledge society*. Bloomfield, CT: Kumarian Press.

Harper, L., English, L. M., & Macdonald, T. E. (2010). Rural feminist activism and religious fundamentalism, Nova Scotia, Canada. In S. Gokal, R. Barbero, & C. Balchin (Eds.), Key learnings from feminists on the frontline: Summaries of case studies on resisting and challenging fundamentalisms. Toronto, Mexico City and Capetown: Association of Women in Development.

Irving, C. J., & English, L. M. (2009). Feminist network activism and education in Canada. *Proceedings of the 28th national annual conference of the Canadian association for the study of adult education*, (pp.122–128), Carleton University. Ottawa, ON.

Irving, C., & English, L. M. (2010). Women, ICTs and lifelong learning. In V. C. X. Wang (Ed.), *Encyclopedia of information communication technologies and adult education integration* (pp.370–376). Chapter 22. Hershey, PA: IGI Global.

Irving, C., & English, L. M. (2011). Community in cyberspace: Gender, social movement learning and the Internet. *Adult Education Quarterly, 61*(3), 262–278. doi 10.1177/0741713610380448

McLuhan, M. (1964). *Understanding media: The extensions of man*. London: Routledge.

Muller, J. (2009). Considering ICT use when energy access is not secured: A case study from rural South Africa. In I. Buskens & A. Webb (Eds.), *African women and ICTs: Investigating technology, gender and empowerment* (pp. 33–43). London: Zed Books.

Postman, N. (1993). *Technopoly: the surrender of culture to technology*. New York: Vintage Books.

Selwyn, N. (2011). *Education and technology: Key issues and debates*. London: Continuum.
Selwyn, N., Gorard, G., & Furlong, J. (2006). *Adult learning in the digital age: Information technology and the learning society*. London: Routledge.
Stross, R. (2008, November 16). What has driven women out of computer science? *New York Times*. Retrieved from http://www.nytimes.com
Van Zoonen, L. (2001). Feminist internet studies. *Feminist Media Studies, 1*(1), 67–72.
Vehviläinen, M., & Brunila, K. (2007). Cartography of gender equality projects in ICT: Liberal equality from the perspective of situated equality. *Information, Communication & Society, 10*(3), 384–403.

AFFILIATIONS

Behrang Foroughi
Assistant professor of adult education at St. Francis Xavier University and Senior Program staff at the Coady International Institute

Leona English
Professor of adult education at St. Francis Xavier University, Antigonish Nova Scotia, Canada

ANTONIA DARDER

12. RADIO AS PUBLIC PEDAGOGY: A CRITICAL ADULT EDUCATION OF THE AIR WAVES[1]

The time has come for educators to develop more engaged systematic political projects in which power, history, and social movements can play an active role in constructing the multiple and shifting political relations and cultural practices necessary for connecting the construction of diverse political constituencies to the revitalization of democratic public life.

Henry Giroux (2003, p. 13)

The revitalization of public democratic life, as articulated in these words by Henry Giroux, speaks to the heart of all efforts linked to forging a public pedagogical practice of adult education. In contrast, it is through both the silencing and dismantling of democratic participatory rights that we are rendered most vulnerable to the destructive impact of neoliberal forces in the world today. At a time when public mainstream discourse touts its self-congratulatory "post-racial" declarations, the policies and practices of the State continue to harshly impact the lives of poor African American and Latinos, as well as other working class people in the U.S. and abroad. Today, few public spaces are found that support genuine public engagement, dialogue, and dissent. Moreover, the disempowering impact of disabling policies and practice of the public sphere is particularly felt among those who can find little relief for the poverty, surveillance, and injustice that thwarts their community participation.

In Champaign-Urbana, the twin-city Midwest university town where I live and teach, community participation is further complicated by the rhetoric of corporate interests, which effectively shroud neoliberal objectives of small university town governance. Within this context, efforts calling for institutional change and municipal reform must be waged by community residents who depend on nomadic, albeit progressive, student and faculty participation. This aspect unfortunately serves as a double edge sword, in that there is a transient quality to public life and the body politic of this Midwest community. Such a politically unstable context requires creative pedagogical interventions by those who will eventually move on, in concert with those who call these twin cities home.

In an effort to support the tenuous nature of community relationships within the confines of a neoliberal university agenda, public pedagogical projects can serve as alternative venues for supporting civic engagement and a critical form of public adult education.

Critical public interventions are of particular importance, within an increasingly conservative culture of scholarship, where neoliberal interests are neatly concealed within an academic rhetoric that furiously prioritizes global concerns, over the needs of local communities. This is the case, particularly, in the current climate of "economic decline," where university "shock doctrine" solutions conveniently signal retrenchment among administrators, faculty, and students, through institutional reliance on "color-blind" neoliberal policies that effectively reinforce traditional structures of privilege and power, negating possibilities for public forms of community education and participation for social change.

THE MEDIA IN THE AGE OF NEOLIBERALISM

Understood as one of neoliberalism rather than simply globalization, the current era seems less the result of uncontrollable natural forces and more as the newest stage of class struggle under capitalism.

Robert McChesney (2001)

It is impossible to speak of the media in the age of neoliberalism without engaging its power to exercise a homogenizing impact on social, political and economic relations at a global level. McChesney insists that *neoliberalism* is a more accurate explanatory term, from which to discuss the overwhelming control of the corporate sector over the public sphere. From this standpoint, "governments are to remain large so as to better serve the corporate interests, while minimizing any activities that might undermine the rule of business and the wealthy...The centerpiece of neoliberal policies is invariably a call for commercial media and communications markets to deregulate" (http://www.monthlyreview.org/301rwm.htm). Moreover, given its privatizing propensity, ownership of the airwaves has become consolidated among a few corporate giants,[2] including General Electric, Time Warner, Univision Communication, and Viacom, who now monopolize the ideological architecture and design of U.S. radio programming.[3]

This power over the airwaves was consolidated following the passage of the Telecommunications Act of 1996, which was the first major reform in the telecommunications law since the Act of 1934. Supposedly, the law was to create greater access to the communications industry by fostering increased market competition for the airwaves. But in reality, the Act radically restructured regulations in such a way as to intensify the market's rule, rather than benefit consumers, as its proponents claimed. As large mighty corporations fought behind the scenes over the wording of the Act, citizen consumers were left completely out of the picture, the majority unaware of the corporatized politics that threaten the democracy of telecommunications in this country. So, although it is true that the Telecommunications Act, indeed, required a radical overhaul, given the dramatic changes in digital technology since 1934, McChesney (1998) argues that the result of the Act of 1996 was a complete disaster.

The results of the Telecommunications Act, with its relaxation of ownership restrictions to promote competition across sectors, have been little short of disastrous. Rather then produce competition, a far-fetched notion in view of the concentrated nature of these markets, the law has paved the way for the greatest period of corporate concentration in US media and communication history. The seven Baby Bells are now four-if the SBC Communications purchase of Ameritech goes through-with more deals on the way. In radio, where ownership restrictions were relaxed the most, the entire industry has been in upheaval, with 4,000 of the 11,000 commercial stations being sold since 1996. In the 50 largest markets, three firms now control access to over half the radio audience. In 23 of those 50 markets, the three largest firms control 80 percent of the radio audience. The irony is that radio, which is relatively inexpensive and thus ideally suited to local independent control, has become perhaps the most concentrated and centralized medium in the United States (http://bostonreview.net/BR23.3/mcchesney.html).

In line with this unprecedented corporate control of the airwaves, radio in conjunction with other media outlets delivers the hidden curriculum of a de facto neoliberal public pedagogy. As Giroux (2004) contends, it "has become thoroughly reactionary as it constructs knowledge, values, and identities through a variety of educational sites and forms of pedagogical address that have largely become the handmaiden of corporate power, religious fundamentalism, and neo-conservative ideology" (497). Hence, in contrast to the old belief that the media should function as a neutral sphere in which different ideas and perspectives can be engaged and interrogated within a democratic context, the mainstream media now, more than ever, is a powerful hegemonic tool that functions in the overriding justification and legitimation of societal inequalities, political exclusions, and environmental demise.

Thus, efforts to counter the pervasiveness of oppression—whether tied to racism, class and gendered inequalities, or stifling homophobic representations—must contend with neoliberal distortions that create confusion and contradictions among even well-meaning people. In the homogenizing script of neoliberal existence, bootstrap accountability returns as a central value of the "good society." Therefore, the stories that move across the mainstream airwaves embrace again notions of self-reliance and self-made individualism. Accordingly, a "rugged individualism" is venerated and social action, outside the marketplace or neoliberal dictates, is deemed either suspect or the product of the weak and whining. Moreover, Giroux (2004b), in *Dissent Voice*, condemns neoliberal ideology for its dehistoricizing and depoliticizing of society, as well as "in its aggressive attempts to destroy all of the public spheres necessary for the defense of a genuine democracy, neoliberalism reproduces the conditions for unleashing the most brutalizing forces of capitalism. Social Darwinism has been resurrected from the ashes of the

19th century sweatshops and can now be seen in full bloom" (http://dissidentvoice.org/Aug04/Giroux0807).

As such, neoliberal sensibilities turn a blind eye to the suffering of the oppressed through a systematic denial of its dehumanizing propensities—propensities that privilege profit and material gain over even the essential human needs of the most vulnerable. The stories of the disenfranchised are systematically silenced and maligned, while their truths are relegated to the political waste basket of corporate dominion. This consistent denial or marginalization of stories that unveil injustice prevents any possibility of truly becoming a democratic society, in that the strength, knowledge, and wisdom of those subjugated are rendered unavailable or nonexistent. This further prevents the genuine integration of disenfranchised populations into the decision-making life of the community. Instead, neoliberalism leaves us all at the mercy of the marketplace, restricting the nature of our very existence, as it unmercifully seeks to shrink and contort our definitions of self and humanity.

In response to the limiting neoliberal priorities of both public universities and municipalities, many communities have begun to explore the use of community radio as an alternative form of adult education, in an effort to both counter the silences and revitalize solidarity across cultural, class, gendered, and sexual differences. Early proponents for the pedagogical use of community radio include the founders of Pacifica in California, which later merged with KPFK, one of the strongest public radio stations in the Western United States.[4] KPFK has been a leader in the use of the airwaves as public pedagogy, regularly airing programming produced by David Barsamian[5] of *Alternative Radio* and Amy Goodman and Juan Gonzalez of *Democracy Now*! KBOO community radio in Portland, Oregon has been broadcasting to diverse communities for over forty years.[6] In a city that is predominantly white, the station focuses its programming by and for marginalized communities in the area. Since 1979, WMNF has brought alternative music, arts, and public affairs programming.[7]

Independent Media Centers around the country have also played an important pedagogical role in championing more democratic access to and control of media resources, including the establishment of low-wave radio stations to serve their local and surrounding communities. One excellent example is the work of Grand Rapids Media Consortium[8] which for over 25 years has maintained technology tools and created media services and community venues to benefit the larger community. Here in the Midwest—just as with the Zapatistas "Voice of the Voiceless" and other community-based radio projects around the world—the use of alternative media has shown the potential to enhance communication, alternative educational opportunities, and social action among disenfranchised communities. WRFU,[9] a project of Champaign-Urbana Independent Media Center[10] has been an important resource for community adult education, through the airing of alternative voices.

An important thread that weaves through the mission of most community radio stations is an emphasis on critical engagement with controversial, neglected, and non-mainstream perspectives, as well as an expressed commitment to social justice and democratic life. No doubt that without community stations such as these, the airwaves would remain completely in the hands of corporate media moguls, eliminating the possibility for alternative programming and dissenting views. Moreover, in light of the growing international consolidation of control over the media, community radio creates an important pedagogical and political space where hegemonic belief systems can be challenged and alternative views can be mobilized for social action. Eronini R. Megwa (2007) asserts, in his writings about community radio in South Africa,

> Community radio gives listeners a sense of community and identity and creates action space for people to have both direct and indirect link with community power structures as well as to have access to resources. Community radio is an integral part of the community in which it is located. It is acceptable to the community as a development tool. Community radio can mobilize communities to act as change agents by engaging groups and organizations to direct their resources in order to actualize strategies at individual, group, and organizational levels (53).

COMMUNITY RADIO AS PUBLIC PEDAGOGY

I attended to the public pedagogy of the free radio airwaves...Between belting out oldies lyrics along with the station disc jockeys who populate the dial, I listened to National Public Radio in its various forms across two time zones. Within one 13-hour jaunt, I learned four lessons that make me a modern American:

Lesson One: Consume above all else, consume,

Lesson Two: Believe experts,

Lesson Three: Romanticize the past, and

Lesson four: Civic life is boring.

Patrick Shannon (2007)[11]

In 1941, twenty years after the first radio news program was aired, George V. Denny, executive director of the League for Political Education, enthusiastically declared that *radio builds democracy*. As a device designed to attract attention and stimulate interest in social and political problems, he surmised that radio could function as an effective medium of public instruction or adult education within a democratic society. Hence, the interrogation of radio as a public sphere for democratic participation has a long history within the educational field. However, initial perspectives were generally grounded upon a modernist assumption that a "neutral" discourse, which presented a variety of sides, was in the best interest of genuine democracy.

Peter G. Mwesige (2009), who studied the promise and limits of radio programming in Uganda, strongly disagrees with any view that essentializes radio as a democratizing public sphere. He argues instead that,

> [R]adio also appears to peddle misinformation and distortions; to invite adulterated debate that excites and inflames rather than informs; to give the public the illusion of influence; and, arguably, to lead to political inertia. At the group level, talk radio may have created an illusion of competition to the extent that it provided voice to oppositional political groups that were otherwise not fully free to participate in the political process. What we have, then, is an imperfect public sphere – but a sort of public sphere nonetheless (221).

Similarly, critical education theorists (Giroux, 2004a; Apple 2004; McLaren 1997; Kellner 1995; Freire 1993) have indeed shattered the assumption of neutrality attached to public media production. Instead, they unveil the hidden curriculum of wealth and power, embedded in discourses of neutrality and meritorious solutions thought to "naturally" arise from the "fair airing" of all sides. In concert, the four lessons garnered by Patrick Shannon during his 13 hours of "free" radio listening shed light not only on the overwhelming adherence of radio to values that bolster neoliberal society, but also the deceptive manner in which the notion of neutrality operates amidst the public airwaves. And, despite claims that listeners are not passive agents, constant repetition of embedded values appear to erode the human agency of unsuspecting audiences, while simultaneously conditioning and priming the mind (Croteau & Hoynes 2002, 1994), as Shannon notes, to equate consumption with freedom; believe in the power of experts over one's own knowledge; objectify the past as romantic ideal; and readily abdicate our right to civic participation in search of pleasure and entertainment. In the midst of convoluted discourses that legitimatize and perpetuate the interest of the powerful and wealthy, critical adult educators and community activists are challenged to establish spaces for counterhegemonic dialogue and alternative public engagement. This entails the development of a critical public pedagogy in which social agency is nurtured and critical faculties of political discernment are activated and stretched, in the interest of social justice and public democratic life.

With this intent, the *Liberacion!*[12] Radio Collective was established in 2005, as a means to apply the principles of critical adult education to the practice of a public pedagogy, within the public sphere of radio programming. As such, critical public pedagogy is defined here as a deliberate and sustained effort to speak through a critical lens of society, in such a way as to inform (and transform) mainstream public discourses and community political practices, in the interest of the disenfranchised. This is of particular significance, as previously noted, within the contemporary neoliberal context in which we struggle to live and resist the market forces of privatization and "accountability," ever encroaching upon our daily lives. More specifically, the work here points to a political pedagogical process within the public life of a small rural university town in the Midwest—a context in which the power of conservative ideologies push forcefully against the forces of difference—forces which call for systematic and structural institutional change, predicated upon the politics of social justice, human rights, and economic democracy.

Nowhere is the battle to control the minds and hearts of the populace ever so contentious and strained as it is within small rural communities, where notions of "tradition" and "insider" entitlement are given reign, over political and cultural forces that seek social inclusion, within the fabric of democratic life. This means, more specifically, to engage from *within* a community context where neoliberal values and the rhetoric of impending economic collapse now offer a respite from what many deem the "bothersome" politics of diversity. Within this deeply entrenched conservative public arena, community radio plays a significant pedagogical role in countering the official transcript of "whiteness," privilege, and conserving ideals of tradition, so blindly embedded in the dominant relationships and discourses of both the university and the larger municipal landscape.

It is precisely in the midst of such a politic that critically engaged radio pedagogy, with an eye toward participation within the public sphere, has been forged as an alternative practice of adult education. This entails a pedagogical process that makes central the significance of public life and recognizes the importance of creating alternative venues for democratic participation, especially for those who have been historically silenced and relegated to the margins of municipal existence. Through a sustained commitment to combine graduate intellectual formation, collective media production, adult education practices, and critical community engagement, the *Liberacion! Radio Collective* was born. Its impetus emerged from an acceptance that democracy is never guaranteed and that, inherent in its possibilities, is the need for on-going interaction and engagement with public issues that require the silences to be broken and the voices of the voiceless and unattended to find themselves at the center of the airwaves.

Hence, progressive, independent media production, tied foremost to the needs of the disenfranchised and oppressed within neoliberal society, encompasses a counterhegemonic pedagogical alternative for community expression and dialogue, as well as political engagement. That is, a form of critical adult education and public engagement that places public media "at the heart of a democratic society" (Aufderheide & McAfee (2005); one that "treats people as active learners in and builders of society...[where] people can assert themselves not only as individuals but also, if they work with others, as decision-makers and mobilizers of the public will."[13]

It is with these key elements in mind, that the radio collective was established to function principally as an avenue for alternative readings of the world, as well as a means to document on-going political struggles—struggles that, although might seem unrelated and disparate, are fundamentally interconnected with the subordination of populations deemed disposable and problematic to neoliberal capitalist dictates. Within small communities, such efforts are especially significant in that fewer public pedagogical venues associated with alternative forms of adult education are available for challenging the distortions and false readings, which flourish about the "Other," who remain underserved and only minimally acknowledged within the public life of the twin cities.

This is important here, in that the radio collective exists within a context where the airwaves, just as the streets, are dominated and policed through a racialized victim-blaming rhetoric that belies the impoverished conditions and lack of opportunities available to marginalized populations in the region. This home of the diehard Indian mascot "tradition" is also home to poor Black and Latino families who contend daily with the impact of poor schooling, high unemployment, lack of health care, poor housing, and increasing homelessness and incarceration. Moreover, it is the site where racialized policing has led, for example, to numerous police shootings of unarmed Black youth; where corporate-inspired relationships permitted a 20 year cover-up of an abandoned toxic waste site in a poor Black community; and where deep homophobic culture has resulted in violent attacks of working-class gay and transgendered people in the campus town area.

A recent incident serves as an illustration of the difficulties and tensions at work in this small rural college town. In October 2009, police shot to death Kiwane Carrington, a 15 year-old poor Black youth, who had lost his mother to cancer two months earlier. The youth, who had forgotten his key to the house in which he was staying, was apprehended when attempting to enter the home through a rear window. Within minutes of the arrival of an officer and the Chief of Police, the boy was gunned down, allegedly for trying to flee from the scene. Although Kiwane was unarmed and there was no evidence of the youth resisting arrest, police entered the scene with pistols drawn—an action which is considered a violation of their own protocols for handling juvenile encounters. Official actions taken after the death of Kiwane and the arrest of the other youth that accompanied him were met by community outcry.

A community coalition, formed in response to the shooting, circulated and then presented to the City with over 1700 signatures from individuals calling for an investigation into the death and the dismissal of a criminal case filed against the other youth. Despite this and a variety of other concerted community efforts, the shooting was ruled "accidental" by the State's Attorney (whose husband is a Champaign police officer). During the months that followed the shooting, the local "news" venues ran stories that seem to both support police actions in the case and belittle community participation in the matter. One editorial that appeared in the *New Gazette* on March 3, 2010, again maligned the community coalition's persistent public involvement.

> The incident is a tragedy both for Carrington's friends and family members as well as the community, and *the event has become a cause celebre for local residents* who feel the shooting reflects an institutional bias by police against members of minority groups. So they have taken up [the arrested youth's] cause, insisting that the charge against him be dismissed. But the [State's

Attorney], quite correctly, refused to do so, *explaining that public opinion plays no role in prosecuting cases...*The justice system would be a shambles *if the prosecution of criminal cases became the subject of popularity contests...* That's why the petition drive... is not just naive, but *an assault on the entire concept of the rule of law...*[The youth being charged] is represented by a lawyer who is working with [the State Attorney's] office to resolve this case *based on its merits.* That is how it has to be. To handle it any other way would turn the entire concept of the judicial system upside down (my emphasis here).

As an active independent community radio project, members of the *Liberacion!* Radio Collective gathered to produce and air two community radio programs on the Kiwane Carrington case, as a contribution to the collective action and an effort to bring alternative voices to bear on the official transcript being circulated by the mainstream media, the courts, and the police department. The radio segments were archived on the *Liberacion!* Website[14] and copies were made and distributed within the community as part of an adult educational campaign. It is important to note at this juncture, that the effectiveness of the *Liberacion!* radio efforts on this issue was only possible, given pre-established working relationships with community residents, members of the *Independent Media Center's* newspaper, the community *Citizens for Peace and Justice* group, and the *Solidarity Committee* of the Graduate Employees Organization (GEO) on campus. Key to this discussion is the impact of the radio production. The two segments on the case were played on both community radio stations and on a variety of other public affairs programs. Copies were burned and circulated widely in the community for use to stimulate further dialogue on the issue at community meetings. Needless to say, the use of radio programming as a pedagogical tool here functioned effectively to expand community awareness about the case and to consolidate the voices of community members, in calling for fundamental change to the policing of African American youth.

What must be underscored here is that public pedagogical actions are most powerful and effective when linked to larger social movement efforts, which support and sustain one another in the collective endeavor of creating public spaces for alternative political discourses. And although the theoretical lens that best informs the praxis of the radio collective is that of a critical public pedagogy, the production process by which mainstream airwaves are disrupted and redefined is firmly anchored upon an art of resistance, with its multiplicity of voices and methods for naming the world.

RESISTANCE AND MULTIDIMENSIONALITY

We chose the title 'The Art of Resistance' as a way of communicating to fans and listeners to stop and think about their lives and the world around them," Cunningham says. *"I'm not a teacher or a politician; I'm an artist, writer and musician, and this is my way of expressing what's on my mind and how I think*

> *I can impact people's lives. I've learned over the years that music can be as powerful a force as politics to bring out issues that need to be addressed, and the things like what we touch on here, like the prison industry and the way children are being raised, will open eyes.*
>
> Caleb Cunningham (2009) Hop Collective Project Lionheart[15]

The art of resistance, as described by the *Project Lionheart* band member above, is shaped by struggles to address in multidimensional ways the underbelly of economic and cultural domination as it manifests within disenfranchised communities, while simultaneously seeking critical solutions that might potentially disrupt its negative impact. There's no doubt that the art of resistance encompasses a deep faith in humanity and the profound capacity of human beings for creativity and resilience, even in the face of suffering and adversity. The art of community resistance then implies that there is an organic and collective quality to the manner in which issues are undertaken and the participatory processes by which the design of *Liberacion!* radio programs are carried out. This posits a formulation of community resistance that inherently redefines the potential power of the airwaves as a form of adult education within the public arena, from that of solely entertainment to that of public pedagogical significance for democratic life. In the Gramscian sense, then, this public media production by the radio collective functions, uncompromisingly, as a counter-narrative to hegemonic discourses of the neoliberal State. It is precisely this quality of counter-narration that supports a space in which dominant political, economic, cultural, and ideological interests and their consequences can be interrogated, unveiled, and potentially transformed.

True to their critical adult education and critical media literacy underpinnings, *Liberacion!* radio segments focus consistently on emancipatory themes and issues raised by community participants themselves, in which the multidimensional aspect of social issues can be engaged by a variety of spokespersons, representing both academic and non-academic praxis. Hence, for example, an interview with a professor who can provide a critical theoretical analysis of incarceration is weaved together with an interview of a parent of an incarcerated youth, with a commentary of an educator who teaches in a prison program, with the poetry of inmates, and the music of *Dead Prez* that challenges the politics of incarceration in the Black community. Through the use of what I term a *multi-intellectual design*, this form of community resistance as public pedagogy is shaped, simultaneously, through multidimensional discursive forms, which break with the tradition of isolated, one-dimensional approaches generally utilized even among progressive radio programmers.

This form of multidimensional community engagement and adult education approach is important to building greater fluidity and a more expansive understanding of political participation and community resistance. Thus, a capacity to willingly and legitimately integrate vastly different perspectives and different articulations of similar societal mechanisms and oppressive structures cannot be undermined nor ignored within critical media production or community resistance efforts. Through multiple discursive engagements with a variety of social and political issues, new public discourses organically emerge to forge new avenues and possibilities for dissent.

From the experiences of the radio collective, new avenues for dialogue, solidarity, and dissent are best achieved through dismantling false competing perspectives that privilege either academic knowledge over community or community knowledge over the academic. This calls for releasing the objectifying strictures perpetuated by anti-intellectual views of disenfranchised community members, as well as debilitating criticisms of elitism projected on to formally-educated comrades. Moreover, it is only through the courage to enter into such a multidimensional praxis of public pedagogy, with humility, dignity and respect, that new relationships of solidarity can be built, anchored upon on-going genuine exchanges of both lived and formally-studied knowledge, technical skills, historical understandings, and community resources—all deeply valuable and vital to the interrogation and transformation of racialized inequalities, class and gendered formations, heterosexist ideations, and other forms of social exclusions in the world.

This is the kind of public pedagogy that embraces an integrated and communal understanding of knowledge; one that is guided by life affirming principles of social justice, human rights, and economic democracy. The intentionality behind this public pedagogical approach with students is fundamentally linked to creating the conditions, through dialogue, reflection, and action, for the development and evolution of political consciousness—a consciousness grounded in organic community relationships and joint political labor. To effectively integrate public pedagogical projects, such as the *Liberacion! Radio Collective*, into the intellectual formation of graduate students, demands that our teaching be rooted in a political process of critical academic praxis.

Within this perspective, the privilege of an education is not predicated upon competing against one another for individual rewards or privileged institutional status. Rather, university education is a politicizing context in which faculty and students must consistently (re)learn together to read the shifting cultural landscapes of power, so that we might sharpen our understanding of institutional constraints that thwart community self-determination. Such formation also challenges deeply held bourgeois notions of "professionalism"[16] tied to traditional academic preparation and, instead, asks students to consider how their intellectual preparation will function in the service of justice.

Within such a context, academic "success" is no longer attached to the material ambitions of individuals and their contribution to bolstering capitalist democracy, but rather to generating academic resources and technical skills that can be shared and utilized, in the collective interest of building alternative adult education opportunities within the community, along with forging together political solidarity and democratic participation across members of universities and communities. And all of this can only be generated and sustained through the unambiguous cultivation of a revolutionary love—a love that enhances our solidarity and commitment to one another, as kin and comrades in our struggle to overcome the debilitating forces of human oppression, through the daily revitalization of democratic public life.

NOTES

1. This chapter was published under the same title in 2011 in Policy Futures in Education, 9(6), 696–705. http://dx.doi.org/10.2304/pfie.2011.9.6.696 Permission granted by publisher.
2. Who owns the News Media <http://www.stateofthemedia.org/2010/media-ownership/dashboard.php>
3. Fear and Favor in the Newsroom, produced by Beth Sanders and Randy Baker in 1996 and narrated by Stud Terkel, provides one of the most powerfully incisive critiques of corporate control of news reporting in the United States. Unfortunately, the documentary was "turned down by virtually every entity in the PBS system. Frontline, Point of View, PBS's independent documentary series, and PBS itself all refused to give the show a national broadcast. Indeed, after viewing an early sample clip of the show, Mark Weiss the Executive Producer of Point of View, told us P.O.V. would not be interested, because the show would not be well received in venues such as Redbook." To learn more about the story of the documentary, see: http://www.albionmonitor.com/9804b/copyright/fearfavor.html and listen to a *Democracy Now!* segment about the film: http://www.democracynow.org/1997/11/18/fear_and_favor_in_the_newsroom
4. Pacifica was established in the late 1940's out of the peace movement surrounding World War II. In 1949 KPFA went on the air from Berkeley, California. KPFK, in Los Angeles, was the second of what would eventually become five Pacifica Stations to go on the air. See: http://www.kpfk.org/aboutkpfkpacifica-.html
5. Alternative Radio, established in 1986, is dedicated to the founding principles of public broadcasting, which urge that programming serve as "a forum for controversy and debate," be diverse and "provide a voice for groups that may otherwise be unheard." The project is entirely independent, sustained solely by individuals who buy transcripts and tapes of programs. See: http://www.alternativeradio.org/
6. See: http://kboo.fm/node/34
7. See: http://www.wmnf.org/station/about
8. To learn more about the work of the Grand Rapids Media Center, see: http://www.grcmc.org/
9. See: http://www.wrfu.net/
10. The Urbana-Champaign Independent Media Center is a grassroots organization committed to using media production and distribution as tools for promoting social and economic justice in the Champaign County area. See http://www.ucimc.org/content/about-uc-imc
11. See: http://www-rohan.sdsu.edu/~rgibson/rouge_forum/shannon.htm
12. I established the *Liberacion!* Radio Collective with graduate students and community members. The intent was to create a space where student could be involved in the practice public pedagogy, in conjunction with community members. For more information on the program and our radio archives, see: http://www.radioliberacion.org/
13. See: http://www.current.org/why/why0517aufdermcafee.shtml
14. To access the radio segment of *The Police Shooting of Kiwane Carrington* 1 & 2, see: http://www.radioliberacion.org/audio/Kiwane.mp3; http://www.radioliberacion.org/audio/Kiwane2.mp3
15. See: http://www.prlog.org/10436445-seattlebased-hiphop-collective-project-lionheart-makes-sound-records-debut.html
16. For an excellent historical discussion and critique of "professionalism" see: *The Culture of Professionalism: The Middle Class and the Development of Higher Education in America* by Burton Bledstein (1978).

REFERENCES

Apple, M. W. (2004). *Ideology and curriculum*, London: Routledge & Kegan Paul.
Croteau, D., & Hoynes, W. (2002). *Media Society: Industries, Images, and Audiences*. Los Angeles/London: Pine Forge Press.
Croteau, D., & Hoynes, W. (1994). *Invitation only: How the media limit political debate*. Monroe, ME: Common Courage Press.
Denny, G. (1941). Radio builds democracy . *Journal of Educational Sociology, 14* (6), 370–377.
Freire, P. (1993). *Pedagogy of the City*. New York: Continuum.

Giroux. H. (2003). Public pedagogy and the politics of resistance: Notes on a critical theory of educational struggle. *Education Theory, 35, 1 (5–16).*
Giroux, H. (2004a). *Public pedagogy and the politics of neo-liberalism: Making the political more pedagogical policy futures in education, 2* (3 & 4).
Giroux, H. (2004b). Neoliberalism and the demise of democracy: Resurrecting hope in dark times. *Dissent voices.* http://dissidentvoice.org/Aug04/Giroux0807.htm
Kellner, D (1995). *Media culture: Cultural studies, identity and politics. Between the modern and the postmodern.* London: Routledge.
McChesney, R. (2001). Global media, neoliberalism, and imperialism. *Monthly Review 52* (10). http://www.monthlyreview.org/301rwm.htm
McLaren, Peter. (1997). *Revolutionary multiculturalism: Pedagogies of dissent for the new millennium.* Boulder, CO: Westview Press.
Megwa, Eronini, R. (2007). Community radio stations as community technology centers: An evaluation of the development impact of technological hybridization on stakeholder communities in South Africa. *Journal of Radio Studies 14*(1), 49–66.
Mweige, P. (2009). The democratic functions and dysfunctions of political talk radio: the case of Uganda. *Journal of African Media Studies*, *1* (2), 221–245.
Shannon, P. (2007). Pedagogies of the oppresors: Critical literacies as counter narratives. Speech presented at the Rouge Forum on March 2. See: http://www-rohan.sdsu.edu/~rgibson/rouge_forum/shannon.htm

AFFILIATION

Antonia Darder
Leavey Presidential Chair of Ethics and Moral Leadership at Loyola
Marymount University,
Los Angeles and is Professor Emerita of Education Policy,
Organization and Leadership at the University of Illinois Urbana Champaign

ASOKE BHATTACHARYA

13. ADULT EDUCATION AND FILM/TELEVISION

INTRODUCTION: FILM AS A MASS COMMUNICATION MEDIUM

When cinema appeared at the end of the nineteenth century, it was just another form of entertainment along with theatre and music. Within no time, however, its technical novelty turned it into a mass communication medium since the same production, however short in duration, could reach many people at the same time across the length and breadth of a country or the world over. With cinema halls proliferating, even remote areas fell under its spell. As more and more people, including those belonging to the lower middle class and the working class, could avail themselves of this entertainment at affordable price, it soon became an instrument for reaching out to a large cross-section of society.

As the medium matured, it developed various characteristics: it became a form of show business. It could be used to propagate important national and societal messages. It also developed its own aesthetics. Social documentary film movements, providing films based on real life issues, also emerged.

The mass appeal of film and the cinema's extraordinary reach throughout society began to haunt adult education practitioners. It was felt that messages having relevant contents could be directed towards the adult learners to impart education for life and a livelihood. It was also believed that, even adult basic education, including literacy, could be imparted through films.

The emergence of television by the end of the Second World War enormously broadened the scope of the audio-visual medium including films. Whereas previously one had to go to a cinema hall to enjoy a film show, television films and other entertainments as well as information began to reach households to entertain as well educate the individual, family and community. The power of this new device was so all-pervasive that adult educationists throughout the world thought of using the medium for education. In the following pages, I will discuss use of television and films for educational purposes. This follows from a brief preamble in which I shall deal briefly with the minimal effect of mass media, if only as proviso to drive home that use of mass media in adult education cannot be regarded as a panacea.

MINIMAL EFFECT OF MASS MEDIA

Two important research findings radically changed the notion that the mass media was all-powerful and could act as a hypodermic needle to influence the targeted population. The first is the result of an analysis of the 1940 U.S. presidential election, also known as the voter study. The work of Lazarsfeld, Berelson and Gaudet discovered that individuals are more influenced in their decisions by relatives or friends than by the mass media. It fore-grounded the theory of a two-step flow of communication.

MASS MEDIA – OPINION LEADERS – INDIVIDUALS

In each society, there are some people whose opinions are respected. These people are more knowledgeable in specific fields, are exposed to the mass media and can motivate others to follow suit. They are *opinion leaders*.

The second discovery is the more important and can be viewed as a watershed in mass communication research. The works of Hovland (1949) and Klapper (1960) suggested that the social categories to which people belonged and individual differences were more instrumental in decision making than the mass media. People defend themselves against the onslaught of media messages in three ways:

- selective exposure
- selective perception
- selective retention.

As for selective exposure, individuals expose themselves selectively more to those items of communication which are akin to their beliefs, ideas and values. When exposed to the overall media message, people perceive only those events, issues and personalities that conform to their latent beliefs, attitudes and wants. People may be exposed to certain messages, may even perceive them but may not recall them in future. In fact, a person can recall only a few messages. This is known as selective retention. These two discoveries on the limited effectiveness of the mass media played a pivotal role in utilizing it for dissemination of development messages.

How do then messages spread in a society, especially innovations? The answer to this question was found in a seminal study by Everett Rogers. Rogers, son of an Iowa farmer, identified the following factors and areas:

1. An innovation is to be considered new by the recipient.
2. It is communicated through certain channels.
3. Among members of a community.
4. Over a certain period of time.

Researched and widely accepted in the United States, the same rule was applied in countries of the Third World. In the middle of the 1970s, half of the diffusion studies (around 800) were being conducted in the developing world. Rogers conceptualized, confirmed and elaborated five stages in the development of an innovation: awareness, interest, evaluation, trial and adoption.

At the awareness stage, an individual is exposed to an innovation but lacks complete information about it. At the interest stage, the person seeks more information. At the evaluation stage, the person evaluates various issues like present compatibility and future needs, as well as her/his means. At the trial stage, with evaluation possible, the person gives this evaluation a trial on a limited scale. If the outcome of the trial is positive, the person adopts the innovation. Needless to mention that these stages are not watertight compartments .Within and between these stages, the person may reject the innovation if her /his exposures to the experiences of others reinforce her/his belief. Research has shown that, at the awareness stage, the mass media plays a decisive role whereas at the evaluation and adoption stages, interpersonal communication and local information sources play a dominant role. In the areas of adult education and community development, the implications of the theories of minimal effect of mass media and diffusion of innovations are enormous.

USE OF TELEVISION AND FILM IN ADULT EDUCATION

Let us first examine the crucial question of the relationship between television and adult education. 'Is television sufficient unto itself to provide a worthwhile educational experience or is it a necessary but not sufficient part of a broader process that includes other techniques for learning?' By and large, the answer to the crucial question is 'no.' Only those using television for foreign language instruction have found the medium sufficient. In all other fields, it exists in combination with other learning resources and experiences, such as monitors and discussion groups, special reading materials and exercises and correspondence work. Television is seldom effective alone.

The Carnegie Commission on Education Television reiterates this observation. The Commission believes ...that the deficiencies in instructional television go far beyond matters of itself and equipment. It is of much greater consequence that instructional television has never been fully integrated into the educational process. Instructional television like instructional radio and instructional motion pictures before it, lies outside the process, put to incidental use as ancillary material... In short, the commission believes that instructional television must be regarded as an element in the total educational process. (Ohliger, 1968). Long before the Open University of the United Kingdom came into existence, we find a report that 'the British were considering a proposal for a "University of the Air" which would combine television, correspondence, listening groups and residence education in degree granting programmes.' (Ohliger,1968). Many research studies conducted at the Chicago Public School which offered credit courses for junior college students via television have shown that 'some parts of the teaching process are best done other than by television and television is more effective when this kind of supplement is provided for it.'(Ohliger, 1968).

One UNESCO publication reports: 'The broadcast media lack the spontaneous interaction of teacher and student; they lack the permanency of the printed work; they tend towards centralization and do not adapt themselves easily to local conditions and pre-occupations; they require a technical infrastructure and suitable maintenance. These and other limitations underlie the importance of combining their use with other media of communication and underpinning them with an organizational and maintenance structure.'(Ohliger, 1968).

On the basis of twenty three case studies in seventeen countries, Schramm and others concluded in a UNESCO study that 'One of the reasons why a high degree of integration is so important is that the effectiveness of the new media is coming more and more to be seen as dependent upon the amount of learning activity that goes on at the receiving end ... it is not productive to think of the media as pouring content into viewers and listeners; A better way is to think of them as stimulating learning activity on the part of their viewers and listeners... The point is that, except in the rarest of instances, the new media cannot be counted to do an adequate educational job by themselves and hardly anywhere in the world are they being asked to do this. Planned guidance for pupils, practice opportunities, and an opportunity for two-way communication, if possible, must be built into the teaching system of which the media are a part.'(Ohliger, 1968).

Groombridge, writing in another publication of UNESCO, concludes, on the basis of studies conducted in Canada, Czechoslovakia and Japan, that 'Perhaps the most important conclusion to draw from these accounts in this study is that television is educationally most valuable when it is employed as a member of a teaching team and least valuable when it has to sustain the entire educational relationship with the viewer. It needs to be thought about much more in terms drawn from education and less as a form of broadcasting... for education by television to succeed ... it is important that the actual programme be reinforced by other educational experiences.'(Ohliger, 1968).

The task of integrating media options with adult education is a difficult one. The ingredients of a comprehensive, multi-media educational programme for adults are usually controlled by different agencies. The job of relating different media in a learning system is formidable. The reason is that when two agencies are collaborating—educational institutions and mass media—in a common endeavour, the project itself is not always of sufficient concern to either party. Each has a fear of the other party determining its objective. This difficulty has been reported over time—in the 1960s as well as in 2004. (Singhal et al, 2009).

Adult education is traditionally concerned with people rather than production. The producer's world is that of output whereas the educator is concerned with the human being. To make television a tool not of the producer but of the human being, to permit active participation of the viewer in the exploration and utilization of the medium of communication is a challenge faced by development communication specialists and adult educators throughout the world over the last fifty years. If, however, a proper matching is achieved, the result can be far-reaching with regard to the development of people's consciousness.

In integrative utilization, two educational techniques are frequently used. These are face to face discussion in small groups and correspondence work. The literature on listening group is extensive. Ohliger prepared a lengthy historical discussion on their use in over 30 countries which contains a bibliography of 800 items. The dissertation was condensed into a monograph published by the Center for Study of Liberal Education for Adults.(Ohliger,1968) The Japanese television system, NHK, started 'The Women's Class' way back in 1959. There were 20,000 groups enrolling 200,000 women. The groups watched and discussed television programmes dealing with various problems in politics, economics and social welfare. (Ohliger,1968). Such groups were also formed in Denmark and were known as 'Study Circles' – shades of Freire here. In India, groups of peasant listeners were successfully formed.

For these groups to be successful, it is necessary to train their lay leaders. Belgium organized an extensive training course for the leaders of the 'tele-clubs' in the 1960s. These clubs were also organized in Togo in Africa. Niger offered a two-week course. The groups are particularly effective when members of the lower middle class and the working class with less educational attainments take part in such programmes. During the period under discussion, the North Carolina Department of Public Instruction conducted a special television discussion course in conjunction with agricultural extension on the use of fertilizer and lime. By organizing television group viewing, it is possible to exploit the capacity of the medium to stimulate a large number of people at a low per capita cost. Such programmes can present to the viewers national and international experts and also materials using the resources of film and studio. Small groups of people spread all over can be stimulated by telecasting these programmes in appropriate slots and channels.

Schramm reported that the combination of mass media and distance learning, previously known as Correspondence Study, was quite effective. 'The combination of broadcasts and correspondence study is clearly an effective one – more effective than either of the components alone, because broadcasting can supply a personal note, the motivation and the time schedule which are most difficult to handle by correspondence and correspondence can supply the two-way communication between student and teacher which broadcasting lacks. Broadcast-correspondence education is also apparently an economical way of teaching. Moreover, it seems able to rescue the students for further education and higher training; without it these students would be lost to education and, likewise, education would be lost to them.'(Ohliger, 1968).

In a rating scale devised by Wedemeyer and Childs with ten criteria totaling 40 points, correspondence study alone rates 25 points and audio-visual teaching 23. The combination achieves 33.

Needless to mention that such observations gave rise to "Open and Distance Learning" when mass media and correspondence study were combined to form an innovative whole. Groombridge says: "television is ... a profoundly educational medium. It socializes viewers in the social-psychologist's sense and is often most influential when at its least self-conscious... when the creative qualities of intelligence, curiosity, wonder or imagination are at work, then many programmes in the general output will educate more effectively than a purpose-built educational series."(Ohliger, 1968).

A very useful publication called 'Using films' edited by Limbacher (1967) has a chapter on utilization of films for adult discussion groups. A UNESCO publication comments that 'Film allows to a much greater extent than television intensive individual work with a group.'(Ohliger, 1968, p.) In a study in which thirty training directors from small, medium and large firms were asked to rate seven processes (lecture, conference, programmed instruction, role playing, sensitivity training, television and film) in terms of knowledge acquisition, films tied with conference in second place. (Ohliger, 1968).

Because they cannot stop, movies cannot replace the book or the study guide for real learning. But with videotapes, cd or vcd all of which can be manipulated at ease, this difficulty can be overcome. Film shows followed by discussion prove quite fruitful in teacher education as has been reported in Algeria. (Ohliger, 1968).

AREAS OF ADULT EDUCATION AND LIFELONG LEARNING

1. Liberal Adult Education

Various authors have suggested that educational television should be used for the growth of democracy. Liberal education frees each citizen of a nation personally and politically. Continuing Liberal Education is necessary to attain such objectives. It has been observed that citizenship education is most served by combining television/ film with correspondence education and distance learning.

2. Public Affairs Education

Based on the assumption that parents watch television with their children, many educators have proposed that teachers encourage children to watch programmes relating to public affairs and discuss them in class.

There is a direct relationship between television broadcasts and informal education.

3. Academic Education

Before the advent of Open and Distance Learning, Japan dedicated a number of days each year for students of correspondence education to spend at school where television programmes were telecast for viewing in groups.

4. Basic Education

Television and films have been used to combat illiteracy. On the televised lessons themselves, it is important to incorporate economic motivation. Most eloquent results are obtained when television is used in conjunction with the instructor. Such encouraging results have been observed in India in the 1990s. Literacy training at the place of employment was available in Latin America, including Brazil, where employers were required by law to provide such education. In such programmes, films and television packages were employed.

5. Business and Industry

Courses for supervisors were introduced way back in the 1960s. South Carolina in the United States enrolled as many as 3100 management personnel in one television course. In Japan, vocational and technical correspondence courses combined with television began in 1960. Thousands of adults enrolled.

6. Continuing Professional Education

Teachers used to enroll in large numbers in such courses. The physicians were the next large group. These courses used the correspondence method coupled with audio-visual programmes.

FILMS FOR LIFELONG LEARNING

Films can be generally categorized as: feature films, short films and documentaries. Feature films are based on novels and stories though scripts are also based on real life incidents. The stories are told in film language which consists mainly of diverse editing techniques including montage, collage etc. Feature films have many things to offer to the audience. These sometimes provide entertainment and sometimes entertainment and education. Both are elements for learning for life. Entertainment is part of life. Good entertainment films enhance the quality of life. If education is added, the film can serve the purpose of both learning for life as well as for livelihood. For example, a detective story may be entertainment to others but educative to the people employed in the police force. As far as entertainment is concerned, Chaplin's films like Gold Rush, City Light etc stand out as shining examples. But they also have a subtle educational dimension. For instance, 'The Great Dictators' and 'Monsieur Verdoux' not only entertain but also educate. In Cuba, during the great literacy campaigns of 1960s, Chaplin's films were shown to the neo-literates. Short films of fiction also serve the same purpose.

Documentary films are made to focus on diverse and important issues of daily life, on environment, on science, sports, cultural issues and events, as well as on any other issue concerning people, society and country. They also focus on important personalities whose life and work inspire or educate the masses. Satyajit Ray made a documentary film on the life of Rabindranath Tagore, the great Indian poet and educationist. One of the earliest documentaries 'Nanook of the North' by Flaherty, on the Eskimoes of Alaska, still enthralls the audience. There are documentaries on the flora and fauna of various regions of the earth, on the inhabitants of the Amazon jungles or on the origin and development of species etc. There are documentaries on HIV AIDS, Malaria, Tuberculosis and many other diseases—the purpose being that of educating the masses on how to take preventive measures and, in the case of their being affected, fight the disease. Even feature films have been made to act as a spur for people to engage in social action.

Films are great tools of social communication. A film called Parama made by an Indian woman director Aparna Sen was the initiator of a debate on women's liberation in the 1980s in India. There are many films which, following their appearance, created a great commotion among the public, triggering debates on the issue among people. Newspapers and magazines publish stories on the subject. Examples abound. The commercial film 'Titanic' released in the nineties still draws attention to safety. Reports that the ship's captain was drunk during the tragedy constantly raise issue regarding safety measures in the contemporary public transportation system.

CONCLUSION

The foregoing indicates that the film and television media constitute important sites of adult learning, an area which draws on a large variety of contemporary provision. They contribute in no small measure to that aspect of adult education called by Henry Giroux, a prolific writer on film and learning, as 'public pedagogy.' And examples of these types of media serving as forms of social purpose adult learning abound from all corners of the world, as my chapter would have indicated by now. They are not just confined to the Western world. I also hope to have shown that, despite the dumbing down' culture that prevails in Western-inspired or packaged contemporary media provision there exist enough pockets of healthy film and television production, with direct or indirect educational dimensions, to fill one with hope concerning the emancipatory potential of these cultural activities. I am using 'emancipatory' here in the sense of their potentially contributing to the creation of a better world, one of the targets of socially transformative adult education.

REFERENCES

Allport, G., & Portman, L. (1947). *The psychology of rumour*, New York: Holt.
Daniels, W. M. (1951). The Point Four Programme, New York: H. H. Wilson.
Felciano, G. (1981). *The educational use of mass media*, New York: The World Bank.
Ghosh, Avik. (2006*)*. *Communication technology and human development*, New Delhi: Sage Publications
Hovland, C. I., Janis, I. L. & Kelly, H. H. (1953). *Communication and persuasion*, New Haven: Yale University Press.
Klapper, J. T. (1960). *The effects of mass communication*, Illinois: Free Press.
Limbacher, J. L (1967). *Using films. A handbook for the program planner*, New York: Educational Film Library Association.
Oliger, J. (1968). *The mass media in adult education*, Syracuse, New York: ERIC Clearing House on Adult Education.
Rogers, E. (1962). *Diffusion of innovation*, New York: The Free Press.
Severin, W., & Tankard, J. (1987). *Communication theories*, New York: Hastings House.

Shah, S. Y. (Ed). (2008). *International perspectives on adult and lifelong education: Selected papers*, New Delhi: International Institute of Adult and Lifelong Education.
Singhal, A., & Dearing, J. W. (2006). *Communication of innovation: A journey with everett Rogers*, New Delhi: Sage Publications.
UNESCO. (2006). 'Literacy initiative for empowerment, 2005–2015: Vision and Strategy Paper', Hamburg: UNESCO
UNESCO. (2009). *Confintea VI: Harnessing the power and potential of adult learning and education for a viable future*, Belem: UNESCO.

AFFILIATION

Asoke Bhattacharya
Formerly Professor of Adult, Continuing Education and Extension,
Jadavpur University, Kolkata, India

JIM ELMBORG

14. LITERACIES, NARRATIVES AND ADULT LEARNING IN LIBRARIES

INTRODUCTION[1]

Librarians in the academy "increasingly see themselves as educators, an evolution in the profession that challenges established definitions of librarianship and of how we generate knowledge about professional values and practices" (Elmborg, 2006a:192). Academic libraries are places where learners come to construct new knowledge through selection of information sources and research literature in print and electronic forms. In order to help students accomplish these important research tasks, academic librarians as educators focus on the development of "information literacy" skills in the library classroom, at the reference desk, and in research consultations with learners.

The Association of College and Research Libraries defines information literacy as the ability to: "determine the extent of information needed; access the needed information effectively and efficiently; evaluate information and its sources critically; incorporate selected information into one's knowledge base; use information effectively to accomplish a specific purpose; understand the economic, legal, and social issues surrounding the use of information, and access and use information ethically and legally" (American Library Association, 2000, p. 2–3). Learners within academic library settings use information resources toward specific ends—-learner constructed research and writing projects that offer new perspectives on particular topics. Such projects may take the form of individual research papers and/or class presentations, literature reviews, theses, e-portfolios, webpages, or collaboratively created mini-documentaries. Learners navigate an information and technology-rich environment and learn skills that contribute significantly to the research and writing process. In this chapter I will reflect on literacies developed within diverse communities of discourse and how these literacies inform the research and writing process as learners construct new knowledge and write/create/present their findings. I will also explore the changing narrative of adult learning in libraries, as well as critical theory informed approaches to information literacy skill development.

LITERACY IN SCHOOLS AND LIBRARIES

As an educator within the field of library science, I work with adult students who are preparing to become librarians and educators within the rapidly changing world of libraries. My background in the field of English and composition studies informs my current work in the field of library science. As the writing process is directly related to the research process, it makes sense that these two areas are closely connected in current academic library practice.

Prior to coming to the field of library science, I taught English for ten years in the public schools. Struggling writers were always a presence in my classrooms. During that time, I increasingly saw teaching and learning English in terms of social class, with students from middle-class homes sliding comfortably into the student role while other students from less privileged homes struggled. Successful students seemed to intuitively understand important things about being in school, some of which are superficial and some more significant. Together, they comprise a suite of practices that we might call school literacies. These students understood how to play the "game" of being a student. Later in my career as an English graduate student teaching composition courses to freshmen, issues of school literacy came into sharper focus. I saw students with good minds and good work ethics fail in their attempts to enter college because they could not sort out these school literacies by themselves. Their work was deemed inappropriate because they didn't understand how to play the college student "game." In the mid-seventies, Composition Studies began to aggressively develop pedagogies that helped students learn to play this game, and these pedagogies informed my earliest efforts to theorize student learning.

Moving to the field of library science, I clearly saw similar issues of pedagogy and social class playing out in professional practices of librarianship, though we tended not to recognize this within the profession. As pragmatic and results-oriented fields of practice, both writing instruction and librarianship have a practical and perhaps instrumental tendency, and many instructors tend to define teaching as transmission of a set of discrete skills. The writing process (Brainstorming, Drafting, Revising, and Editing) was originally considered revolutionary pedagogy in the field of composition studies because it shifted the focus from product to process to support students who had to learn basic academic skills (i.e., how to play the game). Carol Kuhlthau's (2004) Research Process within libraries (Task Initiation, Topic Selection, Pre-focus Exploration, Focus Formulation, Information Collection, Search Closure) was strongly related to the writing process and had the same pedagogical goals. These models were developed by researchers, who observed the work of successful students and created models to describe what they saw. In order to successfully play the game, the theory goes, unsuccessful students need to learn to emulate successful students. As a consequence, process was detached from inquiry, and writing and research were defined as a set of reified tasks, separate from any meaning the student hoped to convey.

While in theory, these pedagogies encouraged the use of process to engage students and to help them construct meaning, in practice, correct process was easy to enforce through graded assignments that punished students for not doing the process correctly. In other words, pedagogy originally designed to relinquish control to the direction of the student evolved into an instrument of power used to discipline students into a visible process. Perhaps more problematic, by insisting that unsuccessful students emulate successful ones, these process models obscured the central role that culture plays in a student's ability and willingness to play this game by these rules. Mary Louse Pratt's concept of the "contact zone" as "social spaces where cultures meet, clash, and grapple with each other, often in contexts of highly asymmetrical relations of power" (2002, p. 4) helps us understand the role culture plays in the learning that takes place in libraries. Each learner brings multiple literacies (formed from a diversity of discourse communities) to the library and encounters new cultural codes which must be mastered to successfully navigate the library and the larger academic world. Librarians as educators need to create critical approaches to pedagogy by employing horizontal rather than vertical/authoritarian communication and teaching practices.

TOWARD CRITICAL INFORMATION LITERACY

As Gee (1999) suggests, we are all members of multiple discourse communities. To be a fully participating member of a discourse community, one must know the codes that insiders of such communities use to communicate. The codes and discourses of academic communities (the college game or the academic library game) can be learned if learners are assisted in joining the communities. The process of exploring how this joining occurs is essential to understanding a critical approach to information literacy. Critical Information Literacy, or Critical Literacy, aims to bring as many newcomers into the game as possible by assisting learners in developing understanding of the codes or language of the academic discourse community. Democratic in impulse, Critical Literacy seeks to empower rather than discipline, raise rather than rank, and include rather than exclude.

Theorists central to this perspective include Lev Vygotsky and Paulo Freire. Lev Vygotsky (1962) argues that the development of thought is not only a measure of cognitive growth but also the development of language shared appropriately with all members of a community. We learn language by talking to other people, by sharing observations about what we see around us, and by mimicking the words, phrases, and patterns we hear from those more advanced. Eventually, as this discourse becomes more natural, this shared communal language becomes integral to how we think. Indeed, Vygotsky argues that such language running in our heads *is* our thinking. We continue to learn throughout our lives by conversing with others, and especially by seeking out others who have more understanding than we do. By talking to these people, we learn how they think by learning how they use language. Our thinking is then shaped by this language.

Academic environments, including libraries, provide a context for this thinking through language. According to Vygotsky, we learn best from those who are within our zone of understanding (he called it a "Zone of Proximal Development"), slightly more advanced, but not so much so that they are incomprehensible to us. Having more advanced peers helps us learn more effectively than having very advanced professors or teachers. Through conversation, we learn to "scaffold" our ideas as we build or construct these ideas. Learners in libraries collaborate with other learners to engage the information and research sources they encounter, scaffolding and learning together.

Paulo Freire (1993) equates literacy with the development of agency. Without literacy, one cannot conceive of being a self who takes meaningful action in the world. The banking system, which Freire denounces, teaches students to bank knowledge and to hoard it as wealth. The way we are taught enacts a value system, which mirrors the capitalist system of Western culture and trains students to work in it. Indeed, the power in Freire is in his comprehensive critique of the "game" itself. Can we ethically focus attention on bringing students into the game if the game itself is corrupt? American educators have imported Freire's pedagogies, but the fit is somewhat awkward. American students are not generally oppressed in the same sense that Brazilian peasants might be. In school, American students have been bribed to be good students with the promise that material success will ensue from the consumption of school knowledge, and it undoubtedly does. They are thus taught to consume both knowledge and products. Particularly in educational settings, they are prepared for lives as consumers and good citizens who work within rather than challenge the status quo.

Freire encourages praxis to move us past instrumental ways of teaching and reified forms of knowledge toward critically engaged positions designed to empower learners and transform our institutions. Professional practice as praxis exists across educational and institutional spectrums. In developing praxis, we are challenged to envision our institutions, including libraries, as sites of knowledge construction. In the library setting, that means avoiding any instinct to hand pre-produced, packaged information to people, even if they seem to want that package. If literacy is defined broadly as the set of skills one needs to get in the game, then we need to work to both teach these skills and also to fix the game itself, to separate ourselves from the machine of cultural production that encourages us to consume and to produce consumers. We want people to own their questions, their minds, and their bodies.

To what extent is such praxis happening in libraries today? This is difficult to measure. Scholars working in the area of Critical Information Literacy explore critical concepts of power, control, and cultural hegemony to question the prevailing practice of librarianship (Accardi, Drabinski & Kumbier, 2010; Green & Macauley, 2007; Jacobs, 2008; Simmons, 2005; Swanson, 2004). While not widely adopted, the approach has clear relevance to daily library practice, and many individual librarians are drawn to seeing their practice in this way. A critical approach to information literacy development means changing the view of education as the transfer of information or "getting the right knowledge into students' heads" to an awareness of each person's agency and ability to make meaning within the library setting (Elmborg, 2006a: 194). This process becomes a political act as learners and educators challenge the structures that privilege the knowledge of those in power. Praxis may not look much different on the surface from traditional library practice. The key to all practice/praxis is conversation. How we talk to other people, whether we see people as learners struggling for meaning, respecting that struggle and helping them scaffold, encouraging them to grow, develop, and challenge the assumptions they hold as well as their given place in the world. These are all ways of working in a library that are largely invisible to outsiders.

A revolutionary reference or research consultation in a library looks very much like a traditional reference interview on the surface (Elmborg 2006b), but the fundamental nature of the conversation differs in many ways when the librarian assumes the role of critical educator. In 1999, I was working at the reference desk in a small college in South Carolina. The state legislature, under great pressure from all directions, was debating removing the Confederate flag from the top of the state house in Columbia. Passions were high on both sides of the question. A young man came to the reference desk at this small private college on a Sunday afternoon and posed a classic reference question. He needed five academic sources that would prove the flag was a symbol of pride not racism. My training as a reference librarian was clear about how I should proceed. My job was to answer that question by doing my best to find those sources. How he might use them was not my concern. However, as an educator, I needed to engage the assumptions behind that question, to talk about symbols and how they work. We needed to talk about proof and how one proves a thesis academically, about multiple perspectives on reality. In essence, his position of privilege was invisible to him and so were the consequences of his argument. I would like to say I enlightened him that afternoon, but I do not know that to be true. I do know that we had a critical discussion of race and cultural symbolism, and that, to an onlooker, the discussion looked the same as any other conversation at a reference desk.

THE TRADITIONAL LIBRARY NARRATIVE

Pre-Internet, we thought of libraries as information utilities and librarians as information authorities who utilized tools, such as indexes, bibliographies, and catalogs. They were the best tools available, but by today's standards, they were pretty crude, difficult to use and hard to actually make work through a process of inquiry. Of course, the tools were not available outside the walls of the library. Librarianship was a bibliographic profession, and we defined it through a bibliographic narrative. George Lakoff (1980) argues that we all live according to internalized narratives, and often these narratives remain unexamined below the level of consciousness. We don't really think about the life stories we accept as models, but these stories govern our values and how we see ourselves and our positions in the narrative. Also, we have metaphors that only make sense if we place them in the context of narrative, but we tend to employ the metaphors as if they reflect universal truths.

Contemporary librarians inherited a bibliographic narrative, a narrative that defines librarians as professionals who collect, manage, study, describe, and provide access to books. Librarianship involved expertise with tools, which librarians made and used expertly. The librarian was positioned, in this narrative, between the books and the people who wanted information. The reference desk was a symbolic place of in-between-ness—mostly between people and books—and it was a symbol of authority, owned by the librarian surrounded by his or her tools. Many underlying assumptions informed this positioning. Librarians assumed that learners had questions and that librarians had answers, or could at least find answers, and that the tools created to answer these questions were fairly infallible. Librarians saw themselves as ethically, morally, and personally neutral, a conduit from question to answer. Perhaps most importantly, librarians saw learners as having a basic void. They came to the library because they lacked information that librarians could provide. Librarians gave them information if users could ask good questions, which was key to the game. In the classroom, librarians did something called bibliographic instruction, teaching the tools of bibliography.

These definitions of librarianship are derived from broader cultural assumptions about what it means to be a professional. They reflect a belief that knowledge resides in experts, and that professionalism is related to the possession of expert knowledge. Professionals have a fiduciary relationship with clients in this model, which means clients must trust that the professional is an honest agent working on their behalf. Professionals act for clients who lack skill and knowledge to act for themselves. They must do so by interviewing the client, understanding his or her need, and then acting for the client's good. Many professions subscribe to this model: bankers, attorneys, physicians. Very little education of the client takes place in this model, and the client is not positioned as a learner. The client wants an outcome. The professional's job is to achieve this outcome for the client. This situation, with the professional librarian at a desk or in a classroom mediating between knowledge/information and people, describes the traditional, bibliographic position of the librarian, a role that I deemed inadequate in discussing the Confederate flag with my student. This view is based on a narrative that is no longer sustainable.

CRITICAL INFORMATION LITERACY AS THE NEW LIBRARY NARRATIVE

Information Literacy forms a new narrative for library practice, and this narrative of information literacy in libraries builds on a larger literacy narrative (Vygotsky, 1962; Freire, 1993; Foucault, 1995; Gee, 1999). In particular, Gee (1999) sees literacy as an entire repertoire of performances appropriate to social situations. Viewed this way, literacy is something mobile and flexible, not just a set of skills with written text. Literacy is the ability to read the codes of our cultures and sub-cultures. Literacy is also the ability to produce codes that are valued in these cultures (Elmborg, 2006b).

Literacy is fundamentally connected to community, and community members are the judges of literacy competency. According to this view, we are all literate, but we are not all literate in the same communities.

For example, when I teach a course called *Literacy and Learning* designed for librarians in training, I start by asking students to identify a community they belong to based on their interests. They describe interests like knitting, ethnic dancing, computer programming, creative anachronism, hand-fishing, gourmet cooking, and video gaming. I ask them to think about the ways community members become insiders in that culture, what it means to perform the insider role, what codes you need to understand, and how one gains status by performing a role, especially a role using language. I ask them to think about that as a kind of literacy. I want them to see how the literacy narrative treats the codes of communication as something we learn as we come into new intellectual and physical spaces.

Librarians need to see information as situated in a community and to see themselves as masters of informational codes. To operate in the literacy metaphor, librarians need to work on the boundaries of their discourse communities, bringing new learners into the community by helping them learn what information they need to function. To do this, librarians need to locate themselves at the boundaries rather than in the centers. Contemporary boundaries are porous. People migrate between communities. In the bibliographic narrative, librarians required newcomers to come to them, where they sat in the center of the traditional circle of power. Librarians didn't come to clients. This position made sense under the expert model because the expert's time could best be used by accepting clients sequentially into the space of the tools. In the new literacy narrative, a person constructing meaning does not lack anything. Rather, that person seeks initiation into a community and its codes. People tend to want to do that on their own by working on the edges. There isn't a problem to solve. There is a community to join.

Back in the bibliographic narrative, librarians performed a kind of sorting function, helping those who could ask good questions, particularly those who made the effort to approach the library and librarian. There is an amazing scene in the film *Sophie's Choice* where Meryl Streep's character approaches the reference desk to ask about the writer "Emile Dickens" (read: Emile Dickinson). She has a heavy European accent, and the reference librarian answers her a question, but in the process, he ridicules her pronunciation, humiliating her and sending her away in tears. Some powerful stereotypes are conveyed here. The librarian, positioned between Streep's character and knowledge or information, makes no effort to meet her in some supportive way, no attempt to see her as someone with knowledge of many worlds and many codes, trying to grow in new directions. The future of libraries and librarianship cannot be between learners and information in this way, but must be alongside learners, especially those who didn't inherit English school literacy. Practicing librarianship this way does not necessarily mean abolishing the reference desk as a physical place (though I find experiments in this direction interesting). "Place" and "Position" are more conceptual than literal. Librarians need to move away from the mediating position and develop strategies to work with people collaboratively, to honor their experiences, and to build bridges from where they are to new literacies. The vehicle for that change is language.

In my experience, too many librarians still think their job is to provide correct answers to questions. To be clear, I do not advocate that we abolish correctness as a standard, but rather that we need a human connection with someone, to understand the way they view the world, where their question or problem is coming from. The librarian can answer questions without really helping people, as I would have by finding five sources to prove the Confederate flag symbolizes pride. In contrast, Critical Information Literacy involves a commitment to social justice within capitalist societies (Wysocki & Johnson-Eilola, 1999). Capitalism has created an amazingly unequal distribution of wealth globally, resulting in economic migration on an unprecedented scale as people uproot themselves from their homes, taking huge risks pursuing work and better lives. The casualties are enormous, and capitalism is a very unforgiving system, cruel in many cases. If librarians treat literacy as the birthright of a privileged few, then leave it to capitalism to sort it all out, we've adopted a Darwinian "survival of the fittest" perspective. Librarians need to be positioned with those who struggle, offering supportive and respectful help. This positioning places the librarian as educator alongside learners. For example, librarians can collaborate with other faculty in engaging students in service learning and civic engagement projects in the community, creating the opportunity for critical reflection about community challenges and fostering learning in and outside the classroom.

IMPLICATIONS FOR ADULT EDUCATION

First of all, it's important for librarians as adult educators to respect the knowledge of the people they work with. Western education is still largely conceived as the process of putting the right content into people's minds—Freire's banking concept. In practice, most educators still focus most of their attention on content, knowing it thoroughly and presenting it clearly. It takes confidence, both on a personal and intellectual level, to relinquish the power that comes from the position of authority, the position of the knowing teacher, and to attempt to connect teaching with learning. One can't ultimately relinquish teaching power absolutely. Being aware of that power and using it carefully is crucial. Taking care to engage learners with a constructivist approach to learning within the library shifts this power dynamic.

Secondly, it's important to take the time to figure out where people are emotionally, intellectually, and cognitively, and to conduct conversations within their Zone of Proximal Development. That means having real conversations that engage people, acknowledging what they know, and attempting to build understanding. I advise educators not to overestimate the usefulness of what we think we know about libraries or information. Everything we think we know is based on our own cultural assumptions, our narrative. If the people we work with don't share those assumptions, we need to realize that what we describe might be alien or might even conflict with what others know or believe. Homi Bhabha (1990) describes the early efforts of Christian missionaries to convert Hindus in India. They talked about the importance of Jesus to salvation and his role as a deity. The Hindus said they were interested in knowing more about Jesus, but not if he ate meat. Here we see the ways that cultural assumptions can't be simply given to people. They lie deep inside us shaping our understandings. What we know about libraries is like that.

Finally, we need to take each day, each person, each situation as it comes. We need to be open to experiencing cultural "otherness" in all its forms. We should try to avoid imposing order or expectations. Librarians are not the center of the library. The collection is not the center of the library. Each person who comes to the library to learn and grow is the center of the library. The librarian's role is to locate that center and to help build and solidify it, putting adults in charge of their own learning, letting them articulate what they want to know and how they want to learn it.

NOTE

[1] This chapter first appeared as Elmborg, J (2010), Literacies, Narratives, and Adult Learning in Libraries, *New Directions for Adult and Continuing Education*, 127, 67–76, ISSN: 1536–0717 Copyright 2010, Wiley. This material is reproduced with permission of John Wiley & Sons, Inc.

The author wishes to acknowledge the significant role played by Marilyn McKinley Parrish in the shaping of this article. Our extensive conversations over many months have played a crucial role in my thinking about this chapter and to my understanding of libraries as cultural institutions crucial to adult education.

REFERENCES

Association of College & Research Libraries (2000). Information literacy competency standards. Chicago: American library association. Retrieved July, 19, 2010 from http://www.ala.org/ala/mgrps/divs/acrl/standards/standards.pdf

Accardi, M., Drabinski, E., & Kumbier, A. (2010). *Critical library instruction theories and methods.* Duluth, Minn: Library Juice Press, 2010.

Bhabha, H. (1990). The third space: Interview with Jonathan Rutherford. In J. Rutherford (Ed.), *Identity: Community, culture, difference,* (pp. 207–221). London: Lawrence & Wishart.

Elmborg, J. (2006a). Critical information literacy: Implications for instructional practice. *The Journal of Academic Librarianship, 32* (2), 192–199.

Elmborg, J. (2006b). Libraries in the contact zone: On the creation of educational space. *Reference and User Services Quarterly, 46* (1) 56–64.

Freire, P. (1993). *Pedagogy of the oppressed.* New York: Continuum.

Foucault, M. (1995). *Discipline and punish.* New York: Vintage.

Gee, J.P. (1999). *An introduction to discourse analysis: Theory and method.* London: Routledge.

Green, R., & Macauley, P. (2007). Doctoral students' engagement with information: An American-Australian perspective. *Portal-Libraries and the Academy, 7* (3), 317–332.

Jacobs, H. L. M. (2008). Information literacy and reflective pedagogical praxis. *The Journal of Academic Librarianship, 34* (3), 256–262.

Kuhlthau, C. C. (2004). *Seeking meaning: A process approach to library an information services.* (2nd ed.) Westport, Conn: Libraries Unlimited.

Lakoff, G (1980). *Metaphors we liveb by.* Chicago: University of Chicago Press.

Pratt, M. L. (2002). Arts of the Contact Zone. In J. M. Wolff (Ed.), *Professing in the Contact Zone*, (pp. 1–18). Urbana, IL: NCTE.
Simmons, M. H. (2005). Librarians as disciplinary discourse mediators. *Portal: Libraries and the Academy, 5* (3), 297–311.
Swanson, T. A. (2004). A radical step: Implementing a critical information literacy model. *Portal: Libraries and the Academy, 4* (2), 259–274.
Vygotsky, L. S. (1962). *Thought and language. Cambridge*, Mass: M. I. T. Press.
Wysocki, A. F., & Johnson-Eilola, J. (1999). Blinded by the letter: Why are we using literacy as a metaphor for everything else? In G.E. Hawisher & Selfe C. L. (Ed.). *Passions, Pedagogies, and 21st Century Technologies*, (pp. 349–368) Utah State University Press and NCTE.

AFFILIATION

Jim Elmborg
Associate Professor of Library and Information Science, the School of Library and Information Science at The University of Iowa

MAE SHAW & ROSIE MEADE

15. COMMUNITY DEVELOPMENT AND THE ARTS: TOWARDS A MORE CREATIVE RECIPROCITY

INTRODUCTION

In some ways 2011 was a bad year for authority figures in Ireland and the UK. Rioting, the drip feed of abuse revelations, the phone-hacking scandals, the Euro currency crisis and the unfolding consequences of financial retrenchment, have concentrated the minds of populations on both sides of the Irish Sea. By way of response, mainstream political and media commentaries invoke the familiar concepts of community, order and control; regarded simultaneously as casualties and solutions to the crises of our day. Community development has been here many times before and there's nothing particularly novel in the expectation that 'communities' should step in wherever the market and state fail. But there is something wilfully disingenuous in the way that mainstream commentaries disregard the extent and consequences of the 'neo-liberalisation' of our times. Public policy and politicians have gravitated towards the consensus that we are all self-interested economic actors: in discourse and practice our capacities for acting and thinking critically and collectively about the worlds we now inhabit are increasingly undermined or denied.

In his book *Ill Fares the Land*, Tony Judt (2010) argues that we are not only unable to respond to the political imperatives of our time, we are also unable to talk about them – and that the two are interconnected. In other words, in these neo-liberal times managerialist and market speak work their way into all spheres of life, dictating how we represent ourselves and others, so that they become naturalised, 'common sense', as it were. The language available to us has become so constricted that questions to do with fairness, justice and morality – the real questions for democratic life, and therefore, for community development – have become depoliticized within a stunted, repetitive and sanitized discourse (Judt, 2010). In this context community development, despite its democratic ethos, too readily becomes framed as a technique to activate 'problem' groups, families and communities. In contrast, this chapter argues for and draws upon alternative discourses; discourses that invoke creativity, imagination and critique. We want to consider how a focus on cultural practice in community settings might help us to think outside the current consensus. We want especially to affirm that creativity and critique may be present beyond the mainstream gaze: that people's everyday and more specialised cultures can embody hopes, frustrations, dreams and demands that should be central to democratic politics.

A concern with culture and the arts is not by any means a peripheral one for community development. Indeed processes of development, regeneration and urban renewal are often premised on the role that artists and arts organisations can play in raising the economic profile or improving the image of particular areas. The risk is that really existing neighbourhoods and communities become further marginalised in these processes as their cultural contribution is ignored or scorned. In this chapter, we consider how community development might catalyse and nourish a more dialectical relationship between the cultural politics of people in communities and the wider political culture of the state.

Malik (2000, p. 46) argues that the arts provide a distinctive space where personal and political roles and relations can be renegotiated and re-imagined partly because of their unique potential to take us out of ourselves, 'to range over the actual, the probable, the possible and even the impossible'. In this sense, the arts have much to offer community development. But the relationship should also be reciprocal. The democratic impulse – if not always the actuality – of participation that is enshrined in anything that calls itself community development may lend weight and depth to what otherwise may be ephemeral or diversionary arts activities. Such a symbiotic relationship may create the conditions in which 'imagination' can be sustained as a dynamic process of communication so that 'meaning-making' begins to replace 'meaning-taking' as a primary objective of community development work.

COMMUNITY DEVELOPMENT AND DEMOCRACY: AN AMBIVALENT RELATIONSHIP

Generally and historically speaking, community development is concerned with the relationship between governments, whether local or national, and citizens (Shaw and Martin, 2000). It is charged variously with strengthening, inducing or 'delivering' participatory democracy. This has become a particularly problematic prospect in the twenty-first century not least because of democracy's own inherent plasticity. As John Gaventa (2007, p. x) puts it:

> Democracy is at once the language of military power, neoliberal market forces, political parties, social movements, donor agencies and NGOs.

Furthermore, aspects of globalisation place new demands and pressures on what Amin (2002, p. 960) calls 'the politics of living together'. A somewhat sceptical and critical approach to the claims made for democracy is therefore necessary in order to locate its ideological deployment in policy, and to appreciate how this translates into community development theory and practice.

Community development occupies a contradictory yet strategic position between the demands of the state – to deliver policy objectives – and the needs and interests of people in diverse communities – to articulate their own experience. Governments in Ireland and across the UK repeatedly draw on community development and its discourses to mobilise, discipline, modify and redirect the behaviours of what are perceived as 'risky' or 'vulnerable' sections of the population (Rose, 1996, see also Mooney & Neal, 2009; Meade, 2011; Shaw, 2011). But, in their turn, community organisations make demands of policy makers and shape or redirect policy delivery on the ground. At its best, participatory democracy, as articulated through community development, has served over time as the crucible for contestation, negotiation and significant reform. Within the neo-liberal paradigm, however, a *genuinely participatory* democracy is largely regarded as a time-wasting irritant or a barrier to economic growth. In other words, there are serious tensions between the authoritarianism of the state's market enforcement (Harvey, 2005, p. 79), its mainstreaming of austerity in both Ireland and the UK, its appeals to community empowerment or the mythical Big Society, and its responsibilities to support individual freedom and social solidarity. Community development therefore embodies, and must navigate some deeply ambivalent ambitions.

Over the last decade or so, the discourses and practices of community development have become inextricably linked with concepts such as 'active citizenship', 'social capital' and 'participatory democracy'. It is generally assumed that the most effective way for citizens to cooperate, voice their opinions or influence governance is through participation in community-based structures and institutions. Although suggestive of community ownership and control, policy discourses typically present citizens as 'targets' for engagement in 'invited' (Gaventa, 2004) rather than 'negotiated' or 'autonomous' structures.

Furthermore, 'community participation's' democratic reach tends to be narrowly defined, in that it continues to be wedded to traditional political concerns such as governance and fixated upon relations with the state. More recently, and in the context of austerity, policy discourses have begun to embody an even more explicitly economistic and disciplinary aspect, as communities are required to demonstrate their value for money, their ability to provide low-cost services and the 'evidence' base for their practices (Meade, 2011; Shaw, 2011).

While engaged interaction between formal political institutions and more informal community networks is important, in this context we want to emphasize a more expansive and expressive concept of democracy. We argue that the idea of democracy needs to be reclaimed as an active social, political and cultural process through which change occurs in different contexts and spaces by means of subversion, opposition and resistance as much as by participation and consent. Therefore, democracy is sustained not by the conformist citizen, but by the agency of the critical and creative citizen. This highlights a crucial role for community development practitioners in finding ways to enhance people's potential for democratic agency by helping to release or resource their capacity to be active and creative; to cultivate their democratic imagination.

By using the term 'democratic imagination' we hope to enliven what can otherwise become a deadly culture of instrumentalism in both the arts and community development fields. Arts and community practices can seek to unleash underexplored possibilities: for entering attentively into the experience of others; for asserting the place of cultural production in the lives of communities; for excavating and exploring the causes of flaws and wounds in society; for thinking critically about structures and relations of power; and for acting creatively and collectively to transform the world for the better (Meade & Shaw, 2007). The relationship between community development and participatory arts needs to be reconsidered in light of these possibilities. In this sense, we would suggest that the concepts of *cultural democracy* and *cultural resistance* can contribute to a more nuanced and less institutionally fixated vision of cultural practice.

CULTURAL DEMOCRACY IN THE MARKETPLACE

Cultural democracy is vibrant, public and discursive (McGonagle, 2007). It asserts that diverse citizens should and do communicate their views and understandings of the world through a range of processes and in multiple spheres. Cultural democracy positions cultural production as both central to human experience and as a necessary site for democratization. In other words, citizens are seen as creators, as opposed to mere audiences or spectators, whose active engagement in the making, consumption and distribution of culture should be acknowledged and supported (Matarasso, 2006).

While it is obvious that all of us are involved in the fashioning and refashioning of culture in its anthropological sense, opportunities to engage in or with the arts are not so broadly distributed. Matarasso (2006, p. 3) points to the persistence of cultural exclusion and the failure of governments to support 'the diversity of cultural expression'. Furthermore, dominant classifications of *the culture* or *the cultures* of a given society typically value individual artefacts over collective enterprise, heritage over ecology, authors over audiences and the heroic over the mundane. The porosity and contested character of culture is overlooked when particular versions, be they consumer or 'High' cultural variants, are promoted to the exclusion of all others.

For example, Peck (2009, p.7) explains how 'the creativity script' in the United States combines cultural libertarianism with neo-liberal economic imperatives: originality and creativity is 'cool' – so long as it sells. The result, in some cases, has been the 'bohemification' of declining inner city areas towards the creation of vibrant metropolitan spaces, only to drive out traditional working class communities who can no longer afford to live in them. In such instances, creativity strategies, be they arts projects or 'street culture', can simply represent commodified assets that reinforce the market's domination of public space and the exclusion of the poor. Similar trends are discernible across the European Union where, according to Marita Muukkonen (2004), the meaning of culture has been appropriated for new and dubious purposes in official policy documents.

Business leaders and management gurus have become as interested in creativity as those who are involved in the arts, reflecting a change from a manufacturing economy to what has been called an 'economy of the imagination' (Mirza, 2006). The rise of 'Brand Ireland' discourses as a reaction to the recession in Ireland further illustrates the point. Mainstream media and policy makers repeatedly assess the value of the arts with reference to their economic and reputational payoffs alone, and the cultural sector is responsibilised to promote Ireland's brand identity internationally (Meade, 2011a).

Ultimately, such policies and discourses place artists in an invidious position and reinforce a deeply conservative understanding of art's social purposes. Government demands that the arts 'build communities, regenerate economies and include marginalised groups' (Selwood, 2006, p. 53) but this can compromise the autonomy and integrity of the work being undertaken. The parallels with community development's own recent experiences are instructive. For one thing, projects that are conceptualized and imposed from above according to limiting funding streams and limited timescales, often fail to attract the very people for whom they are intended. Ironically, this may leave community arts projects even more vulnerable in the face of public expenditure cuts. In a wider sense, there is a danger that community identity and experience is marketed – as distinct from articulated – in terms associated with the heritage or tourist industries: offering commodified or sanitized versions of social reality under the banner of traditional culture. When populism and consumerism are allowed to stand in for sustained democratic engagement, community development and the arts can lose their critical edge and their functions become determined by the market.

In talking about cultural democracy, we need to look more carefully at what constitutes popular or democratic culture in the current context, and by what authority. If community development is to act purposefully in this terrain, the following might be useful considerations. First, let's talk about popular cultures rather than popular culture, appreciating that class, place and other affiliations inflect the cultural lives of citizens. Second, let's try to look beyond the artefacts and experiences that people buy, to consider their own flashes of artistry and productivity. Of course these may be difficult to track, particularly when they involve no obvious commercial exchange or occur in lowly venues or in private spaces. Third, we might consider whether and how state and market forces misrecognize popular cultures: by denying them status, audiences or channels of distribution. Finally, we may ask what, if anything, communities need in order to make and do culture better. In raising this we might keep in mind Paul Willis's warning against condescension and presumption: not starting with the question 'why are their cultures not as we think they should be?' but rather with 'what are their cultures?' (Willis, 1990, p. 5) and maybe, even, with 'what would they like them to be?'

CULTURAL INVASION AND RESISTANCE

It has become almost a commonplace fact that life in many post-industrial democracies is more unequal than at any time since World War II (Wilkinson &

Pickett, 2009). This appears to be true on a range of indicators, including income, mobility, health, education, and morbidity. The obduracy of social and economic hierarchies should therefore make us wary of overstating the transcendent power of the arts. And it is important to remember the potential of the cultural sphere to provide a convenient means of political displacement; distracting attention from inequality and its associated political and social compromises. In this regard, Frankfurt theorists Theodor Adorno and Max Horkheimer, writing during the mid-twentieth century, presciently described how the 'culture industry' bound individuals to the repressive logic of capitalism, effectively hollowing out our intellects (Kellner, 1995, pp. 28–31). Given the ubiquity of 'reality TV' which seeks to satirise and demean the poor rather than question poverty, it would be easy to concur with their pessimistic appraisal.

Nevertheless, and while keeping in mind their scope for ideological complicity, we would argue that the arts and cultural practices can and do speak out against oppression and domination. For example, sociologists Eyerman and Jamison (1998) have analysed the long-standing significance of song in helping social movements in the United States to frame issues, memorialize grievances and victories, and to demonstrate and create internal solidarity. Recognizing the historically significant and 'political' role of the arts also forces us to look beyond the tired formulae for democratic communication that characterise much community development practice. Furthermore, if we were to adopt a more organic approach to popular culture we would surely find that citizens use culture to interrogate, inflect, oppose and exceed their social situations in surprising ways.

Stephen Duncombe (2003, p. 5) defines cultural resistance as 'culture that is used, consciously or unconsciously, effectively or not, to resist and/or change the dominant political, economic and/or social structure'. If, as he goes on to argue, politics is essentially a cultural discourse derived from socially constructed rituals, symbols and understandings, it follows that cultural practice may be utilized to subvert or challenge the norms of political discourse. This is an important point for community development, in particular. Rather than assuming that communities and individuals, with their low rates of participation in electoral or development processes, are pathologically apathetic or disengaged, we need to pay closer attention to their practices of everyday life in order to discern the values and commentaries that infuse them (de Certeau, 1984). We need, in other words, to grasp what captures people's imagination rather than to lament or penalize their passivity towards normative democratic practices from which they are to a large extent excluded.

Cultural resistance theorists draw attention to the covert or implicit tactics through which social actors articulate a sense of self or contest both low-level and grand scale oppressions (Kelley 1996). What Duncombe (2003) characterises as a 'politics that doesn't look like politics' incorporates cultural practices – including style, attitude, jokes, participation in gangs, graffiti, outlaw status – through which oppositional identities may be nurtured and expressed. In other words, oppositional solidarities may be forged and reinforced in those comparatively privatized or 'invisible' spheres where the force of dominant power relations is felt less acutely or in which politics becomes deeply personal. Theories of cultural resistance, therefore, force us to interrogate if and how community development may be overly prescriptive in its efforts to engineer democracy. They also remind us of the importance of deep and open-minded engagement with communities and of the necessity to create mutually respectful relationships. Ironically, the interventionist gaze may be too superficial and too myopic to recognize the questioning and critical intelligences that animate these cultural gestures.

CONSUMERISM AND CONSUMPTION

Concepts of cultural democracy and resistance are attractive insofar as they highlight the creative and activist potentialities of citizens and, as such, they also suggest that people can transcend that great enemy of activism – consumerism. It is often assumed, for example, that while people are buying, watching or selecting, they are not making or doing or even being. Certainly, the sheer pervasiveness of consumerism in contemporary life means that previously sequestered spaces – the body, the school, or even childhood itself – are now seen as fair game for marketing (Cook, 2007). Moral panics and health campaigns remind us that our mental and physical health is endangered as our hedonistic consumption culminates in an 'obesity crisis' and the 'scourge of binge drinking'. However, these moralizing discourses rarely take sufficient account of the structural, economic, political and geographical factors that shape individual behaviour (Linehan, 2006). For example, urban development and community regeneration processes have been instrumental in reorienting and rebranding cities around consumption (Valentine, 2001; see also Linehan, 2006; Minton, 2009). Consumerism may be bad for the culture but it is consistently represented as an imperative for the economy. Indeed, contemporary theorists of consumer society argue that we occupy a distinct historical period in which 'consumption' has become the primary frame of reference for our behaviours and emotions (Bauman, 2007, 2007a; Gilbert, 2008). As Bauman notes, it is largely through consumption that our social identities are forged and it is increasingly difficult – if not impossible – to conceive of human desires, emotions or needs as 'prior to', 'outside of' or 'distinct from' consumer relationships.

In our view there may be less deterministic ways of seeing consumer culture. In these terms, community arts and development processes can contribute to a more nuanced understanding of how ordinary people navigate their identities in consumer society. Contemporary cultural products may have degraded origins, their substance and presentation may owe more to the profit motive than any aesthetic vision, and they may be designed for easy disposal and replacement, but that does not mean that their use or applications can be reliably predicted. Among recognized or aspiring artists the previously controversial use of 'found objects' is now commonplace. Bland or uninteresting mass-produced items are re-appropriated and remade when they are invested with unexpected meaning: Duchamp's humble 'Fountain' or Oppenheim's

'Object' spring to mind. In the context of the gallery, where we are conscious of being addressed by 'artists', it is easier to recognize as purposeful such efforts to reanimate consumer goods. However, the capacity to subvert or appropriate might be traceable across our societies, discernible in more low-key and everyday contexts (Willis, 1990). In any case, if consumerism is all pervasive, if it cuts through all aspects of our social and cultural lives, then it is an impossibly tall order for individuals and communities – particularly those who are most marginalized or alienated – to stand firm against the tide.

It may be that critiques of consumer society may dismiss consumption too readily as an inherently passive role. For advocates of cultural democracy, a remaining challenge is to recognize and critically engage with more artful and active forms of consumption, as ordinary people negotiate and redefine the purposes of the objects they buy or, indeed, the democratic arrangements they are sold (see Willis, 1990). Otherwise we are at risk of repeating the fallacy that there is little meaningful going on in communities save what is delivered or unleashed by well meaning interventions.

CONCLUSION

Clearly the arts cannot hope to transcend the socio-economic context by force of will alone, but they can awaken people to both the negative and positive spaces that they open up. We are reminded of Dewey's comparison of the aesthetic with the 'anaesthetic' (numb, imperturbable, unmoveable), and the power of art to 'break through the crust of conventionality [...] reject the static, the automatic, the merely habitual' (Dewey, 1934, p. 48). At best, the arts can enable those most removed from the formal structures and institutions of power to communicate to those in power on their own terms in their own interests – precisely what is claimed for community development.

In exploring the potential of and for socially committed arts practice, we would therefore argue that there is a need to invigorate the concept of 'cultural democracy'. In our view, culture must be defined in broad and inclusive terms as the making of meaning through everyday living, as well as through more specialized intellectual or artistic processes (Williams, [1958] 1989). Therefore, our conception of cultural democracy accepts that cultural production is central to human experience not just by right, but as an 'evolutionary necessity' (Fyfe, 2007). It is also informed by a recognition of the centrality of consumption in contemporary society, where consumer impulses are less a matter of moral character than they are responses to a complex web of structural and social forces. To put it another way, while we may have some choice regarding the specifics of what we consume, we may have little choice but to *be* consumers. In this context to reassert the values of collectivity and productivity – values that are central to cultural democracy – is to strike a note of opposition against the current hegemony.

Such a conception of cultural democracy allows for the possibility that the multiple practices of resistance that occur within communities may contain an (albeit latent) political dimension. Without committed attention to identifying and exploring such practices, they may remain invisible or be dismissed as deviant or pathological. In this sense, we recognize that through their everyday lives and within the parameters of their consumer role, citizens will artfully and imaginatively react to, reclaim and refashion commodities and experiences. The challenge is to locate the transformative and collective potential in such practices. We therefore hope that community development can serve as a space within which otherwise atomized or individualized resistances might be supported to become part of a *common* democratic culture. Community arts practice and community development may have much to offer each other in cultivating and sustaining the kind of democratic imagination which is necessary for this task.

REFERENCES

Amin, A. (2002). Ethnicity and the multicultural city. *Environment and Planning*, 34(6), 959–980.

Bauman, Z. (2007). Liquid arts. *Theory, Culture and Society*, 24(1), 117–126.

Bauman, Z. (2007a). *Consuming life*, Cambridge: Polity Press.

Cook, D. (2007). The disempowering empowerment of children's consumer "Choice". *Society and Business Review*, 2(1), 37–52.

de Certeau, M. (1984). *The practice of everyday life*, Berkeley: University of California Press.

Dewey, J. (1934). *Art as experience*, New York: Milton, Balch & Company.

Duncombe, S. (2003). *The cultural resistance reader*, London: Verso.

Eyerman, R., & Jamison, A. (1998). *Music and social movements*, Cambridge: Cambridge University Press.

Fyfe, H. (2007). Keynote speech. *Critical connections conference*, Edinburgh: Queen Margaret University (unpublished).

Gaventa, J. (2004). 'Towards participatory local governance: Assessing the transformative potential.' In S. Hickey & G. Mohan (Eds.), *Participation: From tyranny to transformation* (pp. 25–42), London: Zed Books.

Gaventa, J. (2007). Foreword. In A. Cornwall & V. S. Soelho (Eds.), *Spaces for change: The politics of citizen participation in new democratic arenas* (pp. x-xviii), London: Zed Books.

Gilbert, J. (2008). Against the commodification of everything; Anti consumerist cultural studies in the age of ecological crisis.*Cultural Studies*, 22(5), 551–566.

Harvey, D. (2005). *A brief history of neo-liberalism*, Oxford: OUP.

Judt, T. (2010). *Ill Fares the land*, London: Allen Lane.

Kelley, R. (1996). *Race rebels*, New York: The Free Press.

Kellner, D. (1995). *Media culture – cultural studies, identity and politics between the modern and postmodern*, London: Routledge.

Linehan, D. (2006). For the way we live today: Consumption, lifestyle and identity in contemporary Ireland. In B. Bartley & R. Kitchin (Eds.), *Ireland: Contemporary Perspectives (pp. 289–300)*, Liverpool: Pluto Press.

Malik, K. (2000). *Man, beast and zombie: What science can and cannot tell us about human nature*, London: Phoenix Books/Weidenfeld and Nelson.

Matarasso, F. (01/11/2006). Amid the affluent traffic: The importance of cultural inclusion. *Presentation to national economic and social forum*, Dublin, 1 November 2006, http://www.nesf.ie/dynamic/pdfs/i.%20Matarasso.pdf (Date Accessed: 18/03/2011)

McGonagle, D. (2007). "A New Deal": art, museums and communities – re-imagining relationships. *Community Development Journal*, 42(4), 425–34.

Meade, R., & Shaw, M. (2007). Editorial. Community development and the arts: Reviving the democratic imagination. *Community Development Journal*, 42(4), 413–21.

Meade, R. (2011). Government and community development in Ireland: the contested subjects of professionalism and expertise *Antipode,* http://onlinelibrary.wiley.com/doi/10.1111/j.1467-8330.2011.00924.x/abstract

Meade, R. (2011a). Brand Ireland: Culture in the crisis. *Concept, 3*(2), 14–20.

Minton, A. (2009). *Ground Control: Fear and Happiness in the 21st Century City*, London: Penguin.

Mirza, M. (2006). The arts as painkiller. In M. Mirza (Ed.), *Culture Vultures: Is UK Arts Policy Damaging the Arts*? (pp. 93–111), London: Policy Exchange..

Mooney, G., & Neal, S. (2009). *Community: Welfare, crime and society*, Oxford: Oxford University Press.

Muukkonen, M. (2004). Between a rock and hard place – the possibilities for contemporary art institutions to function as critical political spaces. *Variant, 2,* 6–10.

Peck, J. (2009). The creativity fix. *Variant, 34,* 5–9.

Rose, N. (1996). The death of the social. *Economy and Society, 25*(3), 327–356.

Selwood, S. (2006). Unreliable evidence: The rhetoric of data collection in the cultural sector. In M. Mirza (Ed.), *Culture Vultures: Is UK Arts Policy Damaging the Arts*? (PP. 38–53), London: Policy Exchange.

Shaw, M., & Martin, I. (2000). Community work, citizenship and democracy: Re-making the connections. *Community Development Journal, 35*(4), 401–414.

Shaw, M. (2011). The big society – what's the big idea? *Concept, 2*(2), 3–6.

Valentine, G. (2001). *Social geographies*, London: Pearson.

Wilkinson, R., & Pickett, K. (2009). The spirit level: Why Equality is Better for Everyone, London: Penguin.

Williams, R. (Ed.). (1989). *Resources of hope*, London: Verso.

Willis, P. (1990). *Common culture*, Milton Keynes: Open University Press.

AFFILIATIONS

Mae Shaw
Senior Lecturer, Institute of Education, Community and Society,
Moray House School of Education,
The University of Edinburgh, Scotland

Rosie Meade
Lecturer, School of Applied Social Studies,
University College Cork, Cork, Ireland

ALEXIS KOKKOS

16. THE USE OF AESTHETIC EXPERIENCE IN UNEARTHING CRITICAL THINKING

INTRODUCTION

The contribution of aesthetic experience – as applied to the systematic exploration of works of art – to the learning process has been increasingly recognized by adult educators. However, the way aesthetic experience can be applied in the adult education framework, depends on the purpose we wish to serve. If the main purpose is to enhance the development of critical thinking and the challenge of the established norms of social reality – a position shared by the author of this chapter – then the use of aesthetic experience in the learning context is connected to the process of the critical approach towards the status quo.

Many contributions on this subject can be found in the relevant literature, developed by Dewey, the Frankfurt School, as well as scholars of critical pedagogy and transformative learning. However, there hasn't been a proposal of a comprehensive method that would embody aesthetic experience in various forms of adult education, focusing on critical consciousness. I have attempted to contribute by suggesting a method termed "Transformative Learning through Aesthetic Experience" (Kokkos, 2010). The method has been applied in several organizations in Greece, such as the Hellenic Open University, Second Chance Schools, Enterprises and the Therapy Center for Dependent Individuals (KETHEA). The method was also applied in Denmark, Romania and Sweden through the European Grundtvig Project *ARTiT: Development of Innovative Methods of Training the Trainers*, for which I am the scientific responsible.

In this report, basic theoretical approaches are presented concerning the use of aesthetic experience in the perspective of the development of critical thinking. Subsequently, the aforementioned method is presented, followed by an extended discourse on the challenges that educators are confronted with during the process of the pilot implementation.

THEORETICAL APPROACHES

Dewey set the foundations for the usefulness of aesthetic experience towards a critical understanding of the established experience. He claimed (1934/1980) that the meeting of our old assumptions with new, alternative ones, which emerge through our contact with art, results in "the reconstruction of the past" (Dewey, 1934 / 1980, p. 284), which strengthens the ability to challenge our ways of comprehension.

The contribution of the scholars of the Frankfurt School is significant (Adorno, 1941/1997, 1970/2000; Horkheimer, 1938/1984; Marcuse, 1978). They claimed that important artworks are in contrast to the instrumental rationality that is incorporated in the mechanisms of social reality. Therefore, the contact with great artworks makes possible the inversion of the alienating assumptions and regenerates the desire for human emancipation.

Additionally, Adorno (1941/1997, 1970/2000) and Horkheimer (1938/1984) determined the criteria which define a piece of art as important:

- *Holistic dimension:* The content (meaning) of a great artwork is functionally expressed through properly shaped morphological elements,[1] which in their turn reflect the essence of the artwork. Through the dialectic relation of form and content an interaction takes place among the structural and contextual elements and among each of the elements and the entire work.[2]
- *Human existence:* The issues which are approached express deep dimensions of human existence.
- *Unconventional texture:* The content and form of great works of art oppose stereotypes, standard models, one-dimensional interpretations.[3]

The trend of critical pedagogy has also contributed to the use of aesthetic experience as a means of enhancing critical consciousness. Freire himself (1970, 1978) used *'codifications'* (sketches created by important painters – see Freire, 1971, p. 114) which contained stimuli in order to discuss critically various aspects of the oppressing reality. Shor (1980, 1992) and others extended the Freireian method by using works of art including theatre, poetry and music.

Finally, during the last fifteen years the scholars who work for the development of the theoretical framework of transformative learning have suggested ways through which the works of art should be used during the learning process. Indicatively, Greene (2000) showed that the analysis of great works of literature allows us to perceive various issues in a different way than the one we tend to consider as given. Dirkx (1997) stated that contact with art is one of the key triggers that can engender the dialogue with the unconscious forces of our inner world. Kegan (2000) analyzed parts of Ibsen's *Doll's House* to show the way in which the heroine transforms her initial assumptions.

THE METHOD: "TRANSFORMATIVE LEARNING THROUGH AESTHETIC EXPERIENCE"

The method that I suggested refers to the way in which aesthetic experience should reinforce the development of critical dimensions of the learning processes, and is based on the ideas of Dewey, Adorno, Horkheimer and Freire.

It involves six stages:

- A determination of the need to critically examine an issue is activated.
- Participants express their ideas about the points of view that need to be examined.
- The educator negotiates with them on which points of view will be eventually put in critical examination and in what order.
- The educator and the participants negotiate on the artworks that should be selected as triggers for the critical approach of the various points of view.
- Critical reflection through aesthetic experience is activated. Within this stage, Perkin's model (1994) is used for the investigation of the meaning of the artworks.[4]
- The educator facilitates a critical reflection on the previous steps.

In the following sections, I will present reflections on two issues, which seemed to be most challenging for the adult educators participating in the pilot application of the method. The first one concerns the criteria according to which the educators and the participants could choose the appropriate artworks for the development of the critical learning processes. The second issue is related to the ways in which educators and learners can have access to high-quality aesthetic experience, especially those not familiar with it.

CRITERIA FOR CHOOSING ARTWORKS FOR EDUCATIONAL PURPOSES

Adult educators often wonder about the criteria which ensure that the artworks chosen are in fact appropriate. This is a complex issue. At the end of the 18th century, Kant (1790/1995) showed that the way we judge the value of artworks is subjective. Our judgment of art cannot be based on evidentiary principles or on universally accepted criteria, but it is defined by our frames of reference. This opinion is highly accepted by art theorists (e.g. Berger, 1972; Danto, 1981; Gazetas, 2000).

Therefore, when an educator wishes to incorporate the goals of critical pedagogy and transformative learning in his or her frame of reference, the criteria for choosing artworks in the learning framework should relate to the fact that the elaboration of those artworks enhances critical thinking.

Previously we examined the specific criteria on which the scholars of the Frankfurt School claim that works of art may unearth emancipatory processes. Let's now examine the examples they give in order to support their argumentation. Adorno, in *Aesthetic Theory* (1970/2000), a compendium of his beliefs on the liberating role of art, includes numerous references to Bach, Beethoven, Mozart, Schubert, Picasso, Rembrandt, Klee, Baudelaire, Euripides, Goethe, Proust, Shakespeare. Marcuse (1978) refers to Beethoven, Aeschylus, Beckett, Baudelaire, Brecht, Goethe, Kafka, Proust, Rimbaud, Shakespeare.

We have also seen other theorists who connect aesthetic experience to the development of critical thinking, referring to many of the aforementioned artists or to others equally acknowledged. For instance, Dewey refers to the works of Cézanne, Goya, Matisse, Rembrandt, Renoir, van Gogh, Keats, Mann, Shakespeare. Perkins

(1994) analyses works of Klee, Matisse, Rembrandt, van Gogh, while Greene (2000) refers mostly to Beethoven, Cézanne, Goya, Monet, Picasso, van Gogh, Velázquez, Camus, Eliot, Flaubert, Joyce, Sartre, Woolf.

It follows from the above that there is a significant convergence of theorists that the great works of visual arts, music, literature and theatre are most suitable as a means of triggering critical reflection in an educational setting.

However, Pierre Bourdieu (1979, 1985, 1969/1991) approached the issue of attitude towards artworks from a different perspective. He highlighted the social causes of aesthetic criteria and preferences. He claimed that social groups with cultural qualifications which are obtained through education but also, imperceptibly, through the friction within the cultural environment, show a positive predisposition towards works of art considered to be great from the dominant value system, as opposed to other social groups. They acknowledge the aesthetic value of those works and have the will to approach them. At the same time, they have developed the capability to decipher the codes of the messages that emerge from such artworks. On the contrary, those who were deprived of educational qualifications in their childhood, usually form a negative or a neutral attitude towards 'significant' works of art, as they find it difficult to comprehend their meaning: "The poorer the educational background, the weaker the informational and audio content of the message actually received by the recipient is more likely to be" (Bourdieu, 1985, p. 384). Therefore, those who do not possess a cultural capital avoid coming in contact with works of art which are considered significant[5]. Thus, the assumption that non-privileged social groups do not have the 'spiritual ability' of the cultivated ones is interiorized in the social consciousness and contributes to the reproduction of social inequality structures.

Based on this rationale, Bourdieu went one step further. He listed the works of art in three categories of *'taste'*, i.e, the expression of aesthetic preference. In the first category, he enlisted the works of artists who correspond to what he calls *'legal taste'*, meaning that they are considered in western contemporary societies to be great (Bourdieu, 1979, p. 14–16). The French scholar enlists for example artworks of Bach, Mahler, Stravinsky, Braque, Goya, Kandinsky, Picasso, Flaubert, Beckett,Pinter. It is quite obvious that the works of art of the *'legal taste'* category correspond to the category that scholars such as Dewey, Adorno, Marcuse, Perkins and Greene believe to trigger critical reflection.

Bourdieu enlists the rest of artworks in two more categories:

a) Those corresponding to *'medium taste'*, meaning works considered to be of lesser significance, although they derive from major forms of art (classical music, visual arts, literature), such as, for instance, Strauss's waltzes, paintings by Utrillo or Buffet, as well as significant works from inferior forms of art (mainstream songs, folk dancing, operettas, etc).

b) The creations corresponding to *'popular taste'*, which refer to mass culture creations which do not wish to belong in the sphere of significant art (for instance, most 'entertaining' songs, melodrama, 'boulevard' theatre, music-hall, etc) and also works of art of the two previous categories whose value has been distorted as they were spread, through commercialized forms of consumption, without any consideration on quality. Examples of works of art being subject to such exploitation are the *Traviata* and *The Blue Danube* (ibid, p. 16).

Bourdieu's contribution on social predispositions towards works of art may be connected to the subject of choosing works of art for educational purposes in two ways. On the one hand, if important works of art are used in the educational process, it is probable to reproduce inequalities among the learners, as these works attract those equipped with the corresponding educational background. On the other hand, Bourdieu's approach does not oppose the argument of those who claim that the great works of art can essentially lead to a process of emancipation against contemporary alienating challenges.

In conclusion, in the framework of adult education that adopts the principles of critical pedagogy and transformative learning, every possible effort should be made to render high-quality aesthetic experience accessible to learners who were deprived of it. They should be positively reinforced towards great works of art in order for them to use the appropriate ones to serve their educational goals. Through this process it is possible to empower their critical attitude towards social-economic norms, but also to diminish the educational inequalities amongst themselves.

How can this be possible? It is important that we provide a comprehensive account of the means whereby educators and learners can be assisted in their familiarization with the liberating force of art. The next section presents some reflections on this matter.

ACCESS TO AESTHETIC EXPERIENCE

The literature shows that scholars concerned with the development of critical thinking through art-based learning (e.g. Dewey, Greene, Perkins) make suggestions, but do not offer specific educational conditions that would help those excluded from a high-level aesthetic experience to gain access to it.

On the other hand, a literature survey on the educational activities that are rapidly developing in museums, art galleries and libraries, shows that, although this movement aims to attract a wide range of social groups by highlighting the relationship of artworks to their social experience, it doesn't emphasize ways to develop their ability to perceive the meaning of works of high aesthetic value (e.g. Illeris, 2011; Sifakakis, 2007; Thompson, 2002).

Finally, the study of Bourdieu contains rare and vaguely formulated references to the way the educational system could reinforce the positive disposition of all social groups towards art. For instance:

> Indeed, only an institution whose special role is to transmit the qualities that define the cultivated human being to most people through learning and practicing, only

> such an institution could counterbalance (at least partially) the lack for those, who don't find the motivation for cultural practice in the context of their families (Bourdieu, 1985, p. 383) [...]. It is known that with the same cost the increase of schooling years or the increase of the hours of teaching art would in the long term lead incomparably more people to museums, theatres and concerts (ibid, p. 385) [...]. However, the ability of using the encrypted code of education can only be reached through the process of systematic learning, organized by an institution especially developed for this purpose (ibid, p. 385–386).

However, Freire's ideas offer answers to the issue at hand. Freire realized that some groups of students found it difficult to study the significant philosophical-political texts in depth, and developed ways that would prompt their familiarization with that form of studying. He mentions, for example:

> Of course, most of the new generation of Brazillian students, don't know how to write in the way demanded by the universities. This is a problem. Some professors say, "I have nothing to do with this because my task here is to teach Hegel. If they are not able to understand Hegel, this is *their* problem *not* mine" (Shor & Freire, 1987, p. 83).

> Then, my rigor and my political position lead me to help the students by teaching them to read. How can I do that? I do that *simultaneously* with reading Hegel! That is, instead of telling the students, you have to read the first chapter of this book by Hegel or this book by Gramsci, I read one chapter with them in the whole time of the seminar. I read with them, without telling them I am teaching them how to read, what it means to read critically, what demands you make on yourself to read, that it's impossible to go to the next page without understanding the page you are on, that if you don't understand some words you have to go to a dictionary. If a normal dictionary does not help you, you have to go to a philosophical dictionary, a sociological dictionary, an etymological dictionary! Reading a book is a kind of permanent research. I do that with the students (ibid, p. 84).

Freire mentions the possibility of introducing significant books to learners, as long as some principles are followed during the educational process, such as the persistent concern of the facilitator to support participants with learning difficulties, the inspirational and participatory way of teaching rather than the sterile academic way, as well as the careful approach to the texts, gradually increasing the level of difficulty.

A series of experiences from the field of adult education has shown that following the above principles can allow participants to gain access to great artworks, even if they were not familiar with them in the past. For instance, in some educational programs for seniors, or at Second Chance Schools and Therapy Centers for Dependent Individuals, participants seemed able to comprehend and enjoy fine artworks when the learning conditions were appropriate (Darrough, 1992; Gibbons, 1985; Myers, 1992; Gogou & Barlos, 2011; Giannakopoulou *et al.*, 2011).

Therefore, it is my contention that Freire's ideas on accessing important works of literature could be applied respectively in the case of learners' accessing of works of fine art. What follows are some suggestions, as well as practice examples from the project *ARTiT*.

FORMING ATTITUDES AND CAPABILITIES OF ADULT EDUCATORS

An issue that should be addressed firstly is how positive the adult educators' attitude is towards significant works of art and how capable they are of evaluating and elaborating on them, in order to coordinate relative processes addressed to learners.

We attempted to explore this issue within the framework of the *ARTiT* project, with the contribution of the sociologist of culture Spyros Sifakakis. 18 adult educators from 6 different organizations implemented the project's art-based methodology.[6] They accepted to answer the question "Which are your three favorite works of art from fine arts, literature/poetry/theater, movies and music? List the title of each artwork and the name of the artist." We evaluated the answers according to the criteria proposed by the Frankfurt school in order to determine if an artwork can unearth critical thinking. The artworks that were mentioned by the educators were graded with 3 if they fully met those criteria, with 2 if they met them fairly and with 1 if they hardly met them. Also graded with 1 was the failure of referring to any work of art, because we considered this to be a strong indication of lacking familiarity with works belonging to the two previous categories. The opinions expressed by 16 of the 18 educators mostly ranked around 2, while the average mark was exactly 2.0.

This approach, although quantitatively limited, offers indications that several adult educators are fairly positive towards great works of art, but have not completely mastered the way of distinguishing them from trivial ones. Therefore, the adult educational organizations should assist educators in developing a positive attitude towards significant works of art, as well as their ability to decipher and use them for educational purposes in a fruitful way.

DEVELOPMENT OF TRAINING THE EDUCATORS

It is crucial for educational organizations to train adult educators on criteria for the evaluation of works of art, as well as on techniques to use them during the learning process. Additionally, educators should learn how to use artworks to critically approach the issues at hand. In the *ARTiT* project, for instance, educators were trained to elaborate critical questions on various issues using an archive of works of art we had developed. For instance, for the subject of "Relationships between genders", critical questions were posed, such as:

a. How do we perceive unpaid work at home?
b. How do men perceive the inequality between the female-male role?
c. What do men think when they realize their spouses actually work more than them?

d. Why are there inequalities between male and female roles?
e. What do we think of men taking over female roles (household chores, raising the children, etc)?
f. What do we think of the 'female mystery' nowadays?
g. Is manhood in danger in our days?
h. How does the gender inequality affect sexuality?

Sixteen works of art were proposed in order to trigger the elaboration of the specific critical questions, as shown in the following table. Participants could select the critical questions they would like to address or create new ones. They could also choose which of the artworks would be used.

Proposed works of art	Suggested Critical Questions							
	a	b	c	d	i	f	g	h
1. *Girl Peeling Vegetables,* Jean-Baptiste-Simeon Chardin **(FA)**	✓	✓	✓	✓	✓			
2. *The Laundress,* Ştefan Luchian **(FA)**	✓	✓	✓	✓	✓			
3. *Rest in the field,* Camil Ressu **(FA)**		✓	✓	✓	✓			
4. *Life,* Pablo Picasso **(FA)**						✓	✓	✓
5. *The Wave,* Camille Claudel **(FA)**						✓		
6. *The Rape,* Edgar Degas **(FA)**				✓			✓	✓
7. *Diego and I,* Frida Kahlo **(FA)**				✓		✓	✓	✓
8. *Ali: Fear eats the soul,* Rainer Werner Fassbinder **(F)**				✓	✓		✓	✓
9. *Dogtooth,* Yiorgos Lanthimos **(F)**						✓	✓	
10. *Ginger & Fred,* Federico Fellini **(F)**						✓	✓	✓
11. *Reconstruction,* Theo Angelopoulos **(F)**	✓	✓		✓	✓	✓	✓	✓
12. *The Bell Jar,* Sylvia Plath **(L)**						✓		
13. *The eyes of the poor,* Charles Baudelaire **(L)**				✓		✓		
14. *Freedom of love,* André Breton **(L)**						✓		
15. *Eveline,* James Joyce **(L)**		✓			✓	✓		✓
16. *Like a rolling stone,* Bob Dylan **(M)**						✓		✓
FA: Fine Arts, **F:** Films, **L:** Literature, **M:** Music								

After the educators were familiarized with this method, they applied it in their educational settings. Learners worked in groups, forming critical questions on several subjects and choosing works of art to be used for the elaboration of those questions.

THE PARTICIPATION OF THE LEARNERS

The active participation of the learners is fundamental in every adult education project in order to create an atmosphere of interaction, mutual understanding and emotional expression, which is a precondition for the development of the learning process. With regard to the increase of participation during the process of choosing works of art, four alternative ways – or combinations of those – were suggested:

- The educators propose several different works of art and participants choose the ones they prefer, as well as the order in which they want to work with them.
- The educators suggest resources for the learners to choose the works of art they prefer.
- The educators offer the criteria for searching and choosing artworks, followed by a discussion with the trainers on the works of art that will be used.
- First, participants propose the works of art of their preference, followed by a discussion with the educators on the works of art that will be used.

Whatever the process of choosing works of art, participants were encouraged to choose those which inspired them, expressed them and related to their experiences. For this reason, before discussing a subject, all the relative chosen artworks were presented to participants, followed by a discourse on which ones would be chosen to be used and in which order.

HANDLING TENSIONS

However, handling a discourse on choosing and elaborating on works of art can be challenging. Some participants disagree with the educators' proposals based on the criteria they endorsed during their socialization, and counter-propose works of art or interpretations which possibly embedded codes of the dominant cultural system. It is also possible that they strongly insist on their opinion, as they are emotionally attached to these artworks.

Several ways of handling possible tensions have been designed in the *ARTiT* framework.

Firstly, it was made clear to the groups of learners that great works of art are not only to be found in exhibitions or encyclopedias, but also many are already known to them from everyday experience. For instance, works from folk poetry can be used, as well as folk dancing and paintings and songs whose music and lyrics are of high aesthetic value.

Secondly, we made sure that the great majority of the artworks that we proposed are of high standards but also to be appreciated in a straightforward manner. On some occasions however, when it is not possible to find works with those characteristics to address an issue, we alternatively proposed other ones that we feel belong to the intermediate level of our 1–3 scale or, alternatively, high-standard works that would possibly require more effort.

Finally, given that the correlation between the content and the elements of the form of a work of art is quite complex, this approach did not take place in the first phases of the elaboration of an artwork, but in the latter ones. On the other hand, participants were encouraged to focus on the elements of the form, in order to give the approach a holistic dimension. The depth of this procedure depended on their mood, as well as on the level of confidence the educators felt could efficiently support the attempt.

SOME RESULTS

The *ARTiT* project offered ample opportunity to apply these specifications. The archive given to the groups of learners consisted of 98 works of art. 73 of those ranked 3 on our scale and 25 ranked 2, with an average of 2.7. Almost all the groups showed a preference to works of high aesthetic value. Within the groups, a total of 49 works were chosen, reaching the same average with the *ARTiT* archive. This is clearly a positive sign, if we compare this data to the preferences the educators had expressed in the beginning of the project, with an average mark of 2.0. Therefore, we can presume that when some requirements are met, it is possible for both educators and learners to develop a positive attitude towards great works of art and prefer those to trivial ones.

The answers of the 186 participants constitute a further indication concerning the development of their attitude towards contact with art. At the beginning of the pilot implementation they were asked "Do you like Art?" and they answered: "a great deal" 24%, "much" 33%, "somewhat" 24%, "little" 17%, "not at all" 2%. At the end of the implementation they were asked "Did you like the training through the use of works of art which was conducted in the framework of ARTiT?" Their answers show a significant evolution of their familiarization with – high standard – aesthetic experience: "a great deal" 37%, "much" 44%, "somewhat" 13%, "little" 3%, "not at all" 3%.

Some characteristic explanations that participants gave in their answers in the latter question were:

- I liked it because it helped me find out more about art in general and the training process helped us describe ourselves and understand better the relations between people.
- I was amazed to see how we can interpret a painting and how we can draw a conclusion to such interesting topics.

– I look art in a different way now.
– Great idea! Art became more interesting for us!

Also, according to the observation task-sheet that the educators filled out, it was noted that they themselves as well as the learners enjoyed the chosen artworks and used them creatively. More specifically, based on the 1–5 Likert scale, the average ranks of the educators' comments were as follows: "The learners liked the lesson": 4.6; "I liked the lesson" 4.7; "The learners appreciated the contribution of art to our discussion": 4.7. It is also quite evident that the use of aesthetic experience contributed in unearthing critical thinking on the issues at hand ("My students re-examined stereotyped ideas or assumptions": 4.3). We hope this last finding will be verified by the results we expect to accrue from the comparative content analysis of the essays composed by participants in the beginning and at the end of the function of their learning groups.

EPILOGUE

Nevertheless, we must be alert against difficulties that may emerge. Critical reflection on taken for granted assumptions, combined with the understanding of art is a complex process. It requires persistence, patience and empathy to meet the goal – an attitude for life – in order to take the next steps. At the end of the journey the reward may be the empowerment of the learners, as they will be able to explore the issues they study holistically and obtain a more open perception of the world. Even we, the adult educators, may encounter some creative sides of ourselves.

NOTES

[1] For example, concerning a film, some of the basic morphological elements are the mode of narration, the visual dimension (frame choice and composition, scale, perspective), the sound design, the editing (continuity, montage, rhythm, etc). Respectively, in a literary text some of the basic structural elements are the narration point of view, the moment or the incidents described, the time period of the characters' life; in music, basic structural elements would be the rhythm, the melody, the musical instruments used, the tempo, etc; in paintings, the color, the shape, the lines, the form, etc.

[2] As an opposite example, Adorno (1941/1997) has stated the characteristics of musical works of the cultural industry: there is no relation between the components; the beginning and the end of each part follow standard patterns; not much importance is given to the whole feeling of the music work – the emphasis is on individual elements, such as effect, style, volume, beat, refrain; the music work in general "exempts from the effort to participate" (ibid, p. 183).

[3] As an example of the difference between a great work of art and a conventional one, we could compare the masterpiece by Kurosawa *The Seven Samurai* to *The Magnificent Seven*, starring Yul Brynner and Steve Mc Queen. The two films are based on the same plot: seven professional fighters agree to save a village from bandits. In the first film, there is a dialectical presentation of numerous diachronic situations of the human experience: The solidarity among the villagers is mixed up with the element of individualism; although they respect the Samurai, they don't trust them; heroism coexists with fear; the reason the Samurai agree to protect the village is to make a living, but at the same time they obey the code of the honorable warrior; love is massacred in this setting (a young woman is brutally punished by her father for having an affair with a Samurai, an action that violates the norms

of the community). The second movie is full of stereotypes, typical of cultural industry products. The contradictions are simplified; the cowboy-saviors are fearless; for them fighting is entertaining; the reason they protect the village is their 'free rider' mentality (they find it more 'interesting' than working at a saloon). The love story has a happy ending (the young woman's father does not appear, she is free to live her life as she wants, and the cowboy lover gives up his reckless life to stay with her).

[4] Perkins's model discusses the way learners are capable of penetrating, through a series of questions posed by the educator, into the meaning of artworks.

[5] For instance, museums in France were visited every year in the 60's by 1% of farmers, 4% of workers, and 45% of 'higher social groups' (Bourdieu, 1969/1991, p15). A recent study verifies that those who are actively interested in art visit museums and are attracted by significant plays and movies are 9% of the population and of high educational background. Conversely, 41% of the population is remotely – if at all – interested in art, and come from social groups of low income and/or education. (Arts Counsil, 2008).

[6] Denmark is represented by Roskilde University and Vucfyn; Greece by the Hellenic Adult Education Association and the Hellenic Open University; Romania by the University of Pitesti and Sweden by ABF.

REFERENCES

Adorno, T. (1941/1997). *The sociology of music* (Trans. T. Loupasakis, G. Sagriotis, F. Terzakis). Athens: Nepheli.
Adorno, T. (1970/2000). *Aesthetic theory* (Trans. L. Anagnostou). Athens: Alexandreia.
Arts Council (2008). *Arts audiences: Insight*. London, U.K.: The Colourhouse.
Berger, J. (1972). *Ways of seeing*. London, U.K.: Penguin Books.
Bourdieu, P., & Darbal, A. (1969/1991). *The love of art: European art museums and their public*. Cambridge: Polity Press.
Bourdieu, P. (1979). *La distinction: Critique sociale du jugement de gout*. Paris: Editions de Minuit.
Bourdieu, P. (1985). The school as a conservative force: Scholastic and cultural inequalities. In A. Fragoudaki (Ed.), *Sociology of Education: Theories on Social Inequalities in School* (pp. 357–391). Athens: Papazisis.
Danto, A. (1981). *The transfiguration of the commonplace*. Harvard University Press.
Darrough, G. P. (1992). Making choral music with older adults. *Music Educators Journal, 79*, 27–29.
Dewey, J. (1934/1980). *Art as experience*. USA: The Penguin Group.
Dirkx, J. (1997). Nurturing soul in adult learning. In P. Cranton (Ed.), *Transformative learning in action: Insights from practice* (pp. 79–88). New Directions for Adult and Continuing Education, no 74. San Francisco, CA: Jossey – Bass.
Freire, P. (1970). *Pedagogy of the oppressed*. New York, N.Y.: Herder and Herder.
Freire, P. (1971). *L'Education: Pratique de la Liberté* [Education: The Practice of Freedom]. Paris: CERF.
Freire, P. (1978). *Lettres à la guinée – Bissau sur l' alphabétisation* [Letters to Guinea – Bissau on Literacy]. Paris: Maspero.
Gazetas, A. (2000). *Imagining selves: The politics of representation, film narratives, and adult education*. New York, N.Y.: Peter Lang Publishing.
Giannakopoulou, M., Deliyannis, D., Ziozias, A., & Chadoulitsi, V. (2011). Educational experimentations at the alternative adult school of KETHEA "EXODOS". In A. Kokkos & Associates (Eds.), *Education through Art* (pp. 138–158). Athens: Metaixmio.
Gibbons, A. C. (1985). Stop babying the elderly. *Music Educators Journal, 71*, 48–51.
Greene, M. (2000). *Releasing the imagination*. San Francisco, C.A.: Jossey-Bass.
Gogou, V., & Barlos, A. (2011). Transforming perceptions through aesthetic experience at the second chance school of larisa. In A. Kokkos & Associates (Eds.), *Education through Art* (pp. 159–190). Athens: Metaixmio.
Horkheimer, M. (1938/1984). Art and mass culture. In T. Adorno et al, *Art and Mass Culture* (Trans. Z. Sarikas) (pp. 49–68). Athens: Ypsilon.
Illeris, H. (2011). Employability or empowerment? – learning in art galleries. *Lifelong Learning in Europe, 2/2011*, 82–95.

Kant, E. (1790/1995). *Critique de la faculté de juger* [Critique of judgement]. Paris: Flammarion.
Kegan, R. (2000). What «Form» Transforms? A constructive-developmental approach to transformative learning. In J. Mezirow & Associates (Eds.) *Learning as Transformation: Critical Perspectives on a Theory in Progress* (pp. 35–70). San Francisco, C.A.: Jossey-Bass.
Kokkos, A. (2010). Transformative learning through aesthetic experience: Towards a comprehensive method. *Journal of Transformative Education, 80*, 155–177. See also *http://jtd.sagepub.com/content/early/2011/06/29/1541344610397663*, 1–23.
Marcuse, H. (1978). *The aesthetic dimension*. Boston, M.A.: Beacon Press.
Myers, D.E. (1992). Teaching learners of all ages. *Music Educators Journal, 79*, 23–26.
Perkins, D. (1994). *The intelligent eye*. Los Angeles, C.A.: Harvard Graduate School of Education.
Shor, I. (1980). *Critical teaching and everyday life*. Montréal, Canada: Black Rose Books.
Shor, I. (1992). *Empowering education*. Chicago, IL: The University of Chicago Press.
Shor, I., & Freire, P. (1987). *A pedagogy for liberation*. New York, N.Y.: Bergin and Garvey.
Sifakakis, S. (2007). Contemporary art's audiences. *European Journal of Cultural Studies, 10*, 203–223.
Thompson, J. (2002). *Bread and roses: Arts, culture and lifelong learning*. Leicester, UK: NIACE.

AFFILIATION

Alexis Kokkos
Professor and Dean of the School of Humanities,
Hellenic Open University, Athens

PALLE RASMUSSEN

17. THE FOLK HIGH SCHOOL: DENMARK'S CONTRIBUTION TO ADULT EDUCATION

INTRODUCTION

The folk high school is a model of adult education, developed in Denmark during the last half of the 19th century. Folk high schools are most often boarding schools offering short or longer non-vocational courses. There is a large variety of teaching subjects, both theoretical and practical. Teaching emphasizes the development of personal, social and civic competencies, and discussion and collaboration have an important role. There are no final exams.

The folk high school model grew out of a special historical situation. In Denmark, as in many other countries, the idea of adult education was initially a by-product of the idea of basic school education for all children. Adult education was included in the plan for a general system of basic public education which was developed by the absolutist monarchy around year 1800. This work was partly inspired by the philosophy of enlightenment, and alongside public basic education for all, the plan made provision for voluntary evening classes for young people and adults. However, by the time the reform was introduced, the state did not have the resources to implement it. The Danish state was bankrupt, having chosen the wrong side in the Napoleonic wars. The basic school system was built up slowly during the first half of 19th century, and the evening classes spread even slower.

The early state initiatives in adult education were in fact overtaken by the folk high schools, which were an education initiative from below, inspired especially by ideas developed by Nikolaj Grundtvig.

THE EDUCATIONAL IDEAS OF NIKOLAJ GRUNDTVIG

Nikolaj F. S. Grundtvig (1783–1872) was a pastor and bishop, but also a poet, philosopher, historian and politician (Lawson 1993). In Grundtvig's early writing the dominant idea was Danish national consolidation based on Lutheran Christianity. Gradually new ideas emerged, not least in articles in the journal 'Danne-Virke' which Grundtvig himself published from 1816. He now refrained from basing the enlightenment of the people in the Christian faith and the revelations described in the Bible. Instead the emphasis was on what he later called 'Christianity as an outlook'. This entails a distinction between on one hand

Christian faith and on the other Christian recognition of the human being as a creation, a recognition that, in Grundtvig's view, can be shared by all spiritual people regardless of their position towards Christianity. He further argued that the Nordic people have special resources for developing a genuine Christian outlook, because they have a tradition of natural religious feeling which manifests itself in deep deference towards what has been inherited and a stable conviction of the presence of an all-mighty god and a governing providence (Grell 1998, p. 15 f.) For Grundtvig this was the elementary humanity on which popular education should be based.

Grundtvig saw popular and human life in the early 19th century as being in a state of crisis. The reason for this was a false conception of humanity, the consequences of which had become evident through the French revolution. During his stay in England in 1829, Grundtvig had also seen symptoms of this crisis. In Oxford and Cambridge he had witnessed a type of scientific thought that he found completely out of touch with the reality of English society, and for that reason also unable to have an impact on social reality. The dominant form of science and its human values had led to disintegration, emptiness and powerlessness in the face of contemporary social reality.

As an alternative, Grundtvig envisaged a type of scientific knowledge that 'not only extends to all that is knowable, but embraces it as a living idea and with a common purpose, which is the enlightenment of human life in all its directions and relationships' (Grundtvig 2011, p. 62). He was well aware that scientific thought is different from popular learning and life, but he claimed that a scientific approach must connect to popular learning in order not to be derailed. The broad mass of people would not be able to unite these two types of thinking, but they should not be allowed to exist in isolation from each other, because scientific thinking would then degenerate into lack of spirituality and popular learning into superficiality. He argued that only through the native tongue can the living historical outlook and through it true humanity manifest itself as a determining element in human being's lives. Through its history and its mother tongue any people has the mission to contribute to a growing understanding of the true relation between the creator and his work. Grundtvig also used the concept of the popular spirit, which has the power to connect a people to its history.

The reorientation of Grundtvig's ideas also led to a clarification of his views on popular education (Grell, 1998). He now saw the school and education as an independent factor in a people's life, alongside the church and the state.

A key text for understanding Grundtvig's views on popular education and the folk high school is 'The Danish Four-leaf Clover or A Partiality for Danishness' published in 1836 (included in Grundtvig, 2011). His argument here includes a distancing from the traditional schooling based on the Latin language and heritage, which dominated Danish as well as European higher education at the time. Latin schooling is described as 'the school of death' in contrast to the school for life, which has its basis in the Christian outlook (rather than faith) and which aims at historically informed learning for the benefit of civic life and society. Learning must establish an educated culture, which will empower the people to manifest influence in the popular council of state.

The high school was envisaged primarily as a school for popular and civic life. However, Grundtvig also described a somewhat different type of high school, the one he proposed for establishment at the Soroe Academy. This was to educate civil servants and representatives elected to the assembly of social estates that had been established by the King.

In the folk high school the most important subjects to be taught were to be the mother tongue and national history. There was also to be teaching in the national constitutional framework and in geography, science and literature.

From around 1845 the increasing tension between Denmark and Germany influenced Grundtvig's views on popular education and prompted him to emphasize the Danish culture as an independent one. 'Danishness' was now seen as true human creation in a popular form. In Denmark the 'popular school' had the upper hand in relation to the 'big machinery', and this benefitted sound thinking not only in relation to 'craft activity' but also in relation to 'life earlier and now' with its virtues and vicissitudes.

The most important text on the high school from this period is probably "A Congratulation to Denmark on the Danish Dimwit and the Danish High School", published in 1847 (included in Grundtvig, 2011). The background was that the King had announced his decision to establish a Danish high school in Soroe, following Grundtvig's proposal (in the end the project was not realized). In this text Grundtvig attacks both Latin education and German culture, but he emphasized that Danishness does not exclude connections to other cultures, and that Danishness 'is happy to welcome, appreciate, extol, and as far as possible acquire all that is so-called 'foreign' (...), so as not to miss out on what is universal and common to all mankind, and in which of course everything that is truly 'of the people' will eventually find its purpose and be illuminated' (Grundtvig 2011, p. 320).

Grundtvig saw a risk that the school could make its student dabblers in scientific thinking. Because of that his preferred students were young people who had already found work in a practical occupation to which they could return after a spell at the high school. In a speech given in the newly established Parliament in 1849 he argues that not childhood but youth is the right age for education and enlightenment. In that phase of life '...all great questions about the calling and mission of human beings' awaken or may be awakened' (Grell 1998, p. 37).

THE DANISH FOLK HIGH SCHOOL MOVEMENT

Grundtvig's model of popular adult education contained a unique combination of elements. The high schools were to enhance young people's commitment to and competence in developing agriculture, but teaching was to be dominated by general and cultural subjects. The schools were to be independent of the state, but a main purpose was to boost national culture and consciousness. Christianity was part of the ideological basis but Grundtvig's kind of Christianity was more open and joyous than mainstream Protestantism. Teaching was to be based on 'the living word', i.e. oral narration and discussion. It was to take place in Danish and be based on Danish culture and literature. There were not to be any examinations and the students were to live-in at the schools so that they shared not only learning but also everyday life and its practical activities.

The folk high school idea achieved great impact and became a kind of social movement (Gundelach 1988, p 115 f.). A main reason for this was that the idea had strong resonance among the Danish farmers, who increasingly manifested themselves as the population group ensuring the economic and social basis of society by means of their work and their ability to organise production (Korsgaard, 2000). This latter quality was demonstrated in the years after 1870, when the growth of free trade in the world market made large quantities of cheep grain from Russia and the United States available in Europe. Danish agriculture managed to survive this crisis by changing fairly quickly from grain to animal products, and it managed to introduce the new products and technologies through co-operative ventures, without giving up small and medium-size farming. This kind of experience made the farmers a self-conscious class; but for several decades, even after the formal introduction of democracy, the landowners and other conservative forces denied them access to political power and the cultural resources of established society.

Another reason for the success of the folk high schools was a widespread sense of national purpose following the war with Prussia in 1864 over the Schleswig-Holstein question. In this war Denmark lost a significant part of its territory, and while there was little prospect of regaining this there was a strong desire to strengthen Danish society in other ways. Enrico Dalgas, who worked to transform moor areas to fertile land, coined the phrase 'what is lost externally must be won internally', and such ideas also spurred efforts in culture and education.

The first folk high school, established in Rødding in 1844, was in fact closely linked to the Schleswig-Holstein question. It was based on funds collected to support Danish culture and language in these mixed German-Danish provinces. The school was inspired by Grundtvig's ideas and led by people subscribing to them, although Grundtvig himself seems to have had little contact with it. The school was situated in the area ceded to Germany and had to close after the war but was re-established in Danish territory as Askov High School, one of the most famous and still existing schools.

From 1860 onwards many folk high schools were established in rural districts all over Denmark. One of the main actors was Christen Kold (Bjerg, 1994). He had grown up in the countryside, attended a teacher training school and worked as house teacher. He was strongly religious, in a more traditional protestant sense, but with his social background he was able to implement Grundtvig's ideas successfully at Ryslinge Folk High School, which opened in 1851.

By 1880 there were 64 folk high schools which were attended by some 3.300 students. Schools were residential, and courses normally lasted between 3 and 5 months. Most schools were co-educational, but often the men went to school in the winter, when there was less work to be done in fields, while the women went in spring and summer.

The folk high schools took part in paving the way for the introduction of parliamentary democracy in Denmark around the turn of the century (Borish,1991). The theory and practice of the folk high schools had a great impact on the Danish educational tradition, not only in the area of adult education but also, for example, in basic school education and teacher training. The high school movement created and spread an educational ideal that was anti-elitist and liberal, that emphasised oral presentation and dialogue, and that linked education to national and local rather than international culture.

The folk high school model also dominated Danish adult education in the years after the turn of the century, but in more differentiated forms. While the first wave of high schools had mainly been associated with Grundtvigian ideology, other religious and political movements now also took up the idea. One of these was the workers' movement, which established residential schools with a view to training the movements' representatives and activists. In the years when the farmers had been struggling to gain political power, the processes of industrialisation and urbanisation had also got under way, and the social democratic party was growing strong.

For the great majority of workers in the towns, a stay at a folk high school was not really an option. They had to find other means of developing their knowledge and improving their qualifications. The adult education that gradually was developed in the towns, for the most part, took the form of evening courses. Some of the early courses were ideologically influenced and organised by the workers' movement and radical intellectuals. One example is the "Students' Association's evening classes for workers", which started in Copenhagen around 1880. There were also courses in general skills like writing and arithmetic, often initiated by employers or local public authorities.

Adult education in the workers' movement was gradually strengthened, and in 1924 the "Workers Educational Association" was established. Activities such as these paved the way for the liberal evening school, which was institutionalised in a unique way in the nineteen forties. A scheme was adopted which allowed and supported teaching by voluntary associations linked to different ideologies and movements. The basic idea was that when a number of people assemble with a teacher and a programme or a subject, they are entitled to support from public funds. All the main political parties have had their own educational associations offering evening courses in both practical subjects (like housekeeping), general subjects (like languages) and ideological issues. In continuation of the folk high school these evening schools had no sharp distinction between cultural and vocational rationality.

The existence of this tradition also meant that when adult education was made part of welfare and labour market policies it retained a strong humanistic dimension (Olesen & Rasmussen, 1996).

INTERNATIONAL IMPACT

Before long the success of the folk high school movement also inspired educators outside Denmark to establish adult education institutions based on the same principles. This happened first in Norway and Sweden, two other Nordic countries with close cultural and historical ties and related languages. The first Norwegian folk high school started in 1864 and the first Swedish school in 1866. Especially in Sweden the schools played a role in developing the civic culture. At the time parts of the liberal elites were focusing on the common cultural origins of the three countries and promoting stronger collaboration among them, including political collaboration. Grundtvig, who had done much work on Nordic history, was one of the intellectuals participating in this venture, and the establishment of folk high schools in Norway and Sweden could be seen as part of a greater common Nordic project.

Another factor that contributed to spreading the folk high school idea to other countries was migration. Around 1900 many Danes migrated to North America, and some of them established adult education activities. Partly because of this, but also through international communication and cooperation among educators, the folk high school model became known in the US and in Canada (Kulich, 1964; Bugge, 1999). In these countries the model was not widely adopted, but a limited number of schools were established. Much later a leading American radical educator, Myles Horton, was to spend time in Denmark and reinvent the idea of the Folk High School in Tennessee. This took the form of an important school for social movement education, including leadership education, known as Highlander Folk High School (Horton & Freire, 1990).

In the years following the First World War the folk high school became known in many countries around the world. A feature of this period was a strong feeling that education should contribute to international and intercultural understanding, and there were many initiatives to collaborate across borders in developing progressive educational practices. The folk high school model fitted this ambition well, and school projects were started in different countries. For instance two folk high schools were established in Japan. However, the growing international tensions that in the end led to the Second World War meant that much of this work was discontinued.

Although the folk high schools established in different countries followed some of the same principles and generally acknowledged their inspiration from Grundtvig, their character and role depended on local needs and conditions. An example is the origin of folk high schools in Poland (Kulich, 2002, p 50 f.). Here the existence of such schools in Denmark and Sweden had become known around 1890, and ten years later two folk high schools were established for rural youth, one for men and one for women. The schools were situated in the part of Poland controlled by Russia;

to obtain permission from the Russian authorities they had to be called 'agricultural courses'. They were not to teach Polish language, literature and history, and books and notes were banned. In fact these subjects were taught anyway and books and notes were hidden when official inspection took place. By 1914 seven such schools were in operation in the Russian part of Poland. There is no doubt that these folk high schools responded not only to the need for general training of rural youth, but also to a growing sense of Polish national identity. The war ended the work of these schools but after 1920 new initiatives were taken, not least by the educator Ignacy Solarez, and more than 20 folk high schools were active in the inter-war years. These had strong links to the Polish peasant movement and some of them were closed by the conservative government.

Another example comes from adult education in Tanzania. Following independence (Tanganyika in 1960 and Zanzibar in 1964), Tanzania embraced the Folk High School concept. During the presidency of Julius Nyerere, the concept was reinvented with a view to developing agricultural colleges in the East African country (Dahlstedt & Nordvall, 2011). These schools, developed in collaboration with Swedish educationalists, were known as Folk Development Colleges and were residential, hosting persons who had been successful in the famed national literacy programme and who were selected by their village community (Bhola, 1984, p. 154; Mayo, 1997, p. 64).

The most important international impact of the Danish folk high school has not been the work of actual schools in different countries, but the widespread knowledge of the educational principles formulated originally by Grundtvig and Kold and developed through the intensive work of the first folk high schools in the last part of the 19th century. Together with other progressive models of adult education the folk high school has given inspiration for education and learning in many contexts (Warren, 1989).

THE DANISH FOLK HIGH SCHOOL TODAY

Historically the tradition of the folk high school has had significant impact on educational practices both in Denmark and elsewhere. And folk high schools are still an important element in Danish education today, although the societal context is obviously very different and has changed much of the rationale for attending these schools.

Denmark is no longer a traditional society with a large rural population. Agriculture now has a subordinate role in the economy, and it is highly mechanized and run by relatively few well educated people. So there is no longer a close connection between a peasant class and the folk high schools. The level of education in the Danish population is generally high, and there is a comprehensive system of adult education including different vocational programmes as well as 'second chance' education in general school subjects. Many of the educational needs originally covered by the folk high schools are thus being filled in other ways.

But the folk high schools are still there. Today there are around 70 folk high schools in Denmark, most of them situated in rural areas or smaller towns and often named after the local district. Some of them, like the Askov, Testrup and Vallekilde schools, are from the founding period around 1860, while others are more recent. Almost all are residential schools with students and staff living, eating, and sharing the same daily routines together for the duration of a course.

The educational activity of folk high schools is regulated by legal framework, but the schools have much freedom regarding the subjects, content and methods of their teaching (Ministry of Children and Education 2012). The courses vary in length from a week to several months. The subjects must be of a broad, general nature for half of the time of a course, but the rest of the time can be spent on going into depth with special subjects and skills. Many schools have and advertise a special profile, either in activities or in ideology. The Danish association of folk high schools lists the following types: Christian or spiritual schools; general and Grundtvigian schools; gymnastics and sports schools; lifestyle schools; schools for senior citizens and youth schools (for the 16–19 age group). The Grundtvigian schools constitute the majority; they have a general commitment to the principles originally set out by Grundtvig, but are different in other respects. Some of them may focus on music and theatre, others on politics and philosophy.

As suggested by the variety of types, modern folk high schools cater for different interests and are attended by different segments of the population. Around 50.000 persons attend a folk high school each year, most of them for short courses. Most students are young adults under the age of 25. The overall gender distribution is fairly equal, although there are some well-known differences like an over-representation of women in courses on housekeeping and needlework. The level of previous education is relatively high, in fact higher than in most other types of adult education. Many of the participants have at least an upper secondary degree. This reflects the fact that courses at these residential schools are often used as a 'waiting period' for young people before entering a career or some kind of full-time vocational education.

A special type of 'waiting period' to which folk high schools have also responded is unemployment. Although labour market authorities generally prefer to have unemployed people upskilled at vocational schools, attending folk high school courses has also been recognized as relevant, especially for developing communicative and other personal skills. Around 1980, when unemployment in Denmark was high, this led to the emergence of a new type of school, the day high schools. These schools are not residential; they try to make the objective of the folk high schools concerning life enlightenment, revival and political education available for unemployed adults, most often low-skilled women or men, who neither can nor wish to leave their normal everyday lives. The framework and function of the education is determined by the labour market and by the form of working life, but content and pedagogy find their inspiration in the tradition of popular enlightenment. There are still a considerable number of these schools, which are generally smaller and less independent than the traditional folk high schools.

The folk high schools of today are in many ways different from the ones that were established during the second half of the 19th century. But it is significant that they still refer to the educational values and principles formulated by Grundtvig and Kold, and that they generally are successful in applying these principles to educational activities for modern individuals.

CONCLUSION

Under the conditions of modernisation the social basis and the cultural significance of learning undergo rapid change. This represents challenges to the folk high school model, which was originally closely connected to different types of collective actors and identities, for instance in local rural communities, in social movements and in labour market organisations. Today these collective actors have a less prominent role, and new types of identity and solidarity are emerging in modern societies. A trivial but nevertheless telling example is the fact that the folk high school tradition strongly emphasised the Danish language as an expression of popular experience and national identity, while modern young Danes embrace American culture and enthusiastically speak English whenever they have the opportunity. This does not mean that the folk high school model and its cultural roots are now irrelevant and should be abandoned. The social and personal aspects of learning, the right to adult education and educational equality are still important values, but they need to be reinterpreted and reaffirmed. As argued by Habermas (for instance in Habermas 1995), open and democratic communication with inclusion of all relevant partners offers a potential way to undertake this.

REFERENCES

Bjerg, J. (1994). Christen mikkelsen kold 1816–70, *Prospects 24* (1–2), 21–35.
Bhola, H. S. (1984). *Campaigning for literacy. Eight national experiences of the twentieth century, with a memorandum to decision makers*, Paris: UNESCO.
Borish, S. (1991). *The land of the living: The danish folk high schools and Denmark's non-violent path to modernization.* Nevada City: Blue Dolphin Press.
Bugge, K. (1999). *Canada and Grundtvig.* Vejle, Denmark: Kroghs Forlag.
Dahlstedt, M., & Nordvall, H. (2011). Paradoxes of solidarity: Democracy and colonial legacies in Swedish popular education, *Adult Education Quarterly, 61* (3), 244–261.
Grell, H. (1998). *Vision og virkeliggørelse [Vision and Realization].* Aarhus University: Center for Grundtvig-studier.
Grundtvig, N. F. S. (1991). *Selected educational writings* (compiled by Max Lawson). Elsinore: International People's College.
Grundtvig, N. F. S. (2011). *The school for life. N. F. S. Grundtvig on education for the people.* Edited by C. Warren and U. Jonas. Aarhus: Aarhus University Press.
Gundelach, P. (1988). *Sociale bevægelser og samfundsændringer [Social Movements and Social Change].* Aarhus: Politica.
Habermas, J. (1997). What does 'Working off the past' mean today? In J. Habermas, *A berlin republic. Writings on Germany*, (pp.17–40). Lincoln: University of Nebraska Press.
Horton, M., & Freire, P. (1990). *We make the road by walking. Conversations on education and social change* (B. Bell; J, Gaventa & J. Peters, Eds.), Philadelphia: Temple University Press.

Korsgaard, O. (2000). Learning and the changing concept of enlightenment: Danish adult education over five centuries. *International Review of Education, 46* (3/4), 305–325.

Kulich, J. (1964). The danish folk high school: Can it be transplanted? The success and failure of the Danish folk high school at home and abroad. *International Review of Education, 10* (4), 417–430.

Kulich, J. (2002). *Grundtvig's educational ideas in central and eastern Europe and the baltic states in the twentieth century.* Copenhagen: Vartov Publishing.

Lawson, M. (1993). N. F. S. Grundtvig. *Prospects: The quarterly review of comparative education* (Paris, UNESCO: International Bureau of Education), *XXIII* (3/4), 613–23.

Mayo, M (1997). *Imagining tomorrow. Adult Education for Transformation*, Leicester: NIACE.

Ministry of Children and Education (2012). *Non-formal adult education. Fact sheet.* Copenhagen: Ministry of Children and Education.

Olesen, H.S. and Rasmussen, P. (1996). Introduction, in H. S Olesen and P. Rasmussen, P (Eds.) *Theoretical Issues in Adult Education. Danish Research and Experiences* (pp.7–22). Frederiksberg: Roskilde University Press

Warren, C. (1989). 'Andragogy and N.F.S. Grundtvig: A critical link'. *Adult Education Quarterly, 39* (4), 211.

AFFILIATION

Palle Rasmussen
Department of Learning and Philosophy,
Aalborg University, Denmark

MARVIN FORMOSA

18. FOUR DECADES OF UNIVERSITIES OF THE THIRD AGE: PAST, PRESENT, FUTURE[1]

INTRODUCTION

The second half of the twentieth century witnessed a proliferation of educational institutions catering exclusively to the learning needs and interests of older adults. The University of the Third Age [U3A], founded in 1972, has become one of the most successful institutions engaged in late-life learning. U3As can be loosely defined as socio-cultural centres where older persons acquire new knowledge of significant issues, or validate the knowledge which they already possess, in an agreeable milieu and in accordance with easy and acceptable methods (Midwinter, 1984). Its target audience are people in the third age of the life course – that is, a life phase "in which there is no longer employment and child-raising to commandeer time, and before morbidity enters to limit activity and mortality brings everything to a close" (Weiss & Bass, 2002, p. 3). The U3A movement has not only withstood the test of time but is also marked by an extensive increase of centres and members all over the five continents. In 2011, Australia and New Zealand included 240 (69,086 members) and 65 (11,336 members) U3As respectively, whilst figures for Britain reached 798 U3As with some 269,750 members (The Third Age Trust, 2011). In 2008, the number of Chinese U3As reached 40,000 with over 4.3 million members (Swindell, 2011). The goal of this article is to take stock of four decades of U3A activity. First, it traces the genealogy of the U3A movement by highlighting its origins, developments, and contemporary structuring. Second, it underlines the successes and achievements of U3As in improving the quality of life of older persons. Third, it goes beyond functionalist rationales by documenting lacunae that may characterise U3As. Finally, it engages a discussion of the possible future roles, opportunities, and directions for U3As.

1972–1980: FRENCH ORIGINS

Following legislation passed by the French government in 1968 which made universities responsible for the provision of lifelong education, the summer of 1972 saw Pierre Vellas coordinating at the University of Toulouse a summer programme of lectures, guided tours, and other cultured activities, for retired persons (Radcliffe, 1984). Surprisingly, when the programme came to end the enthusiasm and determination of the participants showed no signs of abating, so that Vellas was 'forced' to launch a new series of lectures for retirees for the forthcoming academic year. Vellas (1997) formulated four key objectives for this new educational enterprise – namely, (i) raising the quality of life of older people, (ii) realising a permanent educational programme for older people in close relational with other younger age groups, (iv) co-ordinating gerontological research programmes, and last but not least, (iv) realising initial and permanent education programmes in gerontology. The first U3A was open to anyone who had reached statutory retirement age in France at that time, and who was willing to fill in a simple enrolment form and pay a nominal fee. Learning activities were scheduled for daylight hours, five days a week, for eight or nine months of the year. After the programme was marketed on a limited basis, 100 older persons attended the opening session for the 1972–1973 academic year (Philibert, 1984). Teachers were highly enthusiastic about the motivation and sheer human warmth displayed by older students, and marvelled at the way they learnt with new techniques such as audio-visual language laboratories. The first U3A curriculum, at Toulouse, focused on a range of gerontological subjects, although in subsequent years subject content became mainly in the humanities and arts (Vellas, 1997).

The Union French University of the Third Age was founded in 1980 and quickly sought to clarify the meaning of the word 'university' in the title, and therefore, which kinds of U3As are eligible to become members (Radcliffe, 1984). The dominant view was that U3As should strive to maintain high academic standards by holding direct links with recognised and established universities, and to uphold the credibility of the label 'university' by increasing the proportion of university academic staff. As a result, although lectures were combined with debates, field trips, and recreational and physical opportunities, the French academic maxim of "teachers lecture, students listen" was constantly upheld (Percy, 1993, p. 28). Indeed, all U3As during the 1970s operated through a more or less a strict 'top-bottom' approach, where the choice of subjects and setting of course curricula was the responsibility of university academics, and with learners expected to show deference to the intellectual eminence of university professors.

In retrospect, there was nothing exceptional about this programme apart from the fact that a section of a large provincial university had taken an interest in ageing and decided to enlist the resources of the university in programmes for senior citizens. Yet, the Toulouse initiative struck a rich vein of motivation so that just three years later U3As were already established in Belgium, Switzerland, Poland, Italy, Spain, and Quebec in Canada (Swindell & Thompson, 1995). The U3A phenomenon struck a rich vein of motivation because retirees perceived such centres as offering them the possibility to continue engaging in physical and cognitive activities even beyond retirement, and to keep abreast of physical, psychological, and social changes occurring in later life (Glendenning, 1985). This may be because the U3A movement was in marked contrast to the tradition of centralised educational management, and provided an opportunity to sow the first seeds of educational innovation and reform. In Radcliffe's (1984, p. 65) words, "the U3A was in some measure an expression of a counter-culture, the resort of those to whom a fair measure of educational opportunity has been denied...a challenge in support of the right to life-long education".

1981–1990: THE BRITISH RENAISSANCE

As the U3A phenomenon gained increasing international recognition, it did not escape the attention of British educators and gerontologists. The first U3A in Britain was established in Cambridge, in July 1981, and quickly replicated in other cities and towns (Midwinter, 2004). The British version underwent a substantial change compared to the original French model, with Midwinter (1984, p. 3) going as far as to describe the use of the title 'U3A' as "an unashamed burglary of the continental usage". Rather than being incorporated within social science, education, or theology faculties within traditional universities, British U3As embraced a self-help approach based upon the principle of reciprocity, of mutual giving and taking. Self-help groups include people coming together to assist each other with common problems, providing mutual support and an exchange of information, whilst being typified by minimal social distance between them (Brownlie, 2005). The self-help model holds immense potential for late-life education since experts of all kinds retire with the skills and interest to successfully increase both the number and range of resources available. The key objectives stipulated for British U3As, according to Peter Laslett (1989), included

> ...to educate British society at large in the facts of its present age constitution and of its permanent situation in respect of ageing...to create an institution for those purposes where there is no distinction between those who teach and those who learn, where as much as possible of the activity is voluntary, freely offered by members of the University...to undertake research on the process of ageing in society, and especially on the position of the elderly in Britain... (p. 177–8)

The hallmarks of British U3As include their sturdy independence and anti-authoritarian stance (Huang, 2006). Aspiring to instigate a democratic movement that enriches the lives of older adults through the development of a range of learning, action, and reflection opportunities, British U3As declined to form part of "the official, state-founded, established structure with its professional teachers and administers" (Laslett, 1989, p. 174). Instead of developing into campus-based organisations (although the Lancaster and London U3As were notable exceptions), British U3as were more akin to Illich's (1973) visions in *Deschooling Society*, which stressed the oppressive and ineffectual nature of institutionalised education, on the basis that whilst institutionalised learning undermines people's confidence and undermines their capacity to solve problems, the so-called experts (that is, teachers) tend to self-select themselves and act as gate-keepers as what should be learnt in life. Illich (ibid.) argued that a more promising education system is characterised by more fluid and flexible forms of learning that include three key purposes: providing easy access to learning resources, facilitating the sharing of knowledge, and creating opportunities for the transferring of skills – all of which are found at the core of the British U3A model. Indeed, programme directors rejected the idea of pre-packaged courses for more or less passive digestion, and instead demanded a kind of intellectual democracy where all members would be expected to participate in teaching and learning. Since in the absence of any financial and administrative support from official authorities sessions often take place in members' own homes, British U3As are also successful in promoting what Illich (1973, p. 110) termed as 'learning webs' – that is, "reticular structures for mutual access...to the public and designed to spread equal opportunity for learning and teaching". In Midwinter's (1984, p. 4) words, the British U3A movement "cocks a perky snook at the conventional university", with the term 'university' used in the medieval sense of fellow students "joined together in the selfless pursuit of knowledge and truth for its own sake".

In retrospect, the French and British U3As models were a product of particular socio-political contexts (Glendenning, 1985). The 'extra-mural' character of the former model followed legislation passed by the French government in 1968 which required universities to provide opportunities for lifelong education in collaboration with all interested parties. Hence, the French U3As had legislation on their side, together with a conviction that education for older adults was a necessary part of universities responsibilities, so that it is not surprising that their key distinguishing feature is their association with established universities and government departments responsible for the welfare of older people. On the other hand, the proposals of the working party on *Education and Older Adults* set up by the British Universities Council for Adult and Continuing Education in 1982 elicited a poor response from universities and political parties (ibid.). Hence, British U3As had no other alternative but to adopt the principles of self-help learning, as evidenced from their strong will to remain free of universities, autonomous from local authorities, and downplay traditional credentials. As one of its co-founders claimed, "our view was always that Third Agers should be liberated to organise their own affairs and invest their own destiny...[U3As] are all about older persons being the creators, not the recipients, of a service" (Midwinter, 2003, p. 1, 2).

1991–2011: CONTEMPORARY DEVELOPMENTS

The U3A movement has gone a long way since its inception. In 2008, the International Association of Universities of the Third Age [IAUTA] included memberships from U3As situated in 23 different countries, although U3As are present in more than 60 countries (Swindell, 2011). IAUTA organises a biennial international congress and encourages collaborative projects between U3As situated in different countries.

Another productive organisation is WorldU3A. Founded in 1997, it encourages international contacts between U3As through internet activity. One of its invaluable projects consists of the ongoing 'technological support' email list moderated by U3A members which provide rapid answers to technology-based problems (ibid.).

Although many centres still follow either the French or British traditions, there are at present four other models: the 'culturally-hybrid', 'French-speaking North American', 'South American', and 'Chinese' types (Levesque, 2006). Culturally-hybrid U3As include both Francophone and British elements. For instance, U3As in Finland are affiliated with a university programme, use university resources, but then rely heavily on 'local learning groups' of older people to define the curricula so that they are characterised by an open door policy and are essentially cooperative unions (Yenerall, 2003).

The U3A in Malta also combines Francophone and Anglophone characteristics by having lectures by university-based professors as well as interest-group sessions under the guidance of members (Formosa, 2012). French-speaking U3As in Canada form part of a traditional university, but then are seriously intent on blurring the distinction between higher education and third-age learning. For instance, the U3A in Montreal established an Bachelor of Arts degree programme to meet the complex needs and interests of the third-age population whereby admission requirements included "appropriate former studies or self-taught knowledge" and "sufficient knowledge of both French and English" (Lemieux, 1995, p. 339). South American U3As are also close to the Francophone model as they are characterised by an institutional link to a host University where the link is regarded as self-evident as much from the University's point of view as from that of the members. However, South American U3As are also typified by a strong concern for the most deprived and vulnerable sectors of the older population (Levesque, 2006) – which is surely very atypical to the Francophone model whose value orientations tend to be apolitical, and at times, even elitist (Formosa, 2007). Finally, Chinese U3As make use of a number of older revered teachers who are paid a stipend, and older and younger unpaid volunteers, to teach a curriculum which covers compulsory subjects such as health and exercise, as well as various academic and leisure courses ranging from languages to philosophy to traditional crafts (Swindell, 2011). U3As in China adopt a holistic perspective towards learning, and hence, are much concerned with the maintenance and development of citizenship, cultural consolidation, philosophical reflection, and bodily harmony. Of course, there are U3As which do not fit either of the models expanded herein. U3As in Taiwan are neither attached to universities nor are they self-help organisations. Instead they have been established, managed and financed by local authorities, with teaching carried out by professional teachers (Huang, 2005).

U3As are no exception to the e-learning revolution. Although initially the primary scope of experimentation with online courses was solely to reach out to older persons who could not join their peers in the classroom-setting such as those living in remote areas and the homebound (Swindell, 2000, 2002), this stance soon changed. As internet connection became a dominant feature of daily living in later life so that in New Zealand, Canada, Sweden, and the United States at least 38 per cent of the population aged 65 plus go online (Pierce, 2008), and once the coming of the Web 2.0 internet revolution – with its Blogs, Wikis, Moodle, and Podcasts – brought the possibility for interactive learning to previously unimaginable levels, it became evident that virtual learning can provide a reliable and valid experience both on its own and to everyone irrespective of social and health status (Swindell, et al., 2011). Success stories include U3A Online coordinated by tutors located in Britain, Australia, and New Zealand, the online courses coordinated by the British federation of U3As, and the Virtual University of the Third Age. The administration of U3A Online, set up in 1998, is carried by volunteers and learning takes place by electronic forum, email and Skype. One strength of volunteer-based virtual learning is that it has few expensive overheads as there are no salaries to pay, no expensive insurance costs, and no health-safety concerns, so that membership costs for U3A Online amount only to A$25 (Swindell, 2011). In early 2011, "39 courses were available to U3A Online members with others in various stages of completion...free to members for self-study and are available 365 days a year" (ibid., p. 46).

CONTRIBUTIONS OF U3AS

Irrespective of the geographical context, U3As must be credited for providing an opportunity for older adults to participate in lifelong learning, and therefore, contributing strongly towards the ongoing construction of societies where people age positively. U3As play a key role in the democratisation of lifelong learning by providing educational opportunities to a sector of the population that is generally left out in the cold as far as learning is concerned. Indeed, one does not have to go back many years to find a time when it was widely thought that intelligence declined with age, and that older adults could not learn anything novel – indeed, the traditional adage of 'you cannot teach an old dog new tricks!'.

Although the United States is a notable exception, for most countries the founding of U3As represented the first real possibility for older citizens to participate in non-formal learning. The burgeoning number of U3As was also instrumental in influencing the inclusion of older adults in 'lifelong learning' policies. The United Nations' International Plan on Action on Ageing states that "the role played by educational institutions for older persons, such as by universities of the third age, needs to be further recognized and supported" (United Nations, 2002, paragraph 47). U3As ensure a higher visibility of third agers as independent, industrious, and creative citizens. They militate against the widespread stereotypes of older persons as a needy and dependent group, as passive takers and recipients of pensions and welfare services. Moreover, the empowering potential of U3As is not to be underestimated since participation in lifelong learning can provide learners with a platform whereby they can voice their opinions. In the Irish context, U3As have been credited for providing a physical space "where ageing groups are getting together...[to] get the government to understand that older people also have a voice" (Blackrock U3A member [Ireland], cited in Bunyan and Jordan, 2005, p. 271).

Various studies applaud U3As for improving the quality of life of members. Admittedly, at present one locates no rigorous research programme investigating the relationship between U3A membership on one hand, and improvement in physical and cognitive well-being on the other. It is surely not the intention here to argue in favour of some strong causational relationship between learning and an improvement in physical/cognitive well-being in later life since, as Withnall (2010) argues, most research in this field has tended to proceed on the basis of a range of clinically unproven assumptions. It remains, however, that there are many valid and reliable studies showing how continued mental stimulation in later life aids learners to, at least, maintain their physical and cognitive health status (Cohen, 2006; National Seniors Australia, 2010). Wrosch and Schulz's (2008) findings that older adults who were proactive and persistent in countering health problems experienced greater physical and mental health benefits augurs well, since most U3As offer various courses on health promotion and illness prevention. In this respect, the fact that Australian elders perceive their U3A membership to have improved their health status is surely encouraging. As documented by one U3A member (cited in Williamson, 1997),

> If you're active, and you're active in your mind then, yes, it does make a difference to your health...but if you were sitting down doing nothing, well your system's not working – the brain's not working. And if the brain starts to get slack or just doing nothing it transmits to the rest of the body and the rest of the body becomes slack. (p. 180)

Sonata and colleagues' (2011) study in Brazil also underlined the role of U3As in augmenting elders' physical health. The Piracicaba U3A was found to function to preserve members' 'fat-free mass' levels by decreasing and improving their levels of inactivity and physical exercise respectively, factors which are crucial to, at least, maintaining, well-being in later life.

U3As also hold a potential to lead learners towards improved levels of psychological capital. Studies have uncovered an association between participation in U3As and improved levels of self-assurance, self-satisfaction, self-esteem and sense of coherence on one hand, and a decline of depressive and anxiety symptoms on the other (Formosa, 2000; Zielińska-Więczkowska et al., 2011, 2012). This implies that engagement at a U3A centre can have therapeutic functions towards the adjustment of older adults with their ageing and retirement transitions. Indeed, a study on the relationship between psychological well-being (autonomy, personal growth, control, positive relationships with others, purpose, personal acceptance, and generativity) and participation in the São Paulo U3A in Brazil concluded that "the students [sic] who had been longer on the program run by the institute studied, exhibited higher levels of subjective and psychological well-being...where the satisfaction and benefits gained [from learning] extend into other areas of life" (Ordonez et al., 2011,

p. 224). Turning our attention again to the Irish context, Whitaker's (2002, cited in Bunyan & Jordan, 2005) research concludes that U3A participation helps to develop confidence as learners realise the value of the knowledge that they share with others. She notes that by participating in U3As members get their life experiences recognised and appreciated, and learn how to get beyond the critical voice that tells us we 'aren't good enough' or 'that we have nothing to say'. Elsewhere, Irish participants also disclosed how U3A helped them to improve their confidence in their abilities in information and communication technology (Bunyan & Jordan, 2005).

U3As are also recommended for resolving the tensions arising from the push towards the productive use of one's free time and the pull of 'liberation' or 'well-earned rest' of retirement. As Walker (1998) affirmed, whilst "for some of its members, U3A may function as a springboard experience...others find their aspirations completely met within U3A activity". Similarly, Ellis & Leahy (2011) report that when members are asked what they gain from their involvement in U3A activities, the first thing that they usually report is not generally related to the learning activities *per se* but the associated social outcomes such as socialising, making new friends who share their interests, having the opportunity to achieve personal growth, and finding a support group which helps them through difficult periods in their personal life. In other words, for many U3A members it is not 'learning' as such that enticed to enrol and keep on participating, but the 'sheer fun' that accompanies such an activity. This is because U3A centres are typified by a sense of vitality and dynamism that go beyond what is usually the case in a normal adult education centre, to the extent that many feel that their membership gave them a new lease of life. For instance, the coordinator of the U3A in Malta noted how during his tenure he witnessed the U3A injecting members with a novel sense of purpose: "retired teachers have gone back to part-time teaching of English to foreign students, others have started hobbies related to their former work, [whilst] others who used to read very little, if at all, have discovered a new world opening up to them" (Schembri, 1994, p. 21). Elsewhere, members in Irish U3As also commented at length on the social aspects of the learning environment:

> What I like is the idea of meeting people from different walks of life, that have been in a different area to what I have been, and different experiences. And it's lovely chatting with somebody and you learn quite a lot from their way of life and what they thought about different things. And I also think in this group there's a warm...friendship...you feel at home (Blackrock U3A member [Ireland], cited in Bunyan & Jordan, 2005, p. 270).

The e-learning travails of the U3A movement has also been providing low-cost learning opportunities for older people. One finds considerable anecdotal evidence showing that this process is making a considerable improvement to the quality of life of individual older adults:

> I'll go as far as to say that being totally absorbed in my most recent online course has saved my sanity this year...I am deaf – communicating online is

wonderful for me. I am sure that is true for other people with disabilities of many kinds. (U3AOnline members, cited in Swindell et al., 2011, p. 130).

Finally, it is noteworthy that the majority of U3As only exist because of time-consuming work on behalf of volunteers. In the UK, the balance of volunteers to staff is overwhelming, with over 250,000 members and only 14 staff at the national office, half of them part-time (Cox, 2011). In Italy, 57 per cent of tutors are volunteers (Principi & Lamura, 2009). The economic value of U3As has been efficiently gauged by Swindell who, instead of modestly letting the record of voluntarism speak for itself, actually calculated an actual monetary figure to the work that third-age volunteers donate to many sectors of the Australian and New Zealander U3As. His latest calculations are of $21 million and $1.9 million for Australian and New Zealand U3As respectively (Swindell et al., 2010). Whilst 22 per cent of volunteering time was generally spent on administrative issues, the remainder consisted of actual tutoring hours. Swindell's estimates provide proof to the claim that the U3A phenomenon enables the government to spend less on welfare and civic programmes targeting the improvement of the quality of life in later years, as well as challenging the orthodox beliefs of ageing as a period of loss and decline, and that older adults are simply recipients of welfare and consumers of public funds.

The U3A phenomenon also problematises Putnam's (2000) argument that civic participation has declined in the latter part of the 20th Century, whilst backing Freedman's (1999, p. 19) claim that older adults have become the "new trustees of civic life". Undoubtedly, U3As are a strong affiliate in the 'civic enterprise' movement. Although U3As are not political enterprises, and thus do not promote any kind of political activism, they do encourage older persons to become involved in helping others in the community. U3As enrich societies with opportunities for greater fulfilment and purpose in later years, and therefore, enable older adults to reach improved levels of active, successful, and productive ageing. Indeed, the U3A approach provides a sustainable policy model for how future governments might capitalise on the productive resources of the increasing numbers of expert retirees.

ISSUES AND PREDICAMENTS

Despite the aforementioned contributions of U3As to society in general and older persons in particular, what appears to be a forthright exercise in facilitating learning opportunities for older adults is also fraught with widespread misconceptions and biases. In some ways, and especially from a logistical perspective, U3As have become victims of their own success. The triumph of U3As in attracting more learners is giving forth to problems in locating suitable venues large enough to accommodate the membership body, and enough volunteers to administer and run courses of study and interest-groups. This is especially the case for U3As following the self-help model who tend not possess sufficient funds to employ administrative staff and who are reluctant to implement or increase enrolment fees as this is perceived to undermine the self-help character of the organisation. Indeed, some U3As had no other option than to cap memberships in order to ensure that members could be accommodated in the already over-stretched facilities of centres, as well as operate waiting lists (Picton & Lidgard, 1997).

Laslett's (1989, p. 178) objective for U3As to "undertake research on the process of ageing in society" has also emerged as a contentious issue. Laslett thought that U3A members are in an ideal situation to undertake research that would counter not only the predominance of ageist literature on the ageing process but would also function "to assail the dogma of intellectual decline with age" (ibid., p. 178). Although initially one witnessed some level of participation on behalf of U3As in a number of research projects, it must be admitted that most U3As neither participate in nor produce research. Most U3A managers are occupied with the demands of day-to-day organisation, and research is not amongst the members' high priorities. As Katz (2009, p. 156) claimed, members "are seeking an education apart from formal accreditation institutions, and Laslett's mandate to create an alternative, Third Age research base [appears] to be daunting".

Although U3As following the Francophone model are more able to access funds, retain nominal enrolment fees (as they make free use of university resources), and implement easily any course that strikes the fancy of members due to the large of pool of teaching personnel at the university/college, they are not devoid of limitations. Lectures generally take place upon university campuses which tend to be far away from village and city centres, and hence, inaccessible for many older adults (Picton & Lidgard, 1997). They are also characterised by a lack of agency over the ethos and direction of the U3A, as usually the academic body has the last say on every matter and total decision-making power on the most fundamental aspects (Formosa, 2000). For instance, the drive behind the founding of the U3A in Malta arose neither from responses to community needs nor from requests by older persons themselves, but from the aspirations of academics working in the field of ageing (ibid.). As a result, it is governed by a 'mission statement' that was written and developed exclusively by university academics without any consultation with age-interest groups or older persons.

Irrespective of the type of organisational model being followed, research has found U3As to incorporate a number of crucial biases. A consistent criticism levelled at U3As is that of elitism as there is a compounding class divide affecting chances to seek membership (Radcliffe, 1984; Swindell, 1993; Picton and Lidgard, 1997; Formosa, 2000, 2007; Alfageme, 2007). Although U3As offer no hindrances or obstacles to membership, membership bodies tend to be exceedingly middle-class. Educators have long commented how "threatened...by elitism and pastime activism, U3As might indulge in narcissism and escapism and miss altogether the highest vocation they should respond to" (Philibert, 1984, p. 57), and how U3As "pandered to the cultural pretentious of an aged bourgeoisie who had already learned to play the system" (Morris, 1984, p. 136). This occurs because older adults who have experienced post-secondary education, and have advanced qualifications and skills, are already convinced of the joy of learning so that their motivation to enrol in U3As is very strong. To middle-class elders, joining means going back to an arena in which they feel confident and self-assured of its outcome and development. On the other hand, working-class elders are apprehensive to join an organisation with such a 'heavy' class baggage in its title. Moreover, the liberal-arts curriculum promoted by most U3As is perceived as alien by working-class elders, who tend to experience 'at-risk-poverty' lifestyles, and are more interested in practical knowledge related to lifelong work practices. Formosa (2000) argues that U3A may actually be serving as a strategy for middle-class elders to offset the class-levelling experience resulting from retirement. In the way that books and paintings are used to impress friends and other social viewers, membership is employed as a strategy of class 'distinction'.

U3As have also been criticised for including gender biases that worked against the interests of both men and women. On one hand, all surveys uncover a positive women to men ratio: 3:1 in the UK and Malta (Midwinter, 1996; National Statistics Office, 2009), 4:1 percent in Australia (Hebestreit, 2006), and 2.5:1 percent in Spain (Alfageme, 2007), to mention some. It may seem that this gender imbalance is because women hold higher life expectancies and leave employment at an earlier age than men. While such explanations do make sense, they fail to explain why older women choose to enrol in U3As and overlook that married women retirees remain accountable for most domestic responsibilities. At the same time, the high participation rates of women do not necessarily imply that U3As are fulfilling some beneficial roles towards them. The reality, in fact, is otherwise, as studies point out how U3As may serve to anchor female members in gender expectations about women's traditional roles. For instance, women tend to be less visible in mixed classes at U3As where male learners are more likely to dominate any discussion even when in the minority (Bunyan and Jordan, 2005). Formosa (2005) also noted how the Maltese U3A was characterised by a 'masculinist' discourse where women are silenced and made passive through their invisibility, an outnumbering of male over female tutors, and a perception of older learners as a homogenous population which contributed towards a 'malestream' learning environment. However, this is not the same as saying that men enjoy preferential treatments in U3As.

The low percentage of men signals strongly that for a number of reasons the organisation is not attractive to them. First, U3As are promoted through avenues – such as during health programmes on the broadcasting media or through leaflets at health centres – where most of the clients are women. Second, U3As are exceedingly 'feminised'. Not only is the membership mostly female, but so are management committees (Williamson, 2000). As Scott and Wenger (1995, p. 162) stated, older men tend not to want to become involved with old people's organisations they perceive to be dominated by women. Third, U3A courses tend to reflect the interests of the female membership. Health promotion courses, despite being open to all, are generally delivered by female tutors with a bias towards women-related health issues such as weight-loss and osteoporosis (Formosa, 2005). U3As, hence, continue to enforce men to relate to a culture that encourages them to cling to traditional roles and patterns of behaviour where it is believed that that engaging in learning is for women rather than for men.

Other predicaments concerning the U3A include the movement's tendency to lack ethnic minorities and fourth agers in its membership body. For instance, both Swindell (1999) and Findsen (2005) point out that given the multi-cultural environment of Australia and New Zealand, one would reasonably expect to see at least some Asian faces plus those of Maori and Pasifika people. This is, however, not the case and memberships of Australasian U3As are heavily represented by members from the Anglo-Saxon community. Findsen concludes that the exclusion of minority groups may not be deliberate, but as the projected ethos of U3As mirrors the values of the dominant groups in society, ethnic minorities feel that they do not have the necessary 'cultural capital' to participate in such learning ventures. At the same time, U3A membership bodies generally do not include older persons experiencing physical and cognitive difficulties. This is surprising considering that there are many old-old persons (aged *circa* 75 plus) facing mobility and mental challenges. Moreover, even at a relatively young age, many a times prior to statutory retirement, various older adults experience complications from strokes, diabetes, and neurological diseases so that their functional mobility and intellectual resources become seriously limited. Indeed, a significant percentage of older adults experience significant mobility and mental problems to the extent of becoming housebound or having to enter residential and nursing care homes. Unfortunately, to-date one locates no distinct efforts by the U3A movement to encompass the learning needs and interests of frail older adults in its aims and objectives.

Vellas (1997) and Laslett (1989) hoped that U3As would play a key role in the strengthening of intergenerational ties. However, most U3As continue to take the form of age-segregated educational programmes, with some even restricting membership to adults who have not yet reached their 60th birthday (Formosa, 2000). This means that U3As are playing a limited role in the quest to ensure a society of all ages. Admittedly, third-age learning provides a greater degree of commonality and likelihood of peer support, as well as convenient daytime scheduling, length and frequency of courses, semesters, and affordable costs (Manheimer et al., 1995). Drawbacks, however, include not responding well to the needs of older adults, being too small to provide differentiated and specialised course programmes, segregating older students from the rest of population, inclined to become 'inferior universities, and embodying low levels in the quality of educational experience and courses offered (van der Veen, 1990). Moreover, age-segregated sessions miss out on the various benefits that arise from the implementation of intergenerational learning. Thomas (2009) stresses the role of intergenerational learning in contributing to the policy areas of 'community cohesion' by breaking down barriers within communities, 'community safety' by mitigating stereotypes and providing positive role model, and 'physical wellbeing' by bringing different generations together to exchange skills and knowledge. With respect to older adults, intergenerational learning challenges the stereotypical images of older people so that it enables them to contribute to society in a meaningful way, and hence, creating an 'age friendly society' where people are enabled to 'live well in later life' (Sánchez & Martinez, 2007).

RENEWING U3As: FUTURE ROLES, OPPORTUNITIES AND DIRECTIONS

As the U3A movement embarks on its fifth decade, it would be a mistake for programme managers to rest on its laurels, as doing so the movement would risk meeting the same fate as the sewing circles of our grandparents' time. The key challenge faced by U3As is to remain in tune and relevant to the life-world of present and incoming older cohorts. The U3A concept emerged in the early 1970s when the life course was divided in three clear and distinct stages: childhood as a time for education, adulthood as a time to raise a family and work, and old age as a brief period characterised by withdrawal from work until frail health and eventually death. During this period the identity of older people existed within the context of the welfare state that embedded them in a culture of dependence through a compulsory pensioner status and near-compulsory entry to residential/nursing care (Townsend, 2007). With the coming of late modernity the social fabric became more fluid in character, so that later life disengaged itself from traditional concepts of retirement to become increasingly complex, differentiated, and experienced in a myriad of ways (Blaikie, 1999). Nowadays, identities in later life take on a 'reflexive organized endeavour', operating on the basis of choice and flexibility, and finding their full expression in material consumption (Gilleard & Higgs, 2000). However, it seems that U3As remain locked in more traditional perceptions of late adulthood and somewhat oblivious to such transformations. James (2008) argues that centres have generally failed to keep pace with what older adults actually do in their lives, what tickles their fancy, and what motivates them to age actively, successfully, and productively. She highlights how the U3A movement tends to be characterised by what Riley and Riley (1994) term as 'structural lag' – namely, a failing on behalf of structural arrangements to meet or be relevant to the needs of a large proportion of its clientele. In Riley and Riley's words, 'structural lag' refers to

> ...the imbalance – or the mismatch – between the strengths and capacities of the mounting numbers of long-lived people and the lack of role opportunities in society to utilize and reward these strengths. This is the problem we call structural lag, because the age structure of social role opportunities has not kept pace with rapid changes in the ways people grow old. (Riley and Riley, 1994, p. 15).

Similarly, Formosa (2012) points out that U3As generally overlook how incoming older cohorts are characterised by diverse generational dispositions when compared to those older adults that Vellas and Laslett had in mind when drafting the movement's principles and objectives. Undoubtedly, the past two decades have brought cultural changes that have altered the norms and values of contemporary older cohorts. Most salient among these changes include an improvement in their wealth, health, and educational status, smaller family circles due to more older women having participated in labour markets, and an increasing readiness to combine part-time employment with leisure pursuits in retirement. The coupling of such transformations to other processes, most notably secularisation and individualisation, has been instrumental in urging third agers to create their own life biographies rather than remain shackled to traditional expectations towards daily living in 'old age'. In such circumstances, it is surely time for U3As to re-appraise their functions and purposes, and demonstrate that the movement remains a forward thinking group which welcomes new ideas and new ways of practice. It would be extremely unfortunate if upcoming and present third agers feel the need to start new organisations simply because of their perception that U3As are no longer relevant to their lives. This section forwards four recommendations for the U3A movement to remain more in tune with the needs and interests of contemporary older adults.

OVERCOMING FRENCH-BRITISH POLARITIES

Contrary to what is generally assumed, studying for pleasure and towards a qualification are not necessarily incompatible, but may even be complimentary. After all, one frequently hears of third agers being emboldened by their U3A experience as to start a university course, and on the other hand, of older undergraduates taking a keen interest or even becoming members in their local U3A. Rather than entrenching the U3A experience in an absolutist vision – advocating either strict autonomy or complete integration with traditional universities – U3as have much to gain from seeking partnerships with tertiary educational sectors working on similar ethos. Whilst partnerships in older adult learning do not have to be formally constituted and grand affairs, the benefits of collaborative approaches include "better information is available to help plan for learning, to deliver it in the best way, to promote engagement with it and to provide progression routes from it" (Gladdish, 2010, p. 26). One successful partnership between a traditional university and a U3A is found between the University of South Australia and the Whyalla U3A (Ellis, 2009; Ellis & Leahy, 2009). The central location and resources of the university provided rent-free premises which allowed their fees to be kept much lower than in other Australian U3As, and easy access for invited speakers and members. U3A members also enjoyed interacting with younger students and the help and encouragement that university staff extended to them. On the other hand, the benefits that the campus received from the U3A included the location of a pool of 'clients' for nursing and social work students, volunteer and administrative help on open days, whilst adding to the cultural and generational diversity present on campus. Another promising partnership constitutes the memorandum of understanding between Third Age Trust and The Open University in Britain which recognises the complementary missions of both organisations, and which may lead to better opportunities for older learners to improved access of library and online facilities, participation in university courses and modules, and registering as students with reduced fees and different entrance qualifications.

QUALITY OF LEARNING

Research studies and rationales focusing on the U3A movement affirm in a equivocal manner that learning holds positive benefits for its members. However, the precise contribution of learning in U3As to an empowerment agenda remains ambiguous. One must ask whether learners at U3A centres are too docile, too passive, as though listening alone were enough. This is certainly the case for U3As following the French model whose members are lectured by professors employed by the traditional university which the centres belong to. In its quest to improve the quality of life of the member body, the U3A movement is to seek a learning environment that is more dynamic in nature, one which facilitates

> learners who are able to take control and direct learning; learners who are enabled to continue learning after a course has finished; learners who, in their daily lives, know how to put into practice learning they have undertaken;...and learners who develop strategies that enable them to know how to go about the business of learning. (Gladdish, 2010, p. 15).

This is possible if learning environments at U3As drop traditional 'top-bottom' approaches in favour of a situation that places the teacher and learner in a dynamic relationship. Although teachers will always keep hold some level of authority on the learning session since it is their responsibility to create and sustain the right environment for learning to occur, older learners should have an opportunity to have a say in directing both the nature and content of the learning that takes place. Following Gladdish (2010), successful learning in later life relies on consideration and consensus to drive activity, one which involves negotiation, advocacy, intervention, promotion, and sometimes compromise. In short, "it is about creating something new with, as well as behalf of other" (ibid. p. 10).

QUALITY OF INSTRUCTION

The quality of instruction is also to be put under scrutiny as it is important that older learners do not fall back on the educational experience of their youth. Top-bottom approaches to educational instruction are to be avoided. Instead, course tutors should enable older adults to foster the control that they may be consciously or unconsciously lacking through encouragement to take responsibility for their learning by choosing those methods and resources by which they want to learn. A useful strategy here is to emphasise the importance of personal goal setting at the beginning of the course schedule and encourage it through activities such as making a personal statement of what the learners want to achieve. Facilitating learning in later life thrives on collaborative and partnership partnership, and is characterised by 'co-operative work' between tutors and learners (Gladdish, 2010). Tutors are also encouraged to draw on the life experiences of learners by allowing them to share examples of their experiences with the class and encouraging them to think about how those examples relate to class information. Course material that is presented in a way that reflects the 'real world', rather than some abstract component, is very popular with older learners. It is important for facilitators to synchronise themselves with the life course experience of learners, born around World War II, and who lived their teenage and early adult years in the fifties and sixties. Nevertheless, U3As must not assume that older learners continue living in some by-gone world. Rather, e-learning has become increasing popular in later life as it offers the opportunity for older learners to access information and communicate with others when and if they want to. For U3As to continue being relevant to contemporary elders, centres must make more effort to embed their learning strategies in the web 2.0 revolution that now provides extremely user-friendly applications. Contrary to its predecessor, web 2.0 uses interactive tools – ranging from Blogs, Wikis, Podcasts, online journals, to virtual picture databases – to offer limitless possibilities for an interactive, empowering, and participatory form of older adult learning.

QUALITY OF CURRICULA

The relevance of taught content warrants careful attention since it tends to influence the extent that older persons are attracted to and benefit from the learning experience. The curriculum at U3As should be as bold and original as possible, negotiated with, and even determined, by the most vital interests of learners. However, this does not mean that U3A centres do not have any part to play in the choice of subjects. As Gladdish (2010, p. 36) affirms, "learning providers must be part of the debate that identifies appropriate curricula for older people, and they need to exercise professional judgement and integrity about their ability or otherwise to contribute to development and delivery". More specifically, there is a real urgency for U3As to include non-liberal and – health related areas of learning such as financial literacy and caregiving, but especially, scientific courses that introduce learners to environmental, botanical, and zoological studies. Since the correlation between later life and illiteracy is well-known, U3As would do well to set up literacy courses for older persons, a move that would help in mitigating the oft mentioned charge of elitism. Moreover, the introduction of new areas of study may function for U3As to become successful in attracting non-typical learners such as older men (e.g. gardening, toy modelling, astronomy) and ethnic minorities (e.g. martial arts, origami, tai-chi). U3As must also coordinate intergenerational learning sessions that include curricula catering for learners from the whole of the life course, and hence, linking third agers with children, teenagers, adults, and even older peers. Specific activities may include book clubs, community work and film screenings, drama, as well as adoptive grandparent-grandchild relations. U3As would also do well to adopt curricula that operate on the principles of situated learning. A promising avenue in the respect is environmental volunteering where U3A can link up with eco-friendly organisations that provide both learning opportunities as well as possibilities for green volunteering. Older persons possess a maturity of judgement, and therefore, are highly apt to highlight the imperative need to create a sustainable society and conserve our natural resources.

UNIVERSITIES OF THE FOURTH AGE

For the U3A movement to be a really valid exemplary of late-life learning, its activities must also branch out to older people who experience health difficulties. In this respect, there is a need for U3As to develop Universities of the Fourth Age [U4A] which would invest in more and better learning opportunities to people whose physical and cognitive limitations lead them to either become housebound or enter residential/nursing homes. On one hand, strategies may include providing adequate transport facilities to and back from the learning centre, having sessions taking place in learners' homes, transmitting sessions either online or on radio and/ or television programmes, coordinating mobile libraries, and ensuring that course material is issued in 'clear/large print'. On the other hand, U3As are encouraged to promote the value of learning residential and nursing homes as a tool for improving well-being, and augmenting a more positive outlook on life. U3As may provide volunteers to work in homes to facilitate or run discussion groups, reading societies, social/cultural outings, as well as perhaps in-house magazine. Another possible activity which U3As may help coordinating is a 'life-history project' where residents record their past, the present, and most importantly, the future in terms of unfulfilled ambitions, dreams, and aspirations, which they can present to their relatives, friends, and case workers. The running of interest-groups – ranging on subjects as diverse as choirs, horticulture therapy, reflexology, keep fit, and sports activities – is surely another area in which U3As can contribute and help.

CONCLUSION

This paper began by tracing the origins and modern developments of the U3A movement. U3As vary in size and resources, and their development is inevitably uneven. However, all are united in their efforts to provide learning opportunities for older adults, as well as increasing the visibility of older generations whose presence and worth is easily undervalued and overlooked. U3As also remind governments and educational bodies of the actual meaning of the words 'lifelong learning', providing a niche for a category of citizens who are left out in the cold as far as learning opportunities are concerned, as governments continue to cling on traditional models of education geared towards production, profitability and employability. However, this paper also brought forward the difficulties that the U3A movement is currently experiencing, and the possible and actual biases that centres may experience. One cannot let the successes of the U3A movement overshadow the fact that the movement cater little for older men, elder from ethnic minorities, and others experiencing physical and cognitive difficulties. To help overcome such lacunae, this paper also provided a number of suggestions for the future role for U3As, ranging from embracing a broader vision of learning, improving the quality of learning, instruction, and curricula, as well as a wider participation agenda that attracts elders experiencing physical and cognitive challenges. Of course, such proposals require a certain amount of human resources and monetary capital to take off. Whilst it is hoped that U3As are successful in attracting more volunteers to their fold, another possible strategy is to turn such projects into formal ventures and apply for funds from public enterprises whose ethos is to improve the physical, social, and psychological well-being of older people. It is noteworthy that both the United Nations' (2002) *Madrid International Action Plan of Action on Ageing* and the European Union's [EU] policy documents on lifelong learning (European Commission, 2006, 2007) include a strong emphasis on the need to improve opportunities for learning in later life. Moreover, the fact that the EU coordinates the Grundtvig Programme which so far has provided funding to many a third-age learning project, and that 2012 has been designated as the European Year for Active Ageing and Solidarity between Generations, should augur well to the successful lobbying of political, intellectual and financial backing.

NOTE

[1] This article has appeared as Marvin Formosa 'Four Decades of Universities of the Third Age: past, present and Future' *Ageining and Society*, available online on CJO 2nd August 2012 doi 10.1017/S0144686X12000797. Permission to republish granted by Cambridge University Press. http://journals.cambridge.org/action/displayAbstract?fromPage=online&aid=8656535.
I am indebted to Dr. Rick Swindell, co-founder and former president of U3A Online at Griffith University, for the Australian and New Zealand figures.

REFERENCES

Alfageme, A. (2007). The clients and functions of spanish university programmes for older people: A sociological analysis, *Aging & Society*, 27(3), 343–361.

Blaikie, A. (1999). *Ageing and popular culture*. Cambridge: Cambridge University Press.

Brady, E. M., Holt, S., & Welt, B. (2003). Peer teaching in lifelong learning institutes. *Educational Gerontology*, 29 (10), 851–868.

Brownlie, K. (2005). Self-help groups. In F.J. Turner (Ed.), *Encyclopedia of Canadian social work*. Wilfred Laurier University Press (pp. 336–7), Ontario, Canada.

Bunyan, K., & Jordan, A. (2005). Too late for the learning: Lessons from older learners, *Research in post-compulsory education*, 10(2), 267–81.

Cohen, G. D. (2006). *The mature mind: The positive power of the aging brain*. New York: Basic Books.

Cox, A. (2011). *Age of opportunity: Older people, volunteering and big society*. London: ResPublica.

Ellis, B. J. (2009). University and seniors working together: Engagement in a regional community, *Australasian Journal of University-Community Engagement*, 4(2), 6–19.

Ellis, B. J. & Leahy, M. J. (2011). A mutually beneficial regional relationship: University of the third age and university campus, *Gateways: International Journal of Community Research and Engagement*, 4, 154–167.

European Commission, (2006). *Adult learning: It is never too late to learn*. COM (2006) 614 final. European Commission, Brussels.

European Commission, (2007). *Action plan of adult learning: It is always a good time to learn*. COM (2007) 558 final. European Commission, Brussels.

Findsen, B. (2005). *Learning later*. Malabar, FL: Krieger.
Formosa, M. (2000). Older adult education in a maltese university of the third age: A critical perspective. *Education and Ageing, 15*(3), 315–339.
Formosa, M. (2005). Feminism and critical educational gerontology: An agenda for good practice. *Ageing International, 30*(4), 396–411.
Formosa, M. (2007). A bourdieusian interpretation of the university of the third age in malta. *Journal of Maltese Education Research, 4*(2), 1–16.
Formosa, M. (2010). Lifelong learning in later life: The universities of the third age, *Lifelong Learning Institute Review*, 5, 1–12.
Formosa, M. (2012). Education and older adults at the university of the third age, *Educational Gerontology, 38*(1), 1–13.
Freedman, M. (1999). *Prime time: How baby boomers will revolutionise retirement and transform America*. New York: Public Affairs.
Gilleard, C., & Higgs, P. (2000). *Cultures of ageing: Self, citizen and the body*. New Jersey: Prentice Hall.
Gladdish, L. (2010). *Learning, participation and choice: A guide for facilitating older learners*. Leicester: NIACE.
Glendenning, F. (1985). Education for older adults in Britain: A developing movement. In F. Glendenning (Ed.), *Educational gerontology: International perspectives* (pp. 100–141). Kent: Croom Helm.
Hebestreit, L. (2008). The role of the university of the third age in meeting the needs of adult learners in victoria, Australia, *Australian Journal of Adult Learning, 48*(3), 547–565.
Huang, C. (2005). The development of a university of the third age in Taiwan: An interpretative perspective, *Educational Gerontology, 31*(7), 503–519.
Huang, C. (2006). The university of the third age in the UK: An interpretative and critical study, *Educational Gerontology, 35*(10), 825–842.
Illich, I. (1973). *Deschooling society*. Hammondsworth: Penguin Books Ltd.
James, K. T. (2008). *Rethinking art education for older adults: An ethnographic study of the university of the third age*. A dissertation in art education submitted in partial fulfilment of the requirements for the degree of Doctor of Philosophy, The Pennsylvania State University, College of Arts and Architecture.
Katz, S. (2007). *Cultural aging: Life course, lifestyles, and senior worlds*. Toronto: University of Toronto Press.
Laslett, P. (1989). *A fresh map of life: The emergence of the third age*. London: Macmillan Press.
Lemieux, A. (1995). The university of the third age: Role of senior citizens, *Educational Gerontology, 21*(4), 337–344.
Levesque, J-L. (2006). *What kinds of futures for U3As*? http://www.aiuta.org/documents/workshopfederici.pdf (Accessed 7 June 2011).
Manheimer, R. J., Snodgrass, D. D., & Moskow-McKenzie, D. (1995). *Older adult education: A guide to research, programs, and policies*. Greenwood, Westport, Connecticut.
Midwinter, E. (1984). Universities of the third age: English version. In E. Midwinter (Ed), *Mutual aid universities* (pp.3–19). London: Croom Helm.
Midwinter, E. (1996). *U3A thriving people*. London: The Third Age Trust.
Midwinter, E. (2003). Happy anniversary! *U3A sources, an educational bulletin*, 19, 1–2.
Midwinter, E. (2004). *500 Beacons: The U3A story*. Third Age Trust, London.
Morris, D. (1984). Universities of the third age, *Adult Education*, 57 (2): 135–139.
National Office of Statistics, (2009). *Demographic review 2008*. Malta: National Statistics Office.
National Seniors Australia 2010. *Later life learning: Unlocking the potential for productive ageing*. Canberra: National Seniors Australia Productive Ageing Centre.
Ordonez, T. N., Lima-Silva, T. B., & Cachioni, M. (2011). Subjective and psychological well-being of students of a university of the third age, *Dementia e Neuropsychologia, 5*(3), 216–225.
Percy, K. (1993). *Working and learning together: European initiatives with older people*. A report of the annual conference of the Association of Educational Gerontology held in 1993, the European Year of Older People and Solidarity between Generations, Glasgow, Scotland, United Kingdom, July, 1–4, 1993.

Philibert, M. (1984). Contemplating the universities of the third age. In E. Midwinter (Ed.), *Mutual aid universities* (pp. 51–60). Kent: Croom Helm.

Picton, C., & Lidgard, C. (1997). Developing U3A, *Third Age Learning International Studies*, 7, 219–24.

Pierce, J. (2008). *World internet project international report 2009*. http://www.digitalcenter.org/WIP2009/WorldInternetProject-FinalRelease.pdf (Accessed on 25 March 2010).

Principi, A., & Lamura, G. (2009). Education for older people in Italy, *Educational Gerontology*, 35(3), 246–259.

Putnam, R. (2000). *Bowling alone: The collapse and revival of American community*. New York: Simon and Schuster.

Radcliffe, D. (1984). The international perspective of U3As. In E. Midwinter (Ed.), *Mutual Aid Universities* (pp. 61–71). Kent: Croom Helm.

Riley, M. W., & Riley, J. Jr. (1994). Structural lag: Past and future. In M. W. Riley, R. L. Kahn, & A. Foner (Eds.), *Age and structural lag*. New York: John Wiley & Sons, Inc. pp. 15–36.

Sánchez, M., & Martinez, A. (2007). A society for all ages. In M. Sánchez (Ed.), *Intergenerational programmes: Towards a society for all ages* (pp. 16–33). www.laCaixa.es/ObraSocial (Accessed at June 12, 2010).

Schembri, A. M. (1994). Educating the elderly, *Bold* 4(2), 18–21.

Scott, A., & Wenger, G. C. (1995). Gender and social support networks in later life. In S. Arber & J. Ginn (Eds.), *Connecting gender and ageing: a sociological approach* (pp. 158–172) Buckingham: Open University Press.

Sonati, J. G., Modenezea, D. M. Vilartaa, R., Macielb, E. S., Boccalettoa, E., & da Silva, C. (2011). Body composition and quality of life of the elderly offered by the 'University third age' in Brazil, *Archives of Gerontology and Geriatrics*, 52(1), 32–35.

Swindell, R. F. (1993). U3A in Australia: A model for successful aging, *Aging & Society*, 13(2), 245–266.

Swindell, R. F. (1999). New directions, opportunities and challenges for New Zealand U3As, *New Zealand Journal of Adult Learning*, 27(1): 41–57.

Swindell, R. F. (2000). U3A Without walls: Using the internet to reach out isolated people, *Education and Ageing*, 15(2), 251–263

Swindell, R. F. (2002). U3A Online: A virtual university of the third age for isolated older people, *International Journal of Lifelong Education*, 21(5), 414–429.

Swindell, R. F. (2011). Successful ageing and international approaches to later-life learning. In G. Boulton-Lewis & M. Tam (Eds.), *Active ageing, active learning* (pp. 35–65). New York: Springer.

Swindell, R., Grimbeek, P., & Heffernan, J. (2011). U3A Online and successful aging: A smart way to help bridge the grey digital divide. In J. Soar, R. F. Swindell and P. Tsang (Eds.), *Intelligent technologies for bridging the grey digital divide* (pp. 122–140). New York: Information Science Reference.

Swindell, R. F., & Thompson, J. (1995). International perspectives on the U3A, *Educational Gerontology*, 21(5): 415–27.

The Third Age Trust, (2011). *The third age trust*. http://www.u3a.org.uk/ (Accessed 5, Jun 2011)

Thomas, M. (2009). *Think community: An exploration of the links between intergenerational practice and informal adult learning*. Leicester: NIACE.

Townsend, P. (2007). Using human rights to defeat ageism: Dealing with policy-induced 'structured dependency. In M. Bernard & T. Scharf (Ed.), *Critical Perspectives on Ageing Societies* (pp. 27–44). Bristol: The Policy Press.

United Nations, (2002). *Report of the second world assembly on ageing, Madrid International Plan of Action in Ageing* (MIPAA). New York: United Nations.

Van der Veen, R. (1990). Third age or inter-age universities? *Journal of Educational Gerontology*, 5(2), 96–105.

Vellas, P. (1997). Genesis and aims of the universities of the third age, *European Network Bulletin*, 1, 9–12.

Walker, J. (1998). Mapping the learning of older adults. *Adults Learning*, 10(2), 14–16.

Weiss, R. S., & Bass, S. A. (2002). Introduction. In R. S. Weiss & S.A. Bass (Eds.), *Challenges of the third age: Meaning and purpose in later life* (pp. 3–12). New York: Oxford University Press, 3–12.

Williamson, A. (1997). 'You're never old to learn': Third-age perspectives on lifelong learning, *International Journal of Lifelong Learning, 16*(1): 173–84.

Williamson, A. (2000). Gender differences in older adults' participation in learning: Viewpoints and experiences of learners at the university of the third age (U3A), *Educational Gerontology, 26*(1), 49–66.

Withnall, A. (2010). *Improving Learning in Later Life*. London: Routledge.

Wrosch, C., & Schulz, R. (2008). Health-engagement control strategies and 2-year changes in older adults' physical health, *Psychological Science, 19*(6): 537–541.

Yenerall, J. (2003). Educating an aging society: The university of the third age in Finland, *Educational Gerontology, 29*(8), 703–716.

Zielińska-Więczkowska, H. Kedziora-Kornatowska, K., & Ciemnoczołowskic, W. (2011). Evaluation of quality of life of students of the university of third age on the basis of socio-demographic factors and health status, *Archives of Gerontology and Geriatrics, 53*(2): 198–202.

Zielińska-Więczkowska, H., Ciemnoczołowski, W., Kedziora-Kornatowska, K., & Marta Muszalik, M. (2012). The sense of coherence as an important determinant of life satisfaction, based on own research, and exemplified by the students of University of the Third Age, *Archives of Gerontology and Geriatrics, 53*(2), 238–241.

AFFILIATION

Marvin Formosa
Senior Lecturer, European Centre for Gerontology,
University of Malta, Malta

JOSEPH GIORDMAINA

19. THE EUROPEAN AGENDA FOR EDUCATION IN PRISON

INTRODUCTION

The purpose of this chapter is to provide an overview of how the Council of Europe (CoE) by means of its various recommendations as well as the European Union (EU) through both its declared policies as well as its partly/fully funded training programmes are mapping the chart for education and training in European Prisons. The chapter argues that irrespective of the goals set by the CoU and the EU regarding education in prison, progress remains slow, and educational provision in prison remains rather limited.

MAKING SENSE OUT OF PRISON TIME

The challenge for prison administrators since practically the 18th century was on how to combine elements of punishment with elements of rehabilitation and preparation for resettlement into society. Discipline became a means of control and reformation of the prisoner with the long term aim that he or she will not reoffend. It was also a means for the crime not to repeat itself – a form of deterrent. Discipline included rewards for good deeds, punishment for failure to conform. This was done under constant surveillance, hence the birth of the panopticon. Attempts at implementing such reforms were the topic of discussions in international conference, as, for example, are described in the Paris Prison Congress 1895 Summary Report that indicates how the World's Prison Congress meets every five years in order to discuss issues related to prison and crime. As is still the case, this meeting comprised speeches by policy setters, including in this case the President of France. Ideas were presented, and visits to the Prisons, Reformatories and Charitable institutions of Paris were organised. A handsome medal with an inscription of the name of each delegate was presented to the participants at the end of the Congress – not that different from what happens today. The goals of education in prison have not changed so much in the last 100 years:

> In the prisons of tomorrow education will be taken as a matter of course, as it is now in progressive communities which seek to offer varied educational opportunities to their citizens. It will not be considered the sole agency of rehabilitation; no exaggerated claims will be made for its efficacy. It will be

recognized as having the same unquestionable place in prisons that it has in the world outside, and as probably having somewhat greater value because of the unusually heavy concentration of under-educated adults presented by our prison population. (MacCormick, 1931, p. 72).

However, the purpose of prison education should be defined not just in terms of its contribution to the reduction of recidivism. It is important to recognise that to provide prison education is important in itself in a civilised society because it is the right thing to do. We should be developing the person as a whole, not just in terms of the qualifications they hold for employment. Education, and the process of engaging in learning, has a value in itself which needs to be recognised. A focus on reducing recidivism without considering the prisoner's right to education more broadly, would not be sufficient. (House of Commons. Education and Skills Committee, 2005, p. 13).

GUIDING TEXTS

There are a number of texts that deal with prisons and the management of prisoners. In most of these one finds reference to the provision of some sort of education for the prisoner. For example The Standard Minimum Rules for the Treatment of Prisoners, adopted by the Economic and Social Council in its resolution 663 c (XXIV) of 31 July 1957 in Part II entitled Rules Applicable to Special Categories (Prisoners under Sentence) dedicates rules 77 and 78 to Education and Recreation.[1] Similarly the United Nations Standard Minimum Rules for the Administration Juvenile Justice of (1985) provides rules that safeguard education in juvenile justice systems. Principle 28 of the Body of Principles for the Protection of All Persons under Any Form of Detention or Imprisonment[2] states that 'A detained or imprisoned person shall have the right to obtain within the limits of available resources, if from public sources, reasonable quantities of educational, cultural and informational material, subject to reasonable conditions to ensure security and good order in the place of detention or imprisonment.'

The more general and basic document that offers a direction with regard to 'education as a right' for everyone, irrespective of age, is surely the Convention for the Protection of Human Rights and Fundamental Freedoms, particularly Article 2 (Council of Europe (2010).[3] The Hamburg Declaration on Adult Education (CONFINTEA V) adopted this recommendation in a more practical way:

Basic education for all means that people, whatever their age, have an opportunity, individually and collectively, to realize their potential. It is not only a right; it is also a duty and a responsibility both to others and to society as a whole. It is essential that the recognition of the right to education throughout life should be accompanied by measures to create the conditions required to exercise this right. The challenges of the twenty-first century cannot be met by governments, organizations or institutions alone; the energy, imagination and genius of people and their full, free and vigorous participation in every aspect of life are also needed. Youth and adult learning is one of the principal means of significantly increasing creativity and productivity, in the widest sense of those terms, and these in turn are indispensable to meeting the complex and interrelated problems of a world beset by accelerating change and growing complexity and risk.[4]

Munoz (2009 p. 5) argues that 'human rights are not relinquished upon imprisonment.' As Special Rapporteur on the right to education of persons in detention, Munoz (2009) identifies prisoners as a marginalised and vulnerable group with regard to discrimination in education. He justifies education in programmes in prison not only as a tool for change (e.g. control of recidivism, reintegration and employability), but 'an imperative in its own right' (p. 4). Munoz draws the point very often forgotten in most literature dealing with education in prison: human dignity. 'Human dignity, core to human rights, implies respect for the individual, in his actuality and also in his potential. As education is uniquely and pre-eminently concerned with learning, fulfilling potential and development, it should be a fundamental concern of education in detention, not simply a utilitarian add-on should resources allow it (p. 7).[5]

COUNCIL OF EUROPE

The recommendation of the Council of Europe that specifically deals with Education in Prison is recommendation R(89)12.[6] This extensive recommendation (accompanied by an explanatory memorandum) commends to governments of member States to implement policies which recognise the following:

1) All prisoners shall have access to education, which is envisaged as consisting of classroom subjects, vocational education, creative and cultural activities, physical education and sports, social education and library facilities;
2) Education for prisoners should be like the education provided for similar age groups in the outside world, and the range of learning opportunities for prisoners should be as wide as possible;
3) Education in prison aims to develop the whole person bearing in mind his or her social, economic and cultural context;
4) All those involved in the administration of the prison system and the management of prisons should facilitate and support education as much as possible;
5) Education should have no less a status than work within the prison regime and prisoners should not lose out financially or otherwise by taking part in education;
6) Every effort should be made to encourage the prisoner to participate actively in all aspects of education;

7) Development programmes should be provided to ensure that prison educators adopt appropriate adult education methods;
8) Special attention should be given to those prisoners with particular difficulties and especially those with reading or writing problems;
9) Vocational education should aim at the wider development of the individual, as well as being sensitive to trends in the labour market;
10) Prisoners should have direct access to a well-stocked library at least once per week;
11) Physical education and sports for prisoners should be emphasised and encouraged;
12) Creative and cultural activities should be given a significant role because these activities have particular potential to enable prisoners to develop and express themselves;
13) Social education should include practical elements that enable the prisoner to manage daily life within the prison, with a view to facilitating the return to society;
14) Wherever possible, prisoners should be allowed to participate in education outside prison;
15) Where education has to take place within the prison, the outside community should be involved as fully as possible;
16) Measures should be taken to enable prisoners to continue their education after release;
17) The funds, equipment and teaching staff needed to enable prisoners to receive appropriate education should be made available.

This is the recommendation that the European Prison Education Association (EPEA) strongly advocates.[7] A quick reading of it indicates that it is dated, and should be updated in order to reflect better the progress made in education, particularly the promotion and use of Information Technology. The focus on this recommendation is education during incarceration. The Council of Europe has published other resolutions in which one finds reference to the importance of continuity of education upon release. Recommendation CM/Rec (2010)1of the Committee of Ministers to member states on the Council of Europe Probation Rules[8] (recommendation 61) states:

> Supervision following early release shall aim to meet the offenders' resettlement needs such as employment, housing, education and to ensure compliance with the release conditions in order to reduce the risks of reoffending and of causing serious harm.

With regard to juvenile prisoners, the Council of Europe recommends that the sanctions or measures that may be imposed on juveniles, as well as the manner of their implementation, shall be specified by law and based on the principles of social integration and education and of the prevention of re-offending.[9] Recommendation 28 of the same document states that:

> The rights of juveniles to benefits in respect of education, vocational training, physical and mental health care, safety and social security shall not be limited by the imposition or implementation of community sanctions or measures.

Interestingly enough the same documents specifies that the relationship between the staff concerned and the juveniles shall be guided by principles of education and development (recommendation 38). The document lists a number of 'regime activities' that aim at education, personal and social development, vocational training, rehabilitation and preparation for release (recommendation 77 and 78).[10] The document also promotes the idea of an Individual Education Plan[11] for each juvenile inmate (recommendation 79).

The European Prison Rules[12] dedicate a particular section to Education (Rule 28).[13] A specific section is dedicated to children under detention:

> 35.1 Where exceptionally children under the age of 18 years are detained in a prison for adults the authorities shall ensure that, in addition to the services available to all prisoners, prisoners who are children have access to the social, psychological and educational services, religious care and recreational programmes or equivalents to them that are available to children in the community.
>
> 35.2 Every prisoner who is a child and is subject to compulsory education shall have access to such education.

The document suggests that sentenced prisoners taking part in education or other programmes during working hours as part of their planned regime should be remunerated as if they had been working (recommendation 105.4). With regard to sentenced prisoners the document states that:

> 106.1 A systematic programme of education, including skills training, with the objective of improving prisoners' overall level of education as well as their prospects of leading a responsible and crime-free life, shall be a key part of regimes for sentenced prisoners.
>
> 106.2 All sentenced prisoners shall be encouraged to take part in educational and training programmes.
>
> 106.3 Educational programmes for sentenced prisoners shall be tailored to the projected length of their stay in prison.[14]

Recommendation No. R (84) 12 of the Committee of Ministers to member states Concerning Foreign Prisoners[15] reminds us that foreign prisoners should have the same access as national prisoners to education and vocational training. This is very important given the fact that in most prisons practically half the population is made up of foreign inmates.[16] The same goes for dangerous prisoners (recommendation

7): to provide education, vocational training, work and leisure-time occupations and other activities to the extent that security permits.[17] Recommendation No. R (82) 16 of the Committee of Ministers to member states on Prison Leave[18] recommends to governments of the member states to grant prison leave to the greatest extent possible on medical, educational, occupational, family and other social grounds (recommendation 1).

THE EUROPEAN UNION

There are a number of documents issued by the European Council that have somehow influenced the direction education is taking in prison. Renewed Social Agenda: Opportunities, Access and Solidarity in 21st century Europe[19] is the communication from the commission that argues that 'the focus for a renewed social agenda should be on empowering and enabling individuals to realise their potential while at the same time helping those who are unable to do so'. The Renewed Social Agenda is based on three interrelated goals of equal importance: Creating Opportunities, Providing Access and Demonstrating Solidarity (p. 6), three goals that one can easily relate to prisoners and education (formal and informal) in prisons. According to the text of the Agenda, its goal is to reinforce the Lisbon Strategy for Growth and Jobs. In the Presidency Conclusions of the Lisbon European Council (23 and 24 March 2000) the texts pointed out that

> Europe's education and training systems need to adapt both to the demands of the knowledge society and to the need for an improved level and quality of employment. They will have to offer learning and training opportunities tailored to target groups at different stages of their lives: young people, unemployed adults and those in employment who are at risk of seeing their skills overtaken by rapid change. This new approach should have three main components: the development of local learning centres, the promotion of new basic skills, in particular in the information technologies, and increased transparency of qualifications.[20]

The research report entitled *Developing Local Learning Centres and Learning Partnerships as part of Member States' targets for reaching the Lisbon goals in the field of education and training: A study of the current situation* (Buiskool, 2005) highlights how, after 5 years, only three such centres had in fact developed in prisons. These centres were set up in Belgium and Portugal where, in the latter, education is provided in prisons with the support of social partners. The Popular University of Palencia (Spain) has, amongst its target groups, unemployed prisoners with whom they promote social participation, education, training and culture. Activities are held both inside and outside penitentiary centres (p. 121).

The Council's conclusions on the role of education and training in the implementation of the 'Europe 2020' strategy[21] draws attention to The Copenhagen Process, whose strategic priorities for the next decade were reviewed at a ministerial meeting in Bruges in December 2010,[22] emphasising that vocational education and training (VET) has a key role to play in supporting the aims of the 'Europe 2020' strategy by providing relevant, high quality skills and competences. Also the document draws attention to the 'agenda for new skills and jobs' initiative that highlights the need to upgrade skills and to boost employability. Direct relevance to the role of education in prison is made in this document:

> In response to the aims of the 'European Platform against Poverty' initiative, greater efforts are also required to provide support and open up opportunities for non-traditional and disadvantaged learners. Factors such as better access to high quality early childhood education and care, the provision of innovative education and training opportunities for disadvantaged groups are important for reducing social inequalities and enabling all citizens to realise their full potential.[23]

EUROPEAN COMMUNITY: DG EDUCATION AND CULTURE

The DG Education and Culture through its initiatives has contributed substantially (but independently of the Council of Europe) to education in prison. The biggest contribution has been funding for projects related to education in prison and the organisation of conferences as well as the commissioning of research. The Compendium of EU-Sponsored Projects Relevant to Prison Education (1995–2004) lists a number of projects supported through the Socrates Programme, mainly through the Grundtvig Programme, the Leonardo Da Vinci Programme as well as the programme referred to as Accompanying Measures. Unfortunately the Compendium,[24] itself the product of another project entitled The ICCEPE (International Conference: Challenges for European Prison Education) Project is simply a list of projects, and in no way does it analyse, group or comment on the validity and successes of these projects. The same compendium lists 67 EQUAL Projects relevant to prison issues. A more recent Compendium: Compendium of Prison Education Projects Funded by The Socrates, Leonardo and Lifelong Learning Programmes has recently been published by GHK, at the request of the European Commission, Directorate General for Education and Culture, with input from the project coordinators.[25]

There are several benefits that these programmes bring about. These include the bringing together of various partitions from a small number of European countries to work together on a common idea, which they develop, implement and evaluate. Most of the budgets are relatively small (for Grundtvig the maximum is often €400,000). Most of this amount goes to travel and working days, and members of the team have to fork out anything between 25% and 30% of the total amount. This in itself often rules out small NGOs who do not have the capital to contribute such a sum. Small NGOs are also not in a financial position to guarantee the total amount for the project, and hence they are precluded from coordinating such projects.[26] To a certain extent, even if their work is of an excellent quality, they are marginalised to the periphery of the project. The effect of these projects is also limited. Very often as soon as the funding stops at the end of the project, the project and its products are no longer supported and the initiative ends there. It is often hard to get copies of the products of such projects, and e-mailing the coordinators of the projects of the listed projects in the compendium yields no results at all. Often one perceives a gap between the high expectations of the project outcomes and the actual achievements/products of such projects. The EU would do well to create a centre where all the results of EU sponsored projects are made available to all prisons interested in using the products. A second and third period of funding should also be considered for successful projects. This should also make it possible to enlarge the partnership group to include more participants and disseminate and implement more the product of successful projects. Basically a strategy of growth for successful projects should be designed and implemented.

The DG Employment, Social Affairs and Inclusion, as well as DG Justice have in their own ways contributed, particularly through their funded projects (e.g. Daphne III programme, the Fundamental Rights and Citizenship Funding Programme, the Civil Justice Programme and the Criminal Justice Support Programme),[27] to education and preparation for employment in prisons. Unfortunately the three main Directorates involved work separately, with lots of overlap between funded projects. As a result, the wheel is being invented and reinvented over and over again.

MISSING IN PRISON: A HOLISTIC APPROACH.

The European agenda is clearly set, and initiatives and projects are in place. But the main question is why are such initiatives not filtering down to the daily inmate's life in prison. Various speculations can be made, all of which need to be backed up by thorough research, which in general is missing from the field (Hawley 2011 p. 27).[28] For example research on the effectiveness of education in prison, as a means of reducing recidivism, is hardly available in Europe.[29]

Most of the documents reviewed above do not explore and define the role of education in prison, and consequently the kind of education one ought to be promoting. In a nutshell there are at least three ways of looking at education in prison: firstly as a way of coping with life in prison (hence designing an education that is wider in scope, more general, and available to all, including lifers), secondly, an education that is a preparation for release and employment and hence designing an education that is mainly vocational in nature, focused for those who are in the last term of their sentence. It has been shown that employment is the factor that mostly reduces re-offending (Bouffard, MacKenzie & Hickman 2000), hence most emphasis on education in prison has been of this kind. Interestingly not enough research has been done to show the correlation between the employment an ex-prison inmate secures on release, and the kind of job training he or she has been provided with prison. Some of the research available indicates that inmates are employed in jobs that are unrelated to the training/education they received in prison (Wilson *et al*, 2000 p. 361).

The third view of education as implemented in prison is that education is a good in itself – it makes us better human beings – and hence should be available to all. If this is the case then one might also consider imposing education as part of the daily programme in prison, similarly to the way prison itself and the punishment it brings with it are imposed. The latter are often justified on the grounds that they are good for both the individual and society at large. After all, compulsory education has always been considered a good in itself, particularly as a process of 'normalisation,' an aim 'correctional' facilities are definitely trying to reach as their very name implies. The probability is that the above three mentioned approaches are not an either/or approach but all three 'philosophies' can take place in parallel, posing serious challenges to the design of a curriculum in prison.

There are other serious hindrances that may explain the lack of proper educational programmes' implementation in prisons in Europe. One of these could be the lack of public support for prisons as institutions for social reformation rather than institutions of seclusion and punishment. Lack of public support is often exchanged in a weak political agenda to change things in prison, particular by governments whose ideology leans to the right. Often governments are signatories of the various resolutions of the Council of Europe and other bodies as indicated in the first part of this article but, when it comes to implementations, the story is a different one indeed. One solution could be for recommendations to be evolved into European Law that all EU members have to abide with.

The way prisons themselves function has also been problematic in implementing education in prisons. For one thing, the prison guards, those closest to the prison inmate, are hardly ever involved in education projects. A holistic approach in the design of an education programme for the prison inmate, as well as in the delivery of the various education provisions, hardly exists in most prisons (Braggins & Talbot 2006).[30]

The Education in Prison agenda has also been to a certain extent heavily influenced by countries in the North of Europe. The realities in Northern European prisons contrast sharply with the realities of prisons in southern and eastern Europe. The image projected is of an ideal towards which all of Europe should strive, something that is, practically, not possible because of cultural and economic differences. The document 'Prison education and Training in Europe – Final Report' (2012) is replete with examples from Norway and the UK. Hardly any examples from other countries with very different social and economic realities are mentioned.

Last but not least the EU should strive to see that the very basics in prisons with regard to health and physical security are met. In reality, the least preoccupation of a sick, hungry and insecure prisoner is education. Overcrowding, abuse and hardship in prison is still the order of the day in some countries. It is ironic that in some prisons in Europe the discussion is on whether the inmate should have access to a tablet, a laptop or a desktop computer, while in others, finding funds for food and basic health provisions is a feat in itself.

NOTES

[1] Education and recreation. 77. (1) Provision shall be made for the further education of all prisoners capable of profiting thereby, including religious instruction in the countries where this is possible. The education of illiterates and young prisoners shall be compulsory and special attention shall be paid to it by the administration. (2) So far as practicable, the education of prisoners shall be integrated with the educational system of the country so that after their release they may continue their education without difficulty. 78. Recreational and cultural activities shall be provided in all institutions for the benefit of the mental and physical health of prisoners.

[2] Adopted by General Assembly resolution 43/173 of 9 December 1988.

[3] Article 2: Right to Education states: No person shall be denied the right to education. In the exercise of any functions which it assumes in relation to education and to teaching, the State shall respect the right of parents to ensure such education and teaching in conformity with their own religious and philosophical convictions.

[4] ://www.unesco.org/education/uie/confintea/declaeng.htm

[5] Munoz (2009) identifies three types of education in prison: the "medical" model, the "cognitive deficient" model and the "opportunistic" model. The medical model focuses on and treats the perceived psychological deficiencies of the criminal; the cognitive deficiency model focuses on the promotion of moral development; and the opportunistic model on linking learning with training for employment.

[6] Education in Prison. Council of Europe Recommendation No. R (89) 12 adopted by the Committee of Ministers of the Council of Europe on 13 October 1989 and explanatory memorandum Strasbourg 1990.

[7] The European Prison Education Association is an organisation made up of prison educators, administrators, governors, researchers and other professionals whose interests lie in promoting and developing education and related activities in prisons throughout Europe in accordance with the recommendations of the Council of Europe. http://www.epea.org/

[8] This recommendation was adopted by the Committee of Ministers on 20 January 2010 at the 1075th meeting of the Ministers' Deputies.

[9] Recommendation CM/Rec(2008)11 of the Committee of Ministers to member states on the European Rules for juvenile offenders subject to sanctions or measures.

[10] 77: Regime activities shall aim at education, personal and social development, vocational training, rehabilitation and preparation for release. These may include:

    a. schooling;
    b. vocational training;
    c. work and occupational therapy;
    d. citizenship training;
    e. social skills and competence training;
    f. aggression-management;
    g. addiction therapy;
    h. individual and group therapy;
    i. physical education and sport;
    j. tertiary or further education;
    k. debt regulation;
    l. programmes of restorative justice and making reparation for the offence;
    m. creative leisure time activities and hobbies;
    n. activities outside the institution in the community, day leave and other forms of leave; and
    o. preparation for release and aftercare.

78.1. Schooling and vocational training, and where appropriate treatment interventions, shall be given priority over work.
78.2. As far as possible arrangements shall be made for juveniles to attend local schools and training centres and other activities in the community.
78.3. Where it is not possible for juveniles to attend local schools or training centres outside the institution, education and training shall take place within the institution, but under the auspices of external educational and vocational training agencies.
78.4. Juveniles shall be enabled to continue their schooling or vocational training while in detention and those who have not completed their compulsory schooling may be obliged to do so.
78.5. Juveniles in detention shall be integrated into the educational and vocational training system of the coun.try so that after their release they may continue their education and vocational training without difficulty.

[11] The Recommendation Rec(2006)2 of the Committee of Ministers to member states on the European Prison Rules (Adopted by the Committee of Ministers on 11 January 2006 at the 952nd meeting of the Ministers' Deputies) suggests Individual Sentence Plans for all prisoners:

103.3 Sentenced prisoners shall be encouraged to participate in drawing up their individual sentence plans.
103.4 Such plans shall as far as is practicable include:

a. work;
b. education;
c. other activities; and
d. preparation for release.

[12] Recommendation Rec(2006)2 of the Committee of Ministers to member states on the European Prison Rules (Adopted by the Committee of Ministers on 11 January 2006 at the 952nd meeting of the Ministers' Deputies).

[13] 28.1 Every prison shall seek to provide all prisoners with access to educational programmes which are as comprehensive as possible and which meet their individual needs while taking into account their aspirations.
28.2 Priority shall be given to prisoners with literacy and numeracy needs and those who lack basic or vocational education.
28.3 Particular attention shall be paid to the education of young prisoners and those with special needs.
28.4 Education shall have no less a status than work within the prison regime and prisoners shall not be disadvantaged financially or otherwise by taking part in education.
28.5 Every institution shall have a library for the use of all prisoners, adequately stocked with a wide range of both recreational and educational resources, books and other media.
28.6 Wherever possible, the prison library should be organised in co-operation with community library services.
28.7 As far as practicable, the education of prisoners shall:

a. be integrated with the educational and vocational training system of the country so that after their release they may continue their education and vocational training without difficulty; and
b. take place under the auspices of external educational institutions.

[14] Recommendation Rec(2003) 23 of the Committee of Ministers to member states on the management by prison administrations of life sentence and other long-term prisoners suggests that Sentence plans should include a risk and needs assessment of each prisoner and be used to provide a systematic approach to:

– the initial allocation of the prisoner;
– progressive movement through the prison system from more to less restrictive conditions with, ideally, a final phase spent under open conditions, preferably in the community;

- participation in work, education, training and other activities that provide for a purposeful use of time spent in prison and increase the chances of a successful resettlement after release;
- interventions and participation in programmes designed to address risks and needs so as to reduce disruptive behaviour in prison and re-offending after release;
- participation in leisure and other activities to prevent or counteract the damaging effects of long terms of imprisonment;
- conditions and supervision measures conducive to a law-abiding life and adjustment in the community after conditional release.

[15] Adopted by the Committee of Ministers on 21 June 1984 at the 374th meeting of the Ministers' Deputies.
[16] See Table 3.2 p. 77: Foreign Prisoners on 1st September 2010. Council of Europe Annual Penal Statistics. Space I Survey 2010 (Strasbourg, 23 March 2012. pc-cp\space\documents\ pc-cp (2012) 1).
[17] Recommendation No. R (82) 17 of the Committee of Ministers to member states concerning Custody and Treatment of Dangerous Prisoners (Adopted by the Committee of Ministers on 24 September 1982 at the 350th meeting of the Ministers' Deputies).
[18] Adopted by the Committee of Ministers on 24 September 1982 at the 350th meeting of the Ministers' Deputies.
[19] Commission of The European Communities Brussels, 2.7.2008. Com(2008) 412 Final Communication from the Commission to The European Parliament, The Council, The European Economic and Social Committee and The Committee of The Regions. Renewed social agenda: Opportunities, access and solidarity in 21st century Europe.
[20] http://consilium.europa.eu/ueDocs/cms_Data/docs/pressData/en/ec/00100-r1.en0.htm
[21] Notices from European Union Institutions, Bodies, Offices and Agencies. Council. Council Conclusions on the Role of Education and Training in the Implementation of The 'Europe 2020' Strategy. (2011/C 70/01) (5).
[22] Bruges, Communiqué on enhanced European cooperation in VET: http://ec.europa.eu/education/lifelong-learning-policy/doc/vocational/ bruges_en.pdf
[23] This note reflects strategic objective 3: Promoting equity, social cohesion and active citizenship as found in the document entitled: Notices From European Union Institutions and Bodies. Council conclusions of 12 May 2009 on a strategic framework for European Cooperation in Education and Training ('ET 2020'), (2009/C 119/02). This strategic objective states: Education and training policy should enable all citizens, irrespective of their personal, social or economic circumstances, to acquire, update and develop over a lifetime both job-specific skills and the key competences needed for their employability and to foster further learning, active citizenship and intercultural dialogue. Educational disadvantage should be addressed by providing high quality early childhood education and targeted support, and by promoting inclusive education. Education and training systems should aim to ensure that all learners — including those from disadvantaged backgrounds, those with special needs and migrants — complete their education, including, where appropriate, through second-chance education and the provision of more personalised learning. Education should promote intercultural competences, democratic values and respect for fundamental rights and the environment, as well as combat all forms of discrimination, equipping all young people to interact positively with their peers from diverse backgrounds.
[24] SEEC, IPEA, FOKO (2005) The ICCEPE Project. International Conference 'Challenges for European Prison Education'. Compendium of EU-Sponsored Projects Relevant to Prison Education 1995–2004. Lovech. Infovision.
[25] GHK (2010)Grundtvig and Leonardo Da Vinci Catalogue of Projects on Prison Education & Training. http://ec.europa.eu/education/grundtvig/confprison_en.htm
[26] A case in point is the EPEA – The European Prison Education Association who itself could never coordinate a project because of this lack of guarantee to the sum provided for the project to take place. In one particular project the EPEA was interested in coordinating (the Training Teachers to Teach in Prison project), the University of Malta had to take its place as coordinator – since as a government entity it could offer the guarantee – and the EPEA ended up as a partner of project.

[27] The Daphne III programme aims to contribute to the protection of children, young people and women against all forms of violence and attain a high level of health protection, well-being and social cohesion. Its specific objective is to contribute to the prevention of, and the fight against all forms of violence occurring in the public or the private domain, including sexual exploitation and trafficking of human beings. It aims to take preventive measures and provide support and protection for victims and groups at risk.
The Fundamental Rights and Citizenship programme aims to promote the development of a European society based on respect for fundamental rights and rights derived from citizenship of the European Union. The Civil Justice programme aims to eliminate obstacles to the smooth functioning of cross-border civil proceedings in EU countries and thereby to improve the daily life of individuals and businesses by fostering access to justice. The Criminal Justice Support Programme was set up to promote judicial cooperation in the field of criminal justice. It provides financial support for projects initiated and managed by the Commission with a European dimension, transnational and national projects implemented by organisations in EU countries as well as activities of NGOs or other entities pursuing an aim of general European interest.
http://ec.europa.eu/justice/newsroom/criminal/grants/index_en.htm

[28] Prison education and training in Europe – a review and commentary of existing literature, analysis and evaluation. Directorate General for Education and Culture, European Commission. Framework Contract No EAC 19/06, Order 130. 6 May 2011 (p. 27). ec.europa.eu/education/grundtvig/doc/confl1/ghk_en.pdf

[29] American research is available in this area, including: Chapell, C. A. (2004). Post-secondary correctional Education and recidivism: A meta-analysis of research conducted 1990–1999. *Journal of Correctional Education*, 55, 148–167 and Bazos, A., & Hausman, J. (2004). Correctional Education as a Crime Control Program. University of California at Los Angeles School of Public Policy and Social Research, – Department of Policy Studies. Available from National Institute of Corrections:http://www.nicic.org/Library/019685

[30] Julia Braggins and Jenny Talbot: Wings of Learning: the role of the prison officer in supporting prisoner education. www.crimeandjustice.org.uk/opus210/wings-of-learning.pdf

REFERENCES

Bazos, A., & Hausman, J. (2004). Correctional education as a crime control program. University of California at Los Angeles school of public policy and social research, – department of policy studies.

Bouffard, J. A., MacKenzie, D. L., & Hickman, L.J. (2000). Effectiveness of vocational education and employment programs for adult offenders: A methodology-based analysis of the literature, in *Journal of Offender Rehabilitation*, Vol. 31 (1/2), pp. 1–41.

Braggins, J., & Talbot, J. (2006). Wings of learning: The role of the prison officer in supporting prisoner education. UK: The centre for crime and justice studies.

Buiskool, Bert-Jan et al. (2005). Developing local learning centres and learning partnerships as part of Member States' targets for reaching the Lisbon goals in the field of education and training: A study of the current situation. Leiden, the Netherlands.

Chapell, C. A. (2004). Post-secondary correctional education and recidivism: A meta-analysis of research conducted 1990–1999. *Journal of Correctional Education*, 55, 148–167.

Commission of the European Communities Brussels, 2.2.2005. COM(2005) 24 final communication to the spring European council. Working together for growth and jobs. A new start for the lisbon strategy. Communication from president Barroso in agreement with Vice-President Verheugen.

Council of Europe (2010). European convention on human rights as amended by Protocols Nos. 11 and 14. Council of Europe treaty series, No. 5. Strasbourg: Council of Europe Publishing.

Council of Europe Recommendation CM/Rec(2010)1 of the Committee of Ministers to member states on the Council of Europe Probation Rules (Adopted by the Committee of Ministers on 20 January 2010 at the 1075th meeting of the Ministers' Deputies)

Fifth International Conference on Adult Education (1997). The hamburg declaration on adult learning and the agenda for the future: Fifth international conference on adult education 14–18 July.

Hawley, J., Murphy, I., & Souto-Otero M. (2012). Survey on prison education and training in europe final report. Order 23 of the DG education and culture framework contract 02/10 – Lot. Birmingham: GHK.
Hawley, J. (2011). Prison education and training in Europe – a review and commentary of existing literature, analysis and evaluation. Directorate General for Education and Culture, European Commission. A report submitted by GHK.
Howard Association (London England) (1895). *The Paris Prison Congress, 1895: summary report.* London: LSE Library.
http://www.unesco.org/education/uie/confintea/pdf/con5eng.pdf
MacCormick, A. H. (1931). Education in the prison of tomorrow. *Annals of the American Academy of Political and Social Science, 157,* 72–77.
Muñoz V., (2009). Promotion and protection of human rights, civil, political, economic, social and cultural rights, including the right to development. The right to education of persons in detention. Report of the special rapporteur on the right to education. United Nations General Assembly.
United Nations (1977). Standard minimum rules for the treatment of prisoners. Adopted by the first united nations congress on the prevention of crime and the treatment of offenders, held at Geneva in 1955, and approved by the Economic and Social Council by its resolutions 663 C (XXIV) of 31 July 1957 and 2076 (LXII) of 13 May 1977.
United Nations (1985). United Nations Standard Minimum Rules for the Administration of Juvenile Justice of (1985). United Nations. Department of Public Information.
United Nations (1988). Body of Principles for the Protection of All Persons under Any Form of Detention or Imprisonment Adopted by General Assembly resolution 43/173 of 9 December 1988.
Wilson, D. B., Gallagher, C. A., & MacKenzie, D. L. (2000). "A meta-analysis of corrections-based education, vocation, and work programs." *Journal of Research in Crime and Delinquency*, 2000; 37: 347–368.

AFFILIATION

Joseph Giordmaina
Senior Lecturer, Department of Education Studies,
University of Malta

PART IV

LEARNING IN EVERYDAY LIFE

PATRICIA CRANTON

20. TRANSFORMATIVE LEARNING

warbride

My mother arrived in Canada in 1948 to marry a Canadian soldier whom she had met when the Canadian army participated in the liberation of the Netherlands. My mother grew up in Amsterdam where she was a part of a large musical and artistic family. That family disowned her when she "ran away to marry a soldier," and my mother was not to see any of them again for more than 20 years, by which time her parents were no longer alive. After a long journey by ship from Amsterdam to Montreal and then by train from Montreal to Alberta, my mother arrived in what she saw as a desolate and isolated rural community of farmers. Money was scarce. There was little music. My mother's English was what she learned in high school, and it did not serve her well in the community. She and my father married in November of 1948, and I was born in September of 1949, followed by three more children within six years.

The nearest neighbor lived one mile away. My father worked on the farm from morning to night. And my mother could not drive a car. She was afraid and lonely. She was afraid of the big open spaces and the huge sky and the silence. She was afraid of the great lumbering beasts that were the farm's cattle. She was afraid to try to learn to drive a car, and so she never did learn.

I tell this story as a way of introducing transformative learning theory. I used to think, with little patience when I was young, that all she needed to do was to "get with it," "to pull herself together." How hard was it to drive a car? I drove the farm trucks when I was tall enough to reach the pedals. It was, to me, a simple mechanical skill.

THE ORIGINS OF TRANSFORMATIVE LEARNING THEORY

Jack Mezirow (1978) conducted a comprehensive study of the experiences of women participating in college re-entry programs. He sent surveys to the administrative staff, counselors, program directions, students, and teachers in 12 community college programs and followed up with further surveys and interviews. This led him to be able to define a ten-phase process which described the women's experiences. He identifies "perspective transformation" as the central process occurring in the personal development of the women participating in the re-entry programs (p. 7). How Mezirow describes the process within the context of the time is interesting: "The process is illustrated in part by consciousness raising, for many the heart of the women's movement. It is ironic that this educational development, which has transformed the perspectives of thousands of women, has never found its way into the literature of adult education" (p. 8). He describes the women in his study as learning to see themselves as products of previously unchallenged and oppressive cultural expectations. He says that, although the women's movement provided support, "the process of negotiating perspective transformation can be painful and treacherous" (p. 11). The woman's very identity is called into question.

Mezirow (1975) originally proposed that a perspective transformation included the phases: a disorienting dilemma, self-examination, assessment of assumptions and a sense of alienation, relating to others, exploring options, building competence and self-confidence, planning a course of action, acquiring the skills for the course of action, trying out new roles, and reintegrating the social context. In preparation for writing this chapter, I reread Mezirow's early work, and this led me to rethink my mother's experience. The nature of her disorienting dilemma and loss of identity are clear—she left everything that was familiar, including her family, culture, and her sense of self in the world. I assume that she engaged in self-examination; she must have questioned the decision she made to come to Canada and examined her loneliness and fears. It was difficult for her to relate to others (to realize that her problem was shared) since the neighbor women did not share her experience, and she was limited in her ability to go to visit anyone. And beyond this, I think the remaining phases were simply out of her reach. Without support, she could not build competence and self-confidence, or plan and implement a course of action.

TRANSFORMATIVE LEARNING: THE COGNITIVE PERSPECTIVE

In 1981, Mezirow used Habermas's (1971) kinds of knowledge as a framework for his work, and in 1991, he combined critical theory and cognitive psychology to create a comprehensive theory of transformative learning. Mezirow periodically adjusted his definition of transformative learning over the years, but essentially it remained the same. In 2003, he wrote: "Transformative learning is learning that transforms problematic frames of reference—sets of fixed assumptions and expectations (habits of mind, meaning perspectives, mindsets)—to make them more inclusive, discriminating, open, reflective, and emotionally able to change. Such frames of reference are better than others because they are more likely to generate beliefs and opinions that will prove more true or justified to guide action" (pp. 58–59). That is, when people encounter an experience or perspective that is discrepant with their beliefs and values, that encounter has the potential to call those beliefs and values into question and to lead to a deep shift in the way people see themselves and/or the world.

Habits of mind are a product of past experiences, knowledge of the world, cultural background, and psychological inclinations. People develop habitual expectations—what happens before is likely to happen again. Mezirow (2000) identified six types of habits of mind. Epistemic habits of mind are those related to knowledge and how we acquire knowledge. Sociolinguistic habits of mind are related to social norms, cultural expectations, and the way language reflects those norms and expectations. Psychological habits of mind have to do with people's self-concept, inhibitions, anxieties, and fears. Moral-ethical habits of mind define good and evil, morality, and the extent to which people see themselves as responsible for advocating for justice in the world. Philosophical habits of mind are based on worldview, political views, and religious doctrine. Aesthetic habits of mind include values, tastes, judgments, and standards about beauty. Habits of mind are not easily accessible: they tend to be deeply embedded and unexamined. As such, they can create constraints that prevent people from learning or critically questioning their perspectives.

I cannot presume to know my mother's habits of mind, but I can speculate about some of them. In terms of epistemic perspectives, she had no knowledge of any of the things in her new world (farming, cattle, or growing crops). Her sociolinguistic habits of mind originated in her family and cultural background (for example, her views of the 'working class'). She was afraid of many things in her new surroundings (psychological habits of mind). I imagine that in terms of moral-ethical habits of mind, she felt guilt about leaving her family and being disowned by them. My mother was a Catholic, but there was no Catholic church that was accessible to her, so she was forced to give up her participation in her religion (philosophical habits of mind). Her family was musical and artistic; there was little or no music or art in her new life (aesthetic habits of mind).

In the recent literature on transformative learning theory, the central concepts include: consciousness-raising in order to make habits of mind conscious, discourse or dialogue with others, critical reflection and critical self-reflection in relation to assumptions and values, support from others, and action on changed perspectives. In contexts where there is a facilitator or educator, consciousness-raising may involve strategies such as role playing, journal writing, critical questioning, experiential activities, and arts-based activities. Consciousness-raising also occurs in self-help groups, online chat groups, blogs, retreats, book club discussions, or in any context where people exchange views related to their perspectives and habits of mind. Mezirow (2003, p. 59) defines discourse as dialogue involving the assessment of beliefs, feelings, and values. Discourse is more formalized than conversation or simple dialogue. The ideal conditions of discourse include: having accurate and complete information, being free from coercion, being able to weigh evidence and assess arguments, being open to alternatives, being able to reflect critically, having equal opportunity to participate, and being able to accept informed consensus as valid (Mezirow, 1991, p. 78). Critical reflection and critical self--reflection involve an examination of the content, process, and premise of a problem or experience. This can be in relation to the outside world (critical reflection) or in relation to one's self (critical self-reflection). Content reflection means asking "What is happening here? What is going on?" Process reflection is an examination of the strategies that are being used to address an issue: "How did this come to be? How did I get to this place?" Premise reflection focuses on the premise underlying the issue: "Why is this important to me in the first place? Why do I care about this?" It is premise reflection that has the greatest potential to lead to transformative learning, and premise reflection usually follows content and process reflection.

TRANSFORMATIVE LEARNING: BEYOND RATIONAL

Independently of Mezirow's development of transformative learning theory, Boyd and Myers (1988; Boyd, 1985; Boyd, 1989) defined transformative education within the context of small group learning. They drew on Jungian concepts such as individuation. Boyd and Myers (1988) describe a positive transformation as "an event which moves a person to psychic integration and active realization of their [sic] true being" (p. 262). They compare their conceptualization of transformative education to Mezirow's (1981) particularly in relation to the role of the ego. In Mezirow's cognitive approach, the goal of transformative learning is to have the ego take control of a person's life, by becoming aware of the constraints and inhibitions in the unconscious. Boyd and Myers see all psychic (psychological) structures as involved in transformation; this follows Jung's ([1921] 1971) description of individuation—a process by which people become aware of the psychic structures of anima, animus, ego, shadow, and the collective unconscious. In doing so, they differentiate themselves from the collective of humanity, while, at the same time, seeing how they are a part of the collective of humanity.

Dirkx (1997, 2006, 2012) contributed extensively to the beyond-rational interpretation of transformative learning theory by elaborating on and extending Boyd and Myers work. Dirkx (2006) writes about emotion-laden images "as a means of .... working through unconscious psychic conflicts and dilemmas associated with the learning task or content, and of fostering opportunities among our learners for meaning making, deep change, and transformation" (p. 16). Dirkx (2012) sees individuation as central to transformative learning, and he stresses "the importance of understanding our 'inner' worlds, of which we may be unaware" (p. 118). The primary focus of soul work is the development of a conscious relationship with the unconscious (Dirkx, 1997, 2012). Soul work is described through examples of experiences—through art, music, film, nature, joy, and suffering. It involves paying attention to everyday experiences and the images that exist therein. Elsewhere, I have written about a student in one of my adult learning groups (Cranton, 2006). Jim was a tradesperson learning to be a teacher of his trade, and he hid his anxiety about being a student by taking on the role of class clown. The group came to depend on Jim for a good joke and a good laugh in every class. One day, he broke out of his role and became angry, resentful, and upset. He shouted, "I can't do this, I can't be a teacher, this was not meant to be, I am quitting now!" It was a summer day. The sun was shining into our classroom windows. I suggested that we take a break and go for a walk in the woods just outside of our building. A few of the other men walked with Jim, and we all wandered along the trails in the woods for 30 minutes or so. Jim's classmates stayed with him for the rest of the afternoon and into the evening. The next day, Jim announced that he would be "ok," and he dropped his clown role. I think this was an example of soul work—the sun shining in the window, Jim's vulnerability and suffering, his classmates' support, and the connection with nature.

It is not only scholars of depth psychology who have contributed to the beyond-rational understanding of transformative learning. O'Sullivan (2012), for example, writes from a planetary and ecological perspective; Schapiro, Wasserman, and Gallegos (2012) describe transformative learning as occurring within and through relationships. Lawrence (2012) sees transformation as a product of arts-based experiences. Jarvis (2012) focuses specifically on the role of romantic fiction as an art form that can stimulate transformation. In all of these approaches it is not the cognitive processes of thinking and reflecting that are central to the learning, but rather intuition, imagination, emotion, narrative, and embodiment.

When I think again about my mother's story, I can see that much of her story was beyond the rational. Her fears of open space, big skies, and silence may have been the result of living for the first 26 years of her life in a big, noisy city, but I suspect it was not that straightforward. She had lost her identity—her family, her culture, her country, her language, her religion, and the art and music that sustained her soul. The big empty sky, the open empty spaces, and the dark silence that can only exist on the prairies could well have symbolized the emptiness that came with the loss of her sense of self. The "great beasts," as she called the cattle, may have been symbolic of the "primitive," which was how she saw much of her surroundings. She knew no one with a similar experience; there was little to hang onto—no support, no alternatives, no way of addressing the situation in which she found herself.

TRANSFORMATIVE LEARNING: SOCIAL CHANGE

Social change has long been a goal of adult education, from the founding of the Antigonish movement in Canada in the late 1920s and the founding of the Highland Folk School in the United States in 1932. Selman (1989) takes this back much further to the Corresponding Societies in Britain in the late 1700s which were interested in political change and the Adult Schools which were dedicated to promoting literacy. Adult educators interested in social reform were seen by many as agitators (promoting literacy empowered people in a time when empowerment of the "masses" was seen as a threat). More than 100 years later, the Antigonish movement was seen, by some, as communist-inspired (Selman), and in the context of the time, this was a strongly negative statement.

There still is a tension in adult education between humanism and critical theory, or a "radical philosophy." And this tension is certainly reflected in transformative learning theory. Those theorists who focus on individuals' transformative learning are criticized as neglecting social change or even as neglecting the social context of individuals' learning. However, Mezirow (2000) distinguishes between the educational goal of helping people become aware of oppressive structures and change them, and the political goal of forcing economic change. In an often quoted passage, Brookfield (2000, p. 143) goes so far as to say that critical reflection without social action is a "self-indulgent form of speculation that makes no real difference to anything." Brookfield (2012) prefers to focus on ideology critique rather than transformative learning in part because he sees transformative learning as no longer having a clear meaning.

Taylor (2009) tries to work out this issue by describing an individual "unit of analysis," where individual growth and learning is the focus and little attention is paid to social context or social change, and a social "unit of analysis," with an emphasis on ideology critique where people "transform society and their own reality" (p. 5). However, this does not help much; the same tension exists. Newman (2012) suggests that transformative learning has come to mean so many things that it is no longer a useful construct; he proposes that we are talking about nothing more than "good teaching."

Transformative *learning* is a learning process. Individual people learn. Organizations and societies and cultures may change, but they do not learn in the way that people learn. Individuals may learn about a variety of things, and they may transform their perspectives in a variety of ways. Some of this learning is inner-oriented and personal (but still always within a social context), and other times this learning may be about social injustice, unveiling oppression, social action, and so forth, but it is the individual who is transforming his or her perspectives on social issues. Transformative learning involves action, so when a person transforms a perspective related to social issues, that person acts on the transformed perspective. And there we join individual transformation and social action.

INTEGRATION

Transformative learning theory is young, not even 40 years old at the time of this writing. In 2000, Mezirow described it as a theory in progress, and he has encouraged others to challenge and elaborate on his work. As a result, transformative learning theory has developed in several directions, and people have come to use the word "transformative" to describe a variety of events and situations some of which are not related to learning at all (for example, when the majority Canadian Conservative government brought down the federal budget for the spring of 2012, it was hailed as a transformative budget). For this reason, scholars such as Brookfield (2012) and Newman (2012) are ready to abandon the terminology or the theory itself. Even within the discourse that is pertinent to adult learning, there is a fragmentation of thought that needs to be addressed.

Taylor (2008) describes several alternative conceptions of transformative learning and sets them up in contrast to each other. He labels Mezirow's approach as psychocritical. He sees Dirkx's work as a psychoanalytic view since it is based on the psychic structures of depth psychology. Taylor describes a psycho-developmental approach as one that looks at continuous, incremental growth over the lifespan. Turning to social change, Taylor says that another alternative perspective is social-emancipatory, rooted in the work of Freire (1970). He then comes up with four more views of transformative learning from the more recent literature: neurobiological (based on the notion that the brain structure changes during learning), cultural-spiritual (which explores a culturally relevant and spiritually grounded approach), race-centric (where people of African descent are put at the center), and planetary (focused on the interconnectedness of the universe, planet, environment, humanity, and the personal world).

If the theory of transformative learning is to continue to develop and inform adult education practice in a meaningful way, scholars need to work toward an integration of theoretical perspectives rather than to continue with further fragmentation. We also need to work toward clarity on what is and what is not transformative learning. To do that, we need to focus on the full phrase—transformative learning—and include only what is related to adult learning and include only the learning that results in a deep shift in perspective, regardless of the process (for example, rational or beyond rational) of getting there. In that way, we can bring together the existing perspectives rather than set them up as dualisms. I interpreted my mother's story through both a rational and a beyond-rational lens, for example. The same person can experience transformative learning in different ways depending on the context and the content of the learning; transformative learning related to my work might be purely cognitive, and transformation related to a personal loss might be primarily beyond rational. And different people might respond to the same situation in diverse ways depending on their personality or learning style preferences. In other words, the rational, beyond rational, and social change perspectives can be a part of the same theoretical framework.

REFERENCES

Boyd, R. D., & Myers, J. B. (1988). Transformative education. *International Journal of Lifelong Education, 7*, 261–284.

Boyd, R. D. (1989). Facilitating personal transformation in small groups. *Small Group Behavior, 20*(4), 459–474.

Boyd, R. D. (1985). Trust in groups: The great mother and transformative education. In L. S. Walker (Ed.), *Proceedings of the annual midwest research-to-practice conference in adult and continuing education.* (pp. 22–26). Ann Arbor: University of Michigan.

Brookfield, S. D. (2012).Critical theory and transformative learning. In E.W. Taylor & P. Cranton (Eds.), *The handbook of transformative learning: Theory, research, and practice* (pp. 131–146). San Francisco: Jossey-Bass.

Cranton, P. (2006). *Understanding and promoting transformative learning: A guide for educators of adults* (2nd ed.). San Francisco: Jossey-Bass.

Dirkx, J. M. (1997). Nurturing soul in adult education. In P. Cranton (Ed.), *Transformative learning in action: Insights from practice* (pp. 79–88). New Directions for Adult and Continuing Education, no. 74. San Francisco: Jossey-Bass.

Dirkx, J. M. (2006). Engaging emotions in adult learning: A Jungian perspective on emotion and transformative learning. In E.W. Taylor (Ed.), *Fostering transformative learning in the classroom: challenges and innovations* (pp. 15–26). New Directions for Adult and Continuing Education, no. 109. San Francisco: Jossey-Bass.

Dirkx, J. M. (2012). A jungian approach to transformative learning. In E.W. Taylor & P. Cranton (Eds.), *The handbook of transformative learning: Theory, research, and practice* (pp. 116–130). San Francisco: Jossey-Bass.

Freire, P. (1970). *Pedagogy of the oppressed.* New York, NY: Seabury.

Habermas, J. (1971). *Knowledge and human interests.* Boston: Beacon Pres.

Jarvis, C. (2012). Fiction and film and transformative learning. In E.W. Taylor & P. Cranton (Eds.), *The handbook of transformative learning: Theory, research, and practice* (pp. 486–502) San Francisco: Jossey-Bass.

Jung, C. (1971). *Psychological types.* Princeton: Princeton University Press. (Originally published in 1921).

Lipson Lawrence, R. (2012). Out of our heads: Transformative learning through artistic expression. In E.W. Taylor & P. Cranton (Eds.), *The handbook of transformative learning: Theory, research, and practice* (pp. 471–485). San Francisco: Jossey-Bass.

Mezirow, J. (1975). *Education for perspective transformation: Women's reentry programs in community colleges.* New York: Center for Adult Education, Teachers College, Columbia University.

Mezirow, J. (1978). Perspective transformation. *Adult Education, 28,* 100–110.

Mezirow, J. (1981). A critical theory of adult learning and education. *Adult Education, 32,* 3–24.

Mezirow, J. (1991). *Transformative dimensions of adult learning.* San Francisco: Jossey-Bass.

Mezirow, J. (2000). Learning to think like an adult. In J. Mezirow & Associates (Eds.), *Learning as transformation: Critical perspectives on a theory in progress* (pp. 3–31). San Francisco: Jossey-Bass.

Mezirow, J. (2003). Transformative learning as discourse. *Journal of Transformative Education, 1*(1), 58–63.

Newman, M. (2012). Calling transformative learning into question: Some mutinous thoughts. *Adult Education Quarterly, 62*(1), 36–55.

O'Sullivan, E. (2012). Ecology and transformation: Forging a planetary context for transformative learning. In E. W. Taylor & P. Cranton (Eds.), *The handbook of transformative learning: Theory, research, and practice* (pp. 162–177). San Francisco: Jossey-Bass.

Schapiro, S., Wasserman, I., & Gallegos, P. (2012). Group work and dialogue: Spaces and processes for transformative learning in relationships. In E.W. Taylor & P. Cranton (Eds.), *The handbook of transformative learning: Theory, research, and practice* (pp. 355–372). San Francisco: Jossey-Bass.

Selman, G. (1989). The enemies of adult education. *Canadian Journal of University Continuing Education, 15,* 68–81.

Taylor, E. W. (2008). Transformative learning theory. In S.B. Merriam (Ed.), *Third update on adult learning theory* (pp. 5–16). New Directions for Adult and Continuing Education, no. 119. San Francisco: Jossey-Bass.

Taylor, E. W. (2009). Fostering transformative learning. In J. Mezirow & E.W. Taylor (Eds.), *Transformative learning in practice: Insights from community, workplace, and higher education* (pp. 3–17). San Francisco: Jossey-Bass.

AFFILIATION

Patricia Cranton
Professor, University of New Bruinswick, Canada

LYN TETT

21. ADULT LITERACIES

WHAT IS MEANT BY ADULT LITERACY?

Definitions of what it means to be literate are always shifting. The common way to think about literacy is by seeing it as a ladder that people climb up. This begins at school where children are ranked according to their examinable achievements and adult literacy is the extension of the process in post-school contexts. The emphasis is, therefore, on standardising literacy accomplishments, tests, core skills, and uniform learning outcomes that are specified in advance of the learning process. People are ranked from bottom to top with the emphasis on what they can't do rather than what they can. This leads to a deficit model where those on the bottom rungs are positioned as lacking the skills that they need. The frameworks used to define this ladder are top-down ones constructed largely in terms of pre-vocational and vocationally relevant literacy requirements that lead to employment. Consequently, they do not recognise the validity of people's own definitions, uses and aspirations for literacy and this means that the literacies people are expected to gain are not negotiable or learner-centred and not locally responsive (see Hamilton *et al*, 2012). They define what counts as 'real literacy' and silence everything else. This is because literacy is socially constructed and must be seen in relation to the interests and powerful forces that seek to fix it in particular ways (Crowther *et al*, 2001).

Some definitions, however, acknowledge the complexity of adult literacy such as that used in Scotland:

- To be literate and numerate is not only to have the mechanical skills of encoding and decoding symbols but also the knowledge, skills and understanding that enable us to do what we want to do in our private, family, community and working lives;
- The key life areas and social contexts in which literacy and numeracy are used are important in deciding on what is to be learned;
- Literacy and numeracy skills are almost always employed for a purpose – such as making decisions or solving problems – and in a particular social context (Learning Connections, 2005: 13).

This definition is based on a view of literacies that emphasises the importance of the context in which people use their abilities (Barton, 2007; Papen, 2005). It also assumes that people are part of social networks and will rely on work colleagues, family or friends to help them with some literacies tasks. Research by Bynner and

Parsons (2006: 10) confirmed this perspective as they found in their analysis of the 1958 and 1970 British birth cohort studies that there was a 'continuing low awareness of literacy and numeracy difficulties, which is not surprising among adults, most of whom manage their lives well and learn to cope with any skills difficulties they have'.

Popular conceptions of literacy can easily stigmatise adults as lacking competence and media panics can lead politicians and policy-makers to address these perceived deficits in stigmatising ways. However, the selection and distribution of literacy to different social groups is not something that happens neutrally because literacy is deeply bound up with producing, reproducing and maintaining unequal arrangements of power. Consequently, the dominant model of literacy systematically fails to address issues of power relations in peoples' lives and what they can do about them.

LITERACIES AND POWER

New research and practice has shown that it is more appropriate to talk about literacies as plural, rather than singular. This approach, known as the New Literacy Studies (as in Barton 2007; Street and Lefstein, 2008), has been at the forefront in undermining the discourse of deficit because it grounds literacies in real peoples' lives and starts from the local, everyday experience of literacy in particular communities of practice. This means that there are different literacy practices in different domains of social life, such as education, religion, workplaces, families, community activities. These change over time and different literacies are supported and shaped by the institutions and social relationships that people are part of and do not transfer easily across contexts. Detailed studies of particular situations are revealing about these differences and in turn these help identify the broader meanings, values and uses that literacy has for people in their day-to-day lives. The new literacy studies dispenses with the idea that there is a single literacy that can be unproblematically taken for granted, rather we have to think in pluralistic terms about the variety of literacies that are used in different contexts in order to make literacies practices meaningful to people.

Another important strand of thinking about literacies has developed from the changes in communication technologies that are also shaping literacy practices. The juxtaposition of icons, imagery and text particularly in the internet is presenting new challenges for the process of communication and the literacies associated with it (see Kress, 2009). In an information rich world there is an increasing gap between those with access to information and those that are denied it. Redistributing information and making it accessible to the 'information poor' is an important educational and political task. Moreover, the demands of a 'knowledge economy' and the so-called 'information society' cannot simply be constrained within the traditional conventions of literacy understanding. Rather than seeing literacy as a tool for organising our knowledge that is consistent with the economistic vision of the global economy (see Tett, 2010), other ways are needed that shift from seeing literacy as a deficit in people to an examination of the literacies that people engage in. This shift needs to recognise difference and diversity and challenges how these differences are viewed in society. From this perspective the deficit, if there is one to be located, is in a society that excludes, reduces and ridicules the rich means of communication that exist amongst its people (see Hamilton et al, 2012).

IMPLICATIONS FOR LEARNING AND TEACHING

Traditional constructs of teaching still frame literacy as the acquisition of a body of standardised reading, writing and mathematical skills that can be formally assessed and compared within and between nations. The International Adult Literacy Surveys (IALS)(OECD, 2000), for example, have spurred governments into channelling funds into literacy and numeracy teaching aimed at remedying these 'deficiencies' and meeting pre-set targets for minimum levels of competence. Behind these initiatives lie ideological assumptions that are germane to this chapter. They are:

- That the statistics provide an accurate account of people's literacies in use
- That formalised teaching of literacy skills will automatically improve competencies in life
- That increases in formally assessed levels of literacy will enhance national economic prosperity
- That responsibility for rectifying the problem of low literacy lies solely with the individual.

The synergistic effect of these unspoken but powerful assumptions positions adult learners as if they were child-like rather than capable independent adults through, for example, describing their skills in terms of children's reading ages (Crowther et al, 2001). In another example, Sir Claus Moser, who headed an enquiry into adult literacy and numeracy in England, suggested 'these people have very limited lives… they can't lead a normal life like you and me' (Claus Moser, BBC Radio 4, 27th March 2000, 'The Great British Secret', presented by Vivian White). Adults are also viewed as people whose deficiencies have a direct and adverse impact on the national good and who therefore pose a problem for the literate 'others'. A front-page article in an American banking journal proclaimed, '*Our* high level of illiteracy is more than a sad set of statistics. It is the Achilles heel of *our* continued prosperity' (RBC Centura Bank 2003) (emphasis added). Such messages are internalised by those who are deemed to be lacking such skills. '[They shape] how they think about themselves and how they act in the world' (Soroke 2004, p 44). As Charlesworth, (2000, p. 243–4) argues:

> Being told that one is not clever is like being told that one is fat or ugly; it is not something about which one can achieve indifference because it is likely to play

a deciding role in one's destiny, particularly in the possibility of a worthwhile life and happiness. Thus we end up with people defined ... as useless, unable, stupid; lacking in the dignities given to the privileged

Thus literacies learners enter the learning situation not as equal, capable adults, but as markedly unequal people. Add to this the negative experiences of education endured by many literacies learners throughout their schooling (Maclachlan & Tett, 2006), together with the fragile learner identities of many learners (Tett & Maclachlan, 2007) and the whole produces an exceptionally 'lopsided' balance of power that is particularly evident in literacies contexts.

In addition there are many complex issues affecting learning including the dominant attitudes prevailing in society about learning at the macro level, as well as the cognitive, the social and the emotional dimensions operating at the individual level (Illeris, 2002). For example, adults interviewed in Maclachlan and colleagues' (2008) study of literacy learners said:

The teachers were more interested in the bright ones; the ones that could get on...They sort of just left me to one side... I tried to do my best, but I just felt that because I wasn't bright and I wasn't brainy that people just didn't want to know.

In English and Maths classes if you got picked on by the teacher ...and when you got it wrong you got hit. So there was fear – no one would put up their hand unless you were 100% sure, and that marks you.

This means it is important that tutors and learners have an awareness of the values of equality and activity in the learning/teaching situation and understand that learning has a variety of dimensions. Rogers (2003) distinguishes the everyday learning that we engage in through living and acting in the world around us from acquisitional or 'task-conscious' learning (p. 16). He maintains, however, that many adults with negative experiences of compulsory education struggle to marry their construction of themselves as capable 'task-conscious' learners with their sense of self as learners in structured educational contexts. Although adults may recognise their competence in relation to the acquisitional learning that they regularly encounter such as caring for children or elders, their perceptions and experience of education inhibit the transfer of this positive self-construct in formalised learning contexts. They can therefore revert to constructing themselves as *not* competent, because they equate learning primarily with formal education.

For these reasons literacies programmes that are based in the life situations of adults and communities in response to issues that are derived from their own knowledge are more likely to be successful. When the emphasis is put on how adults can and want to use their literacies then the focus moves to what people have, rather than what they lack, what motivates them rather than what is seen by others as something they need (see Tett et al, 2006). In addition, where the power to determine the content of the curriculum lies primarily with the participants, rather than the provider, then it can be instrumental in challenging these imbalances in deciding what is to be learnt. Interventions that aim to promote initial participation and continuing retention in adult literacies provision should therefore take cognizance of all these dimensions if learners are to have positive, successful experiences of learning.

For example, one project studied by Maclachlan and colleagues, (2008) demonstrated the importance of the emotional and social dimensions of learning and how working together helped participants to see learning as both possible and valuable. For example, interviewees said 'being part of the group has helped me to keep going even when things were really difficult at home' and 'the others knew I didn't like writing on the flip-chart because my spelling isn't good but with their encouragement I did it and after that I felt really proud of myself'. Good relationships between and amongst tutors and learners created an atmosphere of trust where support, encouragement and constructive feedback helped people to take risks. This in turn enabled the learners to become more autonomous in their learning and develop the ability to use their own judgement regarding the quality of their work. For example, 'the first version of my letter to the council about the graffiti was all muddled up so I rewrote it four times before I was satisfied it said what I wanted' and 'I was asked to do a reading by my Church so I got the others in the group to listen to me and tell me how it sounded and gradually learned that I had to say it really slowly if people were going to understand me'. Participants and tutors together formed a community of practice that acted as a 'locus of engagement in action, interpersonal relations, shared knowledge, and negotiation [that are] mediated by the communities in which their meanings are negotiated in practice' (Wenger, 1998, p. 85). Where there is a sense of shared experiences and values amongst class members, as another learner in this project noted: 'you feel at ease, you feel good. Most people's problems are worse than mine... No one throws stones at anyone else, – we're all in the same boat but for different reasons'.

Another important factor is the pedagogy and practice of the education providers. This involves developing a flexible curriculum that places participants at the centre of practice where learning activities are chosen or adapted to learners' goals, personal interests or immediate lives. For example, in another project studied by Maclachlan and colleagues, (2008) a participant said: 'the tutors here offer me lots of choice and help me to move on to the next thing when I'm ready'. In addition, a major part of providing successful learning opportunities is through tutors creating a supportive atmosphere where learners are treated with respect and equality within relationships of warmth and trust in the classroom. In sharing experiences participants also learn that they are not different and not deficient, but are instead capable learners in their own right. They also begin to recognise that they are not 'the only one with literacy problems' and that not 'everyone else' is better than them, because they are involved in the mutual learning that characterises the process of becoming part of a learning group. These social communities shift the emphasis from learning as transmission to learning as doing, as a social activity where 'collaborative practices mediate opportunities for learning' (Guile and Young, 2001 p 59). Finally positive tutor-student relationships are very important. For example: 'it motivates me that the tutors are working so hard to help me. I've already been able to write a letter and had a good result from it. I feel it's the first time anyone's reacted to anything I've said' (Maclachlan et al, 2008).

OUTCOMES OF PARTICIPATION

In this section I draw on a large-scale study of over six hundred learners participating in literacies education in Scotland carried out by Tett and colleagues in 2006. The key finding from this study (Tett et al, 2006; Tett and Maclachlan, 2007) was that participating built confidence that then enabled people to do things differently. The study found that there were *psychological* differences in how people felt about themselves. Students reported: increases in their self-esteem; a greater belief in their own potential and achievements; they had greater independence; they were happier; more able to voice their opinions; more aware of others. Confidence was also related to *increasing skills*. For example students reported that they were more able to: speak to other people confidently; use computers; read newspapers and books; fill in forms; go shopping and calculate the best value items. Students also reported changes in *facets of their lives* such as: approaching strangers for information; feeling safer in their neighbourhood; more able to deal with conflict and stand up for themselves; able to engage in conversations without needing an interpreter.

Below are specific illustrations of the changes that students reported:

I'm not crabbit [bad tempered] anymore because I'm not avoiding problems I'm tackling them head on.

I don't need to depend on others and have changed to being very hopeful and helpful.

There's no more fighting with my daughter when it's homework time because I can help her with it, which I couldn't do in the past.

I'm more confident in speaking to others so I'm not scared to go to interviews now.

I am now a union representative at work...people now come to me for advice with problems with staff.

This study also found that learning was dynamic because benefits gained in one domain, such as education, impacted on other domains, such as family and community. Many people detailed the variety of ways in which their participation in adult literacies had helped them to do a better job as a parent, and had improved relationships generally within their families. These positive changes in attitudes to education and family life are likely to result in benefits for the wider family and community as well as the individual concerned.

These findings show the importance of providing good quality teaching to enable literacies learners to progress and sustain their learning. However, education cannot on its own affect large-scale social transformation, but it is a necessary and pivotal component of such change. It causes adults to think and act differently and this chapter has illustrated how a positive learning experience was the catalyst in enabling adult literacy learners to do just that.

CONCLUSION

It is known that the literacy process itself, and the wider cultural action for freedom born in the context of learning to read and write (see Freire, 1972), need to reflect the values of equality and activity if literacies tutors are to be part of a radical tradition rather than a conservative force preventing change. Freire (1972) talks of reading the world in reading the word and sees such literacy learning as enabling adults to learn, not their place in society, but about their place in society so that they may collectively act to change it for the better. In learning communities where power and meaning are mutually negotiated learners do begin to recognise their personal worth and power and its impact in the wider world. However, critical, radical adult learning extends beyond the parameters of individual change. It is a collective process whereby people who begin to see themselves differently as individuals, also question together the asymmetrical power relationships that have marginalised them and their practices, and act to change them. If the emphasis is put on how adults can and want to use the many varieties of literacies then the focus moves to what people have, rather than what they lack, what motivates them rather than what is seen as something they need.

Learning provides a space where the discourse of deficit can potentially be challenged, first within the group and then in the wider world (see Rogers, 2003). We make meaning with others because learning is a social activity as well as a cognitive process, and part of that meaning for literacies learners is learning who they are, that they are not different or alone in struggling to master the technicalities of our literacies conventions. As Heaney (1995) points out, '[when] learning is defined as an individual's ongoing negotiation with communities of practice [this] ultimately gives definition to both self and that practice [and] explains adult learning in a variety of social groups and settings'. Adult literacies groups can provide the opportunity for learners to share their apprehensions, their experiences of literacies, of being labelled as 'wanting' and of the effects that this has had upon their sense of self. Astin (1993) has shown that the strongest single source of influence on cognitive and affective development is a student's peer group because working together enables people to learn from each other. Moreover, in the adult literacies context, the diverse experiences and the different literacies abilities that participants' possess are important sources for learning (see Zepke & Leach, 2006). In sharing experiences they will also learn that they are not different and not deficient, but are instead capable learners in their own right.

The curriculum should therefore lead to the development of a critical understanding of the social, political and economic factors that shape experience. The challenge is to capture the positive belief in the power of learning and in the potential of all people that comes from engaging in more democratic decision-making about what is important knowledge. This type of learning would provide some real choices about what being a citizen means and show how everyone can contribute to democratic processes.

Faced with a dominant discourse that blames people for the poverty that they suffer it is easy for these feelings of failure to be internalised and so confidence and self-esteem are lost. When people are excluded from participation in decision-making as well as access to employment and material resources then individual action that will change their circumstances becomes almost impossible. Working together on local issues can, however, lead to the development of a political culture that focuses on the fundamentally unequal nature of society rather than people's individual deficits. Emphasising the importance of the redistribution of resources shows that there are alternatives to increasing inequalities. These alternatives will grow out of the local politics that are founded in civil society.

REFERENCES

Astin, A. (1993). *What matters in college? Four critical years revisited* San Francisco, CA: Jossey Bass

Barton, D. (2007). *Literacy: An introduction to the ecology of written language 2nd edition*, Oxford: Blackwell.

Bynner, J., & Parsons, S. (2006). *New light on literacy and numeracy*. London: National Research and Development centre for adult literacy.

Charlesworth, S. J. (2000). *A phenomenology of working class experience*, Cambridge: Cambridge University Press.

Crowther, J. Hamilton, M., & Tett, L. (Eds.) (2001). *Powerful literacies*, Leicester: NIACE.

Crowther, J., & Tett, L. (2011). 'Critical and social literacy practices from the Scottish adult literacy experience: Resisting deficit approaches to learning', *Literacy, 45*(3) pp. 126–131.

Freire, P. (1972). *Pedagogy of the oppressed*, Harmondsworth: Penguin.

Guile, D., & Young, M. (2001). Apprenticeship as a conceptual basis for a social theory of learning. In C. Paechter et al (Eds.), *Knowledge, power and learning*. (pp. 56–62) London, P Chapman and the Open University Press.

Hamilton, M., Tett, L., & Crowther, J. (2012). 'Introduction' in L. Tett, M. Hamilton & J. Crowther, *More Powerful Literacies*, (pp. 31–57) Leicester: NIACE

Heaney, T. (1995). Learning to control democratically. Cited in Merriam, S et al. (2003). On becoming a witch: Learning in a marginalized community of practice. *Adult Education Quarterly*, May 2003, 170–188.

Illeris K. (2002). *The three dimensions of learning: Contemporary learning theory in the tension field between the cognitive, the emotional and the social* leicester, UK: NIACE.

Kress, G. (2009). *Multimodality: Exploring contemporary methods of communication*. London: Routledge.

Learning Connections (2005). *Report on the adult literacy and numeracy strategy, 2004–5*, Edinburgh: Scottish Executive.

Learning Connections (2005). *An adult literacy and numeracy curriculum framework for Scotland*, http://www.aloscotland.com/alo/files/ALNCurriculumFramework.pdf

Maclachlan, K. Hall, S. Tett, L. Crowther, J., & Edwards, V. (2008). *Motivating adult learners to persist, progress and achieve: Literacies learners at risk of non-completion of learning targets*. Edinburgh, Scottish Government.

Maclachlan, K., & Tett, L. (2006). 'Learning to change or changing the learning: Adult literacy and numeracy in Scotland', *Journal of adult and continuing education, 12*(2), 195–206.

Organization of Economic Co-operation and Development. (2000). *Literacy in the information age: Final report of the international adult literacy survey.* Paris: OECD.

Papen, U. (2005). *Adult literacy as social practice: More than skills,* London: Routledge

RBC Centura Bank (2003). *Charlotte Business Journal,* www.bizjournals.com/charlotte/stories/2003/05/05/editorial2.html

Rogers, A. (2003). *What is the difference? A new critique of adult learning and teaching.* Leicester: NIACE.

Soroke, B. (2004). *Doing freedom: An ethnography of an adult literacy centre.* MA thesis, Faculty of Education, University of British Columbia.

Street B., & Lefstein, A. (2008). *Literacy: An advanced resource for students.* London: Routledge.

Tett, L. Maclachlan, K. Hall, S., Edwards, V. Thorpe, G., & Garside, L. (2006). *Evaluation of the Scottish adult literacy and numeracy strategy,* Glasgow: Scottish Executive <http://www.scotland.gov.uk/Publications/2006/03/20102141/0>

Tett, L., & Maclachlan, (2007). Adult literacy and numeracy, social capital, learner identities and self-confidence. *Studies in the Education of Adults, 39* (2), 150–167.

Tett, L. (2010). *Community education, learning and development,* Edinburgh: Dunedin Academic Press

Wenger, E. (1998). Communities of practice: learning, meaning and identity Cambridge: Cambridge University Press.

Zepke N., & Leach, L. (2006). Improving learner outcomes in lifelong education: Formal pedagogies in non-formal learning contexts? *International Journal of Lifelong Education, 25*(5), 507–518.

AFFILIATION

Lyn Tett
Professor of Community Education,
School of Education and Professional Development,
University of Huddersfield, England

KAELA JUBAS

22. LEARNING (THROUGH) CONSUMPTION: SHOPPING AS A SITE OF ADULT EDUCATION

INTRODUCTION

I began connecting shopping and adult learning in 2005, during my doctoral studies. At that time, a range of shopping-related movements came to the fore in the city where I lived – Vancouver, on Canada's West Coast. From the farmers' market where vendors talked about food security, to a "say no to Walmart" campaign orchestrated by small business owners and other community members, to cafes providing fair trade, organic coffee and information about the conditions of coffee production and trade, my shopping engaged me in critical practices and learning. I came to see shopping as a process through which adults experience, understand and (re-)construct identity, globalization and social transformation continually and intimately.

In this chapter, I review ideas explored elsewhere (Jubas, 2008, 2010, 2011). Consistent with this collection, I work from a critical theory perspective, and insert elements of feminist and poststructural scholarship. I am influenced greatly by the writing of Antonio Gramsci (1971), whose view of the everyday as a site of learning is central. His emphasis on dialectic, or irresolvable tension between materiality and culture or ideology, is helpful in exploring tensions that emerge for consumer-learners. In that regard, the ideology of consumerism, which portrays shopping and consumption as manifestations of democratic freedom and pathways to preferred sense of self, bolsters hegemonically structured relations of class, gender and race.

Although shopping and consumption are not synonymous, they are deeply intertwined and often used interchangeably. Today, shopping occurs in stores and market stalls, sales in community centre halls and backyards or garages, and online commercial sites and classifieds. It involves cash, credit, bartering and, sometimes, free give-aways. It begins before one enters a commercial site, and involves seeking, recognizing and considering options, acquiring goods, services and experiences, and, sometimes, foregoing a purchase. Using consumption in its expansive sense, to include shopping, I concur with Hearn and Roseneil's (1999) explanation:

> Consumption is one of the basic ways in which society is structured and organised, usually unequally, sometimes incredibly so. Differential powers,

> resources and life chances are routinely produced and reproduced by and through consumption patterns. Consumption not only takes place within culture and thus within specific cultures; it also produces culture and cultures.... Furthermore, consumption also constructs, even consumes, the consumer. Just as production produces both products and the producer, the worker, so too consumption has a dialectical form. People do consumption, are "done to", constructed, consumed by that consumption. Consumption is a structure, process and agency. (p. 1)

In thinking about how shopping functions pedagogically, I turn to the five pillars of education outlined by UNESCO. Four of these pillars – learning to know, learning to do, learning to live together and learning to be – were introduced by UNESCO in 1972 and retained in later documents (Delors et al., 1996). The fifth pillar – learning to transform oneself and society – was inserted into UNESCO's work focused on education for sustainability ("Education for sustainable development," 2012), and extended thinking in a critical direction. Together, these principles offer a familiar framework for thinking about lifelong learning, which I use to illustrate how shoppers can engage in learning. Following an outline of my conceptualization of adult learning, I discuss shopping in relation to each of the pillars.

CONCEPTUALIZING LEARNING

I begin with a Gramscian perspective on culture-as-pedagogy. This understanding is consistent with the commonly accepted constructivist view which sees learning as a process through which adults build knowledge in a sociocultural context, rather than have abstract knowledge transferred by teachers. In this framework, knowledge is "the meaning that people make out of their experiences" (Merriam & Brockett, 2007, p. 46).

Associated with a constructivist perspective is the well accepted dictum in adult education that everyday life is an important site of learning. That belief invites adult educators to attend seriously to apparently mundane arenas as "classrooms without boundaries" (hooks, 2003, p. 13). As I explore here and elsewhere (Jubas, 2008, 2010, 2011), shopping and consumption are parts of everyday life in which adults learn "informally," without preset instruction, curriculum or assessment, and "incidentally," without any expectation or recognition (Foley, 2001; Hrimech, 2005). Thanks largely to the work of consumption-related social movements, some of that learning can be politically oriented.

Formal adult consumer education is often aimed at women in the field of home economics or so-called life skills segments of curriculum for marginalized learners. In contrast, all consumers encounter informal education delivered through entertainment and advertising industries. Together, these pedagogies often bolster a hegemonic consumerist ideology by teaching people that, in a capitalist democracy, spending power signals freedom and individual shoppers are responsible for learning to make "good" shopping decisions (Sandlin, 2004). Increasingly, a range of oppositional voices are encouraging a more critical approach to shopping and consumption. Such potential critical learning is complicated and complex, though; as I establish in later sections, even the most critical shoppers and consumers are implicated in ideologies and structures that they try to disrupt.

Learning is also holistic, involving emotions as well as intellect. In this sense, affect is not something that disrupts learning and needs to be managed (Dirkx, 2001; hooks, 2003). Both mainstream marketing and advertising, and alternative movements and campaigns play on people's emotions in helping them understand their shopping and consumption options and in influencing understandings of choices and shopping behaviour. In the sections below, I apply the pillars outlined by UNESCO to shopping, to illustrate how adult learning can be seen as multidimensional, formal, informal and incidental, and instrumental and critical – a truly complex process.

PILLAR ONE: LEARNING TO KNOW

This pillar articulates the traditional liberal purpose of education. It recognizes breadth and depth in education and learning, along with "learning to learn, so as to benefit from the opportunities education provides throughout life" (Delors et al., 1996, p. 37). The emphasis is on learning for the sake of learning, as a process of individual and human betterment.

As they shop for and consume items and experiences, adults continuously engage in learning. Most obviously, they learn how to interpret information encountered while they shop. From "best before" dates, to nutritional details and claims, to icons providing directions for care or signalling organic or fair trade certification, adults develop a "shopping-related literacy" (Jubas, 2010, 2011). Like all literacies, this one has instrumental and critical potential. Shoppers can interpret information provided on labels or in advertisements as facts seen as useful in making purchasing and consumption decisions, and even life-saving details for people with severe allergies. Alternatively, shoppers can question claims presented by producers, advertisers and retailers, and seek information which signals a correspondence between options available in the marketplace and their own values.

Learning about options and what they might mean is an ongoing process, because shoppers are presented with ever-changing possibilities, information and sources of information, including advertisements, staff in a shop, consumer education publications and personal acquaintances. Notable additions to these more traditional information sources are the growing number of books, organizations, documentary films and new social movements which push back against mainstream consumerist rhetoric extolling the virtues of consumption. Part of what shoppers learn, then, is which sources of information are useful and trustworthy, and how to make use of them; this is a form of learning how to learn and developing oneself through learning.

PILLAR TWO: LEARNING TO DO

The second pillar focuses on learning to develop competencies, as individuals and team members, within and outside paid employment. The skill and knowledge that adults build as shoppers relates to this pillar for several reasons. First, learning about how to research options and make decisions can be applied in settings beyond shopping. Second, many adults are responsible for making purchases as part of their jobs; to the extent that their own shopping processes help them develop in this area, shoppers are better prepared for and capable at work. Third, shopping is a process that adults undertake in a solitary and a group manner, as family members, flat-mates or friends. Shopping, then, is a learning process that begins early in life and continues throughout adulthood, and is individualized and shared.

PILLAR THREE: LEARNING TO LIVE TOGETHER

This pillar emphasizes learning "to manage conflicts – in a spirit of respect for the values of pluralism, mutual understanding and peace" (Delors, 1996, p. 37). This purpose of learning is invoked in discussions about education for civic development or citizenship education. The fanciful Paris shopping arcades and world fairs of the late 1800s taught "people to adapt to the brave new world around them, but they also made the crucial link between pedagogy and commerce that is with us to this day" (Hoechsmann, 2010, p. 24). Scholars such as Cohen (2003) trace twentieth-century American discourses and practices of consumer-citizenship. Early in the century, the consumer was seen as an individual citizen-as-worker and citizen-as-customer who deserved both fair wages and prices. During the Depression, a more collectivist impulse led to protective measures such as price controls and agricultural subsidies. In the Cold War decades, the so-called free market was attached to democratic rights, and the image of the loyal, freedom-loving American consumer-citizen emerged (see also Spring, 2003). Over the century, emphasis shifted away from states as responsible for the welfare of their citizens, toward individual consumers as responsible for the success of their states.

That notion remains recognizable, if also challenged. Reports that US political leaders beckoned Americans to go shopping shortly after 9/11, a position openly criticised by Toni Morrison and others, on the grounds that people were called on to act as consumers rather citizens, exaggerate actual remarks at the time. A few years later, however, President George W. Bush did "encourage you all to go shopping more" ("President Bush holds a news conference," 2006, p. 29) as an antidote to an anticipated recession. As that statement suggests, shopping has been invoked to aid in the construction of a unified and diverse citizenry. In this regard, shopping functions in the same way as print media in its early days, when it aided in the construction of an idealized nationally "imagined community" (Anderson, 1991).

As Anderson (1991) notes, though, this national (or global) community remains a figment, and the ideal at its centre is tied to hegemonic interests, reflected in class, gender and race relations. In the example of shopping, the directive to spend freely cannot be fulfilled by members of the lower classes, and promises that consumers can enjoy unending possibilities for new identities and status remain empty. Historically charged with overseeing shopping and consumption on behalf of their families, female shoppers who are perceived as emotional and weak are seen as embodiments of the stereotype of women as "flighty" (Bowlby, 2001, p. 119), "silly shopper[s]" (Bowlby, 2001, p.133). Like citizenship, consumption is contested terrain, and the notion of learning to live in harmony and unity that this pillar implies says more about the impact of humanist philosophy on imagining social life than about realizing it.

PILLAR FOUR: LEARNING TO BE

This pillar emphasizes learning through which individuals develop a sense of self, so that they can "act with ever greater autonomy, judgement and personal responsibility" (Delors et al., 1996, p. 37). Mainstream consumer education holds that learning skills such as budgeting and self-restraint can help adults realize those qualities. That message is complemented by the pedagogy of the advertiser and the marketplace, or "marketalkracy" (Stasko & Norris in Sandlin, Burdick, & Norris, 2012, p. 148), which teaches shoppers that they are what they buy and consume. As Sandlin, Burdick and Norris note, "we pedagogically *become* Ford truck owners, Marlboro [cigarette] men and women, and Macs rather than PCs" (p. 144, emphasis in original). That process of learning to self-identify or self-brand is driven as much by emotional and psychic concerns about social status and acceptance as it is by intellectual concerns about the safety of trucks and cigarettes or the affordability and usefulness of computer products.

Of course, not all shoppers acquiesce to "marketalkracy" in a straightforward manner. Other forces, from spiritual teachings, experiences and convictions to social movements and messages, offer alternative pedagogies. Learning to be as a shopper can be fulfilling or insidious.

PILLAR FIVE: LEARNING TO TRANSFORM ONESELF AND SOCIETY

This pillar emerged in UNESCO's environmental education platform. It proposes shifting to more fair and viable practices, and "teaching people to reflect critically on their own communities…[and] to assume responsibility for creating and enjoying a sustainable future" ("Education for sustainable development," 2012, p. 6). Movements such as fair trade, organics and locavore adhere to these aims. Fair trade aims to improve the conditions of producers in the Global South, strengthen their communities, and connect them to consumers – primarily in the Global North.

289

Organic farming of food or crops used for textiles adopts an ecological approach to sustainability. For locavores, "knowing who made your food and where it hails from...is a political imperative" (Flowers & Swan, 2011, p. 236). Beyond food, this movement encourages shoppers to buy locally made goods so that community-based producers and retailers remain viable, and transport-related environmental damage is minimized. Such social movements are emerging in the context of and disrupt hegemonic, globalized consumerism which portrays the free market as the rightful determinant of production, trade and consumption practices. They help adults understand the complexities and seriousness of their shopping decisions, develop more critical shopping practices, and connect local conditions to globalized systems.

These trends are not as recent as the term new social movements implies. Marginalized groups and their allies have long used consumer power to express their demands as citizens. By the late 1780s, British abolitionists protested slavery by boycotting slave-produced sugar from the colonies (Jubas, 2008; Klotz, 2002; Sussman, 2000). In addition to their abolitionist aim, these boycotts represented attempts by women, who lacked most formal citizenship rights, to enter into public policy debates through a proverbial back door – their socially determined role as shoppers and consumers in the service of the family. Much later, African Americans and other activists in the 1960s' civil rights movement employed boycotts and so-called buycotts – the preference for supportive producers and retailers – to advance their agenda (Cohen, 2003). Boycotts were used to similar effect internationally to press for the end of apartheid in South Africa (Klotz, 2002). Recent decades have seen calls for the integration of minority groups into representations of the good consumer (Spring, 2003). In these ways, adults have been called upon as shoppers and have attempted to use that role to spur social change.

CONSUMER-LEARNING IN A TIME OF POSTMODERN GLOBALIZATION: POTENTIAL AND CAUTIONS

In this chapter, I use the common referent of consumer-citizen and propose a new, albeit related, term – consumer-learner – to suggest the connections between shopping and learning. Resulting learning is especially important in adulthood, as core values and self-identity become clearer and the ability to connect one's actions to wider outcomes becomes more sophisticated. It is emotionally as well as intellectually based, because needs and wants are determined as much by culturally and socially guided aspirations as they are by material circumstances or health and safety concerns.

Critical shopping does or, at least, can fulfill some positive purposes; however, as I have also suggested, shopping, adult learning and transformation are complex and complicated. Greenwood (2010) articulates one conundrum:

> In a world where much of the story of consumption is socially unjust and ecologically irresponsible, where this story is concealed from view in places

we do not know, and where the story is hidden deep within selves full of paradox and contradiction, it is not always easy to know what action to take or what parts of ourselves need to change. (p. 194)

Shopping thoughtfully might aid adults learn critically about the processes and structures which unite *and* divide people and places; however, altering these processes and structures is beyond the capacity of individual shoppers. To the extent that learning about and through shopping helps people challenge what Gramsci (1971) describes as ideologically based "common sense," it can contribute to their inclinations to engage in community-based and global movements for change.

It is also important to remember the complications and limitations of the movements themselves. In redefining good shopping practice, movements such as fair trade, organics and locavore reiterate, even as they challenge, fundamentally hegemonic ideas and structures. One prevalent idea behind these movements is that shopping and consumption are expressions of democracy; that is articulated in the colloquialism "vote with your dollar." Moreover, shopping-related actions seem to garner the attention of the middle and upper classes (Connelly & Prothero, 2008; Jubas, 2008, 2010; Klotz, 2002), an unsurprising finding given the reality that the options that they promote carry greater financial costs than conventional options.

To muddy matters further, movements are being "mainstreamed," so that certified products become available in multinational chain stores which hold so much power over unjust, unsustainable global systems. Ironically, these oppositional movements reinforce elements of consumerism and problematic ideals of citizenship, and illustrate the complexity of hegemony and social transformation. Without romanticizing these movements, adult educators and learners can bring them into their classrooms, and recognize them as sites of rich, albeit it confusing, informal and incidental learning. A final lesson for the consumer-learner is that the uncertainties and complications which imbue the postmodern sensibility pervade shopping and adult learning.

REFERENCES

Anderson, B. (1991). *Imagined communities: Reflections on the origin and spread of nationalism* (Rev. ed.). London & New York: Verso (Original work published 1983).

Bowlby, R. (2001). *Carried away: The invention of modern shopping.* New York & Chichester, UK: Columbia University Press.

Cohen, L. (2003). *A consumers' republic: The politics of mass consumption in postwar America.* New York: Alfred A. Knopf.

Connelly, J., & Prothero, A. (2008). Green consumption: Life-politics, risks and contradictions. *Journal of Consumer Culture, 8*(1), 117–145.

Delors, J., Mufti, I. A., Amagi, I., Carneiro, R., Chung, F., Geremek, B., Gorham, W., Kornhauser, A., Manley, M., Quero, M. P., Savané, M.-A., Singh, K., Stavenhagen, R., Suhr, M. W., Nazhou, Z. (1996). *Learning: The treasure within. Report to UNESCO of the international commission on education for the twenty-first century (highlights).* Retrieved from http://unesdoc.unesco.org/images/0010/001095/109590eo.pdf

Dirkx, J. M. (2001). The power of feelings: Emotion, imagination, and the construction of meaning in adult education. *New Directions for Adult and Continuing Education, 89,* 63–72.

Flowers, R., & Swan, E. (2011). "Eating at us": Representations of knowledge in the activist documentary film *Food, Inc. Studies in the Education of Adults, 43*(2), 234–250.

Foley, G. (2001). Radical adult education and learning. *International Journal of Lifelong Education, 20*(1/2), 71–88.

Gramsci, A. (1971). *Selections from the prison notebooks* (Q. Hoare & G. Nowell Smith, Eds. and Trans.). New York: International Publishers.

Greenwood, D. A. (2010). Chocolate, place, and a pedagogy of consumer privilege. In J.A. Sandlin & P. McLaren (Eds.), *Critical pedagogies of consumption: Living and learning in the shadow of the Shopocalypse*. New York: Routledge.

Hearn, J., & Roseneil, S. (1999). Consuming cultures: Power and resistance. In J. Hearn & S. Roseneil (Eds.), *Consuming cultures: Power and resistance* (pp. 1–13). London: MacMillan Press Ltd., New York: St. Martin's Press, Inc.

Hoechsmann, M. (2010). Rootlessness, reenchantment, and educating desire: A brief history of the pedagogy of consumption. In J.A. Sandlin & P. McLaren (Eds.), *Critical pedagogies of consumption: Living and learning in the shadow of the "Shopocalypse"* (pp. 23–35). New York & London: Routledge.

hooks, b . (2003). *Teaching community: A pedagogy of hope*. New York: Routledge.

Hrimech, M. (2005). Informal learning. In L.M. English (Ed.), *International encyclopedia of adult education* (pp. 310–312). New York: Palgrave Macmillan.

Jubas, K. (2008). Adding human rights to the shopping list: British women's abolitionist boycotts as radical learning and practice. *Convergence, 41*(1), 77–94.

Jubas, K. (2010). *The politics of shopping: What consumers learn about identity, globalization and social change*. Walnut Creek, CA: Left Coast Press.

Jubas, K. (2011). Everyday scholars: Exploring shopping as a site of adult learning. *Adult Education Quarterly, 61*(3), 225–243.

Klotz, A. (2002). Transnational activism and global transformation: The anti-apartheid and abolitionist experiences. *European Journal of International Relations, 8*(1), 49–76.

Learning to transform oneself and society. (2012). Retrieved from http://www.unesco.org/new/en/education/themes/leading-the-international-agenda/education-for-sustainable-development/education-for-sustainable-development/five-pillars-of-learning/learning-to-transform/

Merriam, S. B., & Brockett, R. G. (2007). *The profession and practice of adult education: An introduction* (updated Ed.). San Francisco: Jossey-Bass.

President Bush holds a news conference. (2006, December 20). Retrieved from http://www.washingtonpost.com/wp-dyn/content/article/2006/12/20/AR2006122000933.html

Sandlin, J. A. (2004). Beyond price comparisons: Towards a more critical consumer education for adults through informal sites of learning. *Adult Learning, 15*(1/2), 30–33.

Sandlin, J. A., Burdick, J., & Norris, T. (2012). Erosion and experience: Education for democracy in a consumer society. *Review of Research in Education, 36*, 139–168.

Spring, J. (2003). *Educating the consumer-citizen: A history of the marriage of schools, advertising, and media*. Malwah, NJ: Lawrence Erlbaum Associates

Sussman, C. (2000). *Consuming anxieties: Consumer protest, gender, and British slavery, 1713–1833*. Stanford, CA: Stanford University Press.

ANTONIA DE VITA & ANNA MARIA PIUSSI

23. SOCIAL CREATION

INTRODUCTION: LEARNING BY CREATING TOGETHER

As scholars who for years have been passionately involved in the politics of education, our aim in this chapter is to highlight the educative and transformative resources of *social creation* at all stages in life and in work with adults, both women and men. We consider it important to propose this approach at a time when the prevalent concept is that education and culture are resources of capital rather than public goods (necessary life-sustaining resources).

In several countries, the 'weak link' of public education, namely adult education, is grossly neglected. It revolves around either the weak politics of excessive welfarism, based on a defective model of human beings, or aggressive neoliberal market economics. Florid and global, it has become part and parcel of an education and knowledge market (Federighi 2006). It is labour-market-oriented and predicated on the politics of 'making people responsible', rendering adult education merely a matter of individual use and responsibility. States and their supranational agencies play an important role in this politics in that they support private interests and sanction what is presented as the inevitable neoliberal social model.

On the contrary, the social creation approach refutes the inevitability of this model and the crisis it brings with it. We increasingly detect numerous signs of awareness of the symbolic and material significance of this crisis. There is a growing belief in the need to extricate oneself from the individualistic and mercantile model of social relations. There is also the desire to re-create the measure of value of one's own singularity and of associated living, learning in the exchange with others to combine in new and creative configurations experience and knowledge, work and politics, need and desire, life and economy.

Our concern is to provide illustrative examples of social creation inspired by a sense of both personal and collective initiatives. These types of practice highlight the notion of persons as subjects engaged in collective endeavour, capable of arousing in others the desire to be active players in modifying contexts and relations as well as in regenerating and enriching public life. At the heart of social creation lies the quest for self- and collective transformation as a lever for social transformation. This therefore entails a process of acquiring awareness and continuous learning from one's own experience and that of others, extracting oneself from the strictly and narrowly economistic notion of competences and measurable efficiency (Mayo, 2009) and taking into account the broader and possibly socially more enriching and fulfilling aspects of reality.

Our theoretical-epistemological background is grounded in the politics of sexual difference, a perspective developed in Italy, France and Spain, and well known in other European countries and further afield, which has enabled us to redefine, as women (and also men), issues, tasks, priorities, and conditions for lifelong education in these difficult and uncertain, but also promising, times. The forced change aimed at fashioning our lives, our inner selves and our desires in the name of modernity and economic competitiveness, are daily losing their credibility and appeal.

We perceive the collapse of an entire way of making sense of the world which, through languages and signifiers, promises and injunctions, has sustained a neoliberal form of capitalism which has sought to regulate social and economic relations to its advantage, conditioning both the material and symbolic worlds. In doing so, it has replaced reality with its own types of simulacra. This model is deaf to the unmistakably human need 'to be', in the first person, i.e. with all one's intrinsic originality and ready to engage in genuinely free relations with others with a view to recreating the world. It is this need or desire that urges people to learn and do research in a transcendental form of human action not attainable via the capitalist market. We know through experience that the best energies are therefore exerted on the process of adapting to what, according to Capitalist discourse, is considered 'appropriate', 'The thing to do'. In other words, this process can help broaden the politics of social change, mapping out positive and creative pathways not geared to a utopian future but, on the contrary, rooted in something that already exists here and now. As shown by the feminist politics of difference, this involves the opening from the inside of the present another present, which is alive and not repetitive and which engenders transformations, extracting itself from the dialectics of opposition and endless criticism. It also avoids the voluntarist foreshadowing a better world to come.

The history of the Madres de Plaza de Mayo is a well-known and enlightening example on how political and socio-economic injusticies can be hindered, and showed a way to learn and teach new measures of humanity and social relations through a process of social creation. These are ordinary, powerless women spurred on by a desire to create. They have managed to carve out a public space for the pursuit of truth and freedom of expression in a country reeling from terror.

This form of social creation has a 'glocal' ring to it. While originating in a local context it has generated a global resonance. It has had a telling effect on small and large cultural and political institutions, social movements and individuals all over the world. Drawing strength from relations which are initially limited but which later become more expansive, through small gestures that are evocative and symbolic, the footsteps of these women in the Plaza de Mayo, repeated and renovated every

Thursday year in year out, are material and symbolic acts. They serve as a classic example of social and political creation. The mothers of the *desaparecidos* have invented new forms of political-symbolic practices capable of overturning dominant conceptions of reality. These practices help to keep the violent power structure in check, with the result that these women continue to be the forbears of a social order based on self-reliance, strong democratic social relations and the will to generate a better social environment.

They derive their strength from a type of practice that transforms lived experience into an understanding of themselves and of the world, a tenacity in terms of desire, powerful relationships and, once again, the ability to overturn the stark reality of their context through symbolic creations. Calling themselves "mothers of all the *desaparecidos*, pregnant once again with their own children and their struggles", they transform their motherhood into a subversive political invention (Morales 2010). They engender a sense of freedom and justice that expands and draws in others in increasingly widening circles. They have revealed the power of the maternal gesture, a 'doing' for themselves and *with* and *for* others.

This symbolic gesture is sustained first by feeling and secondarily by thought. Pursuing their policy of starting from themselves and their free relationship with others, they have 'given birth' (in the sense of *partum* – this is their own choice of expression which underlines the practical politics of maternal language) to a popular university in Buenos Aires, re-launching popular education – at high levels of implementation and in an original manner – centered around Freire's notion of critical literacy, on 'reading the word and the world'. This constitutes a kind of social creation where knowledge derived from their experience of struggle intermeshes with knowledge that is useful for the purpose of transforming human relations in order to render the world's marginalized contexts liveable. Young people (female and male) hailing from different parts of the world are received as if they were new offspring, frequenting the various courses delivered by teachers from different countries. The competences for education are shared and refined in a process of co-investigation where everything becomes useful. Significant is the workshop "Cocinando política ....sin que se queme" ("Cooking politics...without getting burnt") held on the 35th year (2012) of the Madres Association. This workshop entails a type of learning characterised by the interlinking of the cultivation of biological orchards and allotments, close links between food and politics, the properties of seeds and fruit and the strengthening of relationships.

What we have is a "legacy of life and freedom" (Padoan 2005, p. 5), the fruit of an intensely subjective experience of the world providing us with scenarios resonating with our lives – many instances of political resurgence in which women and young people from different parts of the world play prominent roles. New political movements are engaged in weaving a new tapestry of civilisation. In so doing they engage, also through intelligent use of the social networks, in new and vibrant forms of self-organisation responsive to contemporary needs (Sennett 2012). What is at stake is not seizing power but the creation of another order and set of relations with oneself, with others and with the world. This constitutes a revolution of the mind and sense with transformative effects on the materiality of individual and collective living. And all this is to form part of a fecund virtuous circle comprising new types of experience and a new symbolic order that furnishes measure. These forms of political action, not constrained by political parties and traditional political organizations, exist at a different level with respect to the oppressor/oppressed dialectic and also the historical dilemma of being either inside or outside existing power structures. They take their cue from practices such as that of starting from themselves and the practice of relations, very much associated with the *feminism of difference*. The latter has been instructive in terms of the *disfare facendo* (undoing by doing) process.

The negative approach of deconstructing through mere antagonistic criticism is replaced by a more positive approach, carried out at another level, involving the actual realization of what is needed and desired (Lonzi 1974, p. 32). A recurring visible and operative theme is the need and desire for practices of freedom that are to be implemented now, in everyday life, and not postponed to a world which has yet to exist. They are implemented in the day-to-day experience of assuming responsibilities, risk-taking and engaging in reciprocal exchanges. These help people to render common everyday life political and help to educate people in the art of conviviality. This resonates with the work of other groups from other parts of the world. For years now these groups have been creating new forms of living based on sobriety, self-production, critical consumption, a social solidarity economy, 'grass-roots' agricultural and sustainable food production, social solidarity modes of urban living and housing, ways of enjoying indispensable resources such as the time and social relations – in short, an economy and a society governed by non-capitalist ways of thinking and now spreading out to and reaching educational institutions, universities and the sphere of scientific research.

A wide constellation of political paths which are also existential subjective paths, never one without the other, is changing the material and symbolic conditions of individual and collective lives. Close to the spirit of women's politics, they put at the centre the reasons of life, love instead of violence and convey a sense of shared vibrant experiences, together with the knowledge they generate. This knowledge is neither instrumental nor specialised and is therefore more precious, useful and irreplaceable –useful knowledge concerning conviviality. The conditions and contexts are therefore created for all to express themselves, desire and imagine. In these contexts, people learn that acquiring awareness or developing consciousness moves things more than critical thinking. Action brings about more authentic modifications than reaction and relational conflict resolves matters more than wars against an enemy.

It involves the coming into effect of processes that enable us to rethink dominant theories and practices associated with life-long and life-wide learning. It also involves generating a freer set of relations between formal, non-formal and informal dimensions. The trend in adult education can be reversed in the direction of one that is social and participative, where the process of self-learning is also a process of learning with others. One can overcome the dichotomies of subject-object in education, institutional-personal, formal-informal, through a breathtakingly all-comprising circle.

Present-day mainstream education, increasingly subservient to the needs of a neoliberal market, conceived of as an individual consumer good, risks becoming merely the preparation of human resources for capital. This education risks being dependent on "too much expertise" (Illich, 2008). Such dependence constitutes a source of instability, contrasting starkly with a type of education that is *empowering* and *enabling*. There are alternative forms of knowledge that are considered 'non-expert' and linked to the life worlds of ordinary people and their manner of coming to grips with their problems. These alternative forms of knowledge entail learning ways to solve these problems through free exchange of experience with others. In the meantime, they are set aside as unnecessary and useless forms of knowledge circulating in everyday life and accessible for free. These forms of knowledge are considered "non-expert", yet they are irreplaceable, because they belong to the life world of ordinary people struggling with problems and to their particular ways of learning and providing possible solutions through free exchange of experience with others.

The practice of social creation can enable us to overcome the view that we are perennially incompetent, inadequate, in debt (to other people's expertise), and deprived of any personal calling. We cling to the view that institutional democracy and educational democracy are the primary responsibilities of national governments and that public service and culture are a common good. At a time, however, when the gap between education and job possibilities is widening, and when educational deficits co-exist with the notorious financial deficits in order to provoke a greater sense of guilt, let us not underestimate the power of the perverse but widespread ideology of an unending process of education which obliges people to seek new opportunities for learning. This is based on the widespread quest for acquiring narrowly defined competences and certification. It is also based on the hankering after an illusory sense of adequacy in this world.

An alternative conceptualization of life-long learning is being realised. We are at a historical conjuncture where politics can once again be allied to a different and better form of education: as long as one recognises the pre-eminence of *politica prima* (politics of everyday life), to use a term coined by the Italian feminism of difference (Libreria delle donne di Milano 1996). This type of politics is women's preferred political option in contrast to that which we conventionally regard as politics, namely the institutional type of politics, which is increasingly impotent in the face of the overriding power of the market. *Politica Prima* lies at the heart of change and transformative learning, since it openly activates individual and collective dimensions (appealing to the individual and collective imagination) and the dimension of the senses. It helps provide a new disposition which transforms relations between oneself and others and the world. It gives rise to significant learning experiences which are not appropriated from outside but stem from within and are enhanced through these relations.

It is the most elementary form of politics, within the reach of everyone. It constitutes a way of life involving daily social relations at work, in the neighbourhood, in the community, in the emotional sphere, and also when thinking. The aim is to make living together more civil.

This form of politics enables one to rename reality with a choice of words capable of regenerating it. It is often hidden from public life but demands a shift in priorities: first and foremost, it embraces the politics espoused by social movements. It involves social action which helps create a polis different from the one dominated by political parties and featuring a representative democracy. And yet a rapport can be established with this kind of official politics. In this connection the unexpected outcome of a case involving the new city council of Milan with regard to the issue of the Roma girls and boys is instructive.

This issue, involving people in Milan over the last two years, is both *commonplace* and *extraordinary*. Fortunately, situations such as these, which are not widely publicised, occasionally occur within our territory and help prevent deep social divisions. And yet it is an extraordinary occurrence which cannot be transferred 'cargo cult'-style but which can still have wider resonance. It has helped generate, within the city, learning, change and 'knowledge of the heart' (Zambrano 1987). Twenty years of public politics characterised by the safeguarding of power blocs and private interests, territorial neglect, and xenophobic tendencies, led the city to face the 2011 city council elections in a state of conflict and social division. The outgoing administration sought consensus and electoral victory by preying on the popular fear and criminalisation of gypsies. The latter live in camps within the territory owing to the lack of socially cohesive policies. Roma families, belonging to one of the oldest peoples in Europe, who sent their children to local schools for the purposes of integration, had become the target of alarmist and exaggerated campaigns.

This was the key feature of the outgoing mayor's electoral campaign. In the space of two years there were no less than four hundred evacuations carried out by the police with clinical coolness and with a disproportionate use of force and money, with caravans lifted by excavators and relocated. As reported by one of the teachers who was to be a protagonist in the turn of events which was to follow, all this was witnessed by children who were stupefied, seeing their world crumble and not knowing why. This crackdown forced the families to undergo continuous relocations and obliged the children to leave their schools. Thanks to the efforts of teachers and mothers, ordinary women, who had stayed away from politics, became political subjects when taking charge of the problem and beginning to speak publically about it, thus giving rise to a solution predicated on civil social relations.

By chance, as they themselves admit, the teachers and mothers found themselves at the heart of a change occurring in their lives and in the life of the city. They did so initially by engaging in minor acts such as looking around for the children and taking them to school, assisting them in their normal desire to develop, learn and play, calling them by name, knowing their mothers, families, life histories, needs, and desires. They thus helped bring down classification barriers which normally serve to create social distance and diffidence: "they were no longer gypsies but persons". They were not motivated by principles or ideals to defend and fight for. "We did not embrace any cause", they said, "nor did we respond to insults, even the gross insults on the part of the institutions; we simply had no time to lose". They thus maintained a practical and creatively symbolic, rather than an antagonistic, stance. This creativity expanded to render the circles even wider, encompassing district residents, voluntary associations, and the local and national press. The points of departure were small but significant, including the organisation of dinners and Sunday get-togethers, searching for homes or accommodating a Roma family in one's own home, creating scholarships for education and training, helping with job searches and giving the lie to the popular misconception that gypsies prefer begging to working.

This represents a symbolic leap in that recognition of the dignity of these families led to the empowerment of subjects and gave rise to healthy exchange relations. A project involving the selling of bread baked by Roma women led to appreciation by the inhabitants of Milan of bread baked by "people who belong to the land" The creation of an adult literacy school for Roma people, involving journalists and university professors from the city, was followed by an initiative sustained by two social promotion associations. This entailed the creation, in the city's outskirts and amidst the gypsy caravans, of the Voyage Museum, a historical-ethnographic museum cum documentation centre, which enables the culture of the Roma and Sinti – their language, music and culture – to be learned and appreciated by the rest of the inhabitants of Milan.

These women were catalysts for the transformations that occurred within the city. A vibrant energy, sustained by new and diffuse sensibilities for issues concerning social justice and the public good, replaced conflict and the need to cower within a defensive shell. The notion that one can be an agent of social change, starting from oneself in concert with others, replaced indifference and the tendency to delegate power to others. This resurgence in the city led to elections resulting in a change of mayor. The new mayor named his election platform a 'gentle revolution' and won on the back of a campaign in which he presented himself and his politics as 'second-level": he placed himself at the service of the *politica prima* capable of really tackling problems because it does not resort to violent short cuts, but relies on the cultivation of social awareness and people's direct engagement with issues, wise and patient mediation and the creation of relationships that enhance the quality of life when people live together. These constitute real, valuable capital – being *with* and *for* others. And the learning which derives from it constitutes a personal transformation that changes the world and leads to the development of powerful symbolic competence, profound individual and collective knowledge, emanating from life itself. This is a type of learning that reconfigures relationships between bodies, spaces, times, stories, words and signifiers in a new way. Such knowledge is a public good *par excellence*.

FROM THE PEDAGOGY OF CAPITAL TO SOCIAL CREATION

Social creation is the name of a theoretical hypothesis born out of the need to state, in a positive and propositional sense, what happens or can happen when relations and contexts manage to reflect their creative dimensions. Once ideas gain substance through an appropriate language and form; a new mode of thinking is born, touched and soiled by the situations and contingencies in which it is embedded. The creations which are of interest to us do not occur *ex nihilo* because their point of origin is something that already exists. One adds to their original form those missing elements in what is a generative process (Bateson, 1989), thus creating something new. What we mean by social creation is that symbolic disposition whereby people become *subjects*. They become the authors of their own knowledge and skills. This occurs within a movement that is inspired by the idea of people as subjects rather than by the capitalist appropriation of knowledge that characterises the 'pedagogy of capital' (De Vita 2009). It is to the latter pedagogy that we have been exposed over the past few decades.

To understand the pedagogy of capital we have to look at the whole set of different modalities and processes that have not only rendered the capitalist mode of production hegemonic but – and this is where we need to sharpen our awareness – have also transformed it into a sophisticated and evolved symbolic educational order that influences our way of producing ideas and making sense. We must be aware of the manner of organizing, re-organizing, recounting and re-recounting experiences, thus establishing accepted modes of articulating human/social relationships and embracing new consumer products.

It is the relationship between educational and social relationships and consumer products and their ramifications for educational activity that is of interest to us. This issue has led to our bringing together two ideologically loaded words, 'pedagogy' and 'capital'. A cautious exploration of the relationship between these two words can shed light on the complexity of the present times and on the difficulties which we encounter daily as educators. New useful theoretical hypotheses may emerge to reconceptualise work of a social and educational nature so as to be able to delineate new approaches to adult learning.

What I call the 'pedagogy of capital' are contemporary capitalist pedagogical postures which have radically redefined the notion and practice of exchange: the intercourse between human/social relationships, goods and consumer products. The relationship between goods, between goods and humans, between goods and language and between goods and experience has changed profoundly over the last thirty years as a result of the spiritual renewal of capitalism. This renewal is paradoxically as well known as it is a matter of mystery, as familiar as it is misunderstood in terms of its radical implications for human exchanges and the educational and social forms of human relationships. Ever present and all pervasive, the 'spirit of capitalism' (Boltansky, Chiapello 1999) has distorted the 'reality landscape' and the contexts of social and educational practice and action. It imposes a view of human/social relationships geared to mercantile exchange, one which is markedly utilitarian (Caillé 1988). This entails excessive individualism, compulsory competitivity, the alien nature of other people's experiences, and the superfluity of relations which are of value only outside the productive domain. We have moved towards a set of relations which is decidedly economistic and which, through its concomitant pedagogy/ideology, are aimed at instructing persons both young and old alike to embrace a view of living in the world which closely resembles that of frequenting a supermarket or of working for a firm, or both. That immense exchange which characterises relations between human beings – giving, having, donating, reciprocating, nurturing interests and desires, living and working in a great economy, everything capable of circulating among us (Godbout, 2007) – is not ignored by the pedagogy of capital, but is used and depotentiated, denied value, and made part of an imposed symbolic order that establishes what is of value and what is not.

The pedagogy of capital, and its associated contradictions and dilemmas, have been addressed and discussed within a branch of educational enquiry, particularly that area known as critical pedagogy. In a text dedicated to life-long education, Schettini (2005) outlined some of the current preoccupations and dilemmas involved in education. He argues that we have witnessed a shift in the discourse from the promising openings of the 70's with regard to emancipatory and political education to one which, as far as adult education is concerned, nowadays risks proving instrumental. The transformation of the discourse of major European and international organisations has led to a neoliberal perspective. In a detailed analysis of key international documents (UNESCO, OECD, EU) on life-long education/learning, Mayo (2004) highlights the shifts that have led us from deeply rooted ideas that were democratic and humanistic, inspired by writers such as Antonio Gramsci and Paulo Freire, to a perspective focussing on the competences purported to be required of individuals in a knowledge society at the service of a global and globalized marketplace. Perhaps, as Piussi maintains, what has been generally lacking is a critique of the manner in which the 'new opportunities' brought about by the neoliberal U-turn are actually transforming themselves into opportunities to "liquidate education" (Piussi 2008, 180), through a view of freedom that is very much skewed in favour of freedom of the market with very little importance attached to the genuinely human freedom of men and women.

The positing of a pedagogy of social creation derives from the need to highlight the virtues of a social pedagogy entailing the spread of practices and contexts that activate and re-activate an economy of genuine human and symbolic exchange. This would be an economy involving an exchange of goods and gestures, that changes and redirects the tendencies and dispositions that characterise the different exchanges proposed and imposed by the neoliberal market. The change being proposed here is intended to free the notion of 'economic' from its capitalist reductionist range of connotations.

Social creation provides examples of contemporary narratives that are manifest in our everyday actions: studying, working, participating, consuming. This sense of 'economic' derives from its theological roots. It is capable of restoring a complex and well articulated order of exchanges in which passions, interests, monetary and extra-monetary gain, lack of instrumental reasoning, motivations, and the search for beauty and happiness can combine freely. These exchanges exist at the furthest remove from the type of relations and contexts currently associated with the restricted notion of exchange as understood from an economistic and utilitarian perspective. Some years ago, when helping with the preparation of adult women involved in the initial period of running small social businesses,[1] we emphasised the importance of creating the right contexts, and the appropriate conditions for meaningful education. In this regard, we coined the term 'social creation' initially regarding it as a neat expression and soon after as the term denoting a new theoretical hypothesis which was to become the subject of years of research.[2]

WORKSHOPS ON DIVERSE ECONOMIES

Among the intuitions that sprung to mind, leading to a study of *diverse economies*, there was one that closely reflected our pedagogical interests: persons, communities and free organisations engaged at different levels. This involves a change in lifestyle. It is a change from a lifestyle characterised by being simply consumers/producers to one in which a contribution is made to the development of an economy that is regarded as a resource for people and not vice versa. New and promising ways of interpreting consumption and production provide the grist to the mill of our workshops on diverse economies (Mance 2000; Coraggio 2011).

Inspired by this approach and together with others, we came into contact with the experiences of women and men involved in the creation of economic processes that place the emphasis on people as social actors in the economy with outcomes that, for the most part, still need to be investigated.

We listened to participants in the so-called GAS groups (Gruppi di Acquisto Solidale[3]), entrepreneurs (both female and male) who have generated work in the agricultural or renewable energy sectors and people who have been voluntarily engaged in cultural work. The material, consisting in narrated experiences and practices as well as insights, derived from listening to these people, is rich and serves to stimulate the creation of new languages and forms of representation of the diverse economies.[4]

When, in fact, this type of change passes the test of everyday life and furnishes opportunities to rethink matters from the inside, from the standpoint of those involved – what we buy and eat, how we work and what we earn besides money, how we spend our money and how all this is related to the search for new human relations and relations between people and their environment, how we intensify or slow down the time factor in our daily lives and, finally, the dreams and utopias which these life and work choices generate – the educational dimension emerges as a factor of primary importance.

Educational issues come into play in the context of the practices of an alternative economy or social-solidarity economy, or diverse economies, the latter being the term we prefer. The educational and self-educational demands and issues are substantial in this context and mainly stem from the concerns of adults, though adolescents and even young children are also not excluded.

SOCIAL CREATION

Day-to-day experience enables us to penetrate into the actual warp and weft of the economy. We are therefore in a position to listen to narratives that testify to an active participation in the economic process, at both an elementary and radical level, since these narratives re-interrogate and re-interpret the intertwining of needs and desires, limits and resources, necessities and luxuries, keeping a firm grip on the search for happiness and a sense of responsibility, with a vision that starts from the smallness of the local but does not lose sight of the big global picture: act locally, think globally, in the words of Vandana Shiva. We are only a small fraction in this world, and yet we are called upon to play our part.

The link between the educational or self-educational dimension and the rethinking of political forms is one of the most interesting features emerging from research concerning diverse economies. Re-appropriating the political and social dimension is allied to research into modes and forms capable of starting with the self and emerging from one's grass roots, that is, from lived experience, from changes in everyday life. This involves not only a lifestyle of one's own but also the idea of what it means to consume, produce, participate, create social links, live the experience within the territory, and recover the ability to be in tune with the rest of humanity and with the cosmos. Adult education and self-education processes featured prominently in all the interviews and focus group research we carried out in different areas of Northern Italy and Sardinia: Parma, Verona, Nuoro and Iglesias. It predominantly consists in educating oneself and educating with a view to human, social and political growth and change. Growing and changing featured prominently in the narratives we listened to. We can also talk about growing in order to foster change: very often, in fact, the great passion for learning shown by adults, both female and male, who, for various reasons, feel actively involved in the construction of diverse economies, is an integrative process of learning encompassing all areas, ranging from education and self-education. This occurs through belonging to a group for social purchasing that practices self-learning at work or within the family. Training and educating oneself results from action with others in generating knowledge and sharing experience.

For the producers, the firm itself provides the main setting for the transverse learning involved, while group for social purchasing and its reality context serve as the transverse learning setting for critical consumers (Social Solidarity Purchasing Groups [GAS], consumer associations, etc.). When discussing the formative and educational dimension of life within an association, one should bear in mind the importance accorded to this by the people involved. Self-education or self-learning constitutes a key transverse element in all the experiences we listened to.

Self-learning in the adult education context is a methodological approach adopted with regard to the Justice Budgets that emerged from discussions within national meetings, and that have proved very successful. We have adopted this concept within the group and are carrying it forward. We first took up this concept rather sporadically but, as of last year, we shave started adopting a more methodological approach, involving the holding of workshops. We felt that this could be a more practical way of engaging in self-learning in order, amongst other things, to circulate existing knowledge. The intention is to put theory into practice. This year, we have held workshops. We tried to hold a workshop on self-care (....) We then held one on information technology and Linux and one on the garden (Interview 05, Verona).

The process of self-learning is quite complex since it involves various different spheres that circulate different forms of knowledge, both popular and expert, emanating from within and from outside. In any event, they enhance the sense of active participation. Adult self-education and learning constitute a circular movement providing reciprocal sustenance that furnishes the right setting for the construction of knowledge or the re-appropriation of marginalised knowledge.

WHAT HAVE WE LEARNT? HOW HAVE WE CHANGED?

The practices of diverse economies can lead to creative dimensions and rich individual and collective learning pathways among producers and critical consumers. A substantial amount of learning took place among the participants in the GAS groups, including the ability to manage and organise, improvise, listen, engage in self-criticism, work within and belong to a group, manage conflict, strengthen already existing skills, enhance the ability to provide shared 'bottom-up' solutions, generate ideas in general, and re-educate oneself to carry out and teach children basic manual tasks.

The GAS experiences, through the group dimensions and relations arising from interaction with other nuclei and ensembles of social relations, underline the great potential for self-learning that occurs within groups and for capacity building among single participants. They highlight how activities, such as making cakes or jam or other products in the context of a shopping group or life within associations, present a value and a certain resonance that was previously lacking in that they were considered too mundane. The work of diverse economy practitioners leads to the valorisation and generation of novel research into material competences in an age in which people are increasingly becoming deskilled in terms of practical competences. We perceive a distinct link, as regards practices such as trimming trouser hems, home bread-making etc., between the quest for sobriety and a conscious process of re-appropriating knowledge and skills and a real awareness of one's own life and existence (Interview 08, Iglesias). This proposed key to interpretation, regarding the re-materialisation of competences and our ability to be and do, conscious of our own life, is interesting and promising with regard to an in-depth understanding of the various types of knowledge that the practices and reflections connected with the diverse economies bring to light. There is a radical need to re-appropriate the kind of life that touches all spheres and dimensions, underlining the urgent search for new, attainable horizons, for new pedagogical hopes, and promises of happiness.

These horizons can enable us to erode and undermine, theoretically and practically, the structural and conceptual dualisms and the collective imagination of Western societies. We are currently paying the price for these dualisms through gross political, social, human and existential imbalances. These dualisms have led to gross disharmonies, among living organisms and on a planetary scale, and to violence involving persons and communities. There is an urgent call for this situation to be put back on an even keel thanks to research regarding relational, environmental and even cosmic harmony. And this is the subtle pattern that we unearthed in the narratives and testimonies that we gathered in the 'diverse economy' workshops where new hypotheses of life and production are conceived. An apt term for this research would be 'being in tune with the living' since it presents itself as offering a pathway seeking to restore such elements as agreement, working together, equilibrium, and acceptance in the lives and life systems suffering this loss. This often results in a restless quest for new relations with the planet and new equilibria in terms of consumption and production.

More radically, it results in a moving away from the roles and identities promoted by the market in order to live once again as women and men who feel intrinsically part of a global system, the living system. In the words of one of the interviewees, this research is meant to discover "new ways of being in tune with one's system of life" embracing all that concerns us. It is also intended to make people aspire to new forms of 'communion' with the Earth, with its elements and all those forms of knowledge that help foster friendship with and respect for it, rather than breeding the violence and rivalry that deny us any such harmony. It also involves the discovery of many different forms of relations: between human beings, other living species and the environment, and between human beings and the divine. They represent attempts at developing educational and self-learning perspectives that do not preclude the levying of criticism, as long as it is done in a creative and constructive manner. In short, it constitutes an attempt to "unmake development in order to remake the world" (AA.VV. 2003).

NOTES

[1] We refer to the training course *Io lavoro nel mio quartiere (I work in my neighbourhood)*, conceived and conducted by the Associazione Mimesis in two successive cycles and partly financed in connection with Law 215/92 on female enterprise.

[2] De Vita shared these nascent intuitions with colleagues from the *Studio Guglielma. Ricerca e creazione sociale*, Mimesis, and particularly with Lucia Bertell. This research focus gained momentum over the years also because it attracted the interest of other researchers and as a result of theoretical reflections grounded in fieldwork (De Vita 2004; De Vita, Bertell 2006; De Vita 2009).

[3] Literal translation: Social Solidarity Purchasing Groups. These are free collectivities of critical buyers/consumers who, by doing their shopping, including buying their everyday necessities, together give rise to new forms of social and political practice. This entails new collectively directed education and self-education processes with a view to creating new lifestyles.

[4] Results of research carried out by the Universities of Verona and Parma (Joint Project) entitled *Diverse Economies. Social and Educational Processes in Emerging Economic Practice*.

REFERENCES

AA. VV. (2003). *Défaire le développement, réfaire le monde*. Paris: L'Aventurine.
Bateson, M. C. (1989). *Composing a life*, New York: Atlantic Monthly Press.
Boltansky, L., & Chiapello, È. (1999). *Le nouvel ésprit du capitalisme*. Paris: Gallimard.
Caillé, A. (1988). *Critique de la raison utilitaire. Manifeste du Mauss*. Paris: La Découverte.
Coraggio, J. L. (2011). Economía social y solidaria. In A. Acosta, E. Martínez (Eds.) *El trabajo antes que el capital*. Quito: Abya Yala.
De Vita, A. (2004). *Imprese d'amore e di denaro. Creazione sociale e filosofia della formazione*. Milano: Guerini e Associati.
De Vita, A., & Bertell, L. (2004). La creazione sociale. In A. M. Piussi (Ed.), *Paesaggi e figure della formazione nella creazione sociale (pp. 60–84)*, Roma: Carocci.
De Vita, A. (2009). *La creazione sociale. Relazioni e contesti per educare*. Roma: Carocci.
Federighi, P. (2006). *Liberare la domanda di formazione*. Roma: Edup.
Godbout, J. T. (2007), *Ce qui circule entre nous. Donner, recevoir, rendre*. Paris: Editions du Seuil.
Illich, I. et al. (2008). *Esperti di troppo. Il paradosso delle professioni disabilitanti*. Gardolo: Erickson.
Libreria delle donne di Milano (1996*)*. E' accaduto non per caso: il patriarcato è finito. *Sottosopra*, gennaio.
Lonzi, C. (1974). *Sputiamo su hegel*. Milano: Scritti di Rivolta femminile.
Mayo, P. (2004). El aprendizaje a lo largo de la vida, *Trabajo futuro: la formación como proyecto político y aprendizaje permanente. Laboratori d'iniciatives sindicals i ciutadanes Ettore Gelpi*, (pp. 17–30), Xativa: CREC
Mayo, P. (2009). The 'competence' discourse in education and the struggle for social agency and critical citizenship. *International Journal of Educational Policies*, *3*(2), 5–16.
Mance, E.A. (2000). *A revolução das redes. A colaboração solidária como uma alternativa pós-capitalista à globalização actual*. Petrópolis, R.J: Vozes.
Morales, V. (2010). *De la cocina a la plaza: La categoría "madre" en el discurso de las madres de Plaza de Mayo.*Villa María: EDUVIM.
Padoan, D. (2005). *Le pazze. Un incontro con le madri di plaza de mayo*. Milano: Bompiani.
Piussi, A. M. (Ed.) (2006). *Paesaggi e figure della formazione nella creazione sociale*. Roma: Carocci.
Piussi, A. M. (2008). *Posibilidad de una escuela de libertad*, in AA. VV., *Figuras y pasajes de la complejidad en educación. Esperiencias de resistencia, creación y potencia*, Xativa/València: Istituto Paulo Freire de España, Crec-Denes.
Schettini, B. (2005). *Un'educazione per il corso della vita*. Napoli: Luciano Editore.
Sennett, R. (2012). *Together. The Rituals, Pleasures and Politics of Cooperation*. New Haven: Yale University Press.
Zambrano, M. (1987). *Hacia un saber del alma*. Madrid: Alianza.

AFFILIATIONS

Antonia De Vita
Professore Aggregato, Department of Philosophy, Education and Psychology,
Scienze della Formazione,
University of Verona, Verona, Italy

Anna Maria Piussi
Professor, Department of Philosophy, Education and Psychology,
Scienze della Formazione,
University of Verona, Verona, Italy

PART V

POLICY AND REGIONS

JULIA PREECE

24. ADULT EDUCATION AND POVERTY REDUCTION

INTRODUCTION

Whilst the links between education and poverty have long been understood (Oxaal, 1997), the policy link between adult education and poverty reduction is more fragile. For instance, adult education and lifelong learning have been cited as key to achieving international development targets (UNESCO-IL, 2009), yet adult education itself is not a development target and national poverty reduction papers rarely mention adult education in their strategies (Education International, 2003). This may be partly because of inadequate understanding of adult education's multidimensional nature. Equally the concept of poverty is constantly changing. This paper reviews various conceptual understandings of poverty and its cumulative consequences on health, crime and social exclusion, followed by a discussion on the role of adult education in reducing poverty. The paper concludes that the interdependence of many factors creates a cycle of learning needs that cannot be addressed by one form of educational input at any one point in time.

CONCEPTUALISING POVERTY

Sachs (2005), in his famous book *The End of Poverty* identified three levels of poverty: extreme or absolute, moderate and relative poverty. For the poorest of the poor, poverty means you are: 'chronically hungry, unable to access health care, lack the amenities of safe drinking water and sanitation, cannot afford education for some or all of the children, and perhaps lack rudimentary shelter' (p. 20). The extreme poor are 'caught in the poverty trap, unable on their own to escape from extreme material deprivation'.

Relative poverty refers to household income level which is below a given proportion of average national income. Those in the relatively poor category, usually living in high income countries, will lack access to cultural goods, entertainment, recreation, quality health care, education and 'other prerequisites for upward social mobility' (p. 20).

Indicators of poverty in developing countries are categorized in human development index terms. They include a country's GDP per capita, the percentage below the national poverty line or living on less than one or two dollars a day, literacy rates, life expectancy, HIV prevalence, primary enrolment figures including gender disaggregated data, infant mortality, maternal mortality and other targets specifically tied to the Millennium Development Goals as agreed internationally in 2000. According to Sachs, the end of poverty means: 'Everybody on Earth can and should enjoy basic standards of nutrition, health, water and sanitation, shelter and other minimum needs for survival, well-being, and participation in society'. It also means everyone has a chance to 'climb the ladder of development' (p. 21).

In Europe poverty has been a concern of policy since the Amsterdam Treaty of 1997. The Lisbon Council in March 2000 and its subsequent Nice European Council in December 2000 identified explicit poverty eradication objectives such as employment, access to basic services, healthcare, education, housing, justice and other services such as culture, sport and leisure. Poverty was linked to primary indicators of social exclusion such as income distribution, unemployment, early school leavers not in education or training, life expectancy at birth and self-defined health status by income level. Low income is classified as below 60 per cent of national equivalent median income (Schuller and Watson, 2009). Secondary indicators include persistence of low income, very long term unemployment and educational attainment rate of level 2 or less for adult age groups. Other indicators relate to housing conditions, homelessness and those living in institutions such as homes for the elderly, prisons, orphanages and people on benefit dependency. Access to health services, disability status, levels of functional literacy and numeracy, including the educational attainment level of parents in relation to intergenerational poverty, are all indicators of poverty in European contexts (Nolan, 2003, p. 75–85). 'Direct' indicators are those that relate to living standards; while 'indirect' indicators refer to the resources which individuals are able to access (Andress 2003, p. 117).

However, Andress (2003) highlights a number of discrepancies in the use of low income as the main indicator of poverty. Whilst recognizing the relevance of income differences in free market economies where almost all necessary goods and services are purchased with money, a simple calculation of household income ignores how that money is being used and who has access to the money. For instance there may be excessive household debts in a high income family, and women or other dependents may not have adequate access to combined income sources. Andress suggests that deprivation measures do not necessarily correlate to income measures: a high degree of income-poor persons are not affected by deprivation and also, conversely, that 'about one-third of the deprivation-poor have an income above median level' (p. 124). Indeed, he suggests that 'a "correct" poverty indicator evidently does not exist' (p. 119).

It makes sense, therefore, to extend our examination of poverty to include criteria for non-economic deprivation and look at the effects of poverty. Sen (1999) described the cumulative effects of such deprivations as an absence of freedom to function or participate in economic or social life. These include access to participation, decision making, self-determination and capability functioning (the reasoning power and resources to pursue the goals one values). In Sen's terms, one is poor if one has 'unfreedoms' of capability and participation.

Capability poverty relates to deprivation in the range of things people can do, including the knowledge and skills needed to act independently for productivity or personal welfare. Poor education and knowledge about how to challenge inequitable systems perpetuates exclusion and isolation. This capability 'unfreedom' creates a dependency role for people who are then locked into a vicious cycle of low skills, knowledge and understanding that prevent better paid employment, thus perpetuating the cycle of need for the next generation.

Participatory poverty refers to deprivation in the range of things people can be in public and social life, including holding participatory roles in social life and decision making processes. Participatory poverty impacts on individual identity, either as a result of attitudes and values that are attached to that person's place in society, or as a result of exclusionary measures that fail to recognize someone's existence because their work is carried out 'invisibly', such as family caring. It is argued that if people's voices are silenced often enough, their self-perceptions of agency and perceived ability to change their situations are also silenced (Preece 1999, 2009).

Fullick (2009) points out that poverty impacts on society as a whole. There is therefore a cost to the public purse in terms of higher demands on health resources, prison services, social services, and on the physical environment. Social problems, poor facilities and failing schools reinforce low confidence and aspirations (p. 18). So it is in everyone's interest to eradicate poverty, however it is defined. There are strong associations of poor levels of education with unemployment, low income, physical and mental illness and crime. Decreased sense of well-being has a spiraling effect resulting in less civic participation, exercise, racial tolerance, trust or cooperation (Fullick, 2009, p. 23).

Field (2009) identifies the cyclical relationship, and economic significance, of ill-, or well-being with poverty, so that, for example, unemployment can impact on mental and physical health: 'unemployment also removes people from an important social network, and harms their sense of worth and self-esteem' (p. 19).

The focus on employment as a route out of poverty, however, is not always an option for many. As Fullick (2009) points out, personal circumstances related to disability, illness, age or caring responsibilities may not make employment an option: 'Most people who live in poverty would be helped if there was a broader conception of employment that placed more value on other kinds of engagement, such as learning, unpaid work, voluntary activities and caring' (p. 21). Similarly low paid work itself can create poverty traps. Women are often the majority in these latter categories, as Burke and Jackson (2007) highlight in the European context.

DYNAMICS OF POVERTY

Sebates (2008) emphasises that poverty can be chronic or temporary, and is closely associated with inequality, disadvantage and social exclusion. But the concept of poverty changes over time and location. Definitions define what is measured and also the strategies to overcome it. Dimensions may include vulnerability (such as disability, illness, single parenthood, immigration status, age), shocks (for example, economic and family crises, disease, natural disaster), assets (including financial, human and social capitals), income, services (such as health and education), and empowerment (for instance having a political say, confidence, or sense of dignity) (pp. 6–7).

Closely linked to this analysis Shaffer (2002) offers a diagrammatic representation of the interlocking dynamics of poverty for developing countries. He shows how negative pressures – stresses (such as life cycle pressures, wages, crop yields) and shock (such as wars, civil violence, drought, floods famines) – can be offset by positive pressures. Positive pressures (opportunities) include aspects such as positive technological change, conflict resolution, real wages, employment, access to productive assets and public services. But the impact of these pressures is dependent on individual and collective coping strategies for stresses and enabling strategies for opportunities. Some of the enabling and coping strategies can be learned, others have to be provided in the form of infrastructure support.

These strategies are resourced through different forms of capital – economic, socio/political, environmental and physiological. The association of capital with the ability to move out of or reduce the risk of poverty has been identified by a number of authors. Different forms of capital have been cut in several different ways. They provide interesting indicators of what constitutes poverty in different contexts and the perceived values attached to different kinds of resources for moving out of poverty.

KINDS OF CAPITAL NEEDED TO RESIST POVERTY

Shaffer's (2002, p. 53) four capitals are economic (being able to access or own land, labour, credit); socio/political (being able to draw on a range of social relations, networks and organizations); environmental (having a natural resource base and control over its management); and physiological (healthy functioning of the human body).

For Sachs (2005), however, the extreme poor lack six major kinds of capital. These are:

- Human – health, nutrition, skills for production
- Business – machinery motorized transport used in agriculture, industry and services
- Infrastructure – roads, power, water and sanitation, airports and seaports, telecommunications systems
- Natural – arable land, healthy soils, biodiversity, well-functioning eco-systems
- Public institutional – commercial law, judicial systems, government services and policies that underpin peaceful and prosperous division of labour
- Knowledge – scientific and technical knowhow to raise productivity and promotion of physical and natural capital

In European contexts, many of these capitals are now givens – such as legal and infrastructure systems. But health and nutrition in Sach's list are placed alongside skills as a form of human capital. It is noticeable that Sachs places little emphasis on social capital, though Shaffer identifies this as a core strategic resource for coping and reducing the impact of negative pressures. Indeed, while poor communities may often have strong communitarian social networks (Preece and Mosweunyane, 2004), their lack of bridging social capital (Field, 2005), especially for women, is widely acknowledged as a key issue (Parthasarathy et al., 2007).

A recent report by Schuller and Watson (2009), for the UK context, narrowed this list down to three capitals, representing both inner resources and resources from other people. These are: human capital – referring to skills and qualifications; social capital, pointing to networks where values are shared and people can contribute to common goals; and identity capital, relating to the ability to maintain healthy self-esteem and sense of meaning and purpose in life. These capitals are acquired through a variety of means. And as the developing country descriptors show more clearly, learned capitals require infrastructures that enable these other capitals to flourish.

Schuller and Watson (2009) emphasize that a range of learning is needed in order to ensure a constant flow of social and identity capitals that in turn will impact on human capital. Since education does not automatically create equality, they argue that a socially just and equality focused learning approach should translate learning opportunities into entitlements, particularly for social and demographic groups that are most at risk or most in need of learning.

A socially just education encourages recognition and respect, leading to self-confidence, dignity and cultural integrity. Cultural integrity embraces bodily integrity (freedom from harassment or violence) and health and emotional integrity (freedom from fear) (Walker, 2006).

THE ROLE OF ADULT EDUCATION IN REDUCING POVERTY

There is evidence that different forms of learning (for example community-based education) can impact on self-esteem, health, well-being, civic participation and progression to other forms of learning (Preece & Houghton, 1999; Schuller & Watson, 2009). When people have more self-confidence, their ability to take more control over their lives also increases.

Schuller and Watson (2009), in the context of the UK, emphasise the impact of learning on well-being, leading to freedoms and capabilities, and the means to acquire a range of capitals that will enhance individual and collective life prospects. Their introduction of identity capital offers an economistic spin on some of the 'softer' skills such as confidence and well-being that, for many adult educators, lie at the heart of adult education, especially for vulnerable groups. This shifts the emphasis away from vocationalism to justification for a more varied range of learning opportunities. These opportunities must translate into recurrent opportunities so that people have several chances to accommodate changing life circumstances at different times.

Their evidence-based recommendations indicate that lifelong and lifewide learning opportunities have a better chance of reducing dependency.

Educated parents are generally seen to produce healthier children with potential consequences for preventing poverty in the next generation. Lamb (2009) emphasizes the positive impact of learning as a family, citing evidence that intergenerational learning draws together communities and groups: 'the quickest route out of child poverty is through improving the employment chances of the parents' (p. 6).

Sebates (2008) confirms that learning has the capacity to affect many dimensions of poverty. Existing measures have variable impacts, however. For instance the current skills for life strategy in the UK results in high attrition rates. Sebates also suggests that training will increase productivity but not always increase earnings. For individuals in employment, improved income only emerges after continuous learning, though this may not necessarily apply to all social groups, such as some women. Sebates recommends an asset building approach to adult education. Financial literacy, for example, enables people to use money more effectively and may reduce intergenerational poverty. Similarly health literacy skills may help people make better health decisions.

Fullick (2009) claims, however, that there continue to be many barriers to learning for people living in poverty. Their own motivation to learn is offset by negative stresses such as poor health, family responsibilities, long working hours and a decreased awareness of the value of learning.

There are certain social groups who are particularly marginalized in terms of educational opportunity and risk of falling into the poverty trap. For example, Schuller (2009) reports that two thirds of prisoners leave prison with no job or training to go to, and their social capital is skewed to offenders networks. Large portions lose relationships, jobs and self-worth following a prison sentence. He recommends a wider curriculum than purely skills training which can support the other dimensions of need in relation to vulnerability and assets. He also argues the case for more relevant training of prison officers to improve inmate relationships and use the officers as motivators for continued learning amongst prisoners.

Similarly there is a strong case for increasing investment in learning for older people. A life course approach to learning is recommended to help older adults remain engaged and active outside the world of work. Other marginalized groups include migrants (McNair, 2009) and people with disabilities (Rule & Modipa in this volume).

Since disadvantaged adults need a range of capitals, the range of learning opportunities and entitlements need to be wide: 'People in poverty need learning that supports all aspects of their lives and develops capital that enhances personal identity and social solidarity as well as human capital' (Fullick, 2009, p. 35). This is a core policy theme that Schuller and Watson (2009) present. They also recommend the introduction of learning leave as an entitlement for all employees, with individual learning accounts serving vulnerable groups and people with low incomes.

There are other ways in which adult education can contribute to poverty reduction. It may seem inconceivable that the 'North' could learn any lessons from low income countries about poverty reduction, but, in terms of collective development and grass roots initiatives, there are adult education examples in the 'South' that demonstrate how people can stimulate, for instance, identity capital or financial capability. One such example may be the way that micro credit (a locally managed low interest and revolving loan system amongst small groups of people) may serve as a resource for helping people move out of poverty (Parthasarathy *et al*, 2007). Another example may be an exploration of the REFLECT approach to literacy learning. This is a community based strategy that uses participatory techniques for literacy learning that engages with community identified needs so that literacy skills evolve organically through problem solving (Attwood, 2007).

CONCLUDING REMARKS

This paper has argued that poverty is the outcome of an accumulated set of circumstances, closely aligned to social deprivation and inequalities, and requiring a multidimensional approach to address a variety of interrelating factors. Adult education can contribute to poverty reduction if a holistic and social justice approach is applied that builds the various forms of capital necessary to address poverty dynamics. But adult education is only a contributory strategy to a multifaceted problem.

ACKNOWLEDGEMENTS

Permission has been granted by Taylor and Francis to reproduce this chapter as an adapted extract from the article 'Response to learning through life: thematic area of poverty reduction' published in the *International Journal of Lifelong Education, 29* (4), 475–486 available at www.tandfonline.com.

REFERENCES

Andress, H-J. (2003). Does low income mean poverty? Some necessary extensions of poverty indicators based on economic resources. In P. Krause, G. Baecker & W. Hanesch (Eds.), *Combating poverty in Europe* (pp. 117–130). Aldershot: Ashgate.

Attwood, G. (2007). An action research study of the REFLECT approach in rural Lesotho. Unpublished PhD Thesis, University of the Witwatersrand.

Burke, P.J. & Jackson, S. (2007). *Reconceptualising lifelong learning: Feminist interventions.* London: Routledge.

Education International (2003). *Education for all: Is commitment enough?* Report No. 1. Brussels: Education International.

Field, J. (2005). *Social capital and lifelong learning.* Bristol: The Policy Press.

Field, J. (2009). *Well-being and happiness.* Thematic paper 4. Leicester: NIACE.

Fullick, L (2009). *Poverty reduction and lifelong learning.* Thematic paper 6. Leicester: NIACE.

Lamb, P. (2009). *The impact of learning as a family: A model for the 21st century.* Thematic paper 9. Leicester: NIACE.
Mcnair, S. (2009). *Migration, communities and lifelong learning.* Thematic paper 3. Leicester: NIACE.
Nolan, B. (2003). Indicators for social inclusion in the European Union. In P. Krause, G. Baecker & W. Hanesch (Eds.) *Combating poverty in Europe* (pp.75–90). Aldershot: Ashgate.
Oxaal, Z. (1997). *Education and poverty: A gender analysis.* Report prepared for the Gender Equality Unit, Swedish International Development Cooperation Agency (SIDA), Institute of Development Studies, University of Sussex.
Parthasarathy, S. K., Sharma, J. & Dwivedi, A. (2007). Women's education, empowerment and micro credit: making the connections. In J. Preece, R. van der Veen & W. N. Raditloaneng (Eds.), *Adult education and poverty reduction: Issues for policy, research and practice* (pp. 121–132). Gaborone: Lentswe La Lesedi Pty Ltd.
Preece, J. (Ed.) (2009). *Non-formal education, poverty reduction and life enhancement: A comparative study.* Gaborone: Lentswe La Lesedi Pty Ltd.
Preece, J. (2006). Education for inclusion. *Convergence, XXXIX*(2–3), 147–166.
Preece, J. (1999). *Combating social exclusion in university adult education.* Aldershot: Ashgate.
Preece, J., & Houghton, A-M. (2000). *Nurturing social capital in excluded communities: A kind of higher education.* Aldershot: Ashgate.
Preece, J. & Mosweunyane, D. (2004). *Perceptions of citizenship responsibility amongst Botswana youth.* Gaborone: Lentswe La Lesedi.
Sachs, J. (2005). *The end of poverty: How we can make it happen in our lifetime.* London: Penguin.
Schuller, T. (2009). *Crime and lifelong learning.* Thematic paper 5. Leicester: NIACE.
Schuller, T., & Watson, D. (2009). *Learning through life: Inquiry into the future for lifelong learning.* Leicester: NIACE.
Sebates, R. (2008). *The impact of lifelong learning on poverty reduction.* Public value paper 1. Leicester: NIACE.
Sen, A. (1999). *Development as freedom.* Oxford: Oxford University Press.
Shaffer, P. (2002). Participatory analysis of poverty dynamics: Reflections on the Myanmar PPA. In K. Brock & R. McGee (Eds.) *Knowing poverty: Critical reflections on participatory research and policy.* (pp. 44–68), London: Earthscan Publications.
UNESCO-IL (2009). *Global report on adult learning.* Hamburg: UNESCO-IL.
Walker, M. (2006). Towards a capability based theory of social justice for education policy making. *Journal of Education Policy, 21*(2), 163–185.

AFFILIATION

Julia Preece
Professor of Adult Education,
University of KwaZulu-Natal in Pietermaritzburg, South Africa

DANIEL SCHUGURENSKY & JOHN P. MYERS

25. CINDERELLA AND THE SEARCH FOR THE MISSING SHOE: 1990S LATIN AMERICAN ADULT EDUCATION POLICY AND PRACTICE

INTRODUCTION

Former President of Tanzania, Julius Nyerere, an adult educator himself, once said that adult education is the Cinderella of government departments (Nyerere 1988). This dictum applies as much to most Latin American countries as it does to Tanzania. Adult education governmental agencies throughout the region are often underfunded, forgotten and marginalized from the education policy realm. Usually relegated to a corner in whatever ministry or secretary they are located, these agencies face the challenges of fulfilling ambitious goals with low budgets, poor facilities, limited support and a labor force of low-paid and unpaid teachers, most without a background in the field. As Garcia Huidobro (1994) noted, adult education in Latin America is a low-status endeavor, a 'poor education for poor people'.

This situation worsened during the nineties. In the post-war history of Latin American adult education, seldom had this sector received so little support at both the national and the international level as in this decade. Although a myriad of local programs remained in place, the large-scale initiatives and the legitimacy of the field characteristic of the previous four decades practically vanished. Despite their occasional rhetoric of lifelong education, the emphasis of the overall education strategy of bilateral and multilateral organizations, national governments, and donor agencies lay almost exclusively on schools rather than on non-formal education, and on children rather than on youth and adults. Moreover, whereas in the past Latin American adult education (and particularly the popular education movement) was a permanent source of innovation and creativity that inspired programs all over the world, it has been argued that during the nineties the most interesting innovations in the region came from the school system (Stromquist 1997, Unesco 2000, La Belle 2000, R.M. Torres 2000 a, b).

What is particularly ironic about this process is that the near abandonment of the field of adult education in Latin America (and for that matter, worldwide) occurred at the same time that there was a clear mandate to revitalize it. Such a mandate was articulated in the Education for All Conference held in 1990 in Jomtien, Thailand, and subsequently ignored during most of the decade both by national governments and by international agencies with influence in Latin American education policy. For the field of adult education, the post-Jomtien decade constitutes a sad example of over-commitment and underachievement, which reflects the gap between an expansive rhetoric and a contracting agenda. Indeed, most educational policies for 'including the excluded' implemented during the last decade have themselves excluded adult education from the repertoire of potential interventions, and have excluded adults from their policy radar.[1]

Although the marginalization of adult education was the result of the overall education strategy – and the corresponding budget allocations – of most international and national institutions during the 1990s, some signals suggest that adult education could return to the policy agenda in the near future. At the international level, among those signals are the explicit calls for support of adult education raised in the 2000 World Education Forum (Dakar), the current internal discussions within the World Bank to reconsider its policy priorities towards the area, and the increasing interest among policy-makers in the promotion of opportunities for lifelong learning. In Latin America, efforts to revitalize the field of adult education are being carried out by a variety of actors, particularly after the Fifth International Conference on Adult Education (CONFINTEA V) held in Hamburg in 1997. These efforts have materialized in a series of follow-up activities to that conference, such as the meetings held in Montevideo, Cochabamba, Patzcuaro, and Santiago de Chile under the auspices of Unesco, and the production of a great number of position papers, research documents and monitoring reports by governmental and non-governmental organizations.

It is against this double dynamic of marginalization and rejuvenation that characterized the Latin American adult education movement of the nineties that this article was written. After outlining the macro-level educational policies that have impacted Latin America during the nineties, we provide an overview of the main issues facing adult education in Latin America and explore some of the reasons for the continuing peripheral status of adult education in policy circles. In the final section, the paper discusses some of the efforts currently carried out by the Latin American adult education community to develop a consensual agenda for the field. These efforts are particularly important in a regional context of increasing income polarization that has 220 million poor (of which 90 million live in extreme poverty), 42 million illiterates and 110 million adults who have not completed primary school.[2]

A caveat is necessary at this point. As in any other article that takes Latin America as its subject, it is not possible to capture all of the diversity of the region.[3] Latin America is a heterogeneous and diverse region, and we would be remiss in assuming a single, monolithic reality of adult education policies and practices, or a single cultural, political and socio-economic context. At the same time, despite these differences, adult education policies in many Latin American countries are affected by similar international and regional developments inside and outside the field, and hence they can be better understood in light of those developments. Having said that, this type of macro perspective should be complemented with specific case studies and comparative analyses.

POLITICAL, SOCIAL, AND ECONOMIC CONTEXT

During the 1990s, the Latin American region faced a number of political, social, and economic challenges that affected adult education policies and practices. On the political front, Latin American countries were still experiencing the difficult transition from predominantly authoritarian regimes to formally democratic ones. In the social arena, poverty, unemployment and income inequality were on the rise. Economically, Latin American countries continued to occupy a position of structural dependency in the world system, not only in terms of trade, but also in terms of research and development. Chronic financial dependency is expressed in the repayment of the external debt and related structural adjustment programs. These programs replaced previous redistributive arrangements – that were part and parcel of the different Latin American expressions of the welfare state – with a set of neoliberal policies promoting deregulation, competition, budget cuts, and privatization of public enterprises. They also replaced the previous development strategy of import substitution industrialization and protectionism (based on high tariffs restricting access to domestic markets by foreign imports in favor of domestic production), with a variety of mechanisms of market liberalization. Although there is no consensus as to the real impact of neoliberal policies in Latin America, several studies contend that they have worsened income distribution and have exacted a disproportionately high social cost to the popular classes.[4]

EDUCATION POLICY AND THE LATIN AMERICAN REGION

During the nineties, the Latin American educational policy agenda was shaped by several overall frameworks initiated and carried out by different agencies. This created a complex and confused situation with overlapping goals and projects. Since 1981, the educational plans for the region were guided by the Proyecto Principal de Educación ('Major Project of Education in Latin America and the Caribbean'), coordinated by UNESCO/OREALC. This project set three goals for the year 2000: universal access to primary schooling, eradication of adult illiteracy, and improvement of the quality and efficiency of education. Many still remember the cynicism among adult education researchers and practitioners in Latin America at that time regarding the proclaimed goal of eradicating adult illiteracy in the region without committing the necessary resources for the task and without addressing the socio-economic roots of illiteracy. This situation was to be repeated for the remaining of the century, declaration after declaration, plan after plan.

As of 1990, the educational agenda had also been guided by the goals agreed upon in Jomtien, which partially coincided with the goals of the Proyecto Principal and which also set the accomplishment of these goals for the year 2000. By 1994, a third policy agenda entered the educational landscape. At the Miami Summit convened by US President Clinton, a 'Plan for Universal Access to Education for 2010' was launched that year, and later ratified as the 'Education Initiative' by the Second Summit that was held in Santiago in 1998. This hemispherical initiative (known as the 'Summits of the Americas') adopted goals for the three educational levels, including tertiary education. This effort is headed by the US government, and is coordinated by the governments of Mexico, Argentina and Chile, with the participation of several national, regional and international organizations (e.g. OAS, World Bank, IDB and USAID).

Adult education priorities in the region during the 1990s were affected by these general strategic frameworks, and also by the agenda set for the sector at the fourth and fifth International Conferences of Adult Education (held in Paris 1985 and in Hamburg 1997, respectively). In April 2000, the World Education Forum added another layer to the equation. This conference, a follow-up to Jomtien, was held in Dakar and convened by five international organizations: UNDP (United Nations Development Program), UNFPA (United Nations Population Fund), UNESCO, UNICEF, and the World Bank. In essence, Dakar ratified the goals set in Jomtien, but postponed the deadline to achieve them by the year 2015.[5]

The reasons for the co-existence of so many (and often overlapping) strategic plans for the Latin American education sector are not clear. Rosa Maria Torres suggests that they reflect changes in the role and power of international agencies. Whereas in the early 1980s Unesco was still the international leader in educational expertise, during the 1990s this leadership was displaced by Washington-based agencies, particularly the World Bank and the OAS. Torres contends that what most of these reform initiatives have in common is a top-down enterprise, which is designed, conducted, and evaluated by international and national political and technocratic elites, with little information or encouragement to participate given to citizens, teachers, or education researchers and specialists (R.M. Torres 1999, 2000).

ADULT EDUCATION IN LATIN AMERICA: THE HARDSHIPS OF CINDERELLA

Latin American adult education faces overwhelming challenges that cannot be separated from larger issues of poverty and inequality. As mentioned above, in spite of continuous efforts, there are still in the region 42 million absolute illiterates. However, the real number is probably higher. In a recent study on literacy in seven Latin American countries[6] directed by Isabel Infante, most adults with five years of schooling were unable to respond correctly to a basic preliminary test that would indicate a first level of literacy. The study concluded that a basic command of literacy and numeracy requires at least seven years of schooling, and a fair level of literacy and numeracy (one that allows for a good performance in the workplace) requires approximately 12 years of schooling (Infante 2000). If one accepts the argument (based on the results of this study) that basic literacy requires at least seven years of formal schooling, it follows that the real illiteracy rates in the region are much higher than the official 11.7%.

In any case, regardless of the classification used, both literacy and adult basic education (ABE) programs in the region are not very effective in addressing the educational needs of this population. In the area of adult basic education, for instance, a large gap exists between actual enrollments and potential demand: in a Unesco study of 13 countries, it was found that the total enrollment in ABE was around three million people. This represents less than 2% of the potential demand, and perhaps less if it is considered that enrollment figures are sometimes exaggerated (Messina 1993). Moreover, dropout rates in ABE fluctuate between 30 and 40%, and are even higher at the lower educational levels. For instance, one longitudinal study showed that only 6% of those who began grade one in 1987 completed grade three in 1989 (Messina 1993). To worsen matters, in addition to low enrollments rates and high dropout rates, enrollments in the region are not growing, and in some cases are decreasing. Graciela Messina (1993) argues that, since this decrease in enrollments cannot be related to a decrease in demand, it can be attributed largely to government policies that are withdrawing support from adult education programs, leading to less funding, reduced personnel, and the closure of adult education centers.

In addition to the external factors pointed out by Messina, low enrollments can also be attributed to the irrelevance, compensatory character, and low quality of many adult basic education programs themselves. A related factor is that most adult education programs provide little attention to the most marginalized groups among the poor. Moreover, the field of adult education in the region is highly fragmented, with a variety of modalities and services operating in isolation from each other or without a common long-term strategy. This low level of coordination is also present among the different levels of government services (municipal, provincial and federal), which results in duplication and waste. It is also noticeable in the scarcity of fruitful relationships between the state and civil society. Not only are these relationships infrequent, but when they do exist, the role of non-governmental organizations is usually reduced to implementing state policies as sub-contractors, overlooking their potential contribution to improving those policies and their related programs. This policy may reduce costs in the short term, but reduces the quality and effectiveness of the programs because it does not promote some of the main strengths of NGOs, such as their flexibility and their understanding of local contexts (Archer 2000). Other unresolved issues include the haphazard relationship between adult education and the formal education system, and the absence of a system of assessment and recognition of the experience and learning of the adult population.

An additional challenge is the training and working conditions of adult educators. In Latin America, the teaching profession is characterized by a segmented labor market: teachers of the formal system and adult educators operate in two different circuits with significant differences in terms of training, salaries, professionalization, certification and social prestige. This segmentation is mirrored within the adult education system, between credentialed teachers on the one hand, and literacy workers and community tutors on the other, many of whom work on a voluntary or semi-voluntary basis. Moreover, there is a scarcity of policies, strategies and programs for the training of adult educators in the region, especially within the new paradigm of learning throughout life advanced in Hamburg and Dakar.

These challenges will be difficult to overcome as long as adult education continues to be the Cinderella of government planning offices. Whether the policy responsibility for adult basic education lies within ministries of education or within other ministries and departments (usually those with a mandate to work with poor communities), it has not yet been taken seriously by policy-makers. Indeed, paragraph 37 of the Dakar Declaration laments the fact that 'the education of adults remains isolated, often at the periphery of national education systems and budgets'. Likewise, Oxenham and Aoki (2000, p. 25) contend that the responsibility of adult education programs 'seems to be isolated from or on the margins of broader educational policy making, as though adult basic education were not an authentic or permanent component of a total education system'. Thus, they claim that policy on adult basic education seems narrowly conceived and limited to a relatively short term.

Evidence for this claim of marginality can be found in education budgets. Few countries, if any, allocate more than one or two per cent of their educational expenditures to adult education (Schmelkes 1994: 10, Oxenham & Aoki 2000, p. 25). The fact that adult education budgets did not increase during the nineties is somewhat surprising, because the 'Education for All' agenda set in Jomtien in 1990 explicitly included adult education as part of the overall strategy. This situation raises a pertinent question: What happened with adult education during the nineties?

THE CONTRACTION OF THE EFA AGENDA: 'EDUCATION FOR ALL' OR 'EXCEPT FOR ADULTS'?

As mentioned above, the education policy agenda of the nineties was greatly shaped by the 1990 World Conference on Education for All. The Jomtien meeting, as it is usually known, was organized by an influential group of international agencies (UNESCO, UNICEF, UNDP, UNFPA and the World Bank) and was attended by 155 government delegations and 125 non-governmental organizations from around the world. In Jomtien, government representatives signed a declaration and a framework for action in which they made a commitment to ensure quality basic education for children, youth and adults. These commitments were expressed in six goals to be achieved in the year 2000: expansion of early childhood care, universal access to basic education, improvements in learning achievement, reduction of adult illiteracy in half, expansion of basic education and training for youth and adults (linking it to health, employment and productivity), and use of media and other communication technologies to promote better living and sustainable development.

However, when the Jomtien declaration was translated into actual policies and programs by national educational agencies, it lost most of its comprehensive, inclusive, innovative and progressive potential. As 'Education' was interpreted solely as school, and 'All' was interpreted only as children (especially children at risk), out-of-school youth and adults were ignored. For Rosa Maria Torres (2000), an acute observer of the post-Jomtien developments, the original concepts, guiding principles and targets of EFA 'shrank' during the nineties, as the policies and programs enacted by most countries were a downscaling of the original proposal. According to her, in their misguided interpretation of the original formulation of the Jomtien proposal, national governments not only limited their policies and programs to children and schools, but also changed the original focus on quality of learning and processes to an emphasis on assessing school performance and on standardized testing.

Along the same vein, a document issued by the Latin American office of Unesco maintains that during the 1990s adult education was left out of the official declarations about the educational reform inspired by the Jomtien Conference. The document points out that, at least in Latin America, the reading of Jomtien's EFA has excluded youth and adults as well as non-formal pedagogical practices and the diversity of out-of-school educational environments such as the family, community and the workplace (Unesco 2000, p. 12, 26). Thomas La Belle (2000), who has been studying Latin American adult education since the 1970s, also agrees that during the nineties the notion that adult education could play a key role in development strategies was abandoned by international and national policy makers. These assessments are confirmed by recent World Bank documents acknowledging that adult education has gradually vanished from the priorities of international lending agencies (World Bank 2000a, b).

For this reason, when the Latin American education community submitted a statement for the Dakar Forum in April 2000, one of the recommended policies was to recuperate the original spirit of Education for All in its 'expanded vision of basic education'. This means 'an education capable of satisfying basic education needs of all (children, youth and adults), both within and outside the school system and throughout life' (Latapi *et al.* 2000, p. 5). However, not much attention was paid to this and other similar requests by policy-makers in Dakar. It is in this context that Maria Lourdes Almazan-Khan, after attending the Dakar Conference as part of the delegation of the International Council of Adult Education (ICAE), asked if EFA, rather than 'Education for All', in reality stands for 'Except for Adults'. Almazan-Khan (2000) raised this question not only around issues of implementation of the Jomtien agenda, but also around the Dakar policy strategy, which was intended to rectify the mistakes of the last ten years. She reported that the commitments emanating from Dakar were not significantly informed by the philosophy of lifelong learning. Instead, they were constrained to a highly compartmentalized, 'functionalist' and reductionist view of education, with an emphasis on primary schooling.[7]

FACTORS UNDERMINING SUPPORT FOR ADULT EDUCATION IN LATIN AMERICA

Why have the goals set in Jomtien in 1990 been unfulfilled in Latin America? Rosa Maria Torres (2000: 52) enumerates some of the most recurrent arguments:

> Arguments already put forward include financial setbacks, structural adjustment processes, foreign debt, natural and social catastrophes, technical and human constraints, change of government and discontinuities of policies, co-ordination problems at all levels, weak public information and communication strategies, lack of participation and consultation, low levels of involvement and motivation of teachers and other change agents, false expectations regarding mass media and modern technologies.

In particular, we are interested in exploring why the field of adult education was relegated to the margins in terms of education policies and budgets during the last decade. Why were the original goals of EFA, which included adult education, forgotten by the national governments? What were the reasons for the gap between the Jomtien proposal and the national responses? As a hypothesis, the marginalization of adult education in the region can be explained by the combination of six related factors: 1) breadth and diversity of the field; 2) fragmentation of the field in autonomous and isolated areas; 3) low social relevance and low quality programs; 4) limited correspondence with the model of economic accumulation and political domination; 5) withdrawal of support by international agencies; and 6) unrealistic goals and local bureaucracies. Some of these factors stem from the internal dynamics of adult education in the region, and some relate to the impact of external dynamics on the field.

1. Breadth and diversity of the field   The mission and the boundaries of the field are not clear, to the extent that many providers of adult education (governmental or not) do not identify themselves as adult educators. This is the case, for instance, among professionals who work in areas such as health promotion, legal education, and agricultural extension, who tend to identify themselves more as health professionals, lawyers, or agronomists than as adult educators. Indeed, there is debate as to whether adult education constitutes an independent and professional field. Unlike in other fields (consider, for instance, medicine, or formal school teaching), there is an absence of professional colleges regulating the entrance to the profession and enforcing codes of professional conduct to their members, there is no standardized training (in fact, very little is known about the training of adult educators in the region), there are no systems linking training to certification, and so on. At the same time, because of the diversity of the field, adult education programs are diffused through a multiplicity of ministries and secretaries (which results in lack of coordination and duplication of results), and in a variety of private institutions, unions, popular organizations, and non-governmental organizations. This lack of coordinated effort and the great variety of spaces of intervention (compare, to continue with the previous example, with the identification of doctors and teachers with hospitals and schools) generate a dispersion of efforts, weakness in advancing collective pressure, and difficulties in generating consensual policies for the sector.

2. Fragmentation of the field in autonomous and isolated areas   Even those who consider themselves adult educators, and who work within the government apparatus (usually within ministries of education), tend to work in separation and isolation from each other, within areas of specialization such as adult basic education, literacy, community development, environmental education, technical-vocational education, and so on. In short, there is little coordination (let alone integration) among adult education actors within the state, and even less between them and those adult educators who work outside the state.

3. Low social relevance and low quality programs   Government-run adult education programs, particularly adult basic education programs, tend to have low social credibility, as large sectors of the community do not perceive them as useful or necessary besides the potential use of the diploma for entry into the labor market. Working with poorly paid and poorly trained teachers and volunteers,[8] with low emphasis on quality and low interest in evaluating results, this type of adult education is perceived as second class education for second class citizens.

4. Limited correspondence with the model of economic accumulation and political domination   The marginal role that Latin American adult education has had in public policy formation has also been attributed to its low correspondence with the model of capitalist accumulation and its little utility for the model of political domination. In this regard, Carlos A. Torres (1990, p. 33) pointed out that the clientele of adult education is socially fragmented, politically disorganized, and economically insignificant in Latin American societies. Applying the concepts of segmented labour market theory, Torres contends that the Latin American economic development strategy has focused on enhancing the productivity of the primary sector of the labour market (with stable, high-skilled, and relatively well-paid jobs). Hence, little attention has been paid to adult education and training for the secondary sector (with unstable, low-wage, and unskilled jobs), in which most of the potential clientele of adult education programs work. This economic marginality is correlated with political weakness to demand educational services. On occasions, however, the need for state political legitimation has led some governments to support large-scale adult education programs. Since budget allocations within education tends to favor those groups that are more willing and capable of exercising political pressure and of articulating the social and economic importance at a particular level, adult education usually tends to be marginalized at the time of deciding allocations. This was particularly true during the nineties, in a context of fiscal austerity and budget cuts.

5. Withdrawal of support by international agencies Against the background outlined above, a decision was taken by some influential international agencies to sideline youth and adult educational policies. One of the most surprising cases was Unesco, a traditional supporter of literacy and adult education during previous decades (Jones 1988, R.M. Torres 2000). To provide a rationale for this decision, which had important implications for program funding, two main arguments were typically advanced. The first is that, in a context of financial constraints, choices and priorities have to be made, as it is impossible to provide adequate funding for both children and adult education. Given that children constitute the future generation, it is more appropriate to invest the scarce resources available in children than in adults. In the words of R. M. Torres (2000, p. 27), 'whereby children have to compete financially with the education of their parents, adult education lost out'. The second argument is based on the claim that adult education programs, particularly literacy campaigns, have a poor track record.

This belief has become common sense in many policy circles, although it has not been supported by a critical mass of evidence derived from scientific research on cost-effectiveness; rather, it is largely the product of anecdotal information and opinions (R.M. Torres 2000). The claim is based on only one study (Abadzi, 1994) that contended that adult literacy campaigns conducted during the previous 30 years had an effectiveness rate of just 13 per cent. While this study may be correct, more research is needed into the costs and benefits of literacy programs before advancing the universal claim that all adult education programs are inefficient and wasteful (World Bank 1995, p. 90). In any case, even if past and current adult education programs were found inefficient, it is not clear why the best solution is to cancel them altogether instead of seeking the best strategies to improve them.

6. Unrealistic goals and traditional local bureaucracies The original goals of EFA on adult education were not only abandoned by international agencies, but also by the very governments that committed to them in 1990. Two main reasons have been advanced to explain the gap between the Jomtien proposal and the national responses. One reason is that local bureaucrats did not understand the philosophy and the implications of the proposal, and were unable to translate it into innovative policies and programs (R.M.Torres 2000). The other argument is that the overly unrealistic goals of the declaration made it condemned to failure from the beginning. For instance, the targets of universalizing primary education and reducing adult illiteracy by half in one decade set in Jomtien were seen as unattainable in local adult education circles because they were not tied to resources, capacity building, and redistributive social policies. Since this type of declaration falls within the realm of 'soft law', governmental fulfillment of these commitments constitutes more a moral than a legal responsibility. Based on the experience of previous world declarations and agendas, many actors and observers suggested immediately after Jomtien that the proclamation of these goals were mere rhetorical exercises. In retrospect, their skepticism was well-founded.

THE RETURN OF AE TO THE POLICY TABLE? INCIPIENT DEVELOPMENTS

In spite of the setback suffered during the nineties, some recent developments at the international level and at the regional level suggest that adult education may soon be returning to the table of educational policy-making. Here we describe three of these developments: the internal discussions within international agencies about the appropriateness of abandoning the field; the International Conference held in Hamburg (CONFINTEA V); and the role of the Latin American adult education community in the follow-up to CONFINTEA V.

INTERNATIONAL AGENCIES

International agencies are in a particularly powerful position regarding whether adult education will become a viable component of educational policy or not. Internal discussions within these organizations, notably the World Bank, point out that the matter is still unsettled. For example, in a study on the effects, benefits, efficiency and cost of adult education programmes conducted with the purpose of informing World Bank policy on this area, Oxenham and Aoki (2000) suggest two policy options: either to accept the available evaluations as sufficient for policy changes, or to seek more information.

If the first option is chosen, the signal for policy would be that the Bank should explicitly raise the priority of adult/youth basic education with literacy within its overall strategy for education and encourage affected member countries to do the same. The Bank would need to move from being simply willing to consider lending for the sub-sector to actively offering to assist its member governments mobilize the necessary additional resources. Oxenham and Aoki (2000) argue that programs of adult basic education are cost-effective, because people who participate in them accrue significant beneficial changes in attitude and behavior. Among other things, participants in literacy programs:

1. show enhanced confidence and autonomy within their families and in their communities
2. are more likely than non-literates to send and keep their children in school and monitor their progress
3. alter their health and nutritional practices to the benefit of their families
4. are more likely to be influenced in reducing their norms on family size
5. augment their production and incomes through using the information provided through the program or accessing information elsewhere
6. participate more strongly in community and political affairs
7. show better understanding of messages disseminated by radio, as well as by printed media
8. develop new and productive social relations through their learning groups
9. retain their skills in literacy and use them to expand their satisfactions in daily life. (Oxenham and Aoki 2000, p. 6)

In their introduction, Oxenham and Aoki (2000, p.2) suggest that 'if the Education Sector Board judges the evidence sufficient for World Bank to attach to adult/ youth basic education a priority similar to that for universal primary education for the attainment of Education for All by 2010, it should establish guidelines for strategies'. Among the strategies they proposed are the following: a) to link adult basic education into the main system of accreditation and continuous self-development; b) to articulate the sector with other interests, such as agricultural and health extension, or cooperative groups; c) to relate literacy and numeracy to life, work, social issues and development programs; d) to promote coordination among all national and international agencies (governmental, voluntary, private, community-based, etc.) dealing with the poor; e) to replace standardized 'nation wide' approaches and materials with a more diversified curriculum; f) to support adult educators with technical, moral and material support; g) to relate children's education, especially those from poor families, with the education of their parents; and h) to promote lifelong learning through literate environments and adult basic education (Oxenham and Aoki 2000, p. 38).

These eight proposed strategies would resonate well among people involved in adult education throughout the world. Hopefully, decision-makers will consider them in the near future. At the same time, as it is suggested in strategy g) above, there is increasing awareness that pitting children's education and adult education against each other is unproductive and assumes a false contradiction. Indeed, the literature on the topic strongly indicates that the education of children and that of their parents are mutually supportive, and that the cultural capital of the parents has a powerful impact on their children's school achievement. Thus, the dichotomy between children's education and adult education that prevailed during the 1990s ignores that children's learnings are highly conditioned by the levels of literacy and schooling of their parents. The fact that investments in adult education and literacy are investments in the education of entire families has been already acknowledged by article 6 of the EFA declaration, by the Mid-Decade Meeting of the EFA Forum, known as the Amman Affirmation (1996), and by Unesco (2000, p. 41). To what extent this acknowledgment is going to be translated into real commitments is still to be seen.

CATALYZING STATE AND CIVIL SOCIETY AROUND AN ADULT EDUCATION AGENDA: CONFINTEA V

In the summer of 1997, more than 1,500 delegates from over 130 countries convened in Hamburg, Germany to analyze the situation of adult education and to formulate the guidelines for policy and action for the first decade of the 21st century. The Fifth International Conference on Adult Education (known as CONFINTEA V), held 14–18 July, marked a radical shift with respect to the four previous International Conferences on Adult Education (Elsinore 1949, Montreal 1960, Tokyo 1972, Paris 1985) in at least two respects. First, there was a strong presence of organized civil society in the deliberation process. Whereas the previous conferences congregated almost exclusively governmental representatives, CONFINTEA V was open to delegates from non-governmental organizations as well: of the 1,507 participants, 478 were NGO representatives. This nurtured new relationships between governmental and non-governmental actors, strengthened the awareness about the connections between adult education, social development and democracy, and helped to promote commitments towards environmental sustainability and gender equity. Secondly, the agenda for CONFINTEA V was not an isolated event, but just a moment in a process that started before and continues still. Indeed, the Hamburg agenda was built from regional preparatory meetings (the main Latin American preparatory meeting was held in Brasilia in January 1997) and its commitments are being followed up in each region through a variety of mechanisms. This is due largely to the existence of information and communication technologies (ICTs) that were not available at the time of the previous conference, as well as to the growing awareness that the principles and commitments advanced in international conferences should translate in real policies and programs.[9]

CONFINTEA V produced two key policy statements: The Hamburg Declaration on Adult Learning and The Agenda for the Future. The Declaration consists of 27 principles, which include declaring adult education a right and endorsing the concept of learning throughout life. In the Declaration, adult education is understood in broad terms:

> Adult education denotes the entire body of ongoing learning processes, formal or otherwise, whereby people regarded as adults by the society to which they belong develop their abilities, enrich their knowledge, and improve their technical or professional qualifications or turn them in a new direction to meet their own needs and those of their society. Adult learning encompasses both formal and continuing education, non-formal learning and the spectrum of informal and incidental learning available in a multicultural learning society, where theory- and practice-based approaches are recognized.

Consistent with the approach of the Delors Report published the previous year, this definition of adult education puts the emphasis on the learning undertaken by adults rather than on the provision of educational services by agencies and teachers. At the same time, the Declaration acknowledges a variety of agents in adult education provision, recognition and accreditation: all ministries (and not only ministries of education, which implies the need of inter-ministerial co-operation), employers, unions, non-governmental and community organizations, indigenous peoples, and women's groups. In another part of the Declaration (principle 3), the role of adult education in creating a society committed to social justice and general well-being is underscored:

> Adult education ...is a key to the twenty-first century. It is both a consequence of active citizenship and a condition for full participation in society. It is a powerful concept for fostering ecologically sustainable development, for promoting democracy, justice, gender equity, and scientific, social and

economic development, and for building a world in which violent conflict is replaced by dialogue and a culture of peace based on justice.

In terms of the impact on the adult education community, this type of statement constitutes a double-edge sword. On the one hand, it makes clear that, in order to be relevant, adult education should contribute to social development and to the construction of a better world. On the other hand, it generates unrealistic expectations about the potential of adult education alone to cure all social problems, which usually leads to frustration and cynicism. Indeed, educational inequalities originate in factors external to the educational systems, and are part and parcel of social inequalities. Moreover, the educational provision (formal or non-formal) for the Latin American poor (children as well as adults) is pauperized, and hence reinforces those preexisting inequalities (Muñoz Izquierdo & Ulloa 1992, Rivero 1999, Youngman 2000). Thus, in terms of policy formulation and implementation for the short term, it may be more pertinent to call for quality adult education than to expect from it so many unattainable goals, especially in light of its available resources. The second document, entitled Agenda for the Future, encompasses a great number of ambitious commitments organized around ten main themes:

1) adult learning and democracy
2) improving the conditions and quality of adult learning
3) ensuring the universal right to literacy and basic education
4) adult learning, gender equality and equity, and the empowerment of women
5) adult learning and the changing world of work
6) adult learning in relation to environment, health, and population
7) adult learning, culture, media, and new information technologies
8) adult learning for all: the rights and aspirations of different groups
9) the economics of adult learning
10) enhancing international co-operation and solidarity

The commitments made in the Agenda for the Future are certainly important guidelines for policy development and are being disseminated widely among adult education communities in many countries. However, it is still questionable to what extent they are going to be honored by those who signed them.[10]

In spite of their limitations, both the Declaration and the Agenda for the Future constitute reference frameworks for the adult education communities in each region of the world. They can, for instance, use them as sources to reconceptualize the meaning and purpose of adult education in their region, adapt the strategies developed in Hamburg to the realities of their region, or put emphasis on the implementation of certain commitments that are considered priorities. In Latin America, this work is already being actively undertaken by a network of governmental and non-governmental actors. The next section describes key initiatives in this regard.

THE LATIN AMERICAN ADULT EDUCATION COMMUNITY
AND THE FOLLOW-UP TO CONFINTEA V

For Latin America, the Hamburg Conference came at a time when it was most needed. By 1997, it had become evident that the EFA goals for adult education set in Jomtien in 1990 had been almost abandoned. By and large, Latin American adult education was left out of the processes of educational reform that took place during the nineties, and even from the official discourse on these processes. Hamburg, then, provided a propitious occasion to ignite a process of collective reflection about the adult education agenda for the region and to establish new styles of cooperation between government and non-governmental agencies.

Latin American participation in CONFINTEA V began before Hamburg through a variety of preparatory meetings, especially the one held in Brasilia in early 1997. In this meeting, which was the departure point for a process that would continue beyond Hamburg, debates around the different locations and actors of Latin American adult education opened the path to serious rethinking. Among other things, it was recognized that the name that characterized the field for many years, Adult Education, was no longer an adequate category to reflect its reality. To better reflect the very high participation of youth in the programs, it was proposed to start using the term 'Education of Youth and Adults' (in Spanish, Educación de Jóvenes y Adultos, or EDJA). In many respects the change of name makes sense, because there is not enough awareness about the specific issues concerning young people, who constitute the majority of users of adult education services in the region. Participants in Brasilia raised criticisms of the 'economicista' approach that, focusing only on cost-benefit analysis, is providing the rationale for current educational policy. In response, adult educators called for the incorporation of approaches that include social well-being, equity and active citizenship as part of the equation.

The Latin American follow-up to CONFINTEA V was coordinated by a consortium of four institutions: UNESCO, CEAAL (Consejo de Educación de Adultos de América Latina, an umbrella organization of over two hundred NGOs that operate within the framework of popular education), CREFAL (Centro Regional de Alfabetización y Educación de Adultos para América Latina y el Caribe) and INEA (Instituto Nacional para la Educación de Adultos). The process consisted of a series of national meetings, three subregional meetings, and a regional meeting. The national meetings had the purpose of discussing the applicability of CONFINTEA V recommendations to the local context, but also of developing follow-up activities and indicators. Incidentally, these national meetings opened new spaces for dialogue and cooperation between governmental and non-governmental organizations. The debates and the proposals from the national meetings were carried over to the three subregional meetings held at the end of 1998 and beginning of 1999: Montevideo (Mercosur countries and Chile); Cochabamba (Andean countries); and Pátzcuaro (countries of the Gulf of Mexico as well Spanish and French-speaking Caribbean countries).[11] Subsequently, a regional meeting with participation of the three subregions was held in Santiago de Chile in August 2000.

Participants in these meetings included international agencies (UNESCO, CREFAL), national governments, and non-governmental organizations, as well as a significant number of planners, researchers, academics and adult educators. In some meetings there were also representatives from groups as varied as teacher unions (e.g. CTERA), women's networks (e.g. REPEM), regional international organizations (e.g. OAS), and international adult education think tanks (e.g. the Hamburg-based Unesco Institute for Education). Such a diversity of participants allowed for a multiplicity of perspectives, generated rich debates, and allowed for the open confrontation of different adult education projects for the region. This made it sometimes difficult to achieve consensus. However, while this long and intense process of deliberation demanded a special effort of organization, understanding and systematization, it was worth it. Although the road to agreement was longer than it would have been with a more homogeneous group, this strategy was certainly more democratic and inclusive, and provided new spaces for inter-institutional work around adult education. Moreover, the Latin American experience has become a model for other regions to emulate in their post-CONFINTEA tasks.[12]

Since the initial meetings, it became clear that the Agenda for the Future drafted in Hamburg had to be adapted to the realities and the demands of the Latin American context. Hence, seven main guiding themes were selected for the region from the ten themes raised in CONFINTEA V:

1. Literacy and adult basic education;
2. Education and work;
3. Education, citizen participation and human rights;
4. Education with peasants and indigenous peoples;
5. Youth education;
6. Education and gender; and
7. Education and sustainable local development.

The fact that in all meetings the debates were organized around these seven themes ensured a high degree of consistency throughout the process. Although each meeting had its specificities, the general tone was marked by a critical stance to neoliberal policies and to the abandonment of adult education by policy-makers. Likewise, in all meetings there were calls to ground adult education in the tradition and principles of popular education. Although this is not entirely surprising given the high participation of non-governmental organizations in these events, it is interesting to note that this approach is returning to center stage in the region after a period of relative impasse. As the report of the three subregional meetings remarks,

> Throughout this process the importance of the tradition of popular education in the education of youth and adults was reaffirmed, and a critical perspective

of the neoliberal model and the educational reforms that gave priority to the education of the new generations and relegated to a second level the education for youth and adults was taken'. (Messina 1999, p. 16; *translation is ours*).

Although the three subregional meetings shared this common framework, each one was characterized by specific debates, priorities and proposals. For example, among the main issues emerging from Montevideo were the need to develop specific public policies for adult and youth education that are oriented towards the most marginalized sectors and that promote social justice and equity while celebrating cultural diversity. There was also a stress on the need to systematize experiences, to professionalize adult educators through in-service training and salary improvements, and to create permanent forums to debate adult education policy at the national and regional levels. In Cochabamba discussions addressed the new relationships between the state and civil society, and on the need to build together a political agenda for adult education. There was also an emphasis on strengthening gender perspectives in adult education (understanding gender as a political category), on focusing on issues of justice and peace, and on producing good quality research on the field. Moreover, participants at this meeting called for the development of indicators to assess the fulfillment of commitments made by governments, but also to critically evaluate areas of progress and difficulty in adult education. In Patzcuaro, the need to better integrate adult education internally and externally was stressed. The former refers to the integration of the different fields of adult education (e.g. gender, education and work, local development) among themselves. The latter refers to the integration of adult education policies and programs with social policies oriented towards poverty alleviation and social inclusion, on the one hand, and with educational reforms, on the other. To bring adult education back to the political and educational agenda of the region, participants at the Patzcuaro meeting decided to organize a meeting of education ministers to discuss the role of adult education in the overall education policy. Another issue of concern was the development of strategies for the training of adult educators, an area in particularly bad shape.

In Santiago, the last meeting of the decade, there was a general recapitulation of the issues raised in the subregional meetings, and a discussion about the most appropriate strategies to face the current challenges. Adult education was again understood as a political and social endeavour, and its mission was linked once again to the equalization of opportunities and to social justice. It was recognized that a new relationship between civil society and the state is slowly being forged in the region, and that adult education can both contribute to and benefit from it. In this meeting, the main goal of the sector was defined as 'to develop youth and adults as autonomous citizens, able to participate and organize collectively, critically and creatively in local spaces and in broader contexts, to engage in self-initiated tasks in the face of changes, and to live together in solidarity' (Unesco et al. 2000b, p. 6).

What is becoming increasingly clear from these regional meetings is that the adult education movement in Latin America is in urgent need of continuing to broaden the dialogue already underway, and to work collectively in the definition of goals, strategies and evaluation mechanisms. In addition, the education of adult educators, the collaboration between academic-based and practice-based research, and the dissemination of that research to decision-makers are particularly important policy issues for the short term.

SUMMARY AND CONCLUSIONS

In this article, we used the Cinderella story to refer to the present situation of Latin American adult education in two senses. First, we used it in the meaning conveyed by Nyerere, to describe the marginal status of adult education in the education world. In spite of the efforts carried out by adult education agencies in the region during the last decade, and in spite of the high expectations derived from the Jomtien Declaration, the field has been marginalized from national and international educational institutions, which have concentrated most of their resources and pedagogical innovations on the school system. Secondly, and less literally, we appealed to the Cinderella metaphor to illustrate the active process undertaken by the Latin American adult education movement to redefine its identity, its agenda and its priorities. Although this process brings about unavoidable identity conflicts, we are confident that, like in the Cinderella story, the missing shoe will appear in due time. For that to happen, however, it is important to collectively reflect over the successes and failures of the past and to undertake creative prospective analysis of future trends.

While many of the factors leading to the marginalization of adult education lie outside the field, without a serious and honest self-reflection of the strengths and weaknesses of adult education programs and practices undertaken by its actors, one cannot help recover the missing shoe. Fortunately, important efforts have been developed by the Latin American adult education community in the last few years to reconceptualize its mission and strategies. The preparatory activities for the Fifth International Adult Education Conference (CONFINTEA V), and the follow-up activities and debates undertaken during the last three years (materialized in the Montevideo, Cochabamba, Patzcuaro, and Santiago meetings, and in a variety of position papers and research documents) clearly reveal that the adult education movement in the region is full of energy and eagerness.

However, supporters of Latin American adult education are trapped in a vicious circle. International agencies and national governments are reluctant to support this sector due to its alleged poor performance, but such a poor performance can only be drastically improved with supportive policies and financial commitments. To break this circle, changes have to occur at both levels simultaneously. Policy-makers have to critically review their ideas around the potential of adult education in the light of the available evidence discussed in this article. At the same time, the adult education community must engage in a deep soul-searching philosophical exercise about the purpose of the field and in a pedagogical discussion about the best ways to ensure quality, relevance and equity in our programs.

In the post-CONFINTEA meetings, the Latin American adult education community started this exercise with passion and methodological rigor. One of the issues that appeared several times in those discussions was the need to clarify the boundaries of the field. The dynamics of the discussions suggest that the Latin American adult education movement is experiencing a momentary identity crisis that is pulling it in the two opposite directions of expansion and contraction. Some adult educators argue that, in order to gain relevance and overcome its current crisis, adult education should expand beyond its traditional activities and programs, and make clear connections with the main issues that affect the lives of youth and adults in the region. This means actively engaging with issues related to human rights, poverty, the environment, gender, ethnicity, democracy, citizenship, employment, rural development, unions, migration, violence, local governance, health, consumers' rights, indigenous autonomy, peace, and the like. Other adult educators counter-argue that this type of agenda puts excessive demands on the field, and inevitably leads to dispersion and frustration. In their view, the solution to the crisis lies in concentrating its scarce resources on the few areas in which there is a history of accumulated expertise, such as literacy, adult basic education and vocational training, and doing these things with efficiency and quality. Only this, they argue, will build confidence in the field among internal and external constituencies.

According to the logic of this debate, the field of adult education appears to be in a catch-22 situation. In order to be more effective and attract more people, literacy and adult basic education programs have to become more relevant to the lives of the learners and their communities. However, the achievement of higher relevance usually implies a diversification of programs, contents and methods, which in turn creates dispersion and reduces effectiveness and quality.

In our view, a strategy to rebuild the field of adult education in Latin America must go beyond the straightjacket of choosing between breadth and depth. The practical choice is not between broad expansion and rigorous contraction. It is between a superficial expansion that spreads the field too thin and ends inevitably in self-exhaustion, dispersion and paralysis, and a well-thought out, creative and collaborative intersectoral expansion that articulates quality and relevant efforts carried out by adult educators in governmental and non-governmental institutions with efforts carried out in other areas. More importantly, this collaborative strategy must actively involve the adults and youth themselves in the definition of goals and strategies. As it was mentioned in the Santiago meeting in reference to indigenous education, the task is not anymore to promote an adult education for the indigenous peoples, but to develop with them an inclusive education movement. The transition from the 'for' to the 'with' mentality is an important step for a field traditionally characterized by top-down approaches, compensatory logics and deficit theories.

A related challenge for the Latin American adult education movement is to continue monitoring the progress of the Dakar commitments, and to put pressure on those who exercise power at the national and international level to provide the adequate means for the fulfillment of those commitments. Adult education alone cannot solve all the social problems, and not even all the problems faced by the 150 million Latin American youth and adults who have never accessed or have been pushed out from school. However, in connection with other actors and initiatives, it can offer a significant contribution to a more sustainable, just and equitable development. In the past, adult education in Latin America has developed innovative and creative approaches that have inspired people and programs throughout the world. Today, when it is evident that 'more of the same' is not enough and that the old educational paradigms are not working, Latin America is showing signs of once again becoming a fresh source of original thinking and practice in adult education.

NOTES

[1] An example of this situation can be found in a recent policy document in which the World Bank outlines its educational strategy and lending policies for Latin America and the Caribbean. In the section on priorities, the WB claims that the overarching goal for Latin America and the Caribbean "is to raise the Region's human capital, especially that of the poor" (World Bank 2000:11). Such statement can raise the hopes of Latin American adult educators for a few seconds, but such optimism would probably evaporate after reading the following paragraphs, in which the Bank describes its six strategic priorities to achieve this goal. Throughout them, there is an absence of references to adult education and non-formal education. Even the discussion of the first priority, which calls for 'including the excluded by, whenever possible, targeting interventions to the poor', makes no allusions to the potential role of adult education programs. There are references to a variety of interventions such as early childhood programs, school feeding, school health programs, improvement of quality of learning and school attendance through financial incentives to poor families, or the expansion of opportunities for secondary and tertiary education through income-contingent scholarships. The other five priorities deal with the quality of teaching and school revitalization, secondary education, decentralization of education ministries, tertiary education reform and educational innovations, especially in the use of education technology.

[2] It is pertinent to note that in the period 1980–2000 the illiteracy rates in the region (for people aged 15 and older) decreased from 20.3% to 11.7%; in absolute terms, the number of illiterates only decreased from 44 to 42 million people.

[3] Extremes in the region include, for example, population from 166 million (Brazil) to 2.8 (Panama) million; infant mortality from 7 (Cuba) to 71 (Haiti); income distribution (Gini index) from 60 (Brazil) to 47 (Costa Rica); adult literacy rates (females) that range from 2 (Uruguay) to 54 (Haiti); and net secondary enrollment rates from 36 (El Salvador) to 85 (Chile).

[4] See, for instance, Rosenzvaig 1997, Morley 1994, Berry 1998, Ocampo 1998, Loser and Guerguil 2000, Rivero 1999. These authors argue that after a decade of structural adjustment medicine, poverty levels and income distribution in Latin America are still worse than before the crisis of the 1980s. For the case of Mexico, Veltmeyer *et al.* (1997: 139–40, 162) show that privatization has intensified the concentration of wealth without increasing economic efficiency through competition. At the same time, unemployment increased (300,000 to 1 million jobs lost), the real value of wages decreased from 35% to 50%, and poverty increased.

5. Interestingly, the draft text of Dakar eliminated any reference to adult literacy, but was reinstated after pressure from NGOs and other social actors.
6. The seven countries were Argentina, Brazil, Colombia, Mexico, Paraguay and Venezuela. The sample included more than thousand adults (ages ranged from 15 to 54 years of age) in urban areas.
7. Although the Framework for Action made references to the concept of lifelong learning, Almazan-Khan reports that in general terms the dominant discourse in Dakar understood adult education only in terms of literacy or skills training.
8. The training of adult educators in Latin America is currently a black box. There is still little accurate information about who trains adult educators in the region, the methods and contents used, their impact, the profile of the educators of adult educators, and the like. Anecdotal information suggests that that pre-service and in-service training of adult educators in the region is still less than adequate.
9. During the conference, a special event was organized to pay tribute to two late Latin American adult educators who deeply influenced the contemporary theory and practice of literacy and adult education: Dame Nita Barrow from Barbados and Paulo Freire from Brazil.
10. Just to provide an example of these difficulties, commitment #57 states that 'within UNESCO, the UNESCO Institute for Education (UIE) in Hamburg should be strengthened in order to become an international reference centre for adult and continuing education'. At the time of writing this article, we learned that the German government is withdrawing its support for the Institute. This development prompts a basic reflection. If Unesco itself, the main organizer of the Hamburg Conference and its follow-up, and one of the world leaders in the field of adult education, cannot ensure the fulfillment of this specific commitment, how realistic is it to expect that national governments are going to do it for all the myriad of commitments included in the Agenda?
11. The Patzcuaro forum provided a space for the participation of two countries that seldom attend these type of subregional meetings: Belize and Haiti.
12. For instance, in the International CONFINTEA V follow-up Forum held in Manila at the end of 1999, both the International Council of Adult Education (ICAE) and the Unesco Institute for Education explicitly pointed out that the strategy developed by Latin America to follow up the Hamburg commitments constituted an example for other regions.

REFERENCES

Abadzi, H. (1994). *What we know about acquisition of adult literacy: Is there hope?* Washington, D.C.: World Bank.

Almazan-Khan, M. L. (2000). Does EFA stand for "Except for adults"? *ICAE News, 55,* 171–174.

Arnove, R., Franz, S., Mollis, M., & Torres, C. A. (1999). Education in Latin America at the end of the 1990s. In R. Arnove & C. A. Torres (Eds.), *Comparative education: The dialectic of the global and the local* (pp. 305–328), Lanham, MD: Rowman and Littlefield.

Berry, A. (1998). Chapter 1: The income distribution threat in Latin America. In A. Berry (Ed.), *Economic reforms, poverty, and income distribution in Latin America* (pp.9–41), Boulder, CO: Lynne Rienner.

CONFINTEA. (1997). Adult education. The Hamburg declaration and the Agenda for the Future. Fifth international conference on adult education 14–18 July, Hamburg: Unesco.

Delors, J. et al. (1996). Learning: A treasure within. Report to Unesco of the international commission on education for the 21st. century. Paris: Unesco.

Garcia Huidobro, J. E. (1994). Los cambios en las concepciones actuales de la educacion de adultos, in Unesco/Unicef (org.) *La Educacion de Adultos en America Latina ante el Proximo Siglo* (pp. 15–50), Santiago de Chile: Unesco.

Jones, P. (1988). *International policies for third world education: UNESCO, Literacy and Developments,* London: Routledge.

Infante, I. (Ed.) (2000). *Alfabetismo funcional en siete paises de America Latina,* Santiago: Unesco.

Kopinak, K. (1995). Gender as a vehicle for subordination of women maquiladora workers in Mexico, *Latin American Perspectives 22*(1), 30–48.

La Belle, T. (2000). The changing nature of non-formal education in Latin America, *Comparative Education. 36*(1), 21–36
Latapí, P., Schmelkes, S., & Torres, R. M. (2000). Latin American statement on 'education for all' on the occasion of the world education forum. *Adult Education and Development 55*, 155–162.
Loser, C. & Gueregil, M. (2000). The long road to financial stability, *Finance and Development*.
Messina, G. (1993). *La Educación Básica de Adultos: La Otra Educación*, Santiago: Unesco.
Morley, S. A. (1994). Poverty and inequality in Latin America: Past evidence, future prospects. Policy Essay No. 13, Washington D. C., Overseas Development Council (ODC).
Muñoz-Izquierdo, C., & Ulloa, M. (1994). Cuatro tesis sobre el origen de las desigualidades educativas, *Revista Latinoamericana de Estudios Educativos. XXII* (2), 11–58
Nyerere, J. (1988). Adult education and development, *Adult Education and Development, 30*, 7–18.
Ocampo, J. (1998). Income distribution, poverty, and social expenditure in Latin America, *CEPAL Review*. No 65, 7–14
Oxenham, J., & Aoki, A. (2000). *Including the 900 million +*. Washington DC: The World Bank.
Rivero, J. (1999). *Educación y Exclusión en America Latina: Reformas en Tiempo de Globalización*, Lima: Tarea.
Rosenzvaig, E. (1997). Neoliberalism: Economic philosophy of postmodern demolition, *Latin American Perspectives. 24* (6), 56–62.
Schmelkes, S. (1994). Research trends in adult education in Latin America. Paper presented at the International Seminar on Research Trends in Adult Education. Paris: Unesco.
Stromquist, N. (1997). *Literacy for citizenship: Gender and grassroots dynamics in Brazil*, Albany, NY: SUNY Press.
Summit of the Americas. (1994). Educational mandate of the second summit of the Americas. Miami, Florida, December 9–11. www.summit-americas.org/miamiplan.htm (accessed October 16, 2000).
Summit of the Americas. (1998). Educational mandate of the second summit of the Americas. Santiago de Chile, Chile, April 18–19. http://www.summit.americas.org/chileplan.htm (accessed October 16, 2000).
Torres, C. A. (1990). *The Politics of nonformal in Latin America*, New York: Praeger.
Torres, R. M. (2000). *One decade of education for all: The challenge ahead*, buenos aires: International institute for educational planning.
Torres, R. M. (1999). Reforma educativa en America Latina y el Caribe a fin de Siglo: Una Region, tres plataformas de acción. Unpublished manuscript.
Torres, R. M. (1995). Niños, padres y docentes: La inseparabilidad entre educación de adultos y educación infantil. Documento de trabajo, New York: Unicef.
Unesco. (2000). Estimated illiteracy rate and illiterate population aged 15 years and over. Statistical yearbook. http://unescostat.unesco.org/en/stats/stats0.htm (accessed October 15, 2000).
Unesco/CEAAL/CREFAL. (2000a). La educacion de Personas Jovenes y Adultas en America Latina y el Caribe. Prioridades de Accion en el Siglo XXI, Santiago: Unesco.
Unesco/CEAAL/CREFAL. (2000b). Marco de accion regional de la educacion de personas jovenes y adultas en America Latina y el caribe. Santiago: Unesco. Report prepared by Graciela Messina.
Unesco-OREALC. (1981). Proyecto principal de educación en América Latina y el Caribe: Sus objetivos, características y modalidades de acción. Santiago: Unesco-OREALC.
U. S. Government. (1998). Words into deeds: Progress since the miami summit. Report on the Implementation of the Decisions Reached at the 1994 Summit of the Americas (Washington: The White House). www.summit-americas.org/WordsintoDeeds-eng.htm (accessed October 16, 2000).
Veltmeyer, H., Petras, J., & Vieux, S. (1997). Neoliberalism and capitalism in Mexico 1983–1995: Model of structural adjustment? In Veltmeyer, H., Petras, J. & Vieux, S. (Eds.) *Neoliberalism and Class Conflict in Latin America. A Comparative Perspective on the Political Economy of Structural Adjustment* (pp.139–164), New York: St. Martin's Press.
World Bank. (1999). *Entering the 21st Century. World Development Report 1999/2000* Washington DC: World Bank.
World Education Forum, Jomtien. (1990). *World declaration on education for all: Meeting basic learning needs*. Paris: Unesco.

World Education Forum, Jomtien. (1990). *Framework for action: Meeting basic learning needs. Guidelines for implementing the world declaration on education for all.* Paris: Unesco.
World Education Forum, Dakar. (2000). *The Dakar framework for action. Education for all: Meeting our collective commitments.* Paris: Unesco.
Youngman, F. (2000). *The Political Economy of Adult Education and Development* New York & London: Zed Books.

AFFILIATIONS

Daniel Schugurensky
Head of Justice and Social Inquiry, School of Social Transformation,
and Professor in the School of Public Affairs at Arizona State University

John P. Myers
Associate Professor of Social Science Education in the College of Education,
Florida State University

EDWARD SHIZHA & ALI A. ABDI

26. ADULT CITIZENSHIP EDUCATION AND POLITICAL ENGAGEMENT IN SUB-SAHARAN AFRICA: CRITICAL ANALYSIS

INTRODUCTION

While Sub-Saharan African economies are currently among the fastest growing in the world, the subcontinent is still the most underdeveloped zone globally and its people are the most economically disadvantaged. In relatively speaking about development (or social development, as it should be comprehensively called), we are, by and large, talking about the cultural, educational, political, economic and technological viability as well as the general well-being of societies and individuals. The continuing development challenges in Africa have social and political consequences for its citizens. Poverty and lack of infrastructure especially place significant limitations on the cognitive skills of ordinary Africans, and thus their ability to act as full democratic citizens (Mattes & Mughogho, 2010). Along with limited access to news media (recently, in Zimbabwe, radios where confiscated from rural people in order to deny them access to external radio stations considered hostile to Zimbabwe African National Union (Patriotic Front) [ZANU (PF)], a party led by President Robert Mugabe), Mattes and Mughogho assert that the extremely low levels of formal education found in many African countries strike at the very core of the skills and information that should enable citizens to assess and access social, economic and political developments, learn the rules of government, form opinions about political performance and care about the survival of democracy. Thus education, particularly citizenship education is greatly needed in the continent to improve political literacy among the continent's citizens.

Education in all its forms (formal, informal and non-formal) plays a vital role in enlightening people about their civil, economic and political rights. Education in its various expressions is also understood to be fundamental to the establishment and formation of a citizenry which recognizes and values the importance of participatory engagement in the process of governance and institutions of government that would be relevant to particular societal arrangements (cf. Dewey, 1926; Abdi, Ellis & Shizha, 2005). This is more so in these times of globalization and the extended belief in global citizenship where Africans have to compete with others all over the world for knowledge acquisition and its attendant politico-economic endowments. For African adult learners therefore, adult citizenship education can become the *sine qua non* of both socio-political and economic democracy harnessing and achievement. Adult citizenship education could be theorized as a means by which adults acquire knowledge, skills, dispositions and attitudes that are vital for political participation or engagement. Globalization and its influence on political and governance debates, has aroused what de Souza-Santos and Arriscano-Nunez (2006) call 'waves of democratization' in the form of citizens' initiatives and popular movements world-wide. The question of whether civic or citizenship education can instill political knowledge, values, and skills among citizens in democratic political systems is fully "on the radar screen of contemporary political science" (Galston, 2001, p. 271). In Sub-Saharan Africa, voting and political participation by adults who are discouraged from civic engagement by corrupt regimes appear to be on the rise. Just like young people, adults are increasingly becoming disengaged from political affairs. Consequently, this calls for increased efforts to mobilize both the youth and adults in democratic political processes to stem out this potentially dysfunctional trend. However, Finkel and Ernst (2005) note that there has been an explosion of civic education programs in the past decade in the newly emerging democracies of Eastern Europe, Africa and Latin America. In Africa, not all countries, though, can be labelled as 'emerging democracies'. Systematic socio-political surveys have indicated that only a minority of African countries can be called committed democrats (Bratton, Mattes & Gyimah-Boadi, 2005). For instance, political repression is rampart in some African countries where millions of people are denied the ability to participate in political activities including elections. Furthermore, in those states where elites compete for control over scarce resources, poorly regulated election processes often lead to surges in violence. This has been the case in Angola, Senegal, Mali, Kenya, Côte d'Ivoire, Nigeria and Zimbabwe. Citizenship education in African countries where oppressive regimes keep justifying their hegemonic actions as the best available alternative, require transformative possibilities of citizenship education to denaturalise the highly uneven development realities between the elite and the masses (Abdi *et al*, 2005). This chapter deals with ways of promoting critical adult citizenship education that motivates adult citizens to participate in political engagement, and by extension, in active possibilities of social development.

THE CONCEPT OF CITIZENSHIP EDUCATION

Citizenship education has varied meanings and is sometimes referred to as civic education, political education or democracy education. Lister (2003) argues that citizenship has contested meanings that vary according to the socio-cultural and historical relationship between individuals and society and among states. It is rooted in civil rights and the belongingness of individuals to a nation-state. These rights include agency, defined as the capacity to make informed choices about actions to take and how to do them, as well as assuming responsibility for their consequences (Torres & Reyes, 2010). According to Abdi *et al*:

> In general, citizenship is associated with national identity as affirmed by membership to a particular nation-state that is itself defined by globally recognized national boundaries. Generally, it is the state that packages and regulates the identities of its citizens and controls individual and social rights and responsibilities. In that setting, individuals or citizens carry identity cards, passports, and driver's licences that attest to national identify (or citizenship) within the confines of their country's frontiers or in other parts of the world. More often than otherwise, citizens do not partake in, or even influence this project of identity packaging. It is the reality of a given state's omnipresent power to legitimate citizen's legal and other statuses that actually gives it so much power to control the overall being of its so-called citizens. (2005, p. 460).

Citizenship entails ideals about participation and equality of status. However, in Sub-Saharan Africa and certainly elsewhere, citizenship does not guarantee equality of status. Governments have control on who gets citizenship, who has civic rights and who participates in socio-political activities. In these more complex times, though, we concur with Davies and Evans (2001) who note that citizenship is a multi-dimensional construct and practice with a wide ranging arenas and intersections of operation and different levels of contestations that are contiguous and continuous. Ndegwa (2001) argues that conditions that permeate African nations have changed very little from authoritarianism (Lesotho, Swaziland, Angola, Uganda, Democratic Republic of Congo, Equatorial Guinea, Somalia, Zimbabwe are examples of such cases) and have been inimical to democratization and consolidation of democratic rule. That is especially the case when any discussion of citizenship cannot be divorced or separated from the polemics of democracy, human rights, the rule of law and social justice (Abdi *et al*, 2005). These areas, therefore, remain sites of struggle within the context of individual Africans and collectivities such as civil society associations with most still fighting for basic political rights, which, as mentioned above, would be the key for any effective reconfiguration of the present African condition.

According to Mhlauli (2012), in Africa, as in other parts of the world, education and schooling in particular have played a pivotal role in the development of citizens during the post-independence era. All education generally involves an element of citizenship training; the learning experiences that equip and empower citizens to actively participate in democratic processes. Citizenship education has recently become topical worldwide. The heightened interest is a result of a political context of perceived disaffection, disengagement, alienation and lack of interest in civic issues in democratic societies. Citizenship education gives citizens the skills, abilities, knowledge and resources needed to participate in the economy and politics. For instance, Verba, Kay and Henry (1995) argue that education not only directly increases levels of participation, but also allows citizens to acquire the civic skills necessary to actively and effectively communicate their concerns to politicians.

Similarly, Rosenstone and Hansen argue that education "imparts the knowledge and skills most essential to a citizen's task....well educated [people] have the skills people need to understand the abstract subject of politics, to follow the political campaign, and to research and evaluate the issues and candidates" (1993, p. 136). In addition, civic education is perceived as the remedy for political apathy where citizens could abdicate their democratic rights to have their voices heard in issues that affect their social, cultural, political and economic rights.

Generally speaking, though, the primary aim of citizenship education is to elevate the level of people's participation in politics (Quigley & Bahmueller, 1991). This participation is probably needed more today in Africa (where dictatorship is still eminent) than any other continent. Citizenship education in Sub-Saharan Africa should create critical consciousness among the adult population who have the role of providing political socialization to children and youth. Neighborhood and family civic contexts play a significant role in the development of civic orientations (Kahne & Sporte, 2008). Thus, young people growing up in families and communities that are civically active and financially better off tend to end up more active themselves (Jennings, Stoker & Bowers, 2001). Critical consciousness also helps people to proactively analyse their socio-economic livelihoods and governance (including leadership issues). It is questionable whether citizens in some African countries such as Zimbabwe (where Robert Mugabe has been in power since 1980), Equatorial Guinea (where Teodoro Obiang Nguema Mbasogo clings on to power which he grabbed through a military coup in 1979), Cameroon (where Paul Biya has been in power since 1982) and Angola (where Jose Eduardo Dos Santos has been in power since 1979) can harness the critical consciousness required to empower themselves with progressive democratic values. The fact that undemocratic leadership in these countries has been maintained for decades without any change of power entails lack of critical democratic values which could be inculcated through critical citizenship education. On the basis of this shortcoming, such citizens can be described as having 'democratic deficit' or a caustic and uncritical citizenship understanding. In this less than active form of citizenship, citizens exhibit higher levels of satisfaction with the quality of governance and the performance of democracy than actually demand to live in a democracy (Mattes & Shenga, 2007). Uncritical citizenship stands in direct contrast to Norris's (1999) concept of a critical citizen who supports the ideals of democracy and is likely to identify weaknesses, shortcomings, inadequacies and gaps in their representative institutions, elected leaders, and the policies they pursue.

In Sub-Saharan Africa, democracy is often dictated by the political elites, not in terms of granting citizens their political rights but through 'mobilized democracy'. According to (Bratton *et al.* 2005), previous research shows that identification with a political party and membership in civic associations are often important determinants of a mobilized, rather than autonomous form of participation and citizenship in most African countries. Adults who have experienced the one-man rule in some of these countries should be actively involved in educational programs that lead to the transformation and activation of critical political engagement. The writings of the late Brazilian philosopher Paulo Freire (1992, 1994, 1998) are important works of citizenship education that provocatively analysed critical literacy and the resulting social conscientization so that the underclass could harness new and transformative programs of political awareness for social development. Political literacy gained through conscientization is critical to engaging political elites and empowering the masses. From the Freirean perspective, there has been a remarkable consistency in how his program of grassroots citizenship has influenced past as well as current formations of popular citizenship consciousness. That is, even if the practical operationalization of critical pedagogy may be limited, the continuing appropriation of his progressive philosophy of critical education for horizontal emancipation, by community and civil society associations in Latin America (Africa should learn from the Latin American experience) and elsewhere, is widely visible and conducive to possible projects of social and political enfranchisement.

DEMOCRACY, DIALOGISM AND POLITICAL ENGAGEMENT

Political knowledge, engagement, and attitudes matter for economic and political outcomes, and this is especially true in Africa (Adhvaryu & Fenske, 2013). In democratic societies, citizens are free to participate in economic, social and political activities without fear or hindrance. Civic engagement builds social capital, which in turn improves incomes (Putnam, 2000). Concerning civic/political engagement, O'Neill (2006) states:

> Civic/political engagement is defined as a larger set of activities that includes political participation, but extends beyond it to include activities in civic affairs such as involvement in community associations, as well as psychological dimensions of engagement such as media consumption and political interest. (p. i)

According to Skocpol and Fiorina (1999, p. 2), political involvement concerns itself with "the network of ties and groups through which people connect to one another and get drawn into community and political affairs." Engagement in politics or civil affairs is a democratic right of every eligible citizen. It also involves the enjoyment of freedoms that citizens expect their governments to uphold. Where freedoms of expression, association and speech are enjoyed, citizens feel that their democratic values, which include the ideal of "rule of, by, and for the people" as well as the "core values of equality of interests, political autonomy and reciprocity" (Brettschneider, 2007, p. 28) are being acknowledged and honoured.

Democracy is grounded on participation rights complemented with freedom from government intervention (Torres & Reyes, 2010). Democracy builds pragmatic and quality public discourses on issues regarding leadership and governance, voting rights and overall participation in the socio-political and economic dispensation that will inculcate the possibility of attainment of what Aina (1999) calls a new understanding of 'development consciousness', or "the ways people perceive, think of, and are conscious of development as a process intended to transform their lives in a positive and beneficial direction and of its contribution to the improvement of material and other well-beings" (p. 69). Democracy entails that the rule of law is observed and the rights of people protected. Democracy and the rule of law are dialectical and, by and large, contain within themselves the not so alien polemics of good governance (Abdi *et al.*, 2005).

Osaghae (1999) explains democratization or transition to democracy as a political process that has to do with the transformation of the state and political society. Participation in political, social and economic decisions by the governed irrespective of their gender, political affiliation, ethnicity, race, and religion, and good governance that respects the rule of law, is more important than political control and protecting ruling class interests (Abdi *et al*, 2005). In Africa, where state-centered politics control economic and social relations, the new imperatives should be ways of strengthening state structures through democratic, accountable, and responsive forms of governance that are tolerant to alternative voices and dialogue.

Perhaps, Sub-Saharan Africa requires radical participatory democracy, which is grounded in human values including participation in public dialogue as equally signifying consciousnesses for the understanding and making of a better world for all (Torres & Reyes, 2010). Radical participatory democracy, according to Freire (2003, 2005), is based on the philosophy of dialogism and radical humanism, by which human beings are entitled to basic rights including self-government and self-determination of the type of world in which they want to live. Dialogue gives citizens direction and the sense of possibility so necessary for counteracting the 'betrayal of democracy' (Giroux, 2004). Dialogue is an element that is non-existent in African 'democracies'. Oppositional politics and civil society are most often left out of the political discourse and dialogue. Ruling parties usually dominate and overcrowd the politico-public space resulting in 'one-party-states'. Critical democracy and citizenship cannot exist without a multiparty public sphere, and "the rule of law cannot be held or maintained without a radical democracy" (Habermas, 1996, p. xiii). Habermas (1996) encourages citizens to be politically educated to vigorously and fearlessly defend their public sphere. For Habermas, the public sphere represents a civic space where citizens freely gather to debate and decide about shared concerns and issues. These public spaces provide avenues for diverse voices to be heard through uninhibited dialogue. Dialogue accelerates participatory democracy, which is a prerequisite to personal, social, economic and overall citizenship development.

Tragically, freedom of expression, alternative information, free and fair elections and freedom of association are anathema to African governments. African governments, with the exception of a few like Botswana, become combative when civil society and opposition political parties challenge their governance and corruption. Political persecution, violence and treason charges are targeted at those threatening the *status quo*. For instance, in Zimbabwe from 2000 to 2003, opposition members of the Movement for Democratic Change (MDC), including its entire top leadership cadre, were arrested for non-existent treason charges (Abdi *et al.*, 2005). The charges were trumped up by the ZANU (PF) government in order to induce fear into movements, associations, unions and civil society that were mobilizing and fighting for the democratization of Zimbabwe. These are political tragedies that make participatory democracy elusive in Africa. Nzongola-Ntalaja and Lee (1998) argue, for example, that democracy from a philosophical, historical and comparative perspective is a universal principle of governance that is a moral imperative, a social process, and a particular type of political practice applicable to all human societies. Nyerere (1998, p. 27) also contends that "democracy means much more than voting on the basis of adult suffrage every few years; it means (among other things) attitudes of toleration and willingness to co-operate with others on terms of equality." Following Jean-Jacques Rousseau, Brettschneider (2007) distinguishes between 'sovereign people' and the 'government'. The latter is legitimate only when its laws and institutions respect people's sovereignty (Torres & Reyes, 2010). A government that does not treat its citizens as 'sovereign' is not sovereign itself and it is therefore not legitimate. The legitimacy of governments and their institutions is derived from the people who vote them into power. According to Brettschneider (2007, p. 55), "The procedure of the majority who exercise their political rights through participating in elections and in political decision making can be useful in identifying the preferences of sovereign people, but these procedures should not be viewed as the final arbiter of legitimacy."

CIVIC/CITIZENSHIP EDUCATION PROGRAMS

Operating from the belief that democracies are most likely to function effectively when the populace endorses the values and norms inherent in democratic regimes, civic education programs among primary and secondary school children, as well as among some adult populations, have become commonplace in developing democracies (Brilliant, 2000; Carothers, 1999). Education, according to Woodruff (2005), plays an important role in the development of citizens' wisdom. As Woodruff explains, "citizen wisdom is what the citizens in a well-run democracy ought to have. It builds on common human abilities to perceive, reason, and judge, but it requires also healthy traditions and good education for all" (2005, p. 154). Adult education, which is life-long learning and should be continuously present in the life of individuals before or past postsecondary education, provides adult learners with the wisdom to make critical judgments about their welfare and community development. The wisdom of citizens is crucial for governance, because it is capable of critically judging expert knowledge. In political matters, then, trust is to be placed in the capacities of ordinary citizens rather than those of experts, particularly given the fact that experts can take positions on issues dictated by self-interest (O'Neill, 2006).

According to Stromquist (2006), the connection between literacy (gained from formal, informal and non-formal education; primary, secondary, postsecondary and adult education) and political engagement is predicated on the assumption that as individuals become more exposed to information about their environment, especially the public institutions and government, they will be more prepared to intervene to make such bodies more responsive to their needs. Basic adult education can have extraordinary impact on political literacy. Research on literacy learners in the United States have examined changes over a reasonable period of time and revealed that the study of four adult basic education (ABE) programs conducted by Greenleigh Associates in 1968 (Stromquist, 2006) found that literacy participants reported an increase in community participation. A Kenyan study conducted by Carron, Mwiria, and Righa (1989) used a sample of 371 literacy graduates and 66 illiterates as a comparison group in five different rural locations in the country and concluded that literacy graduates did better in a wide variety of behavioral and attitudinal indicators that included participation in elections and local associations. In another study conducted in Turkey, Kagitcibasi, Goksen, and Gulgoz (2005) used an urban sample of 95 women in an assessment carried out immediately after program participation and a subset of 50 women in a follow-up after one year of program participation. The researchers found that literacy program participants did better than non-participants in the social participation scale and that over time, gains in self-efficacy increased considerably while gains in social participation increased only slightly. Egbo (2000) compared non-literate women to literate women (possessing varying levels of reading proficiency and thus formal education) in Nigeria and found that literate women reported being confident enough to participate in community meetings, considered they knew their rights better than the non-literate women, and felt more confident to make autonomous decisions.

CIVIL SOCIETY AND CITIZENSHIP EDUCATION

Civil society plays an important role in educating adults in citizenship education. The role of civil society is to mobilize citizens through civic/citizenship/political education for greater economic, social and political participation. Civil society is the mechanism by which corruption can be reduced and it engages citizens in the development of a democratic political culture and in the implementation of civic education programs (Finkel, 2000). Most civil society organizations in Africa get financial and material assistance and other supports from international non-governmental organizations (NGOs). These NGOs with their own agendas devote considerable resources to civic education as part of their larger efforts to provide democracy assistance and strengthen civil society in emerging democracies around the world (Carothers, 1999; Diamond 1997). For example, the United States Agency for International Development's (USAID) strategic framework states explicitly that it seeks (a) to strengthen democratic political culture, (b) to promote acceptance by both citizens and political elites of a shared system of democratic norms and values, and (c) to encourage citizens to obtain knowledge about their system of government and act upon their values by participating in the political and policy process (USAID Democracy Strategic Framework, 1998). In Sub-Saharan Africa and in other emerging democracies, there are now a "plethora of public and private international actors involved in these efforts" (Quigley, 1997, p. 564). Research and scholarship in both advanced and developing democracies have emphasized the role of active mobilization efforts in stimulating individual political behavior. For example, in Zambia, Bratton (1999) found that after the civic education provided by civil societies and NGOs, memberships in parties and voluntary associations became stronger predictors of participation than economic status.

In Africa, adult civic education in political mobilization and engagement is conducted overwhelmingly through secondary groups and associations, sometimes by labor, church or trade associations (Abdi, Shizha & Ellis, 2010) but more frequently by what Carothers (1999) refers to as 'advocacy NGOs'. The Electoral Institute for Sustainable Democracy in Africa (EISA), Lawyers for Human Rights in South Africa, Constitutional and Reform Education Consortium in Kenya, Zimbabwe Election Support Network (ZESN), Zimbabwe NGO Human Rights Forum and Open Society Initiative for West Africa (OSIWA) are some of the civil societies supported by international NGOs to achieve their purpose of political socialization. These groups are public interest or reformist groups that are funded by the U.S. and European donors in the hopes that they can become part of a "diverse, active, and independent civil society that articulates the interests of citizens and holds government accountable" (Carothers, 1999, p. 87). In Senegal, for instance, civil society is at the heart of Senegal's new 'alternance', the political change the country is experiencing. Similarly, in Zimbabwe, civil society is at the centre of the political discourse for change that is gaining voice although the Government of Zimbabwe (particularly ZANU (PF) that partnered with the MDC formations in the current Government of National Unity) has been persecuting civil society leaders (e.g., the arrest of the director of the Zimbabwe Human Rights Association (ZimRights), Okay Machisa in January this year for allegedly conducting illegal voter registration and fraud). In Zambia, civil society groups participated heavily and actively in the democratic political change which brought into power the Movement of Multi-Party Democracy (MMD under the late President Frederick Chiluba) in 1991. As Abdi *et al* (2010) point out:

> Zambia is one among several Sub-Saharan African countries where domestic mobilization led to democratic governance, the rethinking of the people was pragmatically responsive to democracy, even if its meaning and central tenets were poorly understood, with expectations that at least, it would lead to better livelihood outcomes for all. (p. 2)

MASS MEDIA AND POLITICAL EDUCATION

Africa, despite the now ubiquitous presence of cell phones and the internet, is a continent of 'low [quality] information societies' characterized by poor communications infrastructure, limited access to news media, low levels of schooling and even lower levels of access to higher education (Mattes & Shenga, 2007). A well-developed mass media that reaches the masses can be a very important vehicle for adult political education and development. The media can play a positive or negative role in the political socialization of citizens. Media should present information that is unbiased for citizens to make critically informed decisions about their political participation and engagement that would affect their livelihoods. Mass media that are widely available to the general public are hampered by their one-way nature that may impose distortions and indoctrinate uncritical citizens. To meet the needs of the present 'revolutionary situation' (particularly in the democratization of politics, education, the economy in Africa) in the education of adults, African countries therefore need to find a range of new and multiple pedagogical ways of promoting participatory tools for adult education. Earlier, Maheu (1968) pointed out how the media can, *inter alia*, provide a continuous flow of information which enables peoples to participate intelligently in civic affairs, and shape discussions on issues of personal concern as well as the decision making process.

Skjelton (2006) reports that in South Africa in 1996, the leaders of South Africa's constituent assembly through their community liaison department worked in close coordination with the constitutional assembly's media department to develop a campaign to raise awareness that a process of making a constitution was happening and encouraged the public to participate. The media campaign emphasized the role of the public in the process, the advertisements included messages such as "It's your right to decide your constitutional rights" and "You've made your mark" (meaning "You voted; now have your say"). According to Skjelton, the community liaison department also provided civic education on the process and on constitutional issues through the use of posters, brochures, leaflets, a bi-weekly constitutional newsletter called 'Constitutional Talk' (160,000 copies were distributed each week), booklets such as "You and Building the New Constitution," comic books, and an official website. A weekly TV program, 'Constitutional Talk', promoted debates on constitutional issues such as the death penalty. However, sometimes civic education programs in Africa fail because some groups are difficult to reach even where media are available. In 1997, in Eritrea, for example, the constitution-making body struggled to communicate with nomads (Medhanie, 2008). It went to great lengths to organize meetings and provided food and water for weeks so that the nomads could stay in one place and talk with constitution-makers in their own language.

Media can also fuel hatred, atrocities and genocide in countries where multipartyism and plural voices from marginalized ethnic groups are suppressed. Usually, government controlled media can promote hostilities against opposition parties or ethnic minorities. For instance, the news media played a crucial role in the 1994 Rwanda genocide. Local media fuelled the killings of Tutsis, while the international media either ignored or seriously misconstrued what was happening (Thompson, 2007). The media should educate the public on tolerance, civility, willingness to listen, negotiate and compromise. It should also inform citizens about governance and development issues. In Ghana, policymakers complain that part of the challenge of communicating about development issues with the public is how little people understand the structure or responsibilities of the various government agencies working on key policy issues like health, education, agriculture, or trade (Bowen, 2010). As one Ghanaian policymaker lamented, very few people know about key elements of the policy process including the decision-making process, budgeting and actual government activities. Many policymakers believe that the media could play an important role in bridging this gap by providing some basic civic education and better coverage of public policy news. Limited public understanding makes it difficult not only for policymakers to serve effectively, but also for citizens to hold them accountable for [un]fulfilling their responsibilities (Bowen, 2010).

COMMUNITY PROGRAMS FOR CIVIC EDUCATION

Adult education programs for civic engagement are most effective when they are conducted within the communities in which the adult learners live. Community-based education programs take into account the socio-economic needs of the communities and place the decision-making process (a form of agency and collectivity) in the hands of the people. The late Julius Nyerere's *Ujamaa* (which means 'extended family' or 'familyhood' in Swahili) in Tanzania, the late Jomo Kenyata's *Harambee* (which means 'all pull together' in Swahili, a form of collectivism or collective self-reliance) in Kenya and *Mushandirapamwe* (which means 'working together for self-reliance' in chiShona) in Zimbabwe are examples of community-based adult education for social development in Africa. The common threads within *Ujamaa*, *Harambee* and *Mushandirapamwe* are (a) work by everyone (b) fair sharing of resources collectively produced and (c) respect for human dignity, which are essential to indigenous African communalism and village life. Developmental villages (*vijiji uya maendeleo*) were introduced in mainland Tanzania over the period 1974–1982 as part of a large-scale resettlement program (Osafo-Kwaako, 2011), while in Zimbabwe they have always been part of community living in rural settlements. The villages are characterized by a community where co-operation and collective advancement are the rationale of every individual's existence.

In many countries today, there is a movement away from simple electoral politics to considering the capacity to participate in everyday engagement in community-level activities and decision-making (Stromquist, 2006). For many disadvantaged groups, this means not only gaining the pertinent information and having the desire to engage in political action, but also having the cultural and physical space to make political action real. The community-based adult education approach is one of the ways in which citizens are empowered to take control of their own socio-economic and political development. Incorporating community-based informal education signifies the recognition of the power of the role of both the individual and the collective agency of change that is found in the potential of using multiple platforms for voicing citizens' concerns.

Community engagement and civic participation are a form of education which expands the individual's freedom. In spite of the political freedom attained in Africa, there still remains a form of imprisonment (Nasongo & Musungu, 2009). As Nyerere (1968) pointed out many years ago, mental liberation is the key to the attainment of genuine humanity. The tasks of education within community engagement are primarily the emancipation of the human person. Robust participation in the life of the community (following community issues, working on community problems, collective engagement with government agencies) is a fundamentally important component of life in a democratic society. Comparatively, national political freedom is of little or no consequence if individuals within the nation-state are oppressed and their citizenship or democratic rights and cognitive freedoms remain fettered.

CONCLUSION

Adult citizenship education has been conducted widely in Africa but with different outcomes. In countries where democracy flourishes, civil society has worked freely to encourage political engagement through citizenship/civic/political education. Citizens need to be empowered with civic knowledge to develop positive attitudes towards governance issues. They should be collectively and openly questioning and challenging political and economic decisions that are made by political elites on their behalf. Civic knowledge, skills, values and dispositions are necessary in a democracy. African governments have the obligations to provide their citizens with a political environment that encourages dialogue and horizontal participation in decision-making processes. Not all citizenship education programs are successful. Few civic education programs have had the time, resources and commitment to reach all citizens including disadvantaged groups effectively. Just to make contact with certain groups may pose significant challenges. Some organizations may be more interested in the money than in achieving the goals of the civic education program. Most civic education programs are conducted with good intentions. The problem lies in their implementation, including unrealistic objectives given time and resource constraints and sometimes a lack of awareness about what the task entails as well as the government's willingness to promote a democratic space for its citizens. Nevertheless, we cannot underestimate the importance of adult citizenship education in advancing political engagement in Africa where the potential formations of critical democracy could usher in more active and inclusive platforms of social development.

REFERENCES

Abdi, Ali A., Ellis, L., & Shizha, E. (2005). Democratic development and the role of citizenship education in Sub-Saharan Africa with a case focus of Zambia. *International Education Journal, 6* (4), 454–466.

Abdi, Ali A., Shizha, E., & Ellis, L. (2010). *Citizenship education and social development in Zambia.* Charlotte, NC: Information Age Publishing Inc.

Adhvaryu, A., & Fenske, J. (2013). *War, resilience and political engagement in Africa.* Preliminary version prepared for the CSAE 2013 Conference in Winnipeg, September 18–20, 2013.

Aina, T. A. (1999). West and central Africa: Social policy for reconstruction and development. In D. Morales-Gomez (Ed.), *Transnational social policies: The new development challenges of globalization* (pp. 679–87). Ottawa: International Development Research Centre.

Bowen, H. (2010). *Media's role in civic education.* New York: AudienceScapes: The InterMedia Knowledge Centre. Retrieved April 20, 2013 from: http://www.audiencescapes.org/medias-role-civic-education-458

Bratton, M. (999). Political participation in a new democracy: Institutional consideration from Zambia. *Comparative Political Studies, 32,* 549–588.

Bratton, M., Mattes, R., & Gyimah-Boadi, E. (2005). *Public opinion, democracy and market reform in Africa.* Cambridge: Cambridge University Press.

Brettschneider, C. (2007). *Democratic rights: The substance of self-government*. Woodstock: Princeton University Press.
Brilliant, F. (2000). *Civic education programming since 1990: A case study based analysis*. Report prepared for U.S. Agency for International Development, Contract No. AEP-I-00-96-90012-00, Task Order No. 10. Management Systems International, Inc.
Carothers, T. (1999). *Aiding democracy abroad: The learning curve*. Washington, D.C.: Carnegie Endowment for International Peace.
Carron, G., Mwiria, K., & Righa, G. (1989). *The functioning and effects of the Kenyan literacy program*. Research Report No. 77. Paris: IIEP.
Davies, I., & Evans, M. (2001). Encouraging active citizenship. *Educational Review, 54*, 69–78.
de Souza-Santos, B., & Arriscano-Nunez, J. (2006). Introduction: Democracy, participation and grassroots movements in contemporary Portugal. In B. de Souza-Santos & J. Arriscano-Nunez (Eds.), *Reinventing Democracy: Grassroots Movements in Portugal* (pp. 1–15). New York: Routledge.
Dewey, J. (1926). *Democracy and education*. New York: Collier.
Diamond, L. (1997). *Consolidating third wave democracies*. Baltimore: Johns Hopkins University Press.
Egbo, B. (2000). *Gender, literacy and life-chances in Sub-Saharan Africa*. Clevedon, U.K.: Multilingual Matters.
Finkel, S. E. (2000). Civic education and the mobilization of political participation in developing democracies. Paper prepared for the conference, 'Political Participation: Building a Research Agenda' Princeton University, October 12–14, 2000.
Finkel, S. E. & Ernst, H.R. (2005). Civic education in post-apartheid South Africa: Alternative paths to the development of political knowledge and democratic values. *Political Psychology, 26*(3), 333–364.
Freire, P. (1992). *Pedagogy of the oppressed*. New York: Continuum.
Freire, P. (1994). *Pedagogy of hope*. New York: Continuum.
Freire, P. (1998). *Teachers as cultural workers: Letters to those who dare teach*. Trans. D. Macedo & A. Oliveira. Boulder, CO: Westview.
Freire, P. (2003). *El grito manso [The gentle shout]*. Buenos aires: Siglo XXI Editores.
Freire. P. (2005). *Pedagogy of indignation*. Boulder, CO: Paradigm Publishers.
Galston, W. A. (2001). Political knowledge, political engagement, and civic education. *Annual Review of Political Science, 4*, 217–34.
Giroux, H. (2004). *The terror of neoliberalism: Authoritarianism and the eclipse of democracy*. Boulder, CO: Paradigm Publishers.
Habermas, J. (1996). *Between facts and norms: Contributions to a discourse theory of democracy*. Cambridge MA: Massachusetts Institute of Technology Press.
Jennings, M. K., Stoker, L. & Bowers, J. (2001). *Politics across the generations: Family transmission reexamined*. Berkeley, CA: Institute of Governmental Studies.
Kagitcibasi, C., Goksen, F., & Gulgoz, S. (2005). Functional adult literacy and empowerment of women: Impact of a functional literacy program in Turkey. *Journal of Adolescent and Adult Literacy, 48*(6), 472–489.
Kahne, J. E., & Sporte, K. E. (2008). Developing citizens: The impact of civic learning opportunities on students' commitment to civic participation. *American Educational Research Journal, 45*(3), 738–766.
Lister, R. (2003). *Citizenship: Feminist perspective*. New York: NYU Press.
Maheu, R. (1968). *Meeting of experts on mass media in adult education and literacy*. A meeting of experts in mass communication and of specialists in adult education, literacy and research held at UNESCO House, Paris, 13–20 November 1967.
Mattes, R., & Mughogho, D. (2010). *The limited impacts of formal education on democratic citizenship in Africa*. Wynberg, South Africa: Centre for Higher Education Transformation.
Mattes, R. & Shenga, C. (2007). *Uncritical citizenship' in a 'low-information' society: Mozambicans in comparative perspective*. Working Paper No. 91. Accra: Afrobarometer. Retrieved April 19, 2013 from: http://www.afrobarometer.org/papers/AfropaperNo91.pdf
Medhanie, T. (2008). *Constitution-making, legitimacy and regional integration: An approach to Eritrea's predicament and relations with Ethiopia*. (Working Paper No. 9), Aalborg University, Denmark: DIIPER Research Series.

Mhlauli, M. V. (2012). The role of education on citizenship development in Africa. *British Journal of Arts and Social Sciences, 4*(1), 104–115.

Nasongo, J. W., & Musungu, L. L. (2009). The implications of Nyerere's theory of education to contemporary education in Kenya. *Educational Research and Reviews, 4*(4), 111–116.

Ndegwa, S. N. (2001). A decade of democracy in Africa. *Journal of the Association of African Studies, XXXVI*, pp. 1–16.

Norris, P. (Ed.) (1999). *Critical citizens: Global support for democratic government*. Oxford: Oxford University Press.

Nyerere, J. (1968). Education for self-reliance. In J. Nyerere *Freedom and socialism: A selection from writings and speeches, 1965–67* (pp. 267–290). London: Oxford University Press.

Nyerere, J. (1998). Governance in Africa. *Southern African political and economic monthly, 11*, 26–28.

Nzongola-Ntalaja, G., & Lee, C. (1998).*Civil society and democracy in Africa*. Asmara: Africa World Press.

O'Neill, B. (2006). *Human capital, civic engagement and political participation: Turning skills and knowledge into engagement and action*. Ottawa: Canadian Policy Research Networks Inc.

Osafo-Kwaako, P. (2011). Long-run effects of villagization in Tanzania. Paper prepared for the NEUDC Conference held at Yale University, November 12–13, 2011.

Osaghae, E. (1999). Democratization in Sub-Saharan Africa: faltering prospects, new hopes. *Journal of Contemporary African Studies, 17*, 5–28.

Putnam, R. D. (2000). *Bowling alone: The collapse and revival of American community*. New York: Simon & Schuster.

Quigley, K. F. F. (1997). Political scientists and assisting democracy: Too tenuous links. *PS: Political Science and Politics, 30*, 564–568.

Quigley, C., & Bahmueller, C. (1991). *Civitas: A framework for civic education*. Calabasas, CA: Center for Civic Education.

Rosenstone, S. J., & Hansen, J. M. (1993). *Mobilization, participation and democracy in America*. New York: MacMillan Publishing Company.

Skjelton, S. (2006). A *people's constitution: Public participation in the South African constitution-making processes*. Midrand, South Africa: Institute for Global Dialogue.

Skocpol, T., & Morris, P. (Eds.) (1999). *Civic engagement in American democracy*. Washington, DC: Brookings Institution Press.

Stromquist, N. P. (2006). The political benefits of adult literacy. Background paper prepared for the *EFA Global Monitoring Report 2006, Literacy for Life*. University of East Anglia, Norwich.

Thompson, A. (2007). *The media and the Rwanda genocide*. New York: Pluto Press.

Torres, M. N., & Reyes, L. V. (2010). Challenges in engaging communities in bottom-up literacies for democratic citizenship. *Education, Citizenship and Social Justice, 5*(3), 191–205.

USAID Democracy Strategic Framework (1998). *Democracy strategic framework*. Washington, D.C.: Global Bureau for Democracy and Governance.

Verba, S., Kay L. S. & Henry E. B. (1995). *Voice and equality: Civic voluntarism in American politics*. Cambridge, MA: Harvard University Press.

Woodruff, P. (2005). *First democracy: The challenge of an ancient idea*. New York: Oxford.

AFFILIATIONS

Edward Shizha
Professor of Contemporary Studies,
Wilfrid Laurier University, Brantford, Canada

Ali A. Abdi
Professor, Department of Education Policy Studies,
Faculty of Education, University of Alberta, Edmonton, Canada

DIDACUS JULES

27. ADULT EDUCATION POLICY IN MICRO-STATES: THE CASE OF THE CARIBBEAN[1]

INTRODUCTION

Among the most prevalent assumptions concerning microstates is the "small is beautiful" stereotype. It is widely assumed that given their small size and small populations, their governance and management are easy and require no special effort. A frequent commentary on small states is that "these countries are so small, they're not even the size of big cities – it ought to be easy to govern and provide services to the people!". To such common assertions I often reply that "the headache of the ant is as massive and bothersome as that of the elephant". Small is definitely not beautiful if you suffer diseconomies of scale in production, infrastructure, marketing, communication (the list is endless…) and have to earn your livelihood in an increasingly competitive international market structurally biased to favor "the big".

Adult education like every other aspect of educational provision reveals the peculiar constraints and limitations faced by small states. Some of these limitations are the products of "smallness" itself; others are a function of dependence, marginality, and the lack of resources; or both. There are still other difficulties which point, not to circumscriptions of size but to the lack of political will, the absence of inventive genius and the preoccupation with traditional approaches and structures with those charged with public policy formation in the micro-state.

A comprehensive study of adult education policy in micro-states would indeed be a welcome undertaking but would require painstaking exegesis of historical trends in the variegated world of small states. Because such an exercise requires extended research, I have chosen to focus on the Caribbean as one of the regions containing the largest number of micro-states and one which – as far as adult education trends are concerned – is marked with sufficient diversity to allow for some theoretical extrapolation.

SMALL STATES IN PERSPECTIVE

The question of small size or "smallness" was first brought to contemporary international focus in the 1920's when the several European microstates attempted to join the League of Nations (Dommen 1985, p. 2). The question again arose in 1967 when the UN Secretary General urged the General Assembly to establish criteria which would take into the consideration the needs of these states. Initially the focus was on *European* small states but then the dramatic increase in independent small states resulting from the process of decolonization has brought attention to the dilemma of underdeveloped countries. There has been intermittent international attention paid to the issue, although economists like William Demas (1965) had been attempting to draw attention to the developmental implications of the issue within their regions.

Since the declaration of the United Nations Decade for International Development, these attempts have gained greater credibility and the notion of small states has gained some international respectability. The idea of "smallness" has stirred some controversy (see Hindmarsh, 1996), giving rise to other distinctions all of which make some claim to theoretical specificity. Those in currency include:- "small landlocked states", "small island states", "micro-states"; although it is generally agreed that there is some arbitrariness in applying empirical measurement to the concept. Among international fora, the issue has gained the greatest prominence in the Commonwealth, within whose ranks are to be found the largest grouping of microstates – the result of the break-up of the British Empire. The impetus for policy action around the peculiar problems of small island states in the Commonwealth can be traced to the 1979 Commonwealth Heads of Government Conference which led to the hosting of a Special Conference in 1981 on the problems and policies of small economies chaired by the UNCTAD Secretary-General Alister McIntyre.

Ultimately the essential issue revolving around these classifications has been the perceived and experienced disadvantages of underdeveloped countries in their international economic and political dealings. The problem of small size is, in the final analysis, a problem of power relations. Within the Commonwealth Caribbean Grenada played a key role in international fora such as the Commonwealth, the Non-Aligned Movement, the OAS in advocacy for consideration of the special problems faced by small island states in the context of the international alignment of power. Maurice Bishop, leader of the Grenada revolution, addressing an *OAS Conference on the Development Problems of Small Island States* in 1981 asserted that:

> We contend that the real problem is not the problem of smallness per se... the real problem that countries like ours face is that, on a day to day basis, we come up against an international system that is organized and geared towards ensuring the continuing exploitation, domination and rape of our economies, our countries and our peoples

This contention has subsequently been articulated using a different language by other writers. Brock (1988) for example, frames the issue in terms of peripherality arguing that this was more than a simple matter of geographic marginality and was in fact rooted in the structural dependency of the periphery on the colonizing center. While it can be argued that the essence of the problem lies in structural inequality on a global scale, there are several key indices which are now commonly accepted – either singly or in combination – as denoting smallness. These include: small populations, limited land mass, low per capita income.

- Small populations – the Commonwealth Secretariat sets a limit of 2 million people as representing the cut-off point for smallness. Brock (1988, p. 167) notes that using this demographic variable "there are 29 full member states of the Commonwealth below this threshold, ranging from Lesotho with 1.35 million to Nauru with about 8,000" and that "if the remaining dependent units of the United Kingdom are added, then a further 16 units come in, ranging from Bermuda with 60,000 to Pitcairn at a miniscule 60". Within the United Nations in 1980, there were 70 countries with populations of less than 2 million people.
- Limited land mass – a more common index is the size of the national territory especially in cases where this territory is landlocked or insular. It was estimated that in 1980, there were 80 states of less than 100,000 square kilometers in size.
- Low per capita income – as indicative of economic constraints but not by itself constituting a classification of size. It is generally accepted that a GNP of less than US$500 per capita constitutes the cut-off point of this category.

That these indices are sometimes problematic is illustrated in several cases in which a particular territory conforms to one or more but not all of the variables. Would Hong Kong, for example, be classified as a micro-state because it has a land size of only 1,000 square kilometers even though its population exceeds 5 million and its GNP places it well above the world median?

The classification of a small state or a micro-state depends to a large extent on the purposes for which this typologizing is being done signifying that the designation of smallness is relative. Hong Kong is not therefore generally classified as a micro-state because of its (relatively) large population and GNP; however when considered in relation to the Chinese mainland, its "smallness" is self-evident. Brock (1988) reports that based on UN data for 1980, there were 37 states which shared all of three characteristics mentioned above. The largest clusters of small states are to be found in the Caribbean, the Indian Ocean and the South Pacific (although the recent events in the Soviet Union and Eastern Europe have unleashed centrifugal forces which are leading to the proliferation of micro-states in that region).

It is also recognized that beyond these broad indicators, delineating which small states constitute microstates involves some arbitrariness since there is no consistent adherence to all of the established criteria. Some theorists (notably Selwyn 1980) have further questioned whether "small island" can be considered a useful category in analytical, predictive or policy terms in relation to small states. For these theorists their "islandness" is not the central issue – what is important are the problems associated with smallness: the peripherality, remoteness, dependence, the diseconomies of small scale both in production and in the provision of social infrastructure.

In this paper, we focus on micro-states and more specifically small island states since the Caribbean is essentially a collection of small island states. It is important to note that small island states have been distinguished from continental microstates. As Dolman (1985) points out continental microstates even where identical in size and population to island states can take advantage of their proximity to larger states in ways which islands cannot (linking in, for example, to their neighbor's infrastructure and markets). There is also the fact observed by Caldwell, Harrison and Quiggin (1980) that islands or coastal enclaves constitute 79% of all microstates in the contemporary world (which makes the Caribbean a useful laboratory for exploring the formation of adult education policy).

A major question facing small island states is the problem of viability. Doumenge (1985, p. 74) described it as being both a static and a dynamic condition and, concurring with Dolman, emphasizes the high degree of vulnerability of these small states:

> Viability is inherently a static condition. It is the combination of the conditions necessary and sufficient for existence and durability. A crisis resulting from a natural catastrophe, demographic collapse, economic setback or geopolitical action may eliminate, temporarily or permanently, any island's viability in a given situation... We have also to look at the dynamics of viability, i.e the conditions required for development in terms of both the maximum utilization of natural resources and the raising of the social and economic living standards of the population. Island territories are particularly sensitive to factors which can produce development or regression, since the small area and population, in conjunction with the effects of isolation, make islands much more malleable and vulnerable than continental territories. Consequently, the viability of small island states is in general subject also to external political forces on which they can exert little influence.

Hein (1985) points to the constraints identified by UNCTAD as representing some of the more detailed problems faced by small (island) states:

> smallness, remoteness, constraints in transport and communications, great distances from market centers, highly limited internal markets, lack of marketing expertise, low resources endowment, lack of natural resources, heavy dependence on a few commodities for their foreign exchange earnings, shortage of administrative personnel and heavy financial burdens.

To this litany of constraints, Dolman (1985, p. 40) adds the "very narrow range of local skills, with a critical shortage of trained manpower, problems of matching skills to available jobs and a heavy reliance on expatriates" – human resource constraints having, as we shall see later, serious implications for adult education policy.

The issue of educational provision has only recently been incorporated into the classification of size. Smawfield (1986) has used university provision as an index of smallness. Bacchus and Brock (1987) have taken educational provision more generally as providing a hierarchy of size profiles (Brock & Smawfield 1988). However none of these classifications have included adult education which has always been a low status dimension of educational provision.

POLICY FORMATION IN SMALL STATES

Torres (1983) has argued that the low priority accorded to adult education in Latin America is largely due to the low socio-economic status of its constituency and their disempowerment in situations of dependent capitalist development (see Schugurensky in this volume). While the same applies to the small island states of the Caribbean, it could be argued that since small or micro-states suffer even greater peripheralization in the world capitalist system than larger nations (Jules, 2008; Bacchus, 2008), the low status of adult education is even more acute in these contexts. Larger dependent nations potentially constitute larger markets; have a larger reserve of labor and their successful incorporation into the global economy necessitates attention to human resource development at least to a level commensurate with the needs of the economy.

In small island economies, productive industry is small scale and their agrarian base does not require sophisticated skilled labor. The openings and opportunities for white-color jobs or occupations requiring more than basic levels of education are limited by the economy which is, in most cases, based on primary agricultural production or basic service industries such as tourism. The micro-state itself is constrained by the limited resources at its disposal and the opportunities for the developing and realizing the potential of its human resource are inhibited by the logic of dependent development. These represent very real constraints on the capacity of the micro-state to formulate and implement policies which are understood to be necessary.

Besides the fact that the resource base for social development is limited and faced with competing demands, there are several other factors affecting policy formation in micro-states. Infrastructural development in these states is relatively more expensive per capita because of the small populations being served. External aid thus plays a significant and proportionately larger role in social and economic development. The character and conditionality of external aid often does not allow for the local determination of needs and the independent conceptualization of appropriate solutions. In education in particular, conformity to the conceptual/ideological dictates of the intellectual-financial complex is a real – even if unstated – pre-condition to donor funding. The prioritization of universal primary education and formal education by agencies such as the World Bank is reflected in the educational policies articulated by the governments of small states.

One result of this dependence has been the neglect of adult education. Lip service by the governments of small island states to the ideals of "continuing education", "human resource development" notwithstanding, adult education provision by the state has been narrow in scope and conception. The notion of the people being the most vital resource of these states has become a well-worn cliche in their development lexicon but there is no evidence that the majority of these states have undertaken the creative imperative of developing a policy and structure which facilitates a more self-reliant direction. In an *Examination of the Particular Needs and Problems of Island Developing Countries* (1985) UNCTAD concluded that:

> island developing countries, like others, would be wise to develop on the basis of the assets they have. One conclusion ... is that human resources are among their most important assets. Further development is likely to be in relatively sophisticated areas, calling for education and training at a high level. Exports, whether of goods or services, are already developing, and will continue to develop, in fields where competition or the sensitivity of developed countries is particularly great. Clever marketing – in a political as well as a commercial sense – will be indispensable, in spite of its high cost for small-scale producers.

The significance of the phrase referring to the *"high cost for small-scale producers"* is important since in the small island states of the Caribbean small-scale producers constitute a substantial segment of producers. In some mono-crop economies such as that of St. Lucia, Dominica, St. Vincent, small-scale producers make up the majority of producers. The unspoken challenge lies therefore not simply in "high level" education and training but in re-training and providing basic education to that numerically and socially significant strata which is likely to pay the full human cost of increased competition.

While one recognizes the objective limitations posed by the nature and scale of the national economies and the restrictions of the resource base, it is essential not to assume an absolute correspondence between the economy and adult education. Limitations of economy only establish general parameters but do not exclude possibilities of a more imaginative re-configuration of existing policies and developmental priorities. An equally important influence is exerted by the developmental vision and the political will of the governments in question.

The historical record points indisputably to the fact that successive Caribbean governments, pursing developmental models based primarily on investment-by-invitation approaches have simply based their educational priorities on what they believe to be the modernizing capacity of universal primary education and the expansion of secondary education in elitist forms. The function of education was therefore seen as meeting the human capital requirements of the modernization thrust. The paradox of these policies is that while universal primary education (UPE) became a much cherished goal and served as a sorting and selection mechanism for access to higher education, adult and continuing education remained a low priority. The "dark side" of UPE were the large numbers of 'professionally unformed' young people – without marketable skills left without any significant opportunities for systematic training or continuation of their education. For hundreds of these young people, the options available were limited to emigration to metropolitan centers seeking employment or further education or the prospect of unchallenging labor or unemployment at home.

In the pursuit of its modernizing mission, the Caribbean small state invested heavily in the construction of the appropriate infrastructure necessary to realize that mission – building roads, expanding communications facilities etc. Much of its effort in agriculture was aimed at improving the production and marketing infrastructure. in spite of these efforts it neglected *the human factor*. Without exception, the highest incidences of illiteracy in these small states were among the most economically productive social strata. The persistence of backward modes of production in that sphere of the economy did not provide the inducement for anything beyond rudimentary worker training. Rather than confronting this reality, educational policy has been based on the fallacious assumption that illiteracy will incrementally disappear as universal primary education is achieved and demographic changes occur.

The failure to develop a strategic adult education policy which focussed on the "human capital" dimension of the modernizing mission is resulting – not only in the failure of that modernization effort in critical core areas of the economy (agriculture and light industry) but a crisis of legitimacy of the small island state itself. Increasing global competitiveness, the reality of a united Europe (see Negt in this volume) with a corresponding loss of preferential access to traditional markets, have exacerbated the uncertainty and the fear that comes with the realization that our principal export industries are unable to compete. The viability and legitimacy of the small island state is thus facing its most severe test.

ADULT EDUCATION POLICY IN MICRO-STATES: CHALLENGES AND OPPORTUNITIES IN THE CARIBBEAN

One consistent response to the crisis of legitimacy of the micro-states at different historical periods has been the migration valve. Although the flow of people from micro-state to metropolis is always occurring, it becomes particularly acute during periods of severe economic stress. The search for economic opportunity and social mobility by these migrants leads to the continuous depletion of an already limited human resource base. One of the leading social demographers in the Caribbean (Massiah, 1976, p. 41) concluded that "emigration has completely dominated the pattern of growth in every Commonwealth Caribbean territory over the past 25 years". The brain drain has necessitated the "importation of certain types of labor to build up the corresponding deficits in their own labor supply due to the apparent inability of the system to generate the quantity and quality of manpower needed for the types of economic strategies being developed".

The implications of migration and the brain drain while noted by governments have never been confronted at the level of policy. Caribbean governments have in practise ignored this issue because the politicians see the migration process as helping to ease the social pressures and demands on the state (see also Baldacchino & Mayo, 1996 with regard to migration and adult education in small states and islands). Migration has become, by default, a compensatory mechanism for the inability of the micro-state to make adequate provision for social needs. However later thinking on the issue by Development economists at the University of the West Indies (Norman Girvan et al.) and the Caribbean Association of Economists has been pointing to the substantial presence of relatively successful Caribbean citizens in major metropolitan centers and has commented on the potential that this represents for alternative development strategies. Calls have been issued for the reconceptualization of the gross national product to incorporate the contribution of this substantial human resource base. The high volume of remittances and the important role of these financial flows to micro-states such as Montserrat and even large small states like Jamaica have already been documented. The challenge – in light of the shrinking of small island economies and the external donor funding available to them – is how to build more structured economic relations between expatriate Caribbean people and their home territories; how to facilitate the repatriation of skills and knowledge to serve the needs of human resource development at home. This challenge presupposes changes in investment policy and requires clear formulation of adult education policies and strategic goals since, as has been argued before, human resource development is among the most critical developmental imperatives of the micro-state.

Understanding what these challenges involve in concrete terms requires an explanation of the current characteristics and configuration of adult education in micro-states. The principal characteristics include fragmentation of initiatives (involving separation of the 'more formal' types of adult education from localized efforts); largely remedial in form; the absence of articulation with the formal education system; and a high level of dependence on private or external funding.

Adult education policy in the micro-states of the Caribbean has only recently been recognized by governments as a legitimate dimension of educational policy. Whatever policies existed up to the late 1950s were an inheritance of British Colonialism in which adult education formed part of the welfare function of the state. Its purpose was essentially ameliorative and its provision was focussed on "lower class needs". In the post-colonial period, the micro-state was faced with rising expectations for increased educational provision including the desire among the newly enfranchised adult population for continuing education opportunities which went beyond welfare. The state's response to these demands was to open these opportunities along selective and elitist lines while either maintaining the welfare forms of adult education or encouraging the assumption of that responsibility by private agencies or civic organizations. The current outcome of this evolution of adult education policy is that adult education policy is now concentrated on the more "formal" types of provision – university extra-mural services, remedial education for secondary-level certification, some technical and vocational training geared to the current but not strategic needs of the lower end of "the labor market".

In this context adult education services in the Caribbean micro-states are far removed from any mass character, even along the lines that the elementary education system is structured. Adult education provision is largely remedial in character and is locked into short term human resource projections with little evidence of a strategic conceptualization of adult education in relation to the requirements for strategic survival and viability of these states. The majority of adult education programs are almost exclusively non-formal and having little – if any – articulation with the formal system or with limited opportunities for career enhancement.

Additionally, these initiatives are fragmented and conducted in isolation from other educational or social development efforts. Because there is no global articulation of adult education policy, these initiatives are also characterized by a great deal of duplication. Many agencies are engaged in different programs with different objectives and priorities but often directed at the same clientele. The Second Caribbean Conference on Adult Education held in Guyana in April 1970, for example, confirmed these problems of adult education in small states. The conference identified the following as being the dominant attributes of adult education in the region at the time:

- the low priority given to adult education by regional governments;
- the predominant emphasis on purely remedial academic work and personal development (which reinforced public perceptions of the second class nature of adult education);
- the absence of structured curricula of any kind; the prevalence of ad hoc approaches and methodologies; the lack of appropriate material and the absence of any articulation with formal education;
- the predominance of private provision by voluntary agencies, community organizations and civic organizations.

A meeting of experts from adult education institutions in the Caribbean held in St. Lucia ten years later (1980) under the auspices of UNESCO and the Government of St. Lucia was still lamenting that "adult education has suffered throughout its history from verbal praises never matched by practical assistance... it has survived and sometimes flourished in spite of receiving meagre official support". Another ten years later (1991) the same pronouncements were still being issued – two of the four major strategies highlighted by the Port of Spain Consensus of the Caribbean Regional Economic Conference as being essential to Caribbean survival in the Twenty-first Century implied the need for a coherent adult education policy: "assignment of the highest priority to human resource development ... and the promotion and enhancement of the democratic traditions and processes especially through the consultative involvement of all social sectors in policy formulation and implementation".

The Second Caribbean Conference on adult education (1970) identified five major types of adult education which ought to have been provided: remedial; vocational, technical and professional; health, welfare and family living; civic, political and community; and self-fulfillment. It also emphasized that, for the provision of an integrated adult education program, it was necessary to upgrade literacy and basic education. There was a clear recognition that "insofar as the updating of people, the retraining of people for employment, the guiding to adjust to new skills because of the new development of technology which is occurring" very little was being done and that this required systematic private and public collaboration (Davis, 1970).

The Conference issued nine critical resolutions all of which remain relevant today. It called for:

- a new integrated strategy related to the socio-economic and cultural needs of the region
- establishment of representative national adult education organizations
- integration of adult education with the formal education system; the harmonization of policies and the demonstration of greater commitment by governments through budgetary provision
- the provision of corresponding private sector and civic material and financial support
- the provision of training for adult educators and the involvement of regional universities in research on adult education issues.

Where traditional sub-systems of adult education are more developed there is a high level of dependence on the global intellectual-financial complex, resulting in conformity to international trends and externally set priorities (in educational financing, curriculum, certification, and policy formation). Examination of any documentation produced by Ministries of Education in Caribbean micro-states shows the extent to which the policy discourse on adult education has been influenced by UNESCO, USAID, the World Bank and other constituents of the intellectual-financial complex. For many micro-states, the adoption of the prescriptions and the rhetoric of the intellectual-financial complex is seen as a strategy for easy access to external funding which also serves the legitimation needs of the state to the extent that programs are funded and appear to have the blessing of international institutions.

Except for cases in which populist regimes have taken a more systematic approach to adult education policy (such as Jamaica under Manley, Grenada under Bishop and the Seychelles), adult education has generally assumed importance to the extent that donor financing has made this possible.

In addition to the characteristics of adult education itself noted above, there are other factors inherent in the composition of the micro-state which are of significance to adult education. A comprehensive survey of the demography of microstates conducted by Caldwell, Harrison and Quiggin (1980, p. 954) has revealed some of these. The survey found that "91% of microstates have a European language as the official language and 87% have a majority of the population able to speak either a European or a Creole language" (my emphases).

Adult education policy in Caribbean micro-states reflects the official preference for European languages by utilizing these as the languages of instruction and until the late 1980's little pedagogical attention was given to the existence of the Creoles which are widely spoken by the working people of the region. This privileging of European languages derives from the persistence of the colonial cultural inheritance and attests to the central role ascribed to communication with metropolitan centers. It also points to the social and linguistic marginalization of large sectors of the population. Numerous studies of the language situation in bi-lingual small states such as St. Lucia have detailed the extent to which the problems of quality and attainment in education have been closely associated with the absence of a language policy and the official neglect of the Creole reality (Carrington, 1984; Alleyne 1961; Issac 1986; Simmons-McDonald 1988). The essential conclusion is that adult education policy in micro-states must include in its frame of reference a language policy which gives due recognition to the language spoken by the majority of the population and which utilizes this language for instructional purposes. No matter how well structured adult education programs might be, unless they deal with the question of indigenous or Creole languages their capacity for human resource development will be severely constrained; this situation also recalls Freire's recommendations regarding the literacy experience in the African small state of Guinea Bissau (Freire & Macedo, 1987).

We have spent some time discussing and elaborating the problems faced by small island and microstates because it is important to understand what the implications of these constraints are for adult education in the context of the search for sustainable development. The objective condition of those states (which is not as much their smallness but their structural dependence) necessitates the most creative exercise of developmental vision. Adult education assumes critical importance as a means, not only of providing new skills and potentials, but more importantly as a mechanism for stimulating creative entrepreneurship (see Baldacchino, 2008), building collective purpose and identity, and envisioning new possibilities for economic survival in a world of hegemonic market forces (Bacchus, 2008).

Adult education policy in micro-states, although neglected,[2] is a field of public policy with immense strategic challenge and creative opportunity. The small population of the micro-state within what is usually a small land area makes national mobilization and internal organization/programming relatively easier to conduct. The opportunities for articulation of adult education with the formal system of education are more attainable. The use of educational infrastructure such as primary schools, technical institutes, libraries for adult education programming can turn a disadvantage of small states – namely the relatively higher per capita cost of social infrastructure – to advantage by avoiding potentially wasteful duplication of facilities and allowing for more cost effective utilization of available resources. In many micro-states, schools often constitute the major social infrastructure in the community and are often used for social events yet few micro-states if any, have deliberately and consciously conceived of the school as a social infrastructure. The implications of these uses of schools and educational facilities for architectural design and the possibilities for securing external assistance funding for the construction of these multi-purpose structures within a more integrated framework combining community development with education of youth and adults are yet to be exploited by small island states. This idea was taken up by the present writer in Trinidad and Tobago and has also inspired more recent literature in the area (Mayo, *et al*, 2008), also leading in Malta to the enshrining of the idea of Schools as community learning centres in the country's 1999 National Curriculum document, without alas being brought into effect, and was retained in Malta's most recent National Curriculum Framework.

The difficulties encountered by small island and micro-states in securing and maintaining the levels of foreign assistance required have, to some extent, resulted from the problems of providing acceptable justification for patterns of educational investment predicated on larger population sizes. Aid donors have therefore tended, in their dealings with micro-states, to express preferences for multi-lateral projects involving groupings of micro-states and/or the provision of regional facilities. In the experience of the micro-states of the Caribbean for example, regional curriculum development or infrastructural development projects such as the UNESCO Multi-island Sectoral Development Project or regional infrastructures such as the University of the West Indies have proven more attractive to donors than individual state initiatives such as the proliferation of State Colleges.

Among the other challenges for adult education policy in micro-states are the opportunities afforded by virtue of size for close interaction between policy makers and implementors – or more fundamentally the possibilities of de-bunking this traditional distinction. The opportunities for democratization of policy formation and implementation as new processes and mechanisms for responding to community need are significantly more rewarding in small states. Brock & Smawfield (1988, p. 232) identify this ease of communication between the different levels and among policy makers and implementors as being a distinct opportunity afforded by "smallness":

> ...in the small country context it is easier for those responsible for policy-making to visualize and subsequently observe the consequences of their decisions, allowing thereby for a greater degree of realism than is often evident in larger systems. Indeed, the effects of change, as a consequence of scale, are likely to be seen more readily and there are likely to be many situations where it is possible to obtain speedier and more effective feedback than might be the case in larger countries.

In adult education policy formation in particular the value of these possibilities go beyond the claims of efficiency. They point to the link between adult education and the deepening of democratic practise within the society as a whole. In addition to developing skills and further education, adult education programs can become mechanisms for participation in developmental processes. The experience of community-based literacy programs throughout the Caribbean (Jules 1990) is replete with examples of participatory approaches to curriculum design, program structuring, and the application of the knowledge and skills gained to community development/improvement. But these experiences have largely been within the voluntary sector and at a community level – there are few instances of their systematization at the level of the state except in the case of Jamaica in the 1970's and Grenada during the 1980's.

The developmental challenge faced by adult education in micro-states also includes the imperative of remedying the educational deficits resulting from elitist educational systems and reversing the limitations imposed by high levels of illiteracy in order to release the human potential of the majority of what is already a small population. With limited populations these states can even less afford the social and economic cost of educational wastage caused by illiteracy or rigid sorting and selection mechanisms in an elitist system. The human cost of high levels of illiteracy is exponentially greater in small states with their limited human resource base than it is in countries with large populations.

In addition to releasing the human potential of the small states, the provision of adult education on a mass scale might well lead to a more emancipatory political practise. This hypothesis must be placed in the historical context of the political culture of the Anglophone Caribbean in which education has been portrayed as a pre-requisite for political enfranchisement. The rights to vote, and to representation were first predicated on property, and then on "educational ability" which remains an unspoken criteria of effective participation. In some cases there are even overt stipulations which associate the right to hold office with educational competence. The articles of incorporation of the St. Lucia Banana Growers Association for example, stipulates that no farmer shall hold office at an executive level if "he (*sic*) is unable to speak and unless incapacitated by blindness or other physical cause, to read the English Language with a degree of proficiency sufficient to enable him to play an active part in the proceedings..." While the need for competence in English is recognized to be essential for the exercise of effective leadership in the organization, it is also clear that as a representative and voluntary federation of agricultural producers, the association has a responsibility of providing opportunities for democratic leadership by *all* members. In small states, the possession or lack of education has thus been effectively used by local elites to restrict access to power and to legitimate their dominance.

One can therefore understand the low priority assigned to adult education and the limited and elitist forms which it has assumed within these micro-states. As Torres observed in the case of Latin America, the low socio-economic status of the adult education constituency and their disempowerment in situations of dependent capitalist development largely accounts for the neglect of that dimension of education. The lack of adequate provision especially on a mass scale in turn serves as a justification for the further disenfranchisement of these social strata. Among small populations, multi-party politics under these conditions has led to deeply ingrained sectarianism and an intensely divisive partisanship. The key to a new politics which utilizes small population size to participatory advantage lies in the broader conception of adult education implied in the critique of a 1980 meeting of experts from adult education institutions in the Caribbean[3]:

> National development also demands that the whole question of functional literacy be examined. There is lack of literacy about economic processes, about the financial process, the lack of literacy about the political process, the lack of literacy about the arts, culture and the changes being brought by science and technology.

Given the economic constraints emanating from small size and small population, the viability of micro-states depends on the creation of a highly educated workforce and the provision of sophisticated skills in areas in which the small state may enjoy a comparative advantage (These are very few but may include services like offshore banking and high tech areas such as computer services/industries). Economic restructuring involves tremendous risks but none of these risks are as ultimately destructive to their viability than the likely outcomes of the present levels of dependence and vulnerability. For micro-states, this project is not simply an issue of market identification and penetration but involves an essential political agenda at both national and international level. Whatever the configuration of the modernizing project undertaken by micro-states, the national political agenda must of necessity include re-distributive equality and economic justice, if it is going to turn smallness to advantage. At the international level, the agenda involves the identification of alliances which will form the natural basis for new forms of production and new "markets" or new patterns of trade and exchange. In other words, micro-states will have to marshall their expatriate populations as a logical resource for accessing new capital, producing new exports, developing new markets.

Adult education assumes tremendous importance in this process as a medium of systematic preparation of people at all levels for new roles, new functions, and the new challenges.

The importance of regionalism as a means of dealing with the constraints of size has often been argued yet the experiences of the micro-states of the Caribbean and the Pacific point to the failure to resolve at a political level, the historical legacy of division. The gradual fragmentation of the University of the West Indies through a purported "re-structuring" exercise which has resulted in greater control of individual campuses by the governments of the territories in which they are located and incurring greater costs to non-campus territories through higher fees and the move by several to establish tertiary institutions of their own is an example of that failure. One unintended benefit of this process has been the establishment by the non-campus territories of community colleges which, to varying degrees, have marshalled the resources of formerly separate tertiary institutions into a single national effort. These institutions are potentially more cost-effective and constitute an important infrastructure for the provision of adult continuing education throughout the region.

Yet the availability of infrastructure is not the sole requirement. Much depends on the ability of the islands to devise strategies for reversing the brain drain, for bringing home locals trained in areas in which the country is economically unable to offer training and to utilize this infrastructure to offer opportunities for systematic training at all levels.

CONCLUSION

In conclusion, what can we learn from micro-states' adult education policies? We have seen in the case of the Caribbean that while there are many constraints of size which affect the chances for less dependent development, there are also constraints which are the result of uncritical acceptance of traditional approaches and the lack of inventive genius among policy makers. A major challenge we conclude is that of turning size to advantage. This requires tremendous innovation but this is not beyond the capacity of micro-states which have significant unutilized human resource reserves especially within the metropolitan countries.

Microstates – by virtue of size – have special opportunities to develop tightly integrated programs of adult education, to design innovative pedagogy using participatory methodologies and are well placed to maximize the creative use of educational infrastructure and resources as part of broader social development initiatives.

Although these opportunities exist, they do not by any means substantiate the "small is beautiful" thesis. The "smallness" of micro-states poses difficulties because these states are structurally dependent and are forced to find mechanisms of survival in a highly competitive and unequal international environment. The tensions resulting from this disadvantaged position exacerbates the crisis of legitimacy of the micro-state but these are dissipated by the significant levels of migration occurring. The emergence of hegemonic trading blocs and the worsening international economic situation demand that new and more imaginative strategies of survival be followed and an essential element of this imperative is the formulation of comprehensive adult education policies. Adult education in the micro-state it is contended should be closely related to the developmental needs of the state and civic society and should promote the expansion of democratic space, social justice and local entrepreneurial creativity.

NOTES

[1] This chapter was previously published as Didacus Jules (1994). Adult education policy in micro-states. The case of the Caribbean. *Policy Studies Review 13* (3 and 4) 415–432.
[2] This has been highlighted in the literature on small states and islands (Rogers, 1996), although a conference on the issue was held in Malta in 1995 and resulted in a special issue of the ICAE's journal, *Convergence 29* (2); a recent special issue of *Comparative Education* on Education in Small States also included a paper on adult education (Mayo *et al*, 2008).
[3] "New Emphases for Adult Education in the Caribbean in the Eighties – Final Report on A Meeting of Experts From Adult Education Institutions in the Caribbean". Castries: UNESCO/Government of St. Lucia 1980. pp. 15.

REFERENCES

Bacchus, M. K. (2008). The education challenges facing small nation states in the increasingly competitive global economy of the twenty-first century. *Comparative Education, 44* (2), 127–145.
Baldacchino, G., & Mayo, P. (1996). Adult continuing education in small and island states. The case of Malta. *Convergence 29* (2), 22–35.
Baldacchino, G. (2008). Entrepreneurship in smaller jurisdictions: Appraising a glocal elite, *Comparative Education, 44*(2), 187–201.
Brock, C. (1988). Beyond the fringe? small states and the provision of education. *Comparative Education, 24*(2), 167–179.
Caldwell, J., Harrison, G., & Quiggin, P. (1980). The demography of micro-states. *World Development, 8*(12), 953–967
CARICOM Secretariat (1991). The port of Spain consensus of the Caribbean regional economic conference.
Davis, H. (1970). A program for adult education in the Caribbean. In *Report on the 2nd Caribbean Conference on Adult Education* (pp. 72–81). Georgetown, Guyana: mimeo.
Dolman, A. (1985). Paradise lost? the past performance and future prospects of small island developing countries. In Dommen & P. Hein (Eds.), *States, microstates and islands* (pp. 40–69). London: Croom Helm.
Doumenge, F. (1985). The viability of small intertropical islands. In E. Dommen & P. Hein (Eds.), *States, microstates and islands* (pp. 70–118). London: Croom Helm.
Freire, P., & Macedo, D (1987), *Literacy. Reading the Word and the World.* Masacusetts: Bergin & Garvey.
Hein, P. (1985). The study of microstates. In E. Dommen & P. Hein (Eds.), *States, microstates and islands* (pp. 16–29). London: Croom Hel.
Hindmarsh, J. H. (1996). How do we define small states and islands? A critical analysis of alternative conceptualisations. *Convergence 29* (2) 36–45.
Jules, D., & Rojas, D. (Eds.) (1982). *Maurice bishop – selected speeches 1979–1981.* Havana: Casa de Las Americas.
Jules, D. (1990). *A review of community-based literacy initiatives in the Caribbean in the 1980's.* St. Lucia: National Research & Development Foundation.
Jules, D. (2008). Rethinking education for the Caribbean: A radical approach, *Comparative Education, 44*(2), 203–214.
Massiah, J. (1976). Reflections on the current demographic position of small states in the Caribbean. In V. Lewis (Ed.). *Size, self-determination and international relations: The Caribbean* (pp. 16–44). Jamaica: Institute of Social & Economic Research.
Mayo, P, Pace, P. J., & Zammit, E. (2008). Adult education in small states: The case of Malta, *Comparative Education, 44*(2), 229–246.
Rogers, A. 1996. Adult continuing education in small states and islands: Concept paper. *Convergence, 29* (2), 8–21.
Selwyn, P. (1980). Smallness and islandness. *World Development, 8*(12), 945–951.
Torres, C. A. (1983). Adult education policy, capitalist development and class alliance: Latin America and Mexico. *International Journal of Political Education 6*(2), 157–173.
UNCTAD (1985). Examination of the particular needs and problems of island developing countries. In E Dommen & P. Hein, (Eds.), *States, microstates and islands* (pp. 119–151). London: Croom Helm.

AFFILIATION

Didacus Jules
The Registrar and Chief Executive Officer of the Caribbean Examinations Council in Barbados

CARMEL BORG & PETER MAYO

28. GLOBALISATION, SOUTHERN EUROPE AND EUROPEAN ADULT EDUCATION POLICY[1]

INTRODUCTION

This chapter explores some of the impacts which the process of the intensification of globalisation is having on the adult education field in Europe. While the authors look at the European field in its larger context, they provide special emphasis on southern Europe for three reasons: (1) this is the region in which they live and operate as academics and practitioners in adult education; (2) it does not feature regularly in the English-language adult education literature; and (3) it is facing, because of its proximity to the shores of North Africa, a specific situation – massive immigration from North and sub-Saharan Africa – which, they argue, is relevant to and needs to be addressed in the adult education field.

TWO TYPES OF GLOBALISATION

Globalisation is conceived of as an all-embracing concept, incorporating both its economic and its cultural dimensions, which are often inextricably intertwined, very much linked to the fact that, in the words of Manuel Castells (1999), 'we live in a global economy' (p. 54). This economy is one 'in which all processes work as a unit on real time throughout the planet; that is, an economy in which capital flows, labor markets, markets, the production process, management, information and technology operate simultaneously at the world level' (Castells, 1999, p. 54). In an interview with Roger Dale & Susan Robertson (2004), Boaventura de Sousa Santos, echoing others (e.g. Marshall, 1997), identified two types of globalisation – hegemonic and 'counterhegemonic globalisation.' The former is the type of globalisation predicated on the ideology of neoliberalism which, in his words, 'is the political form of globalization resulting from US type of capitalism, a type that bases competitiveness on technological innovation coupled with low levels of social protection' (Dale & Robertson, 2004, p. 151). He goes on to state: 'The aggressive imposition of this model by the international financial institutions worldwide not only forces abrupt changes in the role of the state and in the rules of the game between the exploiter and the exploited ... but also changes the rules of the game among the other kinds of developed capitalism' (de Sousa Santos, in Dale & Robertson, 2004, p. 151).

Counter-hegemonic 'globalization' (de Sousa Santos, in Dale & Robertson, 2004, p. 150) or 'globalization from below' (Marshall, 1997) 'consists of resistance against hegemonic globalization organized (through local/global linkages) by movements, initiatives and NGO's, on behalf of classes, social groups and regions victimized by the unequal exchanges produced on a global scale by neoliberal globalization' (de Sousa Santos, in Dale & Robertson, 2004, p. 150). We state at the outset that we prefer 'globalisation from below' to 'counter-hegemonic globalisation' to avoid the kind of binary opposites which, we feel, any discussion of hegemony should avoid (Gramsci himself never used the term 'counter-hegemony'). This second type of globalisation also comprises different movements, previously identified with a rather fragmentary identity and specific issue politics, coming together 'on a scale previously unknown' (Rikowski, 2001, p. 16) to target global capitalism and the meetings of the institutions that support it, such as the International Monetary Fund (IMF), the World Bank and the World Trade Organization (WTO). It also includes, as Carnoy (1999, p. 78) and others have indicated, movements who resist globalisation by asserting fundamentalist interpretations of their religious texts and other movements that seek to assert essentialist notions of identity in the face of threats, posed by globalisation, to these firmly entrenched notions. These notions include a 'fixed' sense of place, belonging and community. A number of exponents of what has come to be regarded as 'Militant Islam', as well as many fundamentalist Christians, would belong to the former category.

Anti-immigrant movements would belong to the second category. Persons can belong to one or more of these categories. All this has a bearing on adult education viewed in its broader context, as we will show in this chapter. Adult education is an amorphous field (Torres, 1987) and takes many forms, extending beyond institutionalised forms of learning and incorporating non-formal and informal learning. It also incorporates the learning activities taking place within social movements themselves, not all of which would prima facie be recognised as a learning activity. Administrative, mobilising and networking (including digital electronic networking) skills are, however, learnt in the process of carrying out such work. Work within movements also entails strategies to create wider public awareness of the matters at issue, and encourage commitment to the struggles involved. These strategies involve processes of education or mis-education (Chomsky, 2000), depending on one's point of view. It would now be appropriate to look at the two types of globalisation more closely, identify some of their features and relate them to the field of adult education, and specifically European adult education.

GLOBALISATION FROM ABOVE

Given the amount of literature that exists concerning neoliberalism and education (see, for instance, Pannu, 1996; Walters, 1997; Burbules and Torres, 2000; Dale and

Robertson, 2004; Giroux, 2004; Olssen, 2004; Jarvis, 2006), it would be futile on our part to engage in an extensive discussion around this issue. We will highlight some of those aspects that, we feel, have a direct bearing on adult education.

The intensification of globalisation, occurring through massive breakthroughs in information and communication technologies, has led to an opening of borders and a liberalisation of services. The highly contested General Agreement on Trade in Services (GATS), which has been debated in the context of the WTO, would, if it had gone through, have had a bearing on all services within the context of education (de Siqueira, 2005; D. Hill & associates, 2005, pp. 21–24; Verger & Bonal, 2006). Much of what would pass for adult education, especially that governed by the market and therefore run on commercial lines, would be seen as a service and would therefore be subject to GATS.

Local entities engaging in this service already face stiff competition from foreign agencies operating in the field, many of which benefit from greater economies of scale. They even enter areas which have hitherto not been catered for by local agencies. Open universities, especially those using the hegemonic English language (see Macedo *et al*, 2003, on the importance of this language in a globalised context), as well as recognised British universities, have been very visible internationally in this area.

The opening of borders and multiple regional markets, a prominent feature of this process, has facilitated mobility of capital (fast-paced economic and financial exchange) and labour, though, as we shall argue, certainly not on a level playing field. This has led to the need for flexible workers and therefore the constant retooling of labour. Lifelong education, which was once promoted by UNESCO, but which had little impact on educational policy despite its having become part of the popular rhetoric, suddenly has been firmly placed on the international policy agenda, albeit with a modification to the terminology. The emphasis now is on 'learning' rather than 'education', a process that takes into consideration the various forms of learning engaged in by persons at all stages of their life. This, however, shifts the emphasis from the state, as a provider of services to which people are entitled, onto individuals, who must be responsible for their own learning. In the case of the European Union (EU), which has adopted this concept as its master-concept (to use the old UNESCO vocabulary), using the term 'learning' instead of 'education' also serves another purpose. Education is regarded within the EU as a matter of national sovereignty. Terms such as 'learning' and 'human resource development' become the choice words in these circumstances.

The need to have flexible workers places the emphasis on learning and skills upgrading being not time-conditioned processes but constants throughout life, given the rapidity with which changes in the labour market are said to take place. Carnoy (1999) argues that globalisation has brought with it a perceived growth in demand for products with high level of skill, thus underlining the importance of skills upgrade through adult education and training (p. 15).This leads countries to engage in spending on education for a more educated, flexible and mobile workforce, in order to attract and maintain investment as well as remain competitive more generally in the global economy. There has been an expansion of higher education and this places pressure on universities and other higher education institutions to provide university continuing education services (see the various contributions to Osborne & Thomas, 2003). In countries not having the right infrastructure to cater for such an increase, including those which only recently established a public university, this could mean buying education services from outside.

Cyprus seems to have had the right infrastructure for higher education expansion. Its public university first opened its doors in 1992. The intake is limited. As a result, pressure is forthcoming from other sources, particularly private institutions, to open shop in Cyprus and, in cases such as the recently renamed University of Nicosia (formerly known as *Intercollege*) and Cyprus College,[2] to be recognised as degree- and diploma-providing institutions. Malta, like Cyprus, a southern EU member state, is also witnessing pressure from private entities offering courses that are accessible to both full-time and part-time evening students and that are being provided by recognised UK universities such as those of Leicester, London and Sheffield Hallam, to name but three.

Other foreign bodies include the Geneva-based European University, which has branches in various countries, including Malta. This occurrence is of great relevance to the issue of the impact of globalisation on university continuing education, especially with respect to established institutions where the 'concern for standards' and the workload of a limited, suitably qualified academic staff precludes them from offering highly sought-after degree courses in the evening. The monopoly of one institution, very much a characteristic of a very small state (and Europe has its share of very small states, including very small island states), is thus challenged. It is often encouraged by governments seeking to boost the country's graduate numbers to enable it to reach 'European levels'. These private institutions, often acting as mediators for recognised foreign bodies, alleviate the government's burden of having to finance the increase in public higher education. Market-driven university continuing education is seen to perform a useful role here.

PRIVATISATION AND ADULT EDUCATION

This situation is also symptomatic of another important feature of globalisation and its underlying neoliberal ideology: increasing privatisation (Hill & associates, 2005, p. 6). This is in keeping with the ideology of the marketplace. Socially oriented adult education was a prime casualty in the shift from public to private sector bias as governments are under pressure to reduce growth of public spending on education. Adult education services are increasingly privatised according to the market, with more emphasis placed on human resource development (HRD) and information technology (IT). The familiar pressure faced by adult education organisers is to search for alternative sources of funding for socially oriented programmes. This often results in their resorting to European funding via the European Social Fund

(ESF), but the emphasis is here placed on 'employability'. Applicants for European Social Funds often use their creative faculties to stretch the meaning of employability to introduce their own specific agendas into this setting.

While certain organisations in Europe, including those in southern Europe, can tap into limited funds from regional governments, the alternative might well be that they opt for a 'quick-fix' solution by turning to the corporate sector. Even here, the agenda would be compromised. The other solution is to join international partnerships involving counterparts from various regions of Europe and apply for funding under the Grundtvig action within what was previously the Socrates Programme (now the Lifelong Learning Programme) or, if they can relate the area to training, what was previously the Leonardo Programme (now subsumed under the Lifelong Learning Programme). Furthermore, in the adult vocational sector, there is now an emphasis on co-funding, often involving employees and their representatives. The widespread presence of and emphasis on information and communication technologies in adult education brings distance and online learning to the fore. As platforms become more versatile and supportive of rich visual and auditory interactions, and faster and more easy to use, we witness the facilitation of the liberalisation and provision of services coming from external centres, including those of former colonial powers. These foreign agencies and their representatives challenge the monopoly of local institutions and fill the gaps not provided by them. The global adult education centre can 'teach' adults anywhere and across time zones.

The area of social purpose adult education is, by and large, the most adversely affected as far as state funding is concerned. And the irony is that, while state funding is decreasing, the onus for such programmes, already placed on individuals, who are constantly called upon to take charge of their own learning, is also being shifted onto non-governmental organisations (NGOs) and community organisations. These organisations are entrusted with the task of helping to build a community's 'social capital'. This term, as employed by James Coleman (1988) and Robert Putnam (2000), is increasingly being used in the adult education discourse. The community organizations are exhorted to enable persons to become more 'entrepreneurial', personally, socially and economically, and less collective and dependent on the state. The debate on rights and responsibilities is rationalised and marketised, with 'autonomous choice' and 'self-help' being advocated for all.[3]

For the state has undergone a transformation of its previous role in reconciling the requirements of capital accumulation with the need to legitimate itself socially and democratically by addressing the demands for social programmes in a variety of social fields. The accumulation/legitimation function that was a characteristic of the state as it was once known (see Baran & Sweezy, 1966; Carnoy & Levin, 1985; Ross & Trachte, 1990) gives way to a new set of functions that are characteristic of the neoliberal state. These include a non-interventionist approach and measures that contribute to the efficiency of the market, such as providing the infrastructure for investment and the mobility of capital, as well as the development of 'human resources'. While advocating for the liberty of the individual, the neoliberal state engages in policing borders and internal areas to control those who fall victim to the ruthlessness of the market – those who become, in Zygmunt Bauman's words, 'the human waste disposal' sector (Bauman, 2006). The image projected by the USA in this regard is that of being very much a 'carceral state', to use the term adapted by Giroux (2004) from Foucault's notion of a 'carceral society'. Perhaps an important function for adult education in this context would be that of stepping up education inside prisons – an area which is increasingly being given importance throughout Europe, and for which EU funding has also been provided – and in 'detention centres' for migrants who reach the shores of Europe. These centres, as has been reported with respect to places such as Malta and Lampedusa (Sicily), [4] have often been denounced for the appalling conditions in which the detainees find themselves. We would consider them to be yet another manifestation of the 'carceral state'.

OLD AGE AS A MARKET

One sector whose security has been jeopardised by this turn of events with respect to the State is that of older adults; we have an ageing population and a decreasing birth rate throughout Europe. The rise of this sector of the population has rendered it an important target for social-oriented adult learning, with NGOs, including those tied to various denominational churches in Europe, playing an important part in this context.

Neoliberal policies and the great demographic shifts that have occurred have led the neoliberal, post-welfare state to consider pensions unsustainable. Suddenly older adults are being regarded as important prospective members of the labour force. The retirement age for certain occupations is being raised and we often come across seminars discussing the feasibility of older adults being gainfully employed past the conventional retirement age. The discourse about adult education for the elderly has shifted from one that focused on non-instrumental learning, including the middleclass- oriented Universities of the Third Age (Formosa, 2000, 2007), the Elderhostels and the more popular community groups, to one that is increasingly becoming vocationalised. It is argued that older adults have much to offer the economy, as long as their labour skills are retooled. As a result, it is further argued, they would no longer be a burden on the state or, we would add, they would now fall prey to the market which is rendering pensions an individual rather than a social concern.

ADULT EDUCATION AND PERFORMANCE INDICATORS

One other feature of globalisation and its impact on education is the emphasis on international quality comparisons – performance indicators, internal and external auditing, accreditation, standardisation, league tables, equivalences and harmonisation. While in the area of marketable skills, 'objective' measurability and comparability are perceived as achievable tasks, these are difficult to achieve in an area where a lot of non-formal and informal learning takes place. Attempts in this regard have, however, been made through the EU's provision of lifelong learning quality indicators and various projects funded by the EU concentrating on classification of competences for adult educators.

GLOBALISATION FROM BELOW

Many consider the more progressive side of adult education to emerge within the context of 'Globalization from below.' And there are those who pin their faith on social movements, given their disenchantment with leftist parties engaging in such action. Progressive social movements, from various parts of the globe, have made their mark in adult education. Apart from numerous NGOs, the anti-global movement that made its presence felt in Seattle, Davos, Genoa and elsewhere has provided a context for the understanding of issues related to international trade and global capitalism in its wider context.

Teach-ins, poster sessions, websites and print literature feature among the pedagogical strategies devised for this purpose. Ongoing developments in information and communication technologies challenge the hegemonic institutions' monopoly of knowledge. NGOs do not need expensive capital investments to relay their messages and engage in education processes. Social movements such as the Frente Zapatista in Chiapas, who make great use of the web as part of their 'Internet war', and the landless peasant movement (MST) in Brazil have also made forms of popular education part of their work. The MST allies political activism and mobilisation with important cultural work, including highly inspiring music and poetry. The MST's extensive educational programme includes courses carried out within the various landless peasants' encampments (Kane, 2001, pp. 40–43) and the movement draws its inspiration from some of the revolutionary figures in Latin America, including Guevara and Freire. This movement has led to support groups emerging in Europe, groups such as the Comitato di Appoggio di Roma al MST (Committee of Support for the MST, Rome), which has produced a variety of resources that shed light on the movement and its concerns (e.g. Stédile & Fernandes, 2001).

FEMINISM AND GRASSROOTS ADULT EDUCATION

The adult education literature also abounds with articles and books relating to grassroots adult education provided within the context of feminism (Thompson, 1983, 1988; Miles, 1998; Hart, 1992; Darmanin, 1997), environmentalism (Hart, 1992; O'Sullivan, 1999; Clover *et al*, 2000), peace activism (Moriarty, 1989) and citizenship movements such as that involved in the 'participatory budget' in Porto Alegre, Brazil (Schugurensky, 2002; Baerle, in Borg & Mayo, 2007), to name a few fields. Some of these topics are dealt with in some depth in separate chapters in the companion volume by Leona English and Peter Mayo (2012).

THE LEARNING DIMENSION

Social movements have a learning dimension to their work (Welton, 1993; Hall & Clover, 2006) and often incorporate adult education projects. However, many activists involved in social movement learning stress that for such learning to be effective it has to be linked with concerns that extend beyond the particular issue highlighted by a specific social movement.

Environmentalist Vincent Caruana (in Borg & Mayo, 2007) elaborates:

> To be more effective (critical) Environmental Education needs to interact and dialogue more with the other so called 'adjectival educations' such as citizenship education, development education and peace education. In other words it needs to actively search for the ecological dimension to citizenship issues, social justice issues and peace issues and raise them as part of the struggle. The current boycott of Coca Cola (www.killercoke.org) is in protest of Coke's murder of indigenous working class organisers in Colombia but there is also an ecological dimension to this struggle – Coke's support for the mass-herbicide poisoning of the entire countryside with Monsanto's Round Up. The current boycott regarding produce from Israel and illegal Israeli settlements in the West Bank and Gaza is about ending the military occupation of Gaza and the West Bank but there is also an ecological dimension to this struggle – the poisonous cloud of pollution (containing high levels of poisonous lead, mercury and PCBs) spread over a third of Lebanon (an area that is home to half its people) from a fire in a bombed fuel tank that burned for 12 days. The same bombing released about four million gallons of oil into the sea, in the largest ever spill in the eastern Mediterranean. The unprecedented response of concerned citizens to the Tsunami disaster is about reconstruction but it is also about re-thinking coastal zone management and respecting the laws of nature. (p. 155)

REGIONAL SOCIAL FORA

One context which allows possibilities for movements to reach out to and act in concert with others is the World Social Forum and its related regional social fora. These fora bring movements together to consolidate the view that 'another world is possible' (see Fisher & Ponniah, 2002). The first Mediterranean social forum, which took place in June 2005, brought women's organisations from various parts of the region together to participate in a Women's Assembly [5] which offers scope for networking and adult learning occurring on a broad international, if regional, scale.

TECHNOLOGY AS LIBERATORY PRACTICE

'Globalisation from below' also involves the use of technology for alternative progressive ends. While a lot of commercially and credentials-driven distance education focuses on areas such as business administration, training, professional courses and IT, we come across learning zones in the humanities, through blogs, on a whole range of subjects, including philosophy, which do not result in credits being awarded but which serve a non-utilitarian educational purpose. They provide a welcome respite from the excessive vocationalism that dominates the neoliberal educational scene. This is to be seen as a learning space. Progressive movements use the Internet, and IT more generally, for transformative ends, and their websites have a strong educational dimension. The Internet is one of the means that serves the interest of what has been termed a 'global civil society'.

If one were to eschew the current meaning attached to the term 'civil society' and adopt the meaning provided by Antonio Gramsci, then a global civil society relates to both forms of globalisation since it constitutes the terrain wherein a lot of the global domination, via global cable networks, information technology, and so on occurs. Once again, however, it creates spaces for progressive action in that it offers the means for progressive groups, located in various parts of the world, to connect electronically or otherwise. IT is a double-edged sword in that, as an instrument of capitalism, it can constitute an effective process of domination, but can also offer progressive possibilities in the fostering of international alliances (Hall, 1993). It can, however, also serve conservative ends since civil society, in both the Gramscian and contemporary uses of the term, is not to be romanticised. As we have shown earlier, it comprises a whole range of groups and movements, including racists and religious fundamentalists.

ADULT EDUCATION IN SOUTHERN EUROPE AND GLOBALISATION FROM BELOW

Inspirational Figures and Grass-Roots Democracy

Several movements mentioned above derive their nourishment from various inspirational figures either through the latter's having served as role models, or because of their activism, or by means of their writings. Prominent among these figures is the Sardinian political leader, activist and theorist Antonio Gramsci, who has a particular following among social movements across the Atlantic and especially in Latin America. In their overview of adult learning within social movements, Hall & Clover (2006) identify him, along with a host of others, as a source of inspiration. Gramsci hails from southern Europe, which is given scant exposure in the international adult education literature in the English language. (see Puigvert, 2004) And yet we would argue that this region furnishes us with a number of experiences, movements and personalities capable of inspiring different forms of progressive adult education. We can point to the Mondragon experience, one of the better-known experiences from the region, with its emphasis on industrial democracy which, together with other attempts at industrial democracy from the region – namely, the Factory Council experience in Turin and the self-management strategies in the old Yugoslavia (then considered a Mediterranean country) – provide interesting contrasts to the fetish of worker management teams within the context of Total Quality Management. Another well-known development from southern Europe is the so-called 150 hours experiment in working-class adult education, where the unions attained the right to paid educational leave not for vocational purposes but for a general education.

We come across an experience of grassroots democracy ('omnicrazia') learning in Italy through the various post-war social orientation centres (Centro di Orientamento Sociale – COS) inspired by the anti-Fascist, Gandhi-inspired peace activist, Aldo Capitini (1899–1968) (Telleri, 2003, p. 97). The Centre for Social Orientation (COS), which Capitini founded in 1944 in his native Perugia, soon after the city's liberation, led to other centres emerging in such towns and cities as Ferrara and small localities in Umbria (Associazione Amici di Aldo Capitini, n.d.). It provided an education intended to empower people to hold those in power accountable and to engage in a form of deliberative democracy. The same can be said of the work of the internationally renowned Danilo Dolci (1924–1997) in Sicily who led by example, giving rise to 'non-violent' collective mobilization and learning for change (including the so-called sciopero alla rovescia – upside-down strike) through such actions on his part as, for instance, hunger strikes (Barone, 2004; Castiglione, 2004). The other important figure whose pedagogical ideas can inspire and sustain progressive work in neoliberal times is the Tuscan radical educator Don Lorenzo Milani (1921–1967). Lorenzo Milani will mostly be remembered for his work with school dropouts at Barbiana. He was, however, also involved in adult and youth education at San Donato di Calenzano (Simeone, 1996).

One of the main emphases in his work, both at San Donato and at Barbiana, is on the collective dimension of learning. This stands in marked contrast to the current neoliberal maxim of individualisation that serves to project persons in two-dimensional terms: producers and consumers. Milani wrote and taught incessantly against the perils of spiralling consumerism, since he was active as an educator during the time of economic boom in Italy. There are also elements of Latin American popular education which made their way into adult education provision in places such as Portugal and Spain.

Apart from various forms of popular education, we notice adult education projects to prepare people in Seville for participation in a 'participatory budget' experiment (Lucio-Villegas Ramos, 2004; CIMAS, 2006; Florindo & Lucio- Villegas Ramos, 2007) along the lines of the Porto Alegre experience. These elements of popular education could be the result of the cultural affinity existing between the Iberian and Latin American contexts. They are also slowly making their presence felt in Italy among social movements there, where they are combined with ideas and tools for community theatre deriving from Augusto Boal. The programmes involved, such as those of the Teatro Giolly, are social justice and community oriented. The Teatro Giolly engages in 'theatre of the oppressed' activities, such as 'forum theatre', where participants act as 'spect-actors' and engage in a process of consciousness raising intended to gain awareness of and confront oppressive structures (Roberto Mazzini, in Borg & Mayo, 2007, p. 100).

A participative form of adult education for social transformation and cultural renewal can be found in Spain. The efforts of CREC (Centre de Recursos I Educació Continua), in Xativa and Valencia, stand in marked contrast to the work of those providing a competence-based adult education. CREC, which is closely connected to the Paulo Freire Institute in Spain, focuses on providing resources for adult educators that centre on substantive wider issues rather than on narrow teaching techniques; there seems to be a preference for theoretical writings rather than 'mix-and-stir' teaching recipes. It provides adult educators with numerous books in Catalan, often translations of major social philosophical, sociological or adult education theoretical works that furnish the reader with a critical social perspective.

GROUPS, MOVEMENTS AND POSSIBILITIES FOR ALLIANCES IN ADULT EDUCATION

The example of CREC and others indicate that it is not only individuals but also groups and movements that ought to be mentioned with regard to adult education. The *Mediterranean Review/Mediterraneo Un Mare di Donne*, a bilingual periodical in Italian and English,[6] provides visibility to women's groups and organisations from the region, that challenge patriarchy at different levels and in different areas. There are other Mediterranean organisations and networks that make women the focus of their attention, and we earlier mentioned the Women's Assembly at the first Mediterranean Social Forum (FSMED). These organisations constitute the basis for a women's movement in the Mediterranean which, once again, like all movements, has a learning dimension in its activities. A question arises (Mayo, 1999): Is there room for an international progressive alliance based on consensus among different movements and organisations?

International fora such as those centering on the ideas of Paulo Freire help bring different activists together so that ideas converge and potential joint projects are devised. Others use the Internet to publicise their ideas and those of the figures and movements who gave rise to them. Some, like the women's organisation *Mediterraneo Un Mare di Donne/Mediterranean Review*, publish their material in both Italian and English, thus providing the conditions to reach out to other groups across the region. Others such as CREC (Centre de Recursos I Educació Contínua) or the Centro di Formazione e Ricerca Don Milani e Scuola di Barbiana provide their material in their own native language, and it therefore has a very limited reach across their boundaries. The main challenge therefore remains that of bringing these forces and the thinking around them together for an international effort to confront the hegemonic form of adult education that pervades contemporary discourse and continues to render the kind of progressive and emancipatory traditions, to which the above movements belong, a repressed historical and contemporary alternative.

HOW MUCH OF THIS IS INCORPORATED INTO EUROPEAN ADULT EDUCATION POLICY?

To what extent are elements connected with 'globalization from below' making their way into European adult education policy? It might be argued that once they become incorporated, these elements blunt their progressive alternative edge. Furthermore, the mainstream system is often adept at incorporating elements of this alternative discourse to secure consent and therefore greater legitimacy as part of what Gramsci would call a 'war of position'. We now look at two European documents, the first of which, the EU Lifelong Learning Memorandum (henceforth EU LLM), is certainly a document intended to provide guidelines for policy-making in adult education and lifelong learning more generally in EU member states. The second document, produced by the European Association for the Education of Adults (EAEA), focuses on the different trends and issues in adult education throughout EU member states. It was commissioned by the EU. The latter is more of an advocacy document than a policy document. We dealt at length with the first document in a series of publications (see Borg & Mayo, 2004, 2005, 2006; Walters et al, 2004). We will provide a synoptic critical commentary on the Memorandum's six key messages. These are: (a) new basic skills; (b) investment in human resources; (c) innovation in teaching and learning; (d) valuing learning; (e) guidance and information; and (f) bringing learning closer to home.

Message 1: New Basic Skills for All

The report published by Cedefop, Eurydice (2001) reveals a range of interpretations of the term 'basic skills'. However, it is becoming increasingly apparent that the dominant discourse on 'basic skills' is labour-market oriented. The net result of this orientation in curriculum reform is that '[a]rrangements for guidance, support and identification of skills needed by the labour market, in cooperation with the social partners, are highly significant aspects of curricular provision' (Cedefop/Eurydice, 2001, p. 15).

Missing from the Memorandum's section on 'basic skills' is the notion of what Freire and others would broadly term 'critical literacy', echoed also in Milani's (2002) insistence on critical readings of contemporary reality and its construction through the media. This attribute would render the discourse on new skills, in the Memorandum, less dominated by the ideology of competitive individualism. Also included in this message is the skill of being able to take charge of one's own learning. However, the notion of 'taking charge of one's own learning' is conceived of in simply individualistic terms that can result in placing the entire responsibility for learning on the individual, with the danger that failure to achieve can be blamed on the victim and not the State.

We reiterate the view that learning is a social act and yet we do not come across, in this message, the 'collectivity' dimension, the important dimension stressed by Freire, Milani and some of the movements from southern Europe to which reference was made earlier on. We should perhaps begin to speak in terms of self- and collectively directed learning.

Key Message 2: Investment in Human Resources

This message's objective is to '[v]isibly raise levels of investment in human resources in order to place priority on Europe's most important asset – its people' (Commission of the European Communities [CEC], 2000, p. 12). This section emphasises the need for a culture of shared responsibility for the education of present and prospective employees. This takes the form of individual incentives such as the opening of learning accounts, subsidised study leave and the affirmation of one's right to training opportunities. It also emphasises the need for more flexible working arrangements that allow employees to learn and upgrade their profile. Once again, the education of workers, in this section, is presented in a manner that suits the interests of the employer by rendering employees partly responsible for their professional upgrading and by relieving employers of part of the responsibility for the provision of training, making the other social partners share the burden. There is little in this section on the rights of employees and their representatives (important social partners) to negotiate paid educational leave for studies in areas which extend beyond the narrow focus of vocational preparation, in the way that, for instance, the steel-metal workers in Italy, through their union representatives, negotiated the right to 150 hours' paid educational leave for a general education.

Key Message 3: Innovation in Teaching and Learning

This message's objective is to '[d]evelop effective teaching and learning methods and contexts for the continuum of lifelong and lifewide learning' (CEC, 2000, p. 13). The message calls for 'a major shift towards user-oriented learning systems with permeable boundaries across sectors and levels'. It refers to the need for 'individuals to become active learners', with the implication being that there is a need to improve existing practices and 'take advantage of the opportunities offered by ICT and by the full range of learning contexts' (CEC, 2000, p. 13). It adds that the '[l]earning systems must adapt to the changing ways in which people live and learn their lives *today*. This is especially important for achieving gender equality and catering to the increasingly active "Third Age" citizenry' (CEC, 2000, p. 14). It also places the emphasis on upgrading the skills of those engaged as educators in formal and non-formal learning environments, be they paid professionals, volunteers or those to whom teaching is a secondary function (CEC, 2000, p. 14). Quite commendable is the sensitivity shown towards social difference based on the recognition of the way traditional teaching ignores such differences and reinforces normalising discourses regarding femininities, masculinities and age. There is an emphasis throughout this and other lifelong learning and lifelong education literature on the need for educators to serve as facilitators, resource persons and so on. While this no doubt results from dissatisfaction with traditional pedagogical methods that are alienating to various categories of students, one must guard against the danger of the pedagogical approach involved degenerating into laissez-faire pedagogy which inevitably favours those who enjoy greater access to resources or, worse, the transmission as 'facilitators' of pre-packaged learning material which the excessive use of IT facilitates. The use of IT in education is naturally given prominence. E-networking is an important development that allows possibilities for collective learning, often with a social purpose, across the globe. On a less optimistic note, however, excessive use of IT in education can continue to render learning an isolated and individualistic activity.

Key Message 4: Valuing Learning

Message 4's objective is to '[s]ignificantly improve the ways in which learning participation and outcomes are understood and appreciated, particularly non-formal and informal learning' (CEC, 2000, p. 15). The message stresses the need to address the current situation where it is stated that '[t]he rising demand for qualified labour by employers and increased competition between individuals to gain and keep employment is leading to a much higher demand for recognised learning than ever before'.One would have expected to find, in this section, the kind of broad philosophical discussion concerning the 'value of learning' reminiscent of the 'old' lifelong education literature. Kenneth Wain states in this regard:

> Indeed the whole tenor of the section could send out the wrong message to governments, institutions, and individuals, that what is valued is only this kind of learning, vocational learning for the purposes of the economy and the job market. While it recognises the great importance of such learning, the committee feels that learning for other than vocational purposes should have been duly recognised and given space in the memorandum especially since the memorandum itself speaks of 'promoting active citizenship' as 'equally important.'[7]

Key Message 5: Rethinking Guidance and Counselling

The objective of Message 5 is to 'Ensure that everyone can easily access good quality information and advice about learning opportunities throughout Europe and throughout their lives' (CEC, 2000, p. 17). This message is of great importance for countries in Europe that still restrict guidance and counselling facilities to schools and tertiary institutions, as well as labour market public and private entities. Given the variegated and broad nature of the field of education, comprising the formal and non-formal sectors, not to mention informal learning, a holistic and lifelong approach to guidance and counselling is being advocated in European Commission documents (Sultana, 2003). The net result of this strategy at the European level is that more and more guidance and counselling provisions are following citizens throughout life; enhancing social inclusion by engaging reluctant learners in educational and training experiences; presenting up-to-date information that responds to client and employer needs; networking with NGOs to address specific needs; and exploiting the potential of technology-based infrastructures for guidance and counselling purposes (Sultana, 2003). The Memorandum should be applauded for attaching importance to the development of such a service intended to be accessible in terms of cost, location and suitability for people of different ages, young and adult alike.

The emphasis on placing 'the client's interests in the forefront' (CEC, 2000, p. 17) is quite appropriate given the learner-centred approach that is continuously advocated in the context of lifelong learning. The Memorandum should also be applauded for warning against the danger of a market-based approach to this area: 'Over the past thirty years, market-based services have mushroomed, especially for the highly qualified. In some Member States, many guidance and counselling services are wholly or partially privatised' (CEC, 2000, p. 18). Rather than simply 'define entitlements' and 'set agreed minimum standards', the public sector should take it upon itself to increase provision in this vital area, quality provision accessible to one and all.

Key Message 6: Bringing Learning Closer to Home

The objective of this message is that of providing 'lifelong learning opportunities as close to learners as possible, in their own communities and supported through ICT-based facilities wherever appropriate' (CEC, 2000, p. 19). This is a very interesting section of the Memorandum that again stresses the notion of outreach, which requires that one draws on the experience garnered in this area by organisations and educators involved in the related fields of community education, action and development, education in prisons, education of older adults and education of the disabled. The section deals with the use of IT in offering 'great potential for reaching scattered and isolated populations' (CEC, 2000, p. 19). It also deals with developing the idea of 'lifelong learning as the driver for local and regional regeneration' and the creation of 'appropriate kinds of learning centres in everyday locations where people gather' (CEC, 2000, p. 19). As with the rest of the document, there is an over-emphasis on the use of IT which no doubt has its merits but, once again, if it is not used carefully and creatively, with educators and learners as important mediators and, better still, co-learners using IT equipment as a complementary resource, it can serve as the vehicle for the transmission of pre-packaged material.

The idea of having 'learning centres in everyday locations' is also to be commended since it is based on the recognition that learning takes place in a variety of settings, many of which constitute sites of much of what passes for 'lifewide education'. The Memorandum refers to lifelong learning as serving as the vehicle for local and regional regeneration. Initiatives connected with Key Message 6 allow scope for partnerships to develop among formal and non-formal, including grassroots, organisations. These partnerships would be justified on the grounds that some of the formal institutions, such as universities, are public institutions supported, for the most part, by public taxes, the taxes of those living within the region. To what extent would the efforts of the grassroots movements improve through greater access to the university's resources? Having said this, there are limits to the kind of regional regeneration and development that is possible in certain contexts, given that uneven levels of development are widely held to be endemic to the capitalist mode of production.

NEOLIBERALISM AND A MARKET-ORIENTED DEFINITION OF SOCIAL VIABILITY

The Memorandum's messages ought to be read in a manner that recognises its underlying market-oriented definition of social viability. In general, although it stresses the need for an education connected with active democratic citizenship, underlines the importance of social difference, and is full of social democratic trappings, the Memorandum is found wanting in its analysis of the effects of neo-liberal, socio-economic policies on educational change. Therefore, while the document refers to 'community', 'citizenship' and 'solidarity', the content is, for the most part, framed by capitalism's latest re-organisational needs: flexibility, mobility, job-related counselling and basic employment-related skills. Rather than rupturing the process of the global auctioning of human services, the Memorandum reinforces the idea that closer links between education and the economy are inevitable. (see Zygmunt Bauman in this volume)

THE EAEA'S 'TRENDS AND ISSUES IN EUROPEAN ADULT EDUCATION'

Later, an EAEA-led consortium carried out work resulting in the document titled 'Adult Education Trends and Issues in Europe.'[8] This 73-page study provides a wide-ranging analysis of the current situation concerning non-formal adult education throughout the continent. Recommendations for the future are formulated in this expansive study. The issues it covers range from immigration to old age, and the authors discuss such topics as funding, regional partnerships and intergenerational learning. The document can be truly inspirational for anyone seeking to influence the development of adult education in his/her own country, region or municipality. In EU member states, this is a very important current occurrence as governments engage in attempts to develop national lifelong learning strategies for which the EU LLM serves as an important source of reference. Particularly striking is the second part of the study concerning certain points made with respect to ageing, decentralisation, partnerships, finance and intergenerational learning. We winced when faced with the term 'human capital' and to a lesser extent 'social capital', since we feel these terms keep us trapped in the logic of capital accumulation. We are more concerned with the first of the two terms, that is unappreciative of the full range of subjectivities that characterise the adult learner. This point is made throughout the study itself, where much emphasis is placed on adult education that extends beyond the simply vocational. We have shown earlier how the term 'social capital' can accommodate neoliberal thinking and discourse. Furthermore, as some studies have shown, greater trust, affiliation and networking, some of the key indicators of 'social capital', can be exclusionary and lead to narrow as opposed to more general social interests.

We now dwell on two crucial issues given adequate importance in the report – the issues of immigration and ageing. These two issues must be central to any report mapping out trends and current issues in European Adult Education in the context of the intensification of globalisation.

Many countries, especially those from southern Europe, have turned from being exporters to being net importers of migrants. These include Greece, Portugal, Italy (including southern Italy), Spain and Malta. Malta's case is worrying since we have a very small state which is a frontier state with regard to North Africa, from where a lot of migrants from sub-Saharan and north Africa cross over the new 'Rio Grande' that is the Mediterranean. The often-expressed fear in Malta is that the small island state, like its nearby Italian island of Lampedusa, will be 'swamped'. This generates xenophobia and racism (evident in many parts of Europe but writ large in these small island contexts under these circumstances), and so there is a need for anti racist adult education to be stepped up in these places and elsewhere, targeting all those engaged in work relating to immigration (e.g. immigration officers, journalists, army, police and so on).

As elsewhere, this occurrence of massive immigration from North Africa has led to the emergence of ultra-right, neofascist movements, and, in Malta, violence has often been perpetrated against immigrants and the property of those who write in favour of or support immigrants and the development of a multi-ethnic society. Anti-racist education should be stepped up across the whole gamut of educational provision in such places. There is also the need for detention centres, where immigrants are kept until a decision is made as to whether they should be granted refugee status or not, to be transformed into 'lifelong learning centres'. These centres would provide programmes in adult education for integration and also resettlement – resettlement into European countries. Small frontier EU member countries cannot tackle this massive immigration situation on their own and require support from other larger European countries that can accommodate migrants. These countries, or some of them, have a *moral obligation* towards migrants from Africa, having been responsible for the underdevelopment of Africa through their colonial policies in the past. This support can include the provision of material and resources for an adult education programme that involves the teaching of such areas as the language and culture of the country or countries where these immigrants can resettle (Borg & Mayo, 2006).

The discussion on the ageing population, in this EAEA study, is enlightening and highlights one of the main issues facing adult education policy makers at present.

The issue of pensions is a crucial one these days and it is one of the areas where social class politics seems to be coming back to the fore. We think the recommendations made in the document are plausible, as indeed there is a key role for adult education to play here. However, the current situation regarding the raising of the retirement age and the need to engage people over 60 in the labour force to counter the perceived non-sustainability of the current pension schemes can lead us to view the education of older adults only in economic terms. There is an urgent need for the provision of general adult education targeting the many *old people's homes* that are mushrooming everywhere in Europe. Adult education should constitute an important feature of activity in these homes that can serve to improve the quality of life of the residents and therefore make the prolongation of life desirable. There is a need for the preparation of a specialised cadre of adult educators who can provide meaningful educational experiences among older adults in these homes.

One other important element missing from this study is a concern with the development of adult education for planetary consciousness, a crucial issue in an age characterized by the intensification of globalisation. There is a felt need for a wide-ranging educational strategy that confronts an ideology where money and profit (the bottom line) are the basic values that render the earth subject to abuse. Biodiversity should be an important concern among adult and popular educators around Europe as we continue to live in a system in which the earth is subjected to rhythms it cannot withstand and the rest of the universe continues to be conceived of as an object of commodification in a predatory and plundering economic system with global tendencies. We need to conceive of active citizenship in terms of improving not only social relations but also human–earth relations. Fortunately there exist movements and organisations that promote this view of learning. Their work needs to be acknowledged and foregrounded.[9] Examples include the Mediterranean NGO Network for Ecology and Sustainable Development, and Greenpeace Mediterranean. Unless we learn to develop a biocentric world view by which we see ourselves as being rooted in rather than in control of nature, we will continue to witness ecological degradation. Mainstream European adult education needs to learn from the work of several NGOs active in transformative ecopedagogical action within the context of the Earth Charter. More efforts should be channelled in the direction of adult education programmes that not only serve to redistribute wealth but enable learners to redefine wealth itself (Milani, 2002) with a view to enhancing the quality of life on and with the rest of the cosmos. Alas, much of the neoliberal discourse that informs many of the documents concerning lifelong learning in Europe militates against this aspect of adult learning. It is a discourse that often promotes market-driven rather than life-centred values.

CONCLUSION

The hegemonic status of neoliberalism has brought about a shift in education policy and in the allocation of funds for education. This chapter illustrated how the privatisation of public services and the State's retreat from its welfare obligations are being reflected in a dominant, glocal discourse in adult education that privileges training for private production, competition and consumption. A sector, adult education, traditionally dominated by public institutions and NGOs, is undergoing a continuing process of privatisation, where the balance is being shifted towards performativity, retooling and employability rather than social engagement and affirmative action. In light of this scenario, and in full knowledge of the fact that hegemony is never complete, we provided various examples of local and global progressive adult education to argue the case for the development of more adult learning spaces that are critical, public and socially committed.

In the face of corporate mediation of social and human–earth relations, we believe that reclaiming adult education sites and policy as possibilities for social agency and critical citizenry should contribute to a moral imagination that transcends the commonsense, market-driven vision of citizens as subjects of consumption. And we feel that there is quite a repressed tradition in adult education, including wonderful and imaginative experiences deriving from southern Europe (alas given scant importance in Northist-dominated international adult education literature in English) that, as we have shown, can provide nourishment for those seeking to reclaim the social purpose of adult education and explore its possibilities for really genuine processes of social empowerment.

NOTES

[1] Previously published as Carmel Borg and Peter Mayo (2008), Globalisation, Southern Europe and European Adult Education Policy, in Policy Futures in Education, 6(6)701-717. Authorisation to republish granted by publisher, Symposium Journals.
[2] We are indebted to Professor Helen Phtiaka for this information.
[3] We are indebted to Professor Margaret Ledwith for this point.
[4] See the report by Matthew Vella, 'MEPs Appalled at Detention Centres', in *MaltaToday*, 26 March 2006. http://www.maltatoday.com.mt/2006/03/26/t15.html See the article by Fabrizio Gatti in *L'Espresso* reproduced at: http://www.metamorfosi.info/infodetail.asp?categoryid=45&infoid=2525 and his book length treatment of the subject (Gatti, 2007)
See also the damning report on treatment of immigrants at the overcrowded Lampedusa detention centre (Centri di Permanenza Temporanea e Assistenza – Centres for Temporary Stay and Assistance) by Amnesty International Italia: http://www.amnesty.it/pressroom/documenti/lampedusaue.html?page=documenti
See also the article by Fabio Raimondi, 'Centri di Permanenza Temporanea' (Administrative Detention Centres) – the new borders of exploitation, with specific reference to the Bossi-Fini law concerning the detention of immigrants, on nolager.org: http://nolager.org/more/display.php?id=14
[5] See the Associazione Donne del Mediterraneo's website: http://www.donnedelmediterraneo.org/intro.php
See the website: http://www.fsmed.info/it/asmujeresfsmed-it.rtf
[6] See http://www.medmedia.org/review/index.htm, updated last on 30 November 2006.
[7] Short paper on message 4 delivered by Kenneth Wain at the National Consultation Conference on Lifelong Learning held in Malta in May 2001.
[8] http://www.eaea.org/doc/eaea/AETIstudyfinal.doc

⁹ See the following websites concerning fora for learning and action that exist in or are focused on Southern Europe and the Mediterranean:
http://www.medforum.org/english/index.htm, http://www.mio-ecsde.org/
http://www.foeme.org/
http://www.foeeurope.org/mednet/about.htm
http://www.greenpeace.org/mediterranean/,
http://www.euromedplatform.org/spip/index.php?lang=en.
We are indebted to Vincent Caruana for this information.

REFERENCES

Associazione Amici di Aldo Capitini (n.d.) *Introducing Aldo Capitini*, DVD.
Baran, P., & Sweezy, P. (1966). *Monopoly capital*. New York: Monthly Review Press.
Barone, G. (2004). *La forza della nonviolenza. Bibliografia e profilo biografico di Danilo Dolci* (The Power of Nonviolence. Bibliography and Biographical Profile of Danilo Dolci). Naples: Dante & Descartes; Partinico: Centro per lo Sviluppo Creativo 'Danilo Dolci'.
Bauman, Z. (2006). The crisis of the human waste disposal industry. In D. Macedo & P. Gounari (Eds.), *The Globalization of Racism* (pp. 36–40). Boulder: Paradigm.
Borg, C., & Mayo, P. (2004). Diluted wine in new bottles: The key messages of the EU memorandum (on lifelong learning), *Lifelong Learning in Europe (LlinE)*, LX(1), 19–25.
Borg, C., & Mayo, P. (2005). The EU memorandum on lifelong learning: Old wine in new bottles? *Globalisation, Societies and Education*, 3(2), 257–278. http://dx.doi.org/10.1080/14767720500167082
Borg, C., & Mayo, P (2006). *Learning and social difference: Challenges for public education and critical pedagogy*. Boulder: Paradigm.
Borg, C., & Mayo, P. (2007). *Public intellectuals, radical democracy and social movements. A book of interviews*. New York: Peter Lang.
Burbules, N. C., & Torres, C. A (Eds.) (2000). *Globalization and education: Critical perspectives*. New York & London: Routledge.
Carnoy, M. (1999). *Globalization and educational reform: What planners need to know*. Paris: UNESCO.
Carnoy, M., & Levin, H (1985). *Schooling and work in the democratic state*. Stanford: Stanford University Press.
Castells, M. (1999). Flows, networks and identities: A critical theory of the information society. In M. Castells, R. Flecha. P. Freire, H. Giroux, D. Macedo & P. Willis (Eds.), *Critical Education in the Information Age* (pp. 37–64). Lanham: Rowman & Littlefield.
Castiglione, A. (Director) (2004). *Danilo Dolci: memory and utopia*. Partencio: Centro per lo Sviluppo Creativo 'Danilo Dolci'. http://www.danilodolci.net
Commission of the European Communities (CEC) (2000). Commission staff working paper: A memorandum on lifelong learning. Brussels: European Commission.
Cedefop, Eurydice (2001). *National actions to implement lifelong learning in Europe*. Thessaloniki and Brussels: Cedefop/Eurydice.
Chomsky, N. (2000). *Chomsky on MisEducation*, ed. D. Macedo. Lanham: Rowman & Littlefield.
CIMAS (Observatorio Internacional de Ciudadania y Medio Ambiente Sostenible) (2006) *La Pedagogía de la Decisión. Aportaciones teóricas y prácticas a la construcción de las Democracias Participativas* (The Pedagogy of Decision. Theoretical and Practical Contributions for the Construction of a Particpatory Democracy). Seville: Ayuntamiento de Sevilla (Delegación de Participación Ciudadana) & CIMAS.
Clover, D., Follen, S. & Hall, B. (2000). *The nature of transformation: Environmental adult education*. Toronto: Department of Adult Education, Community Development and Counselling Psychology.
Coleman, J. (1988). Social capital in the creation of human capital, *American Journal of Sociology*, 94, 95–120. http://dx.doi.org/10.1086/228943
Dale, R., & Robertson, S. (2004). Interview with Boaventura de sousa santos, *Globalization, Societies and Education*, 2(2), 147–160. http://dx.doi.org/10.1080/14767720410001733629

Darmanin, M. (1997). Women's studies in adult education. In G. Baldacchino & P. Mayo (Eds.) *Beyond schooling: Adult education in malta* (pp. 409–438). Malta: Mireva.

de Siqueira, A. C. (2005). The regulation of education through the WTO/GATS, *Journal for Critical Education Policy Studies*, 3(1). http://www.jceps.com/?pageID=article&articleID=41.

Fisher, W. F., & Ponniah, T. (Eds.) (2002). *Another World is Possible: popular alternatives to globalization at the World Social Forum*. London: Zed Books.

Florindo, A. G., & Lucio-Villegas Ramos, E (2007). Presentation of material at Presupuestos Participativos, Educación Ciudadana y Movimientos Sociales (Participatory Budget, Citizenship Education and Social Movements) seminar, Facultad de Ciencias del Trabajo y E.U. Trabajo Social, University of Huelva (El Carmen Campus), 7 May, Huelva, Spain.

Formosa, M. (2000). Older adult education in a maltese university of the third age: A critical perspective, *Education and Ageing*, 15(3), 315–339.

Formosa, M. (2007). A bourdieusian interpretation of a university of the third age in malta, *Journal of Maltese Education Research*, 4(2), 1–16.

Gatti, F. (2007). *Bilal. Viaggiare, lavorare, morire da clandestini* (Bilal. Travelling,Working , dying as Illegal Immigrants), Milan: BUR-Rizzoli

Giroux, H. A. (2004). *The terror of neoliberalism: Authoritarianism and the eclipse of democracy*. Boulder: Paradigm.

Hall, B.L. (1993). Learning and Global Civil Society: electronic networking in international non-governmental organisations, *International Journal of Computers in Adult Education and Training*, 3(3), 5–24.

Hall, B. L., & Clover, D. (2006). Social movement learning. In R. Veira de Castro, A.V. Sancho & P. Guimarães (Eds.), *Adult Education: new routes in a new landscape* (pp. 159–166). Braga: University of Minho.

Hart, M. (1992). *Working and educating for life: Feminist and international perspectives on adult education*. London & New York: Routledge.

Hill, D., & associates (2005). Education Services Liberalisation. In E. Rosskam (Ed.), *Winners or Losers? Liberalizing Public Services* (pp. 3–54). Geneva: International Labour Office.

Jarvis, P. (2006). Globalisation, knowledge and lifelong learning. In R. Veira de Castro, A.V. Sancho & P. Guimarães (Eds.) *Adult Education: new routes in a new landscape* (pp.15–30). Braga: University of Minho.

Kane, L. (2001). *Popular education and social change in Latin America*. London: Latin American Bureau.

English, L., & Mayo, P. (2012). *Learning with adults. A critical pedagogical introduction*. Rotterdam & Taipei: Sense Publishers.

Lucio-Villegas Ramos, E. (2004). Tejiendo la ciudadania desde la educación (Fostering citizenship through education). In E. Lucio-Villegas Ramos & P. Aparicio Guadas (Eds.) *Educación, democracia y emancipación* (Education, democracy and emancipation) (pp. 15–29). Xativa: Dialogos.

Macedo, D., Dendrinos, B., & Gounari, P. (2003). *The hegemony of english*. Boulder: Paradigm.

Marshall, J. (1997). Globalization from below: The trade union connections. In S. Walters (Ed.), *Globalization, Adult Education and Training: impacts and issues* (pp. 57–68). London: Zed Books.

Mayo, P. (1999). *Gramsci, freire and adult education: Possibilities for transformative action*. London: Zed Books.

Milani, B. (2002). From opposition to alternatives: Postindustrial potentials and transformative learning. In E. O'Sullivan, A. Morrell & M. A. O'Connor (Eds.), *Expanding the Boundaries of Transformative Learning: essays on theory and praxis* (pp. 47–58). New York & Basingstoke: Palgrave.

Miles, A. (1998). Learning from the women's movement in the neo-liberal period. In S. M. Scott, B. Spencer & A. Thomas (Eds.), *Learning for Life: Canadian readings in adult education* (pp. 250–258). Toronto: Thompson Educational Publishing.

Moriarty, P (1989). A Freirean Approach to Peacemaking. *Convergence*, XXII(1), 25–36.

Olssen, M. (2004). Neoliberalism, Globalization, Democracy: challenges for education, *Globalization, Societies and Education*, 2(2), 231–276. http://dx.doi.org/10.1080/14767720410001733665

Osborne, M., & Thomas, E. J. (Eds.) (2003). *Lifelong Learning in a Changing Continent: continuing education in the universities of Europe*. Leicester: National Institute of Adult Continuing Education (NIACE).

O'Sullivan, E. (1999). *Transformative Learning: education for the 21st century*. London & New York: Zed Books; Toronto: University of Toronto Press.
Pannu, R. S. (1996). Neoliberal Project of Globalization: prospects for democratisation of education, *Alberta Journal of Educational Research, XLII*(2), 87–101.
Puigvert, L. (2004). North-South/South-North Relations in Adult Education. In D. Caruana & P. Mayo (Eds.), *Perspectives on Lifelong Learning in the Mediterranean. Proceedings of the Conference 'Lifelong Learning in the Mediterranean' Malta, 13–16 September, 2003* (pp. 18–21), Bonn: IIZ/DVV.
Putnam, R. D. (2000). *Bowling alone: The collapse and revival of American community*. New York: Simon & Schuster.
Rikowski, G. (2001). *The battle in seattle: Its significance for education*. London: Tufnell Press.
Ross, R., & Trachte, K. C. (1990). *Global capitalism – the new leviathan*. New York: SUNY Press.
Schugurensky, D. (2002). Transformative learning and transformative politics: The pedagogical dimension of participatory democracy and social action. In E. O'Sullivan., A. Morrell & M.A. O'Connor (Eds.) *Expanding the Boundaries of Transformative Learning: essays on theory and praxis*, (pp. 59–76). New York & Basingstoke: Palgrave.
Simeone, D. (1996). *Verso la scuola di barbiana. L'esperienza pastorale educativa di don Lorenzo milani a S. donato di calenzano* (Towards the school of barbiana. The educational pastoral experience of don lorenzo milani at s. lorenzo di calenzano). San Pietro in Cariano (Verona): Il Segno dei Gabrielli Editori.
Stédile, J. P., & Fernandes, B. M. (2001). *Brava gente. La Lunga Marcia del Movimento Senza Terra del Brasile dal 1984 al 2000* (Good people. The long march of brazil's landless peasant movement from 1984 till 2000). Rome: Rete Radié Resch.
Sultana, R. G. (2003). *Guidance policies in the knowledge society: Trends, challenges and responses across Europe*. Thessalnoniki: CEDEFOP.
Telleri, F. (2003). *Educarsi per educare. teorie e prassi*. Sassari: Carlo Delfino Editore.
Thompson, J. L. (1983). *Learning liberation – women's response to men's education* London: Croom Helm.
Thompson, J. L. (1988). Adult education and the women's movement. In T. Lovett (Ed.), *Radical Approaches to Adult Education – a reader.*(pp. 181–201). London: Routledge.
Torres, C. A. (1987). Towards a political sociology of adult education: An agenda for research on adult education policy making. Occasional paper series, Centre for International Educational Development, University of Alberta, Edmonton, Canada.
Verger, A., & Bonal, X. (2006). Against GATS: The sense of a global struggle, *Journal for Critical Education Policy Studies, 4*(1). http://www.jceps.com/?pageID=article&articleID=55.
Walters, S. (Ed.) (1997). *Globalization, adult education and training: Impacts & issues*. London: Zed Books.
Walters, S., Borg, C., Mayo, P., & Foley, G. (2004). Economics, politics and adult education. In G. Foley (Ed.), *Dimensions of adult learning: Adult education and training in a global era*. (pp. 137–152) Sydney: Allen & Unwin.
Welton, M. (1993). Social revolutionary learning: The new social movements as learning sites, *Adult Education Quarterly, 43*(3), 152–164. http://dx.doi.org/10.1177/0741713693043003002

AFFILIATION

Carmel Borg
Associate Professor, Department of Education Studies, Faculty of Education,
University of Malta

Peter Mayo
Professor, Department of Education Studies, Faculty of Education,
University of Malta

NAME INDEX

Abdi, A., 5, 14, 149, 166, 341, 342, 343, 346, 349, 352, 354
Adorno, T., 4, 200, 206, 207, 208, 215, 216
Aeschylus, 207
Ahtisaari, M., 113, 114
Aitchison, J., 57, 64, 73
Almazan-Khan, M.L., 323, 337
Amin, A., 196, 203
Amin, S., 132
Andress, H.J., 310, 315
Aoki, A., 322, 327, 328, 338
Apple, M., 85, 166, 172
Arlacchi, P., 101, 110, 111
Arnold, D., 51, 132, 146, 147
Aristotle, 127
Armstrong, P., 63, 73
Augustine (of Hippo), 119, 130

Baatjes, I., 57, 64, 73, 74
Bach, J.S., 207, 208
Baker, R., 172
Barnes, C., 59–62, 65, 74, 131, 147
Barrow, N., 337
Barsamian, D., 164
Baudelaire, C., 207, 212
Bauman, Z., 3, 18, 201, 203, 376, 386, 390
Becket, S., 207, 208
Beethoven, L.V., 207, 208
Belloc, H., 10
Bennholdt-Thomsen, V., 103, 110, 111
Bertell, L., 305, 306
Bhabha, H., 193
Bhattacharya, A., 4, 175–182, 183
Biya, P., 344
Boal, A., 380

Borg, C., 5, 13, 14, 18, 377, 378, 381, 382, 387, 389, 390, 392
Bourdieu, P., 121, 130, 208, 209, 210, 216
Braggins, J., 259, 263
Braque, G., 208
Brecht, B., 207
Brookfield, S.D., 83, 84, 272, 273
Buffet, J., 208
Bush, G.W., 288, 292

Caldwell, J., 358, 364, 370
Camus, A., 208
Campani, G., 104, 110, 111
Capitini, A., 380, 390
Carnoy, M., 157, 159, 372, 373, 375, 390
Carrington, K., 168, 169, 172, 365
Caruana, V., 378, 390, 392
Castro, F., 4
Casey White, E., 3, 86
Cezanne, P., 207, 208
Chatterjee, P., 132, 137–142, 148
Clark, M., 59, 69, 74
Clinton, B., 320
Clover, D., 93, 96, 377, 378, 379, 390, 391
Coleman, J., 375, 390
Cunningham, C., 169, 170
Cranton, P., 5, 216, 270, 273, 274

Dahrendorf, R., 123, 130
Dalgas, E., 222
Dale, R., 371, 372, 390
Darder, A., 4, 173
de Leifde, P., 1
des Villers, V., 102
De Vita, A., 4, 300, 305, 306
Delors, J., 30, 88, 95, 96, 286–289, 291, 329, 337

NAME INDEX

Denny, G.V., 165, 172
Dewey, J., 4, 202, 203, 205–209, 216, 341, 353
Dirkx, J., 206, 216, 270, 273, 274, 287, 291
Dolci, D., 380, 390
Dos Santos, J.E., 344
Duchamp, M., 201
Duncombe, S., 200, 203
Durkheim, E., 115, 130

Edwards, M., 157, 158, 159
Eliot, T.S., 208
Ellis, J., 91, 236, 242, 246, 341, 349
Elmborg, J., 4, 185, 189, 190, 193, 194
Engels, F., 34, 52
English, L., 1, 4, 5, 84, 85, 153, 156, 159, 160, 292, 377, 391
Euripides, 207

Field, J., 141, 145, 311, 313, 315
Flaubert, G., 208
Formosa, M., 4, 233, 235, 238–241, 246, 247, 249, 376, 391
Foroughi, B., 4, 160
Forrester, V., 115, 130
Foucault, M., 190, 193, 376
Franco, F., 122
Franklin, U., 156, 159
Freire, P., 4, 5, 50, 69, 74, 88, 96, 143, 155, 159, 166, 172, 179, 187, 188, 190, 192, 193, 206, 210, 211, 216, 217, 224, 227, 273, 274, 281, 282, 295, 301, 306, 337, 345, 346, 353, 365, 370, 377, 381, 382, 383, 390, 391
Freud, S., 120, 130
Fullick, L., 311, 314, 315

Gallegos, P., 271, 274
Gandhi, M., 380
Gates, B., 157
Gates, M., 157

Gee, J., 187, 190, 193
Giroux, H.A., 16, 18, 161, 163, 164, 166, 173, 182, 346, 353, 373, 376, 390, 391
Gladdish, L., 242, 243, 244, 247
Goethe, J.W., 207
Gonzales, J., 164
Goodman, A., 164
Gaventa, J., 196, 197
Goya, F., 207, 208
Gramsci, A., 4, 5, 131, 132, 137, 147, 149, 170, 210, 285, 286, 291, 292, 301, 372, 379, 382, 391
Greene, M., 206, 208, 209, 216
Grundtvig, N.F.S., 4, 205, 219–228, 246, 257, 262, 375
Guha, R., 132, 135, 143, 144, 147, 148

Habermas, J., 121, 130, 227, 268, 274, 346, 353
Hall, S., 142, 148, 282, 283
Hardiman, D., 144
Harrison, G., 358, 364, 370
Hearn, J., 285, 292
Hegel, G.F., 113, 130, 210
Herskovits, M.J., 99, 110, 112
Hill, R.J., 88, 90–93, 96, 97, 98
Hippocrates, 121
Hitler, A., 113
Horkheimer, M., 4, 200, 206, 216
Horton, M., 224, 227
Houghton, T., 64, 73
Hussein, S., 17

Ibsen, H., 206
Illich, I., 37, 52, 231, 232, 247, 297, 306
Infante, I., 320, 337

Jackson, R.W.B., 52
Jamison, J., 200, 203
Joyce, J., 208, 212

Jubas, K., 4, 155, 159, 285, 286, 287, 290, 291, 292
Judt, T., 195, 203
Jules, D., 5, 359, 366, 369, 370

Kafka, F., 207
Kandinsky, W., 208
Kant, E., 121, 130, 207, 217
Kapoor, D., 3, 131–150
Karsten, M.E., 102, 110, 112
Keats, J., 207
Ki-moon, B., 89
Knowles, C., 104, 111, 112
Knowles, M., 78, 82–85
Knowlton, B., 17
Kokkos, A., 4, 205, 216, 217
Kolakowski, L., 11, 18
Kold, K., 4, 222, 225, 227
Kuhlthau, C., 186, 193
Kurosawa, A., 215

La Belle, T., 317, 323, 338
Lakoff, G., 61, 74, 78, 85, 189, 193
Laslett, P., 231, 238, 240, 241, 247
Linton, R., 99, 110
Livingstone, D.W., 3, 4, 38–50, 52, 53

Machisa, O., 349
Maclachlan, K., 278, 279, 280, 282, 283
McChesney, R., 162, 173
Mahler, G., 208
Malik, K., 196, 203
Mandela, N., 4
Mann, T., 207
Marcuse, H., 4, 206, 207, 208, 217
Marx, K., 136, 141, 144, 147
Matarasso, F., 198, 203
Mattes, R. 341, 342, 344, 349, 352, 353
Matisse, H., 207, 208
Mayo, P., iii, v, 1–6, 13, 14, 18, 84, 85, 147, 149, 225, 228, 294, 298, 301, 306, 361, 366, 369–392

Mbasogo, T.O.N., 344
Mead, R., 3, 197, 198, 199, 203, 204
Megwa, E.R., 165, 173
Mercer, S., 104, 111, 112
Mezirow, J., 5, 69, 75, 83, 84, 85, 217, 267–270, 272, 274
Midwinter, E., 229, 231, 232, 239, 247, 248
Milani, L., 380–383, 388, 391
Milbraith, L., 51, 53
Modipa T.R., 3, 76, 314
Moser, C., 277
Mozart, W.A., 207
Mugabe, R., 341, 344
Mughogho, D., 341, 353
Muukkonen, M., 198, 204
Muller, J., 157, 159
Munoz, V., 253, 260, 264
Myers, J., 5, 270, 273, 339

Nicholson, L., 77, 85
Negt, O., 3, 118, 124, 126, 130, 361
Newman, M., 272, 274
Nyerere, J.K., 5, 225, 317, 334, 338, 347, 351, 354

O'Sullivan, E., 271, 274, 377, 391, 392
Oliver, M., 59, 60, 61, 65, 74, 75
Oppenheim, 201
Oxenham, J., 322, 327, 328, 338

Pandey, G., 132
Pratt, M.L., 187, 194
Pemberton, C.L., 3, 86
Picasso, P., 207, 208, 212
Pinter, H., 208
Piselli, F., 101, 110, 112
Pitkin, H.F., 78, 85
Piussi, A.M., 4, 301, 305, 306
Plato, 127
Postman, N., 154, 159
Preece, J., 5, 311, 313, 316

NAME INDEX

Proust, M., 207
Putnam, R., 37, 53, 237, 248, 345, 354, 375, 392

Quiggin, P., 358, 364, 370
Quijano, A., 132, 150

Rasmussen, P., 4, 129, 130, 224, 228
Ray, S., 181
Redfield, R., 99, 112
Reding, V., 13
Rembrandt Van Rijn., 207, 208
Renoir, A., 207
Rerrich, M., 104, 110, 112
Rimbaud, A., 207
Robertson, S., 371, 372, 373, 390
Rogers, A., 176, 182, 183
Rogers , E., 278, 281, 283, 369, 370
Roseneil, S., 285, 292
Rousseau, J.J., 347
Rule, P., 3, 76, 314
Rychen, D.S., 15, 18

Sachs, J., 309, 310, 312, 313, 316
Salazar, A d O., 122
Sanders, B., 172
Santos de Morais, C., 50
Sartre, J.P., 208
Scott, J., 143, 150
Schapiro, S., & Gallegos, P., 271, 274
Schettini, B., 301, 306
Schubert, F., 207
Schugurensky, D., 5, 339, 359, 377, 392
Schuller, T., 310, 313, 314, 316
Scully, J., 60, 61, 64, 75
Sebates, R., 311, 314, 316
Selman, G., 271, 274
Selwyn, N., 154, 156, 160, 357
Sen, A., 182, 310, 311, 316
Sennett, R., 118, 130, 295, 306
Shah, A., 141, 144, 150
Shakespeare, W., 207
Shannon, P., 165, 166, 173

Shaw, M., 3, 196, 197, 198, 203, 204
Shiva, V., 303
Shizha, E., 5, 148, 149, 341, 349, 352, 354
Sibelius, J., 125
Sifakakis, S., 209, 211, 217
Simone Rychen, D., 15, 18
Stravinsky, I., 208
Streep, M., 191

Tagore, R., 181
Talbot, J., 259, 263
Taravella, L., 100, 110, 112
Tett, L., 5, 277, 278, 280, 282, 283
Thomas, L., 12
Torres, C.A., 61, 75, 325, 337, 338, 359, 367, 370, 372, 390, 392
Torres, R.M., 3, 19, 26, 27, 30, 31, 317, 320, 323, 324, 326, 338
Tough, A., 37, 53
Toynbee, A., 51, 53
Tuckett, A., 91

Utrillo, M., 208

Van Gogh, V., 207, 208
Velázquez, D., 208
Vellas, P., 229, 230, 240, 241, 248
Vygotsky, L., 187, 188, 190, 194

Wain, K., v, 13, 50, 53, 384, 389
Watson, D., 110, 112, 310, 313, 314, 316
Wasserman, I., 271, 274
Willis, P., 199, 202, 204, 390
Wilpert, C., 102
Wojciechowski, J., 11, 12, 18
Woodruff, P., 347, 354
Woolf, V., 208
Wrosch, C., 235, 249

Zille, H., 117

SUBJECT INDEX

Academic, 11, 24, 61, 77, 107, 117, 133, 134, 162, 170, 171, 180, 185, 186, 187, 188, 189, 210, 230, 233, 238, 363, 371, 374,
Accessible/ility, 28, 155, 269, 276, 297, 374, 385
Act, 9, 80, 88, 89, 110, 117, 126, 135, 162, 163, 165, 175, 182, 189, 190, 199, 231, 277, 281, 288, 289, 303, 311, 341, 348, 378, 380, 383
Accumulation, 116, 324, 325, 375, 387
ADEA, 133, 134, 135, 138–142, 145, 146
Adivasis, 3, 131, 135, 136, 138
Adult basic education, 57, 58, 63, 65, 71, 175, 321, 322, 325, 327, 328, 332, 335, 348
Aesthetic/s, 205–215
Africa, 2, 5, 34, 57, 58, 59, 64, 87, 153, 154, 157, 341–352, 371, 387
Age, 162–165, 229–246, 376
Agenda, 251–260
Agriculture/al, 34, 139, 142, 222, 225, 312, 350, 361
Aid, 34, 118, 120, 288, 291, 359
AIDS, 59, 182
Algerian, 102
Andragogy, 83
Anglocentric, 2
Anomie, 102, 115
Apple Ltd., 155
Argentina/ian, 4, 20, 320
Armenia, 87
Art/s Gallery/ies, 209
Asian, 143, 240
Assembly, 89, 93, 94, 95, 221, 350, 355, 378, 381
Association of College and Research Libraries, 185

Audiovisual, 21, 23
Autonomy/ous, 22, 99, 102, 110, 143, 144, 146, 197, 199, 232, 235, 242, 279, 289, 324, 325, 327, 333, 335, 344, 345, 348
Austria/n, 125

Ballistic, 9, 10
Banking concept of education, 120, 188, 192, 277, 368
Barbiana, 380, 381
Belém, 92, 95
Bengal/I, 4, 136
Berber, 103
Blogs/blogging, 156, 234, 244, 269, 379
Bioethics, 121
Body, 60, 62, 65, 66, 67, 68, 69, 70, 72–73, 83, 92, 121, 155, 161, 201, 235, 237, 238, 240, 243, 252, 277, 312, 329, 350
Bourgeois/ie, 114, 116, 119, 132, 140, 141, 143, 171, 238
Brazil/ian, 20, 21, 23, 24, 25, 89, 92, 94, 119, 181, 235, 377
Britain/ish, 100, 104, 229, 231, 234, 242, 271
Brussels, 102, 103, 114
Budget, 23, 29, 57, 272, 318, 329, 325, 377, 380, 391
Bureau, 39
Bureaucracy/critic, 24, 37, 127, 135, 140, 324, 326
Business, 13, 14, 107, 115, 142, 162, 175, 181, 199, 285, 312, 379

Calabrian, 101
Campaign, 5, 25, 29, 57, 59, 127, 169, 285, 298, 299, 344, 350

SUBJECT INDEX

Canada/ian
Capital, 4, 38, 39, 40, 42, 43, 44, 93, 178, 224, 230, 233, 234, 267, 268, 271
Carceral, 376
Career, 12, 102, 103, 108, 109, 110, 154, 186, 226, 363
Caribbean, 2, 5, 19, 20, 26, 27, 28, 93, 319, 331, 336, 355–369
Cash crop/ping, 135
CEAAL, 331
Cedefop, 13, 382
Center/centre, 25, 41, 78, 80, 133, 135, 142, 156, 167, 179, 191, 193, 205, 273, 332, 356
Chicago, 177
Chile/ean, 19, 21, 25, 318, 320, 331, 332
Chinese, 10, 229, 233, 357
Civic, 348–349, 351–352
Civil society, 115–117, 328–330, 348–349
Civilisation, 295
Citizen/ship, 341–352
Coady Institute, 4
Cognitive/ition, 38, 39, 61, 69, 119, 120, 187, 230, 235, 240, 245, 246, 268–270, 271, 273, 278, 281, 341, 352
Coke/coca cola, 378
Collaborative Research Centre, 104
Collective/ly, 37, 139, 195, 198, 252, 281, 333, 334, 351, 383
Colombia/an, 378
Colonial/ism, 132, 134, 143, 362
Colony/ies, 99, 101, 102, 106, 131, 139, 141
Commission, 10, 12, 13, 15, 21, 88, 89, 95, 113, 114, 177, 246, 256, 257, 385
Commission for European Communities, 10, 12, 13, 15, 21, 114, 246, 385

Commonwealth, 100, 356, 357, 361
Communication/s, 12, 13, 14, 106, 122, 127, 129, 153, 154, 162, 163, 164, 175–182, 187, 191, 196, 200, 224, 227, 236, 256, 276, 277, 324, 329, 55, 365, 366, 373, 375, 377
Community/ies, 67–69, 165–169, 195–203, 257–258, 331–334, 351–352
Competiveness/competitivity, 12, 13, 14, 25, 26, 28, 294, 361, 371
Composition studies, 186
Cooperative/s, 21, 118, 125, 233, 328
Computers, 21, 119, 154, 157, 280
Conference, 13, 14, 20, 29, 90, 92, 93, 117, 180, 251, 257, 288, 317, 318, 320, 322, 323, 327, 328, 329, 331, 334, 356, 363, 364
CONFINTEA, 19, 20, 22, 23, 24, 25, 26, 28, 29, 30, 90–93, 94, 95, 318, 327, 328–334
Consume/consumption/consumerism, 199, 201–202, 285, 290, 291, 380
Consumer, 16, 198, 201, 202, 203, 285, 286, 287, 288, 289, 290, 290–291, 297, 300, 303
Continuing (professional) education, 1, 15, 36, 37, 50, 64, 65, 80, 109, 154, 180, 181, 232, 276, 279, 329, 359, 360, 362, 368, 374
Convention, 58, 71, 136, 252
Cooperative/s, 118, 233, 328
Corporate/ism, 4, 14, 40, 45, 73, 136, 138, 142, 143, 161, 162, 163, 164, 165, 168, 375, 389
Costs, 22, 23, 117, 120, 125, 234, 240, 291, 321, 326, 368
Creation, 4, 41, 62, 71, 94, 114, 126, 129, 158, 198, 220, 221, 293–305
Credential/s/ling, 42, 45, 46, 47, 48, 50
CREFAL, 331, 332
Creole, 364, 365

SUBJECT INDEX

Critical Information Literacy, 187–189, 190–192
Critical Literacy, 187, 295, 345, 382,
Critical Theory, 4, 67, 185, 268, 271, 285
Curriculum, 13, 37, 58, 65, 71, 163, 166, 230, 233, 239, 244, 259, 278, 279, 286, 314, 328, 364, 366, 382
Cyprus, 374
Czechoslovakia, 178

Dakar, 26, 318, 320, 322, 323, 336
Dalits, 3, 131, 133, 135, 136
Danish, 4, 124, 219, 220, 221–227
Darwinism, 163
Data, 29, 39, 50, 61–70, 72, 73, 133, 134, 214, 310, 357
Declaration, 24, 89, 92, 94, 95, 252, 319, 322, 323, 326, 328, 329, 330, 334, 356
Deficit/model/theory, 275
Delors report, 88, 95, 329
Democracy/democracy now!, 164, 167
Denmark, 219–227
Development, 131–146
Desaparecidos, 4, 295
Difference, 3, 44, 62, 67, 93, 95, 104, 167, 215, 235, 272, 277, 294, 296, 297, 383, 386
Differentiation, 78, 100
Digital, 23, 153, 155, 162, 372
Disabling, 141, 147, 161
Discrimination/atory, 24, 27, 57, 58, 67, 68, 71, 73, 79, 80, 81, 87, 88, 89
Disenfranchised, 88, 91, 164, 166, 167, 170, 171
Displacement, 92, 131, 134, 137, 140, 141, 144, 200
Disposable, 10, 167
Dispossession, 117, 131–146

DNA, 34
Domestic, 47, 48, 88, 101, 103, 104, 156, 239, 319, 349

EAEA, 382, 386, 387
Earth, 121, 124, 181, 305, 310, 388, 389
Ecological/ecology, 51, 94, 109, 115, 127, 134, 135, 141, 144, 145, 198, 271, 282, 290, 329, 378, 388
Economy/ies, 3, 4, 12, 13, 15, 21, 38, 39, 41, 48, 50, 51, 100, 112, 115, 116, 118, 123, 127, 139, 145, 199, 201, 225, 276, 277, 293, 296, 301–305, 343, 350, 359, 360, 361, 371, 374, 376, 384, 386
EFA (Education for All), 19, 20, 26, 29, 31, 317, 322, 323, 324, 326, 328, 331
Efficiency, 12, 13, 28, 294, 319, 327, 335, 366, 375
Egypt/ian, 35, 153
Elderly, 24, 28, 71, 120, 231, 310, 376
Elsinore, 328
Empire, 119, 132, 356
Empowerment/ing, 15, 16, 60, 61, 70, 83, 90, 143, 153, 197, 203, 215, 234, 243, 244, 256, 271, 297, 299, 312, 330, 345, 389
Enable, 58, 62–65, 69, 71, 72, 73, 118, 120, 158, 202, 237, 243, 254, 262, 275, 281, 296, 297, 304, 313, 341, 367, 374, 375, 388
English, 1, 2, 4, 19, 20, 58, 64, 71, 84, 104, 124, 186, 191, 220, 227, 233, 236, 267, 278, 367, 371, 373, 379, 381, 389, 390
Enlightenment, 127, 140, 219, 220, 221, 226

SUBJECT INDEX

Entrepreneurship/entrepreneurial, 365, 369, 375
Environment/al, 33, 34, 37, 48, 49, 51, 60, 61, 62, 68, 78, 79, 83, 90, 94, 127, 138, 143, 145, 158, 163, 181, 185, 208, 236, 239, 240, 243, 244, 262, 273, 289, 290, 295, 302, 305, 311, 312, 325, 329, 330, 335, 347, 352, 369, 378
Equality, 27, 89, 91, 113, 127, 227, 278, 279, 281, 313, 330, 343, 345, 347, 368, 383
Equity, 12, 28, 29, 35, 77, 80–83, 87, 92, 140, 262, 329, 330, 331, 333, 335
Eritrea, 350
Ethnic, 36, 47, 92, 99, 101–104, 106–109, 114, 134, 139, 142, 147, 191, 240, 244, 245, 335, 346, 350, 387
Eurocentric, 140
European Commissioner, 13
European Parliament, 114, 262
European social fund (ESF), 374, 375
European Union, 3, 12, 198, 246, 251, 256, 262, 263, 373
Experience, 1, 4, 5, 23, 25, 28, 42, 46, 47, 57–73

Facebook, 155
Factory Council, 379
Family, 25, 30, 35, 49, 51, 63, 65, 66, 67, 70, 71, 78, 88, 99–103, 106–109, 117–120, 123, 124, 126, 168, 175, 241, 242, 256, 267, 268, 269, 271, 275, 280, 288, 290, 299, 303, 310, 311, 312, 314, 323, 327, 344, 351, 363
Farmer/s, 94, 136, 138, 142, 176, 216, 222, 223, 267, 285, 367
Fashion, 9, 11, 128, 209
Fee/s, 23, 49, 230, 237, 238, 242, 368

Feminine/inity/inism, 5, 111, 156, 296, 297, 377, 384
Films, 1, 4, 102, 103, 175–182, 191, 212, 237, 244, 270, 287
Finance/financial, 23, 28, 29, 64, 65, 80, 103, 106, 147, 153, 154, 195, 232, 233, 244, 246, 253, 257, 261, 291, 297, 312, 314, 315, 319, 324, 326, 334, 344, 348, 358, 359, 362, 364, 368, 371, 373, 374, 386
Finland/nish, 12, 30, 113, 124, 129, 233
First world, 116, 224
First-generation, 101, 105, 106
Fitness, 81, 82
Flexible/ility, 49, 50, 123, 190, 232, 279, 373, 383
Folk/s, 1, 4, 62, 81, 94, 142, 208, 213, 219–227, 271
Folk High Schools, 1, 4, 219–227
Food, 133, 134, 139, 141, 260, 285, 290, 295, 296, 350
Ford, 157, 289
Foreign Direct Investment, 136
Formation, 11, 30, 167, 171, 325, 341, 355, 358, 359, 360, 361, 364, 366
France/French, 30, 34, 101, 102, 107, 113, 115, 116, 124, 125, 208, 215, 220, 229–233, 242, 243, 251, 294, 331
Frankfurt, 3, 4, 110, 112, 200, 205, 206, 207, 211
Freedom, 11, 88, 92, 106, 116, 117, 132, 140, 166, 197, 212, 226, 281, 285, 287, 288, 294, 295, 296, 301, 310, 313, 345, 346, 351, 352
Frente Zapatista, 377
Funding, 23, 58, 64, 121, 157, 199, 246, 257, 258, 321, 326, 359, 362, 364, 365, 374, 375, 376, 386
Further education, 12, 36, 37, 43, 44, 45, 48, 129, 179, 260, 361, 366

SUBJECT INDEX

GAS, 302, 303, 304
GATS, 373
Gaza, 378
General Electric, 162
Generation/s, 24, 39, 40, 42, 61, 65, 81, 99–102, 105–108, 113, 115, 119, 120, 136, 137, 158, 210, 240, 245, 246, 304, 311, 314, 326, 333
German/y/, 3, 90, 100–109, 111, 113, 115, 116, 117, 119, 122, 124, 125, 130, 146, 221, 222, 277, 337
Gerontology, 230, 249
Ghana, 154, 350
Girls, 67, 68, 70, 77–84, 101, 102, 103, 108, 212, 298
Glocal, 294, 389
GNP, 29, 357
Governance, 51, 143, 161, 197, 335, 341, 342, 344–347, 349, 350, 352, 355
Gramscian, 5, 132, 147, 170, 286, 379
Grassroots, 4, 172, 345, 377, 380, 386
Grundtvig programme/project, 205, 246, 257
Guyana, 97, 363

Hamburg, 20, 90, 91, 92, 109, 110, 252, 318, 320, 322, 327–332, 337
Hegemony, 143, 188, 202, 291, 372, 389
Hellenic Open University, 4, 205, 216, 217
Higher education, 105, 154, 220, 233, 349, 360, 374
History, 11, 15, 33, 35, 41, 88, 105, 113–116, 120, 122, 128, 144, 146, 161, 163, 165, 220, 221, 224, 225, 245, 294, 317, 335, 363
HIV, 57, 58, 59, 87, 182, 309
Holistic, 29, 60, 62, 206, 214, 215, 233, 258, 259, 287, 315, 384

Homo eligens, 11
Human capital, 13, 48, 50, 125, 313, 314, 336, 360, 361, 386
Humanist, 129, 224, 289, 301
Humanity, 11, 16, 115, 120, 164, 170, 220, 270, 273, 294, 303, 351
Human Resources, 14, 15, 246, 297, 358–363, 365, 367, 369, 373, 374, 375, 382, 383
Human Rights, 87, 88, 89, 90, 93, 94, 95, 135, 138, 141–144, 154, 167, 171, 252, 253, 332, 335, 343, 349

Iberian, 380
ICAE, 3, 92, 93, 94, 95, 323, 337, 369
Illiteracy, 20, 22, 24, 25, 26, 29, 65, 180, 244, 277, 319, 321, 322, 326, 336, 361, 367
Imagination, 11, 123, 180, 195, 196, 197, 199, 203, 253, 271, 297, 304, 389
IMF, 372
Imperial/ism, 116, 132, 135, 159
Income, 12, 49, 65, 103, 107, 200, 216, 309–312, 314, 315, 318, 319, 327, 336, 345, 357
India/n/s, 2, 4, 131, 132, 134–141, 143, 144, 147, 153, 157, 168, 179, 181, 182, 183, 193, 357
Indigenous, 23, 24, 63, 90, 91, 92, 94, 100, 105, 109, 131, 133, 141, 143, 157, 158, 329, 332, 335, 351, 365, 378
Industry, 34, 136, 154, 162, 163, 170, 181, 200, 215, 216, 312, 359, 361
Informal, 36, 37, 38, 40, 41–45, 49, 51, 91, 107, 129, 153, 154, 155, 180, 197, 256, 286, 287, 291, 296, 297, 329, 341, 347, 351, 377, 384
Information society, 120, 276

401

SUBJECT INDEX

Information Communication Technology, 159, 160
Infrastructure, 22, 116, 178, 312, 313, 341, 349, 355, 357, 358, 361, 365, 366, 368, 369, 374, 375, 385
Integrated National Disability Strategy, 59
Instruction/al, 14, 35, 37, 165, 177, 179, 180, 186, 190, 243, 246, 260, 286, 364, 365
Intellectual, 36, 78, 106, 144, 158, 167, 170, 171, 191, 192, 202, 223, 224, 230, 232, 238, 240, 246, 289, 290, 359, 364
Interaction, 16, 38, 41, 72, 77, 78, 79, 83, 154, 156, 167, 178, 197, 206, 213, 304, 366, 375
Intercultural, 22, 23, 24, 99, 109, 224, 262
Islam/ic, 87, 93, 104, 372
Island/s, 5, 11, 93, 356–362, 365, 366, 368, 369, 374, 387
Italy/Italian, 4, 101, 104, 118, 124, 125, 131, 230, 237, 294, 303, 306, 380, 383, 387

Jomtein, 26, 317–320, 322, 323, 324, 326, 331, 334
Jurisdiction, 370
Justice, 53, 88, 89, 91, 94, 95, 119, 127, 128, 140, 142, 143, 147, 165, 166, 167, 169, 171, 172, 192, 195, 252, 258, 260-263, 269, 295, 299, 303, 310, 315, 329, 330, 333, 339, 343, 368, 369, 378, 380

Kha Ri Gude, 57
Knowledge (based) economy, 3, 276
Knowledge society, 12, 13, 256, 301
Kondh, 133, 134, 138, 139, 145, 146

KwaZulu-Natal, 57–73, 76, 316

Labour, 12, 13, 14, 34–37, 39, 40, 42, 44, 45, 47–51, 100, 101, 103, 104, 106, 108, 109, 131, 136, 142, 143, 147, 224, 226, 227, 242, 254, 293, 312, 325, 373, 376, 382, 384, 388
Language, 2, 15, 19, 28, 31, 33, 71, 78, 79, 90, 91, 92, 108, 124, 177, 181, 187, 188, 191, 192, 195, 196, 220, 222–225, 227, 230, 233, 269, 271, 294, 295, 299, 300, 302, 350, 356, 364, 365, 367, 371, 373, 379, 381, 387
Lecture/s, 52, 79, 154, 180, 229, 230, 233, 238
LGBTQ, 92
Liberal/s, 42, 51, 129, 179, 180, 223, 224, 239, 287
Library/ies, 1, 4, 22, 51, 153, 185–193, 194, 209, 242, 245, 253, 254, 261, 263, 365
Life-wide, 296, 314, 383
Lithuania, 88
Learning organizations, 41
Learning society, v, 1, 2, 3, 5, 7, 33–52, 120, 329
Left/ist, 106, 136, 143, 377
Leisure, 36, 37, 125, 233, 242, 256, 260, 262, 310
Leonardo programme, 375
Liberacion!, 166, 167, 169–172
Liquid, 3, 9, 10, 11, 13, 15–18, 203, 301
Living together, 196, 298
Locavores, 290

Madres, 4, 294, 295
Mafia, 101, 138
Maghreb, 103

SUBJECT INDEX

Malta, iii, v, 6, 13, 233, 236, 238, 239, 262, 264, 366, 369, 374, 376, 387, 389
Management/manager/s, 11, 13, 14, 38–41, 45, 46, 49, 64, 117, 119, 129, 135, 140, 181, 199, 230, 238, 239, 241, 252, 253, 260, 261, 312, 355, 371, 378, 379, 380
Marketplace, 116, 163, 164, 198, 287, 289, 301, 374
Marxist/ian, 136, 141, 144, 147
Masculine/inity, 79, 384
Medical Model, 59, 60, 260
Mediterranean, 5, 156, 378, 379, 381, 387, 388, 390
Memorandum, 13, 110, 136, 242, 253, 260, 382, 384, 385, 386
Memory, 11, 15, 113, 118, 124
MEP/s, 389
Mexico/an, 19, 20, 21, 24, 25, 29, 30, 153, 320, 331, 336, 337
Micro-state/s, 1, 355–369
Middle class, 104, 140, 175, 179, 186, 238, 239
Migrant, 21, 92, 99, 101, 102, 103, 107, 108
Milan, 298, 299,
Millennium Development Goals (MDGs), 310
Mineral ore/s, 135, 136
Mining, 132, 136, 137, 138, 139, 143
Missile, 9, 10
Missionaries, 143, 193
Modernisation, 99, 100, 105, 106, 110, 135, 140, 227
Modernity, 3, 10, 100, 140, 241, 294
Monsanto, 378
Morocco/an, 103
Mothers, 68–71, 102, 103, 105, 168, 220, 221, 267, 268, 269, 271, 273, 295, 298
MST, 377

Multiple literacies, 187
Munich, 104
Museum, 125, 209, 210, 216, 299
Music, 125, 164, 169, 170, 175, 206, 208, 209, 211, 212, 213, 215, 226, 267, 269, 270, 271, 299, 377
Muslim, 101, 102, 103

Nation/Nation-state, 94, 96, 108, 113, 115, 124, 180, 328, 342, 343, 352
Neighborhood/s, 344
Neoliberal/ism, 132, 136, 142, 161, 162–167, 170, 196, 293, 294, 297, 301, 332, 333, 371, 372, 374, 375, 376, 379, 380, 386, 387, 388
New approaches to lifelong earning (NALL), 42, 44
Nicosia, 374
Non-formal, 24, 89, 234, 296, 317, 323, 329, 330, 336, 341, 347, 363, 372, 377, 383, 384, 386
Nongovernmental organization (NGO), 20, 23, 26, 58, 64, 90, 140–143, 145, 147, 196, 257, 263, 321, 329, 331, 337, 348, 349, 372, 375, 376, 377, 385, 388, 389
North/ist, 2, 26, 59, 93, 103, 127, 141, 179, 181, 224, 233, 259, 289, 315, 371, 387, 389
North Africa, 103, 371, 387
Nuclear, 17, 33

OAS, 21, 73, 138, 145, 285, 320, 332, 356, 358, 378
OECD, 19, 50, 128, 277, 301
Offender/s, 254, 260, 314
On the job, 159
Online, 79, 96, 153–157, 233, 234, 236, 237, 242, 244, 245, 246, 269, 285, 375
Opinion leaders, 176, 177

SUBJECT INDEX

Oppression/oppressed, 60, 61, 67–71, 87, 104, 131, 163, 164, 167, 171, 188, 200, 272, 296, 352, 380
Orissa, 131, 132, 135, 136, 138, 143, 145, 146
Out-of-school, 22, 323

Pacific, 93, 164, 357, 368
Paid employment/work, 36, 37, 38, 42, 44, 47, 49, 50, 117, 288, 311
Paidea, 9
Participatory Action Research, 133
Participatory budget, 377, 380
Participatory democracy, 196, 197, 346, 347
Peace, 90, 91, 113, 114, 116, 143, 154, 169, 172, 288, 312, 330, 333, 335, 377, 378, 380, 388, 391
Peasant, 24, 35, 131, 136, 142, 143–147, 179, 188, 225, 332, 377
Pedagogy, 4, 83, 88, 95, 99, 144, 145, 146, 161–171, 172, 182, 186, 187, 205, 206, 207, 209, 226, 279, 286, 288, 289, 300, 301, 302, 345, 369, 384
Performance Indicators, 376,
Physical education/PE, 253, 254, 260
Planet, 16, 51, 271, 273, 305, 371, 388
Planning, 10, 15, 17, 29, 38, 48, 60, 83, 107, 109, 268, 322
Plantation, 137, 139, 142
Plaza de Mayo, 294
Polish, 11, 225
Politica prima, 297, 299
Popular, 13, 42, 93, 117, 133, 139, 144, 146, 153, 156, 169, 199, 200, 208, 220, 221, 226, 227, 244, 256, 276, 295, 298, 299, 304, 317, 319, 324, 331, 332, 342, 345, 373, 376, 377, 380, 388
Porto Alegre, 377, 380

Portugal/Portuguese, 19, 92, 109, 122, 256, 380, 387
Postcolonial, 140
Post-secondary, 42, 43, 45, 46, 238, 263
Power/ful/less/lessness, 13, 16, 21, 33, 103, 116, 117, 129, 144, 163, 166, 169, 170, 175, 191, 220, 275, 277, 294, 295, 299, 327, 328, 329
Praxis, 60, 132, 134, 142, 143, 144, 155, 169, 170, 171, 188, 189
Privatisation, 123, 374–376, 389
Profession, 11, 27, 87, 185, 186, 189, 190, 321, 324
Public intellectual/s, 158
Public pedagogy, 4, 161–171, 172, 182
Public sphere, 94, 161, 162, 163, 165–167, 346
Public space/s, 15, 72, 161, 169, 198, 294, 346

Qualification/s, 40, 42, 45, 46, 92, 104, 106, 108, 128, 208, 223, 238, 242, 252, 256, 313, 329
Quality, 12, 14, 21, 22, 25, 27, 28, 29, 37, 50, 72, 77, 78, 90, 107, 127, 156, 161, 170, 181, 207, 209, 222, 229, 230, 235, 236, 237, 240, 243, 244, 246, 256, 257, 262, 279, 281, 299, 309, 319, 321–325, 330, 333, 335, 336, 344, 345, 349, 361, 365, 377, 380, 384, 385, 388

Race, 48, 51, 67, 73, 80, 104, 110, 114, 157, 189, 273, 285, 289, 346
Racial, 47, 87, 103, 132, 139, 142, 161, 168, 171, 311
Racism, 3, 24, 111, 163, 189, 387
Rationality, 9, 10, 118, 206, 223

SUBJECT INDEX

Recidivism, 252, 253, 258, 263
Responsibility/responsible, 11, 14, 15, 17, 37, 39, 69, 81, 102, 108, 116, 117, 119, 129, 142, 205, 229, 230, 232, 243, 252, 255, 269, 277, 287, 288, 289, 293, 303, 322, 326, 343, 362, 366, 367, 373,382, 383, 387
Resistance, 88, 94, 95, 101, 132, 134, 135, 136, 139, 169, 170, 171, 197–202, 372
Rhine-Main, 101
Roma people, 4, 229
Rural, 22, 23, 24, 57, 64, 70, 72, 101, 131, 132, 134–137, 139, 143, 146, 147, 157, 159, 167, 168, 222, 224–227, 267, 315, 335, 341, 348, 351
Rwanda, 350

San Donato, 380
Scaffold/ing, 81, 188, 189
Scandinavia/n/s, 42, 125
Second world, 116, 175, 224
Self-concept, 269,
Self-directed learning, 37
Senior citizen/s, 226, 230
Services, 10, 23, 36, 38, 39, 45, 46, 47, 77, 81, 103, 104, 105, 117, 118, 120, 124, 143, 158, 164, 171
Shopping, 280, 285–291, 304, 305
Social capital, 37, 197, 312, 313, 314, 345, 375, 386, 387
Social class, 156, 157, 186, 388
Social forum, 378, 381
Social Model, 59, 60, 293
Social system/s, 116, 124
Sociology/ist/ical, 2, 3, 4, 18, 99, 101, 104, 111, 115, 122, 125, 130, 200, 210, 211, 381
Socrates programme, 257, 375

Solidarity, 4, 73, 90, 104, 114, 118, 122, 124, 133, 134, 140, 141, 164, 169, 171, 197, 200, 215, 227, 246, 256, 262, 296, 302, 303, 305, 314, 330, 333, 386
Sophie's choice, 191
South Africa, 57, 58, 59, 64, 73, 76, 87, 165, 290, 316, 349, 350
South/ern, 2, 5, 113, 124, 259, 371, 374, 375, 379, 380, 383, 387, 389, 390
Southern Europe, 2, 5, 371–389, 390
Soviet Union, 116, 357
Spain/Spanish, 19, 20, 27, 30, 122, 230, 239, 256, 294, 331, 363, 380, 381, 387
Spiritual/ity, 69, 72, 117, 140, 144, 208, 220, 226, 273, 289, 300
Sport, 1, 2, 3, 77–84, 103, 181, 226, 245, 253, 254, 260, 310
St. Gil, 103
St. Lucia Banana Growers Association, 367
Statistics, 25, 39, 40, 57, 77, 101, 102, 104, 239, 277
Status Quo, 4, 188, 205, 346
Sub-Saharan, 157, 341–352, 371, 387
Subaltern, 3, 4, 131–146, 147
Subordination, 30, 47, 102, 103, 104, 146, 147, 167
Sustainable/development, 286, 289, 322, 329, 365, 388
Switzerland/swiss, 102, 230
Symbols/ism, 34, 93, 113, 189, 190, 192, 200, 275,

Tanzania, 34, 225, 317, 351
Taste, 208, 269
Tax/es/ation, 113, 116, 125, 386
Technical, 10, 16, 25, 27, 28, 38, 92, 107, 117, 119, 120, 123, 125, 153, 171, 175, 178, 181, 281, 312, 324, 325, 328, 329, 362, 363, 365

SUBJECT INDEX

Technocrat, 320
Telecommunications, 162, 163, 312
Television, 117, 158, 175–182, 245
Temporary, 100, 102, 105, 311, 389
Text/ing, 1, 13, 78, 153, 190, 215, 220, 221, 256, 276, 301, 337
Theatre, 113, 154, 175, 206, 208, 209, 210, 226, 380
Third Age, 4, 24, 229–246, 376, 383
Third World, 104, 116, 176
Time Warner, 162
Togo, 179
Torino (Turin), 103, 110, 379
Trade /union/s, 2, 51, 105, 106, 116, 118, 119, 121, 122, 124, 125, 126
Transformation, 5, 9, 60, 66, 69, 70, 71, 88, 94, 95, 137, 140, 171, 241, 242, 267, 268, 270–273, 281, 285, 290, 291, 293, 294, 299, 301, 344, 346, 375, 381
Twitter, 153, 155
Turkey/ish, 87, 103, 108, 114, 348

Uganda, 91, 93, 154, 166, 343
Underdeveloped, 341, 356
UNESCO, 20, 21, 26, 50, 88, 90, 94, 95, 178, 180, 286, 287, 289, 301, 309, 319, 320, 322, 331, 332, 337, 363, 364, 366, 369, 373
United Kingdom, 40, 41, 59, 107, 177, 195, 197, 237, 239, 259, 313, 314, 357, 374
United Nations (UN), 24, 26, 58, 71, 87–90, 92, 94, 101, 131, 137, 234, 246, 252, 320, 355, 356, 357
University of the West Indies, 362, 366, 368
Universal, 11, 27, 31, 35, 88, 89, 95, 103, 126, 143, 190, 207, 221, 319, 320, 322, 326, 328, 330, 347, 359, 360, 361

Universal Declaration of Human Rights, 88
Univision, 162
Unpaid, 36, 37, 47, 48, 51, 211, 233, 311, 317
Utkal Alumina Industrial Limited, 136, 138, 140
USA, 98, 99, 104, 154, 376
USAID, 320, 348, 364

Video/s/gaming, 180, 191
Vocational /ism, 13, 25, 28, 35, 39, 50, 51, 58, 107, 118, 123, 125, 126, 127, 129, 181, 219, 223, 225, 226, 253–258, 260, 261, 262, 275, 313, 325, 335, 362, 363, 375, 376, 379, 380, 383, 384, 387
Voest-Alpine, 125
Voice/s, 4, 17, 59, 68, 69, 70, 71, 87, 92, 95, 96, 133, 156, 163, 164, 166, 167, 169, 172, 197, 234, 235, 236, 280, 287, 311, 344, 346, 349, 350
Voluntary, 48, 51, 129, 219, 223, 231, 299, 311, 322, 328, 349, 363, 367
Vulnerability, 23, 271, 312, 314, 358, 368

Welfare, 80, 137, 179, 224, 232, 234, 237, 241, 288, 311, 319, 347, 362, 363, 376, 389
Wellbeing, 29, 91, 240
West Bank, 378
Western, 35, 61, 99, 100, 116, 119, 134, 140, 153, 157, 159, 164, 182, 188, 192, 208, 305
Work/force/fare, 13, 27, 41, 47, 49, 368
Workers, 2, 38, 39, 41, 42, 44–47, 50, 88, 91, 104, 105, 107, 124, 126, 127, 216, 223, 245, 286, 288, 322, 361, 373, 380, 383

Working class, 106, 161, 168, 175, 179, 198, 239, 269, 378, 380
Workplace, 15, 37, 38, 41, 48, 49, 50, 124, 276, 320, 323
Workshops, 37, 45, 71, 72, 92, 93, 395, 302–305
World Bank, 19, 26, 143, 157, 318, 320, 322, 323, 326, 327, 328, 336, 359, 364, 372
WTO, 372, 373

Xenophobia, 387

Youth, 19–30, 35, 68, 84, 90, 94, 95, 100, 101, 168, 169, 170, 221, 224, 225, 226, 243, 253, 317, 322, 323, 326, 327, 328, 331, 332, 333, 335, 336, 342, 344, 366, 380
Yugoslavia, 101, 113, 114, 379

Zambia, 153, 157, 349
ZANU, 341, 346, 349
Zimbabwe, 341–344, 346, 347, 349, 351
Zone/s of Proximal Development, 188, 192
Zulu, 58

CPSIA information can be obtained at www.ICGtesting.com
Printed in the USA
LVOW04s0730250515

439710LV00005B/120/P

9 789462 093331

INTERNATIONAL ISSUES IN ADULT EDUCATION

Learning with Adults

A Reader

Peter Mayo (Ed.)
University of Malta, Malta

This anthology brings together some of the finest writers on different aspects of adult education and related areas to provide a complementary reader to the introductory text by Leona English and Peter Mayo *Learning with Adults: A Critical Pedagogical Introduction*. Areas tackled include Disability, Prisons, Third Age Universities, Lifelong Learning Policy, Learning Society, Poverty, LGBTQ, Sport, Women, Literacy, Transformative Learning, Community Arts, Aesthetics, Consumption, Migration, Libraries, Folk High Schools, Adult Education Policy, Subaltern Southern Social Movements, Social Creation, Community Radio, Social Film. Contexts focused on include Africa, Caribbean, Europe, Latin America, Asia (India), small island states. Over thirty authors involved including Zygmunt Bauman, Rosa Maria Torres, Oskar Negt, Antonia Darder, Jim Elmborg, D. W. Livingstone, Palle Rasmussen, Mae Shaw, Leona English, Asoke Bhattacharya, Cynthia L. Pemberton, Eileen Casey White, Daniel Schugurensky, Dip Kapoor, Peter Rule, John Myers, Joseph Giordmaina, Antonia De Vita, Alexis Kokkos, Marvin Formosa, Carmel Borg, Julia Preece, Patricia Cranton, Lyn Tett, Ali A. Abdi, Anna Maria Piussi, Behrang Foroughi, Taadi Ruth Modipa, Robert Hill, Edward Shizha, Kaela Jubas, Ursula Apitzsch, Didacus Jules and Peter Mayo.

... *Learning with Adults: A Reader* constitutes the most valuable practical and theoretical reflection on adult education I have seen in a long time.

Nelly P. Stromquist, Professor, International Education Policy, College of Education University of Maryland, College Park

... This book provides an opportunity at a very appropriate moment to discuss adult education issues during challenging times.

Paula Guimarães, University of Lisbon

... Read and savour delights and surprises.

Michael Welton, UBC and Athabasca University

This book satisfies everything one could desire of a reader on the subject.

Kenneth Wain, University of Malta

Cover picture by Alessio Surian

ISBN 978-94-6209-333-1

SensePublishers   ADUL 13